THE VOYAGE OF THE BEAGLE

Principal Tracks of H.M.S. Beagle 1831-36

THE VOYAGE
OF THE BEAGLE

CHARLES DARWIN

ANNOTATED AND WITH AN INTRODUCTION
BY LEONARD ENGEL

Illustrated with maps, drawings, and
photographs

PUBLISHED IN CO-OPERATION WITH
THE AMERICAN MUSEUM OF NATURAL HISTORY

THE NATURAL HISTORY LIBRARY
ANCHOR BOOKS
DOUBLEDAY & COMPANY, INC.
GARDEN CITY, NEW YORK

The Natural History Library edition is the first publication of *The Voyage of the Beagle*, edited and with an introduction by Leonard Engel.

Natural History Library Edition: 1962

ILLUSTRATIONS REDRAWN BY Nancy Gahan

MAPS DRAWN BY Stephen Kraft

EDITOR'S FOREWORD

The inclusion of *The Voyage of the Beagle* in the Natural History Library needs no justification. It is not only one of *the* great classics of natural history and a key work in the evolution of modern thought: it is also first-rate as literature.

The text is from the edition of 1860, the last to be revised by Darwin. I have also added an introduction which, I hope, puts Darwin and the voyage of the *Beagle* in perspective. In addition, a number of footnotes have been added to the text. My notes are clearly distinguished from Darwin's own, and were added to provide a variety of supplementary information. For example, numerous interesting sidelights on the voyage are to be found in the account of the cruise by Fitz Roy—the captain of the *Beagle*—and in the diary and notebooks Darwin kept while on board, as well as in books like E. Lucas Bridges' fascinating account of life in Tierra del Fuego, *The Uttermost Part of the Earth*. Other notes identify the naturalists, biologists, and travelers Darwin quotes most often; give a bit of background; and render the modern names (where the names have changed) of places visited by Darwin, and English names of species referred to by Darwin in Latin only. Finally, in the century and a quarter since the writing of *The Voyage of the Beagle*, scientific opinion has changed on some of the points Darwin discusses: I have indicated a few of these changes.

In working on this edition of the *Voyage*, I received help and advice from many individuals. I would like particularly to acknowledge my debt to Maurice Ewing, director of the Lamont Geological Observatory, Columbia University, for making it possible for me to see some of the Darwin terrain myself by inviting me aboard the Columbia research schooner *Vema;* to Charles L. Drake of Lamont, for much helpful information; and to Donald Fleming, Professor of History at Harvard University, for advice on the reading list at the end of the volume.

LEONARD ENGEL

Larchmont, New York
July 1961

DARWIN AND THE *BEAGLE*

BY LEONARD ENGEL

In its influence on modern man's outlook upon the world, no voyage since Columbus matches the voyage described in this book. The *Beagle* was a ten-gun brig, a class of small warships used by the British Navy for a wide variety of duties a century and a third ago. In 1831, the *Beagle*—refitted for the occasion as a three-masted bark—was sent to complete a survey of the South American coast and to carry out a chain of longitude measurements around the world. There were many similar survey voyages during the nineteenth century. The *Beagle's* stands out for a single reason. A remarkable young man who was "extremely fond of geology and indeed all branches of natural history" accompanied her as ship's naturalist to take advantage of the opportunity for "collecting, observing and noting anything worthy to be noted in natural history." The youthful naturalist was Charles Darwin. It was the vast and changing panorama of life, both living and extinct, observed by Darwin during the *Beagle's* cruise that set him on the road to *The Origin of Species*. As we shall see later, *The Voyage of the Beagle*—which is also one of the greatest scientific travel adventure tales ever written—plainly foreshadows the revolutionary line along which Darwin's thought was to develop.

When the *Beagle* sailed from Devonport in southwestern England—not to return for four years, nine months and two days—Darwin was not quite twenty-three. Until then, he had been little more than a gentleman idler. He had failed at medicine (he couldn't bear the sight of pain); his family hoped, as the best of an unhappy situation, that he might make a country parson. He hardly seemed an individual destined to make a revolution in science and human thought. Indeed, it took several unexpected—not to say beneficent—turns of fate to put him aboard the *Beagle,* and start him on his life work.

Charles Robert Darwin was born at Shrewsbury in the west of England on February 12, 1809—the day Abraham Lincoln was born in the Kentucky wilderness on the other side of the sea. Unlike Lincoln, Darwin had great advantages of birth. His father, Robert, was a widely known physician. His grandfathers (both of whom died before he was born) were, on his father's side, the celebrated Erasmus Darwin, physician and an early theorist of evolution; and on his mother's side, Josiah Wedgwood, founder of the great Wedgwood pottery works. Darwin's interest in natural history appeared early. By the time he was eight, he later wrote in his autobiography, "my taste for natural history, and more especially for collecting, was well-developed. I tried to make out the names of plants, and collected all sorts of things, shells, seals, franks, coins, and minerals." However, his schooling was in the rigorously classical mold of the time and Darwin got relatively little out of it. At sixteen, he was sent to Edinburgh to study medicine. When it became clear that medicine was not for him, his father (who was a religious skeptic) sent him to Cambridge with the idea that he might enter the ministry. By his own account, the three years he spent at Cambridge were also largely wasted. He disliked most of his formal studies, though he did well enough to stand tenth on the list of those receiving degrees in January 1831. A passion for hunting and riding led him to fall in with a "sporting set, including some dissipated low-minded young men." But he continued his interest in "collecting" (especially beetles) and he became very friendly with the professor of botany, John S. Henslow.

During the summer of 1831, Henslow arranged for Darwin to accompany the professor of geology at Cambridge, Adam Sedgwick—one of the great pioneers of modern geology—on a field trip through Wales. When he returned home, Darwin found a letter from Henslow asking whether he would care to go as naturalist on a forthcoming survey voyage of H.M.S. *Beagle* to Tierra del Fuego and returning to England by way of the South Sea islands and the Indian archipelago. The post carried no pay, but Darwin would be free (as was then the custom) to sell any collections he made.

As Darwin soon learned, he was actually the third choice for the post. It had originally been offered to Henslow, who would have accepted but for his wife's misery at the prospect of his long absence from home. Henslow's brother-in-law, a clergy-man-naturalist named Leonard Jenyns, had reached the point of packing a chest for the trip and then changed his mind.

Darwin was eager to go. But his father objected; he said that he would give his consent only if Charles found "any man of common sense" who advised him to go. The next morning, Darwin—who lived in an age when even college-graduate sons seldom questioned a father's authority—wrote Henslow declining the offer. He then rode off to Maer, the estate of his uncle Josiah Wedgwood (the son of the potter) for the start of the shooting season. The next day, Darwin told his uncle of the offer and its rejection. To Darwin's surprise, Wedgwood said that he should have accepted. Wedgwood thereupon wrote out a point-by-point refutation of Robert Darwin's objections. Later that day, Wedgwood called Charles back from the hunt to drive the thirty miles to Shrewsbury with him to put the case to Robert Darwin in person. Since Wedgwood met the test of "a man of common sense"—he was a substantial businessman—Robert Darwin agreed that his son might go.

The next few weeks were weeks of feverish uncertainty for Darwin. The idea of taking a naturalist along had originated with the *Beagle's* captain, Robert Fitz Roy, a young man only four years Darwin's senior. When Darwin reached London, it developed that Fitz Roy—a man of mercurial changes of temperament—had changed his mind and now wished a personal friend to accompany him in the berth reserved for the naturalist. Fitz Roy received word that his friend had been refused leave from his job just a few minutes before Darwin met him for his first interview. Even then the coast was not clear. Fitz Roy believed strongly that character could be judged by the outline of a man's features. Darwin's nose, he thought, bespoke lack of energy. The day was won for Darwin by a letter from a nephew of Lord Londonderry, a friend and distant relative of Fitz Roy, assuring the *Beagle's* captain that Darwin was a gentleman. There were also doubts about the ship's orders. For a time, it appeared that the *Beagle*—to Darwin's dismay—might go only as far as South America. Darwin held off buying the books and instruments he would need until the last possible moment.

Preparation of the *Beagle* meanwhile went on apace. The survey vessel had returned just a year before from a similar voyage to South America. When examined for her new cruise, her deck and many of her timbers were found rotten. She accordingly underwent a thorough reconstruction at the Devonport naval dockyard. Fitz Roy, though young, was an experienced and skillful seaman, who had had command of the *Beagle* during two years of the previous voyage, and knew exactly what was needed. A third mast was added for a fore-and-aft sail to make her handle easier. The new deck was raised to provide a little more room inside and make her safer in heavy weather. A sheath of fir planking was laid over her bottom and a layer of felt and new copper plates over the planking. Lightning conductors of a newly invented type were installed on her masts and bowsprit. Four of her guns were removed to help make room for stores, of which there were an astonishing quantity: over 6000 cases of tinned meat and vegetables (then the newest thing in ship's stores), barrels of lime juice and other antiscorbutics, medicines, an ample supply of preservatives for any specimens the ship's naturalist might obtain. As refitted, the *Beagle* had a burden (carrying capacity) of 242 tons; ready for sea, her displacement (total tonnage) must have been about 500 tons.

About the middle of September, Darwin journeyed to the dockyard to see the *Beagle*. He was appalled at her small size and the small space allotted to him. His "office" was to be a corner of the chart table in the poop cabin at the stern of the ship. His bed would be a hammock over the chart table, where Fitz Roy was also to sling his hammock since the captain's cabin was overcrowded with instruments. A few small drawers in the corner of the poop cabin would have to do Darwin for stowing his clothing. (When he moved into his quarters aboard the ship, he discovered when he slung his hammock that he had to remove the top drawer to allow room for his feet.) Subsequently, he obtained a cabin under the forecastle and additional drawer space in the poop cabin for storing specimens.

It took the *Beagle* three tries to get off on her cruise. Twice she was driven back to port by violent southwest gales before she finally made good her departure as the year 1831 was drawing to a close. Aboard were no less than 74 persons. The regular crew numbered 65, including Fitz Roy as Commander and Surveyor, twelve officers and petty officers, a surgeon and assistant surgeon, two midshipmen, thirty-four seamen, eight marines, and six boys. Nine "supernumeraries" were also on the ship's list: three natives of Tierra del Fuego who had been brought to England on the *Beagle's* previous cruise and who were being returned to their native land; a missionary on his way out to Tierra del Fuego; an artist and an instrument maker brought along at Fitz Roy's personal expense; Darwin; and personal servants for Fitz Roy and Darwin. (The servants were paid for by their masters. Darwin taught his man taxidermy and used him chiefly for collecting and preparing specimens.)

Darwin discovered within a few hours of the *Beagle's* first attempt at departure that he was—as he feared he would be—extremely prone to seasickness. In fact, he suffered from it nearly constantly throughout the voyage, partly because the poop cabin was the roughest-riding section of the ship. He got his work done nevertheless and pulled his weight in other chores as well. A lanky six-footer, he took his regular turn in the harness for towing the ship's boats up the swift-running Santa Cruz River in Patagonia; he stood watch at shore camps in dangerous areas; he willingly utilized his skill with a gun to augment the ship's meat supply; he undertook a grueling search for water when others in a landing party lay crippled by thirst. Unassuming and gentle in manner withal, he became extremely popular with his shipmates, who nicknamed him "the Fly-catcher" and "the Philosopher." "I think he was the only man I ever knew," one of the midshipmen aboard recalled years later, "against whom I never heard a word said; and as people when shut up in a ship for five years are apt to get cross with each other, that is saying a good deal."

A letter to his sister Susan in July 1832—after he had been at sea for half a year—tells how a typical day passed. "We breakfast at eight o'clock," he wrote. "The invariable maxim is to throw away all politeness—that is, never to wait for each other, and bolt off the minute one has done eating, &c. At sea, when the weather is calm, I work at marine animals, with which the whole ocean abounds. If there is any sea up I am either sick or contrive to read some voyage or travels. At one we dine. You shoregoing people are lamentably mistaken about the manner of living on board. We have never yet (nor shall we) dined off salt meat. Rice and peas and *calavanses* [chick-peas] are excellent vegetables, and, with good bread, who could want more? Judge Alderson could not be more temperate, as nothing but water comes on the table. At five we have tea. The midshipman's berth have all their meals an hour before us, and the gun room an hour afterwards."

On naval vessels, ancient custom decrees that the captain eats alone. Darwin was flattered therefore when Fitz Roy invited him to mess with him. (Although he was carried on the ship's ration list, Darwin insisted on paying his share—30 pounds a year—toward the captain's mess bill.) Darwin soon found eating with the captain something of a trial, for Fitz Roy was a narrow-minded autocrat with an unpredictable temper.

Robert Fitz Roy was a singular individual. He was the grandson of a duke and the nephew of a powerful earl (Lord Castlereagh) and very much a member of the aristocracy as well as a naval officer. As Darwin wrote in his autobiography, Fitz Roy "was devoted to his duty, generous to a fault, bold, determined, and indomitably energetic, and an ardent friend to all under his sway. He would undertake any sort of trouble to assist those whom he thought deserved assistance." He accomplished a prodigious amount of work on the cruise. The Beagle brought back to England no less than 82 coastal sheets and 80 plans and 40 views of harbors. Fitz Roy was also an early student of meteorology and became head of a pioneer British weather service.

Unfortunately, Fitz Roy's very qualities also got him into serious difficulties. Thus, he did not hesitate to spend large sums, without authorization from the Admiralty, for the charter and purchase of vessels to aid the Beagle in her survey; he was sure the Admiralty would approve and reimburse him. When word of the Admiralty's disapproval reached the Beagle in Valparaiso, he was crushed, financially and psychologically. The cruise almost ended right there. The letter from the Admiralty plus overwork so depressed Fitz Roy that he turned over command to his first lieutenant who, under the ship's orders, would have had to sail the Beagle directly back to England. It took days of pleading by all his officers to persuade him to resume command and continue the voyage. (Similar well-meaning extravagance led to Fitz Roy's recall years later as governor of New Zealand. And when he died in 1865—by suicide—a public subscription was needed to pay his debts.)

Worse still for anyone living at close quarters with him was Fitz Roy's tendency to regard disagreement with him as a personal affront. One day early in the voyage, for instance, he told Darwin of a visit to a Brazilian slaveowner, who called in many of the slaves and asked them whether they wished to be free: all had answered "No." Darwin, who abominated slavery, asked Fitz Roy whether the answer of slaves in the presence of their master was worth anything. Fitz Roy thereupon lost his temper and told Darwin that the naturalist could no longer share his mess as he had doubted his word. A few hours later,

Fitz Roy apologized and insisted that Darwin rejoin him in the captain's mess. Darwin, who detested quarreling, simply learned to avoid subjects on which he and the captain disagreed.

One of these was the Biblical story of Creation. Fitz Roy was a deeply religious, zealous fundamentalist. In fact, one of his purposes in inviting a naturalist to accompany the *Beagle* had been the hope that the naturalist might obtain geological evidence to refute evolutionary views (such as those of Lamarck) that were beginning to gain favor in Europe. When Darwin boarded the *Beagle,* he also was a believer in the Bible's story of Creation. But he took with him the first volume of Sir Charles Lyell's *Principles of Geology,* which advanced the revolutionary thesis that the earth's physical features were a product of geological forces acting over immense periods of time—periods incomparably greater than the few thousand years since Creation allowed by the Old Testament. (The second volume of Lyell was not yet out when the *Beagle* left England and did not reach Darwin until mid-1832.) The Lyell book and his observations of the fossil record nibbled away at Darwin's Creationist beliefs throughout the voyage. By the third year, he probably held them no longer. But he refrained from voicing much of what he thought in order to avoid giving offense.

The book *The Voyage of the Beagle* grew out of notebooks and a diary kept by Darwin through the nearly five years of the *Beagle's* cruise. There was, first of all, a series of small pocket notebooks—eighteen in all were filled by the time the *Beagle* returned home—for daily entries. One of these pocket notebooks, together with a volume of Milton's poetry, accompanied Darwin wherever he went. In them may be found hastily scribbled scientific observations ("on the coast about 12 feet high, and in the conglomerate, teeth and thigh bones"), comments on towns and other places visited ("museum, civil manners"), instructions for his servant ("shoe mule"), a record of his expenses, lists of necessaries for inland excursions ("nightcaps, black ribbon, pillboxes, Bramah pens, 2 lbs. common soap, tobacco"). The daily jottings were raw material for two other sets of notes. One, contained in a series of large notebooks that eventually totaled 2000 manuscript pages, recorded Darwin's scientific observations in detail. The other was a diary, written out in quiet intervals aboard ship.

Soon after leaving England, it occurred to Darwin that he might write a book on the geology of the various places he visited. (He eventually wrote three volumes of *Beagle* geology: one on coral reefs, one on volcanic islands, and one on the geology of South America.) But he had no idea of publishing a journal of the cruise until one day during the last year of the voyage, when Fitz Roy made the suggestion after reading a part of the diary. Later, Fitz Roy proposed that Darwin allow use of sections of the diary in an official account of the voyage that Fitz Roy was to prepare. Although Darwin was agreeable, this plan happily fell through. Instead, arrangements were made to publish the Darwin journal as a separate volume in *Voyages of His Majesty's Ships Adventure and Beagle,* the official narrative of the *Beagle* voyage and of an earlier surveying cruise to South America by the *Beagle* and the *Adventure.*

The *Voyages* came out in 1839, three years after the *Beagle's* return home. The volumes by Fitz Roy and Philip Parker King (who had been captain of the *Adventure*) met with the usual fate of official history. Darwin's volume was an instant success. Two additional printings were needed within the first year, and a new edition was brought out by another publisher in 1845.

The diary and the versions of it published in the official *Voyages* and the 1845 edition are not identical. In preparing the diary for publication, Darwin cut out trivia, consolidated descriptions of places visited two or more times, and added extensively from his scientific notebooks. In the process, the diary grew from an original length of 189,000 words (about twice the length of a 300-page novel) to 224,000 words. In revising it again for the 1845 edition, Darwin rephrased some passages to accord with his nascent ideas on evolution and added further from his scientific notebooks, but compressed purely narrative sections so as to bring the whole down to 213,000 words. The book that has come to be known as *The Voyage of the Beagle* is the 1845 version. (The original text of the diary was not published until 1933.)

When the *Voyage* was first published, it bore a typically ponderous nineteenth-century title, *Narrative of the Surveying Voyages of His Majesty's Ships Adventure and Beagle, between the years 1826 and 1836, describing their examination of the Southern Shores of South America, and the Beagle's Circumnavigation of the Globe. Vol. III. Journal and Remarks, 1832–1836.* In the 1845 edition, this became *Journal of Researches into the Natural History and Geology of the countries visited during the Voyage of H.M.S. Beagle round the world under the Command of Capt. Fitz Roy, R.N.* Later editions saw various other permutations such as *Naturalist's Voyage Round the World* until the book finally became simply *The Voyage of the Beagle.*

Although Darwin complains, like many modern authors, that the *Voyage* earned him little money (he owed the publisher of the first edition £21. 10s. for copies purchased for friends), no other book of his gave him the same satisfaction. "The success of this, my first literary child," he wrote late in life, "always tickles my vanity more than that of any of my other works." Readers have made it a favorite for more than a century for several reasons. One is its simple, engaging style; it is much more gracefully written than Darwin's more formal scientific works. Another reason for its popularity is the picture it gives of a great field naturalist at work. For Darwin was a great field naturalist—one of the greatest that ever lived.

As the *Beagle* worked her way around the world, no detail of the lands and waters she visited was too small to escape the sharp eye of the young man in the poop cabin. Searching for marine animals in the Cape Verde Islands, he notices that cuttlefish often betray their hiding places by squirting out a jet of water. In the Pampas, he notes the changes in grasses wrought by the coming of civilized man. In Patagonia, he finds the bones of great extinct quadrupeds and wonders what could have brought about their extinction. In Chile, he lives through an earthquake and finds marine fossils at an altitude of 12,000 feet in the Andes—proof that the world's second highest mountain range was once under water. In the Keeling Islands, he marvels at a crab that opens coconuts.

Darwin's voyage produced two main results. In point of time, the first was his celebrated theory of the formation of coral atolls and reefs. The theory is presented both in Chapter XX of *The Voyage of the Beagle* and in one of the *Beagle* geologies, "The Structure and Distribution of Coral Reefs." In his autobiography, Darwin relates that he thought of his hypothesis while the *Beagle* was still on the South American coast and before he had ever seen a coral island. The essence of his theory is that coral atolls arise upon the flanks of sinking volcanic islands; coral polyps build up as the island slowly sinks beneath the sea. Several decades after the publication of Darwin's theory, a British oceanographer, Sir John Murray, discovered islands in the East Indies with layers of coral interspersed between layers of ocean sediment. Murray argued that Darwin was wrong and that coral reefs and atolls formed on platforms of sediment atop sunken (not sinking) volcanoes. Murray's challenge to Darwin divided nineteenth-century geologists into two hostile camps and led the Royal Society to send out an expedition to Funafuti atoll in 1901 to resolve the dispute by drilling down through the coral until it struck either sediment or volcanic rock. The drillers gave up (coral rock is tough) at 1100 feet without bringing up anything but coral. The question was not settled until shortly after World War II, when an American drilling crew bored down through the coral of Eniwetok. At 4500 feet, the bit crunched into volcanic rock. Although some coral reefs have been formed on sedimentary platforms, the coral islands of the deep ocean are formed as Darwin's brilliant hypothesis of a century and a third ago said they were—upon the flanks of sinking island volcanoes.

The other main product of Darwin's voyage was, of course, his theory of evolution. When the *Beagle* returned to England (in October 1836), Darwin took lodgings in London and settled down to the task of editing his journal and working up the enormous mass of notes and material he had brought with him. By the spring of 1837, he had become completely convinced of the mutability of species, and in July, he began a new series of notebooks for collecting the evidence of evolution and the laws of evolution. By 1842, he had formulated his ideas on natural selection and the struggle for survival in a preliminary essay. But he published nothing until the famous joint publication with Alfred Russell Wallace in 1858, and he did not complete the *Origin of Species* until 1859.

The observations that provided the turning point in Darwin's thinking were made in the rocky, barren Galapagos Islands. Here in the Galapagos, on the equator 600 miles off the west coast of South America, Darwin found "a little world in itself" with inhabitants found nowhere else. Giant tortoises clanking along pathways they themselves had made over the years to the few pools of fresh water. Great lizards that feed, unlike any others of their kind, on seaweed. Mockingbirds very different from those found on the South American mainland. A unique family of drab, finchlike birds (since named Darwin's finches) with no close relatives anywhere in the world except for a single species on an isolated Pacific island 350 miles to the northeast. John Gould, an ornithologist to whom Darwin sent specimens he had taken, recognized them as comprising several different species (thirteen altogether are now known from the Galapagos), each with a distinctive beak adapting it to a different diet and a different part of the island habitat.

Darwin did not appreciate the significance of the odd creatures he saw in the Galapagos at first. But an entry in a diary he kept after his return home reveals that their strangeness nagged him for months. Finally, he saw it plainly: the unusual species of the Galapagos were the descendants of mainland species, reshaped by a new habitat. The isolated Galapagos Islands were a "laboratory" in which evolutionary processes could be watched at work with a clarity never possible in the confusing babel of species on the mainland. A reading of Malthus' *Essay on Population* in October 1838 led him to recognize the struggle for survival and natural selection as the force that drove the evolutionary process.

Why Darwin held off publishing his ideas for two decades has been a puzzle to many writers. The simplest and most probable explanation is a wish to make his case as airtight as possible. Although the name associated with organic evolution is pre-eminently that of Darwin, the fact is that many of the ideas Darwin was to advance, as well as other evolutionary doctrines, had already been put forward by numerous others. The fate of many of these ideas was such as to impress upon a man of Darwin's temperament the need for the most careful, thorough kind of documentation.

One of Darwin's most important predecessors was his grandfather Erasmus, who hit upon natural selection in all but name, though Erasmus Darwin did not make it a central part of his system. (Curiously, Charles Darwin says he was little influenced by his grandfather's writings. But Malthus—who did influence Charles Darwin—obtained some of his key ideas from Erasmus Darwin.) Another prominent pre-Darwinian was Lamarck, who sought to reduce another of Erasmus Darwin's ideas—evolution by the use and disuse of bodily parts—to specifics. Unfortunately, Lamarck chose the giraffe as an illustration for his thesis; the giraffe, he argued, had acquired its long neck by stretching for the higher branches of trees. All Europe laughed, not only at Lamarck, but at the very idea of evolution as well. In 1813, three English physicians independently put forward evolutionary theories rejecting Lamarckian inheritance of acquired characteristics and based explicitly upon natural selection. One, William C. Wells, died before his essay was published. The second, James C. Prichard, later backwa-

tered toward Lamarck. The third, William Lawrence, stirred
official wrath by remarking, in his book, that the aristocracy
of Europe had ruined itself by a kind of selective breeding in
reverse. Lawrence's book was denied a copyright by Britain's
Lord Chancellor as contrary to Scripture; and Lawrence himself was confronted with the blunt choice of suppressing his
book or giving up his medical practice. Darwin certainly knew
of Lawrence's fate, for he refers to the book (of which there
were several illicit editions) in his writings. There were also
other evolutionists, whose work was denounced or ignored, as
well as such odd fish as Robert Chambers, author of an anony-
mous book, *The Vestiges of Creation,* that put forward evolutionary ideas amid a welter of rambling comment best described as claptrap; though enormously popular with the public, *The Vestiges* appalled naturalists by its numerous glaring
fallacies.

Whatever the reason, Darwin steadily piled up a mountain
of data on evolution, but published only the *Beagle* zoology
and geology volumes and monographs such as his well-known
studies of barnacles. Early in 1839, he married his cousin
Emma Wedgwood. The marriage not only brought him finan-
cial security and freedom to pursue his studies (his father settled £13,000 on him, and his wife brought a dowry of £5000
plus an annual allowance of £400, giving Darwin an assured
income of well over £1000 a year). Emma Darwin was an
unusual woman who delighted in ministering to what became
one of Darwin's principal preoccupations and problems—the
famous bouts of illness that afflicted him almost daily after the
Beagle to the end of his life and that sometimes prevented him
from doing any work at all for weeks on end. In recent years,
it has been the fashion to describe Darwin's illness as psycho-
somatic and to imply that it somehow sprang from a desire to
put off his work on evolution. This unflattering opinion has
gained force because no contemporary physician ever arrived
at a specific diagnosis. In the middle of the nineteenth century,
however, the means of medical diagnosis were elementary. In
1959, a distinguished expert in tropical diseases, S. Adler of
Hebrew University, Jerusalem, pointed out that Darwin's symptoms were those of Chagas' disease, a prolonged, debilitating
ailment caused by a South American cousin of the parasite responsible for African sleeping sickness. Darwin, Adler noted,
visited Mendoza, a province of Argentina in which evidence of
Chagas' disease can be found in as much as 60 per cent of the

population. And in Luxan, a town in Mendoza, where he stayed overnight, Darwin was subjected to a night-long attack of the "great black bug of the Pampas" (called the Reduvius by Darwin and now known as *Triatoma infestans*), the insect that has been identified as the principal carrier of Chagas' disease. Darwin's description of the attack is on page 331; his encounter with the "great black bug of the Pampas" could well have been the cause of his 40 years of invalidism.

Darwin remained in London for three and a half years after his marriage. During this period, Darwin was secretary of the Geological Society and was on friendly terms with many of the most famous men in English life, both scientific and nonscientific. Two men—Lyell, the geologist whose book had been so influential in opening Darwin's eyes to geology, and the great botanist Joseph Dalton Hooker—became particularly intimate friends. But Darwin's frail health could not stand the strain. So, in September, 1842, Darwin and his family moved to Down, a village in Kent not many miles from London. Here, he lived in seclusion with his family (he had ten children, of whom seven survived to maturity) for the rest of his life. He received visitors but rarely, his old intimates Lyell and Hooker excepted. Save for very occasional trips to watering places for his health, he never traveled again.

In 1854, Darwin finally began sorting and arranging the monumental pile of notes on the transmutation of species he had been collecting since 1837. Two years later, at the urging of Lyell, who warned him that others were also inquiring into evolution and would precede him in print, Darwin began to write out a detailed exposition of his ideas. Typically, this was to be on a massive scale—three or four volumes at least, though (Darwin complains) "only an abstract of the materials I had collected." He was about halfway through this undertaking when one day early in the summer of 1858, he received a letter from Alfred Russell Wallace, a naturalist traveling in Malaya, soliciting Darwin's opinion of an essay Wallace enclosed, entitled "On the Tendency of Varieties to Depart Indefinitely from the Original Type." The ideas the essay set forth were those of Darwin himself.

Darwin's first inclination was to withdraw in favor of Wallace. He was persuaded by Lyell and Hooker, however, to allow them to arrange for a joint presentation before the Linnaean Society. These are the famous Darwin-Wallace papers published in the *Journal of the Proceedings of the Linnaean So-*

ciety for August 20, 1858. They consist of four documents altogether: an extract from an unpublished essay by Darwin, a letter from Darwin to Asa Gray of Harvard summarizing Darwin's ideas; the Wallace essay; and a covering letter by Hooker and Lyell.

Darwin now set to work in earnest to put his ideas in book form. He scrapped his plans for a work in several volumes and substituted for it a single volume. This was *The Origin of Species*. It took him thirteen months and ten days of "hard labour" and was published in November 1859. Although the Linnaean Society presentation had attracted no particular attention, *The Origin* was instantly on everyone's lips. A printing of 1250 copies—large for a scientific work in those days—sold out on the day of publication.

This is not the place to record the details of the ideological struggle that followed the appearance of *The Origin*. Suffice it to say that Darwinism (a term for the theory of evolution gallantly proposed by Wallace) won the day with surprising speed. Darwin himself pointed out one reason why. "Innumerable well-observed facts," he wrote in his autobiography, "were stored in the minds of naturalists ready to take their proper places as soon as any theory which would receive them was sufficiently explained." Moreover, the original edition of *The Origin* had none of the confusing obscurities that Darwin, who was an incurable reviser, introduced into later editions in an effort to answer questions raised in the debate over evolution. (Some of these questions, as to just how the mechanics of evolution work, have not been answered yet.) The original *Origin* presented a straightforward, overwhelming mass of facts attesting to the grand fact of evolution. And this was the great accomplishment of the gentle Englishman who had set out on the adventure of the *Beagle* nearly thirty years before. *The Origin* changed the question of evolution from *whether* to *how*.

Darwin continued to live, to study plants and animals, and to write for another twenty-three years. He died at Down on April 19, 1882, and was buried in Westminster Abbey. Interestingly, his old companion, the *Beagle*, continued to serve the pursuit of knowledge for many years, too. She was employed on survey voyages to Australia and New Zealand until 1845; she was thereupon transferred to coast guard duty, in which she served until 1870, when she was finally sold out of the British Navy.

DARWIN'S PREFACE

I have stated in the preface to the first Edition of this work, and in the Zoology of the Voyage of the *Beagle*, that it was in consequence of a wish expressed by Captain Fitz Roy, of having some scientific person on board, accompanied by an offer from him of giving up part of his own accommodations, that I volunteered my services, which received, through the kindness of the hydrographer, Captain Beaufort, the sanction of the Lords of the Admiralty. As I feel that the opportunities which I enjoyed of studying the Natural History of the different countries we visited, have been wholly due to Captain Fitz Roy, I hope I may here be permitted to repeat my expression of gratitude to him; and to add that, during the five years we were together, I received from him the most cordial friendship and steady assistance. Both to Captain Fitz Roy and to all the Officers of the *Beagle*[1] I shall ever feel most thankful for the undeviating kindness with which I was treated during our long voyage.

This volume contains, in the form of a Journal, a history of our voyage, and a sketch of those observations in Natural History and Geology, which I think will possess some interest for the general reader. I have in this edition largely condensed and corrected some parts, and have added a little to others, in order to render the volume more fitted for popular reading; but I trust that naturalists will remember, that they must refer for details to the larger publications, which comprise the scientific results of the Expedition. The Zoology of the Voyage of the

[1] [Darwin] I must take this opportunity of returning my sincere thanks to Mr. Bynoe, the surgeon of the *Beagle*, for his very kind attention to me when I was ill at Valparaiso.

Beagle includes an account of the Fossil Mammalia, by Professor Owen; of the Living Mammalia, by Mr. Waterhouse; of the Birds, by Mr. Gould; of the Fish, by the Rev. L. Jenyns; and of the Reptiles, by Mr. Bell. I have appended to the descriptions of each species an account of its habits and range. These works, which I owe to the high talents and disinterested zeal of the above distinguished authors, could not have been undertaken, had it not been for the liberality of the Lords Commissioners of Her Majesty's Treasury, who, through the representation of the Right Honourable the Chancellor of the Exchequer, have been pleased to grant a sum of one thousand pounds towards defraying part of the expenses of publication.

I have myself published separate volumes on the "Structure and Distribution of Coral Reefs"; on the "Volcanic Islands visited during the Voyage of the *Beagle*"; and on the "Geology of South America." The sixth volume of the "Geological Transactions" contains two papers of mine on the Erratic Boulders and Volcanic Phenomena of South America. Messrs. Waterhouse, Walker, Newman, and White, have published several able papers on the Insects which were collected, and I trust that many others will hereafter follow. The plants from the southern parts of America will be given by Dr. J. Hooker, in his great work on the Botany of the Southern Hemisphere. The Flora of the Galapagos Archipelago is the subject of a separate memoir by him, in the "Linnean Transactions." The Reverend Professor Henslow has published a list of the plants collected by me at the Keeling Islands; and the Reverend J. M. Berkeley has described my cryptogamic plants.

I shall have the pleasure of acknowledging the great assistance which I have received from several other naturalists, in the course of this and my other works; but I must be here allowed to return my most sincere thanks to the Reverend Professor Henslow, who, when I was an under-graduate at Cambridge, was one chief means of giving me a taste for Natural History,—who, during my absence, took charge of the collections I sent home, and by his correspondence directed my endeavours,—and who, since my return, has constantly rendered me every assistance which the kindest friend could offer.

Down, Bromley, Kent.
June, 1845.

DARWIN'S POSTSCRIPT

I take the opportunity of a new edition of my Journal to correct a few errors. At page 84 I have stated that the majority of the shells which were embedded with the extinct mammals at Punta Alta, in Bahia Blanca, were still living species. These shells have since been examined (see "Geological Observations in South America," p. 83) by M. Alcide d'Orbigny, and he pronounces them all to be recent. M. Aug. Bravard has lately described, in a Spanish work ("Observaciones Geologicas," 1857), this district, and he believes that the bones of the extinct mammals were washed out of the underlying Pampean deposit, and subsequently became embedded with the still existing shells; but I am not convinced by his remarks. M. Bravard believes that the whole enormous Pampean deposit is a sub-aërial formation, like sand-dunes: this seems to me to be an untenable doctrine.

At page 379 I give a list of the birds inhabiting the Galapagos Archipelago. The progress of research has shown that some of these birds, which were then thought to be confined to the islands, occur on the American continent. The eminent ornithologist, Mr. Sclater, informs me that this is the case with the Strix punctatissima and Pyrocephalus nanus; and probably with the Otus galapagoensis and Zenaida galapagoensis: so that the number of endemic birds is reduced to twenty-three, or probably to twenty-one. Mr. Sclater thinks that one or two of these endemic forms should be ranked rather as varieties than species, which always seemed to me probable.

The snake mentioned at page 382, as being, on the authority of M. Bibron, the same with a Chilian species, is stated by Dr. Günter (Zoolog. Soc., Jan. 24th, 1859) to be a peculiar species, not known to inhabit any other country.

Feb. 1st, 1860.

CONTENTS

CHAPTER I

CHAPTER II

CHAPTER III

CHAPTER IV

CHAPTER X

CHAPTER XI

CHAPTER XII

CHAPTER XIII

CHAPTER XIV

THE VOYAGE OF THE BEAGLE

JOURNAL

CHAPTER I

ST. JAGO—CAPE DE VERD ISLANDS

Porto Praya — Ribeira Grande — Atmospheric Dust with Infusoria — Habits of a Sea-slug and Cuttle-fish — St. Paul's Rocks, non-volcanic — Singular Incrustations — Insects the first Colonists of Islands — Fernando Noronha — Bahia — Burnished Rocks — Habits of a Diodon — Pelagic Confervæ and Infusoria — Causes of discoloured Sea

After having been twice driven back by heavy south-western gales, Her Majesty's ship *Beagle,* a ten-gun brig, under the command of Captain Fitz Roy, R.N., sailed from Devonport on the 27th of December, 1831. The object of the expedition was to complete the survey of Patagonia and Tierra del Fuego, commenced under Captain King in 1826 to 1830—to survey the shores of Chile, Peru, and of some islands in the Pacific—and to carry a chain of chronometrical measurements[1] round the World. On the 6th of January we reached Teneriffe, but were prevented landing, by fears of our bringing the cholera:

[1] [Editor] Needed to fix longitudes. Longitude—angular distance east or west on the earth's surface—is measured by determining the difference between local time and time at the Royal Observatory, Greenwich, England (by international agreement, the location of the zero longitude meridian). Basic procedure is to note the time of the sun's highest ascent (local noon) on a clock kept at Greenwich time. Local noon will be one hour earlier or later for every 15 degrees east or west of Greenwich. Accurate clocks are indispensable to determining longitude; an error of 5 seconds in a ship's chronometer can result in a longitude error of as much as a mile and a third. Today, navigation chronometers are kept accurate with the aid of time signals from such radio stations as WWV, the station of the U. S. National Bureau of Standards.

the next morning we saw the sun rise behind the rugged outline of the Grand Canary island, and suddenly illumine the
Peak of Teneriffe, whilst the lower parts were veiled in fleecy
clouds. This was the first of many delightful days never to be
forgotten. On the 16th of January, 1832, we anchored at Porto
Praya, in St. Jago, the chief island of the Cape de Verd archipelago.

The neighbourhood of Porto Praya, viewed from the sea,
wears a desolate aspect. The volcanic fires of a past age, and
the scorching heat of a tropical sun, have in most places rendered the soil unfit for vegetation. The country rises in successive steps of table-land, interspersed with some truncate conical
hills, and the horizon is bounded by an irregular chain of more
lofty mountains. The scene, as beheld through the hazy atmosphere of this climate, is one of great interest; if, indeed,
a person, fresh from sea, and who has just walked, for the
first time, in a grove of cocoa-nut trees, can be a judge of
anything but his own happiness. The island would generally be
considered as very uninteresting; but to any one accustomed
only to an English landscape, the novel aspect of an utterly
sterile land possesses a grandeur which more vegetation might
spoil. A single green leaf can scarcely be discovered over wide
tracts of the lava plains; yet flocks of goats, together with a
few cows, contrive to exist. It rains very seldom, but during a
short portion of the year heavy torrents fall, and immediately
afterwards a light vegetation springs out of every crevice. This
soon withers; and upon such naturally formed hay the animals live. It had not now rained for an entire year. When the
island was discovered, the immediate neighbourhood of Porto
Praya was clothed with trees,[2] the reckless destruction of
which has caused here, as at St. Helena, and at some of the

Before radio, ships had to depend on the intrinsic accuracy of
their chronometers.

Fitz Roy was fond of and expert in the use of chronometers.
He put 22 aboard the *Beagle*, plus an instrument maker to look
after them. The *Beagle* also carried instruments which were to be
put ashore whenever the *Beagle* was in port for lunar transit and
other astronomical observations intended as a check on the chronometers. Fitz Roy obtained many accurate longitude determinations though these astronomical observations were not his cup of
tea and he seldom carried them out.

[2] [Darwin] I state this on the authority of Dr. E. Dieffenbach,
in his German translation of the first edition of this Journal.

Canary islands, almost entire sterility. The broad, flat-bottomed valleys, many of which serve during a few days only in the season as watercourses, are clothed with thickets of leafless bushes. Few living creatures inhabit these valleys. The commonest bird is a kingfisher (Dacelo Iagoensis), which tamely sits on the branches of the castor-oil plant, and thence darts on grasshoppers and lizards. It is brightly coloured, but not so beautiful as the European species: in its flight, manners, and place of habitation, which is generally in the driest valley, there is also a wide difference.

One day, two of the officers and myself rode to Ribeira Grande, a village a few miles eastward of Porto Praya. Until we reached the valley of St. Martin, the country presented its usual dull brown appearance; but here, a very small rill of water produces a most refreshing margin of luxuriant vegetation. In the course of an hour we arrived at Ribeira Grande, and were surprised at the sight of a large ruined fort and cathedral. This little town, before its harbour was filled up, was the principal place in the island: it now presents a melancholy, but very picturesque appearance. Having procured a black Padre for a guide, and a Spaniard who had served in the Peninsular war as an interpreter, we visited a collection of buildings, of which an ancient church formed the principal part. It is here the governors and captain-generals of the islands have been buried. Some of the tombstones recorded dates of the sixteenth century.[8] The heraldic ornaments were the only things in this retired place that reminded us of Europe. The church or chapel formed one side of a quadrangle, in the middle of which a large clump of bananas were growing. On another side was a hospital, containing about a dozen miserable-looking inmates.

We returned to the Vênda to eat our dinners. A considerable number of men, women, and children, all as black as jet, collected to watch us. Our companions were extremely merry; and everything we said or did was followed by their hearty laughter. Before leaving the town we visited the cathedral. It does not appear so rich as the smaller church, but boasts of a little organ, which sent forth singularly inharmonious cries. We presented the black priest with a few shillings, and the Spaniard, patting him on the head, said, with much candour, he thought his colour made no great difference. We

[8] [Darwin] The Cape de Verd Islands were discovered in 1449. There was a tombstone of a bishop with the date of 1571; and a crest of a hand and dagger, dated 1497.

then returned, as fast as the ponies would go, to Porto Praya.

Another day we rode to the village of St. Domingo, situated near the centre of the island. On a small plain which we crossed, a few stunted acacias were growing; their tops had been bent by the steady trade-wind, in a singular manner—some of them even at right angles to their trunks. The direction of the branches was exactly N.E. by N., and S.W. by S., and these natural vanes must indicate the prevailing direction of the force of the trade-wind. The travelling had made so little impression on the barren soil, that we here missed our track, and took that to Fuentes. This we did not find out till we arrived there; and we were afterwards glad of our mistake. Fuentes is a pretty village, with a small stream; and everything appeared to prosper well, excepting, indeed, that which ought to do so most—its inhabitants. The black children, completely naked, and looking very wretched, were carrying bundles of firewood half as big as their own bodies.

Near Fuentes we saw a large flock of guinea-fowl—probably fifty or sixty in number. They were extremely wary, and could not be approached. They avoided us, like partridges on a rainy day in September, running with their heads cocked up; and if pursued, they readily took to the wing.

The scenery of St. Domingo possesses a beauty totally unexpected, from the prevalent gloomy character of the rest of the island. The village is situated at the bottom of a valley, bounded by lofty and jagged walls of stratified lava. The black rocks afford a most striking contrast with the bright green vegetation, which follows the banks of a little stream of clear water. It happened to be a grand feast-day, and the village was full of people. On our return we overtook a party of about twenty young black girls, dressed in excellent taste; their black skins and snow-white linen being set off by coloured turbans and large shawls. As soon as we approached near, they suddenly all turned round, and covering the path with their shawls, sung with great energy a wild song, beating time with their hands upon their legs. We threw them some vintéms, which were received with screams of laughter, and we left them redoubling the noise of their song.

One morning the view was singularly clear; the distant mountains being projected with the sharpest outline, on a heavy bank of dark blue clouds. Judging from the appearance, and from similar cases in England, I supposed that the air was saturated with moisture. The fact, however, turned out quite the contrary. The hygrometer gave a difference of 29.6 degrees, between the temperature of the air, and the point at which dew was precipitated. This difference was nearly double that which I had observed on the previous mornings. This unusual degree of atmospheric dryness was accompanied by continual flashes of lightning. Is it not an uncommon case, thus to find a remarkable degree of aerial transparency with such a state of weather?

Generally the atmosphere is hazy; and this is caused by the falling of impalpably fine dust, which was found to have slightly injured the astronomical instruments. The morning before we anchored at Porto Praya, I collected a little packet of this brown-coloured fine dust, which appeared to have been filtered from the wind by the gauze of the vane at the masthead. Mr. Lyell has also given me four packets of dust which fell on a vessel a few hundred miles northward of these islands. Professor Ehrenberg[4] finds that this dust consists in great part of infusoria with siliceous shields, and of the siliceous tissue of plants. In five little packets which I sent him, he has ascertained no less than sixty-seven different organic forms! The infusoria, with the exception of two marine species, are all inhabitants of fresh-water. I have found no less than fifteen different accounts of dust having fallen on vessels when far out in the Atlantic. From the direction of the wind whenever it has fallen, and from its having always fallen during those months when the harmattan is known to raise clouds of dust high into the atmosphere, we may feel sure that it all comes from Africa. It is, however, a very singular fact, that, although Professor Ehrenberg knows many species of infusoria peculiar to Africa, he finds none of these in the dust which I sent him: on the other hand, he finds in it two species which hitherto he knows as living only in South America. The dust falls in such quantities as to dirty everything on board, and to hurt people's eyes; vessels even have run on shore owing to the obscurity of the atmosphere. It has often fallen on ships when several hun-

---

[4] [Darwin] I must take this opportunity of acknowledging the great kindness with which this illustrious naturalist has examined many of my specimens. I have sent (June, 1845) a full account of the falling of this dust to the Geological Society. [Christian Gottfried Ehrenberg was a German naturalist, born 1795 at Delitzsch, Prussia, died 1876 in Berlin, and noted particularly for his studies of microscopic plants and animals, which nineteenth-century biologists grouped under the name infusoria.—Ed.]

dred, and even more than a thousand miles from the coast of Africa, and at points sixteen hundred miles distant in a north and south direction. In some dust which was collected on a vessel three hundred miles from the land, I was much surprised to find particles of stone above the thousandth of an inch square, mixed with finer matter. After this fact one need not be surprised at the diffusion of the far lighter and smaller sporules of cryptogamic plants.

The geology of this island is the most interesting part of its natural history. On entering the harbour, a perfectly horizontal white band in the face of the sea cliff, may be seen running for some miles along the coast, and at the height of about forty-five feet above the water. Upon examination, this white stratum is found to consist of calcareous matter, with numerous shells embedded, most or all of which now exist on the neighbouring coast. It rests on ancient volcanic rocks, and has been covered by a stream of basalt, which must have entered the sea when the white shelly bed was lying at the bottom. It is interesting to trace the changes, produced by the heat of the overlying lava, on the friable mass, which in parts has been converted into a crystalline limestone, and in other parts into a compact spotted stone. Where the lime has been caught up by the scoriaceous fragments of the lower surface of the stream, it is converted into groups of beautifully radiated fibres resembling arragonite. The beds of lava rise in successive gently-sloping plains, towards the interior, whence the deluges of melted stone have originally proceeded. Within historical times, no signs of volcanic activity have, I believe, been manifested in any part of St. Jago. Even the form of a crater can but rarely be discovered on the summits of the many red cindery hills; yet the more recent streams can be distinguished on the coast, forming lines of cliffs of less height, but stretching out in advance of those belonging to an older series: the height of the cliffs thus affording a rude measure of the age of the streams.

During our stay, I observed the habits of some marine animals. A large Aplysia is very common. This sea-slug is about five inches long; and is of a dirty-yellowish colour, veined with purple. On each side of the lower surface, or foot, there is a broad membrane, which appears sometimes to act as a ventilator, in causing a current of water to flow over the dorsal branchiæ or lungs. It feeds on the delicate sea-weeds which grow among the stones in muddy and shallow water; and I found in its stomach several small pebbles, as in the gizzard of a bird. This slug, when disturbed, emits a very fine purplish-red fluid, which stains the water for the space of a foot around. Besides this means of defence, an acrid secretion, which is spread over its body, causes a sharp, stinging sensation, similar to that produced by the Physalia, or Portuguese man-of-war.

I was much interested, on several occasions, by watching the habits of an Octopus, or cuttle-fish. Although common in the pools of water left by the retiring tide, these animals were not easily caught. By means of their long arms and suckers, they could drag their bodies into very narrow crevices; and when thus fixed, it required great force to remove them. At other times they darted tail first, with the rapidity of an arrow, from one side of the pool to the other, at the same instant discolouring the water with a dark chestnut-brown ink. These animals also escape detection by a very extraordinary, chameleon-like power of changing their colour. They appear to vary their tints according to the nature of the ground over which they pass: when in deep water, their general shade was brownish purple, but when placed on the land, or in shallow water, this dark tint changed into one of a yellowish green. The colour, examined more carefully, was a French grey, with numerous minute spots of bright yellow: the former of these varied in intensity; the latter entirely disappeared and appeared again by turns. These changes were effected in such a manner, that clouds, varying in tint between a hyacinth red and a chestnut-brown,[5] were continually passing over the body. Any part, being subjected to a slight shock of galvanism, became almost black: a similar effect, but in a less degree, was produced by scratching the skin with a needle. These clouds, or blushes as they may be called, are said to be produced by the alternate expansion and contraction of minute vesicles containing variously coloured fluids.[6]

[5] [Darwin] So named according to Patrick Symes's nomenclature.

[6] [Darwin] See Encyclop. of Anat. and Physiol., article *Cephalopoda*. [As Darwin relates, the color changes of the cuttlefish are produced by the alternate expansion and contraction of minute sacs—now called chromatophores—in the skin. Modern study has shown, however, that the chromatophores contain pigment granules rather than colored fluids. Three types of chromatophore—one containing a yellow pigment, one red and one brown or black—are present. Together with another type of cell, the iridocyte, which has a pearly white sheen, the chromatophores give the cuttlefish a range of color change that is still something to marvel at.—Ed.]

This cuttle-fish displayed its chameleon-like power both during the act of swimming and whilst remaining stationary at the bottom. I was much amused by the various arts to escape detection used by one individual, which seemed fully aware that I was watching it. Remaining for a time motionless, it would then stealthily advance an inch or two, like a cat after a mouse; sometimes changing its colour: it thus proceeded, till having gained a deeper part, it darted away, leaving a dusky train of ink to hide the hole into which it had crawled.

While looking for marine animals, with my head about two feet above the rocky shore, I was more than once saluted by a jet of water, accompanied by a slight grating noise. At first I could not think what it was, but afterwards I found out that it was this cuttle-fish, which, though concealed in a hole, thus often led me to its discovery. That it possesses the power of ejecting water there is no doubt, and it appeared to me that it could certainly take good aim by directing the tube or siphon on the under side of its body. From the difficulty which these animals have in carrying their heads, they cannot crawl with ease when placed on the ground. I observed that one which I kept in the cabin was slightly phosphorescent in the dark.

St. Paul's Rocks.—In crossing the Atlantic we hove-to, during the morning of February 16th, close to the island of St. Paul's. This cluster of rocks is situated in 0° 58′ north latitude, and 29° 15′ west longitude. It is 540 miles distant from the coast of America, and 350 from the island of Fernando Noronha. The highest point is only fifty feet above the level of the sea, and the entire circumference is under three-quarters of a mile. This small point rises abruptly out of the depths of the ocean. Its mineralogical constitution is not simple; in some parts the rock is of a cherty, in others of a felspathic nature, including thin veins of serpentine. It is a remarkable fact, that all the many small islands, lying far from any continent, in the Pacific, Indian, and Atlantic Oceans, with the exception of the Seychelles and this little point of rock, are, I believe, composed either of coral or of erupted matter. The volcanic nature of these oceanic islands is evidently an extension of that law, and the effect of those same causes, whether chemical or mechanical, from which it results that a vast majority of the volcanoes now in action stand either near sea-coasts or as islands in the midst of the sea.

The rocks of St. Paul appear from a distance of a brilliantly white colour. This is partly owing to the dung of a vast multitude of seafowl, and partly to a coating of a hard glossy substance with a pearly lustre, which is intimately united to the surface of the rocks. This, when examined with a lens, is found to consist of numerous exceedingly thin layers, its total thickness being about the tenth of an inch. It contains much animal matter, and its origin, no doubt, is due to the action of the rain or spray on the birds' dung. Below some small masses of guano at Ascension, and on the Abrolhos Islets, I found certain stalactitic branching bodies, formed apparently in the same manner as the thin white coating on these rocks. The branching bodies so closely resembled in general appearance certain nulliporæ (a family of hard calcareous sea-plants), that in lately looking hastily over my collection I did not perceive the difference. The globular extremities of the branches are of a pearly texture, like the enamel of teeth, but so hard as just to scratch plate-glass. I may here mention, that on a part of the coast of Ascension, where there is a vast accumulation of shelly sand, an incrustation is deposited on the tidal rocks, by the water of the sea, resembling, as represented in the woodcut, certain cryptogamic plants (Marchantiæ) often seen on damp walls. The surface of the fronds is beautifully glossy; and those parts formed where fully exposed to the light, are of a jet black colour, but those shaded under ledges are only grey. I have shown specimens of this incrustation to several geologists, and they all thought that they were of volcanic or igneous origin!

In its hardness and translucency—in its polish, equal to that of the finest oliva-shell—in the bad smell given out, and loss of colour under the blow-pipe—it shows a close similarity with living sea-shells. Moreover, in sea-shells, it is known that the parts habitually covered and shaded by the mantle of the animal, are of a paler colour than those fully exposed to the light, just as is the case with this incrustation. When we remember that lime, either as a phosphate or carbonate, enters into the composition of the hard parts, such as bones and shells, of all living animals, it is an interesting physiological fact[7] to find substances harder than the enamel of teeth, and coloured surfaces as well polished as those of a fresh shell, reformed through inorganic means from dead organic matter—mocking, also, in shape some of the lower vegetable productions.

We found on St. Paul's only two kinds of birds—the booby and the noddy. The former is a species of gannet, and the latter a tern. Both are of a tame and stupid disposition, and are so unaccustomed to visitors, that I could have killed any number of them with my geological hammer. The booby lays her eggs on the bare rock; but the tern makes a very simple nest with seaweed. By the side of many of these nests a small flying-fish was placed; which, I suppose, had been brought by the male bird for its partner. It was amusing to watch how quickly a large and active crab (Graspus), which inhabits the crevices of the rock, stole the fish from the side of the nest, as soon as we had disturbed the parent birds. Sir W. Symonds, one of the few persons who have landed here, informs me that he saw the crabs dragging even the young birds out of their nests, and devouring them. Not a single plant, not even a lichen, grows on this islet; yet it is inhabited by several insects and spiders. The following list completes, I believe, the terrestrial fauna: a fly (Olfersia) living on the booby, and a tick which must have come here as a parasite on the birds; a small brown moth, belonging to a genus that feeds on feathers; a beetle (Quedius)

---

[7] [Darwin] Mr. Horner and Sir David Brewster have described (Philosophical Transactions, 1836, p. 65) a singular "artificial substance resembling shell." It is deposited in fine, transparent, highly polished, brown-coloured laminæ, possessing peculiar optical properties, on the inside of a vessel, in which cloth, first prepared with glue and then with lime, is made to revolve rapidly in water. It is much softer, more transparent, and contains more animal matter, than the natural incrustation at Ascension; but we here again see the strong tendency which carbonate of lime and animal matter evince to form a solid substance allied to shell.

and a woodlouse from beneath the dung; and lastly, numerous spiders, which I suppose prey on these small attendants and scavengers of the waterfowl. The often repeated description of the stately palm and other noble tropical plants, then birds, and lastly man, taking possession of the coral islets as soon as formed, in the Pacific, is probably not quite correct; I fear it destroys the poetry of this story, that feather and dirt-feeding and parasitic insects and spiders should be the first inhabitants of newly-formed oceanic land.

The smallest rock in the tropical seas, by giving a foundation for the growth of innumerable kinds of sea-weed and compound animals, supports likewise a large number of fish. The sharks and the seamen in the boats maintained a constant struggle which should secure the greater share of the prey caught by the fishing-lines. I have heard that a rock near the Bermudas, lying many miles out at sea, and at a considerable depth, was first discovered by the circumstance of fish having been observed in the neighbourhood.

FERNANDO NORONHA, *Feb. 20th.*—As far as I was enabled to observe, during the few hours we stayed at this place, the constitution of the island is volcanic, but probably not of a recent date. The most remarkable feature is a conical hill, about one thousand feet high, the upper part of which is exceedingly steep, and on one side overhangs its base. The rock is phonolite, and is divided into irregular columns. On viewing one of these isolated masses, at first one is inclined to believe that it has been suddenly pushed up in a semi-fluid state. At St. Helena, however, I ascertained that some pinnacles, of a nearly similar figure and constitution, had been formed by the injection of melted rock into yielding strata, which thus had formed the moulds for these gigantic obelisks. The whole island is covered with wood; but from the dryness of the climate there is no appearance of luxuriance. Halfway up the mountain, some great masses of the columnar rock, shaded by laurel-like trees, and ornamented by others covered with fine pink flowers but without a single leaf, gave a pleasing effect to the nearer parts of the scenery.

BAHIA, OR SAN SALVADOR. BRAZIL, *Feb. 29th.*[8]—The day has passed delightfully. Delight itself, however, is a weak term to

8 [Editor] When the *Beagle* anchored at Bahia, Brazil was in the tenth year of independence. As in other Latin American countries, the early years of her nationhood were turbulent. Brazil became

express the feelings of a naturalist who, for the first time, has wandered by himself in a Brazilian forest. The elegance of the grasses, the novelty of the parasitical plants, the beauty of the flowers, the glossy green of the foliage, but above all the general luxuriance of the vegetation, filled me with admiration. A most paradoxical mixture of sound and silence pervades the shady parts of the wood. The noise from the insects is so loud, that it may be heard even in a vessel anchored several hundred yards from the shore; yet within the recesses of the forest a universal silence appears to reign. To a person fond of natural history, such a day as this brings with it a deeper pleasure than he can ever hope to experience again. After wandering about for some hours, I returned to the landing-place; but, before reaching it, I was overtaken by a tropical storm. I tried to find shelter under a tree, which was so thick that it would never have been penetrated by common English rain; but here, in a couple of minutes, a little torrent flowed down the trunk. It is to this violence of the rain that we must attribute the verdure at the bottom of the thickest woods: if the showers were like those of a colder clime, the greater part would be absorbed or evaporated before it reached the ground. I will not at present attempt to describe the gaudy scenery of this noble bay, because, in our homeward voyage, we called here a second time, and I shall then have occasion to remark on it.

Along the whole coast of Brazil, for a length of at least 2000 miles, and certainly for a considerable space inland, wherever solid rock occurs, it belongs to a granitic formation. The circumstance of this enormous area being constituted of materials which most geologists believe to have been crystallized when heated under pressure, gives rise to many curious reflections. Was this effect produced beneath the depths of a profound ocean? or did a covering of strata formerly extend over it,

---

independent of Portugal in 1822 through a revolt led by Dom Pedro, son of the king of Portugal; Dom Pedro then became emperor of Brazil. He had no greater talent for governing, however, than other members of Portugal's ruling House of Braganza, and soon had Brazil embroiled in a disastrous war with Argentina over Uruguay. In 1831, he abdicated in favor of his five-year-old son, Dom Pedro II. A regency ruled in the child-emperor's name until 1840, when the parliament, weary of a long succession of provincial revolts and cabals under the regency, handed rule over to the fourteen-year-old emperor himself. Dom Pedro II reigned until 1889, when Brazil finally became a republic.

which has since been removed? Can we believe that any power, acting for a time short of infinity, could have denuded the granite over so many thousand square leagues?

On a point not far from the city, where a rivulet entered the sea, I observed a fact connected with a subject discussed by Humboldt.[9] At the cataracts of the great rivers Orinoco, Nile, and Congo, the syenitic rocks are coated by a black substance, appearing as if they had been polished with plumbago. The layer is of extreme thinness; and on analysis by Berzelius it was found to consist of the oxides of manganese and iron. In the Orinoco it occurs on the rocks periodically washed by the floods, and in those parts alone where the stream is rapid; or, as the Indians say, "the rocks are black where the waters are white." Here the coating is of a rich brown instead of a black colour, and seems to be composed of ferruginous matter alone. Hand specimens fail to give a just idea of these brown burnished stones which glitter in the sun's rays. They occur only within the limits of the tidal waves; and as the rivulet slowly trickles down, the surf must supply the polishing power of the cataracts in the great rivers. In like manner, the rise and fall of the tide probably answer to the periodical inundations; and thus the same effects are produced under apparently different but really similar circumstances. The origin, however, of these coatings of metallic oxides, which seem as if cemented to the rocks, is not understood; and no reason, I believe, can be assigned for their thickness remaining the same.

One day I was amused by watching the habits of the Diodon

9 [Darwin] Pers. Narr., vol. v, pt. 1, p. 18. [The Humboldt cited by Darwin is Friedrich Heinrich Alexander, Baron von Humboldt —better known simply as Alexander von Humboldt, the greatest naturalist and scientific traveler of his day. Born at Berlin in 1769, he recieved an education in languages and sciences at five universities that uniquely fitted him for one of history's great journeys of exploration—his trip of 1799 to 1804 to Mexico and South America. During the journey, he explored the Orinoco, climbed the Andes, laid the basis for the scientific study of tropical storms, introduced isothermal lines as a means of comparing climate in different countries and at different altitudes in mountain regions, and discovered that the earth's magnetic field gradually weakens as the equator is neared. A universal genius, he was equally at home in the zoology laboratory, the astronomical observatory and the fashionable salon, and he was also successful as a diplomat. He became the most famous person in Europe after Napoleon. He died in Berlin in 1859, six months short of his ninetieth birthday.—Ed.]

antennatus, which was caught swimming near the shore. This fish, with its flabby skin, is well known to possess the singular power of distending itself into a nearly spherical form. After having been taken out of the water for a short time, and then again immersed in it, a considerable quantity both of water and air is absorbed by the mouth, and perhaps likewise by the branchial orifices. This process is effected by two methods: the air is swallowed, and is then forced into the cavity of the body, its return being prevented by a muscular contraction which is externally visible: but the water enters in a gentle stream through the mouth, which is kept wide open and motionless; this latter action must, therefore, depend on suction. The skin about the abdomen is much looser than that on the back; hence, during the inflation, the lower surface becomes far more distended than the upper; and the fish, in consequence, floats with its back downwards. Cuvier doubts whether the Diodon in this position is able to swim; but not only can it thus move forward in a straight line, but it can turn round to either side. This latter movement is effected solely by the aid of the pectoral fins; the tail being collapsed, and not used. From the body being buoyed up with so much air, the branchial openings are out of water, but a stream drawn in by the mouth constantly flows through them.

The fish, having remained in this distended state for a short time, generally expelled the air and water with considerable force from the branchial apertures and mouth. It could emit, at will, a certain portion of the water; and it appears, therefore, probable that this fluid is taken in partly for the sake of regulating its specific gravity. This Diodon possessed several means of defence. It could give a severe bite, and could eject water from its mouth to some distance, at the same time making a curious noise by the movement of its jaws. By the inflation of its body, the papillæ, with which the skin is covered, become erect and pointed. But the most curious circumstance is, that it secretes from the skin of its belly, when handled, a most beautiful carmine-red fibrous matter, which stains ivory and paper in so permanent a manner, that the tint is retained with all its brightness to the present day: I am quite ignorant of the nature and use of this secretion. I have heard from Dr. Allan of Forres, that he has frequently found a Diodon, floating alive and distended, in the stomach of the shark; and that on several occasions he has known it eat its way, not only through the coats of the stomach, but through the sides of the monster, which has thus been killed. Who would ever have imagined that a little soft fish could have destroyed the great and savage shark?

March 18*th*.—We sailed from Bahia. A few days afterwards, when not far distant from the Abrolhos Islets,[10] my attention was called to a reddish-brown appearance in the sea. The whole surface of the water, as it appeared under a weak lens, seemed as if covered by chopped bits of hay, with their ends jagged. These are minute cylindrical confervæ,[11] in bundles or rafts of from twenty to sixty in each. Mr. Berkeley informs me that they are the same species (Trichodesmium erythræum) with that found over large spaces in the Red Sea, and whence its name of Red Sea is derived.[12] Their numbers must be infinite: the ship passed through several bands of them, one of which was about ten yards wide, and, judging from the mud-like colour of the water, at least two and a half miles long. In almost every long voyage some account is given of these confervæ. They appear especially common in the sea near Australia; and off Cape Leeuwin I found an allied, but smaller and apparently different species. Captain Cook, in his third voyage, remarks, that the sailors gave to this appearance the name of sea-sawdust.

Near Keeling Atoll, in the Indian Ocean, I observed many little masses of confervæ a few inches square, consisting of long cylindrical threads of excessive thinness, so as to be barely visible to the naked eye, mingled with other rather larger bodies, finely conical at both ends. Two of these are shown in the

woodcut united together. They vary in length from .04 to .06, and even to .08 of an inch in length; and in diameter from .006 to .008 of an inch. Near one extremity of the cylindrical part, a green septum, formed of granular matter, and thickest in the middle, may generally be seen. This, I believe, is the bottom of a most delicate, colourless sac, composed of a pulpy substance, which lines the exterior case, but does not extend

10 [Editor] A group of small, low islands off the Brazilian coast, halfway from Bahia to Rio de Janeiro.

11 [Editor] A nineteenth-century term for filamentous algae.

12 [Darwin] M. Montagne, in Comptes Rendus, &c., Juillet, 1844; and Annal. des Scienc. Nat., Dec. 1844.

within the extreme conical points. In some specimens, small but perfect spheres of brownish granular matter supplied the places of the septa; and I observed the curious process by which they were produced. The pulpy matter of the internal coating suddenly grouped itself into lines, some of which assumed a form radiating from a common centre; it then continued, with an irregular and rapid movement, to contract itself, so that in the course of a second the whole was united into a perfect little sphere, which occupied the position of the septum at one end of the now quite hollow case. The formation of the granular sphere was hastened by any accidental injury. I may add, that frequently a pair of these bodies were attached to each other, as represented above, cone beside cone, at that end where the septum occurs.

I will here add a few other observations connected with the discoloration of the sea from organic causes. On the coast of Chile, a few leagues north of Concepcion, the *Beagle* one day passed through great bands of muddy water, exactly like that of a swollen river; and again, a degree south of Valparaiso, when fifty miles from the land, the same appearance was still more extensive. Some of the water placed in a glass was of a pale reddish tint; and, examined under a microscope, was seen to swarm with minute animalcula darting about, and often exploding. Their shape is oval, and contracted in the middle by a ring of vibrating curved ciliæ. It was, however, very difficult to examine them with care, for almost the instant motion ceased, even while crossing the field of vision, their bodies burst. Sometimes both ends burst at once, sometimes only one, and a quantity of coarse, brownish, granular matter was ejected. The animal an instant before bursting expanded to half again its natural size; and the explosion took place about fifteen seconds after the rapid progressive motion had ceased: in a few cases it was preceded for a short interval by a rotatory movement on the longer axis. About two minutes after any number were isolated in a drop of water, they thus perished. The animals move with the narrow apex forwards, by the aid of their vibratory ciliæ, and generally by rapid starts. They are exceedingly minute, and quite invisible to the naked eye, only covering a space equal to the square of the thousandth of an inch. Their numbers were infinite; for the smallest drop of water which I could remove contained very many. In one day we passed through two spaces of water thus stained, one of which alone must have extended over several square miles.

What incalculable numbers of these microscopical animals! The colour of the water, as seen at some distance, was like that of a river which has flowed through a red clay district; but under the shade of the vessel's side it was quite as dark as chocolate. The line where the red and blue water joined was distinctly defined. The weather for some days previously had been calm, and the ocean abounded, to an unusual degree, with living creatures.[13]

In the sea around Tierra del Fuego, and at no great distance from the land, I have seen narrow lines of water of a bright red colour, from the number of crustacea, which somewhat resemble in form large prawns. The sealers call them whale-food. Whether whales feed on them I do not know; but terns, cormorants, and immense herds of great unwieldy seals derive, on some parts of the coast, their chief sustenance from these swimming crabs.[14] Seamen invariably attribute the discoloration of the water to spawn; but I found this to be the case only on one occasion. At the distance of several leagues from the Archipelago of the Galapagos, the ship sailed through three strips of a dark yellowish, or mud-like water; these strips were some miles long, but only a few yards wide, and they were separated from the surrounding water by a sinuous yet distinct margin. The colour was caused by little gelatinous balls, about the fifth of an inch in diameter, in which numerous minute spherical ovules were embedded: they were of two distinct kinds, one being of a reddish colour and of a different shape from the other. I cannot form a conjecture as to what two kinds of animals these belonged. Captain Colnett remarks, that

[13] [Darwin] M. Lesson (Voyage de la *Coquille,* tom. i. p. 255) mentions red water off Lima, apparently produced by the same cause. Peron, the distinguished naturalist, in the Voyage aux Terres Australes, gives no less than twelve references to voyagers who have alluded to the discoloured waters of the sea (vol. ii. p. 239). To the references given by Peron may be added, Humboldt's Pers. Narr., vol. vi. p. 804; Flinders' Voyage, vol. i. p. 92; Labillardière, vol. i. p. 287; Ulloa's Voyage; Voyage of the *Astrolabe* and of the *Coquille;* Captain King's Survey of Australia, &c.

[14] [Editor] Darwin's "swimming crabs" are now known as Euphausid shrimp. Great masses of Euphausid shrimp or krill (as whalers call them) are found in the Antarctic, where they constitute the principal food of the 100 to 150 ton blue whale, the greatest creature in the sea, and its not-much-smaller cousin, the fin whale. Unhappily, modern whaling has brought both the blue and the fin whale near extinction.

this appearance is very common among the Galapagos Islands, and that the direction of the bands indicates that of the currents; in the described case, however, the line was caused by the wind. The only other appearance which I have to notice, is a thin oily coat on the water which displays iridescent colours. I saw a considerable tract of the ocean thus covered on the coast of Brazil; the seamen attributed it to the putrefying carcass of some whale, which probably was floating at no great distance. I do not here mention the minute gelatinous particles, hereafter to be referred to, which are frequently dispersed throughout the water, for they are not sufficiently abundant to create any change of colour.

There are two circumstances in the above accounts which appear remarkable: first, how do the various bodies which form the bands with defined edges keep together? In the case of the prawn-like crabs, their movements were as coinstantaneous as in a regiment of soldiers; but this cannot happen from any thing like voluntary action with the ovules, or the confervæ, nor is it probable among the infusoria. Secondly, what causes the length and narrowness of the bands? The appearance so much resembles that which may be seen in every torrent, where the stream uncoils into long streaks the froth collected in the eddies, that I must attribute the effect to a similar action either of the currents of the air or sea. Under this supposition we must believe that the various organized bodies are produced in certain favourable places, and are thence removed by the set of either wind or water. I confess, however, there is a very great difficulty in imagining any one spot to be the birthplace of the millions of millions of animalcula and confervæ: for whence come the germs at such points?—the parent bodies having been distributed by the winds and waves over the immense ocean. But on no other hypothesis can I understand their linear grouping. I may add that Scoresby remarks, that green water abounding with pelagic animals is invariably found in a certain part of the Arctic Sea.

CHAPTER II

RIO DE JANEIRO

Rio de Janeiro — Excursion north of Cape Frio — Great Evaporation — Slavery — Botofogo Bay — Terrestrial Planariæ — Clouds on the Corcovado — Heavy Rain — Musical Frogs — Phosphorescent Insects — Elater, springing powers of — Blue Haze — Noise made by a Butterfly — Entomology — Ants — Wasp killing a Spider — Parasitical Spider — Artifices of an Epeira — Gregarious Spider — Spider with an unsymmetrical Web

April 4th to July 5th, 1832.[1]—A few days after our arrival I became acquainted with an Englishman who was going to visit his estate, situated, rather more than a hundred miles from the capital, to the northward of Cape Frio. I gladly accepted his kind offer of allowing me to accompany him.

April 8th.—Our party amounted to seven. The first stage was very interesting. The day was powerfully hot, and as we passed through the woods, every thing was motionless, excepting the large and brilliant butterflies, which lazily fluttered about. The view seen when crossing the hills behind Praia Grande was most beautiful; the colours were intense, and the prevailing tint a dark blue; the sky and the calm waters of the bay vied with each other in splendour. After passing through some cultivated country, we entered a forest, which in the grandeur of all its parts could not be exceeded. We arrived by midday at Ithacaia; this small village is situated on a plain, and round the central house are the huts of the negroes. These, from their regular form and position, reminded me of the drawings of the Hottentot habitations in Southern Africa. As the moon

[1] [Editor] During this three-month interval, the *Beagle* made a trip back to Bahia to check its longitude determinations. Darwin rejoined the ship when it returned to Rio.

rose early, we determined to start the same evening for our
sleeping-place at the Lagoa Marica. As it was growing dark
we passed under one of the massive, bare, and steep hills of
granite which are so common in this country. This spot is notorious from having been, for a long time, the residence of
some runaway slaves,[2] who, by cultivating a little ground near
the top, contrived to eke out a subsistence. At length they were
discovered, and a party of soldiers being sent, the whole were
seized with the exception of one old woman, who, sooner than
again be`led into slavery, dashed herself to pieces from the
summit of the mountain. In a Roman matron this would have
been called the noble love of freedom: in a poor negress it is
mere brutal obstinacy. We continued riding for some hours.
For the few last miles the road was intricate, and it passed
through a desert waste of marshes and lagoons. The scene by
the dimmed light of the moon was most desolate. A few fireflies flitted by us; and the solitary snipe, as it rose, uttered its
plaintive cry. The distant and sullen roar of the sea scarcely
broke the stillness of the night.

April 9th.—We left our miserable sleeping-place before sunrise. The road passed through a narrow sandy plain, lying between the sea and the interior salt lagoons. The number of
beautiful fishing birds, such as egrets and cranes, and the succulent plants assuming most fantastical forms, gave to the scene
an interest which it would not otherwise have possessed. The
few stunted trees were loaded with parasitical plants, among
which the beauty and delicious fragrance of some of the or-
chidæ were most to be admired. As the sun rose, the day
became extremely hot, and the reflection of the light and heat
from the white sand was very distressing. We dined at Mandetiba; the thermometer in the shade being 84°. The beautiful
view of the distant wooded hills, reflected in the perfectly calm
water of an extensive lagoon, quite refreshed us. As the vênda[3]
here was a very good one, and I have the pleasant, but rare
remembrance, of an excellent dinner, I will be grateful and
presently describe it, as the type of its class. These houses are
often large, and are built of thick upright posts, with boughs
interwoven, and afterwards plastered. They seldom have floors,

[2] [Editor] Although Brazil signed a treaty with England to end
the slave trade in 1826, the importation of slaves into Brazil was
not ended until 1853, and slavery itself was not finally ended
until 1888.

[3] [Darwin] Vênda, the Portuguese name for an inn.

and never glazed windows; but are generally pretty well roofed. Universally the front part is open, forming a kind of verandah, in which tables and benches are placed. The bedrooms join on each side, and here the passenger may sleep as comfortably as he can, on a wooden platform, covered by a thin straw mat. The vênda stands in a courtyard, where the horses are fed. On first arriving, it was our custom to unsaddle the horses and give them their Indian corn; then, with a low bow, to ask the senhôr to do us the favour to give us something to eat. "Any thing you choose, sir," was his usual answer. For the few first times, vainly I thanked providence for having guided us to so good a man. The conversation proceeding, the case universally became deplorable. "Any fish can you do us the favour of giving?"—"Oh! no, sir."—"Any soup?"—"No, sir." —"Any bread?"—"Oh! no, sir."—"Any dried meat?"—"Oh! no, sir." If we were lucky, by waiting a couple of hours, we obtained fowls, rice, and farinha. It not unfrequently happened, that we were obliged to kill, with stones, the poultry for our own supper. When, thoroughly exhausted by fatigue and hunger, we timorously hinted that we should be glad of our meal, the pompous, and (though true) most unsatisfactory answer was, "It will be ready when it is ready." If we had dared to remonstrate any further, we should have been told to proceed on our journey, as being too impertinent. The hosts are most ungracious and disagreeable in their manners; their houses and their persons are often filthily dirty; the want of the accommodation of forks, knives, and spoons is common; and I am sure no cottage or hovel in England could be found in a state so utterly destitute of every comfort. At Campos Novos, however, we fared sumptuously; having rice and fowls, biscuit, wine, and spirits, for dinner; coffee in the evening, and fish with coffee for breakfast. All this, with good food for the horses, only cost 2s. 6d. per head. Yet the host of this vênda, being asked if he knew any thing of a whip which one of the party had lost, gruffly answered, "How should I know? why did you not take care of it?—I suppose the dogs have eaten it."

Leaving Mandetiba, we continued to pass through an intricate wilderness of lakes; in some of which were fresh, in others salt water shells. Of the former kind, I found a Limnæa in great numbers in a lake, into which, the inhabitants assured me that the sea enters once a year, and sometimes oftener, and makes the water quite salt. I have no doubt many interesting facts, in relation to marine and fresh water animals, might be observed in this chain of lagoons, which skirt the coast of Brazil. M. Gay[4] has stated that he found in the neighbourhood of Rio, shells of the marine genera solen and mytilus, and fresh water ampullariæ, living together in brackish water. I also frequently observed in the lagoon near the Botanic Garden, where the water is only a little less salt than in the sea, a species of hydrophilus, very similar to a water-beetle common in the ditches of England: in the same lake the only shell belonged to a genus generally found in estuaries.

Leaving the coast for a time, we again entered the forest. The trees were very lofty, and remarkable, compared with those of Europe, from the whiteness of their trunks. I see by my note-book, "wonderful and beautiful, flowering parasites," invariably struck me as the most novel object in these grand scenes. Travelling onwards we passed through tracts of pasturage, much injured by the enormous conical ants' nests, which were nearly twelve feet high. They gave to the plain exactly the appearance of the mud volcanos at Jorullo, as figured by Humboldt. We arrived at Engenhodo after it was dark, having been ten hours on horseback. I never ceased, during the whole journey, to be surprised at the amount of labour which the horses were capable of enduring; they appeared also to recover from any injury much sooner than those of our English breed. The Vampire bat is often the cause of much trouble, by biting the horses on their withers. The injury is generally not so much owing to the loss of blood, as to the inflammation which the pressure of the saddle afterwards produces. The whole circumstance has lately been doubted in England; I was therefore fortunate in being present when one (Desmodus d'orbignyi, Wat.) was actually caught on a horse's back. We were bivouacking late one evening near Coquimbo, in Chile, when my servant, noticing that one of the horses was very restive, went to see what was the matter, and fancying he could distinguish something, suddenly put his hand on the beast's withers, and secured the vampire. In the morning the spot where the bite had been inflicted was easily distinguished from being slightly swollen and bloody. The third day afterwards we rode the horse, without any ill effects.

April 13*th*.—After three days' travelling we arrived at Socêgo, the estate of Senhôr Manuel Figuireda, a relation of one of our party. The house was simple, and, though like a

[4] [Darwin] Annales des Sciences Naturelles for 1833.

barn in form, was well suited to the climate. In the sitting-room gilded chairs and sofas were oddly contrasted with the white-washed walls, thatched roof, and windows without glass. The house, together with the granaries, the stables, and workshops for the blacks, who had been taught various trades, formed a rude kind of quadrangle; in the centre of which a large pile of coffee was drying. These buildings stand on a little hill, over-looking the cultivated ground, and surrounded on every side by a wall of dark green luxuriant forest. The chief produce of this part of the country is coffee. Each tree is supposed to yield annually, on an average, two pounds; but some give as much as eight. Mandioca or cassada is likewise cultivated in great quantity. Every part of this plant is useful: the leaves and stalks are eaten by the horses, and the roots are ground into a pulp, which, when pressed dry and baked, forms the farinha, the principal article of sustenance in the Brazils. It is a curious, though well-known fact, that the juice of this most nutritious plant is highly poisonous. A few years ago a cow died at this Fazênda, in consequence of having drunk some of it. Senhôr Figuireda told me that he had planted, the year before, one bag of feijaô or beans, and three of rice; the former of which pro-duced eighty, and the latter three hundred and twenty fold. The pasturage supports a fine stock of cattle, and the woods are so full of game, that a deer had been killed on each of the three previous days. This profusion of food showed itself at dinner, where, if the tables did not groan, the guests surely did: for each person is expected to eat of every dish. One day, hav-ing, as I thought, nicely calculated so that nothing should go away untasted, to my utter dismay a roast turkey and a pig appeared in all their substantial reality. During the meals, it was the employment of a man to drive out of the room sundry old hounds, and dozens of little black children, which crawled in together, at every opportunity. As long as the idea of slavery could be banished, there was something exceedingly fascinating in this simple and patriarchal style of living: it was such a per-fect retirement and independence from the rest of the world. As soon as any stranger is seen arriving, a large bell is set tolling, and generally some small cannon are fired. The event is thus announced to the rocks and woods, but to nothing else. One morning I walked out an hour before daylight to admire the solemn stillness of the scene; at last, the silence was broken by the morning hymn, raised on high by the whole body of the blacks; and in this manner their daily work is generally begun.

On such fazêndas as these, I have no doubt the slaves pass happy and contented lives. On Saturday and Sunday they work for themselves, and in this fertile climate the labour of two days is sufficient to support a man and his family for the whole week.

April 14th.—Leaving Socêgo, we rode to another estate on the Rio Macâe, which was the last patch of cultivated ground in that direction. The estate was two and a half miles long, and the owner had forgotten how many broad. Only a very small piece had been cleared, yet almost every acre was capable of yielding all the various rich productions of a tropical land. Considering the enormous area of Brazil, the proportion of cultivated ground can scarcely be considered as any thing, compared to that which is left in the state of nature: at some future age, how vast a population it will support! During the second day's journey we found the road so shut up, that it was necessary that a man should go ahead with a sword to cut away the creepers. The forest abounded with beautiful objects; among which the tree ferns, though not large, were, from their bright green foliage, and the elegant curvature of their fronds, most worthy of admiration. In the evening it rained very heavily, and although the thermometer stood at 65°, I felt very cold. As soon as the rain ceased, it was curious to observe the extraordinary evaporation which commenced over the whole extent of the forest. At the height of a hundred feet the hills were buried in a dense white vapour, which rose like columns of smoke from the most thickly-wooded parts, and especially from the valleys. I observed this phenomenon on several occasions: I suppose it is owing to the large surface of foliage, previously heated by the sun's rays.

While staying at this estate, I was very nearly being an eye-witness to one of those atrocious acts which can only take place in a slave country. Owing to a quarrel and a law-suit, the owner was on the point of taking all the women and children from the male slaves, and selling them separately at the public auction at Rio. Interest, and not any feeling of compassion, prevented this act. Indeed, I do not believe the inhumanity of separating thirty families, who had lived together for many years, even occurred to the owner. Yet I will pledge myself, that in humanity and good feeling he was superior to the common run of men. It may be said there exists no limit to the blindness of interest and selfish habit. I may mention one very trifling anecdote, which at the time struck me more forcibly than any story of cruelty. I was crossing a ferry with a negro, who was uncommonly stupid. In endeavouring to make him understand, I talked loud, and made signs, in doing which I passed my hand near his face. He, I suppose, thought I was in a passion, and was going to strike him; for instantly, with a frightened look and half-shut eyes, he dropped his hands. I shall never forget my feelings of surprise, disgust, and shame, at seeing a great powerful man afraid even to ward off a blow, directed, as he thought, at his face. This man had been trained to a degradation lower than the slavery of the most helpless animal.

April 18*th*.—In returning we spent two days at Socêgo, and I employed them in collecting insects in the forest. The greater number of trees, although so lofty, are not more than three or four feet in circumference. There are, of course, a few of much greater dimension. Senhôr Manuel was then making a canoe 70 feet in length from a solid trunk, which had originally been 110 feet long, and of great thickness. The contrast of palm trees, growing amidst the common branching kinds, never fails to give the scene an intertropical character. Here the woods were ornamented by the Cabbage Palm—one of the most beautiful of its family. With a stem so narrow that it might be clasped with the two hands, it waves its elegant head at the height of forty or fifty feet above the ground. The woody creepers, themselves covered by other creepers, were of great thickness: some which I measured were two feet in circumference. Many of the older trees presented a very curious appearance from the tresses of a liana hanging from their boughs, and resembling bundles of hay. If the eye was turned from the world of foliage above, to the ground beneath, it was attracted by the extreme elegance of the leaves of the ferns and mimosæ. The latter, in some parts, covered the surface with a brushwood only a few inches high. In walking across these thick beds of mimosæ, a broad track was marked by the change of shade, produced by the drooping of their sensitive petioles. It is easy to specify the individual objects of admiration in these grand scenes; but it is not possible to give an adequate idea of the higher feelings of wonder, astonishment, and devotion, which fill and elevate the mind.

April 19*th*.—Leaving Socêgo, during the two first days, we retraced our steps. It was very wearisome work, as the road generally ran across a glaring hot sandy plain, not far from the coast. I noticed that each time the horse put its foot on the fine siliceous sand, a gentle chirping noise was produced.

On the third day we took a different line, and passed through the gay little village of Madre de Deôs. This is one of the principal lines of road in Brazil; yet it was in so bad a state that no wheel vehicle, excepting the clumsy bullock-waggon, could pass along. In our whole journey we did not cross a single bridge built of stone; and those made of logs of wood were frequently so much out of repair, that it was necessary to go on one side to avoid them. All distances are inaccurately known. The road is often marked by crosses, in the place of milestones, to signify where human blood has been spilled. On the evening of the 23rd we arrived at Rio, having finished our pleasant little excursion.

During the remainder of my stay at Rio, I resided in a cottage at Botofogo Bay.[5] It was impossible to wish for anything more delightful than thus to spend some weeks in so magnificent a country. In England any person fond of natural history enjoys in his walks a great advantage, by always having something to attract his attention; but in these fertile climates, teeming with life, the attractions are so numerous, that he is scarcely able to walk at all.

The few observations which I was enabled to make were almost exclusively confined to the invertebrate animals. The existence of a division of the genus Planaria, which inhabits the dry land, interested me much. These animals are of so simple a structure, that Cuvier has arranged them with the intestinal worms, though never found within the bodies of other animals. Numerous species inhabit both salt and fresh water; but those to which I allude were found, even in the drier parts of the forest, beneath logs of rotten wood, on which I believe they feed. In general form they resemble little slugs, but are very much narrower in proportion, and several of the species are beautifully coloured with longitudinal stripes. Their struc-

[5] [Editor] In moving to the cottage, Darwin nearly lost all his instruments. The incident is recorded as follows in his diary:

"*April 25th.* Moved all my things from the *Beagle* to Botofogo. Whilst landing on the beach, I suffered on a small scale, sufficient, however, to paint some of the horrors of shipwreck. Two or three heavy seas swamped the boat, & before my affrighted eyes were floating books, instruments & gun cases & everything which was most useful to me. Nothing was lost & nothing completely spoiled, but most of them injured.

"*26th.* Employed all day in restoring the effects of yesterday's disaster."

ture is very simple: near the middle of the under or crawling surface there are two small transverse slits, from the anterior one of which a funnel-shaped and highly irritable mouth can be protruded. For some time after the rest of the animal was completely dead from the effects of salt water or any other cause, this organ still retained its vitality.

I found no less than twelve different species of terrestrial Planariæ in different parts of the southern hemisphere.[6] Some specimens which I obtained at Van Diemen's Land,[7] I kept alive for nearly two months, feeding them on rotten wood. Having cut one of them transversely into two nearly equal parts, in the course of a fortnight both had the shape of perfect animals. I had, however, so divided the body, that one of the halves contained both the inferior orifices, and the other, in consequence, none. In the course of twenty-five days from the operation, the more perfect half could not have been distinguished from any other specimen. The other had increased much in size; and towards its posterior end, a clear space was formed in the parenchymatous mass, in which a rudimentary cup-shaped mouth could clearly be distinguished; on the under surface, however, no corresponding slit was yet open. If the increased heat of the weather, as we approached the equator, had not destroyed all the individuals, there can be no doubt that this last step would have completed its structure. Although so well-known an experiment, it was interesting to watch the gradual production of every essential organ, out of the simple extremity of another animal. It is extremely difficult to preserve these Planariæ; as soon as the cessation of life allows the ordinary laws of change to act, their entire bodies become soft and fluid, with a rapidity which I have never seen equalled.

I first visited the forest in which these Planariæ were found, in company with an old Portuguese priest who took me out to hunt with him. The sport consisted in turning into the cover a few dogs, and then patiently waiting to fire at any animal which might appear. We were accompanied by the son of a neighbouring farmer—a good specimen of a wild Brazilian youth. He was dressed in a tattered old shirt and trousers, and had his head uncovered: he carried an old-fashioned gun and a large knife. The habit of carrying the knife is universal; and in traversing a thick wood it is almost necessary, on account of

6 [Darwin] I have described and named these species in the 'Annals of Nat. Hist.,' vol. xiv. p. 241.

7 [Editor] An old name for Tasmania.

the creeping plants. The frequent occurrence of murder may be partly attributed to this habit. The Brazilians are so dexterous with the knife, that they can throw it to some distance with precision, and with sufficient force to cause a fatal wound. I have seen a number of little boys practising this art as a game of play, and from their skill in hitting an upright stick, they promised well for more earnest attempts. My companion, the day before, had shot two large bearded monkeys. These animals have prehensile tails, the extremity of which, even after death, can support the whole weight of the body. One of them thus remained fast to a branch, and it was necessary to cut down a large tree to procure it. This was soon effected, and down came tree and monkey with an awful crash. Our day's sport, besides the monkey, was confined to sundry small green parrots and a few toucans. I profited, however, by my acquaintance with the Portuguese padre, for on another occasion he gave me a fine specimen of the Yagouaroundi cat.[8]

Every one has heard of the beauty of the scenery near Botofogo. The house in which I lived was seated close beneath the well-known mountain of the Corcovado. It has been remarked, with much truth, that abruptly conical hills are characteristic of the formation which Humboldt designates as gneiss-granite. Nothing can be more striking than the effect of these huge rounded masses of naked rock rising out of the most luxuriant vegetation.

I was often interested by watching the clouds, which, rolling in from seaward, formed a bank just beneath the highest point of the Corcovado. This mountain, like most others, when thus partly veiled, appeared to rise to a far prouder elevation than its real height of 2300 feet. Mr. Daniell has observed, in his meteorological essays, that a cloud sometimes appears fixed on a mountain summit, while the wind continues to blow over it. The same phenomenon here presented a slightly different appearance. In this case the cloud was clearly seen to curl over, and rapidly pass by the summit, and yet was neither diminished nor increased in size. The sun was setting, and a gentle southerly breeze, striking against the southern side of the rock, mingled its current with the colder air above; and the vapour was thus condensed: but as the light wreaths of cloud passed over the ridge, and came within the influence of the warmer atmosphere of the northern sloping bank, they were immediately re-dissolved.

[8] [Editor] A wildcat found from Paraguay to southern Texas.

The climate, during the months of May and June, or the beginning of winter, was delightful. The mean temperature, from observations taken at nine o'clock, both morning and evening, was only 72°. It often rained heavily, but the drying southerly winds soon again rendered the walks pleasant. One morning, in the course of six hours, 1.6 inches of rain fell. As this storm passed over the forests which surround the Corcovado, the sound produced by the drops pattering on the countless multitude of leaves was very remarkable; it could be heard at the distance of a quarter of a mile, and was like the rushing of a great body of water. After the hotter days, it was delicious to sit quietly in the garden and watch the evening pass into night. Nature, in these climes, chooses her vocalists from more humble performers than in Europe. A small frog, of the genus Hyla, sits on a blade of grass about an inch above the surface of the water, and sends forth a pleasing chirp: when several are together they sing in harmony on different notes. I had some difficulty in catching a specimen of this frog. The genus Hyla has its toes terminated by small suckers; and I found this animal could crawl up a pane of glass, when placed absolutely perpendicular. Various cicadæ and crickets, at the same time, keep up a ceaseless shrill cry, but which, softened by the distance, is not unpleasant. Every evening after dark this great concert commenced; and often have I sat listening to it, until my attention has been drawn away by some curious passing insect.

At these times the fireflies are seen flitting about from hedge to hedge. On a dark night the light can be seen at about two hundred paces distant. It is remarkable that in all the different kinds of glowworms, shining elaters, and various marine animals (such as the crustacea, medusæ, nereidæ, a coralline of the genus Clytia, and Pyrosoma), which I have observed, the light has been of a well-marked green colour. All the fireflies, which I caught here, belonged to the Lampyridæ (in which family the English glowworm is included), and the greater number of specimens were of Lampyris occidentalis.[9] I found that this insect emitted the most brilliant flashes when irritated: in the intervals, the abdominal rings were obscured. The flash was almost coinstantaneous in the two rings, but it was just perceptible first in the anterior one. The shining matter was

[9] [Darwin] I am greatly indebted to Mr. Waterhouse for his kindness in naming for me this and many other insects, and in giving me much valuable assistance.

fluid and very adhesive: little spots, where the skin had been torn, continued bright with a slight scintillation, whilst the un-injured parts were obscured. When the insect was decapitated the rings remained uninterruptedly bright, but not so brilliant as before: local irritation with a needle always increased the vividness of the light. The rings in one instance retained their luminous property nearly twenty-four hours after the death of the insect. From these facts it would appear probable, that the animal has only the power of concealing or extinguishing the light for short intervals, and that at other times the display is involuntary. On the muddy and wet gravel-walks I found the larvæ of this lampyris in great numbers: they resembled in general form the female of the English glowworm. These lar-væ possessed but feeble luminous powers; very differently from their parents, on the slightest touch they feigned death, and ceased to shine; nor did irritation excite any fresh display. I kept several of them alive for some time: their tails are very singular organs, for they act, by a well-fitted contrivance, as suckers or organs of attachment, and likewise as reservoirs for saliva, or some such fluid. I repeatedly fed them on raw meat; and I invariably observed, that every now and then the ex-tremity of the tail was applied to the mouth, and a drop of fluid exuded on the meat, which was then in the act of being consumed. The tail, notwithstanding so much practice, does not seem to be able to find its way to the mouth; at least the neck was always touched first, and apparently as a guide.

When we were at Bahia, an elater or beetle (Pyrophorus luminosus, Illig.) seemed the most common luminous insect. The light in this case was also rendered more brilliant by irrita-tion. I amused myself one day by observing the springing pow-ers of this insect, which have not, as it appears to me, been properly described.[10] The elater, when placed on its back and preparing to spring, moved its head and thorax backwards, so that the pectoral spine was drawn out, and rested on the edge of its sheath. The same backward movement being continued, the spine, by the full action of the muscles, was bent like a spring; and the insect at this moment rested on the extremity of its head and wing-cases. The effort being suddenly relaxed, the head and thorax flew up, and in consequence, the base of the wing-cases struck the supporting surface with such force, that the insect by the reaction was jerked upwards to the height of one or two inches. The projecting points of the thorax, and

[10] [Darwin] Kirby's Entomology, vol. ii. p. 317.

the sheath of the spine, served to steady the whole body during the spring. In the descriptions which I have read, sufficient stress does not appear to have been laid on the elasticity of the spine: so sudden a spring could not be the result of simple muscular contraction, without the aid of some mechanical contrivance.

On several occasions I enjoyed some short but most pleasant excursions in the neighbouring country. One day I went to the Botanic Garden, where many plants, well known for their great utility, might be seen growing. The leaves of the camphor, pepper, cinnamon, and clove trees were delightfully aromatic; and the bread-fruit, the jaca, and the mango, vied with each other in the magnificence of their foliage. The landscape in the neighbourhood of Bahia almost takes its character from the two latter trees. Before seeing them, I had no idea that any trees could cast so black a shade on the ground. Both of them bear to the evergreen vegetation of these climates the same kind of relation which laurels and hollies in England do to the lighter green of the deciduous trees. It may be observed, that the houses within the tropics are surrounded by the most beautiful forms of vegetation, because many of them are at the same time most useful to man. Who can doubt that these qualities are united in the banana, the cocoa-nut, the many kinds of palm, the orange, and the bread-fruit tree?

During this day I was particularly struck with a remark of Humboldt's, who often alludes to "the thin vapour which, without changing the transparency of the air, renders its tints more harmonious, and softens its effects." This is an appearance which I have never observed in the temperate zones. The atmosphere, seen through a short space of half or three quarters of a mile, was perfectly lucid, but at a greater distance all colours were blended into a most beautiful haze, of a pale French grey, mingled with a little blue. The condition of the atmosphere between the morning and about noon, when the effect was most evident, had undergone little change, excepting in its dryness. In the interval, the difference between the dew point and temperature had increased from 7°.5 to 17°.

On another occasion I started early and walked to the Gavia, or topsail mountain. The air was delightfully cool and fragrant; and the drops of dew still glittered on the leaves of the large liliaceous plants, which shaded the streamlets of clear water. Sitting down on a block of granite, it was delightful to watch the various insects and birds as they flew past. The humming-bird seems particularly fond of such shady retired spots. Whenever I saw these little creatures buzzing round a flower, with their wings vibrating so rapidly as to be scarcely visible, I was reminded of the sphinx moths: their movements and habits are indeed in many respects very similar.

Following a pathway I entered a noble forest, and from a height of five or six hundred feet, one of those splendid views was presented, which are so common on every side of Rio. At this elevation the landscape attains its most brilliant tint; and every form, every shade, so completely surpasses in magnificence all that the European has ever beheld in his own country, that he knows not how to express his feelings. The general effect frequently recalled to my mind the gayest scenery of the Opera-house or the great theatres. I never returned from these excursions empty-handed. This day I found a specimen of a curious fungus, called Hymenophallus. Most people know the English Phallus, which in autumn taints the air with its odious smell: this, however, as the entomologist is aware, is to some of our beetles a delightful fragrance. So was it here; for a Strongylus, attracted by the odour, alighted on the fungus as I carried it in my hand. We here see in two distant countries a similar relation between plants and insects of the same families, though the species of both are different. When man is the agent in introducing into a country a new species, this relation is often broken: as one instance of this I may mention, that the leaves of the cabbages and lettuces, which in England afford food to such a multitude of slugs and caterpillars, in the gardens near Rio are untouched.

During our stay at Brazil I made a large collection of insects. A few general observations on the comparative importance of the different orders may be interesting to the English entomologist. The large and brilliantly-coloured Lepidoptera bespeak the zone they inhabit, far more plainly than any other race of animals. I allude only to the butterflies; for the moths, contrary to what might have been expected from the rankness of the vegetation, certainly appeared in much fewer numbers than in our own temperate regions. I was much surprised at the habits of Papilio feronia. This butterfly is not uncommon, and generally frequents the orange-groves. Although a high flier, yet it very frequently alights on the trunks of trees. On these occasions its head is invariably placed downwards; and its wings are expanded in a horizontal plane, instead of being folded vertically, as is commonly the case. This is the only butterfly which I have ever seen, that uses its legs for running. Not being aware of this fact, the insect, more than once, as I cautiously approached with my forceps, shuffled on one side just as the instrument was on the point of closing, and thus escaped. But a far more singular fact is the power which this species possesses of making a noise.[11] Several times when a pair, probably male and female, were chasing each other in an irregular course, they passed within a few yards of me; and I distinctly heard a clicking noise, similar to that produced by a toothed wheel passing under a spring catch. The noise was continued at short intervals, and could be distinguished at about twenty yards' distance: I am certain there is no error in the observation.

I was disappointed in the general aspect of the Coleoptera. The number of minute and obscurely-coloured beetles is exceedingly great.[12] The cabinets of Europe can, as yet, boast only of the larger species from tropical climates. It is sufficient to disturb the composure of an entomologist's mind, to look forward to the future dimensions of a complete catalogue. The carnivorous beetles, or Carabidæ, appear in extremely few numbers within the tropics: this is the more remarkable when compared to the case of the carnivorous quadrupeds, which are so abundant in hot countries. I was struck with this observation both on entering Brazil, and when I saw the many elegant and active forms of the Harpalidæ re-appearing on the temperate plains of La Plata. Do the very numerous spiders

[11] [Darwin] Mr. Doubleday has lately described (before the Entomological Society, March 3rd, 1845) a peculiar structure in the wings of this butterfly, which seems to be the means of its making its noise. He says, "It is remarkable for having a sort of drum at the base of the fore wings, between the costal nervure and the subcostal. These two nervures, moreover, have a peculiar screw-like diaphragm or vessel in the interior." I find in Langsdorff's travels (in the years 1803–7, p. 74) it is said, that in the island of St. Catherine's on the coast of Brazil a butterfly called Februa Hoffmanseggi, makes a noise, when flying away, like a rattle.

[12] [Darwin] I may mention, as a common instance of one day's (June 23rd) collecting, when I was not attending particularly to the Coleoptera, that I caught sixty-eight species of that order. Among these, there were only two of the Carabidæ, four Brachelytra, fifteen Rhyncophora, and fourteen of the Chrysomelidæ. Thirty-seven species of Arachnidæ, which I brought home, will be sufficient to prove that I was not paying overmuch attention to the generally favoured order of Coleoptera.

and rapacious Hymenoptera supply the place of the carnivorous beetles? The carrion-feeders and Brachelytera are very uncommon; on the other hand, the Rhyncophora and Chrysomelidæ, all of which depend on the vegetable world for subsistence, are present in astonishing numbers. I do not here refer to the number of different species, but to that of the individual insects; for on this it is that the most striking character in the entomology of different countries depends. The orders Orthoptera and Hemiptera are particularly numerous; as likewise is the stinging division of the Hymenoptera; the bees, perhaps, being excepted. A person, on first entering a tropical forest, is astonished at the labours of the ants: well-beaten paths branch off in every direction, on which an army of never-failing foragers may be seen, some going forth, and others returning, burdened with pieces of green leaf, often larger than their own bodies.

A small dark-coloured ant sometimes migrates in countless numbers. One day, at Bahia, my attention was drawn by observing many spiders, cockroaches, and other insects, and some lizards, rushing in the greatest agitation across a bare piece of ground. A little way behind, every stalk and leaf was blackened by a small ant. The swarm having crossed the bare space, divided itself, and descended an old wall. By this means many insects were fairly enclosed; and the efforts which the poor little creatures made to extricate themselves from such a death were wonderful. When the ants came to the road they changed their course, and in narrow files re-ascended the wall. Having placed a small stone so as to intercept one of the lines, the whole body attacked it, and then immediately retired. Shortly afterwards another body came to the charge, and again having failed to make any impression, this line of march was entirely given up. By going an inch round, the file might have avoided the stone, and this doubtless would have happened, if it had been originally there: but having been attacked, the lion-hearted little warriors scorned the idea of yielding.

Certain wasp-like insects, which construct in the corners of the verandahs clay cells for their larvæ, are very numerous in the neighbourhood of Rio. These cells they stuff full of half-dead spiders and caterpillars, which they seem wonderfully to know how to sting to that degree as to leave them paralysed but alive, until their eggs are hatched; and the larvæ feed on the horrid mass of powerless, half-killed victims—a sight which has been described by an enthusiastic naturalist[13] as curious and pleasing! I was much interested one day by watching a deadly contest between a Pepsis and a large spider of the genus Lycosa. The wasp made a sudden dash at its prey, and then flew away: the spider was evidently wounded, for, trying to escape, it rolled down a little slope, but had still strength sufficient to crawl into a thick tuft of grass. The wasp soon returned, and seemed surprised at not immediately finding its victim. It then commenced as regular a hunt as ever hound did after fox; making short semicircular casts, and all the time rapidly vibrating its wings and antennæ. The spider, though well concealed, was soon discovered; and the wasp, evidently still afraid of its adversary's jaws, after much manœuvring, inflicted two stings on the under side of its thorax. At last, carefully examining with its antennæ the now motionless spider, it proceeded to drag away the body. But I stopped both tyrant and prey.[14]

The number of spiders, in proportion to other insects, is here compared with England very much larger; perhaps more so than with any other division of the articulate animals. The variety of species among the jumping spiders appears almost infinite. The genus, or rather family of Epeira, is here characterized by many singular forms; some species have pointed coriaceous shells, others enlarged and spiny tibiæ. Every path in the forest is barricaded with the strong yellow web of a species, belonging to the same division with the Epeira clavipes of Fabricius, which was formerly said by Sloane to make, in the West Indies, webs so strong as to catch birds. A small and pretty kind of spider, with very long fore-legs, and which appears to belong to an undescribed genus, lives as a parasite on almost every one of these webs. I suppose it is too insignificant to be noticed by the great Epeira, and is therefore allowed

[13] [Darwin] In a MS. in the British Museum by Mr. Abbott, who made his observations in Georgia; see Mr. A. White's paper in the 'Annals of Nat. Hist.,' vol. vii. p. 472. Lieut. Hutton has described a sphex with similar habits in India, in the 'Journal of the Asiatic Society,' vol. i. p. 555.

[14] [Darwin] Don Felix Azara (vol. i. p. 175), mentioning a hymenopterous insect, probably of the same genus, says, he saw it dragging a dead spider through tall grass, in a straight line to its nest, which was one hundred and sixty-three paces distant. He adds that the wasp, in order to find the road, every now and then made "demi-tours d'environ trois palmes." ["half-turns of about three handbreadths."—Ed.]

to prey on the minute insects, which, adhering to the lines, would otherwise be wasted. When frightened, this little spider either feigns death by extending its front legs, or suddenly drops from the web. A large Epeira of the same division with Epeira tuberculata and conica is extremely common, especially in dry situations. Its web, which is generally placed among the great leaves of the common agave, is sometimes strengthened near the centre by a pair or even four zigzag ribbons, which connect two adjoining rays. When any large insect, as a grasshopper or wasp, is caught, the spider, by a dexterous movement, makes it revolve very rapidly, and at the same time emitting a band of threads from its spinners, soon envelops its prey in a case like the cocoon of a silkworm. The spider now examines the powerless victim, and gives the fatal bite on the hinder part of its thorax; then retreating, patiently waits till the poison has taken effect. The virulence of this poison may be judged of from the fact that in half a minute I opened the mesh, and found a large wasp quite lifeless. This Epeira always stands with its head downwards near the centre of the web. When disturbed, it acts differently according to circumstances: if there is a thicket below, it suddenly falls down; and I have distinctly seen the thread from the spinners lengthened by the animal while yet stationary, as preparatory to its fall. If the ground is clear beneath, the Epeira seldom falls, but moves quickly through a central passage from one to the other side. When still further disturbed, it practises a most curious manœuvre: standing in the middle, it violently jerks the web, which is attached to elastic twigs, till at last the whole acquires such a rapid vibratory movement, that even the outline of the spider's body becomes indistinct.

It is well known that most of the British spiders, when a large insect is caught in their webs, endeavour to cut the lines and liberate their prey, to save their nets from being entirely spoiled. I once, however, saw in a hothouse in Shropshire a large female wasp caught in the irregular web of a quite small spider; and this spider, instead of cutting the web, most perseveringly continued to entangle the body, and especially the wings, of its prey. The wasp at first aimed in vain repeated thrusts with its sting at its little antagonist. Pitying the wasp, after allowing it to struggle for more than an hour, I killed it and put it back into the web. The spider soon returned; and an hour afterwards I was much surprised to find it with its jaws buried in the orifice, through which the sting is protruded by the living wasp. I drove the spider away two or three times, but for the next twenty-four hours I always found it again sucking at the same place. The spider became much distended by the juices of its prey, which was many times larger than itself.

I may here just mention, that I found, near St. Fé Bajada,[15] many large black spiders, with ruby-coloured marks on their backs, having gregarious habits. The webs were placed vertically, as is invariably the case with the genus Epeira: they were separated from each other by a space of about two feet, but were all attached to certain common lines, which were of great length, and extended to all parts of the community. In this manner the tops of some large bushes were encompassed by the united nets. Azara[16] has described a gregarious spider in Paraguay, which Walckenaer thinks must be a Theridion, but probably it is an Epeira, and perhaps even the same species with mine. I cannot, however, recollect seeing a central nest as large as a hat, in which, during autumn, when the spiders die, Azara says the eggs are deposited. As all the spiders which I saw were of the same size, they must have been nearly of the same age. This gregarious habit, in so typical a genus as Epeira, among insects, which are so bloodthirsty and solitary that even the two sexes attack each other, is a very singular fact.

In a lofty valley of the Cordillera, near Mendoza, I found another spider with a singularly-formed web. Strong lines radiated in a vertical plane from a common centre, where the insect had its station; but only two of the rays were connected by a symmetrical mesh-work; so that the net, instead of being, as is generally the case, circular, consisted of a wedge-shaped segment. All the webs were similarly constructed.

[15] [Editor] Now called Paraná. A city on the Paraná River and capital of Entre Rios, a province of northern Argentina. Mendoza, mentioned in the next paragraph, was the capital of a virtually autonomous state, also named Mendoza, when Darwin visited it in 1835; today, it is the chief city of one of Argentina's western provinces. Mendoza is in the foothills of the Andes, which Darwin —like most nineteenth-century writers—usually called the Cordillera.

[16] [Darwin] Azara's Voyage, vol. i. p. 213. [Felix de Azara, born 1746, died 1811, Spanish naturalist and traveler. As one of the commissioners appointed to settle the boundaries between the American possessions of Portugal and Spain, he spent twenty years in Paraguay. When he returned to Europe in 1801, he wrote an account of his travels and of Paraguayan geography, history, and zoology, published in Paris in 1809 under the title, *Voyage dans l'Amérique méridionale.*—Ed.]

CHAPTER III

MALDONADO

Monte Video — Maldonado — Excursion to R. Polanco — Lazo and Bolas — Partridges — Absence of Trees — Deer — Capybara, or River Hog — Tucutuco — Molothrus, cuckoo-like habits — Tyrant Flycatcher — Mocking-bird — Carrion Hawks — Tubes formed by Lightning — House struck

July 5th, 1832.—In the morning we got under way, and stood out of the splendid harbour of Rio de Janeiro. In our passage to the Plata, we saw nothing particular, excepting on one day a great shoal of porpoises, many hundreds in number. The whole sea was in places furrowed by them; and a most extraordinary spectacle was presented, as hundreds, proceeding together by jumps, in which their whole bodies were exposed, thus cut the water. When the ship was running nine knots an hour, these animals could cross and recross the bows with the greatest ease, and then dash away right ahead. As soon as we entered the estuary of the Plata, the weather was very unsettled. One dark night we were surrounded by numerous seals and penguins, which made such strange noises, that the officer on watch reported he could hear the cattle bellowing on shore. On a second night we witnessed a splendid scene of natural fireworks; the masthead and yard-arm-ends shone with St. Elmo's light; and the form of the vane could almost be traced, as if it had been rubbed with phosphorus. The sea was so highly luminous, that the tracks of the penguins were marked by a fiery wake, and the darkness of the sky was momentarily illuminated by the most vivid lightning.

When within the mouth of the river, I was interested by observing how slowly the waters of the sea and river mixed. The latter, muddy and discoloured, from its less specific gravity, floated on the surface of the salt water. This was curiously exhibited in the wake of the vessel, where a line of blue water was seen mingling in little eddies, with the adjoining fluid.

July 26th.—We anchored at Monte Video. The *Beagle* was employed in surveying the extreme southern and eastern coasts of America, south of the Plata, during the two succeeding years. To prevent useless repetitions, I will extract those parts of my journal which refer to the same districts, without always attending to the order in which we visited them.[1]

[1] [Editor] A chronology of the *Beagle's* movements is given both in Fitz Roy's journal and Darwin's diary. From Montevideo, the *Beagle* went across and up the Rio de la Plata or River Plate—the great estuary formed by the Paraná and Uruguay Rivers—to Buenos Aires, but was fired upon and turned back because of reports of cholera in England. (The *Beagle* had then been at sea for seven months.) When she returned to Montevideo, the police chief asked for help in keeping order during a local troop mutiny; Fitz Roy landed thirty-two sailors and marines, who stayed ashore overnight. (Darwin went along to see what was going on.) The *Beagle* then sailed down the Argentine coast to Bahia Blanca, where Fitz Roy chartered and refitted two small schooners, the *La Paz* and the *Libré*, to help in coastal surveying. After revisiting Buenos Aires and Montevideo (with less trouble this time), the *Beagle* sailed to Tierra del Fuego to return three Fuegian natives who were aboard (see Chapter X) to their own country. The next stop was the Falkland Islands, where Fitz Roy purchased a schooner, renamed the *Adventure* after the *Beagle's* companion on her earlier voyage, to replace the *La Paz* and *Libré*, which had been chartered for a year only and were too small for work away from shore. (Fitz Roy paid for the charter of the *La Paz* and *Libré* and the purchase of the *Adventure* out of his own pocket; he was forced to sell the *Adventure* at Callao, Peru, when the British Admiralty refused to reimburse him for the purchase price or put the crew on the *Beagle's* pay list.)

The spring of 1833 found the *Beagle* sailing up the Argentine coast to Maldonado—a small seaport down the Rio de la Plata from Montevideo—where she spent over two months, while her crew refitted the *Adventure*. This is the visit to Maldonado described by Darwin in this chapter.

Late in June, Darwin rejoined the *Beagle,* which, paid another visit to Montevideo and then sailed for the Rio Negro, one of the principal rivers of Patagonia. Here Darwin left the ship again, first to spend a week in the Rio Negro area, then to go overland to Bahia Blanca and on to Buenos Aires. When he finally reached Montevideo —to which the *Beagle* had worked her way meanwhile—Darwin found that the *Beagle* would be occupied for several weeks around

MALDONADO is situated on the northern bank of the Plata, and not very far from the mouth of the estuary. It is a most quiet, forlorn, little town; built, as is universally the case in these countries, with the streets running at right angles to each other, and having in the middle a large plaza or square, which, from its size, renders the scantiness of the population more evident. It possesses scarcely any trade; the exports being confined to a few hides and living cattle. The inhabitants are chiefly land owners, together with a few shopkeepers and the necessary tradesmen, such as blacksmiths and carpenters, who do nearly all the business for a circuit of fifty miles round. The town is separated from the river by a band of sand-hillocks, about a mile broad: it is surrounded, on all other sides, by an open slightly-undulating country, covered by one uniform layer of fine green turf, on which countless herds of cattle, sheep, and horses graze. There is very little land cultivated even close to the town. A few hedges, made of cacti and agave, mark out where some wheat or Indian corn has been planted. The features of the country are very similar along the whole northern bank of the Plata. The only difference is, that here the granitic hills are a little bolder. The scenery is very uninteresting; there is scarcely a house, an enclosed piece of ground, or even a tree, to give it an air of cheerfulness. Yet, after being imprisoned for some time in a ship, there is a charm in the unconfined feeling of walking over boundless plains of turf. Moreover, if your view is limited to a small space, many objects possess beauty. Some of the smaller birds are brilliantly coloured; and the bright green sward, browsed short by the cattle, is ornamented by dwarf flowers, among which a plant, looking like

---

the Rio de la Plata and in preparing charts. So he made two additional trips—one up the Paraná to Rosario and Sante Fé, and the other into the interior of Uruguay. He rejoined the *Beagle,* and the ship left the Rio de la Plata for Patagonia and the Strait of Magellan early in December.

March 1834, found Darwin and the *Beagle* both in the Falkland Islands. During April and May, the *Beagle* anchored off the Santa Cruz River in Patagonia, and a party from the ship worked its way up the river to within sight of the Andes. On June 1, the *Beagle* arrived at Port Famine on its second entry into the Strait of Magellan. On June 10, 1834, the *Beagle* entered the Pacific, the Atlantic portion of her survey behind her.

Darwin was away from the ship about seven months during this period of nearly two years. All of his excursions are described in the next several chapters.

the daisy, claimed the place of an old friend. What would a florist say to whole tracts so thickly covered by the Verbena melindres, as, even at a distance, to appear of the most gaudy scarlet?

I staid ten weeks at Maldonado, in which time a nearly perfect collection of the animals, birds, and reptiles, was procured. Before making any observations respecting them, I will give an account of a little excursion I made as far as the river Polanco, which is about seventy miles distant, in a northerly direction. I may mention, as a proof how cheap everything is in this country, that I paid only two dollars a day, or eight shillings, for two men, together with a troop of about a dozen riding-horses. My companions were well armed with pistols and sabres; a precaution which I thought rather unnecessary; but the first piece of news we heard was, that, the day before, a traveller from Monte Video had been found dead on the road, with his throat cut. This happened close to a cross, the record of a former murder.

On the first night we slept at a retired little country-house; and there I soon found out that I possessed two or three articles, especially a pocket compass, which created unbounded astonishment. In every house I was asked to show the compass, and by its aid, together with a map, to point out the direction of various places. It excited the liveliest admiration that I, a perfect stranger, should know the road (for direction and road are synonymous in this open country) to places where I had never been. At one house a young woman, who was ill in bed, sent to entreat me to come and show her the compass. If their surprise was great, mine was greater, to find such ignorance among people who possessed their thousands of cattle, and "estancias" of great extent. It can only be accounted for by the circumstance that this retired part of the country is seldom visited by foreigners. I was asked whether the earth or sun moved; whether it was hotter or colder to the north; where Spain was, and many other such questions. The greater number of the inhabitants had an indistinct idea that England, London, and North America, were different names for the same place; but the better informed well knew that London and North America were separate countries close together, and that England was a large town in London! I carried with me some promethean matches, which I ignited by biting; it was thought so wonderful that a man should strike fire with his teeth, that it was usual to collect the whole family to see it: I was once offered a dollar for a single one. Washing my face in the morning caused much speculation at the village of Las Minas; a superior tradesman closely cross-questioned me about so singular a practice; and likewise why on board we wore our beards; for he had heard from my guide that we did so. He eyed me with much suspicion; perhaps he had heard of ablutions in the Mahomedan religion, and knowing me to be a heretick, probably he came to the conclusion that all hereticks were Turks. It is the general custom in this country to ask for a night's lodging at the first convenient house. The astonishment at the compass, and my other feats in jugglery, was to a certain degree advantageous, as with that, and the long stories my guides told of my breaking stones, knowing venomous from harmless snakes, collecting insects, etc., I repaid them for their hospitality. I am writing as if I had been among the inhabitants of central Africa: Banda Oriental[2] would not be flattered by the comparison; but such were my feelings at the time.

The next day we rode to the village of Las Minas. The country was rather more hilly, but otherwise continued the same; an inhabitant of the Pampas no doubt would have considered it as truly Alpine. The country is so thinly inhabited, that during the whole day we scarcely met a single person. Las Minas is much smaller even than Maldonado. It is seated on a little plain, and is surrounded by low rocky mountains. It is of the usual symmetrical form; and with its whitewashed church standing in the centre, had rather a pretty appearance. The outskirting houses rose out of the plain like isolated beings, without the accompaniment of gardens or courtyards. This is generally the case in the country, and all the houses have, in consequence, an uncomfortable aspect. At night we stopped at a pulperia, or drinking-shop. During the evening a great number of Gauchos came in to drink spirits and smoke cigars: their appearance is very striking; they are generally tall and handsome; but with a proud and dissolute expression of coun-

---

[2] [Editor] An old name for Uruguay, meaning the land on the east bank of the Uruguay River. In 1817, Uruguay was seized from Spain by Portuguese troops and attached to Brazil, then the seat of the Portuguese empire. When Brazil declared its independence in 1822, Uruguay revolted against Brazil. The revolt was supported by Argentina and led to a war between Brazil and Argentina, from which Uruguay emerged as an independent country in 1827. Uruguay was proclaimed a republic in 1830, two years before Darwin's first visit.

tenance. They frequently wear their moustaches, and long black hair curling down their backs. With their brightly-coloured garments, great spurs clanking about their heels, and knives stuck as daggers (and often so used) at their waists, they look a very different race of men from what might be expected from their name of Gauchos, or simple countrymen. Their politeness is excessive; they never drink their spirits without expecting you to taste it; but whilst making their exceedingly graceful bow, they seem quite as ready, if occasion offered, to cut your throat.

On the third day we pursued rather an irregular course, as I was employed in examining some beds of marble. On the fine plains of turf we saw many ostriches (Struthio rhea). Some of the flocks contained as many as twenty or thirty birds. These, when standing on any little eminence, and seen against the clear sky, presented a very noble appearance. I never met with such tame ostriches in any other part of the country: it was easy to gallop up within a short distance of them; but then, expanding their wings, they made all sail right before the wind, and soon left the horse astern.

At night we came to the house of Don Juan Fuentes, a rich landed proprietor, but not personally known to either of my companions. On approaching the house of a stranger, it is usual to follow several little points of etiquette: riding up slowly to the door, the salutation of Ave Maria is given, and until somebody comes out and asks you to alight, it is not customary even to get off your horse: the formal answer of the owner is, "sin pecado concebida"—that is, conceived without sin. Having entered the house, some general conversation is kept up for a few minutes, till permission is asked to pass the night there. This is granted as a matter of course. The stranger then takes his meals with the family, and a room is assigned him, where with the horsecloths belonging to his recado (or saddle of the Pampas) he makes his bed. It is curious how similar circumstances produce such similar results in manners. At the Cape of Good Hope the same hospitality, and very nearly the same points of etiquette, are universally observed. The difference, however, between the character of the Spaniard and that of the Dutch boor is shown, by the former never asking his guest a single question beyond the strictest rules of politeness, whilst the honest Dutchman demands where he has been, where he is going, what is his business, and even how many brothers, sisters, or children he may happen to have.

Shortly after our arrival at Don Juan's, one of the large herds of cattle was driven in towards the house, and three beasts were picked out to be slaughtered for the supply of the establishment. These half-wild cattle are very active; and knowing full well the fatal lazo, they led the horses a long and laborious chase. After witnessing the rude wealth displayed in the number of cattle, men, and horses, Don Juan's miserable house was quite curious. The floor consisted of hardened mud, and the windows were without glass; the sitting-room boasted only of a few of the roughest chairs and stools, with a couple of tables. The supper, although several strangers were present, consisted of two huge piles, one of roast beef, the other of boiled, with some pieces of pumpkin: besides this latter there was no other vegetable, and not even a morsel of bread. For drinking, a large earthenware jug of water served the whole party. Yet this man was the owner of several square miles of land, of which nearly every acre would produce corn, and, with a little trouble, all the common vegetables. The evening was spent in smoking, with a little impromptu singing, accompanied by the guitar. The signoritas all sat together in one corner of the room, and did not sup with the men.

So many works have been written about these countries, that it is almost superfluous to describe either the lazo or the bolas. The lazo consists of a very strong, but thin, well-plaited rope, made of raw hide. One end is attached to the broad surcingle, which fastens together the complicated gear of the recado, or saddle used in the Pampas; the other is terminated by a small ring of iron or brass, by which a noose can be formed. The Gaucho, when he is going to use the lazo, keeps a small coil in his bridle-hand, and in the other holds the running noose, which is made very large, generally having a diameter of about eight feet. This he whirls round his head, and by the dexterous movement of his wrist keeps the noose open; then, throwing it, he causes it to fall on any particular spot he chooses. The lazo, when not used, is tied up in a small coil to the after part of the recado. The bolas, or balls, are of two kinds: the simplest, which is chiefly used for catching ostriches, consists of two round stones, covered with leather, and united by a thin plaited thong, about eight feet long. The other kind differs only in having three balls united by the thongs to a common centre. The Gaucho holds the smallest of the three in his hand, and whirls the other two round and round his head; then, taking aim, sends them like chain shot revolving through the air. The balls no sooner strike any object, than, winding round it, they cross each other, and become firmly hitched. The size and weight of the balls varies, according to the purpose for which they are made: when of stone, although not larger than an apple, they are sent with such force as sometimes to break the leg even of a horse. I have seen the balls made of wood, and as large as a turnip, for the sake of catching these animals without injuring them. The balls are sometimes made of iron, and these can be hurled to the greatest distance. The main difficulty in using either lazo or bolas is to ride so well as to be able at full speed, and while suddenly turning about, to whirl them so steadily round the head, as to take aim: on foot any person would soon learn the art. One day, as I was amusing myself by galloping and whirling the balls round my head, by accident the free one struck a bush; and its revolving motion being thus destroyed, it immediately fell to the ground, and like magic caught one hind leg of my horse; the other ball was then jerked out of my hand, and the horse fairly secured. Luckily he was an old practised animal, and knew what it meant; otherwise he would probably have kicked till he had thrown himself down. The Gauchos roared with laughter; they cried out that they had seen every sort of animal caught, but had never before seen a man caught by himself.

During the two succeeding days, I reached the furthest point which I was anxious to examine. The country wore the same aspect, till at last the fine green turf became more wearisome than a dusty turnpike road. We everywhere saw great numbers of partridges (Nothura major). These birds do not go in coveys, nor do they conceal themselves like the English kind. It appears a very silly bird. A man on horseback by riding round and round in a circle, or rather in a spire, so as to approach closer each time, may knock on the head as many as he pleases. The more common method is to catch them with a running noose, or little lazo, made of the stem of an ostrich's feather, fastened to the end of a long stick. A boy on a quiet old horse will frequently thus catch thirty or forty in a day. In Arctic North America[3] the Indians catch the Varying Hare by walking spirally round and round it, when on its form: the middle of the day is reckoned the best time, when the sun is high, and the shadow of the hunter not very long.

On our return to Maldonado, we followed rather a different

3 [Darwin] Hearne's Journey, p. 383.

line of road. Near Pan de Azucar, a landmark well known to all those who have sailed up the Plata, I stayed a day at the house of a most hospitable old Spaniard. Early in the morning we ascended the Sierra de las Animas. By the aid of the rising sun the scenery was almost picturesque. To the westward the view extended over an immense level plain as far as the Mount, at Monte Video, and to the eastward, over the mammillated country of Maldonado. On the summit of the mountain there were several small heaps of stones, which evidently had lain there for many years. My companion assured me that they were the work of the Indians in the old time. The heaps were similar, but on a much smaller scale, to those so commonly found on the mountains of Wales. The desire to signalize any event, on the highest point of the neighbouring land, seems an universal passion with mankind. At the present day, not a single Indian, either civilized or wild, exists in this part of the province; nor am I aware that the former inhabitants have left behind them any more permanent records than these insignificant piles on the summit of the Sierra de las Animas.

The general, and almost entire absence of trees in Banda Oriental is remarkable. Some of the rocky hills are partly covered by thickets, and on the banks of the larger streams, especially to the north of Las Minas, willow-trees are not uncommon. Near the Arroyo Tapes I heard of a wood of palms; and one of these trees, of considerable size, I saw near the Pan de Azucar, in lat. 35°. These, and the trees planted by the Spaniards, offer the only exceptions to the general scarcity of wood. Among the introduced kinds may be enumerated poplars, olives, peach, and other fruit trees: the peaches succeed so well, that they afford the main supply of firewood to the city of Buenos Ayres. Extremely level countries, such as the Pampas, seldom appear favourable to the growth of trees. This may possibly be attributed either to the force of the winds, or the kind of drainage. In the nature of the land, however, around Maldonado, no such reason is apparent; the rocky mountains afford protected situations, enjoying various kinds of soil; streamlets of water are common at the bottoms of nearly every valley; and the clayey nature of the earth seems adapted to retain moisture. It has been inferred with much probability, that the presence of woodland is generally determined[4] by the annual amount of moisture; yet in this prov-

4 [Darwin] Maclaren, art. 'America,' Encyclop. Britann.

ince abundant and heavy rain falls during the winter; and the summer, though dry, is not so in any excessive degree.[5] We see nearly the whole of Australia covered by lofty trees, yet that country possesses a far more arid climate. Hence we must look to some other and unknown cause.

Confining our view to South America, we should certainly be tempted to believe that trees flourished only under a very humid climate; for the limit of the forest-land follows, in a most remarkable manner, that of the damp winds. In the southern part of the continent, where the western gales, charged with moisture from the Pacific, prevail, every island on the broken west coast, from lat. 38° to the extreme point of Tierra del Fuego, is densely covered by impenetrable forests. On the eastern side of the Cordillera, over the same extent of latitude, where a blue sky and a fine climate prove that the atmosphere has been deprived of its moisture by passing over the mountains, the arid plains of Patagonia support a most scanty vegetation. In the more northern parts of the continent, within the limits of the constant south-eastern trade-wind, the eastern side is ornamented by magnificent forests; whilst the western coast, from lat. 4° S. to lat. 32° S., may be described as a desert: on this western coast, northward of lat. 4° S., where the trade-wind loses its regularity, and heavy torrents of rain fall periodically, the shores of the Pacific, so utterly desert in Peru, assume near Cape Blanco the character of luxuriance so celebrated at Guyaquil and Panama. Hence in the southern and northern parts of the continent, the forest and desert lands occupy reversed positions with respect to the Cordillera, and these positions are apparently determined by the direction of the prevalent winds. In the middle of the continent there is a broad intermediate band, including central Chile and the provinces of La Plata, where the rain-bringing winds have not to pass over lofty mountains, and where the land is neither a desert nor covered by forests. But even the rule, if confined to South America, of trees flourishing only in a climate rendered humid by rain-bearing winds, has a strongly marked exception in the case of the Falkland Islands. These islands, situated in the same latitude with Tierra del Fuego and only between two and three hundred miles distant from it, having a nearly similar climate,

[5] [Darwin] Azara says, "Je crois que la quantité annuelle des pluies est, dans toutes ces contrées, plus considérable qu'en Espagne." ["I believe that the annual rainfall in all these countries is greater than in Spain."—Ed.] Vol. i. p. 36.

with a geological formation almost identical, with favourable situations and the same kind of peaty soil, yet can boast of few plants deserving even the title of bushes; whilst in Tierra del Fuego it is impossible to find an acre of land not covered by the densest forest. In this case, both the direction of the heavy gales of wind and of the currents of the sea are favourable to the transport of seeds from Tierra del Fuego, as is shown by the canoes and trunks of trees drifted from that country, and frequently thrown on the shores of the Western Falkland. Hence perhaps it is, that there are many plants in common to the two countries: but with respect to the trees of Tierra del Fuego, even attempts made to transplant them have failed.

During our stay at Maldonado I collected several quadrupeds, eighty kinds of birds, and many reptiles, including nine species of snakes. Of the indigenous mammalia, the only one now left of any size, which is common, is the Cervus campestris. This deer is exceedingly abundant, often in small herds, throughout the countries bordering the Plata and in Northern Patagonia. If a person crawling close along the ground, slowly advances towards a herd, the deer frequently, out of curiosity, approach to reconnoitre him. I have by this means killed, from one spot, three out of the same herd. Although so tame and inquisitive, yet when approached on horseback, they are exceedingly wary. In this country nobody goes on foot, and the deer knows man as its enemy only when he is mounted and armed with the bolas. At Bahia Blanca, a recent establishment in Northern Patagonia, I was surprised to find how little the deer cared for the noise of a gun: one day I fired ten times from within eighty yards at one animal; and it was much more startled at the ball cutting up the ground than at the report of the rifle. My powder being exhausted, I was obliged to get up (to my shame as a sportsman be it spoken, though well able to kill birds on the wing) and halloo till the deer ran away.

The most curious fact with respect to this animal, is the overpoweringly strong and offensive odour which proceeds from the buck. It is quite indescribable: several times whilst skinning the specimen which is now mounted at the Zoological Museum, I was almost overcome by nausea. I tied up the skin in a silk pocket-handkerchief, and so carried it home: this handkerchief, after being well washed, I continually used, and it was of course as repeatedly washed; yet every time, for a space of one year and seven months, when first unfolded, I distinctly perceived the odour. This appears an astonishing instance of the permanence of some matter, which nevertheless in its nature must be most subtile and volatile. Frequently, when passing at the distance of half a mile to leeward of a herd, I have perceived the whole air tainted with the effluvium. I believe the smell from the buck is most powerful at the period when its horns are perfect, or free from the hairy skin. When in this state the meat is, of course, quite uneatable; but the Gauchos assert, that if buried for some time in fresh earth, the taint is removed. I have somewhere read that the islanders in the north of Scotland treat the rank carcasses of the fish-eating birds in the same manner.

The order Rodentia is here very numerous in species: of mice alone I obtained no less than eight kinds.[6] The largest gnawing animal in the world, the Hydrochærus capybara (the water-hog), is here also common. One which I shot at Monte Video weighed ninety-eight pounds: its length, from the end of the snout to the stump-like tail, was three feet two inches; and its girth three feet eight. These great Rodents occasionally frequent the islands in the mouth of the Plata, where the water is quite salt, but are far more abundant on the borders of freshwater lakes and rivers. Near Maldonado three or four generally live together. In the daytime they either lie among the aquatic plants, or openly feed on the turf plain.[7] When viewed at a distance, from their manner of walking and colour they

[6] [Darwin] In South America I collected altogether twenty-seven species of mice; and thirteen more are known from the works of Azara and other authors. Those collected by myself have been named and described by Mr. Waterhouse at the meetings of the Zoological Society. I must be allowed to take this opportunity of returning my cordial thanks to Mr. Waterhouse, and to the other gentlemen attached to that Society, for their kind and most liberal assistance on all occasions. [George Robert Waterhouse, an otherwise obscure 19th century mammalogist, published a *Natural History of Mammalia* in 1846 and wrote a paper on the South American mice collected by Darwin and the section "Recent Mammalia" in *The Zoology of H.M.S. Beagle,* the series of volumes covering Darwin's zoological collections and findings during the voyage.—Ed.]

[7] [Darwin] In the stomach and duodenum of a capybara which I opened, I found a very large quantity of a thin yellowish fluid, in which scarcely a fibre could be distinguished. Mr. Owen informs me that a part of the œsophagus is so constructed that nothing much larger than a crowquill can be passed down. Certainly the broad teeth and strong jaws of this animal are well fitted to grind into pulp the aquatic plants on which it feeds.

resemble pigs: but when seated on their haunches, and attentively watching any object with one eye, they re-assume the
appearance of their congeners, cavies and rabbits. Both the
front and side view of their head has quite a ludicrous aspect,
from the great depth of their jaw. These animals, at Maldonado, were very tame; by cautiously walking, I approached
within three yards of four old ones. This tameness may probably be accounted for, by the Jaguar having been banished for
some years, and by the Gaucho not thinking it worth his while
to hunt them. As I approached nearer and nearer they frequently made their peculiar noise, which is a low abrupt grunt,
not having much actual sound, but rather arising from the sudden expulsion of air: the only noise I know at all like it, is the
first hoarse bark of a large dog. Having watched the four from
almost within arm's length (and they me) for several minutes,
they rushed into the water at full gallop with the greatest impetuosity, and emitted at the same time their bark. After diving
a short distance they came again to the surface, but only just
showed the upper part of their heads. When the female is
swimming in the water, and has young ones, they are said to
sit on her back. These animals are easily killed in numbers; but
their skins are of trifling value, and the meat is very indifferent.
On the islands in the Rio Parana they are exceedingly abundant, and afford the ordinary prey to the Jaguar.

The Tucutuco (Ctenomys Brasiliensis) is a curious small
animal, which may be briefly described as a Gnawer, with the
habits of a mole. It is extremely numerous in some parts of the
country, but is difficult to be procured, and never, I believe,
comes out of the ground. It throws up at the mouth of its
burrows hillocks of earth like those of the mole, but smaller.
Considerable tracts of country are so completely undermined
by these animals, that horses in passing over, sink above their
fetlocks. The tucutucos appear, to a certain degree, to be gregarious: the man who procured the specimens for me had
caught six together, and he said this was a common occurrence.
They are nocturnal in their habits; and their principal food is
the roots of plants, which are the object of their extensive and
superficial burrows. This animal is universally known by a very
peculiar noise which it makes when beneath the ground. A person, the first time he hears it, is much surprised; for it is not
easy to tell whence it comes, nor is it possible to guess what
kind of creature utters it. The noise consists in a short, but not
rough, nasal grunt, which is monotonously repeated about four

times in quick succession;[8] the name Tucutuco is given in imitation of the sound. Where this animal is abundant, it may be heard at all times of the day, and sometimes directly beneath one's feet. When kept in a room, the tucutucos move both slowly and clumsily, which appears owing to the outward action of their hind legs; and they are quite incapable, from the socket of the thigh-bone not having a certain ligament, of jumping even the smallest vertical height. They are very stupid in making any attempt to escape; when angry or frightened they utter the tucu-tuco. Of those I kept alive several, even the first day, became quite tame, not attempting to bite or to run away; others were a little wilder.

The man who caught them asserted that very many are invariably found blind. A specimen which I preserved in spirits was in this state; Mr. Reid considers it to be the effect of inflammation in the nictitating membrane. When the animal was alive I placed my finger within half an inch of its head, and not the slightest notice was taken: it made its way, however, about the room nearly as well as the others. Considering the strictly subterranean habits of the tucutuco, the blindness, though so common, cannot be a very serious evil; yet it appears strange that any animal should possess an organ frequently subject to be injured. Lamarck would have been delighted with this fact, had he known it, when speculating[9] (probably with more truth than usual with him) on the gradually-*acquired* blindness of the Aspalax, a Gnawer living under ground, and of the Proteus, a reptile living in dark caverns filled with water; in both of which animals the eye is in an almost rudimentary state, and is covered by a tendinous membrane and skin. In the common mole the eye is extraordinarily small but perfect, though many anatomists doubt whether it is connected with the true optic nerve; its vision must certainly be imperfect, though probably useful to the animal when it leaves its burrow. In the tucutuco, which I believe never comes to the surface of the ground, the eye is rather larger, but often rendered blind and useless,

8 [Darwin] At the R. Negro, in Northern Patagonia, there is an animal of the same habits, and probably a closely allied species, but which I never saw. Its noise is different from that of the Maldonado kind; it is repeated only twice instead of three or four times, and is more distinct and sonorous: when heard from a distance it so closely resembles the sound made in cutting down a small tree with an axe, that I have sometimes remained in doubt concerning it.

9 [Darwin] Philosoph. Zoolog., tom. i. p. 242.

though without apparently causing any inconvenience to the animal: no doubt Lamarck would have said that the tucutuco is now passing into the state of the Aspalax and Proteus.

Birds of many kinds are extremely abundant on the undulating grassy plains around Maldonado. There are several species of a family allied in structure and manners to our Starling: one of these (Molothrus niger) is remarkable from its habits. Several may often be seen standing together on the back of a cow or horse; and while perched on a hedge, pluming themselves in the sun, they sometimes attempt to sing, or rather to hiss; the noise being very peculiar, resembling that of bubbles of air passing rapidly from a small orifice under water, so as to produce an acute sound. According to Azara, this bird, like the cuckoo, deposits its eggs in other birds' nests. I was several times told by the country people, that there certainly is some bird having this habit; and my assistant in collecting, who is a very accurate person, found a nest of the sparrow of this country (Zonotrichia matutina), with one egg in it larger than the others, and of a different colour and shape. In North America there is another species of Molothrus (M. pecoris),[10] which has a similar cuckoo-like habit, and which is most closely allied in every respect to the species from the Plata, even in such trifling peculiarities as standing on the backs of cattle; it differs only in being a little smaller, and in its plumage and eggs being of a slightly different shade of colour. This close agreement in structure and habits, in representative species coming from opposite quarters of a great continent, always strikes one as interesting, though of common occurrence.

Mr. Swainson has well remarked,[11] that with the exception of the Molothrus pecoris, to which must be added the M. niger, the cuckoos are the only birds which can be called truly parasitical; namely, such as "fasten themselves, as it were, on another living animal, whose animal heat brings their young into life, whose food they live upon, and whose death would cause theirs during the period of infancy." It is remarkable that some of the species, but not all, both of the Cuckoo and Molothrus, should agree in this one strange habit of their parasitical propagation, whilst opposed to each other in almost every other habit: the molothrus, like our starling, is eminently sociable, and lives on the open plains without art or disguise: the cuckoo,

[10] [Editor] The common cowbird, which now bears the species name of Molothrus ater.

[11] [Darwin] Magazine of Zoology and Botany, vol. i. p. 217.

as every one knows, is a singularly shy bird; it frequents the most retired thickets, and feeds on fruit and caterpillars. In structure also these two genera are widely removed from each other. Many theories, even phrenological theories, have been advanced to explain the origin of the cuckoo laying its eggs in other birds' nests. M. Prévost alone, I think, has thrown light by his observations[12] on this puzzle: he finds that the female cuckoo, which, according to most observers, lays at least from four to six eggs, must pair with the male each time after laying only one or two eggs. Now, if the cuckoo was obliged to sit on her own eggs, she would either have to sit on all together, and therefore leave those first laid so long, that they probably would become addled; or she would have to hatch separately each egg or two eggs, as soon as laid: but as the cuckoo stays a shorter time in this country than any other migratory bird, she certainly would not have time enough for the successive hatchings. Hence we can perceive in the fact of the cuckoo pairing several times, and laying her eggs at intervals, the cause of her depositing her eggs in other birds' nests, and leaving them to the care of foster-parents. I am strongly inclined to believe that this view is correct, from having been independently led (as we shall hereafter see) to an analogous conclusion with regard to the South American ostrich, the females of which are parasitical, if I may so express it, on each other; each female laying several eggs in the nests of several other females, and the male ostrich undertaking all the cares of incubation, like the strange foster-parents with the cuckoo.

I will mention only two other birds, which are very common, and render themselves prominent from their habits. The Saurophagus sulphuratus is typical of the great American tribe of tyrant-flycatchers. In its structure it closely approaches the true shrikes, but in its habits may be compared to many birds. I have frequently observed it, hunting a field, hovering over one spot like a hawk, and then proceeding on to another. When seen thus suspended in the air, it might very readily at a short distance be mistaken for one of the Rapacious order; its stoop, however, is very inferior in force and rapidity to that of a hawk. At other times the Saurophagus haunts the neighbourhood of water, and there, like a kingfisher, remaining stationary, it catches any small fish which may come near the margin. These birds are not unfrequently kept either in cages or in

12 [Darwin] Read before the Academy of Science in Paris. L'Institut, 1834, p. 418.

courtyards, with their wings cut. They soon become tame, and are very amusing from their cunning odd manners, which were described to me as being similar to those of the common magpie. Their flight is undulatory, for the weight of the head and bill appear too great for the body. In the evening the Saurophagus takes its stand on a bush, often by the road-side, and continually repeats without change a shrill and rather agreeable cry, which somewhat resembles articulate words: the Spaniards say it is like the words "Bien te veo" (I see you well), and accordingly have given it this name.

A mocking-bird (Mimus orpheus), called by the inhabitants Calandria, is remarkable, from possessing a song far superior to that of any other bird in the country: indeed, it is nearly the only bird in South America which I have observed to take its stand for the purpose of singing. The song may be compared to that of the Sedge warbler, but is more powerful; some harsh notes and some very high ones, being mingled with a pleasant warbling. It is heard only during the spring. At other times its cry is harsh and far from harmonious. Near Maldonado these birds were tame and bold; they constantly attended the country houses in numbers, to pick the meat which was hung up on the posts or walls: if any other small bird joined the feast, the Calandria soon chased it away. On the wide uninhabited plains of Patagonia another closely allied species, O. Patagonica of d'Orbigny, which frequents the valleys clothed with spiny bushes, is a wilder bird, and has a slightly different tone of voice. It appears to me a curious circumstance, as showing the fine shades of difference in habits, that judging from this latter respect alone, when I first saw this second species, I thought it was different from the Maldonado kind. Having afterwards procured a specimen, and comparing the two without particular care, they appeared so very similar, that I changed my opinion; but now Mr. Gould says that they are certainly distinct; a conclusion in conformity with the trifling difference of habit, of which, however, he was not aware.

The number, tameness, and disgusting habits of the carrion-feeding hawks of South America make them pre-eminently striking to any one accustomed only to the birds of Northern Europe. In this list may be included four species of the Caracara or Polyborus, the Turkey buzzard, the Gallinazo, and the Condor. The Caracaras are, from their structure, placed among the eagles: we shall soon see how ill they become so high a rank. In their habits they well supply the place of our carrion-crows, magpies, and ravens; a tribe of birds widely distributed over the rest of the world, but entirely absent in South America. To begin with the Polyborus Brasiliensis: this is a common bird, and has a wide geographical range; it is most numerous on the grassy savannahs of La Plata (where it goes by the name of Carrancha), and is far from unfrequent throughout the sterile plains of Patagonia. In the desert between the rivers Negro and Colorado, numbers constantly attend the line of road to devour the carcasses of the exhausted animals which chance to perish from fatigue and thirst. Although thus common in these dry and open countries, and likewise on the arid shores of the Pacific, it is nevertheless found inhabiting the damp impervious forests of West Patagonia and Tierra del Fuego. The Carranchas, together with the Chimango, constantly attend in numbers the estancias and slaughtering-houses. If an animal dies on the plain the Gallinazo commences the feast, and then the two species of Polyborus pick the bones clean. These birds, although thus commonly feeding together, are far from being friends. When the Carrancha is quietly seated on the branch of a tree or on the ground, the Chimango often continues for a long time flying backwards and forwards, up and down, in a semicircle, trying each time at the bottom of the curve to strike its larger relative. The Carrancha takes little notice, except by bobbing its head. Although the Carranchas frequently assemble in numbers, they are not gregarious; for in desert places they may be seen solitary, or more commonly by pairs.

The Carranchas are said to be very crafty, and to steal great numbers of eggs. They attempt, also, together with the Chimango, to pick off the scabs from the sore backs of horses and mules. The poor animal, on the one hand, with its ears down and its back arched; and, on the other, the hovering bird, eyeing at the distance of a yard, the disgusting morsel, form a picture, which has been described by Captain Head with his own peculiar spirit and accuracy. These false eagles most rarely kill any living bird or animal; and their vulture-like, necrophagous habits are very evident to any one, who has fallen asleep on the desolate plains of Patagonia, for when he wakes, he will see, on each surrounding hillock, one of these birds patiently watching him with an evil eye: it is a feature in the landscape of these countries, which will be recognized by every one who has wandered over them. If a party of men go out hunting with dogs and horses, they will be accompanied, during the day, by several of these attendants. After feeding, the uncovered craw protrudes; at such times, and indeed generally, the Carrancha is an inactive, tame, and cowardly bird. Its flight is heavy and slow, like that of an English rook. It seldom soars; but I have twice seen one at a great height gliding through the air with much ease. It runs (in contradistinction to hopping), but not quite so quickly as some of its congeners. At times the Carrancha is noisy, but is not generally so: its cry is loud, very harsh and peculiar, and may be likened to the sound of the Spanish guttural *g*, followed by a rough double *r r;* when uttering this cry it elevates its head higher and higher, till at last, with its beak wide open, the crown almost touches the lower part of the back. This fact, which has been doubted, is quite true; I have seen them several times with their heads backwards in a completely inverted position. To these observations I may add, on the high authority of Azara, that the Carrancha feeds on worms, shells, slugs, grasshoppers, and frogs; that it destroys young lambs by tearing the umbilical cord; and that it pursues the Gallinazo, till that bird is compelled to vomit up the carrion it may have recently gorged. Lastly, Azara states that several Carranchas, five or six together, will unite in chace of large birds, even such as herons. All these facts show that it is a bird of very versatile habits and considerable ingenuity.

The Polyborus Chimango is considerably smaller than the last species. It is truly omnivorous, and will eat even bread; and I was assured that it materially injures the potato-crops in Chiloe[13], by stocking up the roots when first planted. Of all the carrion-feeders it is generally the last which leaves the skeleton of a dead animal; and may often be seen within the ribs of a cow or horse, like a bird in a cage. Another species is the Polyborus Novæ Zelandiæ, which is exceedingly common in the Falkland Islands. These birds in many respects resemble in their habits the Carranchas. They live on the flesh of dead animals and on marine productions; and on the Ramirez rocks their whole sustenance must depend on the sea. They are extraordinarily tame and fearless, and haunt the neighbourhood of houses for offal. If a hunting party kills an animal, a number soon collect and patiently await, standing on the ground on all sides. After eating, their uncovered craws are largely protruded, giving them a disgusting appearance. They readily at-

13 [Editor] An island off the Chilean coast, later visited by Darwin.

tack wounded birds: a cormorant in this state having taken to the shore, was immediately seized on by several, and its death hastened by their blows. The *Beagle* was at the Falklands only during the summer, but the officers of the *Adventure*, who were there in the winter, mention many extraordinary instances of the boldness and rapacity of these birds. They actually pounced on a dog that was lying fast asleep close by one of the party; and the sportsmen had difficulty in preventing the wounded geese from being seized before their eyes. It is said that several together (in this respect resembling the Carranchas) wait at the mouth of a rabbit-hole, and together seize on the animal when it comes out. They were constantly flying on board the vessel when in the harbour; and it was necessary to keep a good look-out to prevent the leather being torn from the rigging, and the meat or game from the stern. These birds are very mischievous and inquisitive; they will pick up almost anything from the ground; a large black glazed hat was carried nearly a mile, as was a pair of the heavy balls used in catching cattle. Mr. Usborne experienced during the survey a more severe loss, in their stealing a small Kater's compass in a red morocco leather case, which was never recovered. These birds are, moreover, quarrelsome and very passionate; tearing up the grass with their bills from rage. They are not truly gregarious; they do not soar, and their flight is heavy and clumsy; on the ground they run extremely fast, very much like pheasants. They are noisy, uttering several harsh cries; one of which is like that of the English rook; hence the sealers always call them rooks. It is a curious circumstance that, when crying out, they throw their heads upwards and backwards, after the same manner as the Carrancha. They build in the rocky cliffs of the sea-coast, but only on the small adjoining islets, and not on the two main islands: this is a singular precaution in so tame and fearless a bird. The sealers say that the flesh of these birds, when cooked, is quite white, and very good eating; but bold must the man be who attempts such a meal.

We have now only to mention the turkey-buzzard (Vultur aura), and the Gallinazo. The former is found wherever the country is moderately damp, from Cape Horn to North America. Differently from the Polyborus Basiliensis and Chimango, it has found its way to the Falkland Islands. The turkey-buzzard is a solitary bird, or at most goes in pairs. It may at once be recognized from a long distance, by its lofty, soaring and most elegant flight. It is well known to be a true carrion-feeder. On

the west coast of Patagonia, among the thickly-wooded islets
and broken land, it lives exclusively on what the sea throws
up, and on the carcasses of dead seals. Wherever these animals
are congregated on the rocks, there the vultures may be seen.
The Gallinazo (Cathartes atratus) has a different range from
the last species, as it never occurs southward of lat. 41°. Azara
states that there exists a tradition that these birds, at the time
of the conquest, were not found near Monte Video, but that
they subsequently followed the inhabitants from more northern districts. At the present day they are numerous in the valley
of the Colorado, which is three hundred miles due south of
Monte Video. Its seems probable that this additional migration
has happened since the time of Azara. The Gallinazo generally
prefers a humid climate, or rather the neighbourhood of fresh
water; hence it is extremely abundant in Brazil and La Plata,
while it is never found on the desert and arid plains of Northern Patagonia, excepting near some stream. These birds frequent the whole Pampas to the foot of the Cordillera, but I
never saw or heard of one in Chile: in Peru they are preserved
as scavengers. These vultures certainly may be called gregarious, for they seem to have pleasure in society, and are not
solely brought together by the attraction of a common prey.
On a fine day a flock may often be observed at a great height,
each bird wheeling round and round without closing its wings,
in the most graceful evolutions. This is clearly performed for
the mere pleasure of the exercise, or perhaps is connected with
their matrimonial alliances.

I have now mentioned all the carrion-feeders, excepting the
condor, an account of which will be more appropriately introduced when we visit a country more congenial to its habits
than the plains of La Plata.

In a broad band of sand-hillocks which separate the Laguna
del Potrero from the shores of the Plata, at the distance of a
few miles from Maldonado, I found a group of those vitrified,
siliceous tubes, which are formed by lightning entering loose
sand. These tubes resemble in every particular those from
Drigg in Cumberland, described in the Geological Transactions.[14] The sand-hillocks of Maldonado, not being protected

14 [Darwin] Geolog. Transact., vol. ii. p. 528. In the Philosoph.
Transact. (1790, p. 294) Dr. Priestley has described some imperfect siliceous tubes and a melted pebble of quartz, found in digging

by vegetation, are constantly changing their position. From this cause the tubes projected above the surface; and numerous fragments lying near, showed that they had formerly been buried to a greater depth. Four sets entered the sand perpendicularly: by working with my hands I traced one of them two feet deep; and some fragments which evidently had belonged to the same tube, when added to the other part, measured five feet three inches. The diameter of the whole tube was nearly equal, and therefore we must suppose that originally it extended to a much greater depth. These dimensions arc however small, compared to those of the tubes from Drigg, one of which was traced to a depth of not less than thirty feet.

The internal surface is completely vitrified, glossy, and smooth. A small fragment examined under the microscope appeared, from the number of minute entangled air or perhaps steam bubbles, like an assay fused before the blowpipe. The sand is entirely, or in greater part, siliceous; but some points are of a black colour, and from their glossy surface possess a metallic lustre. The thickness of the wall of the tube varies from the thirtieth to a twentieth of an inch, and occasionally even equals a tenth. On the outside the grains of sand are rounded, and have a slightly glazed appearance: I could not distinguish any signs of crystallization. In a similar manner to that described in the Geological Transactions, the tubes are generally compressed, and have deep longitudinal furrows, so as closely to resemble a shrivelled vegetable stalk, or the bark of the elm or cork tree. Their circumference is about two inches, but in some fragments, which are cylindrical and without any furrows, it is as much as four inches. The compression from the surrounding loose sand, acting while the tube was still softened from the effects of the intense heat, has evidently caused the creases or furrows. Judging from the uncompressed fragments, the measure or bore of the lightning (if such a term may be used), must have been about one inch and a quarter. At Paris, M. Hachette and M. Beudant[15] succeeded in making tubes, in most respects similar to these fulgurites, by passing very strong shocks of galvanism through finely-powdered glass: when salt was added, so as to increase its fusibility, the tubes were larger in every dimension. They failed both with

into the ground, under a tree, where a man had been killed by lightning.

[15] [Darwin] Annales de Chimie et de Physique, tom. xxxvii. p. 319.

powdered felspar and quartz. One tube, formed with pounded glass, was very nearly an inch long, namely .982, and had an internal diameter of .019 of an inch. When we hear that the strongest battery in Paris was used, and that its power on a substance of such easy fusibility as glass was to form tubes so diminutive, we must feel greatly astonished at the force of a shock of lightning which, striking the sand in several places, has formed cylinders, in one instance of at least thirty feet long, and having an internal bore, where not compressed, of full an inch and a half; and this in a material so extraordinarily refractory as quartz!

The tubes, as I have already remarked, enter the sand nearly in a vertical direction. One, however, which was less regular than the others, deviated from a right line, at the most considerable bend, to the amount of thirty-three degrees. From this same tube, two small branches, about a foot apart, were sent off; one pointed downwards, and the other upwards. This latter case is remarkable, as the electric fluid must have turned back at the acute angle of 26°, to the line of its main course. Besides the four tubes which I found vertical, and traced beneath the surface, there were several other groups of fragments, the original sites of which without doubt were near. All occurred in a level area of shifting sand, sixty yards by twenty, situated among some high sand-hillocks, and at the distance of about half a mile from a chain of hills four or five hundred feet in height. The most remarkable circumstance, as it appears to me, in this case as well as in that of Drigg, and in one described by M. Ribbentrop in Germany, is the number of tubes found within such limited spaces. At Drigg, within an area of fifteen yards, three were observed, and the same number occurred in Germany. In the case which I have described, certainly more than four existed within the space of the sixty by twenty yards. As it does not appear probable that the tubes are produced by successive distinct shocks, we must believe that the lightning, shortly before entering the ground, divides itself into separate branches.

The neighbourhood of the Rio Plata seems peculiarly subject to electric phenomena. In the year 1793,[16] one of the most destructive thunderstorms perhaps on record happened at Buenos Ayres: thirty-seven places within the city were struck by lightning, and nineteen people killed. From facts stated in

[16] [Darwin] Azara's Voyage, vol. i. p. 36.

several books of travels, I am inclined to suspect that thunder-storms are very common near the mouths of great rivers. Is it not possible that the mixture of large bodies of fresh and salt water may disturb the electrical equilibrium? Even during our occasional visits to this part of South America, we heard of a ship, two churches, and a house, having been struck. Both the church and the house I saw shortly afterwards: the house belonged to Mr. Hood, the consul-general at Monte Video. Some of the effects were curious: the paper, for nearly a foot on each side of the line where the bell-wires had run, was blackened. The metal had been fused, and although the room was about fifteen feet high, the globules, dropping on the chairs and furniture, had drilled in them a chain of minute holes. A part of the wall was shattered as if by gunpowder, and the fragments had been blown off with force sufficient to dent the wall on the opposite side of the room. The frame of a looking-glass was blackened, and the gilding must have been volatil-ized, for a smelling-bottle, which stood on the chimney-piece, was coated with bright metallic particles, which adhered as firmly as if they had been enamelled.

CHAPTER IV

RIO NEGRO TO BAHIA BLANCA

Rio Negro — Estancias attacked by the Indians — Salt Lakes —
Flamingoes — R. Negro to R. Colorado — Sacred Tree — Pata-
gonian Hare — Indian Families — General Rosas — Proceed to
Bahia Blanca — Sand Dunes — Negro Lieutenant — Bahia Blanca
— Saline Incrustations — Punta Alta — Zorillo

July 24th, 1833.—The *Beagle* sailed from Maldonado, and on
August the 3rd she arrived off the mouth of the Rio Negro.
This is the principal river on the whole line of coast between
the Strait of Magellan and the Plata. It enters the sea about
three hundred miles south of the estuary of the Plata. About
fifty years ago, under the old Spanish government, a small
colony was established here; and it is still the most southern
position (lat. 41°) on this eastern coast of America, inhabited
by civilized man.

The country near the mouth of the river is wretched in the
extreme: on the south side a long line of perpendicular cliffs
commences, which exposes a section of the geological nature
of the country. The strata are of sandstone, and one layer was
remarkable from being composed of a firmly-cemented conglomerate of pumice pebbles, which must have travelled more
than four hundred miles, from the Andes. The surface is everywhere covered up by a thick bed of gravel, which extends far
and wide over the open plain. Water is extremely scarce, and,
where found, is almost invariably brackish. The vegetation is
scanty; and although there are bushes of many kinds, all are
armed with formidable thorns, which seem to warn the stranger not to enter on these inhospitable regions.

The settlement is situated eighteen miles up the river. The
road follows the foot of the sloping cliff, which forms the

northern boundary of the great valley, in which the Rio Negro flows. On the way we passed the ruins of some fine "estancias," which a few years since had been destroyed by the Indians. They withstood several attacks. A man present at one gave me a very lively description of what took place. The inhabitants had sufficient notice to drive all the cattle and horses into the "corral"[1] which surrounded the house, and likewise to mount some small cannon. The Indians were Araucanians from the south of Chile; several hundreds in number, and highly disciplined. They first appeared in two bodies on a neighbouring hill; having there dismounted, and taken off their fur mantles, they advanced naked to the charge. The only weapon of an Indian is a very long bamboo or chuzo, ornamented with ostrich feathers, and pointed by a sharp spear-head. My informer seemed to remember with the greatest horror the quivering of these chuzos as they approached near. When close, the cacique Pincheira hailed the besieged to give up their arms, or he would cut all their throats. As this would probably have been the result of their entrance under any circumstances, the answer was given by a volley of musketry. The Indians, with great steadiness, came to the very fence of the corral: but to their surprise they found the posts fastened together by iron nails instead of leather thongs, and, of course, in vain attempted to cut them with their knives. This saved the lives of the Christians: many of the wounded Indians were carried away by their companions; and at last one of the under caciques being wounded, the bugle sounded a retreat. They retired to their horses, and seemed to hold a council of war. This was an awful pause for the Spaniards, as all their ammunition, with the exception of a few cartridges, was expended. In an instant the Indians mounted their horses, and galloped out of sight. Another attack was still more quickly repulsed. A cool Frenchman managed the gun; he stopped till the Indians approached close, and then raked their line with grape-shot: he thus laid thirty-nine of them on the ground; and, of course, such a blow immediately routed the whole party.

The town is indifferently called El Carmen or Patagones.[2]

1 [Darwin] The corral is an enclosure made of tall and strong stakes. Every estancia, or farming estate, has one attached to it.

2 [Editor] Now called Carmen de Patagones, one of two twin towns, the other being Viedma, on opposite banks of the Rio Negro, 18 miles above its mouth. Both are small ports, with a population of about 5000 each today.

It is built on the face of a cliff which fronts the river, and
many of the houses are excavated even in the sandstone. The
river is about two or three hundred yards wide, and is deep
and rapid. The many islands, with their willow-trees, and the
flat headlands, seen one behind the other on the northern
boundary of the broad green valley, form, by the aid of the
bright sun, a view almost picturesque. The number of the inhabitants does not exceed a few hundreds. These Spanish colonies do not, like our British ones, carry within themselves the
elements of growth. Many Indians of pure blood reside here:
the tribe of the Cacique Lucanee constantly have their Toldos[3]
on the outskirts of the town. The local government party supplies them with provisions, by giving them all the old worn-out
horses, and they earn a little by making horse-rugs and other
articles of riding-gear. These Indians are considered civilized;
but what their character may have gained by a lesser degree
of ferocity, is almost counterbalanced by their entire immoral-
ity. Some of the younger men are, however, improving; they
are willing to labour, and a short time since a party went on
a sealing-voyage, and behaved very well. They were now enjoying the fruits of their labour, by being dressed in very gay,
clean clothes, and by being very idle. The taste they showed
in their dress was admirable; if you could have turned one of
these young Indians into a statue of bronze, his drapery would
have been perfectly graceful.

One day I rode to a large salt-lake, or Salina, which is distant fifteen miles from the town. During the winter it consists
of a shallow lake of brine, which in summer is converted into
a field of snow-white salt. The layer near the margin is from
four to five inches thick, but towards the centre its thickness
increases. This lake was two and a half miles long, and one
broad. Others occur in the neighbourhood many times larger,
and with a floor of salt, two and three feet in thickness, even
when under water during the winter. One of these brilliantly-
white and level expanses, in the midst of the brown and desolate plain, offers an extraordinary spectacle. A large quantity
of salt is annually drawn from the salina; and great piles, some
hundred tons in weight, were lying ready for exportation. The
season for working the salinas forms the harvest of Patagones;
for on it, the prosperity of the place depends. Nearly the whole
population encamps on the bank of the river, and the people

[3] [Darwin] The hovels of the Indians are thus called.

are employed in drawing out the salt in bullock-waggons. This salt is crystallized in great cubes, and is remarkably pure: Mr. Trenham Reeks has kindly analyzed some for me, and he finds in it only 0.26 of gypsum and 0.22 of earthy matter. It is a singular fact, that it does not serve so well for preserving meat as sea-salt from the Cape de Verd islands; and a merchant at Buenos Ayres told me that he considered it as fifty per cent. less valuable. Hence the Cape de Verd salt is constantly imported, and is mixed with that from these salinas. The purity of the Patagonian salt, or absence from it of those other saline bodies found in all sea-water, is the only assignable cause for this inferiority: a conclusion which no one, I think, would have suspected, but which is supported by the fact lately ascertained,[4] that those salts answer best for preserving cheese which contain most of the deliquescent chlorides.

The border of the lake is formed of mud: and in this numerous large crystals of gypsum, some of which are three inches long, lie embedded; whilst on the surface others of sulphate of soda lie scattered about. The Gauchos call the former the "Padre del sal," and the latter the "Madre;" they state that these progenitive salts always occur on the borders of the salinas, when the water begins to evaporate. The mud is black, and has a fetid odour. I could not at first imagine the cause of this, but I afterwards perceived that the froth which the wind drifted on shore was coloured green, as if by confervæ: I attempted to carry home some of this green matter, but from an accident failed. Parts of the lake seen from a short distance appeared of a reddish colour, and this perhaps was owing to some infusorial animalcula. The mud in many places was thrown up by numbers of some kind of worm, or annelidous animal. How surprising it is that any creatures should be able to exist in brine, and that they should be crawling among crystals of sulphate of soda and lime! And what becomes of these worms when, during the long summer, the surface is hardened into a solid layer of salt? Flamingoes in considerable numbers inhabit this lake, and breed here; throughout Patagonia, in Northern Chile, and at the Galapagos Islands, I met with these birds wherever there were lakes of brine. I saw them here wading about in search of food—probably for the worms which burrow in the mud; and these latter probably feed on infusoria or confervæ. Thus we have a little living world within itself,

4 [Darwin] Report of the Agricult. Chem. Assoc. in the Agricult. Gazette, 1845, p. 93.

adapted to these inland lakes of brine. A minute crustaceous animal (Cancer salinus) is said[5] to live in countless numbers in the brine-pans at Lymington; but only in those in which the fluid has attained, from evaporation, considerable strength— namely, about a quarter of a pound of salt to a pint of water. Well may we affirm, that every part of the world is habitable! Whether lakes of brine, or those subterranean ones hidden beneath volcanic mountains—warm mineral springs—the wide expanse and depths of the ocean—the upper regions of the atmosphere, and even the surface of perpetual snow—all support organic beings.

To the northward of the Rio Negro, between it and the inhabited country near Buenos Ayres, the Spaniards have only one small settlement, recently established at Bahia Blanca. The distance in a straight line to Buenos Ayres is very nearly five hundred British miles. The wandering tribes of horse Indians, which have always occupied the greater part of this country, having of late much harassed the outlying estancias, the government at Buenos Ayres equipped some time since an army under the command of General Rosas[6] for the purpose of exterminating them. The troops were now encamped on the

[5] [Darwin] Linnæan Trans., vol. xi. p. 205. It is remarkable how all the circumstances connected with the salt-lakes in Siberia and Patagonia are similar. Siberia, like Patagonia, appears to have been recently elevated above the waters of the sea. In both countries the salt-lakes occupy shallow depressions in the plains; in both the mud on the borders is black and fetid; beneath the crust of common salt, sulphate of soda or of magnesia occurs, imperfectly crystallized; and in both, the muddy sand is mixed with lentils of gypsum. The Siberian salt-lakes are inhabited by small crustaceous animals; and flamingoes (Edin. New Philos. Jour., Jan. 1830) likewise frequent them. As these circumstances, apparently so trifling, occur in two distant continents, we may feel sure that they are the necessary results of common causes. See *Pallas's Travels,* 1793 to 1794, pp. 129–134.

[6] [Editor] Juan Manual Rosas, born in Buenos Aires in 1793 and died in England in 1877, began life as a gaucho (by choice —he refused to accept money from his well-to-do father) and ended it in exile. In between, Rosas became a well-known Indian fighter, a wealthy landowner, governor of the province of Buenos Aires (Argentina's chief province) and dictator of all Argentina (1835–52). Argentines concede that he held Argentina together, but he was an oppressive tyrant who was finally overthrown by a revolt aided by Uruguay and Brazil.

banks of the Colorado; a river lying about eighty miles north-ward of the Rio Negro. When General Rosas left Buenos Ayres he struck in a direct line across the unexplored plains: and as the country was thus pretty well cleared of Indians, he left behind him, at wide intervals, a small party of soldiers with a troop of horses (*a posta*), so as to be enabled to keep up a communication with the capital. As the *Beagle* intended to call at Bahia Blanca, I determined to proceed there by land; and ultimately I extended my plan to travel the whole way by the postas to Buenos Ayres.

August 11th.—Mr. Harris, an Englishman residing at Pata-gones, a guide, and five Gauchos, who were proceeding to the army on business, were my companions on the journey. The Colorado, as I have already said, is nearly eighty miles distant: and as we travelled slowly, we were two days and a half on the road. The whole line of country deserves scarcely a better name than that of a desert. Water is found only in two small wells; it is called fresh; but even at this time of the year, during the rainy season, it was quite brackish. In the summer this must be a distressing passage; for now it was sufficiently deso-late. The valley of the Rio Negro, broad as it is, has merely been excavated out of the sandstone plain; for immediately above the bank on which the town stands, a level country commences, which is interrupted only by a few trifling valleys and depressions. Everywhere the landscape wears the same sterile aspect; a dry gravelly soil supports tufts of brown with-ered grass, and low scattered bushes, armed with thorns.

Shortly after passing the first spring we came in sight of a famous tree, which the Indians reverence as the altar of Wal-leechu. It is situated on a high part of the plain, and hence is a landmark visible at a great distance. As soon as a tribe of Indians come in sight of it, they offer their adorations by loud shouts. The tree itself is low, much branched, and thorny: just above the root it has a diameter of about three feet. It stands by itself without any neighbour, and was indeed the first tree we saw; afterwards we met with a few others of the same kind, but they were far from common. Being winter the tree had no leaves, but in their place numberless threads, by which the various offerings, such as cigars, bread, meat, pieces of cloth, &c. had been suspended. Poor Indians, not having anything better, only pull a thread out of their ponchos, and fasten it to the tree. Richer Indians are accustomed to pour spirits and maté into a certain hole, and likewise to smoke upwards, thinking thus to afford all possible gratification to Walleechu. To complete the scene, the tree was surrounded by the bleached bones of horses which had been slaughtered as sacrifices. All Indians of every age and sex make their offerings; they then think that their horses will not tire, and that they themselves shall be prosperous. The Gaucho who told me this, said that in the time of peace he had witnessed this scene, and that he and others used to wait till the Indians had passed by, for the sake of stealing from Walleechu the offerings.

The Gauchos think that the Indians consider the tree as the god itself; but it seems far more probable, that they regard it as the altar. The only cause which I can imagine for this choice, is its being a landmark in a dangerous passage. The Sierra de la Ventana is visible at an immense distance; and a Gaucho told me that he was once riding with an Indian a few miles to the north of the Rio Colorado, when the Indian commenced making the same loud noise, which is usual at the first sight of the distant tree; putting his hand to his head, and then pointing in the direction of the Sierra. Upon being asked the reason of this, the Indian said in broken Spanish, "First see the Sierra." About two leagues beyond this curious tree we halted for the night: at this instant an unfortunate cow was spied by the lynx-eyed Gauchos, who set off in full chace, and in a few minutes dragged her in with their lazos, and slaughtered her. We here had the four necessaries of life "en el campo,"—pasture for the horses, water (only a muddy puddle), meat and fire-wood. The Gauchos were in high spirits at finding all these luxuries; and we soon set to work at the poor cow. This was the first night which I passed under the open sky, with the gear of the recado for my bed. There is high enjoyment in the independence of the Gaucho life—to be able at any moment to pull up your horse, and say, "Here we will pass the night." The death-like stillness of the plain, the dogs keeping watch, the gipsy-group of Gauchos making their beds round the fire, have left in my mind a strongly-marked picture of this first night, which will never be forgotten.

The next day the country continued similar to that above described. It is inhabited by few birds or animals of any kind. Occasionally a deer, or a Guanaco (wild Llama) may be seen; but the Agouti (Cavia Patagonica) is the commonest quadruped. This animal here represents our hares. It differs, however, from that genus in many essential respects; for instance, it has only three toes behind. It is also nearly twice the size, weighing from twenty to twenty-five pounds. The Agouti is a true friend of the desert; it is a common feature in the landscape to see two or three hopping quickly one after the other in a straight line across these wild plains. They are found as far north as the Sierra Tapalguen (lat. 37° 30′), where the plain rather suddenly becomes greener and more humid; and their southern limit is between Port Desire and St. Julian, where there is no change in the nature of the country. It is a singular fact, that although the Agouti is not now found as far south as Port St. Julian, yet that Captain Wood, in his voyage in 1670, talks of them as being numerous there. What cause can have altered, in a wide, uninhabited, and rarely-visited country, the range of an animal like this? It appears also from the number shot by Captain Wood in one day at Port Desire, that they must have been considerably more abundant there formerly than at present. Where the Bizcacha lives and makes its burrows, the Agouti uses them; but where, as at Bahia Blanca, the Bizcacha is not found, the Agouti burrows for itself. The same thing occurs with the little owl of the Pampas (Athene cunicularia), which has so often been described as standing like a sentinel at the mouth of the burrows; for in Banda Oriental, owing to the absence of the Bizcacha, it is obliged to hollow out its own habitation.

The next morning, as we approached the Rio Colorado, the appearance of the country changed; we soon came on a plain covered with turf, which, from its flowers, tall clover, and little owls, resembled the Pampas. We passed also a muddy swamp of considerable extent, which in summer dries, and becomes incrusted with various salts; and hence is called a salitral. It was covered by low succulent plants, of the same kind with those growing on the sea-shore. The Colorado, at the pass where we crossed it, is only about sixty yards wide; generally it must be nearly double that width. Its course is very tortuous, being marked by willow-trees and beds of reeds: in a direct line the distance to the mouth of the river is said to be nine leagues, but by water twenty-five. We were delayed crossing in the canoe by some immense troops of mares, which were swimming the river in order to follow a division of troops into the interior. A more ludicrous spectacle I never beheld than the hundreds and hundreds of heads, all directed one way, with pointed ears and distended snorting nostrils, appearing just above the water like a great shoal of some amphibious animal. Mare's flesh is the only food which the soldiers have when on an expedition. This gives them a great facility of movement; for the distance to which horses can be driven over these plains is quite surprising: I have been assured that an unloaded horse can travel a hundred miles a day for many days successively.

The encampment of General Rosas was close to the river. It consisted of a square formed by waggons, artillery, straw huts, &c. The soldiers were nearly all cavalry; and I should think such a villanous, banditti-like army was never before collected together. The greater number of men were of a mixed breed, between Negro, Indian, and Spaniard. I know not the reason, but men of such origin seldom have a good expression of countenance. I called on the Secretary to show my passport. He began to cross-question me in the most dignified and mysterious manner. By good luck I had a letter of recommendation from the government of Buenos Ayres[7] to the Commandant of Patagones. This was taken to General Rosas, who sent me a very obliging message; and the Secretary returned all smiles and graciousness. We took up our residence in the *rancho*, or hovel, of a curious old Spaniard, who had served with Napoleon in the expedition against Russia.

We stayed two days at the Colorado; I had little to do, for the surrounding country was a swamp, which in summer (December), when the snow melts on the Cordillera, is overflowed by the river. My chief amusement was watching the Indian families as they came to buy little articles at the rancho where we stayed. It was supposed that General Rosas had about six hundred Indian allies. The men were a tall, fine race, yet it was afterwards easy to see in the Fuegian savage the same countenance rendered hideous by cold, want of food, and less civilization. Some authors, in defining the primary races of mankind, have separated these Indians into two classes; but this is certainly incorrect. Among the young women or chinas, some deserve to be called even beautiful. Their hair was coarse, but bright and black; and they wore it in two plaits hanging down to the waist. They had a high colour, and eyes that glistened with brilliancy; their legs, feet, and arms were small and elegantly formed; their ankles, and sometimes their waists, were ornamented by broad bracelets of blue beads.

---

[7] [Darwin] I am bound to express, in the strongest terms, my obligation to the Government of Buenos Ayres for the obliging manner in which passports to all parts of the country were given me, as naturalist of the *Beagle*.

Nothing could be more interesting than some of the family groups. A mother with one or two daughters would often come to our rancho, mounted on the same horse. They ride like men, but with their knees tucked up much higher. This habit, perhaps, arises from their being accustomed, when travelling, to ride the loaded horses. The duty of the women is to load and unload the horses; to make the tents for the night; in short to be, like the wives of all savages, useful slaves. The men fight, hunt, take care of the horses, and make the riding gear. One of their chief indoor occupations is to knock two stones together till they become round, in order to make the bolas. With this important weapon the Indian catches his game, and also his horse, which roams free over the plain. In fighting, his first attempt is to throw down the horse of his adversary with the bolas, and when entangled by the fall to kill him with the chuzo. If the balls only catch the neck or body of an animal, they are often carried away and lost. As the making the stones round is the labour of two days, the manufacture of the balls is a very common employment. Several of the men and women had their faces painted red, but I never saw the horizontal bands which are so common among the Fuegians. Their chief pride consists in having everything made of silver; I have seen a cacique with his spurs, stirrups, handle of his knife, and bridle made of this metal: the head-stall and reins being of wire, were not thicker than whipcord; and to see a fiery steed wheeling about under the command of so light a chain, gave to the horsemanship a remarkable character of elegance.

General Rosas intimated a wish to see me; a circumstance which I was afterwards very glad of. He is a man of an extraordinary character, and has a most predominant influence in the country, which it seems probable he will use to its prosperity and advancement.[8] He is said to be the owner of seventy-four square leagues of land, and to have about three hundred thousand head of cattle. His estates are admirably managed, and are far more productive of corn than those of others. He first gained his celebrity by his laws for his own estancias, and by disciplining several hundred men, so as to resist with success the attacks of the Indians. There are many stories current about the rigid manner in which his laws were enforced. One of these was, that no man, on penalty of being put into the stocks, should carry his knife on a Sunday: this

[8] [Darwin] This prophecy has turned out entirely and miserably wrong. 1845.

being the principal day for gambling and drinking, many quarrels arose, which from the general manner of fighting with the knife often proved fatal. One Sunday the Governor came in great form to pay the estancia a visit, and General Rosas, in his hurry, walked out to receive him with his knife, as usual, stuck in his belt. The steward touched his arm, and reminded him of the law; upon which turning to the Governor, he said he was extremely sorry, but that he must go into the stocks, and that till let out, he possessed no power even in his own house. After a little time the steward was persuaded to open the stocks, and to let him out, but no sooner was this done, than he turned to the steward and said, "You now have broken the laws, so you must take my place in the stocks." Such actions as these delighted the Gauchos, who all possess high notions of their own equality and dignity.

General Rosas is also a perfect horseman—an accomplishment of no small consequence in a country where an assembled army elected its general by the following trial: A troop of unbroken horses being driven into a corral, were let out through a gateway, above which was a cross-bar: it was agreed whoever should drop from the bar on one of these wild animals, as it rushed out, and should be able, without saddle or bridle, not only to ride it, but also to bring it back to the door of the corral, should be their general. The person who succeeded was accordingly elected; and doubtless made a fit general for such an army. This extraordinary feat has also been performed by Rosas.

By these means, and by conforming to the dress and habits of the Gauchos, he has obtained an unbounded popularity in the country, and in consequence a despotic power. I was assured by an English merchant, that a man who had murdered another, when arrested and questioned concerning his motive, answered, "He spoke disrespectfully of General Rosas, so I killed him." At the end of a week the murderer was at liberty. This doubtless was the act of the general's party, and not of the general himself.

In conversation he is enthusiastic, sensible, and very grave. His gravity is carried to a high pitch: I heard one of his mad buffoons (for he keeps two, like the barons of old) relate the following anecdote: "I wanted very much to hear a certain piece of music, so I went to the general two or three times to ask him; he said to me, 'Go about your business, for I am engaged.' I went a second time; he said, 'If you come again I will punish you.' A third time I asked, and he laughed. I rushed out of the tent, but it was too late; he ordered two soldiers to catch and stake me. I begged by all the Saints in heaven he would let me off; but it would not do;—when the general laughs he spares neither mad man nor sound." The poor flighty gentleman looked quite dolorous, at the very recollection of the staking. This is a very severe punishment; four posts are driven into the ground, and the man is extended by his arms and legs horizontally, and there left to stretch for several hours. The idea is evidently taken from the usual method of drying hides. My interview passed away without a smile, and I obtained a passport and order for the government post-horses, and this he gave me in the most obliging and ready manner.

In the morning we started for Bahia Blanca, which we reached in two days. Leaving the regular encampment, we passed by the toldos of the Indians. These are round like ovens, and covered with hides; by the mouth of each, a tapering chuzo was stuck in the ground. The toldos were divided into separate groups, which belonged to the different caciques' tribes, and the groups were again divided into smaller ones, according to the relationship of the owners. For several miles we travelled along the valley of the Colorado. The alluvial plains on the side appeared fertile, and it is supposed that they are well adapted to the growth of corn. Turning northward from the river, we soon entered on a country, differing from the plains south of the river. The land still continued dry and sterile; but it supported many different kinds of plants, and the grass, though brown and withered, was more abundant, as the thorny bushes were less so. These latter in a short space entirely disappeared, and the plains were left without a thicket to cover their nakedness. This change in the vegetation marks the commencement of the grand calcareo-argillaceous deposit, which forms the wide extent of the Pampas, and covers the granitic rocks of Banda Oriental. From the Strait of Magellan to the Colorado, a distance of about eight hundred miles, the face of the country is everywhere composed of shingle: the pebbles are chiefly of porphyry, and probably owe their origin to the rocks of the Cordillera. North of the Colorado this bed thins out, and the pebbles become exceedingly small, and here the characteristic vegetation of Patagonia ceases.

Having ridden about twenty-five miles, we came to a broad belt of sand-dunes, which stretches, as far as the eye can reach, to the east and west. The sand-hillocks resting on the clay, allow small pools of water to collect, and thus afford in this dry country an invaluable supply of fresh water. The great advantage arising from depressions and elevations of the soil, is not often brought home to the mind. The two miserable springs in the long passage between the Rio Negro and Colorado were caused by trifling inequalities in the plain; without them not a drop of water would have been found. The belt of sand-dunes is about eight miles wide; at some former period, it probably formed the margin of a grand estuary, where the Colorado now flows. In this district, where absolute proofs of the recent elevation of the land occur, such speculations can hardly be neglected by any one, although merely considering the physical geography of the country. Having crossed the sandy tract, we arrived in the evening at one of the post-houses; and, as the fresh horses were grazing at a distance, we determined to pass the night there.

The house was situated at the base of a ridge, between one and two hundred feet high—a most remarkable feature in this country. This posta was commanded by a negro lieutenant, born in Africa: to his credit be it said, there was not a rancho between the Colorado and Buenos Ayres in nearly such neat order as his. He had a little room for strangers, and a small corral for the horses, all made of sticks and reeds; he had also dug a ditch round his house, as a defence in case of being attacked. This would, however, have been of little avail, if the Indians had come; but his chief comfort seemed to rest in the thought of selling his life dearly. A short time before, a body of Indians had travelled past in the night; if they had been aware of the posta, our black friend and his four soldiers would assuredly have been slaughtered. I did not any where meet a more civil and obliging man than this negro; it was therefore the more painful to see that he would not sit down and eat with us.

In the morning we sent for the horses very early, and started for another exhilarating gallop. We passed the Cabeza del Buey, an old name given to the head of a large marsh, which extends from Bahia Blanca. Here we changed horses, and passed through some leagues of swamps and saline marshes. Changing horses for the last time, we again began wading through the mud. My animal fell, and I was well soused in black mire—a very disagreeable accident, when one does not possess a change of clothes. Some miles from the fort we met a man, who told us that a great gun had been fired, which is a signal that Indians are near. We immediately left the road, and followed the edge of a marsh, which when chased offers the best mode of escape. We were glad to arrive within the walls, when we found all the alarm was about nothing, for the Indians turned out to be friendly ones, who wished to join General Rosas.

Bahia Blanca scarcely deserves the name of a village. A few houses and the barracks for the troops are enclosed by a deep ditch and fortified wall. The settlement is only of recent standing (since 1828); and its growth has been one of trouble. The government of Buenos Ayres unjustly occupied it by force, instead of following the wise example of the Spanish Viceroys, who purchased the land near the older settlement of the Rio Negro, from the Indians. Hence the need of the fortifications; hence the few houses and little cultivated land without the limits of the walls: even the cattle are not safe from the attacks of the Indians beyond the boundaries of the plain, on which the fortress stands.[9]

The part of the harbour where the *Beagle* intended to anchor being distant twenty-five miles, I obtained from the Commandant a guide and horses, to take me to see whether she had arrived. Leaving the plain of green turf, which extended along the course of a little brook, we soon entered on a wide level waste consisting either of sand, saline marshes, or bare mud. Some parts were clothed by low thickets, and others with those succulent plants, which luxuriate only where salt abounds. Bad as the country was, ostriches, deer, agoutis, and armadilloes, were abundant. My guide told me, that two months before he had a most narrow escape of his life: he was out hunting with two other men, at no great distance from this part of the country, when they were suddenly met by a party of Indians, who giving chace, soon overtook and killed his two friends. His own horse's legs were also caught by the bolas; but he jumped off, and with his knife cut them free: while doing this he was obliged to dodge round his horse, and received two severe wounds from their chuzos. Springing on the saddle, he managed, by a most wonderful exertion, just to keep ahead of the long spears of his pursuers, who followed him to within sight

[9] [Editor] Bahia Blanca, near the mouth of a river emptying into a bay also named Bahia Blanca, has become one of Argentina's chief ports, with a population of more than 100,000. Puerto Belgrano, the principal base of the Argentine Navy, is on the bay itself, not far from where the *Beagle* anchored.

of the fort. From that time there was an order that no one should stray far from the settlement. I did not know of this when I started, and was surprised to observe how earnestly my guide watched a deer, which appeared to have been frightened from a distant quarter.

We found the *Beagle* had not arrived, and consequently set out on our return, but the horses soon tiring, we were obliged to bivouac on the plain. In the morning we had caught an armadillo, which, although a most excellent dish when roasted in its shell, did not make a very substantial breakfast and dinner for two hungry men. The ground at the place where we stopped for the night, was incrusted with a layer of sulphate of soda, and hence, of course, was without water. Yet many of the smaller rodents managed to exist even here, and the tucutuco was making its odd little grunt beneath my head, during half the night. Our horses were very poor ones, and in the morning they were soon exhausted from not having had any thing to drink, so that we were obliged to walk. About noon the dogs killed a kid, which we roasted. I ate some of it, but it made me intolerably thirsty. This was the more distressing as the road, from some recent rain, was full of little puddles of clear water, yet not a drop was drinkable. I had scarcely been twenty hours without water, and only part of the time under a hot sun, yet the thirst rendered me very weak. How people survive two or three days under such circumstances, I cannot imagine: at the same time, I must confess that my guide did not suffer at all, and was astonished that one day's deprivation should be so troublesome to me.

I have several times alluded to the surface of the ground being incrusted with salt. This phenomenon is quite different from that of the salinas, and more extraordinary. In many parts of South America, wherever the climate is moderately dry, these incrustations occur; but I have nowhere seen them so abundant as near Bahia Blanca. The salt here, and in other parts of Patagonia, consists chiefly of sulphate of soda with some common salt. As long as the ground remains moist in these salitrales (as the Spaniards improperly call them, mistaking this substance for saltpetre), nothing is to be seen but an extensive plain composed of a black, muddy soil, supporting scattered tufts of succulent plants. On returning through one of these tracts, after a week's hot weather, one is surprised to see square miles of the plain white, as if from a slight fall of snow, here and there heaped up by the wind into little drifts.

This latter appearance is chiefly caused by the salts being drawn up, during the slow evaporation of the moisture, round blades of dead grass, stumps of wood, and pieces of broken earth, instead of being crystallized at the bottoms of the puddles of water. The salitrales occur either on level tracts elevated only a few feet above the level of the sea, or on alluvial land bordering rivers. M. Parchappe[10] found that the saline incrustation on the plain, at the distance of some miles from the sea, consisted chiefly of sulphate of soda, with only seven per cent. of common salt; whilst nearer to the coast, the common salt increased to 37 parts in a hundred. This circumstance would tempt one to believe that the sulphate of soda is generated in the soil, from the muriate, left on the surface during the slow and recent elevation of this dry country. The whole phenomenon is well worthy the attention of naturalists. Have the succulent, salt-loving plants, which are well known to contain much soda, the power of decomposing the muriate? Does the black fetid mud, abounding with organic matter, yield the sulphur and ultimately the sulphuric acid?[11]

Two days afterwards I again rode to the harbour: when not far from our destination, my companion, the same man as before, spied three people hunting on horseback. He immediately dismounted, and watching them intently, said, "They don't ride like Christians, and nobody can leave the fort." The three hunters joined company, and likewise dismounted from their horses. At last one mounted again and rode over the hill out of sight. My companion said, "We must now get on our horses: load your pistol;" and he looked to his own sword. I asked, "Are they Indians?"—"Quien sabe? (who knows?) if there are no more than three, it does not signify." It then struck me, that the one man had gone over the hill to fetch the rest of his tribe. I suggested this; but all the answer I could extort was, "Quien sabe?" His head and eye never for a minute ceased scanning slowly the distant horizon. I thought his uncommon coolness too good a joke, and asked him why he did not return home. I was startled when he answered, "We are returning, but in a line so as to pass near a swamp, into which we can

10 [Darwin] Voyage dans l'Amérique Mérid. par M. A. d'Orbigny. Part. Hist. tom. i. p. 664.

11 [Editor] Sulfate deposits, such as Darwin found in Patagonia, are believed today to arise chiefly through physical and chemical action.

gallop the horses as far as they can go, and then trust to our own legs; so that there is no danger." I did not feel quite so confident of this, and wanted to increase our pace. He said, "No, not until they do." When any little inequality concealed us, we galloped; but when in sight, continued walking. At last we reached a valley, and turning to the left, galloped quickly to the foot of a hill; he gave me his horse to hold, made the dogs lie down, and then crawled on his hands and knees to reconnoitre. He remained in this position for some time, and at last, bursting out in laughter, exclaimed, "Mugeres!" (women!) He knew them to be the wife and sister-in-law of the major's son, hunting for ostrich's eggs. I have described this man's conduct, because he acted under the full impression that they were Indians. As soon, however, as the absurd mistake was found out, he gave me a hundred reasons why they could not have been Indians; but all these were forgotten at the time. We then rode on in peace and quietness to a low point called Punta Alta, whence we could see nearly the whole of the great harbour of Bahia Blanca.

The wide expanse of water is choked up by numerous great mud-banks, which the inhabitants call Cangrejales, or *crabberies*, from the number of small crabs. The mud is so soft that it is impossible to walk over them, even for the shortest distance. Many of the banks have their surfaces covered with long rushes, the tops of which alone are visible at high water. On one occasion, when in a boat, we were so entangled by these shallows that we could hardly find our way. Nothing was visible but the flat beds of mud: the day was not very clear, and there was much refraction, or as the sailors expressed it, "things loomed high." The only object within our view which was not level was the horizon; rushes looked like bushes unsupported in the air, and water like mud-banks, and mud-banks like water.

We passed the night in Punta Alta, and I employed myself in searching for fossil bones; this point being a perfect catacomb for monsters of extinct races. The evening was perfectly calm and clear; the extreme monotony of the view gave it an interest even in the midst of mud-banks and gulls, sand-hillocks and solitary vultures. In riding back in the morning we came across a very fresh track of a Puma, but did not succeed in finding it. We saw also a couple of Zorillos, or skunks,—odious animals, which are far from uncommon. In general appearance the Zorillo resembles a polecat, but it is rather larger, and much thicker in proportion. Conscious of its power, it roams by day about the open plain, and fears neither dog nor man. If a dog is urged to the attack, its courage is instantly checked by a few drops of the fetid oil, which brings on violent sickness and running at the nose. Whatever is once polluted by it, is for ever useless. Azara says the smell can be perceived at a league distant; more than once, when entering the harbour of Monte Video, the wind being off shore, we have perceived the odour on board the *Beagle*. Certain it is, that every animal most willingly makes room for the Zorillo.

CHAPTER V

BAHIA BLANCA

Bahia Blanca — Geology — Numerous gigantic extinct Quadrupeds — Recent Extinction — Longevity of Species — Large Animals do not require a luxuriant Vegetation — Southern Africa — Siberian Fossils — Two Species of Ostrich — Habits of Oven-bird — Armadilloes — Venomous Snake, Toad, Lizard — Hybernation of Animals — Habits of Sea-Pen — Indian Wars and Massacres — Arrowhead, Antiquarian Relic

The *Beagle* arrived here on the 24th of August, and a week afterwards sailed for the Plata. With Captain Fitz Roy's consent I was left behind, to travel by land to Buenos Ayres. I will here add some observations, which were made during this visit and on a previous occasion, when the *Beagle* was employed in surveying the harbour.[1]

[1] [Editor] During the *Beagle's* first visit to the Bahia Blanca bay, in September 1832, a party from the ship, including Darwin and Fitz Roy, made a trip to the settlement, then called Fortress Argentino (miscalled "Argentina" by Fitz Roy). Here is an account of the visit, slightly abridged, from Fitz Roy's journal:

"Sept. 7. Messrs. Darwin, Rowlett, and Harris set out with me to visit the Buenos Ayrean settlement, called Argentina. Mr. Harris undertook to be our guide, but after two hours' sailing and pulling we found ourselves near the head of a creek, between two soft mud-banks, where we could neither row nor turn the boat. We could not land because the mud was too soft to bear our weight, so there we staid till the tide flowed. About two hours after this stoppage there was water enough for us to cross a large bank, and gain the right channel, from which we had deviated, and then, with a flowing tide, we made rapid progress, until the 'Guardia' was announced to us. This was a small hut near the water side, but to reach it we had to wind along a tortuous canal, between banks

The plain, at the distance of a few miles from the coast, belongs to the great Pampean formation, which consists in part of a reddish clay, and in part of a highly calcareous marly rock. Nearer the coast there are some plains formed from the wreck of soft mud: and when we arrived at the landing-place seven hours had been passed among rushy mud-banks, surrounded by which we were often prevented from seeing any solid land. The water was every where salt, the tide running strongly, and the boat often aground.

"Waiting to meet us was an assemblage of grotesque figures, which I shall not easily forget—a painter would have been charmed with them. A dark visaged Quixotic character, partly in uniform, mounted on a large lean horse, and attended by several wild looking, but gaily dressed gauchos, was nearest to us. Behind him, a little on one side, were a few irregular soldiers, variously armed, and no two dressed alike, but well mounted, and desperate-looking fellows; while on the other side, a group of almost naked Indian prisoners sat devouring the remains of a half roasted horse; and as they scowled at us savagely, still holding the large bones they had been gnawing, with their rough hair and scanty substitutes for clothing blown about by the wind, I thought I had never beheld a more singular group.

"The tall man in uniform was the commandant of the settlement, or fortress, called Argentina: he and his soldiers had arrived to welcome us, supposing that we were bringing supplies from Buenos Ayres for the needy colony. The Indian prisoners had been brought to work, and assist in carrying the supplies which were expected. Finding that we were neither Buenos Ayreans, nor traders from any other place, it was supposed that we must be spies sent to reconnoitre the place previous to a hostile attack. Neither the explanations nor assertions of Mr. Harris had any weight, for as he was our countryman, they naturally concluded he was in league with us; yet, as the commandant had some idea that we might, by possibility, be what we maintained we were, he disregarded the whispers and suggestions of his people, and offered to carry us to the settlement for a night's lodging.

"Leaving the boat's crew to bivouac, as usual, I accepted a horse offered to me, and took the purser up behind; Mr. Darwin and Harris being also mounted behind two gaucho soldiers, away we went across a flat plain to the settlement. Mr. Darwin was carried off before the rest of the party, to be cross-questioned by an old major, who seemed to be considered the wisest man of the detachment, and he, poor old soul, thought we were very suspicious characters, especially Mr. Darwin, whose objects seemed most mysterious.

"In consequence, we were watched, though otherwise most hospitably treated; and when I proposed to return, next morning, to

of the upper plain, and from mud, gravel, and sand thrown up
by the sea during the slow elevation of the land, of which elevation we have evidence in upraised beds of recent shells, and in
rounded pebbles of pumice scattered over the country. At

the boat, trifling excuses were made about the want of horses and
fear of Indians arriving, by which I saw that the commandant
wished to detain us, but was unwilling to do so forcibly; telling
him, therefore, I should walk back, and setting out to do so, I
elicited an order for horses, maugre the fears and advice of his
major, who gave him all sorts of warnings about us. However, he
sent an escort with us, and a troop of gaucho soldiers were that
very morning posted upon the rising grounds nearest to the *Beagle,*
to keep a watch on our movements.

"We afterwards heard, that the old major's suspicions had been
very much increased by Harris's explanation of Mr. Darwin's occupation. 'Un naturalista' was a term unheard of by any person
in the settlement, and being unluckily explained by Harris as meaning 'a man that knows every thing,' any further attempt to quiet
anxiety was useless.

"As this small settlement has seldom been visited by strangers,
I will describe its primitive state. In the midst of a level country,
watered by several brooks, and much of it thickly covered with
a kind of trefoil, stands a mud-walled erection, dignified with the
sounding appellation of 'La fortaleza protectora Argentina.' It is
a polygon, 282 yards in diameter, having about twenty-four sides,
and surrounded by a narrow ditch. In some places the walls are
almost twenty feet high, but in others I was reminded of the brothers' quarrel at the building of ancient Rome, for there is a mere
ditch, over which a man could jump. It is, however, said by the
gauchos, that a ditch six feet wide will stop a mounted Indian, and
that their houses require no further defence from attacks of the
aborigines. How, or why it is that such excellent horsemen do not
teach their horses to leap, I cannot understand.

"Within, and outside the fort, were huts (ranchos) and a few
small houses:—more were not required for the inhabitants, who,
including the garrison, only amounted to four hundred souls. Some
half-dozen brass guns were in a serviceable condition; and two or
three other pieces occupied old carriages, but did not seem to be
trustworthy. . . .

"We returned to the *Beagle* without another delay among the
mud-banks, and found the rising grounds (heights they could not
be called), nearest the ship, occupied by the troop of gaucho soldiers. As they did not interfere with us, our surveying operations
were begun, and carried on as usual. Mr. Darwin, and those who
could be spared from duties afloat, roamed about the country; and
a brisk trade was opened with the soldiers for ostriches and their
eggs, for deer, cavies, and armadilloes."

Punta Alta we have a section of one of these later-formed little plains, which is highly interesting from the number and extraordinary character of the remains of gigantic land-animals embedded in it. These have been fully described by Professor Owen,[2] in the Zoology of the voyage of the *Beagle*, and are deposited in the College of Surgeons. I will here give only a brief outline of their nature.

First, parts of three heads and other bones of the Megatherium, the huge dimensions of which are expressed by its name. Secondly, the Megalonyx, a great allied animal. Thirdly, the Scelidotherium, also an allied animal, of which I obtained a nearly perfect skeleton. It must have been as large as a rhinoceros: in the structure of its head it comes, according to Mr. Owen, nearest to the Cape Anteater, but in some other respects it approaches to the armadilloes. Fourthly, the Mylodon Darwinii, a closely related genus of little inferior size. Fifthly, another gigantic edental quadruped. Sixthly, a large animal, with an osseous coat in compartments, very like that of an armadillo. Seventhly, an extinct kind of horse, to which I shall have again to refer. Eighthly, a tooth of a Pachydermatous animal, probably the same with the Macrauchenia, a huge beast with a long neck like a camel, which I shall also refer to again. Lastly, the Toxodon, perhaps one of the strangest animals ever discovered: in size it equalled an elephant or megatherium, but the structure of its teeth, as Mr. Owen states, proves indisputably that it was intimately related to the Gnawers, the order which, at the present day, includes most of the smallest quadrupeds: in many details it is allied to the Pachydermata: judging from the position of its eyes, ears, and nostrils, it was probably aquatic, like the Dugong and Manatee, to which it is also allied. How wonderfully are the different Orders, at the present time so well separated, blended together in different points of the structure of the Toxodon!

The remains of these nine great quadrupeds, and many detached bones were found embedded on the beach, within the space of about 200 yards square. It is a remarkable circum-

[2] [Editor] Sir Richard Owen, English surgeon, paleontologist, and comparative anatomist, born in Lancaster, 1804, died in London, 1892. Discoverer of *Trichinella spiralis*, the parasite responsible for trichinosis, and of "Owen's lines," growth lines in tooth dentin. Became head of the natural history department of the British Museum in 1856. Prepared a report on the fossil animals sent back from the *Beagle* by Darwin.

stance that so many different species should be found together;
and it proves how numerous in kind the ancient inhabitants of
this country must have been. At the distance of about thirty
miles from P. Alta, in a cliff of red earth, I found several fragments of bones, some of large size. Among them were the
teeth of a gnawer, equalling in size and closely resembling those
of the Capybara, whose habits have been described; and therefore, probably, an aquatic animal. There was also part of the
head of a Ctenomys; the species being different from the
Tucutuco, but with a close general resemblance. The red earth,
like that of the Pampas, in which these remains were embedded, contains, according to Professor Ehrenberg, eight
fresh-water and one salt-water infusorial animalcule; therefore,
probably, it was an estuary deposit.

The remains at Punta Alta were embedded in stratified
gravel and reddish mud, just such as the sea might now wash
up on a shallow bank. They were associated with twenty-three
species of shells, of which thirteen are recent and four others
very closely related to recent forms; whether the remaining
ones are extinct or simply unknown, must be doubtful, as few
collections of shells have been made on this coast. As, however,
the recent species were embedded in nearly the same proportional numbers with those now living in the bay, I think there
can be little doubt, that this accumulation belongs to a very
late tertiary period. From the bones of the Scelidotherium, including even the knee-cap, being intombed in their proper relative positions, and from the osseous armour of the great
armadillo-like animal being so well preserved, together with
the bones of one of its legs, we may feel assured that these
remains were fresh and united by their ligaments, when deposited in the gravel together with the shells. Hence we have
good evidence that the above enumerated gigantic quadrupeds,
more different from those of the present day than the oldest of
the tertiary quadrupeds of Europe, lived whilst the sea was
peopled with most of its present inhabitants; and we have confirmed that remarkable law so often insisted on by Mr. Lyell,
namely, that the "longevity of the species in the mammalia is
upon the whole inferior to that of the testacea."[3]

The great size of the bones of the Megatheroid animals,
including the Megatherium, Megalonyx, Scelidotherium, and

[3] [Darwin] Principles of Geology, vol. iv. p. 40. [Although the
term Testacea is now confined to an order of protozoa, in Darwin's
day it meant any shelled invertebrate.—Ed.]

Mylodon, is truly wonderful. The habits of life of these animals were a complete puzzle to naturalists, until Professor Owen[4] lately solved the problem with remarkable ingenuity. The teeth indicate, by their simple structure, that these Megatheroid animals lived on vegetable food, and probably on the leaves and small twigs of trees; their ponderous forms and great strong curved claws seem so little adapted for locomotion, that some eminent naturalists have actually believed, that, like the sloths, to which they are intimately related, they subsisted by climbing back downwards on trees, and feeding on the leaves. It was a bold, not to say preposterous, idea to conceive even antediluvian trees, with branches strong enough to bear animals as large as elephants. Professor Owen, with far more probability, believes that, instead of climbing on the trees, they pulled the branches down to them, and tore up the smaller ones by the roots, and so fed on the leaves. The colossal breadth and weight of their hinder quarters, which can hardly be imagined without having been seen, become, on this view, of obvious service, instead of being an incumbrance: their apparent clumsiness disappears. With their great tails and their huge heels firmly fixed like a tripod on the ground, they could freely exert the full force of their most powerful arms and great claws. Strongly rooted, indeed, must that tree have been, which could have resisted such force! The Mylodon, moreover, was furnished with a long extensile tongue like that of the giraffe, which, by one of those beautiful provisions of nature, thus reaches with the aid of its long neck its leafy food. I may remark, that in Abyssinia the elephant, according to Bruce, when it cannot reach with its proboscis the branches, deeply scores with its tusks the trunk of the tree, up and down and all round, till it is sufficiently weakened to be broken down.

The beds including the above fossil remains, stand only from fifteen to twenty feet above the level of high-water; and hence the elevation of the land has been small (without there has been an intercalated period of subsidence, of which we have no evidence) since the great quadrupeds wandered over the surrounding plains; and the external features of the country must then have been very nearly the same as now. What, it may naturally be asked, was the character of the vegetation at that period; was the country as wretchedly sterile as it now

[4] [Darwin] This theory was first developed in the Zoology of the Voyage of the *Beagle*, and subsequently in Professor Owen's Memoir on Mylodon robustus.

is? As so many of the co-embedded shells are the same with
those now living in the bay, I was at first inclined to think that
the former vegetation was probably similar to the existing one;
but this would have been an erroneous inference, for some of
these same shells live on the luxuriant coast of Brazil; and generally, the character of the inhabitants of the sea are useless as
guides to judge of those on the land. Nevertheless, from the
following considerations, I do not believe that the simple fact
of many gigantic quadrupeds having lived on the plains round
Bahia Blanca, is any sure guide that they formerly were clothed
with a luxuriant vegetation: I have no doubt that the sterile
country a little southward, near the Rio Negro, with its scattered thorny trees, would support many and large quadrupeds.

That large animals require a luxuriant vegetation, has been
a general assumption which has passed from one work to another; but I do not hesitate to say that it is completely false,
and that it has vitiated the reasoning of geologists on some
points of great interest in the ancient history of the world. The
prejudice has probably been derived from India, and the Indian
islands, where troops of elephants, noble forests, and impenetrable jungles, are associated together in every one's mind. If,
however, we refer to any work of travels through the southern
parts of Africa, we shall find allusions in almost every page
either to the desert character of the country, or to the numbers
of large animals inhabiting it. The same thing is rendered evident by the many engravings which have been published of
various parts of the interior. When the *Beagle* was at Cape
Town, I made an excursion of some days' length into the country, which at least was sufficient to render that which I had
read more fully intelligible.

Dr. Andrew Smith, who, at the head of his adventurous
party, has lately succeeded in passing the Tropic of Capricorn,
informs me that, taking into consideration the whole of the
southern part of Africa, there can be no doubt of its being a
sterile country. On the southern and south-eastern coasts there
are some fine forests, but with these exceptions, the traveller
may pass for days together through open plains, covered by a
poor and scanty vegetation. It is difficult to convey any accurate
idea of degrees of comparative fertility; but it may be safely
said that the amount of vegetation supported at any one time[5]

[5] [Darwin] I mean by this to exclude the total amount, which
may have been successively produced and consumed during a given
period.

by Great Britain, exceeds, perhaps even tenfold, the quantity on an equal area, in the interior parts of Southern Africa. The fact that bullock-waggons can travel in any direction, excepting near the coast, without more than occasionally half an hour's delay in cutting down bushes, gives, perhaps, a more definite notion of the scantiness of the vegetation. Now, if we look to the animals inhabiting these wide plains, we shall find their numbers extraordinarily great, and their bulk immense. We must enumerate the elephant, three species of rhinoceros, and probably, according to Dr. Smith, two others, the hippopotamus, the giraffe, the bos caffer[6]—as large as a full-grown bull, and the elan—but little less, two zebras, and the quaccha, two gnus, and several antelopes even larger than these latter animals. It may be supposed that although the species are numerous, the individuals of each kind are few. By the kindness of Dr. Smith, I am enabled to show that the case is very different. He informs me, that in lat. 24°, in one day's march with the bullock-waggons, he saw, without wandering to any great distance on either side, between one hundred and one hundred and fifty rhinoceroses, which belonged to three species: the same day he saw several herds of giraffes, amounting together to nearly a hundred; and that, although no elephant was observed, yet they are found in this district. At the distance of a little more than one hour's march from their place of encampment on the previous night, his party actually killed at one spot eight hippopotamuses, and saw many more. In this same river there were likewise crocodiles. Of course it was a case quite extraordinary, to see so many great animals crowded together, but it evidently proves that they must exist in great numbers. Dr. Smith describes the country passed through that day, as "being thinly covered with grass, and bushes about four feet high, and still more thinly with mimosa-trees." The waggons were not prevented travelling in a nearly straight line.

Besides these large animals, every one the least acquainted with the natural history of the Cape, has read of the herds of antelopes, which can be compared only with the flocks of migratory birds. The numbers indeed of the lion, panther, and hyæna, and the multitude of birds of prey, plainly speak of the abundance of the smaller quadrupeds: one evening seven lions were counted at the same time prowling round Dr. Smith's encampment. As this able naturalist remarked to me, the carnage each day in Southern Africa must indeed be ter-

[6] [Editor] The African cape buffalo.

rific! I confess it is truly surprising how such a number of animals can find support in a country producing so little food. The larger quadrupeds no doubt roam over wide tracts in search of it; and their food chiefly consists of underwood, which probably contains much nutriment in a small bulk. Dr. Smith also informs me that the vegetation has a rapid growth; no sooner is a part consumed, than its place is supplied by a fresh stock. There can be no doubt, however, that our ideas respecting the apparent amount of food necessary for the support of large quadrupeds are much exaggerated: it should have been remembered that the camel, an animal of no mean bulk, has always been considered as the emblem of the desert.

The belief that where large quadrupeds exist, the vegetation must necessarily be luxuriant, is the more remarkable, because the converse is far from true. Mr. Burchell[7] observed to me that when entering Brazil, nothing struck him more forcibly than the splendour of the South American vegetation contrasted with that of South Africa, together with the absence of all large quadrupeds. In his Travels,[8] he has suggested that the comparison of the respective weights (if there were sufficient data) of an equal number of the largest herbivorous quadrupeds of each country would be extremely curious. If we take on the one side, the elephant,[9] hippopotamus, giraffe,

[7] [Editor] William John Burchell, British naturalist, born 1782(?), died 1863. Appointed botanist to the East India Company, he was sent to St. Helena in 1810, and in 1811 went to Capetown, from which he carried out one of the earliest scientific explorations of South Africa.

[8] [Darwin] Travels in the Interior of South Africa, vol. ii. p. 207.

[9] [Darwin] The elephant which was killed at Exeter Change was estimated (being partly weighed) at five tons and a half. The elephant actress, as I was informed, weighed one ton less; so that we may take five as the average of a full-grown elephant. I was told at the Surrey Gardens, that a hippopotamus which was sent to England cut up into pieces was estimated at three tons and a half; we will call it three. From these premises we may give three tons and a half to each of the five rhinoceroses; perhaps a ton to the giraffe, and half to the bos caffer as well as to the elan (a large ox weighs from 1200 to 1500 pounds). This will give an average (from the above estimates) of 2.7 of a ton for the ten largest herbivorous animals of Southern Africa. In South America, allowing 1200 pounds for the two tapirs together, 550 for the guanaco and vicuna, 500 for three deer, 300 for the capybara, peccari, and a monkey, we shall have an average of 250 pounds, which I believe is overstating the result. The ratio will therefore be as 6048 to 250, or 24 to 1, for the ten largest animals from the two continents.

bos caffer, elan, certainly three, and probably five species of rhinoceros; and on the American side, two tapirs, the guanaco, three deer, the vicuna, peccari, capybara (after which we must choose from the monkeys to complete the number), and then place these two groups alongside each other, it is not easy to conceive ranks more disproportionate in size. After the above facts, we are compelled to conclude, against anterior probability,[10] that among the mammalia there exists no close relation between the *bulk* of the species, and the *quantity* of the vegetation, in the countries which they inhabit.

With regard to the number of large quadrupeds, there certainly exists no quarter of the globe which will bear comparison with Southern Africa. After the different statements which have been given, the extremely desert character of that region will not be disputed. In the European division of the world, we must look back to the tertiary epochs, to find a condition of things among the mammalia, resembling that now existing at the Cape of Good Hope. Those tertiary epochs, which we are apt to consider as abounding to an astonishing degree with large animals, because we find the remains of many ages accumulated at certain spots, could hardly boast of more large quadrupeds than Southern Africa does at present. If we speculate on the condition of the vegetation during those epochs, we are at least bound so far to consider existing analogies, as not to urge as absolutely necessary a luxuriant vegetation, when we see a state of things so totally different at the Cape of Good Hope.

We know[11] that the extreme regions of North America,

[10] [Darwin] If we suppose the case of the discovery of a skeleton of a Greenland whale in a fossil state, not a single cetaceous animal being known to exist, what naturalist would have ventured conjecture on the possibility of a carcass so gigantic being supported on the minute crustacea and mollusca living in the frozen seas of the extreme North?

[11] [Darwin] See Zoological Remarks to Capt. Back's Expedition, by Dr. Richardson. He says, "The subsoil north of latitude 56° is perpetually frozen, the thaw on the coast not penetrating above three feet, and at Bear Lake, in latitude 64°, not more than twenty inches. The frozen substratum does not of itself destroy vegetation, for forests flourish on the surface, at a distance from the coast." [Sir John Richardson, born 1787 in Scotland, died in England in 1865, British naturalist and explorer. A Navy surgeon, he was appointed naturalist and surgeon to the first two Arctic expeditions of Sir John Franklin, and also served in the same roles on Arctic expeditions led by George Back and Edward Parry (the first man to

many degrees beyond the limit where the ground at the depth of a few feet remains perpetually congealed, are covered by forests of large and tall trees. In a like manner, in Siberia, we have woods of birch, fir, aspen, and larch, growing in a latitude[12] (64°), where the mean temperature of the air falls below the freezing point, and where the earth is so completely frozen, that the carcass of an animal embedded in it is perfectly preserved. With these facts we must grant, as far as *quantity alone* of vegetation is concerned, that the great quadrupeds of the later tertiary epochs might, in most parts of Northern Europe and Asia, have lived on the spots where their remains are now found. I do not here speak of the *kind* of vegetation necessary for their support; because, as there is evidence of physical changes, and as the animals have become extinct, so may we suppose that the species of plants have likewise been changed.

These remarks, I may be permitted to add, directly bear on the case of the Siberian animals preserved in ice. The firm conviction of the necessity of a vegetation possessing a character of tropical luxuriance, to support such large animals, and the impossibility of reconciling this with the proximity of perpetual congelation, was one chief cause of the several theories of sudden revolutions of climate, and of overwhelming catastrophes, which were invented to account for their entombment. I am far from supposing that the climate has not changed since the period when those animals lived, which now lie buried in the ice. At present I only wish to show, that as far as *quantity* of food *alone* is concerned, the ancient rhinoceroses might have roamed over the *steppes* of central Siberia (the northern parts probably being under water) even in their present condition, as well as the living rhinoceroses and elephants over the *Karros* of Southern Africa.[13]

---

try to reach the Pole). He closed his career as an explorer by commanding one of the several expeditions sent out to search for Sir John Franklin's ill-fated 1845 expedition in search of the Northwest Passage.—Ed.]

[12] [Darwin] See Humboldt, Fragmens Asiatiques, p. 386: Barton's Geography of Plants: and Malte Brun. In the latter work it is said that the limit of the growth of trees in Siberia may be drawn under the parallel of 70°.

[13] [Editor] Little was known of the Ice Ages at the time Darwin wrote. Louis Agassiz advanced the hypothesis that there had been Ice Ages in *Etudes sur les Glaciers* in 1840, in the interval between

I will now give an account of the habits of some of the more interesting birds which are common on the wild plains of Northern Patagonia; and first for the largest, or South American ostrich. The ordinary habits of the ostrich are familiar to every one. They live on vegetable matter, such as roots and grass; but at Bahia Blanca I have repeatedly seen three or four come down at low water to the extensive mud-banks which are then dry, for the sake, as the Gauchos say, of feeding on small fish. Although the ostrich in its habits is so shy, wary, and solitary, and although so fleet in its pace, it is caught without much difficulty by the Indian or Gaucho armed with the bolas. When several horsemen appear in a semicircle, it becomes confounded, and does not know which way to escape. They generally prefer running against the wind; yet at the first start they expand their wings, and like a vessel make all sail. On one fine hot day I saw several ostriches enter a bed of tall rushes, where they squatted concealed, till quite closely approached. It is not generally known that ostriches readily take to the water. Mr. King informs me that at the Bay of San Blas, and at Port Valdes in Patagonia, he saw these birds swimming several times from island to island. They ran into the water both when driven down to a point, and likewise of their own accord when not frightened: the distance crossed was about two hundred yards. When swimming, very little of their bodies appear above water; their necks are extended a little forward, and their progress is slow. On two occasions I saw some ostriches swimming across the Santa Cruz river, where its course was about four hundred yards wide, and the stream rapid. Captain Sturt,[14] when descending the Murrumbidgee, in Australia, saw two emus in the act of swimming.

The inhabitants of the country readily distinguish, even at a distance, the cock bird from the hen. The former is larger and darker-coloured,[15] and has a bigger head. The ostrich, I believe the cock, emits a singular, deep-toned, hissing note: when first I heard it, standing in the midst of some sand-hillocks, I thought it was made by some wild beast, for it is a sound that

---

the publication of the first two editions of *The Voyage of the Beagle*. Agassiz' first detailed exposition of the hypothesis, "Système glaciare," was published in 1847, two years after publication of the second and only revised edition of the *Voyage*.

[14] [Darwin] Sturt's Travels, vol. ii. p. 74.

[15] [Darwin] A Gaucho assured me that he had once seen a snow-white or Albino variety, and that it was a most beautiful bird.

one cannot tell whence it comes, or from how far distant. When we were at Bahia Blanca in the months of September and October, the eggs, in extraordinary numbers, were found all over the country. They lie either scattered and single, in which case they are never hatched, and are called by the Spaniards huachos; or they are collected together into a shallow excavation, which forms the nest. Out of the four nests which I saw, three contained twenty-two eggs each, and the fourth twenty-seven. In one day's hunting on horseback sixty-four eggs were found; forty-four of these were in two nests, and the remaining twenty, scattered huachos. The Gauchos unanimously affirm, and there is no reason to doubt their statement, that the male bird alone hatches the eggs, and for some time afterwards accompanies the young. The cock when on the nest lies very close; I have myself almost ridden over one. It is asserted that at such times they are occasionally fierce, and even dangerous, and that they have been known to attack a man on horseback, trying to kick and leap on him. My informer pointed out to me an old man, whom he had seen much terrified by one chasing him. I observe in Burchell's travels in South Africa, that he remarks, "Having killed a male ostrich, and the feathers being dirty, it was said by the Hottentots to be a nest bird." I understand that the male emu in the Zoological Gardens takes charge of the nest; this habit, therefore, is common to the family.

The Gauchos unanimously affirm that several females lay in one nest. I have been positively told that four or five hen birds have been watched to go in the middle of the day, one after the other, to the same nest. I may add, also, that it is believed in Africa, that two or more females lay in one nest.[16] Although the habit at first appears very strange, I think the cause may be explained in a simple manner. The number of eggs in the nest varies from twenty to forty, and even to fifty; and according to Azara, sometimes to seventy or eighty. Now although it is most probable, from the number of eggs found in one district being so extraordinarily great in proportion to the parent birds, and likewise from the state of the ovarium of the hen, that she may in the course of the season lay a large number, yet the time required must be very long. Azara states,[17] that a female in a state of domestication laid seventeen eggs, each at the interval of three days one from another. If the hen was obliged to hatch her own eggs, before the last was laid the

16 [Darwin] Burchell's Travels, vol. i. p. 280.
17 [Darwin] Azara, vol. iv. p. 173.

first probably would be addled; but if each laid a few eggs at successive periods, in different nests, and several hens, as is stated to be the case, combined together, then the eggs in one collection would be nearly of the same age. If the number of eggs in one of these nests is, as I believe, not greater on an average than the number laid by one female in the season, then there must be as many nests as females, and each cock bird will have its fair share of the labour of incubation; and that during a period when the females probably could not sit, from not having finished laying.[18] I have before mentioned the great numbers of huachos, or deserted eggs; so that in one day's hunting twenty were found in this state. It appears odd that so many should be wasted. Does it not arise from the difficulty of several females associating together, and finding a male ready to undertake the office of incubation? It is evident that there must at first be some degree of association between at least two females; otherwise the eggs would remain scattered over the wide plains, at distances far too great to allow of the male collecting them into one nest: some authors have believed that the scattered eggs were deposited for the young birds to feed on. This can hardly be the case in America, because the huachos, although often found addled and putrid, are generally whole.

When at the Rio Negro in Northern Patagonia, I repeatedly heard the Gauchos talking of a very rare bird which they called Avestruz Petise. They described it as being less than the common ostrich (which is there abundant), but with a very close general resemblance. They said its colour was dark and mottled, and that its legs were shorter, and feathered lower down than those of the common ostrich. It is more easily caught by the bolas than the other species. The few inhabitants who had seen both kinds, affirmed they could distinguish them apart from a long distance. The eggs of the small species appeared, however, more generally known; and it was remarked, with surprise, that they were very little less than those of the Rhea, but of a slightly different form, and with a tinge of pale blue. This species occurs most rarely on the plains bordering the Rio Negro; but about a degree and a half further south they

[18] [Darwin] Lichtenstein, however, asserts (Travels, vol. ii. p. 25) that the hens begin sitting when they have laid ten or twelve eggs; and that they continue laying, I presume, in another nest. This appears to me very improbable. He asserts that four or five hens associate for incubation with one cock, who sits only at night.

are tolerably abundant. When at Port Desire, in Patagonia (lat. 48°), Mr. Martens shot an ostrich; and I looked at it, forgetting at the moment, in the most unaccountable manner, the whole subject of the Petises, and thought it was a not full-grown bird of the common sort. It was cooked and eaten before my memory returned. Fortunately the head, neck, legs, wings, many of the larger feathers, and a large part of the skin, had been preserved; and from these a very nearly perfect specimen has been put together, and is now exhibited in the museum of the Zoological Society. Mr. Gould, in describing this new species, has done me the honour of calling it after my name.

Among the Patagonian Indians in the Strait of Magellan, we found a half Indian, who had lived some years with the tribe, but had been born in the northern provinces. I asked him if he had ever heard of the Avestruz Petise? He answered by saying, "Why there are none others in these southern countries." He informed me that the number of eggs in the nest of the petise is considerably less than in that of the other kind, namely, not more than fifteen on an average; but he asserted that more than one female deposited them. At Santa Cruz we saw several of these birds. They were excessively wary: I think they could see a person approaching when too far off to be distinguished themselves. In ascending the river few were seen; but in our quiet and rapid descent, many, in pairs and by fours or fives, were observed. It was remarked that this bird did not expand its wings, when first starting at full speed, after the manner of the northern kind. In conclusion I may observe, that the Struthio rhea inhabits the country of La Plata as far as a little south of the Rio Negro in lat. 41°, and that the Struthio Darwinii takes its place in Southern Patagonia; the part about the Rio Negro being neutral territory. M. A. d'Orbigny,[19] when at the Rio Negro, made great exertions to procure this bird, but never had the good fortune to succeed. Dobrizhoffer[20] long ago was aware of there being two kinds of ostriches; he

[19] [Darwin] When at the Rio Negro, we heard much of the indefatigable labours of this naturalist. M. Alcide d'Orbigny, during the years 1825 to 1833, traversed several large portions of South America, and has made a collection, and is now publishing the results on a scale of magnificence, which at once places himself in the list of American travellers second only to Humboldt.

[20] [Darwin] Account of the Abipones, A.D. 1749, vol. i. (English translation), p. 314.

says, "You must know, moreover, that Emus differ in size and habits in different tracts of land; for those that inhabit the plains of Buenos Ayres and Tucuman are larger, and have black, white, and grey feathers; those near to the Strait of Magellan are smaller and more beautiful, for their white feathers are tipped with black at the extremity, and their black ones in like manner terminate in white."

A very singular little bird, Tinochorus rumicivorus, is here common: in its habits and general appearance, it nearly equally partakes of the characters, different as they are, of the quail and snipe. The Tinochorus is found in the whole of southern South America, wherever there are sterile plains, or open dry pasture land. It frequents in pairs or small flocks the most desolate places, where scarcely another living creature can exist. Upon being approached they squat close, and then are very difficult to be distinguished from the ground. When feeding they walk rather slowly, with their legs wide apart. They dust themselves in roads and sandy places, and frequent particular spots, where they may be found day after day: like partridges, they take wing in a flock. In all these respects, in the muscular gizzard adapted for vegetable food, in the arched beak and fleshy nostrils, short legs and form of foot, the Tinochorus has a close affinity with quails. But as soon as the bird is seen flying, its whole appearance changes; the long pointed wings, so different from those in the gallinaceous order, the irregular manner of flight, and plaintive cry uttered at the moment of rising, recall the idea of a snipe. The sportsmen of the *Beagle* unanimously called it the short-billed snipe. To this genus, or rather to the family of the Waders, its skeleton shows that it is really related.

The Tinochorus is closely related to some other South American birds. Two species of the genus Attagis are in almost every respect ptarmigans in their habits; one lives in Tierra del Fuego, above the limits of the forest land; and the other just beneath the snow-line on the Cordillera of Central Chile. A bird of another closely allied genus, Chionis alba, is an inhabitant of the antarctic regions; it feeds on sea-weed and shells on the tidal rocks. Athough not web-footed, from some unaccountable habit, it is frequently met with far out at sea. This small family of birds is one of those which, from its varied relations to other families, although at present offering only difficulties to the systematic naturalist, ultimately may assist in revealing the grand scheme, common to the present and past ages, on which organized beings have been created.

The genus Funarius contains several species, all small birds, living on the ground, and inhabiting open dry countries. In structure they cannot be compared to any European form. Ornithologists have generally included them among the creepers, although opposed to that family in every habit. The best known species is the common oven-bird of La Plata, the Casara or housemaker of the Spaniards. The nest, whence it takes its name, is placed in the most exposed situations, as on the top of a post, a bare rock, or on a cactus. It is composed of mud and bits of straw, and has strong thick walls: in shape it precisely resembles an oven, or depressed beehive. The opening is large and arched, and directly in front, within the nest, there is a partition, which reaches nearly to the roof, thus forming a passage or antechamber to the true nest.

Another and smaller species of Furnarius (F. cunicularius), resembles the oven-bird in the general reddish tint of its plumage, in a peculiar shrill reiterated cry, and in an odd manner of running by starts. From its affinity, the Spaniards call it Casarita (or little housebuilder), although its nidification is quite different. The Casarita builds its nest at the bottom of a narrow cylindrical hole, which is said to extend horizontally to nearly six feet under ground. Several of the country people told me, that when boys, they had attempted to dig out the nest, but had scarcely ever succeeded in getting to the end of the passage. The bird chooses any low bank of firm sandy soil by the side of a road or stream. Here (at Bahia Blanca) the walls round the houses are built of hardened mud; and I noticed that one, which enclosed a courtyard where I lodged, was bored through by round holes in a score of places. On asking the owner the cause of this, he bitterly complained of the little casarita, several of which I afterwards observed at work. It is rather curious to find how incapable these birds must be of acquiring any notion of thickness, for although they were constantly flitting over the low wall, they continued vainly to bore through it, thinking it an excellent bank for their nests. I do not doubt that each bird, as often as it came to daylight on the opposite side, was greatly surprised at the marvellous fact.

I have already mentioned nearly all the mammalia common in this country. Of armadilloes three species occur, namely, the Dasypus minutus or *pichy*, the D. villosus or *peludo*, and the *apar*. The first extends ten degrees further south than any other kind: a fourth species, the *Mulita,* does not come as far south as Bahia Blanca. The four species have nearly similar habits; the *peludo,* however, is nocturnal, while the others wander by day over the open plains, feeding on beetles, larvæ, roots, and even small snakes. The *apar,* commonly called *mataco,* is remarkable by having only three moveable bands; the rest of its tesselated covering being nearly inflexible. It has the power of rolling itself into a perfect sphere, like one kind of English woodlouse. In this state it is safe from the attack of dogs; for the dog not being able to take the whole in its mouth, tries to bite one side, and the ball slips away. The smooth hard covering of the *mataco* offers a better defence than the sharp spines of the hedgehog. The *pichy* prefers a very dry soil; and the sand-dunes near the coast, where for many months it can never taste water, is its favourite resort: it often tries to escape notice, by squatting close to the ground. In the course of a day's ride, near Bahia Blanca, several were generally met with. The instant one was perceived, it was necessary, in order to catch it, almost to tumble off one's horse; for in soft soil the animal burrowed so quickly, that its hinder quarters would almost disappear before one could alight. It seems almost a pity to kill such nice little animals, for as a Gaucho said, while sharpening his knife on the back of one, "Son tan mansos" (they are so quiet).

Of reptiles there are many kinds: one snake (a Trigonocephalus, or Cophias), from the size of the poison channel in its fangs, must be very deadly. Cuvier, in opposition to some other naturalists, makes this a sub-genus of the rattlesnake, and intermediate between it and the viper. In confirmation of this opinion, I observed a fact, which appears to me very curious and instructive, as showing how every character, even though it may be in some degree independent of structure, has a tendency to vary by slow degrees. The extremity of the tail of this snake is terminated by a point, which is very slightly enlarged; and as the animal glides along, it constantly vibrates the last inch; and this part striking against the dry grass and brushwood, produces a rattling noise, which can be distinctly heard at the distance of six feet. As often as the animal was irritated or surprised, its tail was shaken; and the vibrations were extremely rapid. Even as long as the body retained its irritability, a tendency to this habitual movement was evident. This Trigonocephalus has, therefore, in some respects the structure of a viper, with the habits of a rattlesnake: the noise, however, being produced by a simpler device. The expression of this snake's face was hideous and fierce; the pupil consisted of a vertical slit in a mottled and coppery iris; the jaws were broad at the base, and the nose terminated in a triangular projection. I do not think I ever saw any thing more ugly, excepting, perhaps, some of the vampire bats. I imagine this repulsive aspect originates from the features being placed in positions, with respect to each other, somewhat proportional to those of the human face; and thus we obtain a scale of hideousness.

Amongst the Batrachian reptiles, I found only one little toad (Phryniscus nigricans), which was most singular from its colour. If we imagine, first, that it had been steeped in the blackest ink, and then, when dry, allowed to crawl over a board, freshly painted with the brightest vermilion, so as to colour the soles of its feet and parts of its stomach, a good idea of its appearance will be gained. If it had been an unnamed species, surely it ought to have been called *Diabolicus*, for it is a fit toad to preach in the ear of Eve. Instead of being nocturnal in its habits, as other toads are, and living in damp obscure recesses, it crawls during the heat of the day about the dry sand-hillocks and arid plains, where not a single drop of water can be found. It must necessarily depend on the dew for its moisture; and this probably is absorbed by the skin, for it is known, that these reptiles possess great powers of cutaneous absorption. At Maldonado, I found one in a situation nearly as dry as at Bahia Blanca, and thinking to give it a great treat, carried it to a pool of water; not only was the little animal unable to swim, but, I think without help it would soon have been drowned.

Of lizards there were many kinds, but only one (Proctotretus multimaculatus) remarkable from its habits. It lives on the bare sand near the sea coast, and from its mottled colour, the brownish scales being speckled with white, yellowish red, and dirty blue, can hardly be distinguished from the surrounding surface. When frightened, it attempts to avoid discovery by feigning death, with outstretched legs, depressed body, and closed eyes: if further molested, it buries itself with great quickness in the loose sand. This lizard, from its flattened body and short legs, cannot run quickly.

I will here add a few remarks on the hybernation of animals in this part of South America. When we first arrived at Bahia Blanca, September 7th, 1832, we thought nature had granted scarcely a living creature to this sandy and dry country. By digging, however, in the ground, several insects, large spiders, and lizards were found in a half torpid state. On the 15th, a few animals began to appear, and by the 18th (three days from the equinox), every thing announced the commencement of spring. The plains were ornamented by the flowers of a pink wood-sorrel, wild peas, œnotheræ, and geraniums; and the birds began to lay their eggs. Numerous Lamellicorn and Heteromerous insects, the latter remarkable for their deeply sculptured bodies, were slowly crawling about; while the lizard tribe, the constant inhabitants of a sandy soil, darted about in every direction. During the first eleven days, whilst nature was dormant, the mean temperature taken from observations made every two hours on board the *Beagle,* was 51°; and in the middle of the day the thermometer seldom ranged above 55°. On the eleven succeeding days, in which all living things became so animated, the mean was 58°, and the range in the middle of the day between sixty and seventy. Here then an increase of seven degrees in mean temperature, but a greater one of extreme heat, was sufficient to awake the functions of life. At Monte Video, from which we had just before sailed, in the twenty-three days included between the 26th of July and the 19th of August, the mean temperature from 276 observations was 58°.4; the mean hottest day being 65°.5, and the coldest 46°. The lowest point to which the thermometer fell was 41°.5, and occasionally in the middle of the day it rose to 69° or 70°. Yet with this high temperature, almost every beetle, several genera of spiders, snails, and land-shells, toads and lizards were all lying torpid beneath stones. But we have seen that at Bahia Blanca, which is four degrees southward, and therefore with a climate only a very little colder, this same temperature with a rather less extreme heat, was sufficient to awake all orders of animated beings. This shows how nicely the stimulus required to arouse hybernating animals is governed by the usual climate of the district, and not by the absolute heat. It is well known that within the tropics, the hybernation, or more properly æstivation, of animals is determined not by the temperature, but by the times of drought. Near Rio de Janeiro, I was at first surprised to observe, that, a few days after some little depressions had been filled with water, they were peopled by numerous full-grown shells and beetles, which must have been lying dormant. Humboldt has related the strange accident of a hovel having been erected over a spot where a young crocodile lay buried in the hardened mud. He adds, "The Indians often find enormous boas, which they call Uji, or water serpents, in the same lethargic state. To reanimate them, they must be irritated or wetted with water."

I will only mention one other animal, a zoophyte (I believe Virgularia Patagonica), a kind of sea-pen. It consists of a thin, straight, fleshy stem, with alternate rows of polypi on each side, and surrounding an elastic stony axis, varying in length from eight inches to two feet. The stem at one extremity is truncate, but at the other is terminated by a vermiform fleshy appendage. The stony axis which gives strength to the stem may be traced at this extremity into a mere vessel filled with granular matter. At low water hundreds of these zoophytes might be seen, projecting like stubble, with the truncate end upwards, a few inches above the surface of the muddy sand. When touched or pulled they suddenly drew themselves in with force, so as nearly or quite to disappear. By this action, the highly elastic axis must be bent at the lower extremity, where it is naturally slightly curved; and I imagine it is by this elasticity alone that the zoophyte is enabled to rise again through the mud. Each polypus, though closely united to its brethren, has a distinct mouth, body, and tentacula. Of these polypi, in a large specimen, there must be many thousands; yet we see that they act by one movement: they have also one central axis connected with a system of obscure circulation, and the ova are produced in an organ distinct from the separate individuals.[21] Well may one be allowed to ask, what is an individual? It is always interesting to discover the foundation of the strange tales of the old voyagers; and I have no doubt but that the habits of

[21] [Darwin] The cavities leading from the fleshy compartments of the extremity, were filled with a yellow pulpy matter, which, examined under a microscope, presented an extraordinary appearance. The mass consisted of rounded, semi-transparent, irregular grains, aggregated together into particles of various sizes. All such particles, and the separate grains, possessed the power of rapid movement; generally revolving around different axes, but sometimes progressive. The movement was visible with a very weak power, but even with the highest its cause could not be perceived. It was very different from the circulation of the fluid in the elastic bag, containing the thin extremity of the axis. On other occasions, when dissecting small marine animals beneath the microscope, I have seen particles of pulpy matter, some of large size, as soon as they were disengaged, commence revolving. I have imagined, I know not with how much truth, that this granulo-pulpy matter was in process of being converted into ova. Certainly in this zoophyte such appeared to be the case.

this Virgularia explain one such case. Captain Lancaster, in his voyage[22] in 1601, narrates that on the sea-sands of the Island of Sombrero, in the East Indies, he "found a small twig growing up like a young tree, and on offering to pluck it up it shrinks down to the ground, and sinks, unless held very hard. On being plucked up, a great worm is found to be its root, and as the tree groweth in greatness, so doth the worm diminish; and as soon as the worm is entirely turned into a tree it rooteth in the earth, and so becomes great. This transformation is one of the strangest wonders that I saw in all my travels: for if this tree is plucked up, while young, and the leaves and bark stripped off, it becomes a hard stone when dry, much like white coral: thus is this worm twice transformed into different natures. Of these we gathered and brought home many."

During my stay at Bahia Blanca, while waiting for the *Beagle*, the place was in a constant state of excitement, from rumours of wars and victories, between the troops of Rosas and the wild Indians. One day an account came that a small party forming one of the postas on the line to Buenos Ayres, had been found all murdered. The next day three hundred men arrived from the Colorado, under the command of Commandant Miranda. A large portion of these men were Indians (*mansos*, or tame), belonging to the tribe of the Cacique Bernantio. They passed the night here; and it was impossible to conceive any thing more wild and savage than the scene of their bivouac. Some drank till they were intoxicated; others swallowed the steaming blood of the cattle slaughtered for their suppers, and then, being sick from drunkenness, they cast it up again, and were besmeared with filth and gore.

> Nam simul expletus dapibus, vinoque sepultus
> Cervicem inflexam posuit, jacuitque per antrum
> Immensus, saniem eructans, ac frusta cruenta
> Per somnum commixta mero.

In the morning they started for the scene of the murder, with orders to follow the "rastro," or track, even if it led them to Chile. We subsequently heard that the wild Indians had escaped into the great Pampas, and from some cause the track had been missed. One glance at the rastro tells these people a whole history. Supposing they examine the track of a thousand horses, they will soon guess the number of mounted ones by seeing how many have cantered; by the depth of the other im-

22 [Darwin] Kerr's Collection of Voyages, vol. viii. p. 119.

pressions, whether any horses were loaded with cargoes; by the irregularity of the footsteps, how far tired; by the manner in which the food has been cooked, whether the pursued travelled in haste; by the general appearance, how long it has been since they passed. They consider a rastro of ten days or a fortnight, quite recent enough to be hunted out. We also heard that Miranda struck from the west end of the Sierra Ventana, in a direct line to the island of Cholechel, situated seventy leagues up the Rio Negro. This is a distance of between two or three hundred miles, through a country completely unknown. What other troops in the world are so independent? With the sun for their guide, mares' flesh for food, their saddle-cloths for beds, —as long as there is a little water, these men would penetrate to the end of the world.

A few days afterwards I saw another troop of these banditti-like soldiers start on an expedition against a tribe of Indians at the small Salinas, who had been betrayed by a prisoner cacique. The Spaniard who brought the orders for this expedition was a very intelligent man. He gave me an account of the last engagement at which he was present. Some Indians, who had been taken prisoners, gave information of a tribe living north of the Colorado. Two hundred soldiers were sent; and they first discovered the Indians by a cloud of dust from their horses' feet, as they chanced to be travelling. The country was mountainous and wild, and it must have been far in the interior, for the Cordillera were in sight. The Indians, men, women, and children, were about one hundred and ten in number, and they were nearly all taken or killed, for the soldiers sabre every man. The Indians are now so terrified that they offer no resistance in a body, but each flies, neglecting even his wife and children; but when overtaken, like wild animals, they fight against any number to the last moment. One dying Indian seized with his teeth the thumb of his adversary, and allowed his own eye to be forced out sooner than relinquish his hold. Another, who was wounded, feigned death, keeping a knife ready to strike one more fatal blow. My informer said, when he was pursuing an Indian, the man cried out for mercy, at the same time that he was covertly loosing the bolas from his waist, meaning to whirl it round his head and so strike his pursuer. "I however struck him with my sabre to the ground, and then got off my horse, and cut his throat with my knife." This is a dark picture; but how much more shocking is the unquestionable fact, that all the women who appear above twenty years old are massacred in cold blood! When I exclaimed that this appeared rather inhuman, he answered, "Why, what can be done? they breed so!"

Every one here is fully convinced that this is the most just war, because it is against barbarians. Who would believe in this age that such atrocities could be committed in a Christian civilized country? The children of the Indians are saved, to be sold or given away as servants, or rather slaves for as long a time as the owners can make them believe themselves slaves; but I believe in their treatment there is little to complain of.

In the battle four men ran away together. They were pursued, one was killed, and the other three were taken alive. They turned out to be messengers or ambassadors from a large body of Indians, united in the common cause of defence, near the Cordillera. The tribe to which they had been sent was on the point of holding a grand council; the feast of mare's flesh was ready, and the dance prepared: in the morning the ambassadors were to have returned to the Cordillera. They were remarkably fine men, very fair, above six feet high, and all under thirty years of age. The three survivors of course possessed very valuable information; and to extort this they were placed in a line. The two first being questioned, answered, "No sé" (I do not know), and were one after the other shot. The third also said "No sé;" adding, "Fire, I am a man and can die!" Not one syllable would they breathe to injure the united cause of their country! The conduct of the above-mentioned cacique was very different: he saved his life by betraying the intended plan of warfare, and the point of union in the Andes. It was believed that there were already six or seven hundred Indians together, and that in summer their numbers would be doubled. Ambassadors were to have been sent to the Indians at the small Salinas, near Bahia Blanca, whom I have mentioned that this same cacique had betrayed. The communication, therefore, between the Indians, extends from the Cordillera to the coast of the Atlantic.

General Rosas's plan is to kill all stragglers, and having driven the remainder to a common point, to attack them in a body, in the summer, with the assistance of the Chilenos. This operation is to be repeated for three successive years. I imagine the summer is chosen as the time for the main attack, because the plains are then without water, and the Indians can

only travel in particular directions. The escape of the Indians
to the south of the Rio Negro, where in such a vast unknown
country they would be safe, is prevented by a treaty with the
Tehuelches to this effect;—that Rosas pays them so much to
slaughter every Indian who passes to the south of the river, but
if they fail in so doing, they themselves are to be exterminated.
The war is waged chiefly against the Indians near the Cordillera; for many of the tribes on this eastern side are fighting
with Rosas. The general, however, like Lord Chesterfield,
thinking that his friends may in a future day become his enemies, always places them in the front ranks, so that their numbers may be thinned. Since leaving South America we have
heard that this war of extermination completely failed.

Among the captive girls taken in the same engagement, there
were two very pretty Spanish ones, who had been carried away
by the Indians when young, and could now only speak the
Indian tongue. From their account they must have come from
Salta, a distance in a straight line of nearly one thousand miles.
This gives one a grand idea of the immense territory over which
the Indians roam: yet, great as it is, I think there will not, in
another half century, be a wild Indian northward of the Rio
Negro. The warfare is too bloody to last; the Christians killing
every Indian, and the Indians doing the same by the Christians.
It is melancholy to trace how the Indians have given way before the Spanish invaders. Schirdel[23] says that in 1535, when
Buenos Ayres was founded, there were villages containing two
and three thousand inhabitants. Even in Falconer's[24] time
(1750) the Indians made inroads as far as Luxan, Areco, and
Arrecife, but now they are driven beyond the Salado. Not only
have whole tribes been exterminated, but the remaining Indians

[23] [Darwin] Purchas's Collection of Voyages. I believe the date
was really 1537.
[24] [Editor] Thomas Falconer (usually spelled Falkner), born
1707, died 1784, British Jesuit missionary. The son of an apothe-
cary, Falkner shipped as surgeon of a slave ship which sailed to
Africa and Buenos Aires. In Buenos Aires, he fell sick and was
cared for by the Jesuits. When he recovered, he joined the order
and became a missionary in Paraguay, Tucumen (northwest Argentina) and Patagonia. "Description of Patagonia," "Botanical,
Mineral and Like Observations on the Products of America" and
other writings of his are an important source of information on
South America in the eighteenth century.

have become more barbarous: instead of living in large villages, and being employed in the arts of fishing, as well as of the chace, they now wander about the open plains, without home or fixed occupation.[25]

I heard also some account of an engagement which took place, a few weeks previously to the one mentioned, at Cholechel. This is a very important station on account of being a pass for horses; and it was, in consequence, for some time the headquarters of a division of the army. When the troops first arrived there they found a tribe of Indians, of whom they killed twenty or thirty. The cacique escaped in a manner which astonished every one. The chief Indians always have one or two picked horses, which they keep ready for any urgent occasion. On one of these, an old white horse, the cacique sprung, taking with him his little son. The horse had neither saddle nor bridle. To avoid the shots, the Indian rode in the peculiar method of his nation; namely, with an arm round the horse's neck, and one leg only on its back. Thus hanging on one side he was seen patting the horse's head, and talking to him. The pursuers urged every effort in the chace; the Commandant three times changed his horse, but all in vain. The old Indian father and his son escaped, and were free. What a fine picture one can form in one's mind,—the naked, bronze-like figure of the old man with his little boy, riding like a Mazeppa on the white horse, thus leaving far behind him the host of his pursuers!

I saw one day a soldier striking fire with a piece of flint, which I immediately recognized as having been a part of the head of an arrow. He told me it was found near the island of Cholechel, and that they are frequently picked up there. It was between two and three inches long, and therefore twice as large as those now used in the Tierra del Fuego: it was made of opake cream-coloured flint, but the point and barbs had been intentionally broken off. It is well known that no Pampas Indians now use bows and arrows. I believe a small tribe in Banda Oriental must be excepted; but they are widely separated from the Pampas Indians, and border close on those

[25] [Editor] Between 17,000 and 20,000 Indians are in Argentina today. Some 15,000 live in reservations near the Bolivian border in the northwest corner of Argentina and work in neighboring tobacco and sugar-cane fields. Between 1500 and 2000—the sole survivors of the once-proud Patagonian tribes—live on reservations in Patagonia.

tribes that inhabit the forest, and live on foot. It appears, therefore, that these arrow-heads are antiquarian[26] relics of the Indians, before the great change in habits consequent on the introduction of the horse into South America.

[26] [Darwin] Azara has even doubted whether the Pampas Indians ever used bows.

CHAPTER VI

BAHIA BLANCA TO BUENOS AYRES

September 8th.—I hired a Gaucho to accompany me on my
ride to Buenos Ayres, though with some difficulty, as the father
of one man was afraid to let him go, and another, who seemed
willing, was described to me as so fearful, that I was afraid
to take him, for I was told that even if he saw an ostrich at a
distance, he would mistake it for an Indian, and would fly like
the wind away. The distance to Buenos Ayres is about four
hundred miles, and nearly the whole way through an uninhabited country. We started early in the morning; ascending a few
hundred feet from the basin of green turf on which Bahia
Blanca stands, we entered on a wide desolate plain. It consists
of a crumbling argillaceo-calcareous rock, which, from the dry
nature of the climate, supports only scattered tufts of withered
grass, without a single bush or tree to break the monotonous
uniformity. The weather was fine, but the atmosphere remarkably hazy; I thought the appearance foreboded a gale, but the
Gauchos said it was owing to the plain, at some great distance
in the interior, being on fire. After a long gallop, having
changed horses twice, we reached the Rio Sauce: it is a deep,
rapid, little stream, not above twenty-five feet wide. The second posta on the road to Buenos Ayres stands on its banks; a
little above there is a ford for horses, where the water does not

reach to the horse's belly; but from that point, in its course
to the sea, it is quite impassable, and hence makes a most useful barrier against the Indians.

Insignificant as this stream is, the Jesuit Falconer, whose information is generally so very correct, figures it as a considerable river, rising at the foot of the Cordillera. With respect
to its source, I do not doubt that this is the case; for the
Gauchos assured me, that in the middle of the dry summer, this
stream, at the same time with the Colorado, has periodical
floods; which can only originate in the snow melting on the
Andes. It is extremely improbable that a stream so small as the
Sauce then was, should traverse the entire width of the continent; and indeed, if it were the residue of a large river, its waters, as in other ascertained cases, would be saline. During the
winter we must look to the springs round the Sierra Ventana
as the source of its pure and limpid stream. I suspect the plains
of Patagonia, like those of Australia, are traversed by many
water-courses, which only perform their proper parts at certain
periods. Probably this is the case with the water which flows
into the head of Port Desire, and likewise with the Rio Chupat,
on the banks of which masses of highly cellular scoriæ[1] were
found by the officers employed in the survey.

As it was early in the afternoon when we arrived, we took
fresh horses, and a soldier for a guide, and started for the Sierra de la Ventana. This mountain is visible from the anchorage
at Bahia Blanca; and Capt. Fitz Roy calculates its height to be
3,340 feet—an altitude very remarkable on this eastern side of
the continent. I am not aware that any foreigner, previous to
my visit, had ascended this mountain; and indeed very few of
the soldiers at Bahia Blanca knew anything about it. Hence we
heard of beds of coal, of gold and silver, of caves, and of
forests, all of which inflamed my curiosity, only to disappoint
it. The distance from the posta was about six leagues, over a
level plain of the same character as before. The ride was, however, interesting, as the mountain began to show its true form.
When we reached the foot of the main ridge, we had much
difficulty in finding any water, and we thought we should have
been obliged to have passed the night without any. At last we
discovered some by looking close to the mountain, for at the
distance even of a few hundred yards, the streamlets were

[1] [Editor] Lava containing large cellular spaces formed by the
escape of volcanic gas while the lava is still viscous; essentially, a
very coarse pumice.

buried and entirely lost in the friable calcareous stone and
loose detritus. I do not think Nature ever made a more solitary,
desolate pile of rock;—it well deserves its name of *Hurtado*,
or separated. The mountain is steep, extremely rugged, and
broken, and so entirely destitute of trees, and even bushes, that
we actually could not make a skewer to stretch out our meat
over the fire of thistle-stalks.[2] The strange aspect of this mountain is contrasted by the sea-like plain, which not only abuts
against its steep sides, but likewise separates the parallel ranges.
The uniformity of the colouring gives an extreme quietness to
the view;—the whitish grey of the quartz rock, and the light
brown of the withered grass of the plain, being unrelieved by
any brighter tint. From custom, one expects to see in the neighbourhood of a lofty and bold mountain, a broken country
strewed over with huge fragments. Here nature shows that the
last movement before the bed of the sea is changed into dry
land may sometimes be one of tranquillity. Under these circumstances I was curious to observe how far from the parent
rock any pebbles could be found. On the shores of Bahia
Blanca, and near the settlement, there were some of quartz,
which certainly must have come from this source: the distance
is forty-five miles.

The dew, which in the early part of the night wetted the
saddle-cloths under which we slept, was in the morning frozen.
The plain, though appearing horizontal, had insensibly sloped
up to a height of between 800 and 900 feet above the sea. In
the morning (9th of September) the guide told me to ascend
the nearest ridge, which he thought would lead me to the four
peaks that crown the summit. The climbing up such rough
rocks was very fatiguing; the sides were so indented, that what
was gained in one five minutes was often lost in the next. At
last, when I reached the ridge, my disappointment was extreme
in finding a precipitous valley as deep as the plain, which cut
the chain transversely in two, and separated me from the four
points. This valley is very narrow, but flat-bottomed, and it
forms a fine horse-pass for the Indians, as it connects the plains
on the northern and southern sides of the range. Having descended, and while crossing it, I saw two horses grazing: I
immediately hid myself in the long grass, and began to reconnoitre; but as I could see no signs of Indians I proceeded cautiously on my second ascent. It was late in the day, and this

[2] [Darwin] I call these thistle-stalks for the want of a more correct name. I believe it is a species of Eryngium.

part of the mountain, like the other, was steep and rugged. I was on the top of the second peak by two o'clock, but got there with extreme difficulty; every twenty yards I had the cramp in the upper part of both thighs, so that I was afraid I should not have been able to have got down again. It was also necessary to return by another road, as it was out of the question to pass over the saddle-back. I was therefore obliged to give up the two higher peaks. Their altitude was but little greater, and every purpose of geology had been answered; so that the attempt was not worth the hazard of any further exertion. I presume the cause of the cramp was the great change in the kind of muscular action, from that of hard riding to that of still harder climbing. It is a lesson worth remembering, as in some cases it might cause much difficulty.

I have already said the mountain is composed of white quartz rock, and with it a little glossy clay-slate is associated. At the height of a few hundred feet above the plain, patches of conglomerate adhered in several places to the solid rock. They resembled in hardness, and in the nature of the cement, the masses which may be seen daily forming on some coasts. I do not doubt these pebbles were in a similar manner aggregated, at a period when the great calcareous formation was depositing beneath the surrounding sea. We may believe that the jagged and battered forms of the hard quartz yet show the effects of the waves of an open ocean.

I was, on the whole, disappointed with this ascent. Even the view was insignificant;—a plain like the sea, but without its beautiful colour and defined outline. The scene, however, was novel, and a little danger, like salt to meat, gave it a relish. That the danger was very little was certain, for my two companions made a good fire—a thing which is never done when it is suspected that Indians are near. I reached the place of our bivouac by sunset, and drinking much maté,[3] and smoking several cigaritos, soon made up my bed for the night. The wind was very strong and cold, but I never slept more comfortably.

---

[3] [Editor] A beverage of Indian origin popular in many parts of South America. Also called Paraguay tea, maté is a stimulant like coffee or tea and is made from the young leaves and shoots of an evergreen related to the holly. Maté is brewed by placing the dried leaves in a cup or a special container (likewise known as a maté) and pouring water over them; the infusion is drunk through a bombilla, a metal straw with a strainer at the lower end. The maté evergreen is grown in Brazil and Paraguay.

September 10*th*.—In the morning, having fairly scudded before the gale, we arrived by the middle of the day at the Sauce posta. On the road we saw great numbers of deer, and near the mountain a guanaco. The plain, which abuts against the Sierra, is traversed by some curious gulleys, of which one was about twenty feet wide, and at least thirty deep; we were obliged in consequence to make a considerable circuit before we could find a pass. We stayed the night at the posta, the conversation, as was generally the case, being about the Indians. The Sierra Ventana was formerly a great place of resort; and three or four years ago there was much fighting there. My guide had been present when many Indians were killed: the women escaped to the top of the ridge, and fought most desperately with great stones; many thus saving themselves.

September 11*th*.—Proceeded to the third posta in company with the lieutenant who commanded it. The distance is called fifteen leagues; but it is only guess-work, and is generally overstated. The road was uninteresting, over a dry grassy plain; and on our left hand at a greater or less distance there were some low hills; a continuation of which we crossed close to the posta. Before our arrival we met a large herd of cattle and horses, guarded by fifteen soldiers; but we were told many had been lost. It is very difficult to drive animals across the plains; for if in the night a puma, or even a fox, approaches, nothing can prevent the horses dispersing in every direction; and a storm will have the same effect. A short time since, an officer left Buenos Ayres with five hundred horses, and when he arrived at the army he had under twenty.

Soon afterwards we perceived by the cloud of dust, that a party of horsemen were coming towards us; when far distant my companions knew them to be Indians, by their long hair streaming behind their backs. The Indians generally have a fillet round their heads, but never any covering; and their black hair blowing across their swarthy faces, heightens to an uncommon degree the wildness of their appearance. They turned out to be a party of Bernantio's friendly tribe, going to a salina for salt. The Indians eat much salt, their children sucking it like sugar. This habit is very different from that of the Spanish Gauchos, who, leading the same kind of life, eat scarcely any: according to Mungo Park,[4] it is people who live on vegetable food who have an unconquerable desire for salt. The Indians

---

[4] [Darwin] Travels in Africa, p. 233.

gave us good-humoured nods as they passed at full gallop, driving before them a troop of horses, and followed by a train of lanky dogs.

September 12th and 13th.—I staid at this posta two days, waiting for a troop of soldiers, which General Rosas had the kindness to send to inform me, would shortly travel to Buenos Ayres; and he advised me to take the opportunity of the escort. In the morning we rode to some neighbouring hills to view the country, and to examine the geology. After dinner the soldiers divided themselves into two parties for a trial of skill with the bolas. Two spears were stuck in the ground thirty-five yards apart, but they were struck and entangled only once in four or five times. The balls can be thrown fifty or sixty yards, but with little certainty. This, however, does not apply to a man on horseback; for when the speed of the horse is added to the force of the arm, it is said that they can be whirled with effect to the distance of eighty yards. As a proof of their force, I may mention, that at the Falkland Islands, when the Spaniards murdered some of their own countrymen and all the Englishmen, a young friendly Spaniard was running away, when a great tall man, by name Luciano, came at full gallop after him, shouting to him to stop, and saying that he only wanted to speak to him. Just as the Spaniard was on the point of reaching the boat, Luciano threw the balls: they struck him on the legs with such a jerk, as to throw him down and to render him for some time insensible. The man, after Luciano had had his talk, was allowed to escape. He told us that his legs were marked by great weals, where the thong had wound round, as if he had been flogged with a whip. In the middle of the day two men arrived, who brought a parcel from the next posta to be forwarded to the general: so that besides these two, our party consisted this evening of my guide and self, the lieutenant, and his four soldiers. The latter were strange beings; the first a fine young negro; the second half Indian and negro; and the two others nondescripts; namely, an old Chilian miner, the colour of mahogany, and another partly a mulatto; but two such mongrels, with such detestable expressions, I never saw before. At night, when they were sitting round the fire, and playing at cards, I retired to view such a Salvator Rosa[5] scene. They were seated under a low cliff, so that I could look down upon them; around the party were lying dogs, arms, remnants of deer and

[5] [Editor] A seventeenth-century Italian painter of the Neapolitan school, noted for his battle scenes.

ostriches; and their long spears were stuck in the turf. Further in the dark background, their horses were tied up, ready for any sudden danger. If the stillness of the desolate plain was broken by one of the dogs barking, a soldier, leaving the fire, would place his head close to the ground, and thus slowly scan the horizon. Even if the noisy teru-tero[6] uttered its scream, there would be a pause in the conversation, and every head, for a moment, a little inclined.

What a life of misery these men appear to us to lead! They were at least ten leagues from the Sauce posta, and since the murder committed by the Indians, twenty from another. The Indians are supposed to have made their attack in the middle of the night; for very early in the morning after the murder, they were luckily seen approaching this posta. The whole party here, however, escaped, together with the troop of horses; each one taking a line for himself, and driving with him as many animals as he was able to manage.

The little hovel, built of thistle-stalks, in which they slept, neither kept out the wind or rain; indeed in the latter case the only effect the roof had, was to condense it into larger drops. They had nothing to eat excepting what they could catch, such as ostriches, deer, armadilloes, &c., and their only fuel was the dry stalks of a small plant, somewhat resembling an aloe. The sole luxury which these men enjoyed was smoking the little paper cigars, and sucking maté. I used to think that the carrion vultures, man's constant attendants on these dreary plains, while seated on the little neighbouring cliffs, seemed by their very patience to say, "Ah! when the Indians come we shall have a feast."

In the morning we all sallied forth to hunt, and although we had not much success, there were some animated chaces. Soon after starting the party separated, and so arranged their plans, that at a certain time of the day (in guessing which they show much skill) they should all meet from different points of the compass on a plain piece of ground, and thus drive together the wild animals. One day I went out hunting at Bahia Blanca, but the men there merely rode in a crescent, each being about a quarter of a mile apart from the other. A fine male ostrich being turned by the headmost riders, tried to escape on one side. The Gauchos pursued at a reckless pace, twisting their horses about with the most admirable command, and each man whirl-

6 [Editor] A small South American bird, described more fully by Darwin a little further on in this chapter.

ing the balls round his head. At length the foremost threw them,
revolving through the air: in an instant the ostrich rolled over
and over, its legs fairly lashed together by the thong.

The plains abound with three kinds of partridge,[7] two of
which are as large as hen pheasants. Their destroyer, a small
and pretty fox, was also singularly numerous; in the course of
the day we could not have seen less than forty or fifty. They
were generally near their earths, but the dogs killed one. When
we returned to the posta, we found two of the party returned
who had been hunting by themselves. They had killed a puma,
and had found an ostrich's nest with twenty-seven eggs in it.
Each of these is said to equal in weight eleven hens' eggs; so
that we obtained from this one nest as much food as 297 hens'
eggs would have given.

September 14*th.*—As the soldiers belonging to the next posta
meant to return, and we should together make a party of five,
and all armed, I determined not to wait for the expected troops.
My host, the lieutenant, pressed me much to stop. As he had
been very obliging—not only providing me with food, but lend-
ing me his private horses—I wanted to make him some remu-
neration. I asked my guide whether I might do so, but he told
me certainly not; that the only answer I should receive, probably would be, "We have meat for the dogs in our country, and
therefore do not grudge it to a Christian." It must not be supposed that the rank of lieutenant in such an army would at all
prevent the acceptance of payment: it was only the high sense
of hospitality, which every traveller is bound to acknowledge
as nearly universal throughout these provinces. After galloping
some leagues, we came to a low swampy country, which extends for nearly eighty miles northward, as far as the Sierra
Tapalguen. In some parts there were fine damp plains, covered
with grass, while others had a soft, black, and peaty soil. There
were also many extensive but shallow lakes, and large beds
of reeds. The country on the whole resembled the better parts
of the Cambridgeshire fens. At night we had some difficulty in
finding, amidst the swamps, a dry place for our bivouac.

September 15*th.*—Rose very early in the morning, and
shortly after passed the posta where the Indians had murdered
the five soldiers. The officer had eighteen chuzo wounds in his
body. By the middle of the day, after a hard gallop, we reached
the fifth posta: on account of some difficulty in procuring

[7] [Darwin] Two species of Tinamus, and *Eudromia elegans* of
A. d'Orbigny, which can only be called a partridge with regard to
its habits.

horses we stayed there the night. As this point was the most exposed on the whole line, twenty-one soldiers were stationed here; at sunset they returned from hunting, bringing with them seven deer, three ostriches, and many armadilloes and partridges. When riding through the country, it is a common practice to set fire to the plain; and hence at night, as on this occasion, the horizon was illuminated in several places by brilliant conflagrations. This is done partly for the sake of puzzling any stray Indians, but chiefly for improving the pasture. In grassy plains unoccupied by the larger ruminating quadrupeds, it seems necessary to remove the superfluous vegetation by fire, so as to render the new year's growth serviceable.

The rancho at this place did not boast even of a roof, but merely consisted of a ring of thistle-stalks, to break the force of the wind. It was situated on the borders of an extensive but shallow lake, swarming with wild fowl, among which the black-necked swan was conspicuous.

The kind of plover, which appears as if mounted on stilts, (Himantopus nigricollis) is here common in flocks of considerable size. It has been wrongfully accused of inelegance; when wading about in shallow water, which is its favourite resort, its gait is far from awkward. These birds in a flock utter a noise, that singularly resembles the cry of a pack of small dogs in full chace: waking in the night, I have more than once been for a moment startled at the distant sound. The teru-tero (Vanellus cayanus) is another bird which often disturbs the stillness of the night. In appearance and habits it resembles in many respects our peewits; its wings, however, are armed with sharp spurs, like those on the legs of the common cock. As our peewit takes its name from the sound of its voice, so does the teru-tero. While riding over the grassy plains, one is constantly pursued by these birds, which appear to hate mankind, and I am sure deserve to be hated for their never-ceasing, unvaried, harsh screams. To the sportsman they are most annoying, by telling every other bird and animal of his approach: to the traveller in the country, they may possibly, as Molina says, do good, by warning him of the midnight robber. During the breeding season, they attempt, like our peewits, by feigning to be wounded, to draw away from their nests dogs and other enemies. The eggs of this bird are esteemed a great delicacy.

September 16*th*.—To the seventh posta at the foot of the Sierra Tapalguen. The country was quite level, with a coarse herbage and a soft peaty soil. The hovel was here remarkably neat, the posts and rafters being made of about a dozen dry thistle-stalks bound together with thongs of hide; and by the support of these Ionic-like columns, the roof and sides were thatched with reeds. We were here told a fact, which I would not have credited, if I had not had partly ocular proof of it; namely, that, during the previous night, hail as large as small apples, and extremely hard, had fallen with such violence, as to kill the greater number of the wild animals. One of the men had already found thirteen deer (Cervus campestris) lying dead, and I saw their *fresh* hides; another of the party, a few minutes after my arrival, brought in seven more. Now I well know, that one man without dogs could hardly have killed seven deer in a week. The men believed they had seen about fifteen dead ostriches (part of one of which we had for dinner); and they said that several were running about evidently blind in one eye. Numbers of smaller birds, as ducks, hawks, and partridges, were killed. I saw one of the latter with a black mark on its back, as if it had been struck with a paving-stone. A fence of thistle-stalks round the hovel was nearly broken down, and my informer, putting his head out to see what was the matter, received a severe cut, and now wore a bandage. The storm was said to have been of limited extent: we certainly saw from our last night's bivouac a dense cloud and lightning in this direction. It is marvellous how such strong animals as deer could thus have been killed; but I have no doubt, from the evidence I have given, that the story is not in the least exaggerated. I am glad, however, to have its credibility supported by the Jesuit Dobrizhoffer,[8] who, speaking of a country much to the northward, says, hail fell of an enormous size and killed vast numbers of cattle: the Indians hence called the place *Lalegraicavalca,* meaning "the little white things." Dr. Malcolmson, also, informs me that he witnessed in 1831 in India, a hailstorm, which killed numbers of large birds and much injured the cattle. These hail-stones were flat, and one was ten inches in circumference, and another weighed two ounces. They ploughed up a gravel-walk like musket-balls, and passed through glass-windows, making round holes, but not cracking them.

Having finished our dinner of hail-stricken meat, we crossed the Sierra Tapalguen; a low range of hills, a few hundred feet in height, which commences at Cape Corrientes.[9] The rock in

---

[8] [Darwin] History of the Abipones, vol. ii. p. 6.

[9] [Editor] A cape halfway between Bahia Blanca and the mouth of the Rio de la Plata.

this part is pure quartz; further eastward I understand it is granitic. The hills are of a remarkable form; they consist of flat patches of table-land, surrounded by low perpendicular cliffs, like the outliers of a sedimentary deposit. The hill which I ascended was very small, not above a couple of hundred yards in diameter; but I saw others larger. One which goes by the name of the "Corral," is said to be two or three miles in diameter, and encompassed by perpendicular cliffs between thirty and forty feet high, excepting at one spot, where the entrance lies. Falconer[10] gives a curious account of the Indians driving troops of wild horses into it, and then by guarding the entrance, keeping them secure. I have never heard of any other instance of table-land in a formation of quartz, and which, in the hill I examined, had neither cleavage nor stratification. I was told that the rock of the "Corral" was white, and would strike fire.

We did not reach the posta on the Rio Tapalguen till after it was dark. At supper, from something which was said, I was suddenly struck with horror at thinking that I was eating one of the favourite dishes of the country, namely, a half-formed calf, long before its proper time of birth. It turned out to be Puma; the meat is very white, and remarkably like veal in taste. Dr. Shaw was laughed at for stating that "the flesh of the lion is in great esteem, having no small affinity with veal, both in colour, taste, and flavour." Such certainly is the case with the Puma. The Gauchos differ in their opinion, whether the Jaguar is good eating, but are unanimous in saying that cat is excellent.

September 17*th.*—We followed the course of the Rio Tapalguen, through a very fertile country, to the ninth posta. Tapalguen itself, or the town of Tapalguen, if it may be so called, consists of a perfectly level plain, studded over, as far as the eye can reach, with the toldos, or oven-shaped huts of the Indians. The families of the friendly Indians, who were fighting on the side of Rosas, resided here. We met and passed many young Indian women, riding by two or three together on the same horse: they, as well as many of the young men, were strikingly handsome,—their fine ruddy complexions being the picture of health. Besides the toldos, there were three ranchos; one inhabited by the Commandant, and the two others by Spaniards with small shops.

We were here able to buy some biscuit. I had now been several days without tasting any thing besides meat: I did not at all dislike this new regimen; but I felt as if it would only have

10 [Darwin] Falconer's Patagonia, p. 70.

agreed with me with hard exercise. I have heard that patients
in England, when desired to confine themselves exclusively to
an animal diet, even with the hope of life before their eyes,
have hardly been able to endure it. Yet the Gaucho in the
Pampas, for months together, touches nothing but beef. But
they eat, I observe, a very large proportion of fat, which is
of a less animalized nature; and they particularly dislike dry
meat, such as that of the Agouti. Dr. Richardson,[11] also, has
remarked, "that when people have fed for a long time solely
upon lean animal food, the desire for fat becomes so insatiable,
that they can consume a large quantity of unmixed and even
oily fat without nausea:" this appears to me a curious physiological fact. It is, perhaps, from their meat regimen that the
Gauchos, like other carnivorous animals, can abstain long from
food. I was told that at Tandeel, some troops voluntarily pursued a party of Indians for three days, without eating or
drinking.

We saw in the shops many articles, such as horsecloths, belts,
and garters, woven by the Indian women. The patterns were
very pretty, and the colours brilliant; the workmanship of the
garters was so good that an English merchant at Buenos Ayres
maintained they must have been manufactured in England, till
he found the tassels had been fastened by split sinew.

September 18*th*.—We had a very long ride this day. At the
twelfth posta, which is seven leagues south of the Rio Salado,
we came to the first estancia with cattle and white women. Afterwards we had to ride for many miles through a country
flooded with water above our horses' knees. By crossing the
stirrups, and riding Arab-like with our legs bent up, we contrived to keep tolerably dry. It was nearly dark when we arrived at the Salado; the stream was deep, and about forty yards
wide; in summer, however, its bed becomes almost dry, and
the little remaining water nearly as salt as that of the sea. We
slept at one of the great estancias of General Rosas. It was
fortified, and of such an extent, that arriving in the dark I
thought it was a town and fortress. In the morning we saw
immense herds of cattle, the general here having seventy-four
square leagues of land. Formerly nearly three hundred men
were employed about this estate, and they defied all the attacks
of the Indians.

September 19*th*.—Passed the Guardia del Monte. This is a

[11] [Darwin] Fauna Boreali-Americana, vol. i. p. 35.

nice scattered little town, with many gardens, full of peach and quince trees. The plain here looked like that around Buenos Ayres; the turf being short and bright green, with beds of clover and thistles, and with bizcacha holes. I was very much struck with the marked change in the aspect of the country after having crossed the Salado. From a coarse herbage we passed on to a carpet of fine green verdure. I at first attributed this to some change in the nature of the soil, but the inhabitants assured me that here, as well as in Banda Oriental, where there is as great a difference between the country around Monte Video and the thinly-inhabited savannahs of Colonia, the whole was to be attributed to the manuring and grazing of the cattle. Exactly the same fact has been observed in the prairies[12] of North America, where coarse grass, between five and six feet high, when grazed by cattle, changes into common pasture land. I am not botanist enough to say whether the change here is owing to the introduction of new species, to the altered growth of the same, or to a difference in their proportional numbers. Azara has also observed with astonishment this change: he is likewise much perplexed by the immediate appearance of plants not occurring in the neighbourhood, on the borders of any track that leads to a newly-constructed hovel. In another part he says,[13] "ces chevaux (sauvages) ont la manie de préférer les chemins, et le bord des routes pour déposer leurs excrémens, dont on trouve des monceaux dans ces endroits."[14] Does this not partly explain the circumstance? We thus have lines of richly-manured land serving as channels of communication across wide districts.

Near the Guardia we find the southern limit of two European plants, now become extraordinarily common. The fennel in great profusion covers the ditch-banks in the neighbourhood of Buenos Ayres, Monte Video, and other towns. But the cardoon (Cynara cardunculus)[15] has a far wider range: it oc-

[12] [Darwin] See Mr. Atwater's account of the Prairies, in Silliman's N. A. Journal, vol. i. p. 117.

[13] [Darwin] Azara's Voyage, vol. i. p. 373.

[14] [Editor] "These horses (wild) have the madness of preferring the roads and the edge of these routes for disposing of their excrement, of which one finds great heaps in these places."

[15] [Darwin] M. A. d'Orbigny (vol. i. p. 474) says that the cardoon [a cactus related to the artichoke—Ed.] and artichoke are both found wild. Dr. Hooker (Botanical Magazine, vol. lv. p. 2862) has described a variety of the Cynara from this part of South America under the name of *inermis*. He states that botanists are now gen-

curs in these latitudes on both sides of the Cordillera, across
the continent. I saw it in unfrequented spots in Chile, Entre
Rios, and Banda Oriental. In the latter country alone, very
many (probably several hundred) square miles are covered by
one mass of these prickly plants, and are impenetrable by man
or beast. Over the undulating plains, where these great beds
occur, nothing else can now live. Before their introduction,
however, the surface must have supported, as in other parts,
a rank herbage. I doubt whether any case is on record of an
invasion on so grand a scale of one plant over the aborigines.
As I have already said, I nowhere saw the cardoon south of
the Salado; but it is probable that in proportion as that country
becomes inhabited, the cardoon will extend its limits. The case
is different with the giant thistle (with variegated leaves) of the
Pampas, for I met with it in the valley of the Sauce. According
to the principles so well laid down by Mr. Lyell, few countries
have undergone more remarkable changes, since the year
1535, when the first colonist of La Plata landed with seventy-
two horses. The countless herds of horses, cattle, and sheep,
not only have altered the whole aspect of the vegetation, but
they have almost banished the guanaco, deer, and ostrich.
Numberless other changes must likewise have taken place; the
wild pig in some parts probably replaces the pecarri; packs of
wild dogs may be heard howling on the wooded banks of the
less frequented streams; and the common cat, altered into a
large and fierce animal, inhabits rocky hills. As M. d'Orbigny
has remarked, the increase in numbers of the carrion-vulture,
since the introduction of the domestic animals, must have been
infinitely great; and we have given reasons for believing that
they have extended their southern range. No doubt many plants,
besides the cardoon and fennel, are naturalized; thus the islands
near the mouth of the Parana are thickly clothed with peach
and orange trees, springing from seeds carried there by the
waters of the river.

---

erally agreed that the cardoon and the artichoke are varieties of
one plant. I may add, that an intelligent farmer assured me that
he had observed in a deserted garden some artichokes changing
into the common cardoon. Dr. Hooker believes that Head's vivid
description of the thistle of the Pampas applies to the cardoon; but
this is a mistake. Captain Head referred to the plant, which I have
mentioned a few lines lower down, under the title of giant thistle.
Whether it is a true thistle, I do not know; but it is quite different
from the cardoon; and more like a thistle properly so called.

While changing horses at the Guardia several people questioned us much about the army,—I never saw any thing like the enthusiasm for Rosas, and for the success of the "most just of all wars, because against barbarians." This expression, it must be confessed, is very natural, for till lately, neither man, woman, nor horse, was safe from the attacks of the Indians. We had a long day's ride over the same rich green plain, abounding with various flocks, and with here and there a solitary estancia, and its one *ombu* tree. In the evening it rained heavily: on arriving at a post-house we were told by the owner that if we had not a regular passport we must pass on, for there were so many robbers he would trust no one. When he read, however, my passport, which began with "El Naturalista Don Carlos," his respect and civility were as unbounded as his suspicions had been before. What a naturalist might be, neither he nor his countrymen, I suspect, had any idea; but probably my title lost nothing of its value from that cause.

September 20th.—We arrived by the middle of the day at Buenos Ayres. The outskirts of the city looked quite pretty, with the agave hedges, and groves of olive, peach, and willow trees, all just throwing out their fresh green leaves. I rode to the house of Mr. Lumb, an English merchant, to whose kindness and hospitality, during my stay in the country, I was greatly indebted.

The city of Buenos Ayres is large;[16] and I should think one of the most regular in the world. Every street is at right angles to the one it crosses, and the parallel ones being equidistant, the houses are collected into solid squares of equal dimensions, which are called quadras. On the other hand, the houses themselves are hollow squares; all the rooms opening into a

[16] [Darwin] It is said to contain 60,000 inhabitants. Monte Video, the second town of importance on the banks of the Plata, has 15,-000. [Buenos Aires is the name both of the city—founded in 1535 as Santa Maria de Buenos Aires—and a province, Argentina's largest. In Darwin's day, it was often used also as a name for the young Argentine nation. Argentina declared its independence of Spain —one of the first Spanish colonies to do so—in 1810, but the Spanish were not finally driven out until 1824. A republic was proclaimed in 1825. However, the separate provinces were virtually independent sutrapies of local caudillos (see Chapter XV, describing Darwin's trip to the "republic" of Mendoza). The Argentine Confederation did not become a reality until two years after Darwin's visit to Buenos Aires, when General Rosas, the Indian fighter, seized power and crushed the caudillos.—Ed.]

neat little courtyard. They are generally only one story high, with flat roofs, which are fitted with seats, and are much frequented by the inhabitants in summer. In the centre of the town is the Plaza, where the public offices, fortress, cathedral, &c., stand. Here also, the old viceroys, before the revolution, had their palaces. The general assemblage of buildings possesses considerable architectural beauty, although none individually can boast of any.

The great *corral,* where the animals are kept for slaughter to supply food to this beef-eating population, is one of the spectacles best worth seeing. The strength of the horse as compared to that of the bullock is quite astonishing: a man on horseback having thrown his lazo round the horns of a beast, can drag it any where he chooses. The animal ploughing up the ground with outstretched legs, in vain efforts to resist the force, generally dashes at full speed to one side; but the horse immediately turning to receive the shock, stands so firmly that the bullock is almost thrown down, and it is surprising that their necks are not broken. The struggle is not, however, one of fair strength; the horse's girth being matched against the bullock's extended neck. In a similar manner a man can hold the wildest horse, if caught with the lazo just behind the ears. When the bullock has been dragged to the spot where it is to be slaughtered, the *matador* with great caution cuts the hamstrings. Then is given the death bellow; a noise more expressive of fierce agony than any I know: I have often distinguished it from a long distance, and have always known that the struggle was then drawing to a close. The whole sight is horrible and revolting: the ground is almost made of bones; and the horses and riders are drenched with gore.

CHAPTER VII

BUENOS AYRES TO ST. FÉ

Excursion to St. Fé — Thistle Beds — Habits of the Bizcacha —
Little Owl — Saline Streams — Level Plains — Mastodon — St. Fé
— Change in Landscape — Geology — Tooth of extinct Horse —
Relation of the Fossil and recent Quadrupeds of North and South
America — Effects of a great Drought — Parana — Habits of the
Jaguar — Scissor-beak — Kingfisher, Parrot, and Scissor-tail —
Revolution — Buenos Ayres — State of Government

September 27th[1]—In the evening I set out on an excursion to
St. Fé, which is situated nearly three hundred English miles
from Buenos Ayres, on the banks of the Parana. The roads in
the neighbourhood of the city, after the rainy weather, were

[1] [Editor] The *Beagle* arrived at Montevideo from Bahia Blanca
a few days before Darwin reached Buenos Aires. Darwin was originally to rejoin the ship. However, Fitz Roy sent Darwin's servant
to Buenos Aires with word that the refit of the small schooner Fitz
Roy had purchased in the Falkland Islands, the *Adventure*, was not
yet complete and that the *Beagle* herself was still not finished with
her survey of the Rio de la Plata and the nearby Argentine coast.
So Darwin sent his servant to the nearby estancia of an Englishman to collect and skin birds, and he himself set off for Santa Fé,
chief city of the province of that name and the oldest city with a
continuous existence in Argentina.

Whenever Darwin made an overland trip, he had to do his own
arranging for horses and guides, and purchase his own supplies.
Almost always, he recorded his purchases in one of the small notebooks that were his constant companions. Here, for example is a
list of his purchases in Buenos Aires before setting out for Santa
Fé (from the notebook entry for September 22–27, 1833):

"Bread, sugar, Yerba, 2 packets cigars.
Tailor—shooting Jacket mended and Trousers—Big bag—

extraordinarily bad. I should never have thought it possible for
a bullock waggon to have crawled along: as it was, they
scarcely went at the rate of a mile an hour, and a man was
kept ahead, to survey the best line for making the attempt.
The bullocks were terribly jaded: it is a great mistake to suppose that with improved roads, and an accelerated rate of
travelling, the sufferings of the animals increase in the same
proportion. We passed a train of waggons and a troop of beasts
on their road to Mendoza. The distance is about 580 geographical miles, and the journey is generally performed in fifty days.
These waggons are very long, narrow, and thatched with reeds;
they have only two wheels, the diameter of which in some cases
is as much as ten feet. Each is drawn by six bullocks, which are
urged on by a goad at least twenty feet long: this is suspended
from within the roof; for the wheel bullocks a smaller one is
kept; and for the intermediate pair, a point projects at right
angles from the middle of the long one. The whole apparatus
looked like some implement of war.

September 28*th*.—We passed the small town of Luxan, where
there is a wooden bridge over the river—a most unusual con-
venience in this country. We passed also Areco. The plains
appeared level, but were not so in fact; for in various places
the horizon was distant. The estancias are here wide apart; for
there is little good pasture, owing to the land being covered by
beds either of an acrid clover, or of the great thistle. The latter,
well known from the animated description given by Sir F.
Head, were at this time of the year two-thirds grown; in some
parts they were as high as the horse's back, but in others they
had not yet sprung up, and the ground was bare and dusty as on
a turnpike-road. The clumps were of the most brilliant green,
and they made a pleasing miniature-likeness of broken forest
land. When the thistles are full grown, the great beds are im-

---

Lindsay, Calle Piedad.
Big bottles—Large Clasp Knife.
Bees wax, Rosin, corks for jars.
Market—fish—Repair lock—Paper for plants.
Bottles small with large mouths.
Woollen stockings—mice and rat traps—Black silk
   handkerchief.
Pills Druggist—Museum see petrification—Snuff box.
Mackintosh—washing bills.
Seeds of grass. Katers compass.
Indigo—gunpowder and shot—Gun—Snuff."

penetrable, except by a few tracks, as intricate as those in a labyrinth. These are only known to the robbers, who at this season inhabit them, and sally forth at night to rob and cut throats with impunity. Upon asking at a house whether robbers were numerous, I was answered, "The thistles are not up yet;"—the meaning of which reply was not at first very obvious. There is little interest in passing over these tracts, for they are inhabited by few animals or birds, excepting the bizcacha and its friend the little owl.

The bizcacha[2] is well known to form a prominent feature in the zoology of the Pampas. It is found as far south as the Rio Negro, in lat. 41°, but not beyond. It cannot, like the agouti, subsist on the gravelly and desert plains of Patagonia, but prefers a clayey or sandy soil, which produces a different and more abundant vegetation. Near Mendoza, at the foot of the Cordillera, it occurs in close neighbourhood with the allied alpine species. It is a very curious circumstance in its geographical distribution, that it has never been seen, fortunately for the inhabitants of Banda Oriental, to the eastward of the river Uruguay: yet in this province there are plains which appear admirably adapted to its habits. The Uruguay has formed an insuperable obstacle to its migration; although the broader barrier of the Parana has been passed, and the bizcacha is common in Entre Rios, the province between these two great rivers. Near Buenos Ayres these animals are exceedingly common. Their most favourite resort appears to be those parts of the plain which during one half of the year are covered with giant thistles, to the exclusion of other plants. The Gauchos affirm that it lives on roots; which, from the great strength of its gnawing teeth, and the kind of places frequented by it, seems probable. In the evening the bizcachas come out in numbers, and quietly sit at the mouths of their burrows on their haunches. At such times they are very tame, and a man on horseback passing by seems only to present an object for their grave contemplation. They run very awkwardly, and when running out of danger, from their elevated tails and short front legs, much resemble great rats. Their flesh, when cooked, is very white and good, but it is seldom used.

[2] [Darwin] The bizcacha (Lagostomus trichodactylus) somewhat resembles a large rabbit, but with bigger gnawing teeth and a long tail: it has, however, only three toes behind, like the agouti. During the last three or four years the skins of these animals have been sent to England for the sake of the fur.

The bizcacha has one very singular habit; namely, dragging every hard object to the mouth of its burrow: around each group of holes many bones of cattle, stones, thistle-stalks, hard lumps of earth, dry dung, &c., are collected into an irregular heap, which frequently amounts to as much as a wheelbarrow would contain. I was credibly informed that a gentleman, when riding on a dark night, dropped his watch; he returned in the morning, and by searching the neighbourhood of every biz-cacha hole on the line of road, as he expected, he soon found it. This habit of picking up whatever may be lying on the ground any where near its habitation, must cost much trouble. For what purpose it is done, I am quite unable to form even the most remote conjecture: it cannot be for defence, because the rubbish is chiefly placed above the mouth of the burrow, which enters the ground at a very small inclination. No doubt there must exist some good reason; but the inhabitants of the country are quite ignorant of it. The only fact which I know analogous to it, is the habit of that extraordinary Australian bird, the Calodera maculata, which makes an elegant vaulted passage of twigs for playing in, and which collects near the spot, land and sea-shells, bones, and the feathers of birds, es-pecially brightly coloured ones. Mr. Gould, who has described these facts, informs me, that the natives, when they lose any hard object, search the playing passages, and he has known a tobacco-pipe thus recovered.

The little owl (Athene cunicularia), which has been so often mentioned, on the plains of Buenos Ayres exclusively inhabits the holes of the bizcacha; but in Banda Oriental it is its own workman. During the open day, but more especially in the evening, these birds may be seen in every direction standing frequently by pairs on the hillock near their burrows. If dis-turbed they either enter the hole, or, uttering a shrill harsh cry, move with a remarkably undulatory flight to a short dis-tance, and then turning round, steadily gaze at their pursuer. Occasionally in the evening they may be heard hooting. I found in the stomachs of two which I opened the remains of mice, and I one day saw a small snake killed and carried away. It is said that snakes are their common prey during the daytime. I may here mention, as showing on what various kinds of food owls subsist, that a species killed among the islets of the Chonos Archipelago, had its stomach full of good-sized crabs. In India[3]

[3] [Darwin] Journal of Asiatic Soc., vol. v. p. 363.

there is a fishing genus of owls, which likewise catches crabs.

In the evening we crossed the Rio Arrecife on a simple raft made of barrels lashed together, and slept at the post-house on the other side. I this day paid horse-hire for thirty-one leagues; and although the sun was glaring hot I was but little fatigued. When Captain Head talks of riding fifty leagues a day, I do not imagine the distance is equal to 150 English miles. At all events, the thirty-one leagues was only 76 miles in a straight line, and in an open country I should think four additional miles for turning would be a sufficient allowance.

29th and 30th.—We continued to ride over plains of the same character. At San Nicolas I first saw the noble river of the Parana. At the foot of the cliff on which the town stands, some large vessels were at anchor. Before arriving at Rozario,[4] we crossed the Saladillo, a stream of fine clear running water, but too saline to drink. Rozario is a large town built on a dead level plain, which forms a cliff about sixty feet high over the Parana. The river here is very broad, with many islands, which are low and wooded, as is also the opposite shore. The view would resemble that of a great lake, if it were not for the linear-shaped islets, which alone give the idea of running water. The cliffs are the most picturesque part; sometimes they are absolutely perpendicular, and of a red colour; at other times in large broken masses, covered with cacti and mimosa-trees. The real grandeur, however, of an immense river like this, is derived from reflecting how important a means of communication and commerce it forms between one nation and another; to what a distance it travels; and from how vast a territory it drains the great body of fresh water which flows past your feet.

For many leagues north and south of San Nicolas and Rozario, the country is really level. Scarcely anything which travellers have written about its extreme flatness, can be considered as exaggeration. Yet I could never find a spot where, by slowly turning round, objects were not seen at greater distances in some directions than in others; and this manifestly proves inequality in the plain. At sea, a person's eye being six feet above the surface of the water, his horizon is two miles and four-fifths distant. In like manner, the more level the plain, the more nearly does the horizon approach within these narrow

4 [Editor] Now Argentina's second city, with a population of over half a million, a university and docks for oceangoing ships though located more than 100 miles up the Paraná River.

limits; and this, in my opinion, entirely destroys that grandeur which one would have imagined that a vast level plain would have possessed.

October 1st.—We started by moonlight and arrived at the Rio Tercero by sunrise. This river is also called the Saladillo, and it deserves the name, for the water is brackish. I stayed here the greater part of the day, searching for fossil bones. Besides a perfect tooth of the Toxodon, and many scattered bones, I found two immense skeletons near each other, projecting in bold relief from the perpendicular cliff of the Parana. They were, however, so completely decayed, that I could only bring away small fragments of one of the great molar teeth; but these are sufficient to show that the remains belonged to a Mastodon, probably to the same species with that, which formerly must have inhabited the Cordillera in Upper Peru in such great numbers. The men who took me in the canoe, said they had long known of these skeletons, and had often wondered how they had got there: the necessity of a theory being felt, they came to the conclusion that, like the bizcacha, the mastodon was formerly a burrowing animal! In the evening we rode another stage, and crossed the Monge, another brackish stream, bearing the dregs of the washings of the Pampas.

October 2nd.—We passed through Corunda, which, from the luxuriance of its gardens, was one of the prettiest villages I saw. From this point to St. Fé the road is not very safe. The western side of the Parana northward, ceases to be inhabited; and hence the Indians sometimes come down thus far, and waylay travellers. The nature of the country also favours this, for instead of a grassy plain, there is an open woodland, composed of low prickly mimosas. We passed some houses that had been ransacked and since deserted; we saw also a spectacle, which my guides viewed with high satisfaction; it was the skeleton of an Indian with the dried skin hanging on the bones, suspended to the branch of a tree.

In the morning we arrived at St. Fé. I was surprised to observe how great a change of climate a difference of only three degrees of latitude between this place and Buenos Ayres had caused. This was evident from the dress and complexion of the men—from the increased size of the ombu-trees—the number of new cacti and other plants—and especially from the birds. In the course of an hour I remarked half-a-dozen birds, which I had never seen at Buenos Ayres. Considering that there is no natural boundary between the two places, and that the character of the country is nearly similar, the difference was much greater than I should have expected.

October 3rd and 4th.—I was confined for these two days to my bed by a headach. A good-natured old woman, who attended me, wished me to try many odd remedies. A common practice is, to bind an orange-leaf or a bit of black plaster to each temple: and a still more general plan is, to split a bean into halves, moisten them, and place one on each temple, where they will easily adhere. It is not thought proper ever to remove the beans or plaster, but to allow them to drop off; and sometimes, if a man, with patches on his head, is asked, what is the matter? he will answer, "I had a headach the day before yesterday." Many of the remedies used by the people of the country are ludicrously strange, but too disgusting to be mentioned. One of the least nasty is to kill and cut open two puppies and bind them on each side of a broken limb. Little hairless dogs are in great request to sleep at the feet of invalids.

St. Fé is a quiet little town, and is kept clean and in good order. The governor, Lopez, was a common soldier at the time of the revolution; but has now been seventeen years in power. This stability of government is owing to his tyrannical habits; for tyranny seems as yet better adapted to these countries than republicanism. The governor's favourite occupation is hunting Indians: a short time since he slaughtered forty-eight, and sold the children at the rate of three or four pounds apiece.

October 5th.—We crossed the Parana to St. Fé Bajada, a town on the opposite shore. The passage took some hours, as the river here consisted of a labyrinth of small streams, separated by low wooded islands. I had a letter of introduction to an old Catalonian Spaniard, who treated me with the most uncommon hospitality. The Bajada is the capital of Entre Rios.[5] In 1825 the town contained 6000 inhabitants, and the province 30,000; yet, few as the inhabitants are, no province has suffered more from bloody and desperate revolutions. They boast here of representatives, ministers, a standing army, and gover-

---

[5] [Editor] As mentioned before, Entre Rios is a province of northern Argentina; and Santa Fé Bajada is now named Paraná. Darwin's forecast for the future proved correct. In 1842, it passed under the stifling control of an ironhanded local warlord, General J. J. Urquiza (who first supported the Argentine dictator, General Rosas, then helped turn him out). Urquiza was assassinated in 1870. A brief period of turbulence followed. Entre Rios then developed rapidly into one of the most prosperous sections of Argentina.

nors: so it is no wonder that they have their revolutions. At some future day this must be one of the richest countries of La Plata. The soil is varied and productive; and its almost insular form gives it two grand lines of communication by the rivers Parana and Uruguay.

I was delayed here five days, and employed myself in examining the geology of the surrounding country, which was very interesting. We here see at the bottom of the cliffs, beds containing sharks' teeth and sea-shells of extinct species, passing above into an indurated marl, and from that into the red clayey earth of the Pampas, with its calcareous concretions and the bones of terrestrial quadrupeds. This vertical section clearly tells us of a large bay of pure salt-water, gradually encroached on, and at last converted into the bed of a muddy estuary, into which floating carcasses were swept. At Punta Gorda,[6] in Banda Oriental, I found an alternation of the Pampæan estuary deposit, with a limestone containing some of the same extinct sea-shells; and this shows either a change in the former currents, or more probably an oscillation of level in the bottom of the ancient estuary. Until lately, my reasons for considering the Pampæan formation to be an estuary deposit were, its general appearance, its position at the mouth of the existing great river the Plata, and the presence of so many bones of terrestrial quadrupeds; but now Professor Ehrenberg has had the kindness to examine for me a little of the red earth, taken from low down in the deposit, close to the skeletons of the mastodon, and he finds in it many infusoria, partly salt-water and partly fresh-water forms, with the latter rather preponderating; and therefore, as he remarks, the water must have been brackish. M. A. d'Orbigny found on the banks of the Parana, at the height of a hundred feet, great beds of an estuary shell, now living a hundred miles lower down nearer the sea; and I found similar shells at a less height on the banks of the Uruguay: this shows that just before the Pampas was slowly elevated into dry land, the water covering it was brackish. Below Buenos Ayres there are upraised beds of sea-shells of existing species, which also proves that the period of elevation of the Pampas was within the recent period.

6 [Editor] The Punta Gorda here is a headland on the Uruguay River, near its junction with the Paraná. Darwin also passed a Punta Gorda on the Paraná on his way back to Buenos Aires from Santa Fé.

In the Pampæan deposit at the Bajada I found the osseous armour of a gigantic armadillo-like animal, the inside of which, when the earth was removed, was like a great cauldron; I found also teeth of the Toxodon and Mastodon, and one tooth of a Horse, in the same stained and decayed state. This latter tooth greatly interested me,[7] and I took scrupulous care in ascertaining that it had been embedded contemporaneously with the other remains; for I was not then aware that amongst the fossils from Bahia Blanca there was a horse's tooth hidden in the matrix: nor was it then known with certainty that the remains of horses are common in North America. Mr. Lyell has lately brought from the United States a tooth of a horse; and it is an interesting fact, that Professor Owen could find in no species, either fossil or recent, a slight but peculiar curvature characterizing it, until he thought of comparing it with my specimen found here: he has named this American horse Equus curvidens. Certainly it is a marvellous fact in the history of the Mammilia, that in South America a native horse should have lived and disappeared, to be succeeded in after ages by the countless herds descended from the few introduced with the Spanish colonists!

The existence in South America of a fossil horse, of the mastodon, possibly of an elephant,[8] and of a hollow-horned ruminant, discovered by MM. Lund and Clausen in the caves of Brazil, are highly interesting facts with respect to the geographical distribution of animals. At the present time, if we divide America, not by the Isthmus of Panama, but by the southern part of Mexico[9] in lat. 20°, where the great table-land presents an obstacle to the migration of species, by affecting the climate, and by forming, with the exception of some valleys and of a fringe of low land on the coast, a broad barrier; we

[7] [Darwin] I need hardly state here that there is good evidence against any horse living in America at the time of Columbus.

[8] [Darwin] Cuvier, Ossemens Fossiles, tom. i. p. 158.

[9] [Darwin] This is the geographical division followed by Lichtenstein, Swainson, Erichson, and Richardson. The section from Vera Cruz to Acapulco, given by Humboldt in the Polit. Essay on Kingdom of N. Spain, will show how immense a barrier the Mexican table-land forms. Dr. Richardson, in his admirable Report on the Zoology of N. America read before the Brit. Assoc. 1836 (p. 157), talking of the identification of a Mexican animal with the Synetheres prehensilis, says, "We do not know with what propriety, but if correct, it is, if not a solitary instance, at least very nearly so, of a rodent animal being common to North and South America."

shall then have the two zoological provinces of North and South America strongly contrasted with each other. Some few species alone have passed the barrier, and may be considered as wanderers from the south, such as the puma, opossum, kinkajou, and peccari. South America is characterized by possessing many peculiar gnawers, a family of monkeys, the llama, peccari, tapir, opossums, and, especially, several genera of Edentata, the order which includes the sloths, ant-eaters, and armadilloes. North America, on the other hand, is characterized (putting on one side a few wandering species) by numerous peculiar gnawers, and by four genera (the ox, sheep, goat, and antelope) of hollow-horned ruminants, of which great division South America is not known to possess a single species. Formerly, but within the period when most of the now existing shells were living, North America possessed, besides hollow-horned ruminants, the elephant, mastodon, horse, and three genera of Edentata, namely, the Megatherium, Megalonyx, and Mylodon. Within nearly this same period (as proved by the shells at Bahia Blanca) South America possessed, as we have just seen, a mastodon, horse, hollow-horned ruminant, and the same three genera (as well as several others) of the Edentata. Hence it is evident that North and South America, in having within a late geological period these several genera in common, were much more closely related in the character of their terrestrial inhabitants than they now are. The more I reflect on this case, the more interesting it appears: I know of no other instance where we can almost mark the period and manner of the splitting up of one great region into two well-characterized zoological provinces. The geologist, who is fully impressed with the vast oscillations of level which have affected the earth's crust within late periods, will not fear to speculate on the recent elevation of the Mexican platform, or, more probably, on the recent submergence of land in the West Indian Archipelago, as the cause of the present zoological separation of North and South America. The South American character of the West Indian mammals[10] seems to indicate that

[10] [Darwin] See Dr. Richardson's Report, p. 157; also L'Institut, 1837, p. 253. Cuvier says the kinkajou is found in the larger Antilles, but this is doubtful. M. Gervais states that the Didelphis crancrivora is found there. It is certain that the West Indies possess some mammifers peculiar to themselves. A tooth of a mastodon has been brought from Bahama: Edin. New Phil. Journ. 1826, p. 395.

this archipelago was formerly united to the southern continent, and that it has subsequently been an area of subsidence.

When America, and especially North America, possessed its elephants, mastodons, horse, and hollow-horned ruminants, it was much more closely related in its zoological characters to the temperate parts of Europe and Asia than it now is. As the remains of these genera are found on both sides of Behring's Straits[11] and on the plains of Siberia, we are led to look to the north-western side of North America as the former point of communication between the Old and so-called New World. And as so many species, both living and extinct, of these same genera inhabit and have inhabited the Old World, it seems most probable that the North American elephants, mastodons, horse, and hollow-horned ruminants migrated, on land since submerged near Behring's Straits, from Siberia into North America, and thence, on land since submerged in the West Indies, into South America, where for a time they mingled with the forms characteristic of that southern continent, and have since become extinct.[12]

While travelling through the country, I received several vivid descriptions of the effects of a late great drought; and the account of this may throw some light on the cases where vast numbers of animals of all kinds have been embedded together. The period included between the years 1827 and 1830 is called the "gran seco," or the great drought. During this time so little rain fell, that the vegetation, even to the thistles, failed; the brooks were dried up, and the whole country assumed the appearance of a dusty high road. This was especially the case in the northern part of the province of Buenos Ayres and the southern part of St. Fé. Very great numbers of birds, wild animals, cattle, and horses perished from the want of food and water. A man told me that the deer[13] used to come into

[11] [Darwin] See the admirable Appendix by Dr. Buckland to Beechey's Voyage; also the writings of Chamisso in Kotzebue's Voyage.

[12] [Editor] Most geologists accept the idea of a land bridge between Asia and North America, and North and South America within the geological period—the Age of Mammals—of which Darwin is speaking. The most modern view, however, is that the West Indies are not sinking, but are an area where new land is slowly being formed.

[13] [Darwin] In Capt. Owen's Surveying Voyage (vol. ii. p. 274) there is a curious account of the effects of a drought on the ele-

his courtyard to the well, which he had been obliged to dig to supply his own family with water; and that the partridges had hardly strength to fly away when pursued. The lowest estimation of the loss of cattle in the province of Buenos Ayres alone, was taken at one million head. A proprietor at San Pedro had previously to these years 20,000 cattle; at the end not one remained. San Pedro is situated in the middle of the finest country; and even now abounds again with animals; yet, during the latter part of the "gran seco," live cattle were brought in vessels for the consumption of the inhabitants. The animals roamed from their estancias, and, wandering far southward, were mingled together in such multitudes, that a government commission was sent from Buenos Ayres to settle the disputes of the owners. Sir Woodbine Parish informed me of another and very curious source of dispute; the ground being so long dry, such quantities of dust were blown about, that in this open country the landmarks became obliterated, and people could not tell the limits of their estates.

I was informed by an eye-witness that the cattle in herds of thousands rushed into the Parana, and being exhausted by hunger they were unable to crawl up the muddy banks, and thus were drowned. The arm of the river which runs by San Pedro was so full of putrid carcasses, that the master of a vessel told me that the smell rendered it quite impassable. Without doubt several hundred thousand animals thus perished in the river: their bodies when putrid were seen floating down the stream; and many in all probability were deposited in the estuary of the Plata. All the small rivers became highly saline, and this caused the death of vast numbers in particular spots; for when an animal drinks of such water it does not recover. Azara describes[14] the fury of the wild horses on a similar occasion, rushing into the marshes, those which arrived first being over-

---

phants, at Benguela (west coast of Africa). "A number of these animals had some time since entered the town, in a body, to possess themselves of the wells, not being able to procure any water in the country. The inhabitants mustered, when a desperate conflict ensued, which terminated in the ultimate discomfiture of the invaders, but not until they had killed one man, and wounded several others." The town is said to have a population of nearly three thousand! Dr. Malcolmson informs me that during a great drought in India the wild animals entered the tents of some troops at Ellore, and that a hare drank out of a vessel held by the adjutant of the regiment.

[14] [Darwin] Travels, vol. i. p. 374.

whelmed and crushed by those which followed. He adds that more than once he has seen the carcasses of upwards of a thousand wild horses thus destroyed. I noticed that the smaller streams in the Pampas were paved with a breccia of bones, but this probably is the effect of a gradual increase, rather than of the destruction at any one period. Subsequently to the drought of 1827 to '32, a very rainy season followed, which caused great floods. Hence it is almost certain that some thousands of the skeletons were buried by the deposits of the very next year. What would be the opinion of a geologist, viewing such an enormous collection of bones, of all kinds of animals and of all ages, thus embedded in one thick earthy mass? Would he not attribute it to a flood having swept over the surface of the land, rather than to the common order of things?[15]

October 12*th.*—I had intended to push my excursion further, but not being quite well, I was compelled to return by a balandra, or one-masted vessel of about a hundred tons' burden, which was bound to Buenos Ayres. As the weather was not fair, we moored early in the day to a branch of a tree on one of the islands. The Parana is full of islands, which undergo a constant round of decay and renovation. In the memory of the master several large ones had disappeared, and others again had been formed and protected by vegetation. They are composed of muddy sand, without even the smallest pebble, and were then about four feet above the level of the river; but during the periodical floods they are inundated. They all present one character; numerous willows and a few other trees are bound together by a great variety of creeping plants, thus forming a thick jungle. These thickets afford a retreat for capybaras and jaguars. The fear of the latter animal quite destroyed all pleasure in scrambling through the woods. This evening I had not proceeded a hundred yards, before finding indubitable signs of the recent presence of the tiger, I was obliged to come back. On every island there were tracks; and as on the former excursion "el rastro de los Indios" had been the subject of conversation, so in this was "el rastro del tigre."

The wooded banks of the great rivers appear to be the favourite haunts of the jaguar; but south of the Plata, I was told that they frequented the reeds bordering lakes: wherever they

[15] [Darwin] These droughts to a certain degree seem to be almost periodical; I was told the dates of several others, and the intervals were about fifteen years.

are, they seem to require water. Their common prey is the capybara, so that it is generally said, where capybaras are numerous there is little danger from the jaguar. Falconer states that near the southern side of the mouth of the Plata there are many jaguars, and that they chiefly live on fish; this account I have heard repeated. On the Parana they have killed many wood-cutters, and have even entered vessels at night. There is a man now living in the Bajada, who, coming up from below when it was dark, was seized on the deck; he escaped, however, with the loss of the use of one arm. When the floods drive these animals from the islands, they are most dangerous. I was told that a few years since a very large one found its way into a church at St. Fé: two padres entering one after the other were killed, and a third, who came to see what was the matter, escaped with difficulty. The beast was destroyed by being shot from a corner of the building which was un-roofed. They commit also at these times great ravages among cattle and horses. It is said that they kill their prey by breaking their necks. If driven from the carcass, they seldom return to it. The Gauchos say that the jaguar, when wandering about at night, is much tormented by the foxes yelping as they follow him. This is a curious coincidence with the fact which is generally affirmed of the jackals accompanying, in a similarly officious manner, the East Indian tiger. The jaguar is a noisy animal, roaring much by night, and especially before bad weather.

One day, when hunting on the banks of the Uruguay, I was shown certain trees, to which these animals constantly recur for the purpose, as it is said, of sharpening their claws. I saw three well-known trees; in front, the bark was worn smooth, as if by the breast of the animal, and on each side there were deep scratches, or rather grooves, extending in an oblique line, nearly a yard in length. The scars were of different ages. A common method of ascertaining whether a jaguar is in the neighbourhood is to examine these trees. I imagine this habit of the jaguar is exactly similar to one which may any day be seen in the common cat, as with outstretched legs and exserted claws it scrapes the leg of a chair; and I have heard of young fruit-trees in an orchard in England having been thus much in-jured. Some such habit must also be common to the puma, for on the bare hard soil of Patagonia I have frequently seen scores so deep that no other animal could have made them. The ob-ject of this practice is, I believe, to tear off the ragged points of their claws, and not, as the Gauchos think, to sharpen them. The jaguar is killed, without much difficulty, by the aid of dogs baying and driving him up a tree, where he is despatched with bullets.

Owing to bad weather we remained two days at our moorings. Our only amusement was catching fish for our dinner: there were several kinds, and all good eating. A fish called the "armado" (a Silurus) is remarkable from a harsh grating noise which it makes when caught by hook and line, and which can be distinctly heard when the fish is beneath the water. This same fish has the power of firmly catching hold of any object, such as the blade of an oar or the fishing-line, with the strong spine both of its pectoral and dorsal fin. In the evening the weather was quite tropical, the thermometer standing at 79°. Numbers of fireflies were hovering about, and the musquitoes were very troublesome. I exposed my hand for five minutes, and it was soon black with them; I do not suppose there could have been less than fifty, all busy sucking.

October 15th.—We got under weigh and passed Punta Gorda, where there is a colony of tame Indians from the province of Missiones. We sailed rapidly down the current, but before sunset, from a silly fear of bad weather, we brought-to in a narrow arm of the river. I took the boat and rowed some distance up this creek. It was very narrow, winding, and deep; on each side a wall thirty or forty feet high, formed by trees intwined with creepers, gave to the canal a singularly gloomy appearance. I here saw a very extraordinary bird, called the Scissor-beak (Rhynchops nigra). It has short legs, web feet, extremely long-pointed wings, and is of about the size of a tern. The beak is flattened laterally, that is, in a plane at right angles to that of a spoonbill or duck. It is as flat and elastic as an ivory paper-cutter, and the lower mandible, differently from every other bird, is an inch and a half longer than the upper. In a lake near Maldonado, from which the water had been nearly drained, and which, in consequence, swarmed with small fry, I saw several of these birds, generally in small flocks, flying rapidly backwards and forwards close to the surface of the lake. They kept their bills wide open, and the lower mandible half buried in the water. Thus skimming the surface, they ploughed it in their course: the water was quite smooth, and it formed a most curious spectacle to behold a flock, each bird leaving its narrow wake on the mirror-like surface. In their flight they frequently twist about with extreme quickness, and dexterously manage with their projecting lower mandible to plough up small fish, which are secured by the upper and shorter half of their scissor-like bills. This fact I repeatedly saw, as, like swallows, they continued to fly backwards and forwards close before me. Occasionally when leaving the surface of the water their flight was wild, irregular, and rapid; they then uttered loud harsh cries. When these birds are fishing, the advantage of the long primary feathers of their wings, in keeping them dry, is very evident. When thus employed, their forms resemble the symbol by which many artists represent marine birds. Their tails are much used in steering their irregular course.

These birds are common far inland along the course of the Rio Parana; it is said that they remain here during the whole year, and breed in the marshes. During the day they rest in flocks on the grassy plains, at some distance from the water. Being at anchor, as I have said, in one of the deep creeks between the islands of the Parana, as the evening drew to a close, one of these scissor-beaks suddenly appeared. The water was quite still, and many little fish were rising. The bird continued for a long time to skim the surface, flying in its wild and irregular manner up and down the narrow canal, now dark with the growing night and the shadows of the overhanging trees. At Monte Video, I observed that some large flocks during the day remained on the mud-banks at the head of the harbour, in the same manner as on the grassy plains near the Parana; and every evening they took flight seaward. From these facts I suspect that the Rhynchops generally fishes by night, at which time many of the lower animals come most abundantly to the surface. M. Lesson states that he has seen these birds opening the shells of the mactræ buried in the sand-banks on the coast of Chile: from their weak bills, with the lower mandible so much projecting, their short legs and long wings, it is very improbable that this can be a general habit.

In our course down the Parana, I observed only three other birds, whose habits are worth mentioning. One is a small kingfisher (Ceryle Americana); it has a longer tail than the European species, and hence does not sit in so stiff and upright a position. Its flight also, instead of being direct and rapid, like the course of an arrow, is weak and undulatory, as among the soft-billed birds. It utters a low note, like the clicking together of two small stones. A small green parrot (Conurus murinus), with a grey breast, appears to prefer the tall trees on the islands to any other situation for its building-place. A number of nests are placed so close together as to form one great mass of sticks. These parrots always live in flocks, and commit great ravages on the corn-fields. I was told that near Colonia 2500 were killed in the course of one year. A bird with a forked tail, terminated by two long feathers (Tyrannus savana), and named by the Spaniards scissor-tail, is very common near Buenos Ayres: it commonly sits on a branch of the *ombu* tree, near a house, and thence takes a short flight in pursuit of insects, and returns to the same spot. When on the wing it presents in its manner of flight and general appearance a caricature-likeness of the common swallow. It has the power of turning very shortly in the air, and in so doing opens and shuts its tail, sometimes in a horizontal or lateral and sometimes in a vertical direction, just like a pair of scissors.

October 16th.—Some leagues below Rozario, the western shore of the Parana is bounded by perpendicular cliffs, which extend in a long line to below San Nicolas; hence it more resembles a sea-coast than that of a fresh-water river. It is a great drawback to the scenery of the Parana, that, from the soft nature of its banks, the water is very muddy. The Uruguay, flowing through a granitic country, is much clearer; and where the two channels unite at the head of the Plata, the waters may for a long distance be distinguished by their black and red colours. In the evening, the wind being not quite fair, as usual we immediately moored, and the next day, as it blew rather freshly, though with a favouring current, the master was much too indolent to think of starting. At Bajada, he was described to me as "hombre muy aflicto"—a man always miserable to get on; but certainly he bore all delays with admirable resignation. He was an old Spaniard, and had been many years in this country. He professed a great liking to the English, but stoutly main-

tained that the battle of Trafalgar was merely won by the
Spanish captains having been all bought over; and that the
only really gallant action on either side was performed by the
Spanish admiral. It struck me as rather characteristic, that this
man should prefer his countrymen being thought the worst of
traitors, rather than unskilful or cowardly.

18*th and* 19*th.*—We continued slowly to sail down the noble
stream: the current helped us but little. We met, during our
descent, very few vessels. One of the best gifts of nature, in so
grand a channel of communication, seems here wilfully thrown
away—a river in which ships might navigate from a temperate
country, as surprisingly abundant in certain productions as destitute of others, to another possessing a tropical climate, and a
soil which, according to the best of judges, M. Bonpland, is
perhaps unequalled in fertility in any part of the world. How
different would have been the aspect of this river if English
colonists had by good fortune first sailed up the Plata! What
noble towns would now have occupied its shores! Till the death
of Francia, the Dictator of Paraguay,[16] these two countries
must remain distinct, as if placed on opposite sides of the globe.
And when the old bloody-minded tyrant is gone to his long
account, Paraguay will be torn by revolutions, violent in proportion to the previous unnatural calm. That country will have
to learn, like every other South American state, that a republic
cannot succeed till it contains a certain body of men imbued
with the principles of justice and honour.

October 20*th.*—Being arrived at the mouth of the Parana,
and as I was very anxious to reach Buenos Ayres, I went on
shore at Las Conchas, with the intention of riding there. Upon
landing, I found to my great surprise that I was to a certain
degree a prisoner. A violent revolution having broken out, all
the ports were laid under an embargo. I could not return to
my vessel, and as for going by land to the city, it was out of
the question. After a long conversation with the commandant,
I obtained permission to go the next day to General Rolor, who
commanded a division of the rebels on this side the capital. In
the morning I rode to the encampment. The general, officers,

---

[16] [Editor] José Gaspar Rodriguez Francia—called "El Supremo"
—was a member of the junta formed to govern Paraguay after
Paraguay's declaration of independence from Spain in 1811. In
1814, he was made dictator for three years, and in 1816, for life.
He died in 1840. Few nineteenth-century dictators matched his repu-
tation for iron-fisted rule.

and soldiers, all appeared, and I believe really were, great villains. The general, the very evening before he left the city, voluntarily went to the Governor, and with his hand to his heart, pledged his word of honour that he at least would remain faithful to the last. The general told me that the city was in a state of close blockade, and that all he could do was to give me a passport to the commander-in-chief of the rebels at Quilmes. We had therefore to take a great sweep round the city, and it was with much difficulty that we procured horses. My reception at the encampment was quite civil, but I was told it was impossible that I could be allowed to enter the city. I was very anxious about this, as I anticipated the *Beagle's* departure from the Rio Plata earlier than it took place. Having mentioned, however, General Rosas's obliging kindness to me when at the Colorado, magic itself could not have altered circumstances quicker than did this conversation. I was instantly told that though they could not give me a passport, if I chose to leave my guide and horses, I might pass their sentinels. I was too glad to accept of this, and an officer was sent with me to give directions that I should not be stopped at the bridge. The road for the space of a league was quite deserted. I met one party of soldiers, who were satisfied by gravely looking at an old passport: and at length I was not a little pleased to find myself within the city.

This revolution was supported by scarcely any pretext of grievances: but in a state which, in the course of nine months (from February to October, 1820), underwent fifteen changes in its government—each governor, according to the constitution, being elected for three years—it would be very unreasonable to ask for pretexts. In this case, a party of men—who, being attached to Rosas, were disgusted with the governor Balcarce—to the number of seventy left the city, and with the cry of Rosas the whole country took arms. The city was then blockaded, no provisions, cattle or horses, were allowed to enter; besides this, there was only a little skirmishing, and a few men daily killed. The outside party well knew that by stopping the supply of meat they would certainly be victorious. General Rosas could not have known of this rising; but it appears to be quite consonant with the plans of his party. A year ago he was elected governor, but he refused it, unless the Sala would also confer on him extraordinary powers. This was refused, and since then his party have shown that no other governor can keep his place. The warfare on both sides was avowedly protracted till it was possible to hear from Rosas. A note arrived a few days after I left Buenos Ayres, which stated that the General disapproved of peace having been broken, but that he thought the outside party had justice on their side. On the bare reception of this, the Governor, ministers, and part of the military, to the number of some hundreds, fled from the city. The rebels entered, elected a new governor, and were paid for their services to the number of 5500 men. From these proceedings, it was clear that Rosas ultimately would become the dictator: to the term king, the people in this, as in other republics, have a particular dislike. Since leaving South America, we have heard that Rosas has been elected, with powers and for a time altogether opposed to the constitutional principles of the republic.

CHAPTER VIII

BANDA ORIENTAL AND PATAGONIA

Excursion to Colonia del Sacramiento — Value of an Estancia — Cattle, how counted — Singular Breed of Oxen — Perforated Pebbles — Shepherd-dogs — Horses broken in, Gauchos Riding — Character of Inhabitants — Rio Plata — Flocks of Butterflies — Aëronaut Spiders — Phosphorescence of the Sea — Port Desire — Guanaco — Port St. Julian — Geology of Patagonia — Fossil gigantic Animal — Types of Organization constant — Change in the Zoology of America — Causes of Extinction

Having been delayed for nearly a fortnight in the city, I was glad to escape on board a packet bound for Monte Video. A town in a state of blockade must always be a disagreeable place of residence; in this case moreover there were constant apprehensions from robbers within. The sentinels were the worst of all; for, from their office and from having arms in their hands, they robbed with a degree of authority which other men could not imitate.

Our passage was a very long and tedious one. The Plata looks like a noble estuary on the map; but is in truth a poor affair. A wide expanse of muddy water has neither grandeur nor beauty. At one time of the day, the two shores, both of which are extremely low, could just be distinguished from the deck. On arriving at Monte Video I found that the *Beagle* would not sail for some time, so I prepared for a short excursion in this part of Banda Oriental. Everything which I have said about the country near Maldonado is applicable to M. Video; but the land, with the one exception of the Green Mount, 450 feet high, from which it takes its name, is far more level. Very little of the undulating grassy plain is enclosed; but near the town there are a few hedge-banks, covered with agaves, cacti, and fennel.

November 14th.—We left Monte Video in the afternoon. I intended to proceed to Colonia del Sacramiento,[1] situated on the northern bank of the Plata and opposite to Buenos Ayres, and thence, following up the Uruguay, to the village of Mercedes on the Rio Negro (one of the many rivers of this name in South America), and from this point to return direct to Monte Video. We slept at the house of my guide at Canelones. In the morning we rose early, in the hopes of being able to ride a good distance; but it was a vain attempt, for all the rivers were flooded. We passed in boats the streams of Canelones, St. Lucia, and San José, and thus lost much time. On a former excursion I crossed the Lucia near its mouth, and I was surprised to observe how easily our horses, although not used to swim, passed over a width of at least six hundred yards. On mentioning this at Monte Video, I was told that a vessel containing some mountebanks and their horses, being wrecked in the Plata, one horse swam seven miles to the shore. In the course of the day I was amused by the dexterity with which a Gaucho forced a restive horse to swim a river. He stripped off his clothes, and jumping on its back, rode into the water till it was out of its depth; then slipping off over the crupper, he caught hold of the tail, and as often as the horse turned round, the man frightened it back by spashing water in its face. As soon as the horse touched the bottom on the other side, the man pulled himself on, and was firmly seated, bridle in hand, before the horse gained the bank. A naked man on a naked horse is a fine spectacle; I had no idea how well the two animals suited each other. The tail of a horse is a very useful appendage; I have passed a river in a boat with four people in it, which was ferried across in the same way as the Gaucho. If a man and horse have to cross a broad river, the best plan is for the man to catch hold of the pommel or mane, and help himself with the other arm.

We slept and stayed the following day at the post of Cufre. In the evening the postman or letter-carrier arrived. He was a day after his time, owing to the Rio Rozario being flooded. It would not, however, be of much consequence; for, although he had passed through some of the principal towns in Banda Oriental, his luggage consisted of two letters! The view from the house was pleasing; an undulating green surface, with dis-

[1] [Editor] A town originally settled by the Portuguese and, in the days of the Spanish and Portuguese empires, a frequent subject of dispute between Spain and Portugal.

tant glimpses of the Plata. I find that I look at this province with very different eyes from what I did upon my first arrival. I recollect I then thought it singularly level; but now, after galloping over the Pampas, my only surprise is, what could have induced me ever to have called it level. The country is a series of undulations, in themselves perhaps not absolutely great, but, as compared to the plains of St. Fé, real mountains. From these inequalities there is an abundance of small rivulets, and the turf is green and luxuriant.

November 17*th*.—We crossed the Rozario, which was deep and rapid, and passing the village of Colla, arrived at mid-day at Colonia del Sacramiento. The distance is twenty leagues, through a country covered with fine grass, but poorly stocked with cattle or inhabitants. I was invited to sleep at Colonia, and to accompany on the following day a gentleman to his estancia, where there were some limestone rocks. The town is built on a stony promontory something in the same manner as at Monte Video. It is strongly fortified, but both fortifications and town suffered much in the Brazilian war.[2] It is very ancient; and the irregularity of the streets, and the surrounding groves of old orange and peach trees, gave it a pretty appearance. The church is a curious ruin; it was used as a powder-magazine, and was struck by lightning in one of the ten thousand thunderstorms of the Rio Plata. Two-thirds of the building were blown away to the very foundation; and the rest stands a shattered and curious monument of the united powers of lightning and gunpowder. In the evening I wandered about the half-demolished walls of the town. It was the chief seat of the Brazilian war;—a war most injurious to this country, not so much in its immediate effects, as in being the origin of a multitude of generals and all other grades of officers. More generals are numbered (but not paid) in the United Provinces of La Plata than in the United Kingdom of Great Britain. These gentlemen have learned to like power, and do not object to a little skirmishing. Hence there are many always on the watch to create disturbance and to overturn a government which as yet has never rested on any stable foundation. I noticed, however, both here and in other places, a very general interest in the ensuing election for the President; and this appears a good sign for the prosperity of this little country. The inhabitants do not require much education in their representatives; I heard some

[2] [Editor] The war between Argentina and Brazil over Uruguay in the first years of the Argentine republic and the Brazilian empire.

men discussing the merits of those for Colonia; and it was said that, "although they were not men of business, they could all sign their names:" with this they seemed to think every reasonable man ought to be satisfied.

18th.—Rode with my host to his estancia, at the Arroyo de San Juan. In the evening we took a ride round the estate: it contained two square leagues and a half, and was situated in what is called a rincon; that is, one side was fronted by the Plata, and the two others guarded by impassable brooks. There was an excellent port for little vessels, and an abundance of small wood, which is valuable as supplying fuel to Buenos Ayres. I was curious to know the value of so complete an estancia. Of cattle there were 3000, and it would well support three or four times that number; of mares 800, together with 150 broken-in horses, and 600 sheep. There was plenty of water and limestone, a rough house, excellent corrals, and a peach orchard. For all this he had been offered 2000l., and he only wanted 500l. additional, and probably would sell it for less. The chief trouble with an estancia is driving the cattle twice a week to a central spot, in order to make them tame, and to count them. This latter operation would be thought difficult, where there are ten or fifteen thousand head together. It is managed on the principle that the cattle invariably divide themselves into little troops of from forty to one hundred. Each troop is recognized by a few peculiarly marked animals, and its number is known: so that, one being lost out of ten thousand, it is perceived by its absence from one of the tropillas. During a stormy night the cattle all mingle together; but the next morning the tropillas separate as before; so that each animal must know its fellow out of ten thousand others.

On two occasions I met with in this province some oxen of a very curious breed, called nata or niata. They appear externally to hold nearly the same relation to other cattle, which bull or pug dogs do to other dogs. Their forehead is very short and broad, with the nasal end turned up, and the upper lip much drawn back; their lower jaws project beyond the upper, and have a corresponding upward curve; hence their teeth are always exposed. Their nostrils are seated high up and are very open; their eyes project outwards. When walking they carry their heads low, on a short neck; and their hinder legs are rather longer compared with the front legs than is usual. Their bare teeth, their short heads, and upturned nostrils give them the most ludicrous self-confident air of defiance imaginable.

Since my return, I have procured a skeleton head, through the kindness of my friend Captain Sulivan, R.N., which is now deposited in the College of Surgeons.[3] Don F. Muniz, of Luxan, has kindly collected for me all the information which he could respecting this breed. From his account it seems that about eighty or ninety years ago, they were rare and kept as curiosities at Buenos Ayres. The breed is universally believed to have originated amongst the Indians southward of the Plata; and that it was with them the commonest kind. Even to this day, those reared in the provinces near the Plata show their less civilized origin, in being fiercer than common cattle, and in the cow easily deserting her first calf, if visited too often or molested. It is a singular fact that an almost similar structure to the abnormal[4] one of the niata breed, characterizes, as I am informed by Dr. Falconer, that great extinct ruminant of India, the Sivatherium. The breed is very *true;* and a niata bull and cow invariably produce niata calves. A niata bull with a common cow, or the reverse cross, produces offspring having an intermediate character, but with the niata characters strongly displayed: according to Señor Muniz, there is the clearest evidence, contrary to the common belief of agriculturists in analogous cases, that the niata cow when crossed with a common bull transmits her peculiarities more strongly than the niata bull when crossed with a common cow. When the pasture is tolerably long, the niata cattle feed with the tongue and palate as well as common cattle; but during the great droughts, when so many animals perish, the niata breed is under a great disadvantage, and would be exterminated if not attended to; for the common cattle, like horses, are able just to keep alive, by browsing with their lips on twigs of trees and reeds; this the niatas cannot so well do, as their lips do not join, and hence they are found to perish before the common cattle. This strikes me as a good illustration of how little we are able to judge from the ordinary habits of life, on what circumstances, occurring only at long intervals, the rarity or extinction of a species may be determined.

November 19th.—Passing the valley of Las Vacas, we slept

[3] [Darwin] Mr. Waterhouse has drawn up a detailed description of this head, which I hope he will publish in some Journal.

[4] [Darwin] A nearly similar abnormal, but I do not know whether hereditary, structure has been observed in the carp, and likewise in the crocodile of the Ganges: Histoire des Anomalies, par M. Isid. Geoffroy St. Hilaire, tom. i. p. 244.

at a house of a North American, who worked a lime-kiln on the Arroyo de las Vivoras. In the morning we rode to a projecting headland on the banks of the river, called Punta Gorda. On the way we tried to find a jaguar. There were plenty of fresh tracks, and we visited the trees, on which they are said to sharpen their claws; but we did not succeed in disturbing one. From this point the Rio Uruguay presented to our view a noble volume of water. From the clearness and rapidity of the stream, its appearance was far superior to that of its neighbour the Parana. On the opposite coast, several branches from the latter river entered the Uruguay. As the sun was shining, the two colours of the waters could be seen quite distinct.

In the evening we proceeded on our road towards Mercedes on the Rio Negro. At night we asked permission to sleep at an estancia at which we happened to arrive. It was a very large estate, being ten leagues square, and the owner is one of the greatest landowners in the country. His nephew had charge of it, and with him there was a captain in the army, who the other day ran away from Buenos Ayres. Considering their station, their conversation was rather amusing. They expressed, as was usual, unbounded astonishment at the globe being round, and could scarcely credit that a hole would, if deep enough, come out on the other side. They had, however, heard of a country where there were six months light and six of darkness, and where the inhabitants were very tall and thin! They were curious about the price and condition of horses and cattle in England. Upon finding out we did not catch our animals with the lazo, they cried out, "Ah, then, you use nothing but the bolas:" the idea of an enclosed country was quite new to them. The captain at last said, he had one question to ask me, which he should be very much obliged if I would answer with all truth. I trembled to think how deeply scientific it would be: it was, "Whether the ladies of Buenos Ayres were not the handsomest in the world." I replied, like a renegade, "Charmingly so." He added, "I have one other question: Do ladies in any other part of the world wear such large combs?" I solemnly assured him that they did not. They were absolutely delighted. The captain exclaimed, "Look there! a man who has seen half the world says it is the case; we always thought so, but now we know it." My excellent judgment in combs and beauty procured me a most hospitable reception; the captain forced me to take his bed, and he would sleep on his recado.

21st.—Started at sunrise, and rode slowly during the whole

day. The geological nature of this part of the province was different from the rest, and closely resembled that of the Pampas. In consequence, there were immense beds of the thistle, as well as of the cardoon: the whole country, indeed, may be called one great bed of these plants. The two sorts grow separate, each plant in company with its own kind. The cardoon is as high as a horse's back, but the Pampas thistle is often higher than the crown of the rider's head. To leave the road for a yard is out of the question; and the road itself is partly, and in some cases entirely, closed. Pasture, of course there is none; if cattle or horses once enter the bed, they are for the time completely lost. Hence it is very hazardous to attempt to drive cattle at this season of the year; for when jaded enough to face the thistles, they rush among them, and are seen no more. In these districts there are very few estancias, and these few are situated in the neighbourhood of damp valleys, where fortunately neither of these overwhelming plants can exist. As night came on before we arrived at our journey's end, we slept at a miserable little hovel inhabited by the poorest people. The extreme though rather formal courtesy of our host and hostess, considering their grade of life, was quite delightful.

November 22nd.—Arrived at an estancia on the Berquelo belonging to a very hospitable Englishman, to whom I had a letter of introduction from my friend Mr. Lumb. I stayed here three days. One morning I rode with my host to the Sierra del Pedro Flaco, about twenty miles up the Rio Negro. Nearly the whole country was covered with good though coarse grass, which was as high as a horse's belly; yet there were square leagues without a single head of cattle. The province of Banda Oriental, if well stocked, would support an astonishing number of animals; at present the annual export of hides from Monte Video amounts to three hundred thousand; and the home consumption, from waste, is very considerable. An estanciero told me that he often had to send large herds of cattle a long journey to a salting establishment, and that the tired beasts were frequently obliged to be killed and skinned; but that he could never persuade the Gauchos to eat of them, and every evening a fresh beast was slaughtered for their suppers! The view of the Rio Negro from the Sierra was more picturesque than any other which I saw in this province. The river, broad, deep, and rapid, wound at the foot of a rocky precipitous cliff: a belt of wood followed its course, and the horizon terminated in the distant undulations of the turf-plain.

When in this neighbourhood, I several times heard of the Sierra de las Cuentas: a hill distant many miles to the northward. The name signifies hill of beads. I was assured that vast numbers of little round stones, of various colours, each with a small cylindrical hole, are found there. Formerly the Indians used to collect them, for the purpose of making necklaces and bracelets—a taste, I may observe, which is common to all savage nations, as well as to the most polished. I did not know what to understand from this story, but upon mentioning it at the Cape of Good Hope to Dr. Andrew Smith, he told me that he recollected finding on the southeastern coast of Africa, about one hundred miles to the eastward of St. John's river, some quartz crystals with their edges blunted from attrition, and mixed with gravel on the sea-beach. Each crystal was about five lines in diameter, and from an inch to an inch and a half in length. Many of them had a small canal extending from one extremity to the other, perfectly cylindrical, and of a size that readily admitted a coarse thread or a piece of fine catgut. Their colour was red or dull white. The natives were acquainted with this structure in crystals. I have mentioned these circumstances because, although no crystallized body is at present known to assume this form, it may lead some future traveller to investigate the real nature of such stones.[5]

While staying at this estancia, I was amused with what I saw and heard of the shepherd-dogs of the country.[6] When riding, it is a common thing to meet a large flock of sheep guarded by one or two dogs, at the distance of some miles from any house or man. I often wondered how so firm a friendship had been established. The method of education consists in separating the puppy, while very young, from the bitch, and in accustoming it to its future companions. An ewe is held three or four

[5] [Editor] There is no certainty as to just what kind of "pebbles" Darwin is referring to, since, as he says, he did not see the stones from the Hill of Beads himself. Uruguay is a source, however, of a curious kind of hollow quartz bead which could well be pierced as described. The beads are formed by the intrusion of quartz or related minerals such as amethyst into gas pockets in lava; the quartz forms a lining around the pocket. When the lava, which is softer than quartz, erodes away, a hollow bead is left. But these beads vary in size and shape and do not seem to be as uniform in size as the "beads" Darwin heard about.

[6] [Darwin] M. A. d'Orbigny has given nearly a similar account of these dogs, tom. i. p. 175.

times a day for the little thing to suck, and a nest of wool is made for it in the sheep-pen; at no time is it allowed to associate with other dogs, or with the children of the family. The puppy is, moreover, generally castrated; so that, when grown up, it can scarcely have any feelings in common with the rest of its kind. From this education it has no wish to leave the flock, and just as another dog will defend its master, man, so will these the sheep. It is amusing to observe, when approaching a flock, how the dog immediately advances barking, and the sheep all close in his rear, as if round the oldest ram. These dogs are also easily taught to bring home the flock, at a certain hour in the evening. Their most troublesome fault, when young, is their desire of playing with the sheep; for in their sport they sometimes gallop their poor subjects most unmercifully.

The shepherd-dog comes to the house every day for some meat, and as soon as it is given him, he skulks away as if ashamed of himself. On these occasions the house-dogs are very tyrannical, and the least of them will attack and pursue the stranger. The minute, however, the latter has reached the flock, he turns round and begins to bark, and then all the house-dogs take very quickly to their heels. In a similar manner a whole pack of the hungry wild dogs will scarcely ever (and I was told by some never) venture to attack a flock guarded by even one of these faithful shepherds. The whole account appears to me a curious instance of the pliability of the affections in the dog; and yet, whether wild or however educated, he has a feeling of respect or fear for those that are fulfilling their instinct of association. For we can understand on no principle the wild dogs being driven away by the single one with its flock, except that they consider, from some confused notion, that the one thus associated gains power, as if in company with its own kind. F. Cuvier has observed, that all animals that readily enter into domestication, consider man as a member of their own society, and thus fulfil their instinct of association. In the above case the shepherd-dog ranks the sheep as its fellow-brethren, and thus gains confidence; and the wild dogs, though knowing that the individual sheep are not dogs, but are good to eat, yet partly consent to this view when seeing them in a flock with a shepherd-dog at their head.

One evening a "domidor" (a subduer of horses) came for the purpose of breaking-in some colts. I will describe the preparatory steps, for I believe they have not been mentioned by other travellers. A troop of wild young horses is driven into the corral, or large enclosure of stakes, and the door is shut. We will suppose that one man alone has to catch and mount a horse, which as yet had never felt bridle or saddle. I conceive, except by a Gaucho, such a feat would be utterly impracticable. The Gaucho picks out a full-grown colt; and as the beast rushes round the circus, he throws his lazo so as to catch both the front legs. Instantly the horse rolls over with a heavy shock, and whilst struggling on the ground, the Gaucho, holding the lazo tight, makes a circle, so as to catch one of the hind legs, just beneath the fetlock, and draws it close to the two front legs: he then hitches the lazo, so that the three are bound together. Then sitting on the horse's neck, he fixes a strong bridle, without a bit, to the lower jaw: this he does by passing a narrow thong through the eye-holes at the end of the reins, and several times round both jaw and tongue. The two front legs are now tied closely together with a strong leathern thong, fastened by a slip-knot. The lazo, which bound the three together, being then loosed, the horse rises with difficulty. The Gaucho now holding fast the bridle fixed to the lower jaw, leads the horse outside the corral. If a second man is present (otherwise the trouble is much greater) he holds the animal's head, whilst the first puts on the horsecloths and saddle, and girths the whole together. During this operation, the horse, from dread and astonishment at thus being bound round the waist, throws himself over and over again on the ground, and, till beaten, is unwilling to rise. At last, when the saddling is finished, the poor animal can hardly breathe from fear, and is white with foam and sweat. The man now prepares to mount by pressing heavily on the stirrup, so that the horse may not lose its balance; and at the moment that he throws his leg over the animal's back, he pulls the slip-knot binding the front legs, and the beast is free. Some "domidors" pull the knot while the animal is lying on the ground, and, standing over the saddle, allow him to rise beneath them. The horse, wild with dread, gives a few most violent bounds, and then starts off at full gallop: when quite exhausted, the man, by patience, brings him back to the corral, where, reeking hot and scarcely alive, the poor beast is let free. Those animals which will not gallop away, but obstinately throw themselves on the ground, are by far the most troublesome. This process is tremendously severe, but in two or three trials the horse is tamed. It is not, however, for some weeks that the animal is ridden with the iron bit and solid ring, for it must learn to associate the will of its rider with the feel of the rein, before the most powerful bridle can be of any service.

Animals are so abundant in these countries, that humanity and self-interest are not closely united; therefore I fear it is that the former is here scarcely known. One day, riding in the Pampas with a very respectable "Estanciero," my horse, being tired, lagged behind. The man often shouted to me to spur him. When I remonstrated that it was a pity, for the horse was quite exhausted, he cried out, "Why not?—never mind—spur him—it is *my* horse." I had then some difficulty in making him comprehend that it was for the horse's sake, and not on his account, that I did not choose to use my spurs. He exclaimed, with a look of great surprise, "Ah, Don Carlos, que cosa!" It was clear that such an idea had never before entered his head.

The Gauchos are well known to be perfect riders. The idea of being thrown, let the horse do what it likes, never enters their head. Their criterion of a good rider is, a man who can manage an untamed colt, or who, if his horse falls, alights on his own feet, or can perform other such exploits. I have heard of a man betting that he would throw his horse down twenty times, and that nineteen times he would not fall himself. I recollect seeing a Gaucho riding a very stubborn horse, which three times successively reared so high as to fall backwards with great violence. The man judged with uncommon coolness the proper moment for slipping off, not an instant before or after the right time; and as soon as the horse got up, the man jumped on his back, and at last they started at a gallop. The Gaucho never appears to exert any muscular force. I was one day watching a good rider, as we were galloping along at a rapid pace, and thought to myself, "surely if the horse starts, you appear so careless on your seat, you must fall." At this moment, a male ostrich sprang from its nest right beneath the horse's nose: the young colt bounded on one side like a stag; but as for the man, all that could be said was, that he started and took fright with his horse.

In Chile and Peru more pains are taken with the mouth of the horse than in La Plata, and this is evidently a consequence of the more intricate nature of the country. In Chile a horse is not considered perfectly broken, till he can be brought up standing, in the midst of his full speed, on any particular spot, for instance, on a cloak thrown on the ground: or, again, he will charge a wall, and rearing, scrape the surface with his hoofs. I have seen an animal bounding with spirit, yet merely reined by a fore-finger and thumb, taken at full gallop across

a courtyard, and then made to wheel round the post of a verandah with great speed, but at so equal a distance, that the rider,
with outstretched arm, all the while kept one finger rubbing
the post. Then making a demi-volte in the air, with the other
arm outstretched in a like manner, he wheeled round, with
astonishing force, in an opposite direction.

Such a horse is well broken; and although this at first may
appear useless, it is far otherwise. It is only carrying that which
is daily necessary into perfection. When a bullock is checked
and caught by the lazo, it will sometimes gallop round and
round in a circle, and the horse being alarmed at the great
strain, if not well broken, will not readily turn like the pivot of
a wheel. In consequence many men have been killed; for if
the lazo once takes a twist round a man's body, it will instantly,
from the power of the two opposed animals, almost cut him
in twain. On the same principle the races are managed; the
course is only two or three hundred yards long, the wish being
to have horses that can make a rapid dash. The race-horses
are trained not only to stand with their hoofs touching a line,
but to draw all four feet together, so as at the first spring to
bring into play the full action of the hind-quarters. In Chile I
was told an anecdote, which I believe was true; and it offers a
good illustration of the use of a well-broken animal. A respectable man riding one day met two others, one of whom was
mounted on a horse which he knew to have been stolen from
himself. He challenged them; they answered him by drawing
their sabres and giving chace. The man, on his good and fleet
beast, kept just ahead: as he passed a thick bush he wheeled
round it, and brought up his horse to a dead check. The pursuers were obliged to shoot on one side and ahead. Then instantly dashing on, right behind them, he buried his knife in the
back of one, wounded the other, recovered his horse from the
dying robber, and rode home. For these feats of horsemanship
two things are necessary: a most severe bit, like the Mameluke,
the power of which, though seldom used, the horse knows
full well; and large blunt spurs, that can be applied either as a
mere touch, or as an instrument of extreme pain. I conceive
that with English spurs, the slightest touch of which pricks the
skin, it would be impossible to break in a horse after the South
American fashion.

At an estancia near Las Vacas large numbers of mares are
weekly slaughtered for the sake of their hides, although worth
only five paper dollars, or about half-a-crown apiece. It seems

at first strange that it can answer to kill mares for such a trifle; but as it is thought ridiculous in this country ever to break in or ride a mare, they are of no value except for breeding. The only thing for which I ever saw mares used, was to tread out wheat from the ear; for which purpose they were driven round a circular enclosure, where the wheat-sheaves were strewed. The man employed for slaughtering the mares happened to be celebrated for his dexterity with the lazo. Standing at the distance of twelve yards from the mouth of the corral, he has laid a wager that he would catch by the legs every animal, without missing one, as it rushed past him. There was another man who said he would enter the corral on foot, catch a mare, fasten her front legs together, drive her out, throw her down, kill, skin, and stake the hide for drying (which latter is a tedious job); and he engaged that he would perform this whole operation on twenty-two animals in one day. Or he would kill and take the skin off fifty in the same time. This would have been a prodigious task, for it is considered a good day's work to skin and stake the hides of fifteen or sixteen animals.

November 26th.—I set out on my return in a direct line for Monte Video. Having heard of some giant's bones at a neighbouring farm-house on the Sarandis, a small stream entering the Rio Negro, I rode there accompanied by my host, and purchased for the value of eighteen pence the head of the Toxodon.[7] When found it was quite perfect; but the boys knocked out some of the teeth with stones, and then set up the head as a mark to throw at. By a most fortunate chance I found a perfect tooth, which exactly fitted one of the sockets in this skull, embedded by itself on the banks of the Rio Tercero, at the distance of about 180 miles from this place. I found remains of this extraordinary animal at two other places, so that it must formerly have been common. I found here, also, some large portions of the armour of a gigantic armadillo-like animal, and part of the great head of a Mylodon. The bones of this head are so fresh, that they contain, according to the analysis by Mr. T. Reeks, seven per cent. of animal matter; and when placed in a spirit-lamp, they burn with a small flame. The number of the remains embedded in the grand estuary deposit which forms the Pampas and covers the granitic rocks

[7] [Darwin] I must express my obligation to Mr. Keane, at whose house I was staying on the Berquelo, and to Mr. Lumb at Buenos Ayres, for without their assistance these valuable remains would never have reached England.

of Banda Oriental, must be extraordinarily great. I believe a
straight line drawn in any direction through the Pampas would
cut through some skeleton or bones. Besides those which I
found during my short excursions, I heard of many others,
and the origin of such names as "the stream of the animal,"
"the hill of the giant," is obvious. At other times I heard of
the marvellous property of certain rivers, which had the power
of changing small bones into large; or, as some maintained,
the bones themselves grew. As far as I am aware, not one of
these animals perished, as was formerly supposed, in the
marshes or muddy river-beds of the present land, but their
bones have been exposed by the streams intersecting the subaqueous deposit in which they were originally embedded. We
may conclude that the whole area of the Pampas is one wide
sepulchre of these extinct gigantic quadrupeds.

By the middle of the day, on the 28th, we arrived at Monte
Video, having been two days and a half on the road. The country for the whole way was of a very uniform character, some
parts being rather more rocky and hilly than near the Plata.
Not far from Monte Video we passed through the village of
Las Pietras, so named from some large rounded masses of sye-
nite. Its appearance was rather pretty. In this country a few
fig-trees round a group of houses, and a site elevated a hundred
feet above the general level, ought always to be called picturesque.

During the last six months I have had an opportunity of
seeing a little of the character of the inhabitants of these provinces. The Gauchos, or countrymen, are very superior to those
who reside in the towns. The Gaucho is invariably most obliging, polite, and hospitable: I did not meet with even one instance of rudeness or inhospitality. He is modest, both respecting himself and country, but at the same time a spirited, bold
fellow. On the other hand, many robberies are committed, and
there is much bloodshed: the habit of constantly wearing the
knife is the chief cause of the latter. It is lamentable to hear
how many lives are lost in trifling quarrels. In fighting, each
party tries to mark the face of his adversary by slashing his
nose or eyes; as is often attested by deep and horrid-looking
scars. Robberies are a natural consequence of universal gambling, much drinking, and extreme indolence. At Mercedes I
asked two men why they did not work. One gravely said the
days were too long; the other that he was too poor. The num-

ber of horses and the profusion of food are the destruction of all industry. Moreover, there are so many feast-days; and again, nothing can succeed without it be begun when the moon is on the increase; so that half the month is lost from these two causes.

Police and justice are quite inefficient. If a man who is poor commits murder and is taken, he will be imprisoned, and perhaps even shot; but if he is rich and has friends, he may rely on it no very severe consequence will ensue. It is curious that the most respectable inhabitants of the country invariably assist a murderer to escape: they seem to think that the individual sins against the government, and not against the people. A traveller has no protection besides his fire-arms; and the constant habit of carrying them is the main check to more frequent robberies.

The character of the higher and more educated classes who reside in the towns, partakes, but perhaps in a lesser degree, of the good parts of the Gaucho, but is, I fear, stained by many vices of which he is free. Sensuality, mockery of all religion, and the grossest corruption, are far from uncommon. Nearly every public officer can be bribed. The head man in the post-office sold forged government franks. The governor and prime minister openly combined to plunder the state. Justice, where gold came into play, was hardly expected by any one. I knew an Englishman, who went to the Chief Justice (he told me that, not then understanding the ways of the place, he trembled as he entered the room), and said, "Sir, I have come to offer you two hundred (paper) dollars (value about five pounds sterling) if you will arrest before a certain time a man who has cheated me. I know it is against the law, but my lawyer (naming him) recommended me to take this step." The Chief Justice smiled acquiescence, thanked him, and the man before night was safe in prison. With this entire want of principle in many of the leading men, with the country full of ill-paid turbulent officers, the people yet hope that a democratic form of government can succeed!

On first entering society in these countries, two or three features strike one as particularly remarkable. The polite and dignified manners pervading every rank of life, the excellent taste displayed by the women in their dresses, and the equality amongst all ranks. At the Rio Colorado some men who kept the humblest shops used to dine with General Rosas. A son of a major at Bahia Blanca gained his livelihood by making paper cigars, and he wished to accompany me, as guide or servant,

to Buenos Ayres, but his father objected on the score of the
danger alone. Many officers in the army can neither read nor
write, yet all meet in society as equals. In Entre Rios, the Sala
consisted of only six representatives. One of them kept a common shop, and evidently was not degraded by the office. All
this is what would be expected in a new country; nevertheless
the absence of gentlemen by profession appears to an Englishman something strange.

When speaking of these countries, the manner in which they
have been brought up by their unnatural parent, Spain, should
always be borne in mind. On the whole, perhaps, more credit
is due for what has been done, than blame for that which may
be deficient. It is impossible to doubt but that the extreme lib-
eralism of these countries must ultimately lead to good results.
The very general toleration of foreign religions, the regard
paid to the means of education, the freedom of the press, the
facilities offered to all foreigners, and especially, as I am bound
to add, to every one professing the humblest pretensions to
science, should be recollected with gratitude by those who have
visited Spanish South America.

December 6th.—The *Beagle* sailed from the Rio Plata, never
again to enter its muddy stream. Our course was directed to
Port Desire, on the coast of Patagonia. Before proceeding any
further, I will here put together a few observations made at sea.

Several times when the ship has been some miles off the
mouth of the Plata, and at other times when off the shores of
Northern Patagonia, we have been surrounded by insects. One
evening, when we were about ten miles from the Bay of San
Blas, vast numbers of butterflies, in bands or flocks of countless myriads, extended as far as the eye could range. Even by
the aid of a telescope it was not possible to see a space free
from butterflies. The seamen cried out "it was snowing butterflies," and such in fact was the appearance. More species than
one were present, but the main part belonged to a kind very
similar to, but not identical with, the common English Colias
edusa. Some moths and hymenoptera accompanied the butterflies; and a fine beetle (Calosoma) flew on board. Other instances are known of this beetle having been caught far out at
sea; and this is the more remarkable, as the greater number of
the Carabidæ seldom or never take wing. The day had been
fine and calm, and the one previous to it equally so, with light
and variable airs. Hence we cannot suppose that the insects

were blown off the land, but we must conclude that they voluntarily took flight. The great bands of the Colias seem at first to afford an instance like those on record of the migrations of another butterfly, Vanessa cardui;[8] but the presence of other insects makes the case distinct, and even less intelligible. Before sunset a strong breeze sprung up from the north, and this must have caused tens of thousands of the butterflies and other insects to have perished.

On another occasion, when seventeen miles off Cape Corrientes, I had a net overboard to catch pelagic animals. Upon drawing it up, to my surprise I found a considerable number of beetles in it, and although in the open sea, they did not appear much injured by the salt water. I lost some of the specimens, but those which I preserved belonged to the genera Colymbetes, Hydroporus, Hydrobius (two species), Notaphus, Cynucus, Adimonia, and Scarabæus. At first I thought that these insects had been blown from the shore; but upon reflecting that out of the eight species four were aquatic, and two others partly so in their habits, it appeared to me most probable that they were floated into the sea by a small stream which drains a lake near Cape Corrientes. On any supposition it is an interesting circumstance to find live insects swimming in the open ocean seventeen miles from the nearest point of land. There are several accounts of insects having been blown off the Patagonian shore. Captain Cook observed it, as did more lately Captain King in the *Adventure*. The cause probably is due to the want of shelter, both of trees and hills, so that an insect on the wing, with an off-shore breeze, would be very apt to be blown out to sea. The most remarkable instance I have known of an insect being caught far from the land, was that of a large grasshopper (Acrydium), which flew on board, when the *Beagle* was to windward of the Cape de Verd Islands, and when the nearest point of land, not directly opposed to the trade-wind, was Cape Blanco on the coast of Africa, 370 miles distant.[9]

On several occasions, when the *Beagle* had been within the mouth of the Plata, the rigging has been coated with the web

8 [Darwin] Lyell's Principles of Geology, vol. iii. p. 63. [Vanessa cardui—now called Pyrameis cardui—is the handsome Painted Lady butterfly of North America and Europe.—Ed.]

9 [Darwin] The flies which frequently accompany a ship for some days on its passage from harbour to harbour, wandering from the vessel, are soon lost, and all disappear.

of the Gossamer Spider. One day (November 1st, 1832) I paid particular attention to this subject. The weather had been fine and clear, and in the morning the air was full of patches of the flocculent web, as on an autumnal day in England. The ship was sixty miles distant from the land, in the direction of a steady though light breeze. Vast numbers of a small spider, about one-tenth of an inch in length, and of a dusky red colour, were attached to the webs. There must have been, I should suppose, some thousands on the ship. The little spider, when first coming in contact with the rigging, was always seated on a single thread, and not on the flocculent mass. This latter seems merely to be produced by the entanglement of the single threads. The spiders were all of one species, but of both sexes, together with young ones. These latter were distinguished by their smaller size and more dusky colour. I will not give the description of this spider, but merely state that it does not appear to me to be included in any of Latreille's genera. The little aëronaut as soon as it arrived on board was very active, running about, sometimes letting itself fall, and then reascending the same thread; sometimes employing itself in making a small and very irregular mesh in the corners between the ropes. It could run with facility on the surface of water. When disturbed it lifted up its front legs, in the attitude of attention. On its first arrival it appeared very thirsty, and with exserted maxillæ drank eagerly of drops of water; this same circumstance has been observed by Strack: may it not be in consequence of the little insect having passed through a dry and rarefied atmosphere? Its stock of web seemed inexhaustible. While watching some that were suspended by a single thread, I several times observed that the slightest breath of air bore them away out of sight, in a horizontal line. On another occasion (25th) under similar circumstances, I repeatedly observed the same kind of small spider, either when placed or having crawled on some little eminence, elevate its abdomen, send forth a thread, and then sail away horizontally, but with a rapidity which was quite unaccountable. I thought I could perceive that the spider, before performing the above preparatory steps, connected its legs together with the most delicate threads, but I am not sure whether this observation was correct.

One day, at St. Fé, I had a better opportunity of observing some similar facts. A spider which was about three-tenths of an inch in length, and which in its general appearance resembled a Citigrade (therefore quite different from the gossamer), while standing on the summit of a post, darted forth four or five threads from its spinners. These, glittering in the sunshine, might be compared to diverging rays of light; they were not, however, straight, but in undulations like films of silk blown by the wind. They were more than a yard in length, and diverged in an ascending direction from the orifices. The spider then suddenly let go its hold of the post, and was quickly borne out of sight. The day was hot and apparently quite calm; yet under such circumstances, the atmosphere can never be so tranquil as not to affect a vane so delicate as the thread of a spider's web. If during a warm day we look either at the shadow of any object cast on a bank, or over a level plain at a distant landmark, the effect of an ascending current of heated air is almost always evident: such upward currents, it has been remarked, are also shown by the ascent of soap-bubbles, which will not rise in an in-doors room. Hence I think there is not much difficulty in understanding the ascent of the fine lines projected from a spider's spinners, and afterwards of the spider itself; the divergence of the lines has been attempted to be explained, I believe by Mr. Murray, by their similar electrical condition. The circumstance of spiders of the same species, but of different sexes and ages, being found on several occasions at the distance of many leagues from the land, attached in vast numbers to the lines, renders it probable that the habit of sailing through the air is as characteristic of this tribe, as that of diving is of the Argyroneta. We may then reject Latreille's supposition, that the gossamer owes its origin indifferently to the young of several genera of spiders: although, as we have seen, the young of other spiders do possess the power of performing aërial voyages.[10]

During our different passages south of the Plata, I often towed astern a net made of bunting, and thus caught many curious animals. Of Crustacea there were many strange and undescribed genera. One, which in some respects is allied to the Notopods (or those crabs which have their posterior legs placed almost on their backs, for the purpose of adhering to the under side of rocks), is very remarkable from the structure of its hind pair of legs. The penultimate joint, instead of terminating in a simple claw, ends in three bristle-like appendages of dissimilar lengths—the longest equalling that of the entire leg. These claws are very thin, and are serrated with the finest

[10] [Darwin] Mr. Blackwall, in his Researches in Zoology, has many excellent observations on the habits of spiders.

teeth, directed backwards: their curved extremities are flattened, and on this part five most minute cups are placed which seem to act in the same manner as the suckers on the arms of the cuttle-fish. As the animal lives in the open sea, and probably wants a place of rest, I suppose this beautiful and most anomalous structure is adapted to take hold of floating marine animals.

In deep water, far from the land, the number of living creatures is extremely small: south of the latitude 35°, I never succeeded in catching anything besides some beroe, and a few species of minute entomostracous crustacea.[11] In shoaler water, at the distance of a few miles from the coast, very many kinds of crustacea and some other animals are numerous, but only during the night. Between latitudes 56° and 57° south of Cape Horn, the net was put astern several times; it never, however, brought up anything besides a few of two extremely minute species of Entomostraca. Yet whales and seals, petrels and albatross, are exceedingly abundant throughout this part of the ocean. It has always been a mystery to me on what the albatross, which lives far from the shore, can subsist; I presume that, like the condor, it is able to fast long; and that one good feast on the carcass of a putrid whale lasts for a long time.[12] The central and inter-tropical parts of the Atlantic swarm with Pteropoda, Crustacea, and Radiata, and with their devourers the flying-fish, and again with their devourers the bonitos and albicores; I presume that the numerous lower pelagic animals feed on the Infusoria, which are now known, from the researches of Ehrenberg, to abound in the open ocean: but on what, in the clear blue water, do these Infusoria subsist?

[11] [Editor] The beroë is a member of the ctenophores, the "comb jellies," a class of berrylike animals of the floating planktonic layer of life in the sea. Entomostracous crustacea form one of the great divisions of the class Crustacea. The Entomostraca are mostly small and include the copepods, a family of tiny planktonic crustacea that are probably the most numerous multicelled animals in the world.

[12] [Editor] Darwin's failure to catch much in the way of marine life in the waters around Cape Horn is puzzling. The cold, wind-churned waters of the South Atlantic and the Antarctic teem with planktonic life—enough to support great numbers of fish and once large populations of such large creatures as the blue whale, a feeder upon planktonic shrimp. The albatross feeds primarily upon fish and cuttlefish.

While sailing a little south of the Plata on one very dark night, the sea presented a wonderful and most beautiful spectacle. There was a fresh breeze, and every part of the surface, which during the day is seen as foam, now glowed with a pale light. The vessel drove before her bows two billows of liquid phosphorus, and in her wake she was followed by a milky train. As far as the eye reached, the crest of every wave was bright, and the sky above the horizon, from the reflected glare of these livid flames, was not so utterly obscure as over the vault of the heavens.

As we proceed further southward the sea is seldom phosphorescent; and off Cape Horn I do not recollect more than once having seen it so, and then it was far from being brilliant. This circumstance probably has a close connexion with the scarcity of organic beings in that part of the ocean. After the elaborate paper[13] by Ehrenberg, on the phosphorescence of the sea, it is almost superfluous on my part to make any observations on the subject. I may however add, that the same torn and irregular particles of gelatinous matter, described by Ehrenberg, seem in the southern as well as in the northern hemisphere, to be the common cause of this phenomenon. The particles were so minute as easily to pass through fine gauze; yet many were distinctly visible by the naked eye. The water when placed in a tumbler and agitated, gave out sparks, but a small portion in a watch-glass scarcely ever was luminous. Ehrenberg states that these particles all retain a certain degree of irritability. My observations, some of which were made directly after taking up the water, gave a different result. I may also mention, that having used the net during one night, I allowed it to become partially dry, and having occasion twelve hours afterwards to employ it again, I found the whole surface sparkled as brightly as when first taken out of the water. It does not appear probable in this case, that the particles could have remained so long alive. On one occasion having kept a jelly-fish of the genus Dianæa till it was dead, the water in which it was placed became luminous. When the waves scintillate with bright green sparks, I believe it is generally owing to minute crustacea. But there can be no doubt that very many other pelagic animals, when alive, are phosphorescent.

On two occasions I have observed the sea luminous at considerable depths beneath the surface. Near the mouth of the

13 [Darwin] An abstract is given in No. IV. of the Magazine of Zoology and Botany.

Plata some circular and oval patches, from two to four yards in diameter, and with defined outlines, shone with a steady but pale light; while the surrounding water only gave out a few sparks. The appearance resembled the reflection of the moon, or some luminous body; for the edges were sinuous from the undulations of the surface. The ship, which drew thirteen feet of water, passed over, without disturbing these patches. Therefore we must suppose that some animals were congregated together at a greater depth than the bottom of the vessel.

Near Fernando Noronha the sea gave out light in flashes. The appearance was very similar to that which might be expected from a large fish moving rapidly through a luminous fluid. To this cause the sailors attributed it; at the time, however, I entertained some doubts, on account of the frequency and rapidity of the flashes. I have already remarked that the phenomenon is very much more common in warm than in cold countries; and I have sometimes imagined that a disturbed electrical condition of the atmosphere was most favourable to its production. Certainly I think the sea is most luminous after a few days of more calm weather than ordinary, during which time it has swarmed with various animals. Observing that the water charged with gelatinous particles is in an impure state, and that the luminous appearance in all common cases is produced by the agitation of the fluid in contact with the atmosphere, I am inclined to consider that the phosphorescence is the result of the decomposition of the organic particles, by which process (one is tempted almost to call it a kind of respiration) the ocean becomes purified.[14]

December 23rd.—We arrived at Port Desire, situated in lat. 47°, on the coast of Patagonia.[15] The creek runs for about

[14] [Editor] As it could not have been guessed in Darwin's day, the phosphorescence of the sea is due to the presence of countless billions of luminescent microscopic creatures, which give off light when disturbed.

[15] [Editor] Technically, the name Patagonia refers to the mainland of South America below the Rio Negro in Argentina and latitude 42 South in Chile, so both Argentina and Chile possess part of Patagonia. The Argentine portion is much larger, however, and the name Patagonia has come to mean Argentine Patagonia only. Although efforts were made to establish European settlements in Patagonia as early as the sixteenth century, all before 1880 were defeated by the difficulties of the country and the resistance of the Patagonian Indians. Today, Patagonia is administered by

twenty miles inland, with an irregular width. The *Beagle* anchored a few miles within the entrance, in front of the ruins of an old Spanish settlement.

The same evening I went on shore. The first landing in any new country is very interesting, and especially when, as in this case, the whole aspect bears the stamp of a marked and individual character. At the height of between two and three hundred feet above some masses of porphyry a wide plain extends, which is truly characteristic of Patagonia. The surface is quite level, and is composed of well-rounded shingle mixed with a whitish earth. Here and there scattered tufts of brown wiry grass are supported, and, still more rarely, some low thorny bushes. The weather is dry and pleasant, and the fine blue sky is but seldom obscured. When standing in the middle of one of these desert plains and looking towards the interior, the view is generally bounded by the escarpment of another plain, rather higher, but equally level and desolate; and in every other direction the horizon is indistinct from the trembling mirage which seems to rise from the heated surface.

In such a country the fate of the Spanish settlement was soon decided; the dryness of the climate during the greater part of the year, and the occasional hostile attacks of the wandering Indians, compelled the colonists to desert their half-finished buildings. The style, however, in which they were commenced shows the strong and liberal hand of Spain in the old time. The result of all the attempts to colonize this side of America south of 41°, have been miserable. Port Famine expresses by its name the lingering and extreme sufferings of several hundred wretched people, of whom one alone survived to relate their misfortunes.[16] At St. Joseph's Bay, on the coast

---

Argentina as a series of national territories, through governors appointed from Buenos Aires. Substantial development has occurred in only one area, Comodoro Rivadavia, site of a major oil field. Otherwise, Patagonia is still nearly empty. A small town and a naval air field now are located at Port Desire (Puerto Deseado in Spanish).

[16] [Editor] In 1583, two Spanish settlements were established in southwest Patagonia. Neither survived. One, named San Felipe, was on a peninsula projecting into the Strait of Magellan, about 60 miles south of the present Chilean city of Punta Arenas. San Felipe was visited in 1587 by Thomas Cavendish, the English sea raider, who found its surviving residents in such desperate straits that he called the town Port Famine.

of Patagonia, a small settlement was made; but during one Sunday the Indians made an attack and massacred the whole party, excepting two men, who remained captives during many years. At the Rio Negro I conversed with one of these men, now in extreme old age.

The zoology of Patagonia is as limited as its Flora.[17] On the arid plains a few black beetles (Heteromera) might be seen slowly crawling about, and occasionally a lizard darted from side to side. Of birds we have three carrion-hawks, and in the valleys a few finches and insect-feeders. An ibis (Theristicus melanops—a species said to be found in central Africa) is not uncommon on the most desert parts: in their stomachs I found grasshoppers, cicadæ, small lizards, and even scorpions.[18] At one time of the year these birds go in flocks, at another in pairs; their cry is very loud and singular, like the neighing of the guanaco.

The guanaco, or wild llama, is the characteristic quadruped of the plains of Patagonia; it is the South American representative of the camel of the East. It is an elegant animal in a state of nature, with a long slender neck and fine legs. It is very common over the whole of the temperate parts of the continent, as far south as the islands near Cape Horn. It generally lives in small herds of from half a dozen to thirty in each; but on the banks of the St. Cruz we saw one herd which must have contained at least five hundred.

They are generally wild and extremely wary. Mr. Stokes told me, that he one day saw through a glass a herd of these animals which evidently had been frightened, and were running away at full speed, although their distance was so great that he could not distinguish them with his naked eye. The sportsman frequently receives the first notice of their presence, by hearing from a long distance their peculiar shrill neighing note of

[17] [Darwin] I found here a species of cactus, described by Professor Henslow, under the name of *Opuntia Darwinii* (Magazine of Zoology and Botany, vol. i. p. 466), which was remarkable by the irritability of the stamens, when I inserted either a piece of stick or the end of my finger in the flower. The segments of the perianth also closed on the pistil, but more slowly than the stamens. Plants of this family, generally considered as tropical, occur in North America (Lewis and Clarke's Travels, p. 221), in the same high latitude as here, namely, in both cases, in 47°.

[18] [Darwin] These insects were not uncommon beneath stones. I found one cannibal scorpion quietly devouring another.

alarm. If he then looks attentively, he will probably see the herd standing in a line on the side of some distant hill. On approaching nearer, a few more squeals are given, and off they set at an apparently slow, but really quick canter, along some narrow beaten track to a neighbouring hill. If, however, by chance he abruptly meets a single animal, or several together, they will generally stand motionless and intently gaze at him; then perhaps move on a few yards, turn round, and look again. What is the cause of this difference in their shyness? Do they mistake a man in the distance for their chief enemy the puma? Or does curiosity overcome their timidity? That they are curious is certain; for if a person lies on the ground, and plays strange antics, such as throwing up his feet in the air, they will almost always approach by degrees to reconnoitre him. It was an artifice that was repeatedly practised by our sportsmen with success, and it had moreover the advantage of allowing several shots to be fired, which were all taken as parts of the performance. On the mountains of Tierra del Fuego, I have more than once seen a guanaco, on being approached, not only neigh and squeal, but prance and leap about in the most ridiculous manner, apparently in defiance as a challenge. These animals are very easily domesticated, and I have seen some thus kept in northern Patagonia near a house, though not under any restraint. They are in this state very bold, and readily attack a man by striking him from behind with both knees. It is asserted that the motive for these attacks is jealousy on account of their females. The wild guanacos, however, have no idea of defence; even a single dog will secure one of these large animals, till the huntsman can come up. In many of their habits they are like sheep in a flock. Thus when they see men approaching in several directions on horseback, they soon become bewildered, and know not which way to run. This greatly facilitates the Indian method of hunting, for they are thus easily driven to a central point, and are encompassed.

The guanacos readily take to the water: several times at Port Valdes they were seen swimming from island to island. Byron, in his voyage, says he saw them drinking salt water. Some of our officers likewise saw a herd apparently drinking the briny fluid from a salina near Cape Blanco. I imagine in several parts of the country, if they do not drink salt water, they drink none at all. In the middle of the day they frequently roll in the dust, in saucer-shaped hollows. The males fight together; two one day passed quite close to me, squealing and trying to bite each other; and several were shot with their hides deeply scored. Herds sometimes appear to set out on exploring parties: at Bahia Blanca, where, within thirty miles of the coast, these animals are extremely unfrequent, I one day saw the tracks of thirty or forty, which had come in a direct line to a muddy salt-water creek. They then must have perceived that they were approaching the sea, for they had wheeled with the regularity of cavalry, and had returned back in as straight a line as they had advanced. The guanacos have one singular habit, which is to me quite inexplicable; namely, that on successive days they drop their dung in the same defined heap. I saw one of these heaps which was eight feet in diameter, and was composed of a large quantity. This habit, according to M. A. d'Orbigny, is common to all the species of the genus; it is very useful to the Peruvian Indians, who use the dung for fuel, and are thus saved the trouble of collecting it.

The guanacos appear to have favourite spots for lying down to die. On the banks of the St. Cruz, in certain circumscribed spaces, which were generally bushy, and all near the river, the ground was actually white with bones. On one such spot I counted between ten and twenty heads. I particularly examined the bones; they did not appear, as some scattered ones which I had seen, gnawed or broken, as if dragged together by beasts of prey. The animals in most cases must have crawled, before dying, beneath and amongst the bushes. Mr. Bynoe informs me that during a former voyage he observed the same circumstance on the banks of the Rio Gallegos. I do not at all understand the reason of this, but I may observe, that the wounded guanacos at the St. Cruz invariably walked towards the river. At St. Jago in the Cape de Verd islands, I remember having seen in a ravine a retired corner covered with bones of the goat; we at the time exclaimed that it was the burial-ground of all the goats in the island. I mention these trifling circumstances, because in certain cases they might explain the occurrence of a number of uninjured bones in a cave, or buried under alluvial accumulations; and likewise the cause why certain animals are more commonly embedded than others in sedimentary deposits.[19]

[19] [Editor] E. Lucas Bridges, son of a British missionary who settled in Tierra del Fuego in 1871, gives a simple explanation of accumulations of guanaco bones in *Uttermost Part of the Earth*, an autobiographical account of life in Tierra del Fuego 75 years ago. Bridges writes:

One day the yawl was sent under the command of Mr. Chaffers with three days' provisions to survey the upper part of the harbour. In the morning we searched for some watering-places mentioned in an old Spanish chart. We found one creek, at the head of which there was a trickling rill (the first we had seen) of brackish water. Here the tide compelled us to wait several hours; and in the interval I walked some miles into the interior. The plain as usual consisted of gravel, mingled with soil resembling chalk in appearance, but very different from it in nature. From the softness of these materials it was worn into many gulleys. There was not a tree, and, excepting the guanaco, which stood on the hill-top a watchful sentinel over its herd, scarcely an animal or a bird. All was stillness and desolation. Yet in passing over these scenes, without one bright object near, an ill-defined but strong sense of pleasure is vividly excited. One asked how many ages the plain had thus lasted, and how many more it was doomed thus to continue.

> None can reply—all seems eternal now.
> The wilderness has a mysterious tongue,
> Which teaches awful doubt.[20]

"There is a belief among certain white men that guanaco, when old and infirm, go—as elephants are said to do—to lay their bones amongst those of their fellows in a selected dying-ground. There is a much more matter-of-fact explanation for the accumulated masses of guanaco bones to be found in Patagonia and Tierra del Fuego. In severe winters those animals forget their differences and join in large groups wherever there is less snow and more chance of finding food. This tendency to congregate is increased by the fact that it is easier to follow beaten tracks than to break fresh ground through very deep snows. In Patagonia and northern Fireland, where there are no forests, a fierce blizzard may force guanaco to seek shelter in some clump of bushes where the wind, sweeping over the hills, piles up deep snow all around them. They will eat the bushes, however hard and thorny, but very soon, having lost all their strength and with a white world of snow stretching for leagues in every direction, they give up hope and, one by one, lie down and die.

"After one very severe winter, not many years ago, I counted the bodies of no fewer than fifty-two guanaco lying in an area of less than an acre on the stumps of the hard bushes they had gnawed to the very ground. Only a few miles from the same spot, a friend of mine once counted over two hundred in like condition.

"Hence the legend of the guanaco cemetery."

20 [Darwin] Shelley, Lines on M. Blanc.

In the evening we sailed a few miles further up, and then pitched the tents for the night. By the middle of the next day the yawl was aground, and from the shoalness of the water could not proceed any higher. The water being found partly fresh, Mr. Chaffers took the dingey and went up two or three miles further, where she also grounded, but in a fresh-water river. The water was muddy, and though the stream was most insignificant in size, it would be difficult to account for its origin, except from the melting snow on the Cordillera. At the spot where we bivouacked, we were surrounded by bold cliffs and steep pinnacles of porphyry. I do not think I ever saw a spot which appeared more secluded from the rest of the world, than this rocky crevice in the wide plain.

The second day after our return to the anchorage, a party of officers and myself went to ransack an old Indian grave, which I had found on the summit of a neighbouring hill. Two immense stones, each probably weighing at least a couple of tons, had been placed in front of a ledge of rock about six feet high. At the bottom of the grave on the hard rock there was a layer of earth about a foot deep, which must have been brought up from the plain below. Above it a pavement of flat stones was placed, on which others were piled, so as to fill up the space between the ledge and the two great blocks. To complete the grave, the Indians had contrived to detach from the ledge a huge fragment, and to throw it over the pile so as to rest on the two blocks. We undermined the grave on both sides, but could not find any relics, or even bones. The latter probably had decayed long since (in which case the grave must have been of extreme antiquity), for I found in another place some smaller heaps, beneath which a very few crumbling fragments could yet be distinguished as having belonged to a man. Falconer states, that where an Indian dies he is buried, but that subsequently his bones are carefully taken up and carried, let the distance be ever so great, to be deposited near the sea-coast. This custom, I think, may be accounted for by recollecting, that before the introduction of horses, these Indians must have led nearly the same life as the Fuegians now do, and therefore generally have resided in the neighbourhood of the sea. The common prejudice of lying where one's ancestors have lain, would make the now roaming Indians bring the less perishable part of their dead to their ancient burial-ground on the coast.

January 9th, 1834.—Before it was dark the *Beagle* anchored in the fine spacious harbour of Port St. Julian, situated about one hundred and ten miles to the south of Port Desire. We remained here eight days. The country is nearly similar to that of Port Desire, but perhaps rather more sterile. One day a party accompanied Captain Fitz Roy on a long walk round the head of the harbour. We were eleven hours without tasting any water, and some of the party were quite exhausted. From the summit of a hill (since well named Thirsty Hill) a fine lake was spied, and two of the party proceeded with concerted signals to show whether it was fresh water. What was our disappointment to find a snow-white expanse of salt, crystallized in great cubes! We attributed our extreme thirst to the dryness of the atmosphere; but whatever the cause might be, we were exceedingly glad late in the evening to get back to the boats. Although we could nowhere find, during our whole visit, a single drop of fresh water, yet some must exist; for by an odd chance I found on the surface of the salt water, near the head of the bay, a Colymbetes not quite dead, which must have lived in some not far distant pool. Three other insects (a Cincindela, like *hybrida,* a Cymindis, and a Harpalus, which all live on muddy flats occasionally overflowed by the sea), and one other found dead on the plain, complete the list of the beetles. A good-sized fly (Tabanus) was extremely numerous, and tormented us by its painful bite. The common horsefly, which is so troublesome in the shady lanes of England, belongs to this same genus. We here have the puzzle that so frequently occurs in the case of musquitoes—on the blood of what animals do these insects commonly feed? The guanaco is nearly the only warm-blooded quadruped, and it is found in quite inconsiderable numbers compared with the multitude of flies.

The geology of Patagonia is interesting. Differently from Europe, where the tertiary formations appear to have accumulated in bays, here along hundreds of miles of coast we have one great deposit, including many tertiary shells, all apparently extinct. The most common shell is a massive gigantic oyster, sometimes even a foot in diameter. These beds are covered by others of a peculiar soft white stone, including much gypsum, and resembling chalk, but really of a pumiceous nature. It is highly remarkable, from being composed, to at least one-tenth part of its bulk, of Infusoria: Professor Ehrenberg has already ascertained in it thirty oceanic forms. This bed extends for

500 miles along the coast, and probably for a considerably greater distance. At Port St. Julian its thickness is more than 800 feet! These white beds are everywhere capped by a mass of gravel, forming probably one of the largest beds of shingle in the world: it certainly extends from near the Rio Colorado to between 600 and 700 nautical miles southward; at Santa Cruz (a river a little south of St. Julian), it reaches to the foot of the Cordillera; half way up the river, its thickness is more than 200 feet; it probably everywhere extends to this great chain, whence the well-rounded pebbles of porphyry have been derived: we may consider its average breadth as 200 miles, and its average thickness as about 50 feet. If this great bed of pebbles, without including the mud necessarily derived from their attrition, was piled into a mound, it would form a great mountain chain! When we consider that all these pebbles, countless as the grains of sand in the desert, have been derived from the slow-falling of masses of rock on the old coast-lines and banks of rivers; and that these fragments have been dashed into smaller pieces, and that each of them has since been slowly rolled, rounded, and far transported, the mind is stupefied in thinking over the long, absolutely necessary, lapse of years. Yet all this gravel has been transported, and probably rounded, subsequently to the deposition of the white beds, and long subsequently to the underlying beds with the tertiary shells.

Everything in this southern continent has been effected on a grand scale: the land, from the Rio Plata to Tierra del Fuego, a distance of 1200 miles, has been raised in mass (and in Patagonia to a height of between 300 and 400 feet), within the period of the now existing sea-shells. The old and weathered shells left on the surface of the upraised plain still partially retain their colours. The uprising movement has been interrupted by at least eight long periods of rest, during which the sea ate deeply back into the land, forming at successive levels the long lines of cliffs or escarpments, which separate the different plains as they rise like steps one behind the other. The elevatory movement, and the eating-back power of the sea during the periods of rest, have been equable over long lines of coast; for I was astonished to find that the step-like plains stand at nearly corresponding heights at far distant points. The lowest plain is 90 feet high; and the highest, which I ascended near the coast, is 950 feet; and of this, only relics are left in the form of flat gravel-capped hills. The upper plain of S. Cruz slopes up to a height of 3000 feet at the foot of the Cordillera.

I have said that within the period of existing sea-shells Patagonia has been upraised 300 to 400 feet: I may add, that within the period when icebergs transported boulders over the upper plain of Santa Cruz,[21] the elevation has been at least 1500 feet. Nor has Patagonia been affected only by upward movements: the extinct tertiary shells from Port St. Julian and Santa Cruz cannot have lived, according to Professor E. Forbes, in a greater depth of water than from 40 to 250 feet; but they are now covered with sea-deposited strata from 800 to 1000 feet in thickness: hence the bed of the sea, on which these shells once lived, must have sunk downwards several hundred feet, to allow of the accumulation of the superincumbent strata. What a history of geological changes does the simply-constructed coast of Patagonia reveal!

At Port St. Julian,[22] in some red mud capping the gravel on the 90-feet plain, I found half the skeleton of the Macrauchenia Patachonica, a remarkable quadruped, full as large as a camel. It belongs to the same division of the Pachydermata with the rhinoceros, tapir, and palæotherium; but in the structure of the bones of its long neck it shows a clear relation to the camel, or rather to the guanaco and llama. From recent sea-shells being found on two of the higher step-formed plains, which must have been modelled and upraised before the mud was deposited in which the Macrauchenia was intombed, it is certain that this curious quadruped lived long after the sea was inhabited by its present shells. I was at first much surprised how a large quadruped could so lately have subsisted, in lat. 49° 15′, on these wretched gravel plains with their stunted vegetation; but the relationship of the Macrauchenia to the guanaco, now an inhabitant of the most sterile parts, partly explains this difficulty.

The relationship, though distant, between the Macrauchenia and the Guanaco, between the Toxodon and the Capybara,—the

[21] [Editor] At several points, Darwin refers to the transport of boulders by icebergs. When the *Voyage* was written, it was not yet clearly understood that glaciers also transport boulders and are in fact responsible for most of the evidence of boulder transport in the world's land areas.

[22] [Darwin] I have lately heard that Capt. Sulivan, R.N., has found numerous fossil bones, embedded in regular strata, on the banks of the R. Gallegos, in lat. 51° 4′. Some of the bones are large; others are small, and appear to have belonged to an armadillo. This is a most interesting and important discovery.

closer relationship between the many extinct Edentata and the living sloths, ant-eaters, and armadilloes, now so eminently characteristic of South American zoology,—and the still closer relationship between the fossil and living species of Ctenomys and Hydrochærus,[23] are most interesting facts. This relationship is shown wonderfully—as wonderfully as between the fossil and extinct Marsupial animals of Australia—by the great collection lately brought to Europe from the caves of Brazil by MM. Lund and Clausen. In this collection there are extinct species of all the thirty-two genera, excepting four, of the terrestrial quadrupeds now inhabiting the provinces in which the caves occur; and the extinct species are much more numerous than those now living; there are fossil ant-eaters, armadilloes, tapirs, peccaries, guanacos, opossums, and numerous South American gnawers and monkeys, and other animals. This wonderful relationship in the same continent between the dead and the living, will, I do not doubt, hereafter throw more light on the appearance of organic beings on our earth, and their disappearance from it, than any other class of facts.

It is impossible to reflect on the changed state of the American continent without the deepest astonishment. Formerly it must have swarmed with great monsters: now we find mere pigmies, compared with the antecedent, allied races. If Buffon had known of the gigantic sloth and armadillo-like animals, and of the lost Pachydermata, he might have said with a greater semblance of truth that the creative force in America had lost its power, rather than that it had never possessed great vigour. The greater number, if not all, of these extinct quadrupeds lived at a late period, and were the contemporaries of most of the existing sea-shells. Since they lived, no very great change in the form of the land can have taken place. What, then, has exterminated so many species and whole genera? The mind at first is irresistibly hurried into the belief of some great catastrophe; but thus to destroy animals, both large and small, in Southern Patagonia, in Brazil, on the Cordillera of Peru, in North America up to Behring's Straits, we must shake the entire framework of the globe. An examination, moreover, of the geology of La Plata and Patagonia, leads to the belief that all the features of the land result from slow and gradual changes. It appears from the character of the fossils in Europe, Asia, Australia, and in North and South America, that those

[23] [Editor] Ctenomys: a South American rodent. Hydrochaerus: the capybara.

conditions which favour the life of the *larger* quadrupeds were lately co-extensive with the world: what those conditions were, no one has yet even conjectured. It could hardly have been a change of temperature, which at about the same time destroyed the inhabitants of tropical, temperate, and arctic latitudes on both sides of the globe. In North America we positively know from Mr. Lyell, that the large quadrupeds lived subsequently to that period, when boulders were brought into latitudes at which icebergs now never arrive: from conclusive but indirect reasons we may feel sure, that in the southern hemisphere the Macrauchenia, also, lived long subsequently to the ice-transporting boulder-period. Did man, after his first inroad into South America, destroy, as has been suggested, the unwieldy Megatherium and the other Edentata? We must at least look to some other cause for the destruction of the little tucutuco at Bahia Blanca, and of the many fossil mice and other small quadrupeds in Brazil. No one will imagine that a drought, even far severer than those which cause such losses in the provinces of La Plata, could destroy every individual of every species from Southern Patagonia to Behring's Straits. What shall we say of the extinction of the horse? Did those plains fail of pasture, which have since been overrun by thousands and hundreds of thousands of the descendants of the stock introduced by the Spaniards? Have the subsequently introduced species consumed the food of the great antecedent races? Can we believe that the Capybara has taken the food of the Toxodon, the Guanaco of the Macrauchenia, the existing small Edentata of their numerous gigantic prototypes? Certainly, no fact in the long history of the world is so startling as the wide and repeated exterminations of its inhabitants.

Nevertheless, if we consider the subject under another point of view, it will appear less perplexing. We do not steadily bear in mind, how profoundly ignorant we are of the conditions of existence of every animal; nor do we always remember, that some check is constantly preventing the too rapid increase of every organized being left in a state of nature. The supply of food, on an average, remains constant; yet the tendency in every animal to increase by propagation is geometrical; and its surprising effects have nowhere been more astonishingly shown, than in the case of the European animals run wild during the last few centuries in America. Every animal in a state of nature regularly breeds; yet in a species long established, any *great* increase in numbers is obviously impossible, and must be checked by some means. We are, nevertheless, seldom able with certainty to tell in any given species, at what period of life, or at what period of the year, or whether only at long intervals, the check falls; or, again, what is the precise nature of the check. Hence probably it is, that we feel so little surprise at one, of two species closely allied in habits, being rare and the other abundant in the same district; or, again, that one should be abundant in one district, and another, filling the same place in the economy of nature, should be abundant in a neighbouring district, differing very little in its conditions. If asked how this is, one immediately replies that it is determined by some slight difference in climate, food, or the number of enemies: yet how rarely, if ever, we can point out the precise cause and manner of action of the check! We are, therefore, driven to the conclusion, that causes generally quite inappreciable by us, determine whether a given species shall be abundant or scanty in numbers.

In the cases where we can trace the extinction of a species through man, either wholly or in one limited district, we know that it becomes rarer and rarer, and is then lost: it would be difficult to point out any just distinction[24] between a species destroyed by man or by the increase of its natural enemies. The evidence of rarity preceding extinction, is more striking in the successive tertiary strata, as remarked by several able observers; it has often been found that a shell very common in a tertiary stratum is now most rare, and has even long been thought to be extinct. If then, as appears probable, species first become rare and then extinct—if the too rapid increase of every species, even the most favoured, is steadily checked, as we must admit, though how and when it is hard to say—and if we see, without the smallest surprise, though unable to assign the precise reason, one species abundant and another closely-allied species rare in the same district—why should we feel such great astonishment at the rarity being carried a step further to extinction? An action going on, on every side of us, and yet barely appreciable, might surely be carried a little further, without exciting our observation. Who would feel any great surprise at hearing that the Megalonyx was formerly rare compared with the Megatherium, or that one of the fossil monkeys was few in number compared with one of the now living monkeys? and yet in this comparative rarity, we should have

[24] [Darwin] See the excellent remarks on this subject by Mr. Lyell, in his Principles of Geology.

the plainest evidence of less favourable conditions for their existence. To admit that species generally become rare before they become extinct—to feel no surprise at the comparative rarity of one species with another, and yet to call in some extraordinary agent and to marvel greatly when a species ceases to exist, appears to me much the same as to admit that sickness in the individual is the prelude to death—to feel no surprise at sickness—but when the sick man dies, to wonder, and to believe that he died through violence.

CHAPTER IX

SANTA CRUZ, PATAGONIA, AND THE FALKLAND ISLANDS

Santa Cruz — Expedition up the River — Indians — Immense Streams of Basaltic Lava — Fragments not transported by the River — Excavation of the Valley — Condor, habits of — Cordillera — Erratic Boulders of great size — Indian Relics — Return to the Ship — Falkland Islands — Wild Horses, Cattle, Rabbits — Wolf-like Fox — Fire made of Bones — Manner of hunting Wild Cattle — Geology — Streams of Stones — Scenes of Violence — Penguin — Geese — Eggs of Doris — Compound Animals

April 13th, 1834.—The *Beagle* anchored within the mouth of the Santa Cruz. This river is situated about sixty miles south of Port St. Julian. During the last voyage Captain Stokes proceeded thirty miles up it, but then, from the want of provisions, was obliged to return. Excepting what was discovered at that time, scarcely anything was known about this large river. Captain Fitz Roy now determined to follow its course as far as time would allow. On the 18th three whale-boats started, carrying three weeks' provisions; and the party consisted of twenty-five souls—a force which would have been sufficient to have defied a host of Indians. With a strong flood-tide and a fine day we made a good run, soon drank some of the fresh water, and were at night nearly above the tidal influence.

The river here assumed a size and appearance which, even at the highest point we ultimately reached, was scarcely diminished. It was generally from three to four hundred yards broad, and in the middle about seventeen feet deep. The rapidity of the current, which in its whole course runs at the rate of from four to six knots an hour, is perhaps its most remarkable feature. The water is of a fine blue colour, but with a slight milky tinge, and not so transparent as at first sight would have been expected. It flows over a bed of pebbles, like those which compose the beach and the surrounding plains. It runs in a winding course through a valley, which extends in a direct line westward. This valley varies from five to ten miles in breadth; it is bounded by step-formed terraces, which rise in most parts, one above the other, to the height of five hundred feet, and have on the opposite sides a remarkable correspondence.

April 19th.—Against so strong a current it was, of course, quite impossible to row or sail: consequently the three boats were fastened together head and stern, two hands left in each, and the rest came on shore to track. As the general arrangements made by Captain Fitz Roy were very good for facilitating the work of all, and as all had a share in it, I will describe the system. The party, including every one, was divided into two spells, each of which hauled at the tracking line alternately for an hour and a half. The officers of each boat lived with, ate the same food, and slept in the same tent with their crew, so that each boat was quite independent of the others. After sunset the first level spot where any bushes were growing, was chosen for our night's lodging. Each of the crew took it in turns to be cook. Immediately the boat was hauled up, the cook made his fire; two others pitched the tent; the coxswain handed the things out of the boat; the rest carried them up to the tents and collected firewood. By this order, in half an hour everything was ready for the night. A watch of two men and an officer was always kept, whose duty it was to look after the boats, keep up the fire, and guard against Indians. Each in the party had his one hour every night.

During this day we tracked but a short distance, for there were many islets, covered by thorny bushes, and the channels between them were shallow.

April 20th.—We passed the islands and set to work. Our regular day's march, although it was hard enough, carried us on an average only ten miles in a straight line, and perhaps fifteen or twenty altogether. Beyond the place where we slept last night, the country is completely *terra incognita,* for it was there that Captain Stokes turned back. We saw in the distance a great smoke, and found the skeleton of a horse, so we knew that Indians were in the neighbourhood. On the next morning (21st) tracks of a party of horse, and marks left by the trailing of the chuzos, or long spears, were observed on the ground. It was generally thought that the Indians had reconnoitred us during the night. Shortly afterwards we came to a spot where, from the fresh footsteps of men, children, and horses, it was evident that the party had crossed the river.

April 22nd.—The country remained the same, and was extremely uninteresting. The complete similarity of the productions throughout Patagonia is one of its most striking characters. The level plains of arid shingle support the same stunted and dwarf plants; and in the valleys the same thorn-bearing bushes grow. Everywhere we see the same birds and insects. Even the very banks of the river and of the clear streamlets which entered it, were scarcely enlivened by a brighter tint of green. The curse of sterility is on the land, and the water flowing over a bed of pebbles partakes of the same curse. Hence the number of waterfowl is very scanty; for there is nothing to support life in the stream of this barren river.

Patagonia, poor as she is in some respects, can however boast of a greater stock of small rodents[1] than perhaps any other country in the world. Several species of mice are externally characterized by large thin ears and a very fine fur. These little animals swarm amongst the thickets in the valleys, where they cannot for months together taste a drop of water excepting the dew. They all seem to be cannibals; for no sooner was a mouse caught in one of my traps than it was devoured by others. A small and delicately-shaped fox, which is likewise very abundant, probably derives its entire support from these small animals. The guanaco is also in his proper district; herds of fifty or a hundred were common; and, as I have stated, we saw one which must have contained at least five hundred. The puma, with the condor and other carrion-hawks in its train, follows and preys upon these animals. The footsteps of the puma were to be seen almost everywhere on the banks of the river; and the remains of several guanacos, with their necks dislocated and bones broken, showed how they had met their death.

April 24th.—Like the navigators of old when approaching an unknown land, we examined and watched for the most trivial sign of a change. The drifted trunk of a tree, or a boulder of primitive rock, was hailed with joy, as if we had seen a forest growing on the flanks of the Cordillera. The top, how-

[1] [Darwin] The deserts of Syria are characterized, according to Volney (tom. i. p. 351), by woody bushes, numerous rats, gazelles, and hares. In the landscape of Patagonia, the guanaco replaces the gazelle, and the agouti the hare.

ever, of a heavy bank of clouds, which remained almost constantly in one position, was the most promising sign, and eventually turned out a true harbinger. At first the clouds were mistaken for the mountains themselves, instead of the masses of vapour condensed by their icy summits.

April 26th.—We this day met with a marked change in the geological structure of the plains. From the first starting I had carefully examined the gravel in the river, and for the two last days had noticed the presence of a few small pebbles of a very cellular basalt. These gradually increased in number and in size, but none were as large as a man's head. This morning, however, pebbles of the same rock, but more compact, suddenly became abundant, and in the course of half an hour we saw, at the distance of five or six miles, the angular edge of a great basaltic platform. When we arrived at its base we found the stream bubbling among the fallen blocks. For the next twenty-eight miles the river-course was encumbered with these basaltic masses. Above that limit immense fragments of primitive rocks, derived from the surrounding boulder-formation, were equally numerous. None of the fragments of any considerable size had been washed more than three or four miles down the river below their parent-source: considering the singular rapidity of the great body of water in the Santa Cruz, and that no still reaches occur in any part, this example is a most striking one, of the inefficiency of rivers in transporting even moderately-sized fragments.

The basalt is only lava, which has flowed beneath the sea; but the eruptions must have been on the grandest scale. At the point where we first met this formation, it was 120 feet in thickness; following up the river course, the surface imperceptibly rose and the mass became thicker, so that at forty miles above the first station it was 320 feet thick. What the thickness may be close to the Cordillera, I have no means of knowing, but the platform there attains a height of about three thousand feet above the level of the sea: we must therefore look to the mountains of that great chain for its source; and worthy of such a source are streams, that have flowed over the gently inclined bed of the sea to a distance of one hundred miles. At the first glance of the basaltic cliffs on the opposite sides of the valley, it was evident that the strata once were united. What power, then, has removed along a whole line of country, a solid mass of very hard rock, which had an average thickness of nearly three hundred feet, and a breadth varying from rather less than two miles to four miles? The river, though it has so little power in transporting even inconsiderable fragments, yet in the lapse of ages might produce by its gradual erosion an effect, of which it is difficult to judge the amount. But in this case, independently of the insignificance of such an agency, good reasons can be assigned for believing that this valley was formerly occupied by an arm of the sea. It is needless in this work to detail the arguments leading to this conclusion, derived from the form and the nature of the step-formed terraces on both sides of the valley, from the manner in which the bottom of the valley near the Andes expands into a great estuary-like plain with sand-hillocks on it, and from the occurrence of a few sea-shells lying in the bed of the river. If I had space I could prove that South America was formerly here cut off by a strait, joining the Atlantic and Pacific oceans, like that of Magellan. But it may yet be asked, how has the solid basalt been removed? Geologists formerly would have brought into play, the violent action of some overwhelming debacle; but in this case such a supposition would have been quite inadmissible; because, the same step-like plains with existing sea-shells lying on their surface, which front the long line of the Patagonian coast, sweep up on each side of the valley of Santa Cruz. No possible action of any flood could thus have modelled the land, either within the valley or along the open coast; and by the formation of such step-like plains or terraces the valley itself has been hollowed out. Although we know that there are tides, which run within the Narrows of the Strait of Magellan at the rate of eight knots an hour, yet we must confess that it makes the head almost giddy to reflect on the number of years, century after century, which the tides, unaided by a heavy surf, must have required to have corroded so vast an area and thickness of solid basaltic lava. Nevertheless, we must believe that the strata undermined by the waters of this ancient strait, were broken up into huge fragments, and these lying scattered on the beach, were reduced first to smaller blocks, then to pebbles, and lastly to the most impalpable mud, which the tides drifted far into the Eastern or Western Ocean.[2]

---

[2] [Editor] Modern studies have confirmed some of Darwin's conclusions regarding the geology of Patagonia, and modified others. The marine fossils found by Darwin were for the most part laid down in inland seas rather than arms of the ocean. Rivers are now believed to have had a greater role in cutting the valleys of Patagonia than Darwin gave them. And there were once many

With the change in the geological structure of the plains the character of the landscape likewise altered. While rambling up some of the narrow and rocky defiles, I could almost have fancied myself transported back again to the barren valleys of the island of St. Jago. Among the basaltic cliffs, I found some plants which I had seen nowhere else, but others I recognized as being wanderers from Tierra del Fuego. These porous rocks serve as a reservoir for the scanty rain-water; and consequently on the line where the igneous and sedimentary formations unite, some small springs (most rare occurrences in Patagonia) burst forth; and they could be distinguished at a distance by the circumscribed patches of bright green herbage.

April 27th.—The bed of the river became rather narrower, and hence the stream more rapid. It here ran at the rate of six knots an hour. From this cause, and from the many great angular fragments, tracking the boats became both dangerous and laborious.

This day I shot a condor. It measured from tip to tip of the wings, eight and a half feet, and from beak to tail, four feet. This bird is known to have a wide geographical range, being found on the west coast of South America, from the Strait of Magellan along the Cordillera as far as eight degrees N. of the equator. The steep cliff near the mouth of the Rio Negro is its northern limit on the Patagonian coast; and they have there wandered about four hundred miles from the great central line of their habitation in the Andes. Further south, among the bold precipices at the head of Port Desire, the condor is not uncommon; yet only a few stragglers occasionally visit the seacoast. A line of cliff near the mouth of the Santa Cruz is frequented by these birds, and about eighty miles up the river, where the sides of the valley are formed by steep basaltic precipices, the condor reappears. From these facts, it seems that the condors require perpendicular cliffs. In Chile, they haunt, during the greater part of the year, the lower country near the shores of the Pacific, and at night several roost together in

straits between the Atlantic and Pacific beside the Strait of Magellan and the strait Darwin describes. Before the uplifting of the Andes (60 million or more years ago), much of South America must have consisted of a string of islands. Had Darwin been able to journey up other Patagonian rivers beside the Santa Cruz, he would have seen that. In fact, he all but suggests that in his discussion of the topography of Chile in Chapter XII.

one tree; but in the early part of summer, they retire to the most inaccessible parts of the inner Cordillera, there to breed in peace.

With respect to their propagation, I was told by the country people in Chile, that the condor makes no sort of nest, but in the months of November and December lays two large white eggs on a shelf of bare rock. It is said that the young condors cannot fly for an entire year; and long after they are able, they continue to roost by night, and hunt by day with their parents. The old birds generally live in pairs; but among the inland basaltic cliffs of the Santa Cruz, I found a spot, where scores must usually haunt. On coming suddenly to the brow of the precipice, it was a grand spectacle to see between twenty and thirty of these great birds start heavily from their resting-place, and wheel away in majestic circles. From the quantity of dung on the rocks, they must long have frequented this cliff for roosting and breeding. Having gorged themselves with carrion on the plains below, they retire to these favourite ledges to digest their food. From these facts, the condor, like the galli-nazo, must to a certain degree be considered as a gregarious bird. In this part of the country they live altogether on the guanacos which have died a natural death, or, as more commonly happens, have been killed by the pumas. I believe, from what I saw in Patagonia, that they do not on ordinary occasions extend their daily excursions to any great distance from their regular sleeping-places.

The condors may oftentimes be seen at a great height, soaring over a certain spot in the most graceful circles. On some occasions I am sure that they do this only for pleasure, but on others, the Chileno countryman tells you that they are watching a dying animal, or the puma devouring its prey. If the condors glide down, and then suddenly all rise together, the Chileno knows that it is the puma which, watching the carcass, has sprung out to drive away the robbers. Besides feeding on carrion, the condors frequently attack young goats and lambs; and the shepherd dogs are trained, whenever they pass over, to run out, and looking upwards to bark violently. The Chilenos destroy and catch numbers. Two methods are used; one is to place a carcass on a level piece of ground within an enclosure of sticks with an opening, and when the condors are gorged, to gallop up on horseback to the entrance, and thus enclose them: for when this bird has not space to run, it cannot give its body sufficient momentum to rise from the ground. The

second method is to mark the trees in which, frequently to
the number of five or six together, they roost, and then at night
to climb up and noose them. They are such heavy sleepers, as
I have myself witnessed, that this is not a difficult task. At
Valparaiso, I have seen a living condor sold for sixpence, but
the common price is eight or ten shillings. One which I saw
brought in, had been tied with rope, and was much injured;
yet, the moment the line was cut by which its bill was secured,
although surrounded by people, it began ravenously to tear a
piece of carrion. In a garden at the same place, between twenty
and thirty were kept alive. They were fed only once a week,
but they appeared in pretty good health.[3] The Chileno countrymen assert that the condor will live, and retain its vigour, between five and six weeks without eating: I cannot answer for
the truth of this, but it is a cruel experiment, which very likely
has been tried.

When an animal is killed in the country, it is well known
that the condors, like other carrion-vultures, soon gain intelligence of it, and congregate in an inexplicable manner. In most
cases it must not be overlooked, that the birds have discovered
their prey, and have picked the skeleton clean, before the flesh
is in the least degree tainted. Remembering the experiments of
M. Audubon, on the little smelling powers of carrion-hawks,
I tried in the above-mentioned garden the following experiment: the condors were tied, each by a rope, in a long row at
the bottom of a wall; and having folded up a piece of meat in
white paper, I walked backwards and forwards, carrying it in
my hand at the distance of about three yards from them, but
no notice whatever was taken. I then threw it on the ground,
within one yard of an old male bird; he looked at it for a
moment with attention, but then regarded it no more. With a
stick I pushed it closer and closer, until at last he touched it
with his beak; the paper was then instantly torn off with fury,
and at the same moment, every bird in the long row began
struggling and flapping its wings. Under the same circumstances, it would have been quite impossible to have deceived
a dog. The evidence in favour of and against the acute smelling
powers of carrion-vultures is singularly balanced. Professor
Owen has demonstrated that the olfactory nerves of the turkey-
buzzard (Cathartes aura) are highly developed; and on the

---

[3] [Darwin] I noticed that several hours before any one of the
condors died, all the lice, with which it was infested, crawled to
the outside feathers. I was assured that this always happened.

evening when Mr. Owen's paper was read at the Zoological
Society, it was mentioned by a gentleman that he had seen the
carrion-hawks in the West Indies on two occasions collect on
the roof of a house, when a corpse had become offensive from
not having been buried: in this case the intelligence could
hardly have been acquired by sight. On the other hand, besides
the experiments of Audubon and that one by myself, Mr. Bachman has tried in the United States many varied plans, showing
that neither the turkey-buzzard (the species dissected by Professor Owen) nor the gallinazo find their food by smell. He
covered portions of highly offensive offal with a thin canvas
cloth, and strewed pieces of meat on it; these the carrion-
vultures ate up, and then remained quietly standing, with their
beaks within the eighth of an inch of the putrid mass, without
discovering it. A small rent was made in the canvas, and the
offal was immediately discovered; the canvas was replaced by
a fresh piece, and meat again put on it, and was again devoured
by the vultures without their discovering the hidden mass on
which they were trampling. These facts are attested by the
signatures of six gentlemen, besides that of Mr. Bachman.[4]

Often when lying down to rest on the open plains, on looking
upwards, I have seen carrion-hawks sailing through the air at
a great height. Where the country is level I do not believe a
space of the heavens, of more than fifteen degrees above the
horizon, is commonly viewed with any attention by a person
either walking or on horseback. If such be the case, and the
vulture is on the wing at a height of between three and four
thousand feet, before it could come within the range of vision,
its distance in a straight line from the beholder's eye, would be
rather more than two British miles. Might it not thus readily
be overlooked? When an animal is killed by the sportsman in
a lonely valley, may he not all the while be watched from above
by the sharp-sighted bird? And will not the manner of its descent proclaim throughout the district to the whole family of
carrion-feeders, that their prey is at hand?

When the condors are wheeling in a flock round and round
any spot, their flight is beautiful. Except when rising from the
ground, I do not recollect ever having seen one of these birds
flap its wings. Near Lima, I watched several for nearly half
an hour, without once taking off my eyes: they moved in large
curves, sweeping in circles, descending and ascending without

4 [Darwin] Loudon's Magazine of Nat. Hist., vol. vii.

giving a single flap. As they glided close over my head, I intently watched from an oblique position, the outlines of the separate and great terminal feathers of each wing; and these separate feathers, if there had been the least vibratory movement, would have appeared as if blended together; but they were seen distinct against the blue sky. The head and neck were moved frequently, and apparently with force; and the extended wings seemed to form the fulcrum on which the movements of the neck, body, and tail acted. If the bird wished to descend, the wings were for a moment collapsed; and when again expanded with an altered inclination, the momentum gained by the rapid descent seemed to urge the bird upwards with the even and steady movement of a paper kite. In the case of any bird *soaring*, its motion must be sufficiently rapid, so that the action of the inclined surface of its body on the atmosphere may counterbalance its gravity. The force to keep up the momentum of a body moving in a horizontal plane in the air (in which there is so little friction) cannot be great, and this force is all that is wanted. The movement of the neck and body of the condor, we must suppose, is sufficient for this. However this may be, it is truly wonderful and beautiful to see so great a bird, hour after hour, without any apparent exertion, wheeling and gliding over mountain and river.

April 29th.—From some high land we hailed with joy the white summits of the Cordillera, as they were seen occasionally peeping through their dusky envelope of clouds. During the few succeeding days we continued to get on slowly, for we found the river-course very tortuous, and strewed with immense fragments of various ancient slaty rocks, and of granite. The plain bordering the valley had here attained an elevation of about 1100 feet above the river, and its character was much altered. The well-rounded pebbles of porphyry were mingled with many immense angular fragments of basalt and of primary rocks. The first of these erratic boulders which I noticed, was sixty-seven miles distant from the nearest mountain; another which I measured was five yards square, and projected five feet above the gravel. Its edges were so angular, and its size so great, that I at first mistook it for a rock *in situ*, and took out my compass to observe the direction of its cleavage. The plain here was not quite so level as that nearer the coast, but yet it betrayed no signs of any great violence. Under these circumstances it is, I believe, quite impossible to explain the transportal of these gigantic masses of rock so many miles from their parent-source, on any theory except by that of floating icebergs.

During the last two days we met with signs of horses, and with several small articles which had belonged to the Indians —such as parts of a mantle and a bunch of ostrich feathers— but they appeared to have been lying long on the ground. Between the place where the Indians had so lately crossed the river and this neighbourhood, though so many miles apart, the country appears to be quite unfrequented. At first, considering the abundance of the guanacos, I was surprised at this; but it is explained by the stony nature of the plains, which would soon disable an unshod horse from taking part in the chace. Nevertheless, in two places in this very central region, I found small heaps of stones, which I do not think could have been accidentally thrown together. They were placed on points, projecting over the edge of the highest lava cliff, and they resembled, but on a small scale, those near Port Desire.

May 4th.—Captain Fitz Roy determined to take the boats no higher. The river had a winding course, and was very rapid; and the appearance of the country offered no temptation to proceed any further. Everywhere we met with the same productions, and the same dreary landscape. We were now one hundred and forty miles distant from the Atlantic, and about sixty from the nearest arm of the Pacific. The valley in this upper part expanded into a wide basin, bounded on the north and south by the basaltic platforms, and fronted by the long range of the snow-clad Cordillera. But we viewed these grand mountains with regret, for we were obliged to imagine their nature and productions, instead of standing, as we had hoped, on their summits. Besides the useless loss of time which an attempt to ascend the river any higher would have cost us, we had already been for some days on half allowance of bread. This, although really enough for reasonable men, was, after a hard day's march, rather scanty food: a light stomach and an easy digestion are good things to talk about, but very unpleasant in practice.

5th.—Before sunrise we commenced our descent. We shot down the stream with great rapidity, generally at the rate of ten knots an hour. In this one day we effected what had cost us five-and-a-half hard days' labour in ascending. On the 8th, we reached the *Beagle* after our twenty-one days' expedition. Every one, excepting myself, had cause to be dissatisfied; but to me the ascent afforded a most interesting section of the great tertiary formation of Patagonia.

On *March 1st*, 1833, and again on *March 16th*, 1834, the *Beagle* anchored in Berkeley Sound, in East Falkland Island. This archipelago is situated in nearly the same latitude with the mouth of the Strait of Magellan; it covers a space of one hundred and twenty by sixty geographical miles, and is a little more than half the size of Ireland. After the possession of these miserable islands had been contested by France, Spain, and England, they were left uninhabited. The government of Buenos Ayres then sold them to a private individual, but likewise used them, as old Spain had done before, for a penal settlement. England claimed her right and seized them. The Englishman who was left in charge of the flag was consequently murdered. A British officer was next sent, unsupported by any power: and when we arrived, we found him in charge of a population, of which rather more than half were runaway rebels and murderers.[5]

The theatre is worthy of the scenes acted on it. An undulating land, with a desolate and wretched aspect, is everywhere covered by a peaty soil and wiry grass, of one monotonous brown colour. Here and there a peak or ridge of grey quartz rock breaks through the smooth surface. Every one has heard of the climate of these regions; it may be compared to that which is experienced at the height of between one and two thousand feet, on the mountains of North Wales; having however less sunshine and less frost, but more wind and rain.[6]

16th.—I will now describe a short excursion which I made round a part of this island. In the morning I started with six horses and two Gauchos: the latter were capital men for the purpose, and well accustomed to living on their own resources. The weather was very boisterous and cold, with heavy hailstorms. We got on, however, pretty well, but, except the geol-

[5] [Editor] Argentina, which calls them the Malvinas, still disputes British possession of the Falklands.

[6] [Darwin] From accounts published since our voyage, and more especially from several interesting letters from Capt. Sulivan, R.N., employed on the survey, it appears that we took an exaggerated view of the badness of the climate of these islands. But when I reflect on the almost universal covering of peat, and on the fact of wheat seldom ripening here, I can hardly believe that the climate in summer is so fine and dry as it has lately been represented.

ogy, nothing could be less interesting than our day's ride. The country is uniformly the same undulating moorland; the surface being covered by light brown withered grass and a few very small shrubs, all springing out of an elastic peaty soil. In the valleys here and there might be seen a small flock of wild geese, and everywhere the ground was so soft that the snipe were able to feed. Besides these two birds there were few others. There is one main range of hills, nearly two thousand feet in height, and composed of quartz rock, the rugged and barren crests of which gave us some trouble to cross. On the south side we came to the best country for wild cattle; we met, however, no great number, for they had been lately much harassed.

In the evening we came across a small herd. One of my companions, St. Jago by name, soon separated a fat cow; he threw the bolas, and it struck her legs, but failed in becoming entangled. Then dropping his hat to mark the spot where the balls were left, while at full gallop, he uncoiled his lazo, and after a most severe chace, again came up to the cow, and caught her round the horns. The other Gaucho had gone on ahead with the spare horses, so that St. Jago had some difficulty in killing the furious beast. He managed to get her on a level piece of ground, by taking advantage of her as often as she rushed at him; and when she would not move, my horse, from having been trained, would canter up, and with his chest give her a violent push. But when on level ground it does not appear an easy job for one man to kill a beast mad with terror. Nor would it be so, if the horse, when left to itself without its rider, did not soon learn, for its own safety, to keep the lazo tight; so that, if the cow or ox moves forward, the horse moves just as quickly forward; otherwise, it stands motionless leaning on one side. This horse, however, was a young one, and would not stand still, but gave in to the cow as she struggled. It was admirable to see with what dexterity St. Jago dodged behind the beast, till at last he contrived to give the fatal touch to the main tendon of the hind leg; after which, without much difficulty, he drove his knife into the head of the spinal marrow, and the cow dropped as if struck by lightning. He cut off pieces of flesh with the skin to it, but without any bones, sufficient for our expedition. We then rode on to our sleeping-place, and had for supper "carne con cuero," or meat roasted with the skin on it. This is as superior to common beef as venison is to mutton. A large circular piece taken from the back is roasted on the embers with the hide downwards and in the form of a saucer, so that none of the gravy is lost. If any worthy alderman had supped with us that evening, "carne con cuero," without doubt, would soon have been celebrated in London.

During the night it rained, and the next day (17th) was very stormy, with much hail and snow. We rode across the island to the neck of land which joins the Rincon del Toro (the great peninsula at the S.W. extremity) to the rest of the island. From the great number of cows which have been killed, there is a large proportion of bulls. These wander about single, or two and three together, and are very savage. I never saw such magnificent beasts; they equalled in the size of their huge heads and necks the Grecian marble sculptures. Capt. Sulivan informs me that the hide of an average-sized bull weighs forty-seven pounds, whereas a hide of this weight, less thoroughly dried, is considered as a very heavy one at Monte Video. The young bulls generally run away for a short distance; but the old ones do not stir a step, except to rush at man and horse; and many horses have been thus killed. An old bull crossed a boggy stream, and took his stand on the opposite side to us; we in vain tried to drive him away, and failing, were obliged to make a large circuit. The Gauchos in revenge determined to emasculate him and render him for the future harmless. It was very interesting to see how art completely mastered force. One lazo was thrown over his horns as he rushed at the horse, and another round his hind legs: in a minute the monster was stretched powerless on the ground. After the lazo has once been drawn tightly round the horns of a furious animal, it does not at first appear an easy thing to disengage it again without killing the beast; nor, I apprehend, would it be so if the man was by himself. By the aid, however, of a second person throwing his lazo so as to catch both hind legs, it is quickly managed: for the animal, so long as its hind legs are kept outstretched, is quite helpless, and the first man can with his hands loosen his lazo from the horns, and then quietly mount his horse; but the moment the second man, by backing ever so little, relaxes the strain, the lazo slips off the legs of the struggling beast, which then rises free, shakes himself, and vainly rushes at his antagonist.

During our whole ride we saw only one troop of wild horses. These animals, as well as the cattle, were introduced by the French in 1764, since which time both have greatly increased.

It is a curious fact, that the horses have never left the eastern end of the island, although there is no natural boundary to prevent them from roaming, and that part of the island is not more tempting than the rest. The Gauchos whom I asked, though asserting this to be the case, were unable to account for it, except from the strong attachment which horses have to any locality to which they are accustomed. Considering that the island does not appear fully stocked, and that there are no beasts of prey, I was particularly curious to know what has checked their originally rapid increase. That in a limited island some check would sooner or later supervene, is inevitable; but why has the increase of the horse been checked sooner than that of the cattle? Capt. Sulivan has taken much pains for me in this inquiry. The Gauchos employed here attribute it chiefly to the stallions constantly roaming from place to place, and compelling the mares to accompany them, whether or not the young foals are able to follow. One Gaucho told Capt. Sulivan that he had watched a stallion for a whole hour, violently kicking and biting a mare till he forced her to leave her foal to its fate. Capt. Sulivan can so far corroborate this curious account, that he has several times found young foals dead, whereas he has never found a dead calf. Moreover, the dead bodies of full-grown horses are more frequently found, as if more subject to disease or accidents, than those of the cattle. From the softness of the ground their hoofs often grow irregularly to a great length, and this causes lameness. The predominant colours are roan and iron-grey. All the horses bred here, both tame and wild, are rather small-sized, though generally in good condition; and they have lost so much strength, that they are unfit to be used in taking wild cattle with the lazo: in consequence, it is necessary to go to the great expense of importing fresh horses from the Plata. At some future period the southern hemisphere probably will have its breed of Falkland ponies, as the northern has its Shetland breed.

The cattle, instead of having degenerated like the horses, seem, as before remarked, to have increased in size; and they are much more numerous than the horses. Capt. Sulivan informs me that they vary much less in the general form of their bodies and in the shape of their horns than English cattle. In colour they differ much; and it is a remarkable circumstance, that in different parts of this one small island, different colours predominate. Round Mount Usborne, at a height of from 1000 to 1500 feet above the sea, about half of some of the herds are mouse or lead-coloured, a tint which is not common in other parts of the island. Near Port Pleasant dark brown prevails, whereas south of Choiseul Sound (which almost divides the island into two parts), white beasts with black heads and feet are the most common: in all parts black, and some spotted animals may be observed. Capt. Sulivan remarks, that the difference in the prevailing colours was so obvious, that in looking for the herds near Port Pleasant, they appeared from a long distance like black spots, whilst south of Choiseul Sound they appeared like white spots on the hill-sides. Capt. Sulivan thinks that the herds do not mingle; and it is a singular fact, that the mouse-coloured cattle, though living on the high land, calve about a month earlier in the season than the other coloured beasts on the lower land. It is interesting thus to find the once domesticated cattle breaking into three colours, of which some one colour would in all probability ultimately prevail over the others, if the herds were left undisturbed for the next several centuries.

The rabbit is another animal which has been introduced, and has succeeded very well; so that they abound over large parts of the island. Yet, like the horses, they are confined within certain limits; for they have not crossed the central chain of hills, nor would they have extended even so far as its base, if, as the Gauchos informed me, small colonies had not been carried there. I should not have supposed that these animals, natives of northern Africa, could have existed in a climate so humid as this, and which enjoys so little sunshine that even wheat ripens only occasionally. It is asserted that in Sweden, which any one would have thought a more favourable climate, the rabbit cannot live out of doors. The first few pair, moreover, had here to contend against pre-existing enemies, in the fox and some large hawks. The French naturalists have considered the black variety a distinct species, and called it Lepus Magellanicus.[7] They imagined that Magellan, when talking of an animal under the name of "conejos" in the Strait of Magellan, referred to

---

[7] [Darwin] Lesson's Zoology of the Voyage of the *Coquille*, tom. i. p. 168. All the early voyagers, and especially Bougainville, distinctly state that the wolf-like fox was the only native animal on the island. The distinction of the rabbit as a species, is taken from peculiarities in the fur, from the shape of the head, and from the shortness of the ears. I may here observe that the difference between the Irish and English hare rests upon nearly similar characters, only more strongly marked.

this species; but he was alluding to a small cavy, which to this day is thus called by the Spaniards. The Gauchos laughed at the idea of the black kind being different from the grey, and they said that at all events it had not extended its range any further than the grey kind; that the two were never found separate; and that they readily bred together, and produced piebald offspring. Of the latter I now possess a specimen, and it is marked about the head differently from the French specific description. This circumstance shows how cautious naturalists should be in making species; for even Cuvier, on looking at the skull of one of these rabbits, thought it was probably distinct!

The only quadruped native to the island[8] is a large wolf-like fox (Canis antarcticus), which is common to both East and West Falkland. I have no doubt it is a peculiar species, and confined to this archipelago; because many sealers, Gauchos, and Indians, who have visited these islands, all maintain that no such animal is found in any part of South America. Molina, from a similarity in habits, thought that this was the same with his "culpeu;"[9] but I have seen both, and they are quite distinct. These wolves are well known, from Byron's account of their tameness and curiosity, which the sailors, who ran into the water to avoid them, mistook for fierceness. To this day their manners remain the same. They have been observed to enter a tent, and actually pull some meat from beneath the head of a sleeping seaman. The Gauchos also have frequently in the evening killed them, by holding out a piece of meat in one hand, and in the other a knife ready to stick them. As far as I am aware, there is no other instance in any part of the world, of so small a mass of broken land, distant from a continent, possessing so large an aboriginal quadruped peculiar to itself. Their numbers have rapidly decreased; they are already banished from that half of the island which lies to the eastward of the neck of land between St. Salvador Bay and Berkeley Sound. Within a very few years after these islands shall have become regularly settled, in all probability this fox

[8] [Darwin] I have reason, however, to suspect that there is a field-mouse. The common European rat and mouse have roamed far from the habitations of the settlers. The common hog has also run wild on one islet: all are of a black colour: the boars are very fierce, and have great tusks.

[9] [Darwin] The "culpeu" is the Canis Magellanicus brought home by Captain King from the Strait of Magellan. It is common in Chile.

will be classed with the dodo, as an animal which has perished
from the face of the earth.

At night (17th) we slept on the neck of land at the head of
Choiseul Sound, which forms the south-west peninsula. The
valley was pretty well sheltered from the cold wind; but there
was very little brushwood for fuel. The Gauchos, however,
soon found what, to my great surprise, made nearly as hot a
fire as coals; this was the skeleton of a bullock lately killed,
from which the flesh had been picked by the carrion-hawks.
They told me that in winter they often killed a beast, cleaned
the flesh from the bones with their knives, and then with the
same bones roasted the meat for their suppers.

18th.—It rained during nearly the whole day. At night we
managed, however, with our saddle-cloths to keep ourselves
pretty well dry and warm; but the ground on which we slept
was on each occasion nearly in the state of a bog, and there
was not a dry spot to sit down on after our day's ride. I have
in another part stated how singular it is that there should be
absolutely no trees on these islands, although Tierra del Fuego
is covered by one large forest. The largest bush in the island
(belonging to the family of Compositæ) is scarcely so tall as
our gorse. The best fuel is afforded by a green little bush about
the size of common heath, which has the useful property of
burning while fresh and green. It was very surprising to see
the Gauchos, in the midst of rain and everything soaking wet,
with nothing more than a tinder-box and piece of rag, immediately make a fire. They sought beneath the tufts of grass and
bushes for a few dry twigs, and these they rubbed into fibres;
then surrounding them with coarser twigs, something like a
bird's nest, they put the rag with its spark of fire in the middle
and covered it up. The nest being then held up to the wind,
by degrees it smoked more and more, and at last burst out in
flames. I do not think any other method would have had a
chance of succeeding with such damp materials.

19th.—Each morning, from not having ridden for some time
previously, I was very stiff. I was surprised to hear the Gauchos,
who have from infancy almost lived on horseback, say that,
under similar circumstances, they always suffer. St. Jago told
me, that having been confined for three months by illness, he
went out hunting wild cattle, and in consequence, for the next
two days, his thighs were so stiff that he was obliged to lie in
bed. This shows that the Gauchos, although they do not appear to do so, yet really must exert much muscular effort in

riding. The hunting wild cattle, in a country so difficult to pass as this is on account of the swampy ground, must be very hard work. The Gauchos say they often pass at full speed over ground which would be impassable at a slower pace; in the same manner as a man is able to skate over thin ice. When hunting, the party endeavours to get as close as possible to the herd without being discovered. Each man carries four or five pair of the bolas; these he throws one after the other at as many cattle, which, when once entangled, are left for some days, till they become a little exhausted by hunger and struggling. They are then let free and driven towards a small herd of tame animals, which have been brought to the spot on purpose. From their previous treatment, being too much terrified to leave the herd, they are easily driven, if their strength last out, to the settlement.

The weather continued so very bad that we determined to make a push, and try to reach the vessel before night. From the quantity of rain which had fallen, the surface of the whole country was swampy. I suppose my horse fell at least a dozen times, and sometimes the whole six horses were floundering in the mud together. All the little streams are bordered by soft peat, which makes it very difficult for the horses to leap them without falling. To complete our discomforts we were obliged to cross the head of a creek of the sea, in which the water was as high as our horses' backs; and the little waves, owing to the violence of the wind, broke over us, and made us very wet and cold. Even the iron-framed Gauchos professed themselves glad when they reached the settlement, after our little excursion.

The geological structure of these islands is in most respects simple. The lower country consists of clay-slate and sandstone, containing fossils, very closely related to, but not identical with, those found in the Silurian formations of Europe; the hills are formed of white granular quartz rock. The strata of the latter are frequently arched with perfect symmetry, and the appearance of some of the masses is in consequence most singular. Pernety[10] has devoted several pages to the description of a Hill of Ruins, the successive strata of which he has justly compared to the seats of an amphitheatre. The quartz rock must have been quite pasty when it underwent such remarkable flexures without being shattered into fragments. As the quartz insen-

10 [Darwin] Pernety, Voyage aux Isles Malouines, p. 526.

sibly passes into the sandstone, it seems probable that the former owes its origin to the sandstone having been heated to such a degree that it became viscid, and upon cooling crystallized. While in the soft state it must have been pushed up through the overlying beds.

In many parts of the island the bottoms of the valleys are covered in an extraordinary manner by myriads of great loose angular fragments of the quartz rock, forming "streams of stones." These have been mentioned with surprise by every voyager since the time of Pernety. The blocks are not waterworn, their angles being only a little blunted; they vary in size from one or two feet in diameter to ten, or even more than twenty times as much. They are not thrown together into irregular piles, but are spread out into level sheets or great streams. It is not possible to ascertain their thickness, but the water of small streamlets can be heard trickling through the stones many feet below the surface. The actual depth is probably great, because the crevices between the lower fragments must long ago have been filled up with sand. The width of these sheets of stones varies from a few hundred feet to a mile; but the peaty soil daily encroaches on the borders, and even forms islets wherever a few fragments happen to lie close together. In a valley south of Berkeley Sound, which some of our party called the "great valley of fragments," it was necessary to cross an uninterrupted band half a mile wide, by jumping from one pointed stone to another. So large were the fragments, that being overtaken by a shower of rain, I readily found shelter beneath one of them.

Their little inclination is the most remarkable circumstance in these "streams of stones." On the hill-sides I have seen them sloping at an angle of ten degrees with the horizon; but in some of the level, broad-bottomed valleys, the inclination is only just sufficient to be clearly perceived. On so rugged a surface there was no means of measuring the angle; but to give a common illustration, I may say that the slope would not have checked the speed of an English mail-coach. In some places, a continuous stream of these fragments followed up the course of a valley, and even extended to the very crest of the hill. On these crests huge masses, exceeding in dimensions any small building, seemed to stand arrested in their headlong course: there, also, the curved strata of the archways lay piled on each other, like the ruins of some vast and ancient cathedral. In endeavouring to describe these scenes of violence one is tempted to pass from one simile to another. We may imagine that streams of white lava had flowed from many parts of the mountains into the lower country, and that when solidified they had been rent by some enormous convulsion into myriads of fragments. The expression "streams of stones," which immediately occurred to every one, conveys the same idea. These scenes are on the spot rendered more striking by the contrast of the low, rounded forms of the neighbouring hills.

I was interested by finding on the highest peak of one range (about 700 feet above the sea) a great arched fragment, lying on its convex side, or back downwards. Must we believe that it was fairly pitched up in the air, and thus turned? Or, with more probability, that there existed formerly a part of the same range more elevated than the point on which this monument of a great convulsion of nature now lies. As the fragments in the valleys are neither rounded nor the crevices filled up with sand, we must infer that the period of violence was subsequent to the land having been raised above the waters of the sea. In a transverse section within these valleys, the bottom is nearly level, or rises but very little towards either side. Hence the fragments appear to have travelled from the head of the valley; but in reality it seems more probable that they have been hurled down from the nearest slopes; and that since, by a vibratory movement of overwhelming force,[11] the fragments have been levelled into one continuous sheet. If during the earthquake[12] which in 1835 overthrew Concepcion, in Chile, it was thought wonderful that small bodies should have been pitched a few inches from the ground, what must we say to a movement which has caused fragments many tons in weight, to move onwards like so much sand on a vibrating board, and find their level? I have seen, in the Cordillera of the Andes, the evident marks where stupendous mountains have been broken into pieces like so much thin crust, and the strata thrown

[11] [Darwin] "Nous n'avons pas été moins saisis d'étonnement à la vûe de l'innombrable quantité de pierres de toutes grandcurs, bouleversées les unes sur les autres, et cependant rangées, comme si elles avoient été amoncelées négligemment pour remplir des ravins. On ne se lassoit pas d'admirer les effets prodigieux de la nature."—*Pernety*, p. 526.

[12] [Darwin] An inhabitant of Mendoza, and hence well capable of judging, assured me that, during the several years he had resided on these islands, he had never felt the slightest shock of an earthquake.

on their vertical edges; but never did any scene, like these "streams of stones," so forcibly convey to my mind the idea of a convulsion, of which in historical records we might in vain seek for any counterpart: yet the progress of knowledge will probably some day give a simple explanation of this phenomenon, as it already has of the so long-thought inexplicable transportal of the erratic boulders, which are strewed over the plains of Europe.

I have little to remark on the zoology of these islands. I have before described the carrion-vulture or Polyborus. There are some other hawks, owls, and a few small land-birds. The waterfowl are particularly numerous, and they must formerly, from the accounts of the old navigators, have been much more so. One day I observed a cormorant playing with a fish which it had caught. Eight times successively the bird let its prey go, then dived after it, and although in deep water, brought it each time to the surface. In the Zoological Gardens I have seen the otter treat a fish in the same manner, much as a cat does a mouse: I do not know of any other instance where dame Nature appears so wilfully cruel. Another day, having placed myself between a penguin (Aptenodytes demersa) and the water, I was much amused by watching its habits. It was a brave bird; and till reaching the sea, it regularly fought and drove me backwards. Nothing less than heavy blows would have stopped him: every inch he gained he firmly kept, standing close before me erect and determined. When thus opposed he continually rolled his head from side to side, in a very odd manner, as if the power of distinct vision lay only in the anterior and basal part of each eye. This bird is commonly called the jackass penguin, from its habit, while on shore, of throwing its head backwards, and making a loud strange noise, very like the braying of an ass; but while at sea, and undisturbed, its note is very deep and solemn, and is often heard in the night-time. In diving, its little wings are used as fins; but on the land, as front legs. When crawling, it may be said on four legs, through the tussocks or on the side of a grassy cliff, it moves so very quickly that it might easily be mistaken for a quadruped. When at sea and fishing, it comes to the surface for the purpose of breathing with such a spring, and dives again so instantaneously, that I defy any one at first sight to be sure that it was not a fish leaping for sport.

Two kinds of geese frequent the Falklands. The upland species (Anas Magellanica) is common, in pairs and in small flocks, throughout the island. They do not migrate, but build on the small outlying islets. This is supposed to be from fear of the foxes: and it is perhaps from the same cause that these birds, though very tame by day, are shy and wild in the dusk of the evening. They live entirely on vegetable matter. The rock-goose, so called from living exclusively on the sea-beach (Anas antarctica), is common both here and on the west coast of America, as far north as Chile. In the deep and retired channels of Tierra del Fuego, the snow-white gander, invariably accompanied by his darker consort, and standing close by each other on some distant rocky point, is a common feature in the landscape.

In these islands a great loggerheaded duck or goose (Anas brachyptera), which sometimes weighs twenty-two pounds, is very abundant. These birds were in former days called, from their extraordinary manner of paddling and splashing upon the water, race-horses; but now they are named, much more appropriately, steamers. Their wings are too small and weak to allow of flight, but by their aid, partly swimming and partly flapping the surface of the water, they move very quickly. The manner is something like that by which the common house-duck escapes when pursued by a dog; but I am nearly sure that the steamer moves its wings alternately, instead of both together, as in other birds. These clumsy, loggerheaded ducks make such a noise and splashing, that the effect is exceedingly curious.

Thus we find in South America three birds which use their wings for other purposes besides flight; the penguin as fins, the steamer as paddles, and the ostrich as sails: and the Apteryx of New Zealand, as well as its gigantic extinct prototype the Deinornis, possess only rudimentary representatives of wings. The steamer is able to dive only to a very short distance. It feeds entirely on shell-fish from the kelp and tidal rocks; hence the beak and head, for the purpose of breaking them, are surprisingly heavy and strong: the head is so strong that I have scarcely been able to fracture it with my geological hammer; and all our sportsmen soon discovered how tenacious these birds were of life. When in the evening pluming themselves in a flock, they make the same odd mixture of sounds which bull-frogs do within the tropics.

In Tierra del Fuego, as well as at the Falkland Islands, I made many observations on the lower marine animals,[13] but they are of little general interest. I will mention only one class of facts, relating to certain zoophytes in the more highly organized division of that class. Several genera (Flustra, Eschara, Cellaria, Crisia, and others)[14] agree in having singular moveable organs (like those of Flustra avicularia, found in the European seas) attached to their cells. The organ, in the greater number of cases, very closely resembles the head of a vulture; but the lower mandible can be opened much wider than in a real bird's beak. The head itself possesses considerable powers of movement, by means of a short neck. In one zoophyte the head itself was fixed, but the lower jaw free: in another it was replaced by a triangular hood, with a beautifully-fitted trapdoor, which evidently answered to the lower mandible. In the greater number of species, each cell was provided with one head, but in others each cell had two.

The young cells at the end of the branches of these corallines contain quite immature polypi, yet the vulture-heads attached to them, though small, are in every respect perfect. When the polypus was removed by a needle from any of the cells, these organs did not appear in the least affected. When one of the vulture-like heads was cut off from a cell, the lower mandible retained its power of opening and closing. Perhaps the most singular part of their structure is, that when there were more than two rows of cells on a branch, the central cells were

[13] [Darwin] I was surprised to find, on counting the eggs of a large white Doris (this sea-slug was three and a half inches long), how extraordinarily numerous they were. From two to five eggs (each three-thousandths of an inch in diameter) were contained in a spherical little case. These were arranged two deep in transverse rows forming a ribbon. The ribbon adhered by its edge to the rock in an oval spire. One which I found, measured nearly twenty inches in length and half in breadth. By counting how many balls were contained in a tenth of an inch in the row, and how many rows in an equal length of the ribbon, on the most moderate computation there were six hundred thousand eggs. Yet this Doris was certainly not very common: although I was often searching under the stones, I saw only seven individuals. *No fallacy is more common with naturalists, than that the numbers of an individual species depend on its powers of propagation.*

[14] [Editor] Genera of bryozoa, a class of coral-like marine invertebrates often called "moss animals" because of the resemblance of incrustations of bryozoa upon tidal rocks to moss.

furnished with these appendages, of only one-fourth the size of the outside ones. Their movements varied according to the species; but in some I never saw the least motion; while others, with the lower mandible generally wide open, oscillated backwards and forwards at the rate of about five seconds each turn; others moved rapidly and by starts. When touched with a needle, the beak generally seized the point so firmly, that the whole branch might be shaken.

These bodies have no relation whatever with the production of the eggs or gemmules, as they are formed before the young polypi appear in the cells at the end of the growing branches; as they move independently of the polypi, and do not appear to be in any way connected with them; and as they differ in size on the outer and inner rows of cells, I have little doubt, that in their functions, they are related rather to the horny axis of the branches than to the polypi in the cells. The fleshy appendage at the lower extremity of the sea-pen (described at Bahia Blanca) also forms part of the zoophyte, as a whole, in the same manner as the roots of a tree form part of the whole tree, and not of the individual leaf or flower-buds.

In another elegant little coralline (Crisia?), each cell was furnished with a long-toothed bristle, which had the power of moving quickly. Each of these bristles and each of the vulture-like heads generally moved quite independently of the others, but sometimes all on both sides of the branch, sometimes only those on one side, moved together coinstantaneously; sometimes each moved in regular order one after another. In these actions we apparently behold as perfect a transmission of will in the zoophyte, though composed of thousands of distinct polypi, as in any single animal. The case, indeed, is not different from that of the sea-pens, which, when touched, drew themselves into the sand on the coast of Bahia Blanca. I will state one other instance of uniform action, though of a very different nature, in a zoophyte closely allied to Clytia,[15] and therefore very simply organized. Having kept a large tuft of it in a basin of salt-water, when it was dark I found that as often as I rubbed any part of a branch, the whole became strongly phosphorescent with a green light: I do not think I ever saw any object more beautifully so. But the remarkable circumstance was, that the flashes of light always proceeded up the branches, from the base towards the extremities.

15 [Editor] Clytia: a hydroid.

The examination of these compound animals was always very interesting to me. What can be more remarkable than to see a plant-like body producing an egg, capable of swimming about and of choosing a proper place to adhere to, which then sprouts into branches, each crowded with innumerable distinct animals, often of complicated organizations? The branches, moreover, as we have just seen, sometimes possess organs capable of movement and independent of the polypi. Surprising as this union of separate individuals in a common stock must always appear, every tree displays the same fact, for buds must be considered as individual plants. It is, however, natural to consider a polypus, furnished with a mouth, intestines, and other organs, as a distinct individual, whereas the individuality of a leaf-bud is not easily realised; so that the union of separate individuals in a common body is more striking in a coralline than in a tree. Our conception of a compound animal, where in some respects the individuality of each is not completed, may be aided, by reflecting on the production of two distinct creatures by bisecting a single one with a knife, or where Nature herself performs the task of bisection. We may consider the polypi in a zoophyte, or the buds in a tree, as cases where the division of the individual has not been completely effected. Certainly in the case of trees, and judging from analogy in that of corallines, the individuals propagated by buds seem more intimately related to each other, than eggs or seeds are to their parents. It seems now pretty well established that plants propagated by buds all partake of a common duration of life; and it is familiar to everyone, what singular and numerous peculiarities are transmitted with certainty, by buds, layers, and grafts, which by seminal propagation never or only casually reappear.

CHAPTER X

TIERRA DEL FUEGO

Tierra del Fuego, first arrival — Good Success Bay — An Account of the Fuegians on board — Interview with the Savages — Scenery of the Forests — Cape Horn — Wigwam Cove — Miserable Condition of the Savages — Famines — Cannibals — Matricide — Religious Feelings — Great Gale — Beagle Channel — Ponsonby Sound — Build Wigwams and settle the Fuegians — Bifurcation of the Beagle Channel — Glaciers — Return to the Ship — Second Visit in the Ship to the Settlement — Equality of Condition amongst the Natives

December 17th, 1832.—Having now finished with Patagonia and the Falkland Islands, I will describe our first arrival in Tierra del Fuego.[1] A little after noon we doubled Cape St. Diego, and entered the famous strait of Le Maire. We kept close to the Fuegian shore, but the outline of the rugged, inhospitable Staten-land was visible amidst the clouds. In the afternoon we anchored in the Bay of Good Success. While entering we were saluted in a manner becoming the inhabitants of this savage land. A group of Fuegians partly concealed by the entangled forest, were perched on a wild point overhanging the sea; and as we passed by, they sprang up and waving

[1] [Editor] As made clear by the dates at the beginning of this chapter and of the section on the Falkland Islands in the last, Darwin paid his first visit to Tierra del Fuego before visiting the Falkland Islands. The Strait of Le Maire is at the southeast corner of Tierra del Fuego, between Tierra del Fuego and Staten Island, a desolate, windswept island belonging to Argentina and later the site, for a time, of a penal settlement. Because of strong prevailing winds, the Strait of Le Maire was very difficult for sailing vessels coming in the direction of the *Beagle* to negotiate.

their tattered cloaks sent forth a loud and sonorous shout. The savages followed the ship, and just before dark we saw their fire, and again heard their wild cry. The harbour consists of a fine piece of water half surrounded by low rounded mountains of clay-slate, which are covered to the water's edge by one dense gloomy forest. A single glance at the landscape was sufficient to show me how widely different it was from any thing I had ever beheld. At night it blew a gale of wind, and heavy squalls from the mountains swept past us. It would have been a bad time out at sea, and we, as well as others, may call this Good Success Bay.

In the morning the Captain sent a party to communicate with the Fuegians. When we came within hail, one of the four natives who were present advanced to receive us, and began to shout most vehemently, wishing to direct us where to land. When we were on shore the party looked rather alarmed, but continued talking and making gestures with great rapidity. It was without exception the most curious and interesting spectacle I ever beheld: I could not have believed how wide was the difference between savage and civilized man: it is greater than between a wild and domesticated animal, inasmuch as in man there is a greater power of improvement. The chief spokesman was old, and appeared to be the head of the family; the three others were powerful young men, about six feet high. The women and children had been sent away. These Fuegians are a very different race from the stunted, miserable wretches farther westward; and they seem closely allied to the famous Patagonians of the Strait of Magellan. Their only garment consists of a mantle made of guanaco skin, with the wool outside; this they wear just thrown over their shoulders, leaving their persons as often exposed as covered. Their skin is of a dirty coppery red colour.

The old man had a fillet of white feathers tied round his head, which partly confined his black, coarse, and entangled hair. His face was crossed by two broad transverse bars; one, painted bright red, reached from ear to ear and included the upper lip; the other, white like chalk, extended above and parallel to the first, so that even his eyelids were thus coloured. The other two men were ornamented by streaks of black powder, made of charcoal. The party altogether closely resembled the devils which come on the stage in plays like Der Freischutz.

Their very attitudes were abject, and the expression of their countenances distrustful, surprised, and startled. After we had presented them with some scarlet cloth, which they immediately tied round their necks, they became good friends. This was shown by the old man patting our breasts, and making a chuckling kind of noise, as people do when feeding chickens. I walked with the old man, and this demonstration of friendship was repeated several times; it was concluded by three hard slaps, which were given me on the breast and back at the same time. He then bared his bosom for me to return the compliment, which being done, he seemed highly pleased. The language of these people, according to our notions, scarcely deserves to be called articulate. Captain Cook has compared it to a man clearing his throat, but certainly no European ever cleared his throat with so many hoarse, guttural, and clicking sounds.

They are excellent mimics: as often as we coughed or yawned, or made any odd motion, they immediately imitated us. Some of our party began to squint and look awry; but one of the young Fuegians (whose whole face was painted black, excepting a white band across his eyes) succeeded in making far more hideous grimaces. They could repeat with perfect correctness each word in any sentence we addressed them, and they remembered such words for some time. Yet we Europeans all know how difficult it is to distinguish apart the sounds in a foreign language. Which of us, for instance, could follow an American Indian through a sentence of more than three words? All savages appear to possess, to an uncommon degree, this power of mimicry. I was told, almost in the same words, of the same ludicrous habit among the Caffres[2]: the Australians, likewise, have long been notorious for being able to imitate and describe the gait of any man, so that he may be recognized. How can this faculty be explained? is it a consequence of the more practised habits of perception and keener senses, common to all men in a savage state, as compared with those long civilized?

When a song was struck up by our party, I thought the Fuegians would have fallen down with astonishment. With equal surprise they viewed our dancing; but one of the young men, when asked, had no objection to a little waltzing. Little accustomed to Europeans as they appeared to be, yet they knew and dreaded our fire-arms; nothing would tempt them

[2] [Editor] Kaffirs, a term for African natives. Used chiefly in South Africa, it now has a derogatory implication.

to take a gun in their hands. They begged for knives, calling them by the Spanish word "cuchilla." They explained also what they wanted, by acting as if they had a piece of blubber in their mouth, and then pretending to cut instead of tear it.

I have not as yet noticed the Fuegians whom we had on board. During the former voyage of the *Adventure* and *Beagle* in 1826 to 1830, Captain Fitz Roy seized on a party of natives, as hostages for the loss of a boat, which had been stolen, to the great jeopardy of a party employed on the survey; and some of these natives, as well as a child whom he bought for a pearl-button, he took with him to England, determining to educate them and instruct them in religion at his own expense. To settle these natives in their own country, was one chief inducement to Captain Fitz Roy to undertake our present voyage; and before the Admiralty had resolved to send out this expedition, Captain Fitz Roy had generously chartered a vessel, and would himself have taken them back. The natives were accompanied by a missionary, R. Matthews; of whom and of the natives, Captain Fitz Roy has published a full and excellent account. Two men, one of whom died in England of the small-pox, a boy and a little girl, were originally taken; and we had now on board, York Minster, Jemmy Button (whose name expresses his purchase-money), and Fuegia Basket. York Minster was a full-grown, short, thick, powerful man: his disposition was reserved, taciturn, morose, and when excited violently passionate; his affections were very strong towards a few friends on board; his intellect good. Jemmy Button was a universal favourite, but likewise passionate; the expression of his face at once showed his nice disposition. He was merry and often laughed, and was remarkably sympathetic with any one in pain: when the water was rough, I was often a little sea-sick, and he used to come to me and say in a plaintive voice, "Poor, poor fellow!" but the notion, after his aquatic life, of a man being sea-sick, was too ludicrous, and he was generally obliged to turn on one side to hide a smile or laugh, and then he would repeat his "Poor, poor fellow!" He was of a patriotic disposition; and he liked to praise his own tribe and country, in which he truly said there were "plenty of trees," and he abused all the other tribes: he stoutly declared that there was no Devil in his land. Jemmy was short, thick, and fat, but vain of his personal appearance; he used to wear gloves, his hair was neatly cut, and he was distressed if his well-polished shoes were dirtied. He was fond of admiring himself in a looking-glass; and a merry-faced little Indian boy from the Rio Negro, whom we had for some months on board, soon perceived this, and used to mock him: Jemmy, who was always rather jealous of the attention paid to this little boy, did not at all like this, and used to say, with rather a contemptuous twist of his head, "Too much skylark." It seems yet wonderful to me, when I think over all his many good qualities, that he should have been of the same race, and doubtless partaken of the same character, with the miserable, degraded savages whom we first met here. Lastly, Fuegia Basket was a nice, modest, reserved young girl, with a rather pleasing but sometimes sullen expression, and very quick in learning anything, especially languages. This she showed in picking up some Portuguese and Spanish, when left on shore for only a short time at Rio de Janeiro and Monte Video, and in her knowledge of English. York Minster was very jealous of any attention paid to her; for it was clear he determined to marry her as soon as they were settled on shore.

Although all three could both speak and understand a good deal of English, it was singularly difficult to obtain much information from them, concerning the habits of their countrymen: this was partly owing to their apparent difficulty in understanding the simplest alternative. Every one accustomed to very young children, knows how seldom one can get an answer even to so simple a question as whether a thing is black *or* white; the idea of black or white seems alternately to fill their minds. So it was with these Fuegians, and hence it was generally impossible to find out, by cross-questioning, whether one had rightly understood anything which they had asserted. Their sight was remarkably acute: it is well known that sailors, from long practice, can make out a distant object much better than a landsman; but both York and Jemmy were much superior to any sailor on board: several times they have declared what some distant object has been, and though doubted by every one, they have proved right, when it has been examined through a telescope. They were quite conscious of this power; and Jemmy, when he had any little quarrel with the officer on watch, would say, "Me see ship, me no tell."

It was interesting to watch the conduct of the savages, when we landed, towards Jemmy Button: they immediately perceived the difference between him and ourselves, and held much conversation one with another on the subject. The old man addressed a long harangue to Jemmy, which it seems was to invite him to stay with them. But Jemmy understood very little of their language, and was, moreover, thoroughly ashamed of his countrymen. When York Minster afterwards came on shore, they noticed him in the same way, and told him he ought to shave; yet he had not twenty dwarf hairs on his face, whilst we all wore our untrimmed beards. They examined the colour of his skin, and compared it with ours. One of our arms being bared, they expressed the liveliest surprise and admiration at its whiteness, just in the same way in which I have seen the ourang-outang do at the Zoological Gardens. We thought that they mistook two or three of the officers, who were rather shorter and fairer, though adorned with large beards, for the ladies of our party. The tallest among the Fuegians was evidently much pleased at his height being noticed. When placed back to back with the tallest of the boat's crew, he tried his best to edge on higher ground, and to stand on tiptoe. He opened his mouth to show his teeth, and turned his face for a side view; and all this was done with such alacrity, that I dare say he thought himself the handsomest man in Tierra del Fuego. After our first feeling of grave astonishment was over, nothing could be more ludicrous than the odd mixture of surprise and imitation which these savages every moment exhibited.

The next day I attempted to penetrate some way into the country. Tierra del Fuego may be described as a mountainous land, partly submerged in the sea, so that deep inlets and bays occupy the place where valleys should exist. The mountain sides, except on the exposed western coast, are covered from the water's edge upwards by one great forest. The trees reach to an elevation of between 1000 and 1500 feet, and are succeeded by a band of peat, with minute alpine plants; and this again is succeeded by the line of perpetual snow, which, according to Captain King, in the Strait of Magellan descends to between 3000 and 4000 feet. To find an acre of level land in any part of the country is most rare. I recollect only one little flat piece near Port Famine, and another of rather larger extent near Goeree Road. In both places, and everywhere else, the surface is covered by a thick bed of swampy peat. Even within the forest, the ground is concealed by a mass of slowly putrefying vegetable matter, which, from being soaked with water, yields to the foot.

Finding it nearly hopeless to push my way through the wood,

I followed the course of a mountain torrent. At first, from the waterfalls and number of dead trees, I could hardly crawl along; but the bed of the stream soon became a little more open, from the floods having swept the sides. I continued slowly to advance for an hour along the broken and rocky banks, and was amply repaid by the grandeur of the scene. The gloomy depth of the ravine well accorded with the universal signs of violence. On every side were lying irregular masses of rock and torn-up trees; other trees, though still erect, were decayed to the heart and ready to fall. The entangled mass of the thriving and the fallen reminded me of the forests within the tropics —yet there was a difference: for in these still solitudes, Death, instead of Life, seemed the predominant spirit. I followed the watercourse till I came to a spot, where a great slip had cleared a straight space down the mountain side. By this road I ascended to a considerable elevation, and obtained a good view of the surrounding woods. The trees all belong to one kind, the Fagus betuloides; for the number of the other species of Fagus and of the Winter's Bark, is quite inconsiderable. This beech keeps its leaves throughout the year; but its foliage is of a peculiar brownish-green colour, with a tinge of yellow. As the whole landscape is thus coloured, it has a sombre, dull appearance; nor is it often enlivened by the rays of the sun.

December 20th.—One side of the harbour is formed by a hill about 1500 feet high, which Captain Fitz Roy has called after Sir J. Banks, in commemoration of his disastrous excursion, which proved fatal to two men of his party, and nearly so to Dr. Solander.[3] The snow-storm, which was the cause of their misfortune, happened in the middle of January, corresponding to our July, and in the latitude of Durham! I was anxious to reach the summit of this mountain to collect alpine plants; for flowers of any kind in the lower parts are few in

[3] [Editor] Sir Joseph Banks, born in London 1743, died there in 1820, naturalist who accompanied Captain Cook on his first expedition to the Pacific. A man of wealth, Banks not only financed the fitting out of Cook's ship, the *Endeavour*, but hired draftsmen and painters to record the expedition's observations. He also persuaded Daniel Solander, a distinguished pupil of Linnaeus, to join the ship. As Darwin notes, Solander was almost killed in an attempt to scale Mount Banks in Tierra del Fuego, which Cook's expedition visited on the way to the Pacific. In 1778, Banks was elected president of the Royal Society and served in that post until his death—for 42 years in all.

number. We followed the same watercourse as on the previous day, till it dwindled away, and we were then compelled to crawl blindly among the trees. These, from the effects of the elevation and of the impetuous winds, were low, thick, and crooked. At length we reached that which from a distance appeared like a carpet of fine green turf, but which, to our vexation, turned out to be a compact mass of little beech-trees about four or five feet high. They were as thick together as box in the border of a garden, and we were obliged to struggle over the flat but treacherous surface. After a little more trouble we gained the peat, and then the bare slate rock.

A ridge connected this hill with another, distant some miles, and more lofty, so that patches of snow were lying on it. As the day was not far advanced, I determined to walk there and collect plants along the road. It would have been very hard work, had it not been for a well-beaten and straight path made by the guanacos; for these animals, like sheep, always follow the same line. When we reached the hill we found it the highest in the immediate neighbourhood, and the waters flowed to the sea in opposite directions. We obtained a wide view over the surrounding country: to the north a swampy moorland extended, but to the south we had a scene of savage magnificence, well becoming Tierra del Fuego. There was a degree of mysterious grandeur in mountain behind mountain, with the deep intervening valleys, all covered by one thick, dusky mass of forest. The atmosphere, likewise, in this climate, where gale succeeds gale, with rain, hail, and sleet, seems blacker than anywhere else. In the Strait of Magellan, looking due southward from Port Famine, the distant channels between the mountains appeared from their gloominess to lead beyond the confines of this world.

December 21*st*.—The *Beagle* got under weigh: and on the succeeding day, favoured to an uncommon degree by a fine easterly breeze, we closed in with the Barnevelts, and running past Cape Deceit with its stony peaks, about three o'clock doubled the weather-beaten Cape Horn. The evening was calm and bright, and we enjoyed a fine view of the surrounding isles. Cape Horn, however, demanded his tribute, and before night sent us a gale of wind directly in our teeth. We stood out to sea, and on the second day again made the land, when we saw on our weather-bow this notorious promontory in its proper form—veiled in a mist, and its dim outline surrounded by a storm of wind and water. Great black clouds were rolling across the heavens, and squalls of rain, with hail, swept by us with such extreme violence, that the Captain determined to run into Wigwam Cove. This is a snug little harbour, not far from Cape Horn; and here, at Christmas-eve, we anchored in smooth water. The only thing which reminded us of the gale outside, was every now and then a puff from the mountains, which made the ship surge at her anchors.

December 25th.—Close by the cove, a pointed hill, called Kater's Peak, rises to the height of 1700 feet. The surrounding islands all consist of conical masses of greenstone, associated sometimes with less regular hills of baked and altered clay-slate. This part of Tierra del Fuego may be considered as the extremity of the submerged chain of mountains already alluded to. The cove takes its name of "Wigwam" from some of the Fuegian habitations; but every bay in the neighbourhood might be so called with equal propriety. The inhabitants, living chiefly upon shell-fish, are obliged constantly to change their place of residence; but they return at intervals to the same spots, as is evident from the piles of old shells, which must often amount to many tons in weight. These heaps can be distinguished at a long distance by the bright green colour of certain plants, which invariably grow on them. Among these may be enumerated the wild celery and scurvy grass, two very serviceable plants, the use of which has not been discovered by the natives.

The Fuegian wigwam resembles, in size and dimensions, a haycock. It merely consists of a few broken branches stuck in the ground, and very imperfectly thatched on one side with a few tufts of grass and rushes. The whole cannot be the work of an hour, and it is only used for a few days. At Goeree Roads I saw a place where one of these naked men had slept, which absolutely offered no more cover than the form of a hare. The man was evidently living by himself, and York Minster said he was "very bad man," and that probably he had stolen something. On the west coast, however, the wigwams are rather better, for they are covered with seal-skins. We were detained here several days by the bad weather. The climate is certainly wretched: the summer solstice was now passed, yet every day snow fell on the hills, and in the valleys there was rain, accompanied by sleet. The thermometer generally stood about 45°, but in the night fell to 38° or 40°. From the damp and boisterous state of the atmosphere, not cheered by a gleam of sunshine, one fancied the climate even worse than it really was.

While going one day on shore near Wollaston Island, we pulled alongside a canoe with six Fuegians. These were the most abject and miserable creatures I anywhere beheld. On the east coast the natives, as we have seen, have guanaco cloaks, and on the west, they possess seal-skins. Amongst these central tribes the men generally have an otter-skin, or some small scrap about as large as a pocket-handkerchief, which is barely sufficient to cover their backs as low down as their loins. It is laced across the breast by strings, and according as the wind blows, it is shifted from side to side. But these Fuegians in the canoe were quite naked, and even one full-grown woman was absolutely so. It was raining heavily, and the fresh water, together with the spray, trickled down her body. In another harbour not far distant, a woman, who was suckling a recently-born child, came one day alongside the vessel, and remained there out of mere curiosity, whilst the sleet fell and thawed on her naked bosom, and on the skin of her naked baby! These poor wretches were stunted in their growth, their hideous faces bedaubed with white paint, their skins filthy and greasy, their hair entangled, their voices discordant, and their gestures violent. Viewing such men, one can hardly make oneself believe that they are fellow-creatures, and inhabitants of the same world. It is a common subject of conjecture what pleasure in life some of the lower animals can enjoy: how much more reasonably the same question may be asked with respect to these barbarians! At night, five or six human beings, naked and scarcely protected from the wind and rain of this tempestuous climate, sleep on the wet ground coiled up like animals. Whenever it is low water, winter or summer, night or day, they must rise to pick shell-fish from the rocks; and the women either dive to collect sea-eggs, or sit patiently in their canoes, and with a baited hair-line without any hook, jerk out little fish. If a seal is killed, or the floating carcass of a putrid whale discovered, it is a feast; and such miserable food is assisted by a few tasteless berries and fungi.

They often suffer from famine: I heard Mr. Low, a sealing-master intimately acquainted with the natives of this country, give a curious account of the state of a party of one hundred and fifty natives on the west coast, who were very thin and in great distress. A succession of gales prevented the women from getting shell-fish on the rocks, and they could not go out in their canoes to catch seal. A small party of these men one morning set out, and the other Indians explained to him, that they were going a four days' journey for food: on their return,

Low went to meet them, and he found them excessively tired, each man carrying a great square piece of putrid whales-blubber with a hole in the middle, through which they put their heads, like the Gauchos do through their ponchos or cloaks. As soon as the blubber was brought into a wigwam, an old man cut off thin slices, and muttering over them, broiled them for a minute, and distributed them to the famished party, who during this time preserved a profound silence. Mr. Low believes that whenever a whale is cast on shore, the natives bury large pieces of it in the sand, as a resource in time of famine; and a native boy, whom he had on board, once found a stock thus buried. The different tribes when at war are cannibals. From the concurrent, but quite independent evidence of the boy taken by Mr. Low, and of Jemmy Button, it is certainly true, that when pressed in winter by hunger, they kill and devour their old women before they kill their dogs: the boy, being asked by Mr. Low why they did this, answered, "Doggies catch otters, old women no." This boy described the manner in which they are killed by being held over smoke and thus choked; he imitated their screams as a joke, and described the parts of their bodies which are considered best to eat. Horrid as such a death by the hands of their friends and relatives must be, the fears of the old women, when hunger begins to press, are more painful to think of; we were told that they then often run away into the mountains, but that they are pursued by the men and brought back to the slaughter-house at their own fire-sides![4]

[4] [Editor] Unfortunately, both Darwin and Fitz Roy were misled on this point, for the Fuegians were not cannibals and honored rather than ate their old women. Old women were in demand as second and third wives—the Fuegians were polygamous—because of their experience in the management of canoes and many duties performed by the Fuegian wife. A form of euthanasia by strangulation was practiced but this was confined to the incurably sick and disabled.

In *The Uttermost Part of the Earth,* Bridges provides a plausible explanation of how Darwin and Fitz Roy came to be misled. Here it is:

"Of the three years these young Yaghans lived amongst English people, half was spent on board the *Beagle* with FitzRoy. During this time they convinced him and others that the Fuegian Indians were cannibals. Even that searcher after truth, Charles Darwin, who was closely associated with the trio during the twelve months' voyage of the *Beagle,* accepted their testimony.

"We who later passed many years of our lives in daily contact

Captain Fitz Roy could never ascertain that the Fuegians have any distinct belief in a future life. They sometimes bury their dead in caves, and sometimes in the mountain forests; we do not know what ceremonies they perform. Jemmy Button would not eat land-birds, because "eat dead men:" they are

with these people can find only one explanation for this shocking mistake. We suppose that, when questioned, York Minster, or Jimmy Button, would not trouble in the least to answer truthfully, but would merely give the reply that he felt was expected or desired. In the early days their limited knowledge of English would not allow them to explain at any length, and, as we know, it is much easier to answer 'yes' and 'no.' So the statements with which these young men and little Fuegia Basket have been credited were, in fact, no more than agreement with suggestions made by their questioners.

"We can imagine their reactions when asked what was, to them, a ridiculous question, such as:

" 'Do you kill and eat men?'

"They would at first be puzzled, but when the enquiry was repeated and they grasped its meaning and realized the answer that was expected, they would naturally agree. The interrogator would follow this with:

" 'What people do you eat?'

"No answer.

" 'Do you eat bad people?'

" 'Yes.'

" 'When there are no bad people, what then?'

"No answer.

" 'Do you eat your old women?'

" 'Yes.'

"Once this game was started and their knowledge of English increased, these irresponsible youngsters, encouraged by having their evidence so readily accepted and noted down as fact, would naturally start inventing on their own. We are told that they described, with much detail, how the Fuegians ate their enemies killed in battle and, when there were no such victims, devoured their old women. When asked if they ate dogs when hungry, they said they did not, as dogs were useful for catching otter, whereas the old women were of no use at all. These unfortunates, they said, were held in the thick smoke till they choked to death. The meat, they stated, was very good.

"This delectable fiction once firmly established, any subsequent attempt at denial would not have been believed, but would have been attributed to a growing unwillingness to confess the horrors in which they had formerly indulged. Accordingly, these young story-tellers allowed their imaginations full rein and vied with each other in the recounting of still more fantastic tales, emboldened by the admiration of the other two."

unwilling even to mention their dead friends. We have no reason to believe that they perform any sort of religious worship; though perhaps the muttering of the old man before he distributed the putrid blubber to his famished party, may be of this nature. Each family or tribe has a wizard or conjuring doctor, whose office we could never clearly ascertain. Jemmy believed in dreams, though not, as I have said, in the devil: I do not think that our Fuegians were much more superstitious than some of the sailors; for an old quarter-master firmly believed that the successive heavy gales, which we encountered off Cape Horn, were caused by our having the Fuegians on board. The nearest approach to a religious feeling which I heard of, was shown by York Minster, who, when Mr. Bynoe shot some very young ducklings as specimens, declared in the most solemn manner, "Oh Mr. Bynoe, much rain, snow, blow much." This was evidently a retributive punishment for wasting human food. In a wild and excited manner he also related, that his brother, one day whilst returning to pick up some dead birds which he had left on the coast, observed some feathers blown by the wind. His brother said (York imitating his manner), "What that?" and crawling onwards, he peeped over the cliff, and saw "wild man" picking his birds; he crawled a little nearer, and then hurled down a great stone and killed him. York declared for a long time afterwards storms raged, and much rain and snow fell. As far as we could make out, he seemed to consider the elements themselves as the avenging agents: it is evident in this case, how naturally, in a race a little more advanced in culture, the elements would become personified. What the "bad wild men" were, has always appeared to me most mysterious: from what York said, when we found the place like the form of a hare, where a single man had slept the night before, I should have thought that they were thieves who had been driven from their tribes; but other obscure speeches made me doubt this; I have sometimes imagined that the most probable explanation was that they were insane.

The different tribes have no government or chief; yet each is surrounded by other hostile tribes, speaking different dialects, and separated from each other only by a deserted border or neutral territory: the cause of their warfare appears to be the means of subsistence.[5] Their country is a broken mass of wild

5 [Editor] Before the white man came there were four tribes of Fuegians—the Alacaloofs, Aush, Onas and Yaghans—numbering some 7000 to 8000 individuals altogether. The last full-blooded

rocks, lofty hills, and useless forests: and these are viewed through mists and endless storms. The habitable land is reduced to the stones on the beach; in search of food they are compelled unceasingly to wander from spot to spot, and so steep is the coast, that they can only move about in their wretched canoes. They cannot know the feeling of having a home, and still less that of domestic affection; for the husband is to the wife a brutal master to a laborious slave. Was a more horrid deed ever perpetrated, than that witnessed on the west coast by Byron, who saw a wretched mother pick up her bleeding dying infant-boy, whom her husband had mercilessly dashed on the stones for dropping a basket of sea-eggs! How little can the higher powers of the mind be brought into play: what is there for imagination to picture, for reason to compare, for judgment to decide upon? to knock a limpet from the rock does not require even cunning, that lowest power of the mind. Their skill in some respects may be compared to the instinct of animals; for it is not improved by experience: the canoe, their most ingenious work, poor as it is, has remained the same, as we know from Drake, for the last two hundred and fifty years.

Whilst beholding these savages, one asks, whence have they come? What could have tempted, or what change compelled a tribe of men, to leave the fine regions of the north, to travel down the Cordillera or backbone of America, to invent and build canoes, which are not used by the tribes of Chile, Peru, and Brazil, and then to enter on one of the most inhospitable countries within the limits of the globe? Although such reflections must at first seize on the mind, yet we may feel sure that they are partly erroneous. There is no reason to believe that the Fuegians decrease in number; therefore we must suppose that they enjoy a sufficient share of happiness, of whatever kind it may be, to render life worth having. Nature by making habit omnipotent, and its effects hereditary, has fitted the Fuegian to the climate and the productions of his miserable country.

After having been detained six days in Wigwam Cove by very bad weather, we put to sea on the 30th of December.

Fuegian died about 1958; and, as of 1961, there were only 100 or so part-Fuegians left. As Darwin surmises, warfare between the tribes was frequent, and got to be quite bloody when, some years after Darwin's visit, the natives began to obtain firearms. However, tuberculosis and other white man's diseases were the main cause of the Fuegians' extinction.

Captain Fitz Roy wished to get westward to land York and Fuegia in their own country. When at sea we had a constant succession of gales, and the current was against us: we drifted to 57° 23′ south. On the 11th of January, 1833, by carrying a press of sail, we fetched within a few miles of the great rugged mountain of York Minster (so called by Captain Cook, and the origin of the name of the elder Fuegian), when a violent squall compelled us to shorten sail and stand out to sea. The surf was breaking fearfully on the coast, and the spray was carried over a cliff estimated at 200 feet in height. On the 12th the gale was very heavy, and we did not know exactly where we were: it was a most unpleasant sound to hear constantly repeated, "keep a good look-out to leeward." On the 13th the storm raged with its full fury: our horizon was narrowly limited by the sheets of spray borne by the wind. The sea looked ominous, like a dreary waving plain with patches of drifted snow: whilst the ship laboured heavily, the albatross glided with its expanded wings right up the wind. At noon a great sea broke over us, and filled one of the whale-boats, which was obliged to be instantly cut away. The poor *Beagle* trembled at the shock, and for a few minutes would not obey her helm; but soon, like a good ship that she was, she righted and came up to the wind again. Had another sea followed the first, our fate would have been decided soon, and for ever. We had now been twenty-four days trying in vain to get westward; the men were worn out with fatigue, and they had not for many nights or days a dry thing to put on. Captain Fitz Roy gave up the attempt to get westward by the outside coast. In the evening we ran in behind False Cape Horn, and dropped our anchor in forty-seven fathoms, fire flashing from the windlass as the chain rushed round it. How delightful was that still night, after having been so long involved in the din of the warring elements!

January 15th, 1833.—The *Beagle* anchored in Goeree Roads. Captain Fitz Roy having resolved to settle the Fuegians, according to their wishes, in Ponsonby Sound, four boats were equipped to carry them there through the Beagle Channel. This channel, which was discovered by Captain Fitz Roy during the last voyage, is a most remarkable feature in the geography of this, or indeed of any other country: it may be compared to the valley of Lochness in Scotland, with its chain of lakes and friths. It is about one hundred and twenty miles long, with an average breadth, not subject to any very great variation, of about two miles; and is throughout the greater part so perfectly

straight, that the view, bounded on each side by a line of mountains, gradually becomes indistinct in the long distance. It
crosses the southern part of Tierra del Fuego in an east and
west line, and in the middle is joined at right angles on the
south side by an irregular channel, which has been called Ponsonby Sound.[6] This is the residence of Jemmy Button's tribe
and family.

19th.—Three whale-boats and the yawl, with a party of
twenty-eight, started under the command of Captain Fitz Roy.
In the afternoon we entered the eastern mouth of the channel,
and shortly afterwards found a snug little cove concealed by
some surrounding islets. Here we pitched our tents and lighted
our fires. Nothing could look more comfortable than this
scene. The glassy water of the little harbour, with the branches
of the trees hanging over the rocky beach, the boats at anchor,
the tents supported by the crossed oars, and the smoke curling
up the wooded valley, formed a picture of quiet retirement.
The next day (20th) we smoothly glided onwards in our little
fleet, and came to a more inhabited district. Few if any of these
natives could ever have seen a white man; certainly nothing
could exceed their astonishment at the apparition of the four
boats. Fires were lighted on every point (hence the name of
Tierra del Fuego, or the land of fire), both to attract our attention and to spread far and wide the news. Some of the men
ran for miles along the shore. I shall never forget how wild and
savage one group appeared: suddenly four or five men came
to the edge of an overhanging cliff; they were absolutely naked,
and their long hair streamed about their faces; they held rugged
staffs in their hands, and, springing from the ground, they
waved their arms round their heads, and sent forth the most
hideous yells.

At dinner-time we landed among a party of Fuegians. At
first they were not inclined to be friendly; for until the Captain
pulled in ahead of the other boats, they kept their slings in
their hands. We soon, however, delighted them by trifling presents, such as tying red tape round their heads. They liked our
biscuit: but one of the savages touched with his finger some
of the meat preserved in tin cases which I was eating, and
feeling it soft and cold, showed as much disgust at it, as I should
have done at putrid blubber. Jemmy was thoroughly ashamed

[6] [Editor] The narrow channel leading south from Beagle Channel is Murray Narrows. Ponsonby Sound is a wider expanse of
water at the southern end of Murray Narrows.

of his countrymen, and declared his own tribe were quite different, in which he was wofully mistaken. It was as easy to please as it was difficult to satisfy these savages. Young and old, men and children, never ceased repeating the word "yammerschooner," which means "give me." After pointing to almost every object, one after the other, even to the buttons on our coats, and saying their favourite word in as many intonations as possible, they would then use it in a neuter sense, and vacantly repeat "yammerschooner." After yammerschoonering for any article very eagerly, they would by a simple artifice point to their young women or little children, as much as to say, "If you will not give it me, surely you will to such as these."

At night we endeavoured in vain to find an uninhabited cove; and at last were obliged to bivouac not far from a party of natives. They were very inoffensive as long as they were few in numbers, but in the morning (21st) being joined by others they showed symptoms of hostility, and we thought that we should have come to a skirmish. An European labours under great disadvantages when treating with savages like these, who have not the least idea of the power of fire-arms. In the very act of levelling his musket he appears to the savage far inferior to a man armed with a bow and arrow, a spear, or even a sling. Nor is it easy to teach them our superiority except by striking a fatal blow. Like wild beasts, they do not appear to compare numbers; for each individual, if attacked, instead of retiring, will endeavour to dash your brains out with a stone, as certainly as a tiger under similar circumstances would tear you. Captain Fitz Roy on one occasion being very anxious, from good reasons, to frighten away a small party, first flourished a cutlass near them, at which they only laughed; he then twice fired his pistol close to a native. The man both times looked astounded, and carefully but quickly rubbed his head; he then stared awhile, and gabbled to his companions, but he never seemed to think of running away. Wc can hardly put ourselves in the position of these savages, and understand their actions. In the case of this Fuegian, the possibility of such a sound as the report of a gun close to his ear could never have entered his mind. He perhaps literally did not for a second know whether it was a sound or a blow, and therefore very naturally rubbed his head. In a similar manner, when a savage sees a mark struck by a bullet, it may be some time before he is able at all to understand how it is effected; for the fact of a body being invisible from its velocity would perhaps be to him an idea totally inconceivable. Moreover, the extreme force of a bullet, that penetrates a hard substance without tearing it, may convince the savage that it has no force at all. Certainly I believe that many savages of the lowest grade, such as these of Tierra del Fuego, have seen objects struck, and even small animals killed by the musket, without being in the least aware how deadly an instrument it is.

22nd.—After having passed an unmolested night, in what would appear to be neutral territory between Jemmy's tribe and the people whom we saw yesterday, we sailed pleasantly along. I do not know anything which shows more clearly the hostile state of the different tribes, than these wide border or neutral tracts. Although Jemmy Button well knew the force of our party, he was, at first, unwilling to land amidst the hostile tribe nearest to his own. He often told us how the savage Oens men "when the leaf red," crossed the mountains from the eastern coast of Tierra del Fuego, and made inroads on the natives of this part of the country. It was most curious to watch him when thus talking, and see his eyes gleaming and his whole face assume a new and wild expression. As we proceeded along the Beagle Channel, the scenery assumed a peculiar and very magnificent character; but the effect was much lessened from the lowness of the point of view in a boat, and from looking along the valley, and thus losing all the beauty of a succession of ridges. The mountains were here about three thousand feet high, and terminated in sharp and jagged points. They rose in one unbroken sweep from the water's edge, and were covered to the height of fourteen or fifteen hundred feet by the dusky-coloured forest. It was most curious to observe, as far as the eye could range, how level and truly horizontal the line on the mountain side was, at which trees ceased to grow: it precisely resembled the high-water mark of drift-weed on a sea-beach.

At night we slept close to the junction of Ponsonby Sound with the Beagle Channel. A small family of Fuegians, who were living in the cove, were quiet and inoffensive, and soon joined our party round a blazing fire. We were well clothed, and though sitting close to the fire were far from too warm; yet these naked savages, though further off, were observed, to our great surprise, to be streaming with perspiration at undergoing such a roasting. They seemed, however, very well pleased, and all joined in the chorus of the seamen's songs: but the manner in which they were invariably a little behindhand was quite ludicrous.

During the night the news had spread, and early in the morning (23rd) a fresh party arrived, belonging to the Tekenika, or Jemmy's tribe. Several of them had run so fast that their noses were bleeding, and their mouths frothed from the rapidity with which they talked; and with their naked bodies all bedaubed with black, white,[7] and red, they looked like so many demoniacs who had been fighting. We then proceeded (accompanied by twelve canoes, each holding four or five people) down Ponsonby Sound to the spot where poor Jemmy expected to find his mother and relatives. He had already heard that his father was dead; but as he had had a "dream in his head" to that effect, he did not seem to care much about it, and repeatedly comforted himself with the very natural reflection— "Me no help it." He was not able to learn any particulars regarding his father's death, as his relations would not speak about it.

Jemmy was now in a district well known to him, and guided the boats to a quiet pretty cove named Woollya,[8] surrounded by islets, every one of which and every point had its proper native name. We found here a family of Jemmy's tribe, but not his relations: we made friends with them; and in the evening they sent a canoe to inform Jemmy's mother and brothers. The cove was bordered by some acres of good sloping land,

[7] [Darwin] This substance, when dry, is tolerably compact, and of little specific gravity: Professor Ehrenberg has examined it: he states (König Akad. der Wissen: Berlin, Feb. 1845) that it is composed of infusoria, including fourteen polygastrica, and four phytolitharia. He says that they are all inhabitants of fresh-water; this is a beautiful example of the results obtainable through Professor Ehrenberg's microscopic researches; for Jemmy Button told me that it is always collected at the bottoms of mountain-brooks. It is, moreover, a striking fact in the geographical distribution of the infusoria, which are well known to have very wide ranges, that all the species in this substance, although brought from the extreme southern point of Tierra del Fuego, are old, known forms.

[8] [Editor] Wulaia—as it is more often spelled—is on the west end of Navarin Island, a large rugged island on the south side of Beagle Channel. Navarin Island now belongs to Chile and boasts the world's southernmost inhabited point (camps and weather stations in the Antarctic excepted)—Puerto William, a military post with about 250 soldiers and inhabitants on the Beagle Channel side of the island.

not covered (as elsewhere) either by peat or by forest-trees.
Captain Fitz Roy originally intended, as before stated, to have
taken York Minster and Fuegia to their own tribe on the west
coast; but as they expressed a wish to remain here, and as the
spot was singularly favourable, Captain Fitz Roy determined
to settle here the whole party, including Matthews, the missionary. Five days were spent in building for them three large
wigwams, in landing their goods, in digging two gardens, and
sowing seeds.

The next morning after our arrival (the 24th) the Fuegians
began to pour in, and Jemmy's mother and brothers arrived.
Jemmy recognized the stentorian voice of one of his brothers
at a prodigious distance. The meeting was less interesting than
that between a horse, turned out into a field, when he joins an
old companion. There was no demonstration of affection; they
simply stared for a short time at each other; and the mother
immediately went to look after her canoe. We heard, however,
through York, that the mother had been inconsolable for the
loss of Jemmy, and had searched everywhere for him, thinking
that he might have been left after having been taken in the
boat. The women took much notice of and were very kind to
Fuegia. We had already perceived that Jemmy had almost forgotten his own language. I should think there was scarcely another human being with so small a stock of language, for his
English was very imperfect. It was laughable, but almost pitiable, to hear him speak to his wild brother in English, and then
ask him in Spanish ("no sabe?") whether he did not understand him.

Everything went on peaceably during the three next days,
whilst the gardens were digging and wigwams building. We
estimated the number of natives at about one hundred and
twenty. The women worked hard, whilst the men lounged about
all day long, watching us. They asked for everything they saw,
and stole what they could. They were delighted at our dancing
and singing, and were particularly interested at seeing us wash
in a neighbouring brook; they did not pay much attention to
anything else, not even to our boats. Of all the things which
York saw, during his absence from his country, nothing seems
more to have astonished him than an ostrich, near Maldonado:
breathless with astonishment he came running to Mr. Bynoe,
with whom he was out walking—"Oh, Mr. Bynoe, oh, bird all
same horse!" Much as our white skins surprised the natives,
by Mr. Low's account a negro-cook to a sealing vessel, did so

more effectually; and the poor fellow was so mobbed and shouted at that he would never go on shore again. Everything went on so quietly, that some of the officers and myself took long walks in the surrounding hills and woods. Suddenly, however, on the 27th, every woman and child disappeared. We were all uneasy at this, as neither York nor Jemmy could make out the cause. It was thought by some that they had been frightened by our cleaning and firing off our muskets on the previous evening: by others, that it was owing to offence taken by an old savage, who, when told to keep further off, had coolly spit in the sentry's face, and had then, by gestures acted over a sleeping Fuegian, plainly showed, as it was said, that he should like to cut up and eat our man. Captain Fitz Roy, to avoid the chance of an encounter, which would have been fatal to so many of the Fuegians, thought it advisable for us to sleep at a cove a few miles distant. Matthews, with his usual quiet fortitude (remarkable in a man apparently possessing little energy of character), determined to stay with the Fuegians, who evinced no alarm for themselves; and so we left them to pass their first awful night.

On our return in the morning (28th) we were delighted to find all quiet, and the men employed in their canoes spearing fish. Captain Fitz Roy determined to send the yawl and one whale-boat back to the ship; and to proceed with the two other boats, one under his own command (in which he most kindly allowed me to accompany him), and one under Mr. Hammond, to survey the western parts of the Beagle Channel, and afterwards to return and visit the settlement. The day to our astonishment was over-poweringly hot, so that our skins were scorched: with this beautiful weather, the view in the middle of the Beagle Channel was very remarkable. Looking towards either hand, no object intercepted the vanishing points of this long canal between the mountains. The circumstance of its being an arm of the sea was rendered very evident by several huge whales[9] spouting in different directions. On one occasion I saw two of these monsters, probably male and female, slowly swimming one after the other, within less than a stone's throw of the shore, over which the beech-tree extended its branches.

[9] [Darwin] One day, off the East coast of Tierra del Fuego, we saw a grand sight in several spermaceti whales jumping upright quite out of the water, with the exception of their tail-fins. As they fell down sideways, they splashed the water high up, and the sound reverberated like a distant broadside.

We sailed on till it was dark, and then pitched our tents in a quiet creek. The greatest luxury was to find for our beds a beach of pebbles, for they were dry and yielded to the body. Peaty soil is damp; rock is uneven and hard; sand gets into one's meat, when cooked and eaten boat-fashion; but when lying in our blanket-bags, on a good bed of smooth pebbles, we passed most comfortable nights.

It was my watch till one o'clock. There is something very solemn in these scenes. At no time does the consciousness in what a remote corner of the world you are then standing, come so strongly before the mind. Everything tends to this effect; the stillness of the night is interrupted only by the heavy breathing of the seamen beneath the tents, and sometimes by the cry of a night-bird. The occasional barking of a dog, heard in the distance, reminds one that it is the land of the savage.

January 29th.—Early in the morning we arrived at the point where the Beagle Channel divides into two arms; and we entered the northern one. The scenery here becomes even grander than before. The lofty mountains on the north side compose the granitic axis, or backbone of the country, and boldly rise to a height of between three and four thousand feet, with one peak above six thousand feet. They are covered by a wide mantle of perpetual snow, and numerous cascades pour their waters, through the woods, into the narrow channel below. In many parts, magnificent glaciers extend from the mountain side to the water's edge. It is scarcely possible to imagine any thing more beautiful than the beryl-like blue of these glaciers, and especially as contrasted with the dead white of the upper expanse of snow. The fragments which had fallen from the glacier into the water, were floating away, and the channel with its icebergs presented, for the space of a mile, a miniature likeness of the Polar Sea. The boats being hauled on shore at our dinner-hour, we were admiring from the distance of half a mile a perpendicular cliff of ice, and were wishing that some more fragments would fall. At last, down came a mass with a roaring noise, and immediately we saw the smooth outline of a wave travelling towards us. The men ran down as quickly as they could to the boats; for the chance of their being dashed to pieces was evident. One of the seamen just caught hold of the bows, as the curling breaker reached it: he was knocked over and over, but not hurt; and the boats, though thrice lifted on high and let fall again, received no damage.[10] This was most fortunate for us, for we were a hundred miles distant from the ship, and we should have been left without provisions or fire-arms. I had previously observed that some large fragments of rock on the beach had been lately displaced; but until seeing this wave, I did not understand the cause. One side of the creek was formed by a spur of mica-slate; the head by a cliff of ice about forty feet high; and the other side by a promontory fifty feet high, built up of huge rounded fragments of granite and mica-slate, out of which old trees were growing. This promontory was evidently a moraine, heaped up at a period when the glacier had greater dimensions.

When we reached the western mouth of this northern branch of the Beagle Channel we sailed amongst many unknown desolate islands, and the weather was wretchedly bad. We met with no natives. The coast was almost everywhere so steep, that we had several times to pull many miles before we could find space enough to pitch our two tents: one night we slept on large round boulders, with putrefying sea-weed between them; and when the tide rose, we had to get up and move our blanket-bags. The farthest point westward which we reached was Stewart Island, a distance of about one hundred and fifty miles from our ship. We returned into the Beagle Channel by the southern arm, and thence proceeded, with no adventure, back to Ponsonby Sound.[11]

February 6th.—We arrived at Woollya. Matthews gave so bad an account of the conduct of the Fuegians, that Captain Fitz Roy determined to take him back to the *Beagle;* and ultimately he was left at New Zealand, where his brother was a missionary. From the time of our leaving, a regular system of plunder commenced; fresh parties of the natives kept arriving: York and Jemmy lost many things, and Matthews almost every thing which had not been concealed underground. Every article seemed to have been torn up and divided by the natives.

[10] [Editor] With characteristic modesty, Darwin neglects to mention that he was one of the men who saved the boats. In his journal, Fitz Roy reports:

"By the exertions of those who grappled them [the boats] or seized their ropes, they were hauled up again out of reach of a second and third roller; and indeed we had good reason to rejoice that they were just saved in time; for had not Mr. Darwin, and two or three of the men, run to them instantly, they would have been swept away from us irrevocably."

[11] [Editor] Darwin also neglects to mention that Fitz Roy named a mountain and a sound discovered on this excursion after the *Beagle's* naturalist.

Matthews described the watch he was obliged always to keep as most harassing; night and day he was surrounded by the natives, who tried to tire him out by making an incessant noise close to his head. One day an old man, whom Matthews asked to leave his wigwam, immediately returned with a large stone in his hand: another day a whole party came armed with stones and stakes, and some of the younger men and Jemmy's brother were crying: Matthews met them with presents. Another party showed by signs that they wished to strip him naked and pluck all the hairs out of his face and body. I think we arrived just in time to save his life. Jemmy's relatives had been so vain and foolish, that they had showed to strangers their plunder, and their manner of obtaining it. It was quite melancholy leaving the three Fuegians with their savage countrymen; but it was a great comfort that they had no personal fears. York, being a powerful resolute man, was pretty sure to get on well, together with his wife Fuegia. Poor Jemmy looked rather disconsolate, and would then, I have little doubt, have been glad to have returned with us. His own brother had stolen many things from him; and as he remarked, "what fashion call that:" he abused his countrymen, "all bad men, no sabe (know) nothing," and, though I never heard him swear before, "damned fools." Our three Fuegians, though they had been only three years with civilized men, would, I am sure, have been glad to have retained their new habits; but this was obviously impossible. I fear it is more than doubtful, whether their visit will have been of any use to them.

In the evening, with Matthews on board, we made sail back to the ship, not by the Beagle Channel, but by the southern coast.[12] The boats were heavily laden and the sea rough, and we had a dangerous passage. By the evening of the 7th we were on board the *Beagle* after an absence of twenty days, during which time we had gone three hundred miles in the open boats. On the 11th, Captain Fitz Roy paid a visit by himself to the Fuegians and found them going on well; and that they had lost very few more things.

On the last day of February in the succeeding year (1834), the *Beagle* anchored in a beautiful little cove at the eastern entrance of the Beagle Channel. Captain Fitz Roy determined

[12] [Editor] A permanent European settlement was not established in the Beagle Channel area, until 1869, when the Rev. Whait H. Stirling, a British missionary, erected a house at Ushuaia on the Beagle Island shore of Tierra del Fuego.

on the bold, and as it proved successful, attempt to beat against
the westerly winds by the same route, which we had followed
in the boats to the settlement at Woollya. We did not see many
natives until we were near Ponsonby Sound, where we were
followed by ten or twelve canoes. The natives did not at all
understand the reason of our tacking, and, instead of meeting
us at each tack, vainly strove to follow us in our zig-zag course.
I was amused at finding what a difference the circumstance of
being quite superior in force made, in the interest of beholding
these savages. While in the boats I got to hate the very sound
of their voices, so much trouble did they give us. The first and
last word was "yammerschooner." When, entering some quiet
little cove, we have looked round and thought to pass a quiet
night, the odious word "yammerschooner" has shrilly sounded
from some gloomy nook, and then the little signal-smoke has
curled up to spread the news far and wide. On leaving some
place we have said to each other, "Thank Heaven, we have
at last fairly left these wretches!" when one more faint halloo
from an all-powerful voice, heard at a prodigious distance,
would reach our ears, and clearly could we distinguish—"yammerschooner." But now, the more Fuegians the merrier; and
very merry work it was. Both parties laughing, wondering,
gaping at each other; we pitying them, for giving us good
fish and crabs for rags, &c.; they grasping at the chance of
finding people so foolish as to exchange such splendid ornaments for a good supper. It was most amusing to see the un-
disguised smile of satisfaction with which one young woman
with her face painted black, tied several bits of scarlet cloth
round her head with rushes. Her husband, who enjoyed the
very universal privilege in this country of possessing two wives,
evidently became jealous of all the attention paid to his young
wife; and, after a consultation with his naked beauties, was
paddled away by them.

Some of the Fuegians plainly showed that they had a fair
notion of barter. I gave one man a large nail (a most valuable
present) without making any signs for a return; but he immediately picked out two fish, and handed them up on the point
of his spear. If any present was designed for one canoe, and it
fell near another, it was invariably given to the right owner. The
Fuegian boy, whom Mr. Low had on board, showed, by going
into the most violent passion, that he quite understood the re-
proach of being called a liar, which in truth he was. We were
this time, as on all former occasions, much surprised at the

little notice, or rather none whatever, which was taken of many things, the use of which must have been evident to the natives. Simple circumstances—such as the beauty of scarlet cloth or blue beads, the absence of women, our care in washing ourselves,—excited their admiration far more than any grand or complicated object, such as our ship. Bougainville has well remarked concerning these people, that they treat the "chef-d'œuvres de l'industrie humaine, comme ils traitent les loix de la nature et ses phénomènes."[13]

On the 5th of March, we anchored in the cove at Woollya, but we saw not a soul there. We were alarmed at this, for the natives in Ponsonby Sound showed by gestures, that there had been fighting; and we afterwards heard that the dreaded Oens men had made a descent. Soon a canoe, with a little flag flying, was seen approaching, with one of the men in it washing the paint off his face. This man was poor Jemmy,—now a thin haggard savage, with long disordered hair, and naked, except a bit of a blanket round his waist. We did not recognize him till he was close to us; for he was ashamed of himself, and turned his back to the ship. We had left him plump, fat, clean, and well dressed;—I never saw so complete and grievous a change. As soon however as he was clothed, and the first flurry was over, things wore a good appearance. He dined with Captain Fitz Roy, and ate his dinner as tidily as formerly. He told us he had "too much" (meaning enough) to eat, that he was not cold, that his relations were very good people, and that he did not wish to go back to England: in the evening we found out the cause of this great change in Jemmy's feelings, in the arrival of his young and nice-looking wife. With his usual good feeling, he brought two beautiful otter-skins for two of his best friends, and some spear-heads and arrows made with his own hands for the Captain. He said he had built a canoe for himself, and he boasted that he could talk a little of his own language! But it is a most singular fact, that he appears to have taught all his tribe some English: an old man spontaneously announced "Jemmy Button's wife." Jemmy had lost all his property. He told us that York Minster had built a large canoe, and with his wife Fuegia,[14] had several months since gone to his

---

[13] [Editor] "Masterworks of human industry as they treat the laws of nature and its phenomenon."

[14] [Darwin] Captain Sulivan, who, since his voyage in the *Beagle*, has been employed on the survey of the Falkland Islands, heard from a sealer in 1842 (?), that when in the western part of the

own country, and had taken farewell by an act of consummate villainy; he persuaded Jemmy and his mother to come with him, and then on the way deserted them by night, stealing every article of their property.

Jemmy went to sleep on shore, and in the morning returned, and remained on board till the ship got under weigh, which frightened his wife, who continued crying violently till he got into his canoe. He returned loaded with valuable property. Every soul on board was heartily sorry to shake hands with him for the last time. I do not now doubt that he will be as happy as, perhaps happier than, if he had never left his own country. Every one must sincerely hope that Captain Fitz Roy's noble hope may be fulfilled, of being rewarded for the many generous sacrifices which he made for these Fuegians, by some shipwrecked sailor being protected by the descendants of Jemmy Button and his tribe! When Jemmy reached the shore, he lighted a signal fire, and the smoke curled up, bidding us a last and long farewell, as the ship stood on her course into the open sea.[15]

The perfect equality among the individuals composing the Fuegian tribes, must for a long time retard their civilization. As we see those animals, whose instinct compels them to live in society and obey a chief, are most capable of improvement, so is it with the races of mankind. Whether we look at it as a cause or a consequence, the more civilized always have the most artificial governments. For instance, the inhabitants of Otaheite, who, when first discovered, were governed by hereditary kings, had arrived at a far higher grade than another

---

Strait of Magellan, he was astonished by a native woman coming on board, who could talk some English. Without doubt this was Fuegia Basket. She lived (I fear the term probably bears a double interpretation) some days on board.

[15] [Editor] Bridges' *The Uttermost Part of the Earth* records the further history of the three Fuegians left by the *Beagle* on Navarin Island. Jimmy Button, who had been so ingratiating aboard the ship, organized the massacre of a party of six missionaries who attempted to found a settlement at Wulaia in 1859. Neither he nor the other participants, however, ever suffered reprisals; the Falkland Island missionaries persuaded the British government to forego a "punitive" expedition. York Minster was killed in retaliation for the killing of another Fuegian. Fuegia Basket, his wife, remarried and was last seen, ill and near her end, by the Rev. Thomas Bridges—Lucas Bridges' father—in 1883, at which time she was about 62 years old.

branch of the same people, the New Zealanders,—who, although benefited by being compelled to turn their attention to agriculture, were republicans in the most absolute sense. In Tierra del Fuego, until some chief shall arise with power sufficient to secure any acquired advantage, such as the domesticated animals, it seems scarcely possible that the political state of the country can be improved. At present, even a piece of cloth given to one is torn into shreds and distributed; and no one individual becomes richer than another. On the other hand, it is difficult to understand how a chief can arise till there is property of some sort by which he might manifest his superiority and increase his power.

I believe, in this extreme part of South America, man exists in a lower state of improvement than in any other part of the world. The South Sea Islanders of the two races inhabiting the Pacific, are comparatively civilized. The Esquimaux, in his subterranean hut, enjoys some of the comforts of life, and in his canoe, when fully equipped, manifests much skill. Some of the tribes of Southern Africa, prowling about in search of roots, and living concealed on the wild and arid plains, are sufficiently wretched. The Australian, in the simplicity of the arts of life, comes nearest the Fuegian: he can, however, boast of his boomerang, his spear and throwing-stick, his method of climbing trees, of tracking animals, and of hunting. Although the Australian may be superior in acquirements, it by no means follows that he is likewise superior in mental capacity: indeed, from what I saw of the Fuegians when on board, and from what I have read of the Australians, I should think the case was exactly the reverse.

CHAPTER XI

STRAIT OF MAGELLAN — CLIMATE OF THE SOUTHERN COASTS

Strait of Magellan — Port Famine — Ascent of Mount Tarn — Forests — Edible Fungus — Zoology — Great Sea-weed — Leave Tierra del Fuego — Climate — Fruit Trees and Productions of the Southern Coasts — Height of Snow-line on the Cordillera — Descent of Glaciers to the Sea — Icebergs formed — Transportal of Boulders — Climate and Productions of the Antarctic Islands — Preservation of Frozen Carcasses — Recapitulation

In the end of May, 1834,[1] we entered for the second time the eastern mouth of the Strait of Magellan. The country on both sides of this part of the Strait consists of nearly level plains, like those of Patagonia. Cape Negro, a little within the second Narrows, may be considered as the point where the land begins to assume the marked features of Tierra del Fuego. On the east coast, south of the Strait, broken park-like scenery in a like manner connects these two countries, which are opposed to each other in almost every feature. It is truly surprising to find in a space of twenty miles such a change in the landscape. If we take a rather greater distance, as between Port Famine and Gregory Bay, that is about sixty miles, the difference is still more wonderful. At the former place, we have rounded mountains concealed by impervious forests, which are drenched with the rain, brought by an endless succession of gales; while at Cape Gregory, there is a clear and bright blue sky over the dry and sterile plains. The atmospheric currents,[2]

[1] [Editor] Darwin and the *Beagle* entered the Strait of Magellan for the first time in January, 1834, en route to their second visit to Tierra del Fuego and Beagle Channel.

[2] [Darwin] The south-westerly breezes are generally very dry. January 29th, being at anchor under Cape Gregory: a very hard

although rapid, turbulent, and unconfined by any apparent limits, yet seem to follow, like a river in its bed, a regularly determined course.

During our previous visit (in January), we had an interview at Cape Gregory with the famous so-called gigantic Patagonians, who gave us a cordial reception. Their height appears greater than it really is, from their large guanaco mantles, their long flowing hair, and general figure: on an average their height is about six feet, with some men taller and only a few shorter; and the women are also tall; altogether they are certainly the tallest race which we anywhere saw. In features they strikingly resemble the more northern Indians whom I saw with Rosas, but they have a wilder and more formidable appearance: their faces were much painted with red and black, and one man was ringed and dotted with white like a Fuegian. Capt. Fitz Roy offered to take any three of them on board, and all seemed determined to be of the three. It was long before we could clear the boat; at last we got on board with our three giants, who dined with the Captain, and behaved quite like gentlemen, helping themselves with knives, forks, and spoons: nothing was so much relished as sugar. This tribe has had so much communication with sealers and whalers, that most of the men can speak a little English and Spanish; and they are half civilized, and proportionally demoralised.

The next morning a large party went on shore, to barter for skins and ostrich-feathers; fire-arms being refused, tobacco was in greatest request, far more so than axes or tools. The whole population of the toldos, men, women, and children, were arranged on a bank. It was an amusing scene, and it was impossible not to like the so-called giants, they were so thoroughly good-humoured and unsuspecting: they asked us to come again. They seem to like to have Europeans to live with them; and old Maria, an important woman in the tribe, once begged Mr. Low to leave any one of his sailors with them. They spend the greater part of the year here; but in summer they hunt along the foot of the Cordillera: sometimes they travel as far as the Rio Negro, 750 miles to the north. They are well stocked

---

gale from W. by S., clear sky with few cumuli; temperature 57°, dew-point 36°,—difference, 21°. On January 15th, at Port St. Julian: in the morning light winds with much rain, followed by a very heavy squall with rain,—settled into heavy gale with large cumuli, —cleared up, blowing very strong from S.S.W. Temperature 60°, dew-point 42°,—difference 18°.

with horses, each man having, according to Mr. Low, six or seven, and all the women, and even children, their one own horse. In the time of Sarmiento[3] (1580), these Indians had bows and arrows, now long since disused; they then also possessed some horses. This is a very curious fact, showing the extraordinarily rapid multiplication of horses in South America. The horse was first landed at Buenos Ayres in 1537, and the colony being then for a time deserted, the horse ran wild;[4] in 1580, only forty-three years afterwards, we hear of them at the Strait of Magellan! Mr. Low informs me, that a neighbouring tribe of foot-Indians is now changing into horse-Indians: the tribe at Gregory Bay giving them their worn-out horses, and sending in winter a few of their best skilled men to hunt for them.

June 1st.—We anchored in the fine bay of Port Famine. It was now the beginning of winter, and I never saw a more cheerless prospect; the dusky woods, piebald with snow, could be only seen indistinctly through a drizzling hazy atmosphere. We were, however, lucky in getting two fine days. On one of these, Mount Sarmiento, a distant mountain 6800 feet high, presented a very noble spectacle. I was frequently surprised, in the scenery of Tierra del Fuego, at the little apparent elevation of mountains really lofty. I suspect it is owing to a cause which would not at first be imagined, namely, that the whole mass, from the summit to the water's edge, is generally in full view. I remember having seen a mountain, first from the Beagle Channel, where the whole sweep from the summit to the base was full in view, and then from Ponsonby Sound across several successive ridges; and it was curious to observe in the latter case, as each fresh ridge afforded fresh means of judging of the distance, how the mountain rose in height.

Before reaching Port Famine, two men were seen running along the shore and hailing the ship. A boat was sent for them. They turned out to be two sailors who had run away from a sealing-vessel, and had joined the Patagonians. These Indians had treated them with their usual disinterested hospitality.

---

[3] [Editor] Pedro Sarmiento de Gambra, born in Spain about 1530, died after 1589, Spanish navigator and explorer. Best known for his careful exploration of southwestern Patagonia and his unsuccessful attempt to plant a colony on the Strait of Magellan. This was San Felipe, the settlement dubbed Port Famine by Cavendish.

[4] [Darwin] Rengger, Natur. der Saeugethiere von Paraguay. S. 334.

They had parted company through accident, and were then proceeding to Port Famine in hopes of finding some ship. I dare say they were worthless vagabonds, but I never saw more miserable-looking ones. They had been living for some days on mussel-shells and berries, and their tattered clothes had been burnt by sleeping so near their fires. They had been exposed night and day, without any shelter, to the late incessant gales, with rain, sleet, and snow, and yet they were in good health.

During our stay at Port Famine, the Fuegians twice came and plagued us. As there were many instruments, clothes, and men on shore, it was thought necessary to frighten them away. The first time a few great guns were fired, when they were far distant. It was most ludicrous to watch through a glass the Indians, as often as the shot struck the water, take up stones, and as a bold defiance, throw them towards the ship, though about a mile and a half distant! A boat was then sent with orders to fire a few musket-shots wide of them. The Fuegians hid themselves behind the trees, and for every discharge of the muskets they fired their arrows; all, however, fell short of the boat, and the officer as he pointed at them laughed. This made the Fuegians frantic with passion, and they shook their mantles in vain rage. At last, seeing the balls cut and strike the trees, they ran away, and we were left in peace and quietness. During the former voyage the Fuegians were here very troublesome, and to frighten them a rocket was fired at night over their wigwams: it answered effectually, and one of the officers told me that the clamour first raised, and the barking of the dogs, was quite ludicrous in contrast with the profound silence which in a minute or two afterwards prevailed. The next morning not a single Fuegian was in the neighbourhood.

When the *Beagle* was here in the month of February, I started one morning at four o'clock to ascend Mount Tarn, which is 2600 feet high, and is the most elevated point in this immediate district. We went in a boat to the foot of the mountain (but unluckily not to the best part), and then began our ascent. The forest commences at the line of high-water mark, and during the first two hours I gave over all hopes of reaching the summit. So thick was the wood, that it was necessary to have constant recourse to the compass; for every landmark, though in a mountainous country, was completely shut out. In the deep ravines, the death-like scene of desolation exceeded all description; outside it was blowing a gale, but in these hollows, not even a breath of wind stirred the leaves of the tallest trees. So gloomy, cold, and wet was every part, that not even the fungi, mosses, or ferns could flourish. In the valleys it was scarcely possible to crawl along, they were so completely barricaded by great mouldering trunks, which had fallen down in every direction. When passing over these natural bridges, one's course was often arrested by sinking knee deep into the rotten wood; at other times, when attempting to lean against a firm tree, one was startled by finding a mass of decayed matter ready to fall at the slightest touch. We at last found ourselves among the stunted trees, and then soon reached the bare ridge, which conducted us to the summit. Here was a view characteristic of Tierra del Fuego; irregular chains of hills, mottled with patches of snow, deep yellowish-green valleys, and arms of the sea intersecting the land in many directions. The strong wind was piercingly cold, and the atmosphere rather hazy, so that we did not stay long on the top of the mountain. Our descent was not quite so laborious as our ascent; for the weight of the body forced a passage, and all the slips and falls were in the right direction.

I have already mentioned the sombre and dull character of the evergreen forests,[5] in which two or three species of trees grow, to the exclusion of all others. Above the forest land, there are many dwarf alpine plants, which all spring from the mass of peat, and help to compose it: these plants are very remarkable from their close alliance with the species growing on the mountains of Europe, though so many thousand miles distant. The central part of Tierra del Fuego, where the clay-slate formation occurs, is most favourable to the growth of trees; on the outer coast the poorer granitic soil, and a situation more exposed to the violent winds, do not allow of their attaining any great size. Near Port Famine I have seen more large trees than anywhere else: I measured a Winter's Bark which was four feet six inches in girth, and several of the beech

---

[5] [Darwin] Captain Fitz Roy informs me that in April (our October), the leaves of those trees which grow near the base of the mountains, change colour, but not those on the more elevated parts. I remember having read some observations, showing that in England the leaves fall earlier in a warm and fine autumn, than in a late and cold one. The change in the colour being here retarded in the more elevated, and therefore colder situations, must be owing to the same general law of vegetation. The trees of Tierra del Fuego during no part of the year entirely shed their leaves.

were as much as thirteen feet. Captain King also mentions a beech which was seven feet in diameter seventeen feet above the roots.

There is one vegetable production deserving notice from its importance as an article of food to the Fuegians. It is a globular, bright-yellow fungus, which grows in vast numbers on the beech-trees. When young it is elastic and turgid, with a smooth surface; but when mature, it shrinks, becomes tougher, and has its entire surface deeply pitted or honey-combed, as represented in the accompanying wood-cut. This fungus belongs to

a new and curious genus;[6] I found a second species on another species of beech in Chile; and Dr. Hooker informs me, that just lately a third species has been discovered on a third species of beech in Van Diemen's Land. How singular is this relationship between parasitical fungi and the trees on which they grow, in distant parts of the world! In Tierra del Fuego the fungus in its tough and mature state is collected in large quantities by the women and children, and is eaten uncooked. It has a mucilaginous, slightly sweet taste, with a faint smell

[6] [Darwin] Described from my specimens, and notes by the Rev. J. M. Berkeley, in the Linnean Transactions (vol. xix. p. 37), under the name of Cyttaria Darwinii: the Chilian species is the C. Berteroii. This genus is allied to Bulgaria.

like that of a mushroom. With the exception of a few berries, chiefly of a dwarf arbutus, the natives eat no vegetable food besides this fungus. In New Zealand, before the introduction of the potato, the roots of the fern were largely consumed; at the present time, I believe, Tierra del Fuego is the only country in the world where a cryptogamic plant affords a staple article of food.

The zoology of Tierra del Fuego, as might have been expected from the nature of its climate and vegetation, is very poor. Of mammalia, besides whales and seals, there is one bat, a kind of mouse (Reithrodon chinchilloides), two true mice, a ctenomys allied to or identical with the tucutuco, two foxes (Canis Magellanicus and C. Azaræ), a sea-otter, the guanaco, and a deer. Most of these animals inhabit only the drier eastern parts of the country; and the deer has never been seen south of the Strait of Magellan. Observing the general correspondence of the cliffs of soft sandstone, mud, and shingle, on the opposite sides of the Strait, and on some intervening islands, one is strongly tempted to believe that the land was once joined, and thus allowed animals so delicate and helpless as the tucutuco and Reithrodon to pass over. The correspondence of the cliffs is far from proving any junction; because such cliffs generally are formed by the intersection of sloping deposits, which, before the elevation of the land, had been accumulated near the then existing shores. It is, however, a remarkable coincidence, that in the two large islands cut off by the Beagle Channel from the rest of Tierra del Fuego, one has cliffs composed of matter that may be called stratified alluvium, which front similar ones on the opposite side of the channel,—while the other is exclusively bordered by old crystalline rocks: in the former, called Navarin Island, both foxes and guanacos occur; but in the latter, Hoste Island, although similar in every respect, and only separated by a channel a little more than half a mile wide, I have the word of Jemmy Button for saying, that neither of these animals are found.

The gloomy woods are inhabited by few birds: occasionally the plaintive note of a white-tufted tyrant-flycatcher (Myiobius albiceps) may be heard, concealed near the summit of the most lofty trees; and more rarely the loud strange cry of a black woodpecker, with a fine scarlet crest on its head. A little, dusky-coloured wren (Scytalopus Magellanicus) hops in a skulking manner among the entangled mass of the fallen and decaying trunks. But the creeper (Oxyurus tupinieri) is the commonest bird in the country. Throughout the beech forests,

high up and low down, in the most gloomy, wet, and impenetrable ravines, it may be met with. This little bird no doubt
appears more numerous than it really is, from its habit of
following with seeming curiosity any person who enters these
silent woods: continually uttering a harsh twitter, it flutters
from tree to tree, within a few feet of the intruder's face. It is
far from wishing for the modest concealment of the true
creeper (Certhia familiaris); nor does it, like that bird, run
up the trunks of trees, but industriously, after the manner of
a willow-wren, hops about, and searches for insects on every
twig and branch. In the more open parts, three or four species
of finches, a thrush, a starling (or Icterus), two Opetiorhynchi,
and several hawks and owls occur.

The absence of any species whatever in the whole class of
Reptiles, is a marked feature in the zoology of this country,
as well as in that of the Falkland Islands. I do not ground this
statement merely on my own observation, but I heard it from
the Spanish inhabitants of the latter place, and from Jemmy
Button with regard to Tierra del Fuego. On the banks of the
Santa Cruz, in 50° south, I saw a frog; and it is not improbable
that these animals, as well as lizards, may be found as far
south as the Strait of Magellan, where the country retains the
character of Patagonia; but within the damp and cold limit of
Tierra del Fuego not one occurs. That the climate would not
have suited some of the orders, such as lizards, might have
been foreseen; but with respect to frogs, this was not so
obvious.

Beetles occur in very small numbers: it was long before I
could believe that a country as large as Scotland, covered with
vegetable productions, and with a variety of stations, could be
so unproductive. The few which I found were alpine species
(Harpalidæ and Heteromidæ) living under stones. The vege-
table-feeding Chrysomelidæ, so eminently characteristic of the
Tropics, are here almost entirely absent;[7] I saw very few flies,

---

[7] [Darwin] I believe I must except one alpine Haltica, and a
single specimen of a Melasoma. Mr. Waterhouse informs me, that
of the Harpalidæ there are eight or nine species—the forms of the
greater number being very peculiar; of Heteromera, four or five
species; of Rhyncophora six or seven; and of the following families
one species in each: Staphylinidæ, Elateridæ, Cebrionidæ, Melo-
lonthidæ. The species in the other orders are even fewer. In all
the orders, the scarcity of the individuals is even more remarkable
than that of the species. Most of the Coleoptera have been carefully described by Mr. Waterhouse in the Annals of Nat. Hist.

butterflies, or bees, and no crickets or Orthoptera. In the pools of water I found but few aquatic beetles, and not any fresh-water shells: Succinea[8] at first appears an exception; but here it must be called a terrestrial shell, for it lives on the damp herbage far from water. Land-shells could be procured only in the same alpine situations with the beetles. I have already contrasted the climate as well as the general appearance of Tierra del Fuego with that of Patagonia; and the difference is strongly exemplified in the entomology. I do not believe they have one species in common; certainly the general character of the insects is widely different.

If we turn from the land to the sea, we shall find the latter as abundantly stocked with living creatures as the former is poorly so. In all parts of the world a rocky and partially protected shore perhaps supports, in a given space, a greater number of individual animals than any other station. There is one marine production, which from its importance is worthy of a particular history. It is the kelp, or Macrocystis pyrifera. This plant grows on every rock from low-water mark to a great depth, both on the outer coast and within the channels.[9] I believe, during the voyages of the *Adventure* and *Beagle,* not one rock near the surface was discovered which was not buoyed by this floating weed. The good service it thus affords to vessels navigating near this stormy land is evident; and it certainly has saved many a one from being wrecked. I know few things more surprising than to see this plant growing and flourishing amidst those great breakers of the western ocean, which no mass of rock, let it be ever so hard, can long resist. The stem is round, slimy, and smooth, and seldom has a diameter of so much as an inch. A few taken together are sufficiently strong to support the weight of the large loose stones, to which in the inland channels they grow attached; and yet some of these stones were so heavy that when drawn to the surface, they could scarcely be lifted into a boat by one person. Captain

---

[8] [Editor] A variety of snail.

[9] [Darwin] Its geographical range is remarkably wide; it is found from the extreme southern islets near Cape Horn, as far north on the eastern coast (according to information given me by Mr. Stokes) as lat. 43°,—but on the western coast, as Dr. Hooker tells me, it extends to the R. San Francisco in California, and perhaps even to Kamtschatka. We thus have an immense range in latitude; and as Cook, who must have been well acquainted with the species, found it at Kerguelen Land, no less than 140° in longitude.

Cook, in his second voyage, says, that this plant at Kerguelen Land rises from a greater depth than twenty-four fathoms; "and as it does not grow in a perpendicular direction, but makes a very acute angle with the bottom, and much of it afterwards spreads many fathoms on the surface of the sea, I am well warranted to say that some of it grows to the length of sixty fathoms and upwards." I do not suppose the stem of any other plant attains so great a length as three hundred and sixty feet, as stated by Captain Cook. Captain Fitz Roy, moreover, found it growing[10] up from the greater depth of forty-five fathoms. The beds of this sea-weed, even when of not great breadth, make excellent natural floating breakwaters. It is quite curious to see, in an exposed harbour, how soon the waves from the open sea, as they travel through the straggling stems, sink in height, and pass into smooth water.

The number of living creatures of all Orders, whose existence intimately depends on the kelp, is wonderful. A great volume might be written, describing the inhabitants of one of these beds of sea-weed. Almost all the leaves, excepting those that float on the surface, are so thickly incrusted with corallines as to be of a white colour. We find exquisitely delicate structures, some inhabited by simple hydra-like polypi, others by more organized kinds, and beautiful compound Ascidiæ. On the leaves, also, various patelliform shells, Trochi, uncovered molluscs, and some bivalves are attached. Innumerable crustacea frequent every part of the plant. On shaking the great entangled roots, a pile of small fish, shells, cuttle-fish, crabs of all orders, sea-eggs, star-fish, beautiful Holuthuriæ, Planariæ, and crawling nereidous animals of a multitude of forms, all fall out together. Often as I recurred to a branch of the kelp, I never failed to discover animals of new and curious structures. In Chiloe, where the kelp does not thrive very well, the numerous shells, corallines, and crustacea are absent; but there yet remain a few of the Flustraceæ, and some compound Ascidiæ; the latter, however, are of different species from those in Tierra del Fuego: we here see the fucus possessing a

[10] [Darwin] Voyages of the *Adventure* and *Beagle,* vol. i. p. 363. —It appears that sea-weed grows extremely quick. Mr. Stephenson found (Wilson's Voyage round Scotland, vol. ii. p. 228) that a rock uncovered only at spring-tides, which had been chiselled smooth in November, on the following May, that is within six months afterwards, was thickly covered with Fucus digitatus two feet, and F. esculentus six feet, in length.

wider range than the animals which use it as an abode. I can only compare these great aquatic forests of the southern hemisphere, with the terrestrial ones in the inter-tropical regions. Yet if in any country a forest was destroyed, I do not believe nearly so many species of animals would perish as would here, from the destruction of the kelp. Amidst the leaves of this plant numerous species of fish live, which nowhere else could find food or shelter; with their destruction the many cormorants and other fishing birds, the otters, seals, and porpoises, would soon perish also; and lastly, the Fuegian savage, the miserable lord of this miserable land, would redouble his cannibal feast, decrease in numbers, and perhaps cease to exist.

June 8th.—We weighed anchor early in the morning and left Port Famine. Captain Fitz Roy determined to leave the Strait of Magellan by the Magdalen Channel, which had not long been discovered. Our course lay due south, down that gloomy passage which I have before alluded to, as appearing to lead to another and worse world. The wind was fair, but the atmosphere was very thick; so that we missed much curious scenery. The dark ragged clouds were rapidly driven over the mountains, from their summits nearly down to their bases. The glimpses which we caught through the dusky mass, were highly interesting; jagged points, cones of snow, blue glaciers, strong outlines, marked on a lurid sky, were seen at different distances and heights. In the midst of such scenery we anchored at Cape Turn, close to Mount Sarmiento, which was then hidden in the clouds. At the base of the lofty and almost perpendicular sides of our little cove there was one deserted wigwam, and it alone reminded us that man sometimes wandered into these desolate regions. But it would be difficult to imagine a scene where he seemed to have fewer claims or less authority. The inanimate works of nature—rock, ice, snow, wind, and water —all warring with each other, yet combined against man—here reigned in absolute sovereignty.

June 9th.—In the morning we were delighted by seeing the veil of mist gradually rise from Sarmiento, and display it to our view. This mountain, which is one of the highest in Tierra del Fuego, has an altitude of 6800 feet. Its base, for about an eighth of its total height, is clothed by dusky woods, and above this a field of snow extends to the summit. These vast piles of snow, which never melt, and seem destined to last as long as the world holds together, present a noble and even sublime spectacle. The outline of the mountain was admirably clear and defined. Owing to the abundance of light reflected from the white and glittering surface, no shadows were cast on any part; and those lines which intersected the sky could alone be distinguished: hence the mass stood out in the boldest relief. Several glaciers descended in a winding course from the upper great expanse of snow to the sea-coast: they may be likened to great frozen Niagaras; and perhaps these cataracts of blue ice are full as beautiful as the moving ones of water. By night we reached the western part of the channel; but the water was so deep that no anchorage could be found. We were in consequence obliged to stand off and on in this narrow arm of the sea, during a pitch-dark night of fourteen hours long.

June 10*th*.—In the morning we made the best of our way into the open Pacific. The Western coast generally consists of low, rounded, quite barren hills of granite and greenstone. Sir J. Narborough called one part South Desolation, because it is "so desolate a land to behold:" and well indeed might he say so. Outside the main islands, there are numberless scattered rocks on which the long swell of the open ocean incessantly rages. We passed out between the East and West Furies; and a little farther northward there are so many breakers that the sea is called the Milky Way. One sight of such a coast is enough to make a landsman dream for a week about shipwrecks, peril, and death; and with this sight we bade farewell for ever to Tierra del Fuego.

The following discussion on the climate of the southern parts of the continent with relation to its productions, on the snow-line, on the extraordinarily low descent of the glaciers, and on the zone of perpetual congelation in the antarctic islands, may be passed over by any one not interested in these curious subjects, or the final recapitulation alone may be read. I shall, however, here give only an abstract, and must refer for details to the Thirteenth Chapter and the Appendix of the former edition of this work.

On the Climate and Productions of Tierra del Fuego and of the South-west Coast.—The following table gives the mean temperature of Tierra del Fuego, the Falkland Islands, and, for comparison, that of Dublin:—

	Latitude.	Summer Temp.	Winter Temp.	Mean of Summer and Winter.
Tierra del Fuego .	. 53° 38′S.	50°	33°.08	41°.54
Falkland Islands .	. 51 30 S.	51	—	—
Dublin	. 53 21 N.	59 .54	39 .2	49 .37

Hence we see that the central part of Tierra del Fuego is colder
in winter, and no less than $9\frac{1}{2}°$ less hot in summer, than Dublin. According to Von Buch the mean temperature of July (not
the hottest month in the year) at Saltenfiord in Norway, is as
high as $57°.8$, and this place is actually $13°$ nearer the pole
than Port Famine![11] Inhospitable as this climate appears to our
feelings, evergreen trees flourish luxuriantly under it. Humming-birds may be seen sucking the flowers, and parrots feeding on the seeds of the Winter's Bark, in lat. $55°$ S. I have
already remarked to what a degree the sea swarms with living
creatures; and the shells (such as the Patellæ, Fissurellæ,
Chitons, and Barnacles), according to Mr. G. B. Sowerby, are
of a much larger size, and of a more vigorous growth, than the
analogous species in the northern hemisphere. A large Voluta
is abundant in southern Tierra del Fuego and the Falkland Islands. At Bahia Blanca, in lat. $39°$ S., the most abundant shells
were three species of Oliva (one of large size), one or two
Volutas, and a Terebra. Now these are amongst the best characterized tropical forms. It is doubtful whether even one small
species of Oliva exists on the southern shores of Europe, and
there are no species of the two other genera. If a geologist were
to find in lat. $39°$ on the coast of Portugal, a bed containing
numerous shells belonging to three species of Oliva, to a Voluta
and Terebra, he would probably assert that the climate at the
period of their existence must have been tropical; but judging
from South America, such an inference might be erroneous.

The equable, humid, and windy climate of Tierra del Fuego
extends, with only a small increase of heat, for many degrees
along the west coast of the continent. The forests, for 600
miles northward of Cape Horn, have a very similar aspect.
As a proof of the equable climate, even for 300 or 400 miles
still further northward, I may mention that in Chiloe (corresponding in latitude with the northern parts of Spain) the peach
seldom produces fruit, whilst strawberries and apples thrive

[11] [Darwin] With respect to Tierra del Fuego, the results are
deduced from the observations by Capt. King (Geographical Journal, 1830), and those taken on board the *Beagle*. For the Falkland
Islands, I am indebted to Capt. Sulivan for the mean of the mean
temperature (reduced from careful observation at midnight, 8 A.M.,
noon, and 8 P.M.) of the three hottest months, viz. December, January, and February. The temperature of Dublin is taken from
Barton.

to perfection. Even the crops of barley and wheat[12] are often brought into the houses to be dried and ripened. At Valdivia (in the same latitude of 40°, with Madrid) grapes and figs ripen, but are not common; olives seldom ripen even partially, and oranges not at all. These fruits, in corresponding latitudes in Europe, are well known to succeed to perfection; and even in this continent, at the Rio Negro, under nearly the same parallel with Valdivia, sweet potatoes (convolvulus) are cultivated; and grapes, figs, olives, oranges, water and musk melons, produce abundant fruit. Although the humid and equable climate of Chiloe, and of the coast northward and southward of it, is so unfavourable to our fruits, yet the native forests, from lat. 45° to 38°, almost rival in luxuriance those of the glowing intertropical regions. Stately trees of many kinds, with smooth and highly coloured barks, are loaded by parasitical monocotyledonous plants; large and elegant ferns are numerous, and arborescent grasses intwine the trees into one entangled mass to the height of thirty or forty feet above the ground. Palmtrees grow in lat. 37°; an arborescent grass, very like a bamboo, in 40°; and another closely allied kind, of great length, but not erect, flourishes even as far south as 45° S.

An equable climate, evidently due to the large area of sea compared with the land, seems to extend over the greater part of the southern hemisphere; and as a consequence, the vegetation partakes of a semi-tropical character. Tree-ferns thrive luxuriantly in Van Diemen's Land (lat. 45°), and I measured one trunk no less than six feet in circumference. An arborescent fern was found by Forster in New Zealand in 46°, where orchideous plants are parasitical on the trees. In the Auckland Islands,[13] ferns, according to Dr. Dieffenbach,[14] have trunks so thick and high that they may be almost called tree-ferns; and in these islands, and even as far south as lat. 55° in the Macquarrie Islands, parrots abound.

On the Height of the Snow-line, and on the Descent of the

[12] [Darwin] Agüeros, Descrip. Hist. de la Prov. de Chiloe, 1791, p. 94.

[13] [Editor] A group of small islands south of New Zealand and a political dependency of New Zealand. Macquarrie Island, mentioned a few lines farther on, is an Australian dependency in the Antarctic southeast of Australia.

[14] [Darwin] See the German Translation of this Journal: and for the other facts Mr. Brown's Appendix to Flinders's Voyage.

Glaciers, in South America.—For the detailed authorities for the following table, I must refer to the former edition:—

Latitude.	Height in feet of Snow-line.	Observer.
Equatorial region; mean result	15,748	Humboldt.
Bolivia, lat. 16° to 18° S.	17,000	Pentland.
Central Chile, lat. 33° S.	14,500 to 15,000	Gillies, and the Author.
Chiloe, lat. 41° to 43° S.	6,000	Officers of the *Beagle*, and the Author.
Tierra del Fuego, 54° S.	3,500 to 4,000	King.

As the height of the plane of perpetual snow seems chiefly to be determined by the extreme heat of the summer, rather than by the mean temperature of the year, we ought not to be surprised at its descent in the Strait of Magellan, where the summer is so cool, to only 3500 or 4000 feet above the level of the sea; although in Norway, we must travel to between lat. 67° and 70° N., that is, about 14° nearer the pole, to meet with perpetual snow at this low level. The difference in height, namely, about 9000 feet, between the snow-line on the Cordillera behind Chiloe (with its highest points ranging from only 5600 to 7500 feet) and in central Chile[15] (a distance of only 9° of latitude), is truly wonderful. The land from the southward of Chiloe to near Concepcion (lat. 37°), is hidden by one dense forest dripping with moisture. The sky is cloudy, and we have seen how badly the fruits of southern Europe succeed. In central Chile, on the other hand, a little northward of Concepcion, the sky is generally clear, rain does not fall for the seven summer months, and southern European fruits succeed admirably; and even the sugar-cane has been cultivated.[16] No doubt the plane of perpetual snow undergoes the above remarkable flexure of 9000 feet, unparalleled in other parts of the world, not far from the latitude of Concepcion, where the

[15] [Darwin] On the Cordillera of central Chile, I believe the snow-line varies exceedingly in height in different summers. I was assured that during one very dry and long summer, all the snow disappeared from Aconcagua, although it attains the prodigious height of 23,000 feet. It is probable that much of the snow at these great heights is evaporated, rather than thawed.

[16] [Darwin] Miers's Chile, vol. i. p. 415. It is said that the sugar-cane grew at Ingenio, lat. 32° to 33°, but not in sufficient quantity to make the manufacture profitable. In the valley of Quillota, south of Ingenio, I saw some large date palm-trees.

PLATE 1a: A reproduction from a drawing of unknown origin found by Prof. Seward in a portfolio of Darwin relics in the cellar of the Cambridge Botany School of 1929. Almost identical with the George Richmond water-color drawing of 1840, and probably a preliminary sketch. It shows Darwin still as a young man, only four years after the return of the *Beagle* (from *Charles Darwin's Diary of the Voyage of H.M.S. Beagle*, ed. by Nora Barlow, Cambridge University Press, 1933).

PLATE 1b: Robert FitzRoy, captain of the *Beagle* (1831-36). Courtesy of the Royal Naval College, Greenwich, England. *Credit: The American Museum of Natural History.*

PLATE 2: H.M.S. BEAGLE in the Straits of Magellan (from Order of the Proceedings at the Darwin Celebration, Cambridge, 1909). *Credit: The American Museum of Natural History.*

PLATE 3: H.M.S. BEAGLE. Model by Lois Darling.
Credit: Lee Bolton.

PLATE 4: Darwin's Finches. Arranged to show the evolutionary tree in their development. *Credit: The American Museum of Natural History.*

PLATE 5: Peppered Moths. Showing protective coloration.
Credit: *The American Museum of Natural History*.

PLATE 6. Darwin's Study at Down House.
Credit: *The American Museum of Natural History*.

Copiapó
Guasco
Coquimbo
Illapel (8)
Quillota   Uspallata Pass
Valparaíso   Mendoza (7)
Santiago
Curico   Portillo Pass

Concepcion
Arauco

Valdivia

(6) S. Carlos
I. CHILOE Castro
Cucao
Chonos
Archipelago

C. Tres
Montes

Port Desire R. Port Desire

R.
Santa Cruz (5)

FALKLAND
IS.

C. Virgins
Str. of Magellan
TIERRA DEL FUEGO
Beagle Ch.
HOSTE I. NAVARIN I. STATEN I.
Str. Le Maire
False Cape Horn Cape Horn

R. paraguay
R. Parana
Corrientes
R. Salado
R. Parana
R. Uruguay
Sta. Fé
Baiada de S. Fe or Parana
Rozario
St. Nicholas Mercedes
(3) (4) Las Minas
Buenos Ayres Maldonado
(2) R. Salado Monte Video
Tapalquen
Sa. Ventana
Argentino C. Corrientes
R. Sauce
(1)
R. Colorado Bahia Blanca
R. Negro
El Carmen or Patagones

Peninsula
de S. Josef

R. Chupat

Gulf of S. George

EIGHT PRINCIPAL
INLAND
EXPEDITIONS

1. El Carmen or Patagones-
   Bahia Blanca AUG. 11-17, 1833

2. Bahia Blanca-Buenos
   Ayres (400 mi.) SEPT. 8-20, 1833

3. Buenos Ayres-Sta Fé
   (nearly 300 mi.) SEPT. 27-OCT. 2, 1833
   (returned down the river)

4. Monte Video-Mercedes
   and return NOV. 14-28, 1833

5. Captain's expedition up
   Santa Cruz R. APR. 18-MAY 8, 1834

6. CHILOE. San Carlos-
   Castro-Cucao Castro-
   San Carlos JAN. 22-28, 1835

7. Valparaiso-Mendoza-
   Santiago MAR. 18-APR. 10, 1835

8. Valparaiso-Coquimbo-
   Copiapo (420 miles)
   APR. 27-JUNE 22, 1835

San Carlos
(Ancud)

Chiloe

Caylin
(Quilan)

CORCOVADO
GULF

Guayatecas I.
(Guaitecas)

Chonos
Archipelago

ADVENTURE BAY

DARWIN BAY

Taitao
Peninsula

Peninsula
Tres Montes

0   50   100
MILES

Chiloe

Tierra del Fuego

Horsburgh I

Port Refuge

Direction I.

Prison I⊙

Clunie I.

Water I.

SOUTH KEELING ISLANDS

Gooseberry I.

Ross I.

Selima or Fairlee or South-east I.

Burial Islet

Keeling Islands

0   1   2   3
MILES

NORTH KEELING ISLAND

Wreck Pt.

North Keeling Island

96°54′45″E.

12°0′S.

South Keeling Islands

land ceases to be covered with forest-trees; for trees in South America indicate a rainy climate, and rain a clouded sky and little heat in summer.

The descent of glaciers to the sea must, I conceive, mainly depend (subject, of course, to a proper supply of snow in the upper region) on the lowness of the line of perpetual snow on steep mountains near the coast. As the snow-line is so low in Tierra del Fuego, we might have expected that many of the glaciers would have reached the sea. Nevertheless I was astonished when I first saw a range, only from 3000 to 4000 feet in height, in the latitude of Cumberland, with every valley filled with streams of ice descending to the sea-coast. Almost every arm of the sea, which penetrates to the interior higher chain, not only in Tierra del Fuego, but on the coast for 650 miles northwards, is terminated by "tremendous and astonishing glaciers," as described by one of the officers on the survey. Great masses of ice frequently fall from these icy cliffs, and the crash reverberates like the broadside of a man-of-war, through the lonely channels. These falls, as noticed in the last chapter, produce great waves which break on the adjoining coasts. It is known that earthquakes frequently cause masses of earth to fall from sea-cliffs: how terrific, then, would be the effect of a severe shock (and such occur here[17]) on a body like a glacier, already in motion, and traversed by fissures! I can readily believe that the water would be fairly beaten back out of the deepest channel, and then returning with an overwhelming force, would whirl about huge masses of rock like so much chaff. In Eyre's Sound, in the latitude of Paris, there are immense glaciers, and yet the loftiest neighbouring mountain is only 6200 feet high. In this Sound, about fifty icebergs were seen at one time floating outwards, and one of them must have been *at least* 168 feet in total height. Some of the icebergs were loaded with blocks of no inconsiderable size, of granite and other rocks, different from the clay-slate of the surrounding mountains. The glacier furthest from the Pole, surveyed during the voyages of the *Adventure* and *Beagle,* is in lat. 46° 50′, in the Gulf of Penas. It is 15 miles long, and in one part 7 broad, and descends to the sea-coast. But even a few miles northward of this glacier, in the Laguna de San Rafael, some Spanish missionaries[18] encountered "many icebergs, some

17 [Darwin] Bulkeley's and Cummin's Faithful Narrative of the Loss of the *Wager.* The earthquake happened August 25, 1741.

18 [Darwin] Agüeros, Desc. Hist. de Chiloe, p. 227.

great, some small, and others middle-sized," in a narrow arm of the sea, on the 22nd of the month corresponding with our June, and in a latitude corresponding with that of the Lake of Geneva!

In Europe, the most southern glacier which comes down to the sea is met with, according to Von Buch, on the coast of Norway, in lat. 67°. Now this is more than 20° of latitude, or 1230 miles, nearer the pole than the Laguna de San Rafael. The position of the glaciers at this place and in the Gulf of Penas, may be put even in a more striking point of view, for they descend to the sea-coast, within 7½° of latitude, or 450 miles, of a harbour, where three species of Oliva, a Voluta, and a Terebra, are the commonest shells, within less than 9° from where palms grow, within 4½° of a region where the jaguar and puma range over the plains, less than 2½° from arborescent grasses, and (looking to the westward in the same hemisphere) less than 2° from orchideous parasites, and within a single degree of tree-ferns!

These facts are of high geological interest with respect to the climate of the northern hemisphere, at the period when boulders were transported. I will not here detail how simply the theory of icebergs being charged with fragments of rock, explains the origin and position of the gigantic boulders of eastern Tierra del Fuego, on the high plain of Santa Cruz, and on the island of Chiloe. In Tierra del Fuego, the greater number of boulders lie on the lines of old sea-channels, now converted into dry valleys by the elevation of the land. They are associated with a great unstratified formation of mud and sand, containing rounded and angular fragments of all sizes, which has originated[19] in the repeated ploughing up of the sea-bottom by the stranding of icebergs, and by the matter transported on them. Few geologists now doubt that those erratic boulders which lie near lofty mountains, have been pushed forward by the glaciers themselves, and that those distant from mountains, and embedded in subaqueous deposits, have been conveyed thither either on icebergs, or frozen in coast-ice. The connexion between the transportal of boulders and the presence of ice in some form, is strikingly shown by their geographical distribution over the earth. In South America they are not found further than 48° of latitude, measured from the southern pole; in North America it appears that the limit of their transportal extends to 53½° from the northern pole; but in Europe to not more than 40° of latitude, measured from the same point. On the other hand, in the intertropical parts of America, Asia, and Africa, they have never been observed; nor at the Cape of Good Hope, nor in Australia.[20]

On the Climate and Productions of the Antarctic Islands.—Considering the rankness of the vegetation in Tierra del Fuego, and on the coast northward of it, the condition of the islands south and south-west of America is truly surprising. Sandwich Land, in the latitude of the north part of Scotland, was found by Cook, during the hottest month of the year, "covered many fathoms thick with everlasting snow;" and there seems to be scarcely any vegetation. Georgia, an island 96 miles long and 10 broad, in the latitude of Yorkshire, "in the very height of summer, is in a manner wholly covered with frozen snow." It can boast only of moss, some tufts of grass, and wild burnet: it has only one land-bird (*Anthus correndera*), yet Iceland, which is 10° nearer the pole, has, according to Mackenzie, fifteen land-birds. The South Shetland Islands, in the same lati-

---

[19] [Darwin] Geological Transactions, vol. vi. p. 415.

[20] [Darwin] I have given details (the first, I believe, published) on this subject in the first edition, and in the Appendix to it. I have there shown that the apparent exceptions to the absence of erratic boulders in certain hot countries, are due to erroneous observations: several statements there given, I have since found confirmed by various authors.

tude as the southern half of Norway, possess only some lichens, moss, and a little grass; and Lieut. Kendall[21] found the bay, in which he was at anchor, beginning to freeze at a period corresponding with our 8th of September. The soil here consists of ice and volcanic ashes interstratified; and at a little depth beneath the surface it must remain perpetually congealed, for Lieut. Kendall found the body of a foreign sailor which had long been buried, with the flesh and all the features perfectly preserved. It is a singular fact, that on the two great continents in the northern hemisphere (but not in the broken land of Europe between them), we have the zone of perpetually frozen under-soil in a low latitude—namely, in 56° in North America at the depth of three feet,[22] and in 62° in Siberia at the depth of twelve to fifteen feet—as the result of a directly opposite condition of things, to those of the southern hemisphere. On the northern continents, the winter is rendered excessively cold by the radiation from a large area of land into a clear sky, nor is it moderated by the warmth-bringing currents of the sea; the short summer, on the other hand, is hot. In the Southern Ocean the winter is not so excessively cold, but the summer is far less hot, for the clouded sky seldom allows the sun to warm the ocean, itself a bad absorbent of heat; and hence the mean temperature of the year, which regulates the zone of perpetually congealed under-soil, is low. It is evident that a rank vegetation, which does not so much require heat as it does protection from intense cold, would approach much nearer to this zone of perpetual congelation under the equable climate of the southern hemisphere, than under the extreme climate of the northern continents.

The case of the sailor's body perfectly preserved in the icy soil of the South Shetland Islands (lat. 62° to 63° S.), in a rather lower latitude than that (lat. 64° N.) under which Pallas found the frozen rhinoceros in Siberia, is very interesting. Although it is a fallacy, as I have endeavoured to show in a former chapter, to suppose that the larger quadrupeds require a luxuriant vegetation for their support, nevertheless it is important to find in the South Shetland Islands, a frozen under-soil within 360 miles of the forest-clad islands near Cape Horn, where, as far as the *bulk* of vegetation is concerned, any number of great quadrupeds might be supported. The perfect pres-

[21] [Darwin] Geographical Journal, 1830, pp. 65, 66.
[22] [Darwin] Richardson's Append. to Back's Exped., and Humboldt's Fragm. Asiat., tom. ii. p. 386.

ervation of the carcasses of the Siberian elephants and rhinoceroses is certainly one of the most wonderful facts in geology; but independently of the imagined difficulty of supplying them with food from the adjoining countries, the whole case is not, I think, so perplexing as it has generally been considered. The plains of Siberia, like those of the Pampas, appear to have been formed under the sea, into which rivers brought down the bodies of many animals; of the greater number of these, only the skeletons have been preserved, but of others the perfect carcass. Now it is known, that in the shallow sea on the arctic coast of America the bottom freezes,[23] and does not thaw in spring so soon as the surface of the land; moreover, at greater depths, where the bottom of the sea does not freeze, the mud a few feet beneath the top layer might remain even in summer below 32°, as is the case on the land with the soil at the depth of a few feet. At still greater depths, the temperature of the mud and water would probably not be low enough to preserve the flesh; and hence, carcasses drifted beyond the shallow parts near an arctic coast, would have only their skeletons preserved: now in the extreme northern parts of Siberia bones are infinitely numerous, so that even islets are said to be almost composed of them;[24] and those islets lie no less than ten degrees of latitude north of the place where Pallas found the frozen rhinoceros. On the other hand, a carcass washed by a flood into a shallow part of the Arctic Sea, would be preserved for an indefinite period, if it were soon afterwards covered with mud, sufficiently thick to prevent the heat of the summer-water penetrating to it; and if, when the sea-bottom was upraised into land, the covering was sufficiently thick to prevent the heat of the summer air and sun thawing and corrupting it.

Recapitulation.—I will recapitulate the principal facts with regard to the climate, ice-action, and organic productions of the southern hemisphere, transposing the places in imagination to Europe, with which we are so much better acquainted. Then, near Lisbon, the commonest sea-shells, namely, three species of Oliva, a Voluta and Terebra, would have a tropical character. In the southern provinces of France, magnificent forests, intwined by arborescent grasses and with the trees loaded with

[23] [Darwin] Messrs. Dease and Simpson, in Geograph. Journ., vol. viii. pp. 218 and 220.

[24] [Darwin] Cuvier (Ossemens Fossiles, tom. i. p. 151), from Billing's Voyage.

parasitical plants, would hide the face of the land. The puma and the jaguar would haunt the Pyrenees. In the latitude of Mont Blanc, but on an island as far westward as central North America, tree-ferns and parasitical Orchideæ would thrive amidst the thick woods. Even as far north as central Denmark, humming-birds would be seen fluttering about delicate flowers, and parrots feeding amidst the evergreen woods; and in the sea there, we should have a Voluta, and all the shells of large size and vigorous growth. Nevertheless, on some islands only 360 miles northward of our new Cape Horn in Denmark, a carcass buried in the soil (or if washed into a shallow sea, and covered up with mud) would be preserved perpetually frozen. If some bold navigator attempted to penetrate northward of these islands, he would run a thousand dangers amidst gigantic icebergs, on some of which he would see great blocks of rock borne far away from their original site. Another island of large size in the latitude of southern Scotland, but twice as far to the west, would be "almost wholly covered with everlasting snow," and would have each bay terminated by ice-cliffs, whence great masses would be yearly detached: this island would boast only of a little moss, grass, and burnet, and a titlark would be its only land inhabitant. From our new Cape Horn in Denmark, a chain of mountains, scarcely half the height of the Alps, would run in a straight line due southward; and on its western flank every deep creek of the sea, or fiord, would end in "bold and astonishing glaciers." These lonely channels would frequently reverberate with the falls of ice, and so often would great waves rush along their coasts; numerous icebergs, some as tall as cathedrals, and occasionally loaded with "no inconsiderable blocks of rock," would be stranded on the outlying islets; at intervals violent earthquakes would shoot prodigious masses of ice into the waters below. Lastly, some Missionaries attempting to penetrate a long arm of the sea, would behold the not lofty surrounding mountains, sending down their many grand icy streams to the sea-coast, and their progress in the boats would be checked by the innumerable floating icebergs, some small and some great; and this would have occurred on our twenty-second of June, and where the Lake of Geneva is now spread out![25]

[25] [Darwin] In the former edition and Appendix, I have given some facts on the transportal of erratic boulders and icebergs in the Antarctic Ocean. This subject has lately been treated excellently by Mr. Hayes, in the Boston Journal (vol. iv. p. 426). The

author does not appear aware of a case published by me (Geographical Journal, vol. ix. p. 528), of a gigantic boulder embedded in an iceberg in the Antarctic Ocean, almost certainly one hundred miles distant from any land, and perhaps much more distant. In the Appendix I have discussed at length, the probability (at that time hardly thought of) of icebergs, when stranded, grooving and polishing rocks, like glaciers. This is now a very commonly received opinion; and I cannot still avoid the suspicion that it is applicable even to such cases as that of the Jura. Dr. Richardson has assured me, that the icebergs off North America push before them pebbles and sand, and leave the submarine rocky flats quite bare: it is hardly possible to doubt that such ledges must be polished and scored in the direction of the set of the prevailing currents. Since writing that Appendix, I have seen in North Wales (London Phil. Mag., vol. xxi. p. 180) the adjoining action of glaciers and of floating icebergs.

CHAPTER XII

CENTRAL CHILE

Valparaiso — Excursion to the Foot of the Andes — Structure of
the Land — Ascend the Bell of Quillota — Shattered Masses of
Greenstone — Immense Valleys — Mines — State of Miners —
Santiago — Hot-baths of Cauquenes — Gold-mines — Grinding-
mills — Perforated Stones — Habits of the Puma — El Turco and
Tapacolo — Humming-birds

July 23rd.—The *Beagle* anchored late at night in the bay of
Valparaiso, the chief seaport of Chile.[1] When morning came,
everything appeared delightful. After Tierra del Fuego, the
climate felt quite delicious—the atmosphere so dry, and the

[1] [Editor] When the *Beagle* and her consort, the *Adventure*—
the small schooner purchased by Fitz Roy—entered the Pacific on
June 10, 1834, they anticipated an end to the storms that had
bedeviled them in the Strait of Magellan and around Tierra del
Fuego. But they soon encountered a succession of furious north
gales—"Never has the *Beagle* had such ill luck!" Darwin exclaims
in his diary—that forced her to put into a port on Chiloé Island for
three days (which Fitz Roy took advantage of for chronometer
observations) before proceeding to Valparaiso.
  The *Beagle* was at Valparaiso until November 10. Part of this
time was utilized to translate the soundings and other data gathered
in Patagonian and Fuegian waters into charts; part was spent in
waiting for Darwin to recover from an illness, which kept him in
bed ashore from the end of September, when he returned from
his excursion to Santiago and the Central Valley of Chile, to the
beginning of November. (Darwin's diary gives no indication of
the cause of the illness, but a letter home attributes it to drinking
some new-made Chilean wine on the Santiago excursion.) In
Valparaiso also, Fitz Roy learned of the Admiralty's refusal to
put the *Adventure's* crew on the *Beagle* pay list; so the schooner

heavens so clear and blue with the sun shining brightly, that all nature seemed sparkling with life. The view from the anchorage is very pretty. The town is built at the very foot of a range of hills, about 1600 feet high, and rather steep. From its position, it consists of one long, straggling street, which runs parallel to the beach, and wherever a ravine comes down, the houses are piled up on each side of it. The rounded hills, being only partially protected by a very scanty vegetation, are worn into numberless little gullics, which expose a singularly bright red soil. From this cause, and from the low whitewashed houses with tile roofs, the view reminded me of St. Cruz in Teneriffe. In a north-easterly direction there are some fine glimpses of the Andes: but these mountains appear much grander when viewed from the neighbouring hills; the great distance at which they are situated, can then more readily be perceived. The volcano of Aconcagua is particularly magnificent. This huge and irregularly conical mass has an elevation greater than that of Chimborazo; for, from measurements made by the officers in the *Beagle*, its height is no less than 23,000 foot. The Cordillera, however, viewed from this point, owe the greater part of their beauty to the atmosphere through which they are seen. When the sun was setting in the Pacific, it was admirable to watch how clearly their rugged outlines could be distinguished, yet how varied and how delicate were the shades of their colour.

---

was sold. This plus overwork so depressed Fitz Roy that he put himself on the sick list and resigned the command of the *Beagle*. This would have compelled the immediate return of the ship to England, without completion of the chain of longitude measurements and other of the ship's missions. So Fitz Roy was persuaded by his officers to withdraw his resignation.

Chile had won independence just a few years before the *Beagle's* visit. The Chilean independence movement had begun with the ousting of the Spanish governor by a Chilean junta in 1810. The Spanish regained control in 1814, and were not finally ousted until 1817–18, when the royalists were defeated by an army organized by José de San Martin, one of the heroes of Argentine independence, and Bernardo O'Higgins, the illegitimate son of an Irish adventurer (Ambrosio O'Higgins) who had entered Spanish service and become viceroy of Peru. In 1834, Chile was governed by General Joaquin Prieto, who had seized power in 1830 as head of a military junta and who had been elected president under a constitution that gave him almost dictatorial power. Valparaiso is today a city of more than a quarter of a million.

I had the good fortune to find living here Mr. Richard Corfield, an old schoolfellow and friend, to whose hospitality and kindness I was greatly indebted, in having afforded me a most pleasant residence during the *Beagle's* stay in Chile. The immediate neighbourhood of Valparaiso is not very productive to the naturalist. During the long summer the wind blows steadily from the southward, and a little off shore, so that rain never falls; during the three winter months, however, it is sufficiently abundant. The vegetation in consequence is very scanty: except in some deep valleys, there are no trees, and only a little grass and a few low bushes are scattered over the less steep parts of the hills. When we reflect, that at the distance of 350 miles to the south, this side of the Andes is completely hidden by one impenetrable forest, the contrast is very remarkable. I took several long walks while collecting objects of natural history. The country is pleasant for exercise. There are many very beautiful flowers; and, as in most other dry climates, the plants and shrubs possess strong and peculiar odours—even one's clothes by brushing through them became scented. I did not cease from wonder at finding each succeeding day as fine as the foregoing. What a difference does climate make in the enjoyment of life! How opposite are the sensations when viewing black mountains half-enveloped in clouds, and seeing another range through the light blue haze of a fine day! The one for a time may be very sublime; the other is all gaiety and happy life.

August 14*th.*—I set out on a riding excursion, for the purpose of geologising the basal parts of the Andes, which alone at this time of the year are not shut up by the winter snow. Our first day's ride was northward along the sea-coast. After dark we reached the Hacienda of Quintero, the estate which formerly belonged to Lord Cochrane. My object in coming here was to see the great beds of shells, which stand some yards above the level of the sea, and are burnt for lime. The proofs of the elevation of this whole line of coast are unequivocal: at the height of a few hundred feet old-looking shells are numerous, and I found some at 1300 feet. These shells either lie loose on the surface, or are embedded in a reddish-black vegetable mould. I was much surprised to find under the microscope that this vegetable mould is really marine mud, full of minute particles of organic bodies.

15*th.*—We returned towards the valley of Quillota. The country was exceedingly pleasant; just such as poets would call pastoral: green open lawns, separated by small valleys with rivulets, and the cottages, we may suppose of the shepherds, scattered on the hill-sides. We were obliged to cross the ridge of the Chilicauquen. At its base there were many fine evergreen forest-trees, but these flourished only in the ravines, where there was running water. Any person who had seen only the country near Valparaiso, would never have imagined that there had been such picturesque spots in Chile. As soon as we reached the brow of the Sierra, the valley of Quillota was immediately under our feet. The prospect was one of remarkable artificial luxuriance. The valley is very broad and quite flat, and is thus easily irrigated in all parts. The little square gardens are crowded with orange and olive trees, and every sort of vegetable. On each side huge bare mountains rise, and this from the contrast renders the patchwork valley the more pleasing. Whoever called "Valparaiso" the "Valley of Paradise," must have been thinking of Quillota. We crossed over to the Hacienda de San Isidro, situated at the very foot of the Bell Mountain.

Chile, as may be seen in the maps, is a narrow strip of land between the Cordillera and the Pacific; and this strip is itself traversed by several mountain-lines, which in this part run parallel to the great range. Between these outer lines and the main Cordillera, a succession of level basins, generally opening into each other by narrow passages, extend far to the southward: in these, the principal towns are situated, as San Felipe, Santiago, San Fernando. These basins or plains, together with the transverse flat valleys (like that of Quillota) which connect them with the coast, I have no doubt are the bottoms of ancient inlets and deep bays, such as at the present day intersect every part of Tierra del Fuego and the western coast. Chile must formerly have resembled the latter country in the configuration of its land and water. The resemblance was occasionally shown strikingly when a level fog-bank covered, as with a mantle, all the lower parts of the country: the white vapour curling into the ravines, beautifully represented little coves and bays; and here and there a solitary hillock peeping up, showed that it had formerly stood there as an islet. The contrast of these flat valleys and basins with the irregular mountains, gave the scenery a character which to me was new and very interesting.

From the natural slope to seaward of these plains, they are very easily irrigated, and in consequence singularly fertile.

Without this process the land would produce scarcely anything, for during the whole summer the sky is cloudless. The mountains and hills are dotted over with bushes and low trees, and excepting these the vegetation is very scanty. Each landowner in the valley possesses a certain portion of hill-country, where his half-wild cattle, in considerable numbers, manage to find sufficient pasture. Once every year there is a grand "rodeo," when all the cattle are driven down, counted, and marked, and a certain number separated to be fattened in the irrigated fields. Wheat is extensively cultivated, and a good deal of Indian corn: a kind of bean is, however, the staple article of food for the common labourers. The orchards produce an overflowing abundance of peaches, figs, and grapes. With all these advantages, the inhabitants of the country ought to be much more prosperous than they are.

16*th*.—The major-domo of the Hacienda was good enough to give me a guide and fresh horses; and in the morning we set out to ascend the Campana, or Bell Mountain, which is 6400 feet high. The paths were very bad, but both the geology and scenery amply repaid the trouble. We reached, by the evening, a spring called the Agua del Guanaco, which is situated at a great height. This must be an old name, for it is very many years since a guanaco drank its waters. During the ascent I noticed that nothing but bushes grew on the northern slope, whilst on the southern slope there was a bamboo about fifteen feet high. In a few places there were palms, and I was surprised to see one at an elevation of at least 4500 feet. These palms are, for their family, ugly trees. Their stem is very large, and of a curious form, being thicker in the middle than at the base or top. They are excessively numerous in some parts of Chile, and valuable on account of a sort of treacle made from the sap. On one estate near Petorca they tried to count them, but failed, after having numbered several hundred thousand. Every year in the early spring, in August, very many are cut down, and when the trunk is lying on the ground, the crown of leaves is lopped off. The sap then immediately begins to flow from the upper end, and continues so doing for some months: it is, however, necessary that a thin slice should be shaved off from that end every morning, so as to expose a fresh surface. A good tree will give ninety gallons, and all this must have been contained in the vessels of the apparently dry trunk. It is said that the sap flows much more quickly on those days when the sun is powerful; and likewise, that it is absolutely necessary to take care, in cutting down the tree, that it should fall with its head upwards on the side of the hill; for if it falls down the slope, scarcely any sap will flow; although in that case one would have thought that the action would have been aided, instead of checked, by the force of gravity. The sap is concentrated by boiling, and is then called treacle, which it very much resembles in taste.

We unsaddled our horses near the spring, and prepared to pass the night. The evening was fine, and the atmosphere so clear, that the masts of the vessels at anchor in the bay of Valparaiso, although no less than twenty-six geographical miles distant, could be distinguished clearly as little black streaks. A ship doubling the point under sail, appeared as a bright white speck. Anson expresses much surprise, in his voyage, at the distance at which his vessels were discovered from the coast; but he did not sufficiently allow for the height of the land, and the great transparency of the air.

The setting of the sun was glorious; the valleys being black, whilst the snowy peaks of the Andes yet retained a ruby tint. When it was dark, we made a fire beneath a little arbour of bamboos, fried our charqui (or dried slips of beef), took our maté, and were quite comfortable. There is an inexpressible charm in thus living in the open air. The evening was calm and still;—the shrill noise of the mountain bizcacha, and the faint cry of a goatsucker, were occasionally to be heard. Besides these, few birds, or even insects, frequent these dry, parched mountains.

August 17th.—In the morning we climbed up the rough mass of greenstone which crowns the summit. This rock, as frequently happens, was much shattered and broken into huge angular fragments. I observed, however, one remarkable circumstance, namely, that many of the surfaces presented every degree of freshness—some appearing as if broken the day before, whilst on others lichens had either just become, or had long grown, attached. I so fully believed that this was owing to the frequent earthquakes, that I felt inclined to hurry from below each loose pile. As one might very easily be deceived in a fact of this kind, I doubted its accuracy, until ascending Mount Wellington, in Van Diemen's Land, where earthquakes do not occur; and there I saw the summit of the mountain similarly composed and similarly shattered, but all the blocks appeared as if they had been hurled into their present position thousands of years ago.

We spent the day on the summit, and I never enjoyed one more thoroughly. Chile, bounded by the Andes and the Pacific, was seen as in a map. The pleasure from the scenery, in itself beautiful, was heightened by the many reflections which arose from the mere view of the Campana range with its lesser parallel ones, and of the broad valley of Quillota directly intersecting them. Who can avoid wondering at the force which has upheaved these mountains, and even more so at the countless ages which it must have required, to have broken through, removed, and levelled whole masses of them? It is well in this case, to call to mind the vast shingle and sedimentary beds of Patagonia, which, if heaped on the Cordillera, would increase its height by so many thousand feet. When in that country, I wondered how any mountain-chain could have supplied such masses, and not have been utterly obliterated. We must not now reverse the wonder, and doubt whether all-powerful time can grind down mountains—even the gigantic Cordillera —into gravel and mud.

The appearance of the Andes was different from that which I had expected. The lower line of the snow was of course horizontal, and to this line the even summits of the range seemed quite parallel. Only at long intervals, a group of points or a single cone, showed where a volcano had existed, or does now exist. Hence the range resembled a great solid wall, surmounted here and there by a tower, and making a most perfect barrier to the country.

Almost every part of the hill had been drilled by attempts to open gold-mines: the rage for mining has left scarcely a spot in Chile unexamined. I spent the evening as before, talking round the fire with my two companions. The Guasos of Chile, who correspond to the Gauchos of the Pampas, are, however, a very different set of beings. Chile is the more civilized of the two countries, and the inhabitants, in consequence, have lost much individual character. Gradations in rank are much more strongly marked: the Guaso does not by any means consider every man his equal; and I was quite surprised to find that my companions did not like to eat at the same time with myself. This feeling of inequality is a necessary consequence of the existence of an aristocracy of wealth. It is said that some few of the greater landowners possess from five to ten thousand pounds sterling per annum: an inequality of riches which I believe is not met with, in any of the cattle-breeding countries eastward of the Andes. A traveller does not here meet that unbounded hospitality which refuses all payment, but yet is so kindly offered that no scruples can be raised in accepting it. Almost every house in Chile will receive you for the night, but a trifle is expected to be given in the morning; even a rich man will accept two or three shillings. The Gaucho, although he may be a cut-throat, is a gentleman; the Guaso is in few respects better, but at the same time a vulgar, ordinary fellow. The two men, although employed much in the same manner, are different in their habits and attire; and the peculiarities of each are universal in their respective countries. The Gaucho seems part of his horse, and scorns to exert himself excepting when on its back; the Guaso may be hired to work as a labourer in the fields. The former lives entirely on animal food; the latter almost wholly on vegetable. We do not here see the white boots, the broad drawers, and scarlet chilipa; the picturesque costume of the Pampas. Here, common trousers are protected by black and green worsted leggings. The poncho, however, is common to both. The chief pride of the Guaso lies in his spurs; which are absurdly large. I measured one which was six inches in the *diameter* of the rowel, and the rowel itself contained upwards of thirty points. The stirrups are on the same scale, each consisting of a square, carved block of wood, hollowed out, yet weighing three or four pounds. The Guaso is perhaps more expert with the lazo than the Gaucho; but, from the nature of the country, he does not know the use of the bolas.

August 18th.—We descended the mountain, and passed some beautiful little spots, with rivulets and fine trees. Having slept at the same hacienda as before, we rode during the two succeeding days up the valley, and passed through Quillota, which is more like a collection of nursery gardens than a town. The orchards were beautiful, presenting one mass of peach-blossoms. I saw, also, in one or two places the date-palm: it is a most stately tree; and I should think a group of them in their native Asiatic or African deserts must be superb. We passed likewise San Felipe, a pretty straggling town like Quillota. The valley in this part expands into one of those great bays or plains, reaching to the foot of the Cordillera, which have been mentioned as forming so curious a part of the scenery of Chile. In the evening we reached the mines of Jajuel, situated in a ravine at the flank of the great chain. I stayed here five days. My host, the superintendent of the mine, was a shrewd but rather ignorant Cornish miner. He had married a Spanish

woman, and did not mean to return home; but his admiration
for the mines of Cornwall remained unbounded. Amongst
many other questions, he asked me, "Now that George Rex is
dead, how many more of the family of Rexes are yet alive?"
This Rex certainly must be a relation of the great author Finis,
who wrote all books!

These mines are of copper, and the ore is all shipped to
Swansea, to be smelted. Hence the mines have an aspect singularly quiet, as compared to those in England: here no smoke,
furnaces, or great steam-engines, disturb the solitude of the
surrounding mountains.

The Chilian government, or rather the old Spanish law, en-
courages by every method the searching for mines. The discoverer may work a mine on any ground, by paying five shillings; and before paying this he may try, even in the garden
of another man, for twenty days.

It is now well known that the Chilian method of mining is
the cheapest. My host says that the two principal improvements introduced by foreigners have been, first, reducing by
previous roasting the copper pyrites—which, being the common ore in Cornwall, the English miners were astounded on
their arrival to find thrown away as useless: secondly, stamping and washing the scoriæ from the old furnaces—by which
process particles of metal are recovered in abundance. I have
actually seen mules carrying to the coast, for transportation
to England, a cargo of such cinders. But the first case is much
the most curious. The Chilian miners were so convinced that
copper pyrites contained not a particle of copper, that they
laughed at the Englishmen for their ignorance, who laughed
in turn, and bought their richest veins for a few dollars. It is
very odd that, in a country where mining had been extensively
carried on for many years, so simple a process as gently roasting the ore to expel the sulphur previous to smelting it, had
never been discovered. A few improvements have likewise
been introduced in some of the simple machinery; but even
to the present day, water is removed from some mines by men
carrying it up the shaft in leathern bags!

The labouring men work very hard. They have little time
allowed for their meals, and during summer and winter they
begin when it is light, and leave off at dark. They are paid one
pound sterling a month, and their food is given them: this for
breakfast consists of sixteen figs and two small loaves of bread;
for dinner, boiled beans; for supper, broken roasted wheat

grain. They scarcely ever taste meat; as, with the twelve pounds per annum, they have to clothe themselves, and support their families. The miners who work in the mine itself have twenty-five shillings per month, and are allowed a little charqui. But these men come down from their bleak habitations only once in every fortnight or three weeks.

During my stay here I thoroughly enjoyed scrambling about these huge mountains. The geology, as might have been expected, was very interesting. The shattered and baked rocks, traversed by innumerable dykes of greenstone, showed what commotions had formerly taken place. The scenery was much the same as that near the Bell of Quillota—dry barren mountains, dotted at intervals by bushes with a scanty foliage. The cactuses, or rather opuntias, were here very numerous. I measured one of a spherical figure, which, including the spines, was six feet and four inches in circumference. The height of the common cylindrical, branching kind, is from twelve to fifteen feet, and the girth (with spines) of the branches between three and four feet.

A heavy fall of snow on the mountains prevented me, during the last two days, from making some interesting excursions. I attempted to reach a lake which the inhabitants, from some unaccountable reason, believe to be an arm of the sea. During a very dry season, it was proposed to attempt cutting a channel from it for the sake of the water, but the padre, after a consultation, declared it was too dangerous, as all Chile would be inundated, if, as generally supposed, the lake was connected with the Pacific. We ascended to a great height, but becoming involved in the snow-drifts failed in reaching this wonderful lake, and had some difficulty in returning. I thought we should have lost our horses; for there was no means of guessing how deep the drifts were, and the animals, when led, could only move by jumping. The black sky showed that a fresh snow-storm was gathering, and we therefore were not a little glad when we escaped. By the time we reached the base the storm commenced, and it was lucky for us that this did not happen three hours earlier in the day.

August 26th.—We left Jajuel and again crossed the basin of S. Felipe. The day was truly Chilian: glaringly bright, and the atmosphere quite clear. The thick and uniform covering of newly-fallen snow rendered the view of the volcano of Aconcagua and the main chain quite glorious. We were now on the road to Santiago, the capital of Chile. We crossed the Cerro del Talguen, and slept at a little rancho. The host, talking about the state of Chile as compared to other countries, was very humble: "Some see with two eyes and some with one, but for my part I do not think that Chile sees with any."

August 27th.—After crossing many low hills we descended into the small land-locked plain of Guitron. In the basins, such as this one, which are elevated from one thousand to two thousand feet above the sea, two species of acacia, which are stunted in their forms, and stand wide apart from each other, grow in large numbers. These trees are never found near the sea-coast; and this gives another characteristic feature to the scenery of these basins. We crossed a low ridge which separates Guitron from the great plain on which Santiago[2] stands. The view was here pre-eminently striking: the dead level surface, covered in parts by woods of acacia, and with the city in the distance, abutting horizontally against the base of the Andes, whose snowy peaks were bright with the evening sun. At the first glance of this view, it was quite evident that the plain represented the extent of a former inland sea. As soon as we gained the level road we pushed our horses into a gallop, and reached the city before it was dark.

I stayed a week in Santiago and enjoyed myself very much. In the morning I rode to various places on the plain, and in the evening dined with several of the English merchants, whose hospitality at this place is well known. A never-failing source of pleasure was to ascend the little hillock of rock (St. Lucia) which projects in the middle of the city. The scenery certainly is most striking, and, as I have said, very peculiar. I am informed that this same character is common to the cities on the great Mexican platform. Of the town I have nothing to say in detail: it is not so fine or so large as Buenos Ayres, but is built after the same model. I arrived here by a circuit to the north; so I resolved to return to Valparaiso by a rather longer excursion to the south of the direct road.

September 5th.—By the middle of the day we arrived at one of the suspension bridges made of hide, which crosses the Maypu, a large turbulent river a few leagues southward of Santiago. These bridges are very poor affairs. The road, following the curvature of the suspending ropes, is made of bundles of sticks placed close together. It was full of holes, and

[2] [Editor] Now not only the capital and chief city of Chile, but the fourth largest city in South America, with a population of a million and a quarter.

oscillated rather fearfully, even with the weight of a man leading his horse. In the evening we reached a comfortable farmhouse, where there were several very pretty señoritas. They were much horrified at my having entered one of their churches out of mere curiosity. They asked me, "Why do you not become a Christian—for our religion is certain?" I assured them I was a sort of Christian; but they would not hear of it —appealing to my own words, "Do not your padres, your very bishops, marry?" The absurdity of a bishop having a wife particularly struck them: they scarcely knew whether to be most amused or horror-struck at such an enormity.

6th.—We proceeded due south, and slept at Rancagua. The road passed over the level but narrow plain, bounded on one side by lofty hills, and on the other by the Cordillera. The next day we turned up the valley of the Rio Cachapual, in which the hot-baths of Cauquenes, long celebrated for their medicinal properties, are situated. The suspension bridges, in the less frequented parts, are generally taken down during the winter when the rivers are low. Such was the case in this valley, and we were therefore obliged to cross the stream on horseback. This is rather disagreeable, for the foaming water, though not deep, rushes so quickly over the bed of large rounded stones, that one's head becomes quite confused, and it is difficult even to perceive whether the horse is moving onward or standing still. In summer, when the snow melts, the torrents are quite impassable; their strength and fury is then extremely great, as might be plainly seen by the marks which they had left. We reached the baths in the evening, and stayed there five days, being confined the two last by heavy rain. The buildings consist of a square of miserable little hovels, each with a single table and bench. They are situated in a narrow deep valley just without the central Cordillera. It is a quiet, solitary spot, with a good deal of wild beauty.

The mineral springs of Cauquenes burst forth on a line of dislocation, crossing a mass of stratified rock, the whole of which betrays the action of heat. A considerable quantity of gas is continually escaping from the same orifices with the water. Though the springs are only a few yards apart, they have very different temperatures; and this appears to be the result of an unequal mixture of cold water: for those with the lowest temperature have scarcely any mineral taste. After the great earthquake of 1822 the springs ceased, and the water did not return for nearly a year. They were also much affected by the earthquake of 1835; the temperature being suddenly changed from 118° to 92°.[3] It seems probable that mineral waters rising deep from the bowels of the earth, would always be more deranged by subterranean disturbances than those nearer the surface. The man who had charge of the baths, assured me that in summer the water is hotter and more plentiful than in winter. The former circumstance I should have expected, from the less mixture, during the dry season, of cold water; but the latter statement appears very strange and contradictory. The periodical increase during the summer, when rain never falls, can, I think, only be accounted for by the melting of the snow: yet the mountains which are covered by snow during that season, are three or four leagues distant from the springs. I have no reason to doubt the accuracy of my informer, who, having lived on the spot for several years, ought to be well acquainted with the circumstance,—which, if true, certainly is very curious: for, we must suppose that the snow-water, being conducted through porous strata to the regions of heat, is again thrown up to the surface by the line of dislocated and injected rocks at Cauquenes; and the regularity of the phenomenon would seem to indicate, that in this district heated rock occurred at a depth not very great.

One day I rode up the valley to the farthest inhabited spot. Shortly above that point, the Cachapual divides into two deep tremendous ravines, which penetrate directly into the great range. I scrambled up a peaked mountain, probably more than six thousand feet high. Here, as indeed everywhere else, scenes of the highest interest presented themselves. It was by one of these ravines, that Pincheira entered Chile and ravaged the neighbouring country. This is the same man whose attack on an estancia at the Rio Negro I have described. He was a renegade half-cast Spaniard, who collected a great body of Indians together and established himself by a stream in the Pampas, which place none of the forces sent after him could ever discover. From this point he used to sally forth, and crossing the Cordillera by passes hitherto unattempted, he ravaged the farm-houses and drove the cattle to his secret rendezvous. Pincheira was a capital horseman, and he made all around him equally good, for he invariably shot any one who hesitated to follow him. It was against this man, and other wandering Indian tribes, that Rosas waged the war of extermination.

[3] [Darwin] Caldcleugh, in Philosoph. Transact. for 1836.

September 13*th*.—We left the baths of Cauquenes, and rejoining the main road slept at the Rio Claro. From this place we rode to the town of S. Fernando. Before arriving there, the last land-locked basin had expanded into a great plain, which extended so far to the south, that the snowy summits of the more distant Andes were seen as if above the horizon of the sea. S. Fernando is forty leagues from Santiago; and it was my farthest point southward; for we here turned at right angles towards the coast. We slept at the gold-mines of Yaquil, which are worked by Mr. Nixon, an American gentleman, to whose kindness I was much indebted during the four days I stayed at his house. The next morning we rode to the mines, which are situated at the distance of some leagues, near the summit of a lofty hill. On the way we had a glimpse of the lake Taguatagua, celebrated for its floating islands, which have been described by Mr. Gay.[4] They are composed of the stalks of various dead plants intertwined together, and on the surface of which other living ones take root. Their form is generally circular, and their thickness from four to six feet, of which the greater part is immersed in the water. As the wind blows, they pass from one side of the lake to the other, and often carry cattle and horses as passengers.

When we arrived at the mine, I was struck by the pale appearance of many of the men, and inquired from Mr. Nixon respecting their condition. The mine is 450 feet deep, and each man brings up about 200 pounds weight of stone. With this load they have to climb up the alternate notches cut in the trunks of trees, placed in a zigzag line up the shaft. Even beardless young men, eighteen and twenty years old, with little muscular development of their bodies (they are quite naked excepting drawers) ascend with this great load from nearly the same depth. A strong man, who is not accustomed to this labour, perspires most profusely, with merely carrying up his own body. With this very severe labour, they live entirely on boiled beans and bread. They would prefer having bread alone; but their masters, finding that they cannot work so hard upon this, treat them like horses, and make them eat the beans. Their pay is here rather more than at the mines of Jajuel, being from 24 to 28 shillings per month. They leave the mine only once in three weeks; when they stay with their

[4] [Darwin] Annales des Sciences Naturelles, March, 1833. M. Gay, a zealous and able naturalist, was then occupied in studying every branch of natural history throughout the kingdom of Chile.

families for two days. One of the rules in this mine sounds very harsh, but answers pretty well for the master. The only method of stealing gold is to secrete pieces of the ore, and take them out as occasion may offer. Whenever the major-domo finds a lump thus hidden, its full value is stopped out of the wages of all the men; who thus, without they all combine, are obliged to keep watch over each other.

When the ore is brought to the mill, it is ground into an impalpable powder; the process of washing removes all the lighter particles, and amalgamation finally secures the gold-dust. The washing, when described, sounds a very simple process; but it is beautiful to see how the exact adaptation of the current of water to the specific gravity of the gold, so easily separates the powdered matrix from the metal. The mud which passes from the mills is collected into pools, where it subsides, and every now and then is cleared out and thrown into a common heap. A great deal of chemical action then commences, salts of various kinds effloresce on the surface, and the mass becomes hard. After having been left for a year or two, and then rewashed, it yields gold; and this process may be repeated even six or seven times; but the gold each time becomes less in quantity, and the intervals required (as the inhabitants say, to generate the metal) are longer. There can be no doubt that the chemical action, already mentioned, each time liberates fresh gold from some combination. The discovery of a method to effect this before the first grinding, would without doubt raise the value of gold-ores many-fold. It is curious to find how the minute particles of gold, being scattered about and not corroding, at last accumulate in some quantity. A short time since a few miners, being out of work, obtained permission to scrape the ground round the house and mill: they washed the earth thus got together, and so procured thirty dollars' worth of gold. This is an exact counterpart of what takes place in nature. Mountains suffer degradation and wear away, and with them the metallic veins which they contain. The hardest rock is worn into impalpable mud, the ordinary metals oxidate, and both are removed; but gold, platina, and a few others are nearly indestructible, and from their weight, sinking to the bottom, are left behind. After whole mountains have passed through this grinding-mill, and have been washed by the hand of nature, the residue becomes metalliferous, and man finds it worth his while to complete the task of separation.

Bad as the above treatment of the miners appears, it is gladly accepted of by them; for the condition of the labouring agriculturists is much worse. Their wages are lower, and they live almost exclusively on beans. This poverty must be chiefly owing to the feudal-like system on which the land is tilled: the landowner gives a small plot of ground to the labourer, for building on and cultivating, and in return has his services (or those of a proxy) for every day of his life, without any wages. Until a father has a grown-up son, who can by his labour pay the rent, there is no one, except on occasional days, to take care of his own patch of ground. Hence extreme poverty is very common among the labouring classes in this country.

There are some old Indian ruins in this neighbourhood, and I was shown one of the perforated stones, which Molina mentions as being found in many places in considerable numbers. They are of a circular flattened form, from five to six inches in diameter, with a hole passing quite through the centre. It has generally been supposed that they were used as heads to clubs, although their form does not appear at all well adapted for that purpose. Burchell[5] states that some of the tribes in Southern Africa dig up roots, by the aid of a stick pointed at one end, the force and weight of which is increased by a round stone with a hole in it, into which the other end is firmly wedged. It appears probable, that the Indians of Chile formerly used some such rude agricultural instrument.

One day, a German collector in natural history, of the name of Renous, called, and nearly at the same time an old Spanish lawyer. I was amused at being told the conversation which took place between them. Renous speaks Spanish so well, that the old lawyer mistook him for a Chilian. Renous, alluding to me, asked him what he thought of the King of England sending out a collector to their country, to pick up lizards and beetles, and to break stones? The old gentleman thought seriously for some time, and then said, "It is not well,—*hay un gato encerrado aqui* (there is a cat shut up here). No man is so rich as to send out people to pick up such rubbish. I do not like it: if one of us were to go and do such things in England, do not you think the King of England would very soon send us out of his country?" And this old gentleman, from his profession, belongs to the better informed and more intelligent classes! Renous himself, two or three years before, left in a house at S. Fernando some caterpillars, under charge of a girl to feed,

5 [Darwin] Burchell's Travels, vol. ii. p. 45.

that they might turn into butterflies. This was rumoured through the town, and at last the Padres and Governor consulted together, and agreed it must be some heresy. Accordingly, when Renous returned, he was arrested.

September 19th.—We left Yaquil, and followed the flat valley, formed like that of Quillota, in which the Rio Tinderidica flows. Even at these few miles south of Santiago the climate is much damper; in consequence there were fine tracts of pasturage, which were not irrigated. (20th.) We followed this valley till it expanded into a great plain, which reaches from the sea to the mountains west of Rancagua. We shortly lost all trees and even bushes; so that the inhabitants are nearly as badly off for firewood as those in the Pampas. Never having heard of these plains, I was much surprised at meeting with such scenery in Chile. The plains belong to more than one series of different elevations, and they are traversed by broad flat-bottomed valleys; both of which circumstances, as in Patagonia, bespeak the action of the sea on gently rising land. In the steep cliffs bordering these valleys, there are some large caves, which no doubt were originally formed by the waves: one of these is celebrated under the name of Cueva del Obispo; having formerly been consecrated. During the day I felt very unwell, and from that time till the end of October did not recover.

September 22nd.—We continued to pass over green plains without a tree. The next day we arrived at a house near Navedad, on the sea-coast, where a rich Haciendero gave us lodgings. I stayed here the two ensuing days, and although very unwell, managed to collect from the tertiary formation some marine shells.

24th.—Our course was now directed towards Valparaiso, which with great difficulty I reached on the 27th, and was there confined to my bed till the end of October. During this time I was an inmate in Mr. Corfield's house, whose kindness to me I do not know how to express.

I will here add a few observations on some of the animals and birds of Chile. The Puma, or South American Lion, is not uncommon. This animal has a wide geographical range; being found from the equatorial forests, throughout the deserts of Patagonia, as far south as the damp and cold latitudes (53° to 54°) of Tierra del Fuego. I have seen its footsteps in the Cordillera of central Chile, at an elevation of at least 10,000 feet. In La Plata the puma preys chiefly on deer, ostriches, bizcacha, and other small quadrupeds; it there seldom attacks cattle or horses, and most rarely man. In Chile, however, it destroys many young horses and cattle, owing probably to the scarcity of other quadrupeds: I heard, likewise, of two men and a woman who had been thus killed. It is asserted that the puma always kills its prey by springing on the shoulders, and then drawing back the head with one of its paws, until the vertebræ break: I have seen in Patagonia, the skeletons of guanacos, with their necks thus dislocated.

The puma, after eating its fill, covers the carcass with many large bushes, and lies down to watch it. This habit is often the cause of its being discovered; for the condors wheeling in the air, every now and then descend to partake of the feast, and being angrily driven away, rise all together on the wing. The Chileno Guaso then knows there is a lion watching his prey—the word is given—and men and dogs hurry to the chace. Sir F. Head says that a Gaucho in the Pampas, upon merely seeing some condors wheeling in the air, cried "A lion!" I could never myself meet with any one who pretended to such powers of discrimination. It is asserted, that if a puma has once been betrayed by thus watching the carcass, and has then been hunted, it never resumes this habit; but that having gorged itself, it wanders far away. The puma is easily killed. In an open country, it is first entangled with the bolas, then lazoed, and dragged along the ground till rendered insensible. At Tandeel (south of the Plata) I was told that within three months one hundred were thus destroyed. In Chile they are generally driven up bushes or trees, and are then either shot, or baited to death by dogs. The dogs employed in this chace belong to a particular breed, called Leoneros: they are weak, slight animals, like long-legged terriers, but are born with a particular instinct for this sport. The puma is described as being very crafty: when pursued, it often returns on its former track, and then suddenly making a spring on one side, waits there till the dogs have passed by. It is a very silent animal, uttering no cry even when wounded, and only rarely during the breeding season.

Of birds, two species of the genus Pteroptochos (megapodius and albicollis of Kittlitz) are perhaps the most conspicuous. The former, called by the Chilenos "el Turco," is as large as a fieldfare,[6] to which bird it has some alliance; but its

[6] [Editor] A member of the thrush family.

legs are much longer, tail shorter, and beak stronger: its colour is a reddish brown. The Turco is not uncommon. It lives on the ground, sheltered among the thickets which are scattered over the dry and sterile hills. With its tail erect, and stilt-like legs, it may be seen every now and then popping from one bush to another with uncommon quickness. It really requires little imagination to believe that the bird is ashamed of itself, and is aware of its most ridiculous figure. On first seeing it, one is tempted to exclaim, "A vilely stuffed specimen has escaped from some museum, and has come to life again!" It cannot be made to take flight without the greatest trouble, nor does it run, but only hops. The various loud cries which it utters when concealed amongst the bushes, are as strange as its appearance. It is said to build its nest in a deep hole beneath the ground. I dissected several specimens: the gizzard, which was very muscular, contained beetles, vegetable fibres, and pebbles. From this character, from the length of its legs, scratching feet, membranous covering to the nostrils, short and arched wings, this bird seems in a certain degree to connect the thrushes with the gallinaceous order.

The second species (or P. albicollis) is allied to the first in its general form. It is called Tapacolo, or "cover your posterior;" and well does the shameless little bird deserve its name; for it carries its tail more than erect, that is, inclined backwards towards its head. It is very common, and frequents the bottoms of hedge-rows, and the bushes scattered over the barren hills, where scarcely another bird can exist. In its general manner of feeding, of quickly hopping out of the thickets and back again, in its desire of concealment, unwillingness to take flight, and nidification, it bears a close resemblance to the Turco; but its appearance is not quite so ridiculous. The Tapacolo is very crafty: when frightened by any person, it will remain motionless at the bottom of a bush, and will then, after a little while, try with much address to crawl away on the opposite side. It is also an active bird, and continually making a noise: these noises are various and strangely odd; some are like the cooing of doves, others like the bubbling of water, and many defy all similes. The country people say it changes its cry five times in the year—according to some change of season, I suppose.[7]

[7] [Darwin] It is a remarkable fact, that Molina, though describing in detail all the birds and animals of Chile, never once mentions this genus, the species of which are so common, and so remarkable in their habits. Was he at a loss how to classify them, and did he

Two species of humming-birds are common; Trochilus forficatus is found over a space of 2500 miles on the west coast, from the hot dry country of Lima, to the forests of Tierra del Fuego—where it may be seen flitting about in snow-storms. In the wooded island of Chiloe, which has an extremely humid climate, this little bird, skipping from side to side amidst the dripping foliage, is perhaps more abundant than almost any other kind. I opened the stomachs of several specimens, shot in different parts of the continent, and in all, remains of insects were as numerous as in the stomach of a creeper. When this species migrates in the summer southward, it is replaced by the arrival of another species coming from the north. This second kind (Trochilus gigas) is a very large bird for the delicate family to which it belongs: when on the wing its appearance is singular. Like others of the genus, it moves from place to place with a rapidity which may be compared to that of Syrphus amongst flies, and Sphinx among moths; but whilst hovering over a flower, it flaps its wings with a very slow and powerful movement, totally different from that vibratory one common to most of the species, which produces the humming noise. I never saw any other bird, where the force of its wings appeared (as in a butterfly) so powerful in proportion to the weight of its body. When hovering by a flower, its tail is constantly expanded and shut like a fan, the body being kept in a nearly vertical position. This action appears to steady and support the bird, between the slow movements of its wings. Although flying from flower to flower in search of food, its stomach generally contained abundant remains of insects, which I suspect are much more the object of its search than honey. The note of this species, like that of nearly the whole family, is extremely shrill.

---

consequently think that silence was the more prudent course? It is one more instance of the frequency of omissions by authors, on those very subjects where it might have been least expected.

CHAPTER XIII

CHILOE AND CHONOS ISLANDS

Chiloe — General Aspect — Boat Excursion — Native Indians —
Castro — Tame Fox — Ascend San Pedro — Chonos Archipelago —
Peninsula of Tres Montes — Granitic Range — Boat-wrecked Sailors
— Low's Harbour — Wild Potato — Formation of Peat — Myopota-
mus, Otter and Mice — Cheucau and Barking-bird — Opetiorhynchus
— Singular Character of Ornithology — Petrels

November 10*th.*—The *Beagle* sailed from Valparaiso to the
south, for the purpose of surveying the southern part of Chile,
the island of Chiloe, and the broken land called the Chonos
Archipelago, as far south as the Peninsula of Tres Montes. On
the 21st we anchored in the bay of S. Carlos,[1] the capital of
Chiloe.

This island is about ninety miles long, with a breadth of
rather less than thirty. The land is hilly, but not mountainous,
and is covered by one great forest, except where a few green
patches have been cleared round the thatched cottages. From
a distance the view somewhat resembles that of Tierra del
Fuego; but the woods, when seen nearer, are incomparably

[1] [Editor] Now called Ancud. The principal town of Chiloé (a
name meaning "part of Chile") Island and capital of Chiloé Province, which also includes a number of other islands and part of the
Chilean mainland. Chiloé Province and Chiloé Island are still only
thinly settled today because of the violent westerly storms and
heavy rainfall to which they are subject. During the war of Chilean
independence, Chiloé Island was the last stronghold of the royalists;
they were not driven from the island until 1826. The *Beagle's* survey
covered not only Chiloé Island and the Chonos Archipelago, but
the Guaytecas (a chain of islands between Chiloé and the Chonos)
and a number of small islands between Chiloé and the mainland.

more beautiful. Many kinds of fine evergreen trees, and plants with a tropical character, here take the place of the gloomy beech of the southern shores. In winter the climate is detestable, and in summer it is only a little better. I should think there are few parts of the world, within the temperate regions, where so much rain falls. The winds are very boisterous, and the sky almost always clouded: to have a week of fine weather is something wonderful. It is even difficult to get a single glimpse of the Cordillera: during our first visit, once only the volcano of Osorno stood out in bold relief, and that was before sunrise; it was curious to watch, as the sun rose, the outline gradually fading away in the glare of the eastern sky.

The inhabitants, from their complexion and low stature, appear to have three-fourths of Indian blood in their veins. They are an humble, quiet, industrious set of men. Although the fertile soil, resulting from the decomposition of the volcanic rocks, supports a rank vegetation, yet the climate is not favourable to any production which requires much sunshine to ripen it. There is very little pasture for the larger quadrupeds; and in consequence, the staple articles of food are pigs, potatoes, and fish. The people all dress in strong woollen garments, which each family makes for itself, and dyes with indigo of a dark blue colour. The arts, however, are in the rudest state;— as may be seen in their strange fashion of ploughing, their method of spinning, grinding corn, and in the construction of their boats. The forests are so impenetrable, that the land is nowhere cultivated except near the coast and on the adjoining islets. Even where paths exist, they are scarcely passable from the soft and swampy state of the soil. The inhabitants, like those of Tierra del Fuego, move about chiefly on the beach or in boats. Although with plenty to eat, the people are very poor: there is no demand for labour, and consequently the lower orders cannot scrape together money sufficient to purchase even the smallest luxuries. There is also a great deficiency of a circulating medium. I have seen a man bringing on his back a bag of charcoal, with which to buy some trifle, and another carrying a plank to exchange for a bottle of wine. Hence every tradesman must also be a merchant, and again sell the goods which he takes in exchange.

November 24th.—The yawl and whale-boat were sent under the command of Mr. (now Captain) Sulivan, to survey the eastern or inland coast of Chiloe; and with orders to meet the *Beagle* at the southern extremity of the island; to which point she would proceed by the outside, so as thus to circumnavigate the whole. I accompanied this expedition, but instead of going in the boats the first day, I hired horses to take me to Chacao, at the northern extremity of the island. The road followed the coast; every now and then crossing promontories covered by fine forests. In these shaded paths it is absolutely necessary that the whole road should be made of logs of wood, which are squared and placed by the side of each other. From the rays of the sun never penetrating the evergreen foliage, the ground is so damp and soft, that except by this means neither man nor horse would be able to pass along. I arrived at the village of Chacao, shortly after the tents belonging to the boats were pitched for the night.

The land in this neighbourhood has been extensively cleared, and there were many quiet and most picturesque nooks in the forest. Chacao was formerly the principal port in the island; but many vessels having been lost, owing to the dangerous currents and rocks in the straits, the Spanish government burnt the church, and thus arbitrarily compelled the greater number of inhabitants to migrate to S. Carlos. We had not long bivouacked, before the barefooted son of the governor came down to reconnoitre us. Seeing the English flag hoisted at the yawl's mast-head, he asked, with the utmost indifference, whether it was always to fly at Chacao. In several places, the inhabitants were much astonished at the appearance of men-of-war's boats, and hoped and believed it was the forerunner of a Spanish fleet, coming to recover the island from the patriot government of Chile. All the men in power, however, had been informed of our intended visit, and were exceedingly civil. While we were eating our supper, the governor paid us a visit. He had been a lieutenant-colonel in the Spanish service, but now was miserably poor. He gave us two sheep, and accepted in return two cotton handkerchiefs, some brass trinkets, and a little tobacco.

25th.—Torrents of rain: we managed, however, to run down the coast as far as Huapi-lenou. The whole of this eastern side of Chiloe has one aspect: it is a plain, broken by valleys and divided into little islands, and the whole thickly covered with one impervious blackish-green forest. On the margins there are some cleared spaces, surrounding the high-roofed cottages.

26th.—The day rose splendidly clear. The volcano of Osorno was spouting out volumes of smoke. This most beautiful mountain, formed like a perfect cone, and white with snow, stands out in front of the Cordillera. Another great volcano, with a saddle-shaped summit, also emitted from its immense crater little jets of steam. Subsequently we saw the lofty-peaked Corcovado—well deserving the name of "el famoso Corcovado." Thus we beheld, from one point of view, three great active volcanoes, each about seven thousand feet high. In addition to this, far to the south, there were other lofty cones covered with snow, which, although not known to be active, must be in their origin volcanic. The line of the Andes is not, in this neighbourhood, nearly so elevated as in Chile; neither does it appear to form so perfect a barrier between the regions of the earth. This great range, although running in a straight north and south line, owing to an optical deception, always appeared more or less curved; for the lines drawn from each peak to the beholder's eye, necessarily converged like the radii of a semi-circle, and as it was not possible (owing to the clearness of the atmosphere and the absence of all intermediate objects) to judge how far distant the farthest peaks were off, they appeared to stand in a flattish semi-circle.

Landing at midday, we saw a family of pure Indian extraction. The father was singularly like York Minster; and some of the younger boys, with their ruddy complexions, might have been mistaken for Pampas Indians. Everything I have seen, convinces me of the close connexion of the different American tribes, who nevertheless speak distinct languages. This party could muster but little Spanish, and talked to each other in their own tongue. It is a pleasant thing to see the aborigines advanced to the same degree of civilization, however low that may be, which their white conquerors have attained. More to the south we saw many pure Indians: indeed, all the inhabitants of some of the islets retain their Indian surnames. In the census of 1832, there were in Chiloe and its dependencies forty-two thousand souls: the greater number of these appear to be of mixed blood. Eleven thousand retain their Indian surnames, but it is probable that not nearly all of these are of a pure breed. Their manner of life is the same with that of the other poor inhabitants, and they are all Christians; but it is said that they yet retain some strange superstitious ceremonies, and that they pretend to hold communication with the devil in certain caves. Formerly, every one convicted of this offence was sent to the Inquisition at Lima. Many of the inhabitants who are not included in the eleven thousand with Indian surnames, cannot be distinguished by their appearance from Indians. Gomez,

the governor of Lemuy, is descended from noblemen of Spain
on both sides; but by constant intermarriages with the natives
the present man is an Indian. On the other hand, the governor
of Quinchao boasts much of his purely kept Spanish blood.

We reached at night a beautiful little cove, north of the island
of Caucahue. The people here complained of want of land.
This is partly owing to their own negligence in not clearing
the woods, and partly to restrictions by the government, which
makes it necessary before buying ever so small a piece, to pay
two shillings to the surveyor, for measuring each quadra (150
yards square), together with whatever price he fixes for the
value of the land. After his valuation, the land must be put up
three times to auction, and if no one bids more, the purchaser
can have it at that rate. All these exactions must be a serious
check to clearing the ground, where the inhabitants are so extremely poor. In most countries, forests are removed without
much difficulty by the aid of fire; but in Chiloe, from the damp
nature of the climate, and the sort of trees, it is necessary first
to cut them down. This is a heavy drawback to the prosperity
of Chiloe. In the time of the Spaniards the Indians could not
hold land; and a family, after having cleared a piece of ground,
might be driven away, and the property seized by the government. The Chilian authorities are now performing an act of
justice by making retribution to these poor Indians, giving to
each man, according to his grade of life, a certain portion of
land. The value of uncleared ground is very little. The government gave Mr. Douglas (the present surveyor, who informed me of these circumstances) eight and a half square
miles of forest near San Carlos, in lieu of a debt; and this he
sold for 350 dollars, or about 70*l.* sterling.

The two succeeding days were fine, and at night we reached
the island of Quinchao. This neighbourhood is the most cultivated part of the Archipelago; for a broad strip of land on the
coast of the main island, as well as on many of the smaller
adjoining ones, is almost completely cleared. Some of the farm-
houses seemed very comfortable. I was curious to ascertain
how rich any of these people might be, but Mr. Douglas says
that no one can be considered as possessing a regular income.
One of the richest landowners might possibly accumulate, in a
long industrious life, as much as 1000*l.* sterling; but should
this happen, it would all be stowed away in some secret corner,
for it is the custom of almost every family to have a jar or
treasure-chest buried in the ground.

November 30*th*.—Early on Sunday morning we reached Castro, the ancient capital of Chiloe, but now a most forlorn and deserted place. The usual quadrangular arrangement of Spanish towns could be traced, but the streets and plaza were coated with fine green turf, on which sheep were browsing. The church, which stands in the middle, is entirely built of plank, and has a picturesque and venerable appearance. The poverty of the place may be conceived from the fact, that although containing some hundreds of inhabitants, one of our party was unable anywhere to purchase either a pound of sugar or an ordinary knife. No individual possessed either a watch or a clock; and an old man, who was supposed to have a good idea of time, was employed to strike the church bell by guess. The arrival of our boats was a rare event in this quiet retired corner of the world; and nearly all the inhabitants came down to the beach to see us pitch our tents. They were very civil, and offered us a house; and one man even sent us a cask of cider as a present. In the afternoon we paid our respects to the governor—a quiet old man, who, in his appearance and manner of life, was scarcely superior to an English cottager. At night heavy rain set in, which was hardly sufficient to drive away from our tents the large circle of lookers on. An Indian family, who had come to trade in a canoe from Caylen, bivouacked near us. They had no shelter during the rain. In the morning I asked a young Indian, who was wet to the skin, how he had passed the night. He seemed perfectly content, and answered, "Muy bien, señor."

December 1*st*.—We steered for the island of Lemuy. I was anxious to examine a reported coal-mine, which turned out to be lignite of little value, in the sandstone (probably of an ancient tertiary epoch) of which these islands are composed. When we reached Lemuy we had much difficulty in finding any place to pitch our tents, for it was spring-tide, and the land was wooded down to the water's edge. In a short time we were surrounded by a large group of the nearly pure Indian inhabitants. They were much surprised at our arrival, and said one to the other, "This is the reason we have seen so many parrots lately; the cheucau (an odd red-breasted little bird, which inhabits the thick forest, and utters very peculiar noises) has not cried 'beware' for nothing." They were soon anxious for barter. Money was scarcely worth anything, but their eagerness for tobacco was something quite extraordinary. After tobacco, indigo came next in value; then capsicum, old clothes, and gunpowder. The latter article was required for a very innocent purpose: each parish has a public musket, and the gunpowder was wanted for making a noise on their saint or feast days.

The people here live chiefly on shell-fish and potatoes. At certain seasons they catch also, in "corrales," or hedges under water, many fish which are left on the mud-banks as the tide falls. They occasionally possess fowls, sheep, goats, pigs, horses, and cattle; the order in which they are here mentioned, expressing their respective numbers. I never saw anything more obliging and humble than the manners of these people. They generally began with stating, that they were poor natives of the place, and not Spaniards, and that they were in sad want of tobacco and other comforts. At Caylen, the most southern island, the sailors bought with a stick of tobacco, of the value of three-halfpence, two fowls, one of which, the Indian stated, had skin between its toes, and turned out to be a fine duck; and with some cotton handkerchiefs, worth three shillings, three sheep and a large bunch of onions were procured. The yawl at this place was anchored some way from the shore, and we had fears for her safety from robbers during the night. Our pilot, Mr. Douglas, accordingly told the constable of the district that we always placed sentinels with loaded arms, and not understanding Spanish, if we saw any person in the dark, we should assuredly shoot him. The constable, with much humility, agreed to the perfect propriety of this arrangement, and promised us that no one should stir out of his house during that night.

During the four succeeding days we continued sailing southward. The general features of the country remained the same, but it was much less thickly inhabited. On the large island of Tanqui there was scarcely one cleared spot, the trees on every side extending their branches over the sea-beach. I one day noticed, growing on the sandstone cliffs, some very fine plants of the panke (Gunnera scabra), which somewhat resembles the rhubarb on a gigantic scale. The inhabitants eat the stalks, which are subacid, and tan leather with the roots, and prepare a black dye from them. The leaf is nearly circular, but deeply indented on its margin. I measured one which was nearly eight feet in diameter, and therefore no less than twenty-four in circumference! The stalk is rather more than a yard high, and each plant sends out four or five of these enormous leaves, presenting together a very noble appearance.

December 6th.—We reached Caylen,[2] called "el fin del Cristiandad." In the morning we stopped for a few minutes at a house on the northern end of Laylec, which was the extreme point of South American Christendom, and a miserable hovel it was. The latitude is 43° 10′, which is two degrees farther south than the Rio Negro on the Atlantic coast. These extreme Christians were very poor, and, under the plea of their situation, begged for some tobacco. As a proof of the poverty of these Indians, I may mention that shortly before this, we had met a man, who had travelled three days and a half on foot, and had as many to return, for the sake of recovering the value of a small axe and a few fish. How very difficult it must be to buy the smallest article, when such trouble is taken to recover so small a debt!

In the evening we reached the island of San Pedro, where we found the *Beagle* at anchor. In doubling the point, two of the officers landed to take a round of angles with the theodolite. A fox (Canis fulvipes), of a kind said to be peculiar to the island, and very rare in it, and which is a new species, was sitting on the rocks. He was so intently absorbed in watching the work of the officers, that I was able, by quietly walking up behind, to knock him on the head with my geological hammer. This fox, more curious or more scientific, but less wise, than the generality of his brethren, is now mounted in the museum of the Zoological Society.

We stayed three days in this harbour, on one of which Captain Fitz Roy, with a party, attempted to ascend to the summit of San Pedro. The woods here had rather a different appearance from those on the northern part of the island. The rock, also, being micaceous slate, there was no beach, but the steep sides dipped directly beneath the water. The general aspect in consequence was more like that of Tierra del Fuego than of Chiloe. In vain we tried to gain the summit: the forest was so impenetrable, that no one who has not beheld it, can imagine so entangled a mass of dying and dead trunks. I am sure that often, for more than ten minutes together, our feet never touched the ground, and we were frequently ten or fifteen feet above it, so that the seamen as a joke called out the soundings. At other times we crept one after another on our hands and knees, under the rotten trunks. In the lower part of the moun-

[2] [Editor] Today called Quilan, a village at the southern tip of Chiloé Island.

tain, noble trees of the Winter's Bark, and a laurel like the
sassafras with fragrant leaves, and others, the names of which
I do not know, were matted together by a trailing bamboo or
cane. Here we were more like fishes struggling in a net than any
other animal. On the higher parts, brushwood takes the place
of larger trees, with here and there a red cedar or an alerce
pine. I was also pleased to see, at an elevation of a little less
than 1000 feet, our old friend the southern beech. They were,
however, poor stunted trees; and I should think that this must
be nearly their northern limit. We ultimately gave up the attempt in despair.

December 10th.—The yawl and whale-boat, with Mr. Sulivan, proceeded on their survey, but I remained on board the
Beagle, which the next day left San Pedro for the southward.
On the 13th we ran into an opening[3] in the southern part of
Guayatecas, or the Chonos Archipelago; and it was fortunate
we did so, for on the following day a storm, worthy of Tierra
del Fuego, raged with great fury. White massive clouds were
piled up against a dark blue sky, and across them black ragged
sheets of vapour were rapidly driven. The successive mountain
ranges appeared like dim shadows; and the setting sun cast on
the woodland a yellow gleam, much like that produced by the
flame of spirits of wine. The water was white with the flying
spray, and the wind lulled and roared again through the rigging: it was an ominous, sublime scene. During a few minutes
there was a bright rainbow, and it was curious to observe the
effect of the spray, which, being carried along the surface of
the water, changed the ordinary semi-circle into a circle—a
band of prismatic colours being continued, from both feet of
the common arch across the bay, close to the vessel's side:
thus forming a distorted, but very nearly entire ring.

We stayed here three days. The weather continued bad; but
this did not much signify, for the surface of the land in all these
islands is all but impassable. The coast is so very rugged that
to attempt to walk in that direction requires continued scrambling up and down over the sharp rocks of mica-slate; and as
for the woods, our faces, hands, and shin-bones all bore witness to the maltreatment we received, in merely attempting to
penetrate their forbidden recesses.

December 18th.—We stood out to sea. On the 20th we bade

[3] [Editor] One of the passages through the Chonos Archipelago
is named Darwin Channel, but neither Darwin nor Fitz Roy reveals
whether this was the passage the *Beagle* took.

farewell to the south, and with a fair wind turned the ship's head northward. From Cape Tres Montes we sailed pleasantly along the lofty weather-beaten coast, which is remarkable for the bold outline of its hills, and the thick covering of forest even on the almost precipitous flanks. The next day a harbour was discovered, which on this dangerous coast might be of great service to a distressed vessel. It can easily be recognized by a hill 1600 feet high, which is even more perfectly conical than the famous sugar-loaf at Rio de Janeiro. The next day, after anchoring, I succeeded in reaching the summit of this hill. It was a laborious undertaking, for the sides were so steep that in some parts it was necessary to use the trees as ladders. There were also several extensive brakes of the Fuchsia, covered with its beautiful drooping flowers, but very difficult to crawl through. In these wild countries it gives much delight to gain the summit of any mountain. There is an indefinite expectation of seeing something very strange, which, however often it may be balked, never failed with me to recur on each successive attempt. Every one must know the feeling of triumph and pride which a grand view from a height communicates to the mind. In these little frequented countries there is also joined to it some vanity, that you perhaps are the first man who ever stood on this pinnacle or admired this view.

A strong desire is always felt to ascertain whether any human being has previously visited an unfrequented spot. A bit of wood with a nail in it, is picked up and studied as if it were covered with hieroglyphics. Possessed with this feeling, I was much interested by finding, on a wild part of the coast, a bed made of grass beneath a ledge of rock. Close by it there had been a fire, and the man had used an axe. The fire, bed, and situation showed the dexterity of an Indian; but he could scarcely have been an Indian, for the race is in this part extinct, owing to the Catholic desire of making at one blow Christians and Slaves. I had at the time some misgivings that the solitary man who had made his bed on this wild spot, must have been some poor shipwrecked sailor, who, in trying to travel up the coast, had here laid himself down for his dreary night.

December 28th.—The weather continued very bad, but it at last permitted us to proceed with the survey. The time hung heavy on our hands, as it always did when we were delayed from day to day by successive gales of wind. In the evening another harbour was discovered, where we anchored. Directly afterwards a man was seen waving his shirt, and a boat was sent which brought back two seamen. A party of six had run away from an American whaling vessel, and had landed a little to the southward in a boat, which was shortly afterwards knocked to pieces by the surf. They had now been wandering up and down the coast for fifteen months, without knowing which way to go, or where they were. What a singular piece of good fortune it was that this harbour was now discovered! Had it not been for this one chance, they might have wandered till they had grown old men, and at last have perished on this wild coast. Their sufferings had been very great, and one of their party had lost his life by falling from the cliffs. They were sometimes obliged to separate in search of food, and this explained the bed of the solitary man. Considering what they had undergone, I think they had kept a very good reckoning of time, for they had lost only four days.[4]

[4] [Editor] Fitz Roy gives a more detailed and somewhat different account of the Yankee castaways and their rescue, as follows:

"While we were furling sails, some men were seen on a point of land near the ship, making signals to us in a very earnest manner. Being dressed as sailors, it was natural for us to conclude that they were some boat's crew left there to collect sealskins. A boat was sent to them, and directly she touched the land they rushed into her, without saying a word, as men would if pursued by a dreaded enemy; and not till they were afloat would they compose themselves enough to tell their story. They were North American sailors, who had deserted from the Frances Henrietta (a whaler of New Bedford), in October 1833. When off Cape Tres Montes, but out of sight of land, and in the middle of the night, these six men lowered a boat and left their ship, intending to coast along until they should arrive at Chiloe. Their first landing was effected on the 18th, but owing to negligence the boat was so badly stove that they could not repair her, and all their hopes of effecting a coasting voyage were thus crushed in the very outset.

"Finding it impossible to penetrate far into the country, on account of its ruggedness, and thick forests, which, though only trifling in height, were almost impervious, they began a pilgrimage along-shore; but it was soon evident, to their dismay, that there were so many arms of the sea to pass round, and it was so difficult to walk, or rather climb, along the rocky shores, that they must abandon that idea also, and remain stationary. To this decision they were perhaps more inclined after the death of one of their number: who, in trying to cross a chasm between two cliffs, failed in his leap, fell, and was dashed to pieces. Their permanent abode was then taken up at the point which shelters Port San Estevan, now called Rescue Point; where they passed a year in anxious hope. Of course the few provisions which their boat had carried ashore

December 30th.—We anchored in a snug little cove at the foot of some high hills, near the northern extremity of Tres Montes. After breakfast the next morning, a party ascended one of these mountains, which was 2400 feet high. The scenery was remarkable. The chief part of the range was composed of grand, solid, abrupt masses of granite, which appeared as if they had been coeval with the beginning of the world. The granite was capped with mica-slate, and this in the lapse of ages had been worn into strange finger-shaped points. These two formations, thus differing in their outlines, agreed in being almost destitute of vegetation. This barrenness had to our eyes a strange appearance, from having been so long accustomed to the sight of an almost universal forest of dark-green trees. I took much delight in examining the structure of these mountains. The complicated and lofty ranges bore a noble aspect of durability—equally profitless, however, to man and to all other animals. Granite to the geologist is classic ground: from its wide-spread limits, and its beautiful and compact texture, few rocks have been more anciently recognized. Granite has given rise, perhaps, to more discussion concerning its origin than any other formation. We generally see it constituting the fundamental rock, and, however formed, we know it is the deepest layer in the crust of this globe to which man has penetrated. The limit of man's knowledge in any subject possesses a high interest, which is perhaps increased by its close neighbourhood to the realms of imagination.

January 1st, 1835.—The new year is ushered in with the ceremonies proper to it in these regions. She lays out no false hopes: a heavy north-western gale, with steady rain, bespeaks the rising year. Thank God, we are not destined here to see the end of it, but hope then to be in the Pacific Ocean, where a blue sky tells one there is a heaven,—a something beyond the clouds above our heads.

The north-west winds prevailing for the next four days, we only managed to cross a great bay, and then anchored in another secure harbour. I accompanied the Captain in a boat to the head of a deep creek. On the way the number of seals which we saw was quite astonishing: every bit of flat rock, and

———

were soon exhausted, and for thirteen months they had lived only upon seals' flesh, shell-fish, and wild celery; yet those five men, when received on board the Beagle, were in better condition, as to healthy fleshiness, colour, and actual health, than any five individuals belonging to our ship."

parts of the beach, were covered with them. They appeared
to be of a loving disposition, and lay huddled together, fast
asleep, like so many pigs; but even pigs would have been
ashamed of their dirt, and of the foul smell which came from
them. Each herd was watched by the patient but inauspicious
eyes of the turkey-buzzard. This disgusting bird, with its bald
scarlet head, formed to wallow in putridity, is very common
on the west coast, and their attendance on the seals shows on
what they rely for their food. We found the water (probably
only that of the surface) nearly fresh: this was caused by the
number of torrents which, in the form of cascades, came tumbling over the bold granite mountains into the sea. The fresh
water attracts the fish, and these bring many terns, gulls, and
two kinds of cormorant. We saw also a pair of the beautiful
black-necked swans, and several small sea-otters, the fur of
which is held in such high estimation. In returning, we were
again amused by the impetuous manner in which the heap of
seals, old and young, tumbled into the water as the boat passed.
They did not remain long under water, but rising, followed us
with outstretched necks, expressing great wonder and curiosity.

7th.—Having run up the coast, we anchored near the northern end of the Chonos Archipelago, in Low's Harbour, where
we remained a week. The islands were here, as in Chiloe, composed of a stratified, soft, littoral deposit; and the vegetation
in consequence was beautifully luxuriant. The woods came
down to the sea-beach, just in the manner of an evergreen
shrubbery over a gravel walk. We also enjoyed from the anchorage a splendid view of four great snowy cones of the
Cordillera, including "el famoso Corcovado:" the range itself
had in this latitude so little height, that few parts of it appeared
above the tops of the neighbouring islets. We found here a
party of five men from Caylen, "el fin del Cristiandad," who
had most adventurously crossed in their miserable boat-canoe,
for the purpose of fishing, the open space of sea which separates Chonos from Chiloe. These islands will, in all probability,
in a short time become peopled like those adjoining the coast
of Chiloe.

The wild potato grows on these islands in great abundance,
on the sandy, shelly soil near the sea-beach. The tallest plant
was four feet in height. The tubers were generally small, but
I found one, of an oval shape, two inches in diameter: they
resembled in every respect, and had the same smell as English
potatoes; but when boiled they shrunk much, and were watery

and insipid, without any bitter taste. They are undoubtedly here indigenous: they grow as far south, according to Mr. Low, as lat. 50°, and are called Aquinas by the wild Indians of that part: the Chilotan Indians have a different name for them. Professor Henslow, who has examined the dried specimens which I brought home, says that they are the same with those described by Mr. Sabine[5] from Valparaiso, but that they form a variety which by some botanists has been considered as specifically distinct. It is remarkable that the same plant should be found on the sterile mountains of central Chile, where a drop of rain does not fall for more than six months, and within the damp forests of these southern islands.

In the central parts of the Chonos Archipelago (lat. 45°), the forest has very much the same character with that along the whole west coast, for 600 miles southward to Cape Horn. The arborescent grass of Chiloe is not found here; while the beech of Tierra del Fuego grows to a good size, and forms a considerable proportion of the wood; not, however, in the same exclusive manner as it does farther southward. Cryptogamic plants here find a most congenial climate. In the Strait of Magellan, as I have before remarked, the country appears too cold and wet to allow of their arriving at perfection; but in these islands, within the forest, the number of species and great abundance of mosses, lichens, and small ferns, is quite extraordinary.[6] In Tierra del Fuego trees grow only on the hill-sides; every level piece of land being invariably covered by a thick bed of peat; but in Chiloe flat land supports the most luxuriant forests. Here, within the Chonos Archipelago, the nature of the climate more closely approaches that of Tierra del Fuego than that of northern Chiloe; for every patch of level ground is covered by two species of plants (Astelia pumila and Donatia

[5] [Darwin] Horticultural Transact., vol. v. p. 249. Mr. Caldcleugh sent home two tubers, which, being well manured, even the first season produced numerous potatoes and an abundance of leaves. See Humboldt's interesting discussion on this plant, which it appears was unknown in Mexico,—in Polit. Essay on New Spain, book iv. chap. ix.

[6] [Darwin] By sweeping with my insect-net, I procured from these situations a considerable number of minute insects, of the family of Staphylinidæ, and others allied to Pselaphus, and minute Hymenoptera. But the most characteristic family in number, both of individuals and species, throughout the more open parts of Chiloe and Chonos, is that of the Telephoridæ.

magellanica), which by their joint decay compose a thick bed of elastic peat.

In Tierra del Fuego, above the region of woodland, the former of these eminently sociable plants is the chief agent in the production of peat. Fresh leaves are always succeeding one to the other round the central tap-root; the lower ones soon decay, and in tracing a root downwards in the peat, the leaves, yet holding their place, can be observed passing through every stage of decomposition, till the whole becomes blended in one confused mass. The Astelia is assisted by a few other plants,— here and there a small creeping Myrtus (M. nummularia), with a woody stem like our cranberry and with a sweet berry, —an Empetrum (E. rubrum), like our heath,—a rush (Juncus grandiflorus), are nearly the only ones that grow on the swampy surface. These plants, though possessing a very close general resemblance to the English species of the same genera, are different. In the more level parts of the country, the surface of the peat is broken up into little pools of water, which stand at different heights, and appear as if artificially excavated. Small streams of water, flowing underground, complete the disorganization of the vegetable matter, and consolidate the whole.

The climate of the southern part of America appears particularly favourable to the production of peat. In the Falkland Islands almost every kind of plant, even the coarse grass which covers the whole surface of the land, becomes converted into this substance: scarcely any situation checks its growth; some of the beds are as much as twelve feet thick, and the lower part becomes so solid when dry, that it will hardly burn. Although every plant lends its aid, yet in most parts the Astelia is the most efficient. It is rather a singular circumstance, as being so very different from what occurs in Europe, that I nowhere saw moss forming by its decay any portion of the peat in South America. With respect to the northern limit, at which the climate allows of that peculiar kind of slow decomposition which is necessary for its production, I believe that in Chiloe (lat. 41° to 42°), although there is much swampy ground, no well characterized peat occurs: but in the Chonos Islands, three degrees farther southward, we have seen that it is abundant. On the eastern coast in La Plata (lat. 35°) I was told by a Spanish resident, who had visited Ireland, that he had often sought for this substance, but had never been able to find any. He showed me, as the nearest approach to it which he had dis-

covered, a black peaty soil, so penetrated with roots as to allow
of an extremely slow and imperfect combustion.

The zoology of these broken islets of the Chonos Archipelago is, as might have been expected, very poor. Of quadrupeds two aquatic kinds are common. The Myopotamus Coypus
(like a beaver, but with a round tail) is well known from its
fine fur, which is an object of trade throughout the tributaries
of La Plata. It here, however, exclusively frequents salt water;
which same circumstance has been mentioned as sometimes
occurring with the great rodent, the Capybara. A small sea-
otter is very numerous; this animal does not feed exclusively
on fish, but, like the seals, draws a large supply from a small
red crab, which swims in shoals near the surface of the water.
Mr. Bynoe saw one in Tierra del Fuego eating a cuttle-fish;
and at Low's Harbour, another was killed in the act of carrying
to its hole a large volute shell. At one place I caught in a trap
a singular little mouse (M. brachiotis); it appeared common
on several of the islets, but the Chilotans at Low's Harbour
said that it was not found in all. What a succession of chances,[7]
or what changes of level must have been brought into play,
thus to spread these small animals throughout this broken
archipelago!

In all parts of Chiloe and Chonos, two very strange birds
occur, which are allied to, and replace, the Turco and Tapacolo
of central Chile. One is called by the inhabitants "Cheucau"
(Pteroptochos rubecula): it frequents the most gloomy and
retired spots within the damp forests. Sometimes, although its
cry may be heard close at hand, let a person watch ever so
attentively he will not see the cheucau; at other times, let him
stand motionless and the red-breasted little bird will approach
within a few feet in the most familiar manner. It then busily
hops about the entangled mass of rotting canes and branches,
with its little tail cocked upwards. The cheucau is held in superstitious fear by the Chilotans, on account of its strange and
varied cries. There are three very distinct cries: one is called
"chiduco," and is an omen of good; another, "huitreu," which
is extremely unfavourable; and a third, which I have forgotten.

[7] [Darwin] It is said that some rapacious birds bring their prey
alive to their nests. If so, in the course of centuries, every now and
then, one might escape from the young birds. Some such agency is
necessary, to account for the distribution of the smaller gnawing
animals on islands not very near each other.

These words are given in imitation of the noises; and the natives are in some things absolutely governed by them. The Chilotans assuredly have chosen a most comical little creature for their prophet. An allied species, but rather larger, is called by the natives "Guid-guid" (Pteroptochos Tarnii), and by the English the barking-bird. This latter name is well given; for I defy any one at first to feel certain that a small dog is not yelping somewhere in the forest. Just as with the cheucau, a person will sometimes hear the bark close by, but in vain may endeavour by watching, and with still less chance by beating the bushes, to see the bird; yet at other times the guid-guid fearlessly comes near. Its manner of feeding and its general habits are very similar to those of the cheucau.

On the coast,[8] a small dusky-coloured bird (Opetiorhynchus Patagonicus) is very common. It is remarkable from its quiet habits; it lives entirely on the sea-beach, like a sandpiper. Besides these birds only few others inhabit this broken land. In my rough notes I describe the strange noises, which, although frequently heard within these gloomy forests, yet scarcely disturb the general silence. The yelping of the guid-guid, and the sudden whew-whew of the cheucau, sometimes come from afar off, and sometimes from close at hand; the little black wren of Tierra del Fuego occasionally adds its cry; the creeper (Oxyurus) follows the intruder screaming and twittering; the humming-bird may be seen every now and then darting from side to side, and emitting, like an insect, its shrill chirp; lastly, from the top of some lofty tree the indistinct but plaintive note of the white-tufted tyrant-flycatcher (Myiobius) may be noticed. From the great preponderance in most countries of certain common genera of birds, such as the finches, one feels at first surprised at meeting with the peculiar forms above enumerated, as the commonest birds in any district. In central Chile two of them, namely, the Oxyurus and Scytalopus, occur, although most rarely. When finding, as in this case, animals which seem to play so insignificant a part in the great scheme of nature, one is apt to wonder why they were created. But it should always be recollected, that in some other country per-

---

[8] [Darwin] I may mention, as a proof of how great a difference there is between the seasons of the wooded and the open parts of this coast, that on September 20th, in lat. 34°, these birds had young ones in the nest, while among the Chonos Islands, three months later in the summer, they were only laying; the difference in latitude between these two places being about 700 miles.

haps they are essential members of society, or at some former period may have been so. If America south of 37° were sunk beneath the waters of the ocean, these two birds might continue to exist in central Chile for a long period, but it is very improbable that their numbers would increase. We should then see a case which must inevitably have happened with very many animals.

These southern seas are frequented by several species of Petrels: the largest kind, Procellaria gigantea, or nelly (quebrantahuesos, or break-bones, of the Spaniards), is a common bird, both in the inland channels and on the open sea. In its habits and manner of flight, there is a very close resemblance with the albatross; and as with the albatross, a person may watch it for hours together without seeing on what it feeds. The "break-bones" is, however, a rapacious bird, for it was observed by some of the officers of Port St. Antonio chasing a diver, which tried to escape by diving and flying, but was continually struck down, and at last killed by a blow on its head. At Port St. Julian these great petrels were seen killing and devouring young gulls. A second species (Puffinus cinereus), which is common to Europe, Cape Horn, and the coast of Peru, is of a much smaller size than the P. gigantea, but, like it, of a dirty black colour. It generally frequents the inland sounds in very large flocks: I do not think I ever saw so many birds of any other sort together, as I once saw of these behind the island of Chiloe. Hundreds of thousands flew in an irregular line for several hours in one direction. When part of the flock settled on the water the surface was blackened, and a noise proceeded from them as of human beings talking in the distance.

There are several other species of petrels, but I will only mention one other kind, the Pelacanoides Berardi, which offers an example of those extraordinary cases, of a bird evidently belonging to one well-marked family, yet both in its habits and structure allied to a very distinct tribe. This bird never leaves the quiet inland sounds. When disturbed it dives to a distance, and on coming to the surface, with the same movement takes flight. After flying by the rapid movement of its short wings for a space in a straight line, it drops, as if struck dead, and dives again. The form of its beak and nostrils, length of foot, and even the colouring of its plumage, show that this bird is a petrel: on the other hand, its short wings and consequent little power of flight, its form of body and shape of tail, the absence of a hind toe to its foot, its habit of diving, and its choice of situation, make it at first doubtful whether its relationship is not equally close with the auks. It would undoubtedly be mistaken for an auk, when seen from a distance, either on the wing, or when diving and quietly swimming about the retired channels of Tierra del Fuego.

CHAPTER XIV

CHILOE AND CONCEPCION: GREAT EARTHQUAKE

San Carlos, Chiloe — Osorno in eruption, contemporaneously with Aconcagua and Coseguina — Ride to Cucao — Impenetrable Forests — Valdivia — Indians — Earthquake — Concepcion — Great Earthquake — Rocks fissured — Appearance of the former Towns — The Sea black and boiling — Direction of the Vibrations — Stones twisted round — Great Wave — Permanent elevation of the Land — Area of Volcanic Phenomena — The connexion between the elevatory and eruptive forces — Cause of Earthquakes — Slow elevation of Mountain-chains

On January the 15th we sailed from Low's Harbour, and three days afterwards anchored a second time in the bay of S. Carlos in Chiloe. On the night of the 19th the volcano of Osorno was in action. At midnight the sentry observed something like a large star, which gradually increased in size till about three o'clock, when it presented a very magnificent spectacle. By the aid of a glass, dark objects, in constant succession, were seen, in the midst of a great glare of red light, to be thrown up and to fall down. The light was sufficient to cast on the water a long bright reflection. Large masses of molten matter seem very commonly to be cast out of the craters in this part of the Cordillera. I was assured that when the Corcovado is in eruption, great masses are projected upwards and are seen to burst in the air, assuming many fantastical forms, such as trees: their size must be immense, for they can be distinguished from the high land behind S. Carlos, which is no less than ninety-three miles from the Corcovado. In the morning the volcano became tranquil.

I was surprised at hearing afterwards that Aconcagua in Chile, 480 miles northwards, was in action on this same night; and still more surprised to hear, that the great eruption of Coseguina (2700 miles north of Aconcagua), accompanied by an earthquake felt over 1000 miles, also occurred within six hours of this same time. This coincidence is the more remarkable, as Coseguina had been dormant for twenty-six years: and Aconcagua most rarely shows any signs of action. It is difficult even to conjecture, whether this coincidence was accidental, or shows some subterranean connexion. If Vesuvius, Etna, and Hecla in Iceland (all three relatively nearer each other, than the corresponding points in South America) suddenly burst forth in eruption on the same night, the coincidence would be thought remarkable; but it is far more remarkable in this case, where the three vents fall on the same great mountain-chain, and where the vast plains along the entire eastern coast, and the upraised recent shells along more than 2000 miles on the western coast, show in how equable and connected a manner the elevatory forces have acted.

Captain Fitz Roy being anxious that some bearings should be taken on the outer coast of Chiloe, it was planned that Mr. King and myself should ride to Castro, and thence across the island to the Capella de Cucao, situated on the west coast. Having hired horses and a guide, we set out on the morning of the 22nd. We had not proceeded far, before we were joined by a woman and two boys, who were bent on the same journey. Every one on this road acts on a "hail fellow well met fashion;" and one may here enjoy the privilege, so rare in South America, of travelling without fire-arms. At first, the country consisted of a succession of hills and valleys: nearer to Castro it became very level. The road itself is a curious affair: it consists in its whole length, with the exception of very few parts, of great logs of wood, which are either broad and laid longitudinally, or narrow and placed transversely. In summer the road is not very bad: but in winter, when the wood is rendered slippery from rain, travelling is exceedingly difficult. At that time of the year, the ground on each side becomes a morass, and is often overflowed: hence it is necessary that the longitudinal logs should be fastened down by transverse poles, which are pegged on each side into the earth. These pegs render a fall from a horse dangerous; as the chance of alighting on one of them is not small. It is remarkable, however, how active custom has made the Chilotan horses. In crossing bad parts, where the logs had been displaced, they skipped from one to the other, almost with the quickness and certainty of a dog. On both hands the road is bordered by the lofty forest-trees, with their bases matted together by canes. When occasionally a long reach of this avenue could be beheld, it presented a curious scene of uniformity: the white line of logs, narrowing in perspective, became hidden by the gloomy forest, or terminated in a zigzag which ascended some steep hill.

Although the distance from S. Carlos to Castro is only twelve leagues in a straight line, the formation of the road must have been a great labour. I was told that several people had formerly lost their lives in attempting to cross the forest. The first who succeeded was an Indian, who cut his way through the canes in eight days, and reached S. Carlos: he was rewarded by the Spanish government with a grant of land. During the summer, many of the Indians wander about the forests (but chiefly in the higher parts, where the woods are not quite so thick), in search of the half-wild cattle which live on the leaves of the cane and certain trees. It was one of these huntsmen who by chance discovered, a few years since, an English vessel, which had been wrecked on the outer coast. The crew were beginning to fail in provisions, and it is not probable that, without the aid of this man, they would ever have extricated themselves from these scarcely penetrable woods. As it was, one seaman died on the march, from fatigue. The Indians in these excursions steer by the sun: so that if there is a continuance of cloudy weather, they cannot travel.

The day was beautiful, and the number of trees which were in full flower perfumed the air; yet even this could hardly dissipate the effect of the gloomy dampness of the forest. Moreover, the many dead trunks that stand like skeletons, never fail to give to these primeval woods a character of solemnity, absent in those of countries long civilized. Shortly after sunset we bivouacked for the night. Our female companion, who was rather good-looking, belonged to one of the most respectable families in Castro: she rode, however, astride, and without shoes or stockings. I was surprised at the total want of pride shown by her and her brother. They brought food with them, but at all our meals sat watching Mr. King and myself whilst eating, till we were fairly shamed into feeding the whole party. The night was cloudless; and while lying in our beds, we enjoyed the sight (and it is a high enjoyment) of the multitude of stars which illumined the darkness of the forest.

January 23rd.—We rose early in the morning, and reached the pretty quiet town of Castro by two o'clock. The old gover-

nor had died since our last visit, and a Chileno was acting in
his place. We had a letter of introduction to Don Pedro, whom
we found exceedingly hospitable and kind, and more disinterested than is usual on this side of the continent. The next day
Don Pedro procured us fresh horses, and offered to accompany
us himself. We proceeded to the south—generally following the
coast, and passing through several hamlets, each with its large
barn-like chapel built of wood. At Vilipilli, Don Pedro asked
the commandant to give us a guide to Cucao. The old gentleman offered to come himself; but for a long time nothing would
persuade him, that two Englishmen really wished to go to such
an out of the way place as Cucao. We were thus accompanied
by the two greatest aristocrats in the country, as was plainly
to be seen in the manner of all the poorer Indians towards
them. At Chonchi we struck across the island, following intricate winding paths, sometimes passing through magnificent
forests, and sometimes through pretty cleared spots, abounding with corn and potato crops. This undulating woody country, partially cultivated, reminded me of the wilder parts of
England, and therefore had to my eye a most fascinating aspect. At Vilinco, which is situated on the borders of the lake of
Cucao, only a few fields were cleared; and all the inhabitants
appeared to be Indians. This lake is twelve miles long, and
runs in an east and west direction. From local circumstances,
the sea-breeze blows very regularly during the day, and during the night it falls calm: this has given rise to strange exag-
gerations, for the phenomenon, as described to us at San Carlos,
was quite a prodigy.

The road to Cucao was so very bad that we determined to
embark in a *periagua*. The commandant, in the most authoritative manner, ordered six Indians to get ready to pull us over,
without deigning to tell them whether they would be paid.
The periagua is a strange rough boat, but the crew were still
stranger: I doubt if six uglier little men ever got into a boat
together. They pulled, however, very well and cheerfully. The
stroke-oarsman gabbled Indian, and uttered strange cries, much
after the fashion of a pig-driver driving his pigs. We started
with a light breeze against us, but yet reached the Capella de
Cucao before it was late. The country on each side of the lake
was one unbroken forest. In the same periagua with us, a cow
was embarked. To get so large an animal into a small boat appears at first a difficulty, but the Indians managed it in a minute. They brought the cow alongside the boat, which was heeled

towards her; then placing two oars under her belly, with their ends resting on the gunwale, by the aid of these levers they fairly tumbled the poor beast, heels over head, into the bottom of the boat, and then lashed her down with ropes. At Cucao we found an uninhabited hovel (which is the residence of the padre when he pays this Capella a visit), where, lighting a fire, we cooked our supper, and were very comfortable.

The district of Cucao is the only inhabited part on the whole west coast of Chiloe. It contains about thirty or forty Indian families, who are scattered along four or five miles of the shore. They are very much secluded from the rest of Chiloe, and have scarcely any sort of commerce, except sometimes in a little oil, which they get from seal-blubber. They are tolerably dressed in clothes of their own manufacture, and they have plenty to eat. They seemed, however, discontented, yet humble to a degree which it was quite painful to witness. These feelings are, I think, chiefly to be attributed to the harsh and authoritative manner in which they are treated by their rulers. Our companions, although so very civil to us, behaved to the poor Indians as if they had been slaves, rather than free men. They ordered provisions and the use of their horses, without ever condescending to say how much, or indeed whether the owners should be paid at all. In the morning, being left alone with these poor people, we soon ingratiated ourselves by presents of cigars and maté. A lump of white sugar was divided between all present, and tasted with the greatest curiosity. The Indians ended all their complaints by saying, "And it is only because we are poor Indians, and know nothing; but it was not so when we had a King."

The next day after breakfast, we rode a few miles northward to Punta Huantamó. The road lay along a very broad beach, on which, even after so many fine days, a terrible surf was breaking. I was assured that after a heavy gale, the roar can be heard at night even at Castro, a distance of no less than twenty-one sea-miles across a hilly and wooded country. We had some difficulty in reaching the point, owing to the intolerably bad paths; for everywhere in the shade the ground soon becomes a perfect quagmire. The point itself is a bold rocky hill. It is covered by a plant allied, I believe, to Bromelia, and called by the inhabitants Chepones. In scrambling through the beds, our hands were very much scratched. I was amused by observing the precaution our Indian guide took, in turning up his trowsers, thinking that they were more delicate than his

own hard skin. This plant bears a fruit, in shape like an artichoke, in which a number of seed-vessels are packed: these
contain a pleasant sweet pulp, here much esteemed. I saw at
Low's Harbour the Chilotans making chichi, or cider, with this
fruit: so true is it, as Humboldt remarks, that almost everywhere man finds means of preparing some kind of beverage
from the vegetable kingdom. The savages, however, of Tierra
del Fuego, and I believe of Australia, have not advanced thus
far in the arts.

The coast to the north of Punta Huantamó is exceedingly
rugged and broken, and is fronted by many breakers, on which
the sea is eternally roaring. Mr. King and myself were anxious
to return, if it had been possible, on foot along this coast; but
even the Indians said it was quite impracticable. We were told
that men have crossed by striking directly through the woods
from Cucao to S. Carlos, but never by the coast. On these
expeditions, the Indians carry with them only roasted corn,
and of this they eat sparingly twice a day.

26th.—Re-embarking in the periagua, we returned across the
lake, and then mounted our horses. The whole of Chiloe took
advantage of this week of unusually fine weather, to clear the
ground by burning. In every direction volumes of smoke were
curling upwards. Although the inhabitants were so assiduous in
setting fire to every part of the wood, yet I did not see a single
fire which they had succeeded in making extensive. We dined
with our friend the commandant, and did not reach Castro till
after dark. The next morning we started very early. After having ridden for some time, we obtained from the brow of a steep
hill an extensive view (and it is a rare thing on this road) of
the great forest. Over the horizon of trees, the volcano of
Corcovado, and the great flat-topped one to the north, stood
out in proud pre-eminence: scarcely another peak in the long
range showed its snow summit. I hope it will be long before
I forget this farewell view of the magnificent Cordillera fronting Chiloe. At night we bivouacked under a cloudless sky, and
the next morning reached S. Carlos. We arrived on the right
day, for before evening heavy rain commenced.

February 4th.—Sailed from Chiloe. During the last week I
made several short excursions. One was to examine a great
bed of now-existing shells, elevated 350 feet above the level of
the sea: from among these shells, large forest-trees were growing. Another ride was to P. Huechucucuy. I had with me a
guide who knew the country far too well; for he would per-

tinaciously tell me endless Indian names for every little point, rivulet, and creek. In the same manner as in Tierra del Fuego, the Indian language appears singularly well adapted for attaching names to the most trivial features of the land. I believe every one was glad to say farewell to Chiloe; yet if we could forget the gloom and ceaseless rain of winter, Chiloe might pass for a charming island. There is also something very attractive in the simplicity and humble politeness of the poor inhabitants.

We steered northward along shore, but owing to thick weather did not reach Valdivia till the night of the 8th. The next morning the boat proceeded to the town, which is distant about ten miles. We followed the course of the river, occasionally passing a few hovels, and patches of ground cleared out of the otherwise unbroken forest; and sometimes meeting a canoe with an Indian family. The town is situated on the low banks of the stream, and is so completely buried in a wood of apple-trees that the streets are merely paths in an orchard. I have never seen any country, where apple-trees appeared to thrive so well as in this damp part of South America: on the borders of the roads there were many young trees evidently self-sown. In Chiloe the inhabitants possess a marvellously short method of making an orchard. At the lower part of almost every branch, small, conical, brown, wrinkled points project: these are always ready to change into roots, as may sometimes be seen, where any mud has been accidentally splashed against the tree. A branch as thick as a man's thigh is chosen in the early spring, and is cut off just beneath a group of these points; all the smaller branches are lopped off, and it is then placed about two feet deep in the ground. During the ensuing summer the stump throws out long shoots, and sometimes even bears fruit: I was shown one which had produced as many as twenty-three apples, but this was thought very unusual. In the third season the stump is changed (as I have myself seen) into a well-wooded tree, loaded with fruit. An old man near Valdivia illustrated his motto, "Necesidad es la madre del invencion," by giving an account of the several useful things he manufactured from his apples. After making cider, and likewise wine, he extracted from the refuse a white and finely flavoured spirit; by another process he procured a sweet treacle, or, as he called it, honey. His children and pigs seemed almost to live, during this season of the year, in his orchard.

February 11*th*.—I set out with a guide on a short ride, in which, however, I managed to see singularly little, either of the geology of the country or of its inhabitants. There is not much cleared land near Valdivia: after crossing a river at the distance of a few miles, we entered the forest, and then passed only one miserable hovel, before reaching our sleeping-place for the night. The short difference in latitude, of 150 miles, has given a new aspect to the forest, compared with that of Chiloe. This is owing to a slightly different proportion in the kinds of trees. The evergreens do not appear to be quite so numerous; and the forest in consequence has a brighter tint. As in Chiloe, the lower parts are matted together by canes: here also another kind (resembling the bamboo of Brazil and about twenty feet in height) grows in clusters, and ornaments the banks of some of the streams in a very pretty manner. It is with this plant that the Indians make their chuzos, or long tapering spears. Our resting-house was so dirty that I preferred sleeping outside: on these journeys the first night is generally very uncomfortable, because one is not accustomed to the tickling and biting of the fleas. I am sure, in the morning, there was not a space on my legs of the size of a shilling, which had not its little red mark where the flea had feasted.

12th.—We continued to ride through the uncleared forest; only occasionally meeting an Indian on horseback, or a troop of fine mules bringing alerce-planks and corn from the southern plains. In the afternoon one of the horses knocked up: we were then on a brow of a hill, which commanded a fine view of the Llanos. The view of these open plains was very refreshing, after being hemmed in and buried in the wilderness of trees. The uniformity of a forest soon becomes very wearisome. This west coast makes me remember with pleasure the free, unbounded plains of Patagonia; yet, with the true spirit of contradiction, I cannot forget how sublime is the silence of the forest. The Llanos are the most fertile and thickly peopled parts of the country; as they possess the immense advantage of being nearly free from trees. Before leaving the forest we crossed some flat little lawns, around which single trees stood, as in an English park: I have often noticed with surprise, in wooded undulatory districts, that the quite level parts have been destitute of trees. On account of the tired horse, I determined to stop at the Mission of Cudico, to the friar of which I had a letter of introduction. Cudico is an intermediate district between the forest and the Llanos. There are a good many cottages, with patches of corn and potatoes, nearly all belonging to Indians. The tribes dependent on Valdivia are "re-ducidos y cristianos." The Indians farther northward, about Arauco and Imperial, are still very wild, and not converted; but they have all much intercourse with the Spaniards. The padre said that the Christian Indians did not much like coming to mass, but that otherwise they showed respect for religion. The greatest difficulty is in making them observe the cere-monies of marriage. The wild Indians take as many wives as they can support, and a cacique will sometimes have more than ten: on entering his house, the number may be told by that of the separate fires. Each wife lives a week in turn with the cacique; but all are employed in weaving ponchos, &c. for his profit. To be the wife of a cacique, is an honour much sought after by the Indian women.

The men of all these tribes wear a coarse woollen poncho: those south of Valdivia wear short trowsers, and those north of it a petticoat, like the chilipa of the Gauchos. All have their long hair bound by a scarlet fillet, but with no other covering on their heads. These Indians are good-sized men; their cheek-bones are prominent, and in general appearance they resemble the great American family to which they belong; but their physiognomy seemed to me to be slightly different from that of any other tribe which I had before seen. Their expression is generally grave, and even austere, and possesses much char-acter: this may pass either for honest bluntness or fierce de-termination. The long black hair, the grave and much-lined features, and the dark complexion, called to my mind old por-traits of James I. On the road we met with none of that humble politeness so universal in Chiloe. Some gave their "mari-mari" (good morning) with promptness, but the greater number did not seem inclined to offer any salute. This independence of manners is probably a consequence of their long wars, and the repeated victories which they alone, of all the tribes in Amer-ica, have gained over the Spaniards.

I spent the evening very pleasantly, talking with the padre. He was exceedingly kind and hospitable; and coming from Santiago, had contrived to surround himself with some few comforts. Being a man of some little education, he bitterly complained of the total want of society. With no particular zeal for religion, no business or pursuit, how completely must this man's life be wasted! The next day, on our return, we met seven very wild-looking Indians, of whom some were caciques that had just received from the Chilian government, their yearly small stipend for having long remained faithful. They were fine-looking men, and they rode one after the other, with most gloomy faces. An old cacique, who headed them, had been, I suppose, more excessively drunk than the rest, for he seemed both extremely grave and very crabbed. Shortly before this, two Indians joined us, who were travelling from a distant mission to Valdivia concerning some law-suit. One was a good-humoured old man, but from his wrinkled beardless face looked more like an old woman than a man. I frequently presented both of them with cigars; and though ready to receive them, and I dare say grateful, they would hardly condescend to thank me. A Chilotan Indian would have taken off his hat, and given his "Dios le page!" The traveling was very tedious, both from the badness of the roads, and from the number of great fallen trees, which it was necessary either to leap over or to avoid by making long circuits. We slept on the road, and next morning reached Valdivia, whence I proceeded on board.

A few days afterwards I crossed the bay with a party of officers, and landed near the fort called Niebla. The buildings were in a most ruinous state, and the gun-carriages quite rotten. Mr. Wickham remarked to the commanding officer, that with one discharge they would certainly all fall to pieces. The poor man, trying to put a good face upon it, gravely replied, "No, I am sure, sir, they would stand two!" The Spaniards must have intended to have made this place impregnable. There is now lying in the middle of the courtyard a little mountain of mortar, which rivals in hardness the rock on which it is placed. It was brought from Chile, and cost 7000 dollars. The revolution having broken out, prevented its being applied to any purpose, and now it remains a monument of the fallen greatness of Spain.

I wanted to go to a house about a mile and a half distant, but my guide said it was quite impossible to penetrate the wood in a straight line. He offered, however, to lead me, by following obscure cattle-tracks, the shortest way: the walk, nevertheless, took no less than three hours! This man is employed in hunting strayed cattle; yet, well as he must know the woods, he was not long since lost for two whole days, and had nothing to eat. These facts convey a good idea of the impracticability of the forests of these countries. A question often occurred to me—how long does any vestige of a fallen tree remain? This man showed me one which a party of fugitive Royalists had cut down fourteen years ago; and taking this as a criterion, I should think a bole a foot and a half in diameter would in thirty years be changed into a heap of mould.

February 20*th*.—This day has been memorable in the annals of Valdivia, for the most severe earthquake experienced by the oldest inhabitant. I happened to be on shore, and was lying down in the wood to rest myself. It came on suddenly, and lasted two minutes, but the time appeared much longer. The rocking of the ground was very sensible. The undulations appeared to my companion and myself to come from due east, whilst others thought they proceeded from south-west: this shows how difficult it sometimes is to perceive the direction of the vibrations. There was no difficulty in standing upright, but the motion made me almost giddy: it was something like the movement of a vessel in a little cross-ripple, or still more like that felt by a person skating over thin ice, which bends under the weight of his body.

A bad earthquake at once destroys our oldest associations: the earth, the very emblem of solidity, has moved beneath our feet like a thin crust over a fluid;—one second of time has created in the mind a strange idea of insecurity, which hours of reflection would not have produced. In the forest, as a breeze moved the trees, I felt only the earth tremble, but saw no other effect. Captain Fitz Roy and some officers were at the town during the shock, and there the scene was more striking; for although the houses, from being built of wood, did not fall, they were violently shaken, and the boards creaked and rattled together. The people rushed out of doors in the greatest alarm. It is these accompaniments that create that perfect horror of earthquakes, experienced by all who have thus seen, as well as felt, their effects. Within the forest it was a deeply interesting, but by no means an awe-inspiring phenomenon. The tides were very curiously affected. The great shock took place at the time of low water; and an old woman who was on the beach told me, that the water flowed very quickly, but not in great waves, to high-water mark, and then as quickly returned to its proper level; this was also evident by the line of wet sand. This same kind of quick but quiet movement in the tide, happened a few years since at Chiloe, during a slight earthquake, and created much causeless alarm. In the course of the evening there were many weaker shocks, which seemed to produce in the harbour the most complicated currents, and some of great strength.

March 4*th*.—We entered the harbour of Concepcion. While the ship was beating up to the anchorage, I landed on the island of Quiriquina. The mayor-domo of the estate quickly rode down to tell me the terrible news of the great earthquake of the 20th:—"That not a house in Concepcion or Talcahuano (the port) was standing; that seventy villages were destroyed; and that a great wave had almost washed away the ruins of Talcahuano." Of this latter statement I soon saw abundant proofs —the whole coast being strewed over with timber and furniture as if a thousand ships had been wrecked. Besides chairs, tables, book-shelves, &c., in great numbers, there were several roofs of cottages, which had been transported almost whole. The store-houses at Talcahuano had been burst open, and great bags of cotton, yerba, and other valuable merchandise were scattered on the shore. During my walk round the island, I observed that numerous fragments of rock, which, from the marine productions adhering to them, must recently have been lying in deep water, had been cast up high on the beach; one of these was six feet long, three broad, and two thick.[1]

The island itself as plainly showed the overwhelming power of the earthquake, as the beach did that of the consequent great wave. The ground in many parts was fissured in north and south lines, perhaps caused by the yielding of the parallel and steep sides of this narrow island. Some of the fissures near the cliffs were a yard wide. Many enormous masses had already fallen on the beach; and the inhabitants thought that when the rains commenced far greater slips would happen. The effect of the vibration on the hard primary slate, which composes the foundation of the island, was still more curious: the superficial parts of some narrow ridges were as completely shivered as if they had been blasted by gunpowder. This effect, which was rendered conspicuous by the fresh fractures and displaced soil, must be confined to near the surface, for otherwise there would not exist a block of solid rock throughout Chile; nor is this improbable, as it is known that the surface of a vibrating body is affected differently from the central part. It is, perhaps, owing to this same reason, that earthquakes do not cause quite such terrific havoc within deep mines as would be expected. I believe this convulsion has been more effectual in lessening the size of the island of Quiriquina, than the ordinary wear-and-tear of the sea and weather during the course of a whole century.

The next day I landed at Talcahuano, and afterwards rode

[1] [Editor] Concepción was also the scene of a devastating earthquake in 1751, and again in May 1960.

to Concepcion. Both towns presented the most awful yet interesting spectacle I ever beheld. To a person who had formerly known them, it possibly might have been still more impressive; for the ruins were so mingled together, and the whole scene possessed so little the air of a habitable place, that it was scarcely possible to imagine its former condition. The earthquake commenced at half-past eleven o'clock in the forenoon. If it had happened in the middle of the night, the greater number of the inhabitants (which in this one province amount to many thousands) must have perished, instead of less than a hundred: as it was, the invariable practice of running out of doors at the first trembling of the ground, alone saved them. In Concepcion each house, or row of houses, stood by itself, a heap or line of ruins; but in Talcahuano, owing to the great wave, little more than one layer of bricks, tiles, and timber, with here and there part of a wall left standing, could be distinguished. From this circumstance Concepcion, although not so completely desolated, was a more terrible, and, if I may so call it, picturesque sight. The first shock was very sudden. The mayor-domo at Quiriquina told me, that the first notice he received of it, was finding both the horse he rode and himself, rolling together on the ground. Rising up, he was again thrown down. He also told me that some cows which were standing on the steep side of the island were rolled into the sea. The great wave caused the destruction of many cattle; on one low island, near the head of the bay, seventy animals were washed off and drowned. It is generally thought that this has been the worst earthquake ever recorded in Chile; but as the very severe ones occur only after long intervals, this cannot easily be known; nor indeed would a much worse shock have made any great difference, for the ruin was now complete. Innumerable small tremblings followed the great earthquake, and within the first twelve days no less than three hundred were counted.

After viewing Concepcion, I cannot understand how the greater number of inhabitants escaped unhurt. The houses in many parts fell outwards; thus forming in the middle of the streets little hillocks of brickwork and rubbish. Mr. Rouse, the English consul, told us that he was at breakfast when the first movement warned him to run out. He had scarcely reached the middle of the courtyard, when one side of his house came thundering down. He retained presence of mind to remember, that if he once got on the top of that part which had already fallen, he would be safe. Not being able from the motion of the ground to stand, he crawled up on his hands and knees; and no sooner had he ascended this little eminence, than the other side of the house fell in, the great beams sweeping close in front of his head. With his eyes blinded, and his mouth choked with the cloud of dust which darkened the sky, at last he gained the street. As shock succeeded shock, at the interval of a few minutes, no one dared approach the shattered ruins; and no one knew whether his dearest friends and relations were not perishing from the want of help. Those who had saved any property were obliged to keep a constant watch, for thieves prowled about, and at each little trembling of the ground, with one hand they beat their breasts and cried "misericordia!" and then with the other filched what they could from the ruins. The thatched roofs fell over the fires, and flames burst forth in all parts. Hundreds knew themselves ruined, and few had the means of providing food for the day.

Earthquakes alone are sufficient to destroy the prosperity of any country. If beneath England the now inert subterranean forces should exert those powers, which most assuredly in former geological ages they have exerted, how completely would the entire condition of the country be changed! What would become of the lofty houses, thickly packed cities, great manufactories, the beautiful public and private edifices? If the new period of disturbance were first to commence by some great earthquake in the dead of the night, how terrific would be the carnage! England would at once be bankrupt; all papers, records, and accounts would from that moment be lost. Government being unable to collect the taxes, and failing to maintain its authority, the hand of violence and rapine would remain uncontrolled. In every large town famine would go forth, pestilence and death following in its train.

Shortly after the shock, a great wave was seen from the distance of three or four miles, approaching in the middle of the bay with a smooth outline; but along the shore it tore up cottages and trees, as it swept onwards with irresistible force. At the head of the bay it broke in a fearful line of white breakers, which rushed up to a height of 23 vertical feet above the highest spring-tides. Their force must have been prodigious; for at the Fort a cannon with its carriage, estimated at four tons in weight, was moved 15 feet inwards. A schooner was left in the midst of the ruins, 200 yards from the beach. The first wave was followed by two others, which in their retreat carried away a vast wreck of floating objects. In one part of the bay, a ship was pitched high and dry on shore, was carried off, again driven on shore, and again carried off. In another part, two large vessels anchored near together were whirled about, and their cables were thrice wound round each other: though anchored at a depth of 36 feet, they were for some minutes aground. The great wave must have travelled slowly, for the inhabitants of Talcahuano had time to run up the hills behind the town;[2] and some sailors pulled out seaward, trusting successfully to their boat riding securely over the swell, if they could reach it before it broke. One old woman with a little boy, four or five years old, ran into a boat, but there was nobody to row it out: the boat was consequently dashed against an anchor and cut in twain; the old woman was drowned, but the child was picked up some hours afterwards clinging to the wreck.[3] Pools of salt-water were still standing amidst the ruins

[2] [Editor] A few pages further on, Darwin correctly notes that tidal waves or tsunamis—as scientists now call earthquake-generated waves, to distinguish them from true tides—often come in series and that succeeding waves are often much more damaging than the first. He is incorrect, however, in assuming that tsunamis travel slowly. They have been clocked at speeds of 400 to 500 miles an hour.

[3] [Editor] Fitz Roy's journal gives these additional details of the devastation in Talcahuano:

"About half an hour after the shock, when the greater part of the population had reached the heights,—the sea having retired so much, that all the vessels at anchor, even those which had been lying in seven fathoms water, were aground, and every rock and shoal in the bay was visible,—an enormous wave was seen forcing its way through the western passage which separates Quiriquina Island from the mainland. This terrific swell passed rapidly along the western side of the Bay of Concepcion, sweeping the steep shores of every thing moveable within thirty feet, (vertically) from high water-mark. It broke over, dashed along, and whirled about the shipping as if they had been light boats; overflowed the greater part of the town, and then rushed back with such a torrent that every moveable which the earthquake had not buried under heaps of ruins was carried out to sea. In a few minutes, the vessels were again aground, and a second great wave was seen approaching, with more noise and impetuosity than the first; but though this was more powerful, its effects were not so considerable—simply because there was less to destroy. Again the sea fell, dragging away quantities of woodwork and the lighter materials of houses, and leaving the shipping aground.

"After some minutes of awful suspense, a third enormous swell was seen between Quiriquina and the mainland, apparently larger of the houses, and children, making boats with old tables and chairs, appeared as happy as their parents were miserable. It was, however, exceedingly interesting to observe, how much more active and cheerful all appeared than could have been

than either of the two former. Roaring as it dashed against every obstacle with irresistible force, it rushed—destroying and over-whelming—along the shore. Quickly retiring, as if spurned by the foot of the hills, the retreating wave dragged away such quantities of household effects, fences, furniture, and other moveables, that after the tumultuous rush was over, the sea appeared to be covered with wreck. Earth and water trembled: and exhaustion appeared to follow these mighty efforts. . . .

"Without explanation it appears astonishing how the shipping escaped destruction. There were three large whale-ships, a bark, two brigs, and a schooner, very near the town, in from four to seven fathoms water: they were lying at single anchor, with a good scope of cable: one only was well moored.

"With the southerly breeze, which was rather fresh at the time of the earthquake, these vessels lay to seaward of their anchors, having their sterns towards the sea; and were left aground in this position. The captain of the port, D. Pablo Delano, was on board one of the whale ships at the time, with the hatches battened down, and dead lights shipped. All hands took to the rigging for safety. The first great wave came in an unbroken swell to the stern of the vessel, broke over and lifted her along without doing any material harm, more than sweeping her decks: and the slack chain dragging over the mud checked her gradually, as the first impetus of the wave diminished. Whirling her round, the water rushed out to sea-ward again, leaving the vessel stranded nearly in her former po-sition. From two fathoms, when aground, the depth alongside in-creased to ten, as the water rose highest during the last swell. The two latter waves approached, and affected the shipping similarly to the former: all withstood their force, though the light anchors were dragged. Some of the vessels were thrown violently against others; and whirled around as if they had been in the vortex of a whirlpool. Previous to the rush of waters, the Paulina and Orion, two merchantmen, were lying a full cable's length apart; and after it had passed they were side by side, with three round turns in their cables. Each vessel had therefore gone round the other with each wave: the bow of one was stove in: to the other little damage was done. A small vessel was on the stocks, almost ready for launch-ing; she was carried by the sea two hundred yards in-shore, and left there unhurt. A little schooner, at anchor before the town, slipped her cable, and ran out in the offing as the water fell. She met the wave, unbroken, and rose over it as an ordinary swell. The Colocolo was under sail near the eastern entrance of the bay—she likewise met the wave, as a large swell, without inconvenience."

expected. It was remarked with much truth, that from the destruction being universal, no one individual was humbled more than another, or could suspect his friends of coldness—that most grievous result of the loss of wealth. Mr. Rouse, and a large party whom he kindly took under his protection, lived for the first week in a garden beneath some apple-trees. At first they were as merry as if it had been a picnic; but soon afterwards heavy rain caused much discomfort, for they were absolutely without shelter.

In Captain Fitz Roy's excellent account of the earthquake, it is said that two explosions, one like a column of smoke and another like the blowing of a great whale, were seen in the bay. The water also appeared every where to be boiling; and it "became black, and exhaled a most disagreeable sulphureous smell." These latter circumstances were observed in the Bay of Valparaiso during the earthquake of 1822; they may, I think, be accounted for, by the disturbance of the mud at the bottom of the sea containing organic matter in decay. In the Bay of Callao, during a calm day, I noticed, that as the ship dragged her cable over the bottom, its course was marked by a line of bubbles. The lower orders in Talcahuano thought that the earthquake was caused by some old Indian women, who two years ago being offended stopped the volcano of Antuco. This silly belief is curious, because it shows that experience has taught them to observe, that there exists a relation between the suppressed action of the volcanoes, and the trembling of the ground. It was necessary to apply the witchcraft to the point where their perception of cause and effect failed; and this was the closing of the volcanic vent. This belief is the more singular in this particular instance, because, according to Captain Fitz Roy, there is reason to believe that Antuco was noways affected.

The town of Concepcion was built in the usual Spanish fashion, with all the streets running at right angles to each other; one set ranging S.W. by W., and the other set N.W. by N. The walls in the former direction certainly stood better than those in the latter: the greater number of the masses of brickwork were thrown down towards the N.E. Both these circumstances perfectly agree with the general idea, of the undulations having come from the S.W.; in which quarter subterranean noises were also heard: for it is evident that the walls running S.W. and N.E. which presented their ends to the point whence the undulations came, would be much less likely to fall than those

walls which, running N.W. and S.E., must in their whole
lengths have been at the same instant thrown out of the perpendicular; for the undulations, coming from the S.W., must
have extended in N.W. and S.E. waves, as they passed under
the foundations. This may be illustrated by placing books edge-
ways on a carpet, and then, after the manner suggested by
Michell, imitating the undulations of an earthquake: it will be
found that they fall with more or less readiness, according as
their direction more or less nearly coincides with the line of
the waves. The fissures in the ground generally, though not
uniformly, extended in a S.E. and N.W. direction; and therefore corresponded to the lines of undulation or of principal
flexure. Bearing in mind all these circumstances, which so
clearly point to the S.W. as the chief focus of disturbance, it
is a very interesting fact that the island of S. Maria, situated
in that quarter, was, during the general uplifting of the land,
raised to nearly three times the height of any other part of the
coast.

The different resistance offered by the walls, according to
their direction, was well exemplified in the case of the Cathedral. The side which fronted the N.E. presented a grand pile
of ruins, in the midst of which door-cases and masses of timber
stood up, as if floating in a stream. Some of the angular blocks
of brickwork were of great dimensions; and they were rolled
to a distance on the level plaza, like fragments of rock at the
base of some high mountain. The side walls (running S.W.
and N.E.), though exceedingly fractured, yet remained standing; but the vast buttresses (at right angles to them, and therefore parallel to the walls that fell) were in many cases cut
clean off, as if by a chisel, and hurled to the ground. Some
square ornaments on the coping of these same walls, were
moved by the earthquake into a diagonal position. A similar
circumstance was observed after an earthquake at Valparaiso,
Calabria, and other places, including some of the ancient
Greek temples.[4] This twisting displacement, at first appears to
indicate a vorticose movement beneath each point thus affected; but this is highly improbable. May it not be caused by a
tendency in each stone to arrange itself in some particular position, with respect to the lines of vibration,—in a manner somewhat similar to pins on a sheet of paper when shaken? Gen-

[4] [Darwin] M. Arago in L'Institut, 1839, p. 337. See also Miers's
Chile, vol. i. p. 392; also Lyell's Principles of Geology, chap. xv.
book ii.

erally speaking, arched doorways or windows stood much better than any other part of the buildings. Nevertheless, a poor lame old man, who had been in the habit, during trifling shocks, of crawling to a certain doorway, was this time crushed to pieces.

I have not attempted to give any detailed description of the appearance of Concepcion, for I feel that it is quite impossible to convey the mingled feelings which I experienced. Several of the officers visited it before me, but their strongest language failed to give a just idea of the scene of desolation. It is a bitter and humiliating thing to see works, which have cost man so much time and labour, overthrown in one minute; yet compassion for the inhabitants was almost instantly banished, by the surprise in seeing a state of things produced in a moment of time, which one was accustomed to attribute to a succession of ages. In my opinion, we have scarcely beheld, since leaving England, any sight so deeply interesting.

In almost every severe earthquake, the neighbouring waters of the sea are said to have been greatly agitated. The disturbance seems generally, as in the case of Concepcion, to have been of two kinds: first, at the instant of the shock, the water swells high up on the beach with a gentle motion, and then as quietly retreats; secondly, some time afterwards, the whole body of the sea retires from the coast, and then returns in waves of overwhelming force. The first movement seems to be an immediate consequence of the earthquake affecting differently a fluid and a solid, so that their respective levels are slightly deranged: but the second case is a far more important phenomenon. During most earthquakes, and especially during those on the west coast of America, it is certain that the first great movement of the waters has been a retirement. Some authors have attempted to explain this, by supposing that the water retains its level, whilst the land oscillates upwards; but surely the water close to the land, even on a rather steep coast, would partake of the motion of the bottom: moreover, as urged by Mr. Lyell, similar movements of the sea have occurred at islands far distant from the chief line of disturbance, as was the case with Juan Fernandez during this earthquake, and with Madeira during the famous Lisbon shock. I suspect (but the subject is a very obscure one) that a wave, however produced, first draws the water from the shore, on which it is advancing to break: I have observed that this happens with the little waves from the paddles of a steam boat. It is remarkable that whilst

Talcahuano and Callao (near Lima), both situated at the head of large shallow bays, have suffered during every severe earthquake from great waves, Valparaiso, seated close to the edge of profoundly deep water, has never been overwhelmed, though so often shaken by the severest shocks. From the great wave not immediately following the earthquake, but sometimes after the interval of even half an hour, and from distant islands being affected similarly with the coasts near the focus of the disturbance, it appears that the wave first rises in the offing; and as this is of general occurrence, the cause must be general: I suspect we must look to the line, where the less disturbed waters of the deep ocean join the water nearer the coast, which has partaken of the movements of the land, as the place where the great wave is first generated; it would also appear that the wave is larger or smaller, according to the extent of shoal water which has been agitated together with the bottom on which it rested.

The most remarkable effect of this earthquake was the permanent elevation of the land; it would probably be far more correct to speak of it as the cause. There can be no doubt that the land round the Bay of Concepcion was upraised two or three feet; but it deserves notice, that owing to the wave having obliterated the old lines of tidal action on the sloping sandy shores, I could discover no evidence of this fact, except in the united testimony of the inhabitants, that one little rocky shoal, now exposed, was formerly covered with water. At the island of S. Maria (about thirty miles distant) the elevation was greater; on one part, Captain Fitz Roy found beds of putrid mussel-shells *still adhering to the rocks,* ten feet above high-water mark: the inhabitants had formerly dived at low-water spring-tides for these shells. The elevation of this province is particularly interesting, from its having been the theatre of several other violent earthquakes, and from the vast numbers of sea-shells scattered over the land, up to a height of certainly 600, and I believe, of 1000 feet. At Valparaiso, as I have remarked, similar shells are found at the height of 1300 feet: it is hardly possible to doubt that this great elevation has been effected by successive small uprisings, such as that which accompanied or caused the earthquake of this year, and likewise by an insensibly slow rise, which is certainly in progress on some parts of this coast.

The island of Juan Fernandez, 360 miles to the N.E., was,

at the time of the great shock of the 20th, violently shaken, so that the trees beat against each other, and a volcano burst forth under water close to the shore: these facts are remarkable because this island, during the earthquake of 1751, was then also affected more violently than other places at an equal distance from Concepcion, and this seems to show some subterranean connexion between these two points. Chiloe, about 340 miles southward of Concepcion, appears to have been shaken more strongly than the intermediate district of Valdivia, where the volcano of Villarica was noways affected, whilst in the Cordillera in front of Chiloe, two of the volcanoes burst forth at the same instant in violent action. These two volcanoes, and some neighbouring ones, continued for a long time in eruption, and ten months afterwards were again influenced by an earthquake at Concepcion. Some men, cutting wood near the base of one of these volcanoes, did not perceive the shock of the 20th, although the whole surrounding Province was then trembling; here we have an eruption relieving and taking the place of an earthquake, as would have happened at Concepcion, according to the belief of the lower orders, if the volcano of Antuco had not been closed by witchcraft. Two years and three quarters afterwards, Valdivia and Chiloe were again shaken, more violently than on the 20th, and an island in the Chonos Archipelago was permanently elevated more than eight feet. It will give a better idea of the scale of these phenomena, if (as in the case of the glaciers) we suppose them to have taken place at corresponding distances in Europe:—then would the land from the North Sea to the Mediterranean have been violently shaken, and at the same instant of time a large tract of the eastern coast of England would have been permanently elevated, together with some outlying islands—a train of volcanoes on the coast of Holland would have burst forth in action, and an eruption taken place at the bottom of the sea, near the northern extremity of Ireland—and lastly, the ancient vents of Auvergne, Cantal, and Mont d'Or would each have sent up to the sky a dark column of smoke, and have long remained in fierce action. Two years and three quarters afterwards, France, from its centre to the English Channel, would have been again desolated by an earthquake, and an island permanently upraised in the Mediterranean.[5]

[5] [Editor] Not all of the upraising caused by the 1835 Chilean earthquake was permanent. In the decades following the quake, Santa Maria and several other uplifted areas gradually settled all the way or nearly all the way back to their original level.

The space, from under which volcanic matter on the 20th was actually erupted, is 720 miles in one line, and 400 miles in another line at right angles to the first: hence, in all probability, a subterranean lake of lava is here stretched out, of nearly double the area of the Black Sea. From the intimate and complicated manner in which the elevatory and eruptive forces were shown to be connected during this train of phenomena, we may confidently come to the conclusion, that the forces which slowly and by little starts uplift continents, and those which at successive periods pour forth volcanic matter from open orifices, are identical. From many reasons, I believe that the frequent quakings of the earth on this line of coast, are caused by the rending of the strata, necessarily consequent on the tension of the land when upraised, and their injection by fluidified rock. This rending and injection would, if repeated often enough (and we know that earthquakes repeatedly affect the same areas in the same manner), form a chain of hills;—and the linear island of St. Mary, which was upraised thrice the height of the neighbouring country, seems to be undergoing this process. I believe that the solid axis of a mountain differs in its manner of formation from a volcanic hill, only in the molten stone having been repeatedly injected, instead of having been repeatedly ejected. Moreover, I believe that it is impossible to explain the structure of great mountain-chains, such as that of the Cordillera, where the strata, capping the injected axis of plutonic rock, have been thrown on their edges along several parallel and neighbouring lines of elevation, except on this view of the rock of the axis having been repeatedly injected, after intervals sufficiently long to allow the upper parts or wedges to cool and become solid;—for if the strata had been thrown into their present highly-inclined, vertical, and even inverted positions, by a single blow, the very bowels of the earth would have gushed out; and instead of beholding abrupt mountain-axes of rock solidified under great pressure, deluges of lava would have flowed out at innumerable points on every line of elevation.[6]

[6] [Darwin] For a full account of the volcanic phenomena which accompanied the earthquake of the 20th, and for the conclusions deducible from them, I must refer to Volume V. of the Geological Transactions.

CHAPTER XV

PASSAGE OF THE CORDILLERA

Valparaiso — Portillo Pass — Sagacity of Mules — Mountain Torrents — Mines, how discovered — Proofs of the gradual Elevation of the Cordillera — Effect of Snow on Rocks — Geological Structure of the two Main Ranges, their distinct Origin and Upheaval — Great Subsidence — Red Snow — Winds — Pinnacles of Snow — Dry and clear Atmosphere — Electricity — Pampas — Zoology of the opposite sides of the Andes — Locusts — Great Bugs — Mendoza — Uspallata Pass — Silicified Trees buried as they grew — Incas Bridge — Badness of the Passes exaggerated — Cumbre — Casuchas — Valparaiso

March 7th, 1835.—We stayed three days at Concepcion, and then sailed for Valparaiso. The wind being northerly, we only reached the mouth of the harbour of Concepcion before it was dark. Being very near the land, and a fog coming on, the anchor was dropped. Presently a large American whaler appeared close alongside of us; and we heard the Yankee swearing at his men to keep quiet, whilst he listened for the breakers. Captain Fitz Roy hailed him, in a loud clear voice, to anchor where he then was. The poor man must have thought the voice came from the shore: such a Babel of cries issued at once from the ship—every one hallooing out, "Let go the anchor! veer cable! shorten sail!" It was the most laughable thing I ever heard. If the ship's crew had been all captains, and no men, there could not have been a greater uproar of orders. We afterwards found that the mate stuttered: I suppose all hands were assisting him in giving his orders.

On the 11th we anchored at Valparaiso, and two days afterwards I set out to cross the Cordillera.[1] I proceeded to San

[1] [Editor] The *Beagle* returned meanwhile to the Concepción area to continue its survey.

tiago, where Mr. Caldcleugh most kindly assisted me in every possible way in making the little preparations which were necessary. In this part of Chile there are two passes across the Andes to Mendoza: the one most commonly used—namely, that of Aconcagua or Uspallata—is situated some way to the north; the other, called the Portillo, is to the south, and nearer, but more lofty and dangerous.

March 18*th*.—We set out for the Portillo pass. Leaving Santiago we crossed the wide burnt-up plain on which that city stands, and in the afternoon arrived at the Maypu, one of the principal rivers in Chile. The valley, at the point where it enters the first Cordillera, is bounded on each side by lofty barren mountains; and although not broad, it is very fertile. Numerous cottages were surrounded by vines, and by orchards of apple, nectarine, and peach trees—their boughs breaking with the weight of the beautiful ripe fruit. In the evening we passed the custom-house, where our luggage was examined. The frontier of Chile is better guarded by the Cordillera, than by the waters of the sea. There are very few valleys which lead to the central ranges, and the mountains are quite impassable in other parts by beasts of burden. The custom-house officers were very civil, which was perhaps partly owing to the passport which the President of the Republic had given me; but I must express my admiration at the natural politeness of almost every Chileno. In this instance, the contrast with the same class of men in most other countries was strongly marked. I may mention an anecdote with which I was at the time much pleased: we met near Mendoza a little and very fat negress, riding astride on a mule. She had a *goître* so enormous that it was scarcely possible to avoid gazing at her for a moment; but my two companions almost instantly, by way of apology, made the common salute of the country by taking off their hats. Where would one of the lower or higher classes in Europe, have shown such feeling politeness to a poor and miserable object of a degraded race?

At night we slept at a cottage. Our manner of traveling was delightfully independent. In the inhabited parts we bought a little firewood, hired pasture for the animals, and bivouacked in the corner of the same field with them. Carrying an iron pot, we cooked and ate our supper under a cloudless sky, and knew no trouble. My companions were Mariano Gonzales, who had formerly accompanied me in Chile, and an "arriero," with his ten mules and a "madrina." The madrina (or godmother) is a most important personage: she is an old steady mare, with a little bell round her neck; and wherever she goes, the mules, like good children, follow her. The affection of these animals for their madrinas saves infinite trouble. If several large troops are turned into one field to graze, in the morning the muleteers have only to lead the madrinas a little apart, and tinkle their bells; and although there may be two or three hundred together, each mule immediately knows the bell of its own madrina, and comes to her. It is nearly impossible to lose an old mule; for if detained for several hours by force, she will, by the power of smell, like a dog, track out her companions, or rather the madrina, for, according to the muleteer, she is the chief object of affection. The feeling, however, is not of an individual nature; for I believe I am right in saying that any animal with a bell will serve as a madrina. In a troop each animal carries on a level road, a cargo weighing 416 pounds (more than 29 stone), but in a mountainous country 100 pounds less; yet with what delicate slim limbs, without any proportional bulk of muscle, these animals support so great a burden! The mule always appears to me a most surprising animal. That a hybrid should possess more reason, memory, obstinacy, social affection, powers of muscular endurance, and length of life, than either of its parents, seems to indicate that art has here outdone nature. Of our ten animals, six were intended for riding, and four for carrying cargoes, each taking turn about. We carried a good deal of food, in case we should be snowed up, as the season was rather late for passing the Portillo.

March 19*th*.—We rode during this day to the last, and therefore most elevated house in the valley. The number of inhabitants became scanty; but wherever water could be brought on the land, it was very fertile. All the main valleys in the Cordillera are characterized by having, on both sides, a fringe or terrace of shingle and sand, rudely stratified, and generally of considerable thickness. These fringes evidently once extended across the valleys, and were united; and the bottoms of the valleys in northern Chile, where there are no streams, are thus smoothly filled up. On these fringes the roads are generally carried, for their surfaces are even, and they rise with a very gentle slope up the valleys: hence, also, they are easily cultivated by irrigation. They may be traced up to a height of between 7000 and 9000 feet, where they become hidden by the irregular piles of debris. At the lower end or mouths of the valleys, they are continuously united to those land-locked plains (also formed of shingle) at the foot of the main Cordillera, which I have described in a former chapter as characteristic of the scenery of Chile, and which were undoubtedly deposited when the sea penetrated Chile, as it now does the more southern coasts. No one fact in the geology of South America interested me more than these terraces of rudely-stratified shingle. They precisely resemble in composition, the matter which the torrents in each valley would deposit, if they were checked in their course by any cause, such as entering a lake or arm of the sea; but the torrents, instead of depositing matter, are now steadily at work wearing away both the solid rock and these alluvial deposits, along the whole line of every main valley and side valley. It is impossible here to give the reasons, but I am convinced that the shingle terraces were accumulated, during the gradual elevation of the Cordillera, by the torrents delivering, at successive levels, their detritus on the beach-heads of long narrow arms of the sea, first high up the valleys, then lower and lower down as the land slowly rose. If this be so, and I cannot doubt it, the grand and broken chain of the Cordillera, instead of having been suddenly thrown up, as was till lately the universal, and still is the common opinion of geologists, has been slowly upheaved in mass, in the same gradual manner as the coasts of the Atlantic and Pacific have risen within the recent period. A multitude of facts in the structure of the Cordillera, on this view receive a simple explanation.

The rivers which flow in these valleys ought rather to be called mountain-torrents. Their inclination is very great, and their water the colour of mud. The roar which the Maypu made, as it rushed over the great rounded fragments, was like that of the sea. Amidst the din of rushing waters, the noise from the stones, as they rattled one over another, was most distinctly audible even from a distance. This rattling noise, night and day, may be heard along the whole course of the torrent. The sound spoke eloquently to the geologist; the thousands and thousands of stones, which, striking against each other, made the one dull uniform sound, were all hurrying in one direction. It was like thinking on time, where the minute that now glides past is irrecoverable. So was it with these stones; the ocean is their eternity, and each note of that wild music told of one more step towards their destiny.

It is not possible for the mind to comprehend, except by a

slow process, any effect which is produced by a cause repeated so often, that the multiplier itself conveys an idea, not more definite than the savage implies when he points to the hairs of his head. As often as I have seen beds of mud, sand, and shingle, accumulated to the thickness of many thousand feet, I have felt inclined to exclaim that causes, such as the present rivers and the present beaches, could never have ground down and produced such masses. But, on the other hand, when listening to the rattling noise of these torrents, and calling to mind that whole races of animals have passed away from the face of the earth, and that during this whole period, night and day, these stones have gone rattling onwards in their course, I have thought to myself, can any mountains, any continent, withstand such waste?

In this part of the valley, the mountains on each side were from 3000 to 6000 or 8000 feet high, with rounded outlines and steep bare flanks. The general colour of the rock was dullish purple, and the stratification very distinct. If the scenery was not beautiful, it was remarkable and grand. We met during the day several herds of cattle, which men were driving down from the higher valleys in the Cordillera. This sign of the approaching winter hurried our steps, more than was convenient for geologising. The house where we slept was situated at the foot of a mountain, on the summit of which are the mines of S. Pedro de Nolasko. Sir F. Head marvels how mines have been discovered in such extraordinary situations, as the bleak summit of the mountain of S. Pedro de Nolasko. In the first place, metallic veins in this country are generally harder than the surrounding strata: hence, during the gradual wear of the hills, they project above the surface of the ground. Secondly, almost every labourer, especially in the northern parts of Chile, understands something about the appearance of ores. In the great mining provinces of Coquimbo and Copiapó, firewood is very scarce, and men search for it over every hill and dale; and by this means nearly all the richest mines have there been discovered. Chanuncillo, from which silver to the value of many hundred thousand pounds has been raised in the course of a few years, was discovered by a man who threw a stone at his loaded donkey, and thinking that it was very heavy, he picked it up, and found it full of pure silver: the vein occurred at no great distance, standing up like a wedge of metal. The miners, also, taking a crowbar with them, often wander on Sundays over the mountains. In this south part of Chile, the men who drive cattle into the Cordillera, and who frequent every ravine where there is a little pasture, are the usual discoverers.

20*th*.—As we ascended the valley, the vegetation, with the exception of a few pretty alpine flowers, became exceedingly scanty; and of quadrupeds, birds, or insects, scarcely one could be seen. The lofty mountains, their summits marked with a few patches of snow, stood well separated from each other; the valleys being filled up with an immense thickness of stratified alluvium. The features in the scenery of the Andes which struck me most, as contrasted with the other mountain chains with which I am acquainted, were,—the flat fringes sometimes expanding into narrow plains on each side of the valleys,—the bright colours, chiefly red and purple, of the utterly bare and precipitous hills of porphyry,—the grand and continuous wall-like dikes,—the plainly-divided strata which, where nearly vertical, formed the picturesque and wild central pinnacles, but where less inclined, composed the great massive mountains on the outskirts of the range,—and lastly, the smooth conical piles of fine and brightly-coloured detritus, which sloped up at a high angle from the base of the mountains, sometimes to a height of more than 2000 feet.

I frequently observed, both in Tierra del Fuego and within the Andes, that where the rock was covered during the greater part of the year with snow, it was shivered in a very extraordinary manner into small angular fragments. Scoresby[2] has observed the same fact in Spitzbergen. The case appears to me rather obscure: for that part of the mountain which is protected by a mantle of snow, must be less subject to repeated and great changes of temperature than any other part. I have sometimes thought, that the earth and fragments of stone on the surface, were perhaps less effectually removed by slowly percolating snow water[3] than by rain, and therefore that the appearance of a quicker disintegration of the solid rock under the snow, was deceptive. Whatever the cause may be, the quantity

[2] [Darwin] Scoresby's Arctic Regions, vol. i. p. 122.
[3] [Darwin] I have heard it remarked in Shropshire, that the water, when the Severn is flooded from long-continued rain, is much more turbid than when it proceeds from the snow melting on the Welsh mountains. D'Orbigny (tom. i. p. 184), in explaining the cause of the various colours of the rivers in South America, remarks that those with blue or clear water have their source in the Cordillera, where the snow melts.

of crumbling stone on the Cordillera is very great. Occasionally in the spring, great masses of this detritus slide down the mountains, and cover the snow-drifts in the valleys, thus forming natural ice-houses. We rode over one, the height of which was far below the limit of perpetual snow.

As the evening drew to a close, we reached a singular basin-like plain, called the Valle del Yeso. It was covered by a little dry pasture, and we had the pleasant sight of a herd of cattle amidst the surrounding rocky deserts. The valley takes its name of Yeso from a great bed, I should think at least 2000 feet thick, of white, and in some parts quite pure, gypsum. We slept with a party of men, who were employed in loading mules with this substance, which is used in the manufacture of wine. We set out early in the morning (21st), and continued to follow the course of the river, which had become very small, till we arrived at the foot of the ridge, that separates the waters flowing into the Pacific and Atlantic Oceans. The road, which as yet had been good with a steady but very gradual ascent, now changed into a steep zigzag track up the great range, dividing the republics of Chile and Mendoza.[4]

I will here give a very brief sketch of the geology of the several parallel lines forming the Cordillera. Of these lines, there are two considerably higher than the others; namely, on the Chilian side, the Peuquenes ridge, which, where the road crosses it, is 13,210 feet above the sea; and the Portillo ridge, on the Mendoza side, which is 14,305 feet. The lower beds of the Peuquenes ridge, and of the several great lines to the westward of it, are composed of a vast pile, many thousand feet in thickness, of porphyries which have flowed as submarine lavas, alternating with angular and rounded fragments of the same rocks, thrown out of the submarine craters. These alternating masses are covered in the central parts, by a great thickness of red sandstone, conglomerate, and calcareous clay-slate, associated with, and passing into, prodigious beds of gypsum. In these upper beds shells are tolerably frequent; and

---

4 [Editor] Mendoza was one of the provinces of Argentina that existed as a virtually independent state in the years following the Argentine war of independence. Originally a province of Chile, the Spanish government transferred it to the viceroyalty of the Rio de la Plata in 1776. Generals José de San Martin and Bernardo O'Higgins took advantage of its remoteness to train the army of Argentine and Chilean patriots that finally drove the Spanish out of Argentina and Chile.

they belong to about the period of the lower chalk of Europe. It is an old story, but not the less wonderful, to hear of shells which were once crawling on the bottom of the sea, now standing nearly 14,000 feet above its level. The lower beds in this great pile of strata, have been dislocated, baked, crystallized and almost blended together, through the agency of mountain masses of a peculiar white soda-granitic rock.

The other main line, namely, that of the Portillo, is of a totally different formation: it consists chiefly of grand bare pinnacles of a red potash-granite, which low down on the western flank are covered by a sandstone, converted by the former heat into a quartz-rock. On the quartz, there rest beds of a conglomerate several thousand feet in thickness, which have been upheaved by the red granite, and dip at an angle of 45° towards the Peuquenes line. I was astonished to find that this conglomerate was partly composed of pebbles, derived from the rocks, with their fossil shells, of the Peuquenes range; and partly of red potash-granite, like that of the Portillo. Hence we must conclude, that both the Peuquenes and Portillo ranges were partially upheaved and exposed to wear and tear, when the conglomerate was forming; but as the beds of the conglomerate have been thrown off at an angle of 45° by the red Portillo granite (with the underlying sandstone baked by it), we may feel sure, that the greater part of the injection and upheaval of the already partially formed Portillo line, took place after the accumulation of the conglomerate, and long after the elevation of the Peuquenes ridge. So that the Portillo, the loftiest line in this part of the Cordillera, is not so old as the less lofty line of the Peuquenes. Evidence derived from an inclined stream of lava at the eastern base of the Portillo, might be adduced to show, that it owes part of its great height to elevations of a still later date. Looking to its earliest origin, the red granite seems to have been injected on an ancient pre-existing line of white granite and mica-slate. In most parts, perhaps in all parts, of the Cordillera, it may be concluded that each line has been formed by repeated upheavals and injections; and that the several parallel lines are of different ages. Only thus can we gain time, at all sufficient to explain the truly astonishing amount of denudation, which these great, though comparatively with most other ranges recent, mountains have suffered.

Finally, the shells in the Peuquenes or oldest ridge, prove, as before remarked, that it has been upraised 14,000 feet since a

Secondary period, which in Europe we are accustomed to consider as far from ancient; but since these shells lived in a moderately deep sea, it can be shown that the area now occupied by the Cordillera, must have subsided several thousand feet—in northern Chile as much as 6000 feet—so as to have allowed that amount of submarine strata to have been heaped on the bed on which the shells lived. The proof is the same with that by which it was shown, that at a much later period since the tertiary shells of Patagonia lived, there must have been there a subsidence of several hundred feet, as well as an ensuing elevation. Daily it is forced home on the mind of the geologist, that nothing, not even the wind that blows, is so unstable as the level of the crust of this earth.

I will make only one other geological remark: although the Portillo chain is here higher than the Peuquenes, the waters, draining the intermediate valleys, have burst through it. The same fact, on a grander scale, has been remarked in the eastern and loftiest line of the Bolivian Cordillera, through which the rivers pass: analogous facts have also been observed in other quarters of the world. On the supposition of the subsequent and gradual elevation of the Portillo line, this can be understood; for a chain of islets would at first appear, and, as these were lifted up, the tides would be always wearing deeper and broader channels between them. At the present day, even in the most retired Sounds on the coast of Tierra del Fuego, the currents in the transverse breaks which connect the longitudinal channels, are very strong, so that in one transverse channel even a small vessel under sail was whirled round and round.

About noon we began the tedious ascent of the Peuquenes ridge, and then for the first time experienced some little difficulty in our respiration. The mules would halt every fifty yards, and after resting for a few seconds the poor willing animals started of their own accord again. The short breathing from the rarefied atmosphere is called by the Chilenos "puna;" and they have most ridiculous notions concerning its origin. Some say "all the waters here have puna;" others that "where there is snow there is puna;"—and this no doubt is true. The only sensation I experienced was a slight tightness across the head and chest, like that felt on leaving a warm room and running quickly in frosty weather. There was some imagination even in this; for upon finding fossil shells on the highest ridge, I entirely forgot the puna in my delight. Certainly the exertion of walking was extremely great, and the respiration became deep and laborious: I am told that in Potosi (about 13,000 feet above the sea) strangers do not become thoroughly accustomed to the atmosphere for an entire year. The inhabitants all recommend onions for the puna; as this vegetable has sometimes been given in Europe for pectoral complaints, it may possibly be of real service:—for my part I found nothing so good as the fossil shells!

When about halfway up we met a large party with seventy loaded mules. It was interesting to hear the wild cries of the muleteers, and to watch the long descending string of the animals; they appeared so diminutive, there being nothing but the bleak mountains with which they could be compared. When near the summit, the wind, as generally happens, was impetuous and extremely cold. On each side of the ridge we had to pass over broad bands of perpetual snow, which were now soon to be covered by a fresh layer. When we reached the crest and looked backwards, a glorious view was presented. The atmosphere resplendently clear; the sky an intense blue; the profound valleys; the wild broken forms; the heaps of ruins, piled up during the lapse of ages; the bright-coloured rocks, contrasted with the quiet mountains of snow; all these together produced a scene no one could have imagined. Neither plant nor bird, excepting a few condors wheeling around the higher pinnacles, distracted my attention from the inanimate mass. I felt glad that I was alone: it was like watching a thunderstorm, or hearing in full orchestra a chorus of the Messiah.

On several patches of the snow I found the Protococcus nivalis, or red snow, so well known from the accounts of Arctic navigators. My attention was called to it, by observing the footsteps of the mules stained a pale red, as if their hoofs had been slightly bloody. I at first thought that it was owing to dust blown from the surrounding mountains of red porphyry; for from the magnifying power of the crystals of snow, the groups of these microscopical plants appeared like coarse particles. The snow was coloured only where it had thawed very rapidly, or had been accidentally crushed. A little rubbed on paper gave it a faint rose tinge mingled with a little brick-red. I afterwards scraped some off the paper, and found that it consisted of groups of little spheres in colourless cases, each the thousandth part of an inch in diameter.

The wind on the crest of the Peuquenes, as just remarked,

is generally impetuous and very cold: it is said[5] to blow steadily from the westward or Pacific side. As the observations have been chiefly made in summer, this wind must be an upper and return current. The Peak of Teneriffe, with a less elevation, and situated in lat. 28°, in like manner falls within an upper return stream. At first it appears rather surprising, that the trade-wind along the northern parts of Chile and on the coast of Peru, should blow in so very southerly a direction as it does; but when we reflect that the Cordillera, running in a north and south line, intercepts, like a great wall, the entire depth of the lower atmospheric current, we can easily see that the trade-wind must be drawn northward, following the line of mountains, towards the equatorial regions, and thus lose part of that easterly movement which it otherwise would have gained from the earth's rotation. At Mendoza, on the eastern foot of the Andes, the climate is said to be subject to long calms, and to frequent though false appearances of gathering rain-storms: we may imagine that the wind, which coming from the eastward is thus banked up by the line of mountains, would become stagnant and irregular in its movements.

Having crossed the Peuquenes, we descended into a mountainous country, intermediate between the two main ranges, and then took up our quarters for the night. We were now in the republic of Mendoza. The elevation was probably not under 11,000 feet, and the vegetation in consequence exceedingly scanty. The root of a small scrubby plant served as fuel, but it made a miserable fire, and the wind was piercingly cold. Being quite tired with my day's work, I made up my bed as quickly as I could, and went to sleep. About midnight I observed the sky became suddenly clouded: I awakened the arriero to know if there was any danger of bad weather; but he said that without thunder and lightning there was no risk of a heavy snow-storm. The peril is imminent, and the difficulty of subsequent escape great, to any one overtaken by bad weather between the two ranges. A certain cave offers the only place of refuge: Mr. Caldcleugh, who crossed on this same day of the month, was detained there for some time by a heavy fall of snow. Casuchas, or houses of refuge, have not been built in this pass as in that of Uspallata, and therefore, during the autumn, the Portillo is little frequented. I may here remark that within the

[5] [Darwin] Dr. Gillies in Journ. of Nat. and Geograph. Science, Aug. 1830. This author gives the heights of the Passes.

main Cordillera rain never falls, for during the summer the
sky is cloudless, and in winter snow-storms alone occur.

At the place where we slept water necessarily boiled, from
the diminished pressure of the atmosphere, at a lower temperature than it does in a less lofty country; the case being the
converse of that of a Papin's digester. Hence the potatoes,
after remaining for some hours in the boiling water, were
nearly as hard as ever. The pot was left on the fire all night,
and next morning it was boiled again, but yet the potatoes were
not cooked. I found out this, by overhearing my two companions discussing the cause; they had come to the simple conclusion, "that the cursed pot (which was a new one) did not
choose to boil potatoes."

March 22nd.—After eating our potato-less breakfast, we
travelled across the intermediate tract to the foot of the Portillo range. In the middle of summer cattle are brought up here
to graze; but they had now all been removed: even the greater
number of the guanacos had decamped, knowing well that if
overtaken here by a snow-storm, they would be caught in a
trap. We had a fine view of a mass of mountains called
Tupungato, the whole clothed with unbroken snow, in the
midst of which there was a blue patch, no doubt a glacier;—
a circumstance of rare occurrence in these mountains. Now
commenced a heavy and long climb, similar to that up the
Peuquenes. Bold conical hills of red granite rose on each hand;
in the valleys there were several broad fields of perpetual snow.
These frozen masses, during the process of thawing, had in
some parts been converted into pinnacles or columns,[6] which,
as they were high and close together, made it difficult for the
cargo mules to pass. On one of these columns of ice, a frozen
horse was sticking as on a pedestal, but with its hind legs
straight up in the air. The animal, I suppose, must have fallen
with its head downward into a hole, when the snow was con-

---

[6] [Darwin] This structure in frozen snow was long since observed
by Scoresby in the icebergs near Spitzbergen, and lately, with more
care, by Colonel Jackson (Journ. of Geograph. Soc., vol. v. p. 12)
on the Neva. Mr. Lyell (Principles, vol. iv. p. 360) has compared
the fissures, by which the columnar structure seems to be determined, to the joints that traverse nearly all rocks, but which are
best seen in the non-stratified masses. I may observe, that in the
case of the frozen snow, the columnar structure must be owing to
a "metamorphic" action, and not to a process during *deposition.*

tinuous, and afterwards the surrounding parts must have been removed by the thaw.

When nearly on the crest of the Portillo, we were enveloped in a falling cloud of minute frozen spicula. This was very unfortunate, as it continued the whole day, and quite intercepted our view. The pass takes its name of Portillo, from a narrow cleft or doorway on the highest ridge, through which the road passes. From this point, on a clear day, those vast plains which uninterruptedly extend to the Atlantic Ocean, can be seen. We descended to the upper limit of vegetation, and found good quarters for the night under the shelter of some large fragments of rock. We met here some passengers, who made anxious inquiries about the state of the road. Shortly after it was dark the clouds suddenly cleared away, and the effect was quite magical. The great mountains, bright with the full moon, seemed impending over us on all sides, as over a deep crevice: one morning, very early, I witnessed the same striking effect. As soon as the clouds were dispersed it froze severely; but as there was no wind, we slept very comfortably.

The increased brilliancy of the moon and stars at this elevation, owing to the perfect transparency of the atmosphere, was very remarkable. Travellers having observed the difficulty of judging heights and distances amidst lofty mountains, have generally attributed it to the absence of objects of comparison. It appears to me, that it is fully as much owing to the transparency of the air confounding objects at different distances, and likewise partly to the novelty of an unusual degree of fatigue arising from a little exertion,—habit being thus opposed to the evidence of the senses. I am sure that this extreme clearness of the air gives a peculiar character to the landscape, all objects appearing to be brought nearly into one plane, as in a drawing or panorama. The transparency is, I presume, owing to the equable and high state of atmospheric dryness. This dryness was shown by the manner in which woodwork shrank (as I soon found by the trouble my geological hammer gave me); by articles of food, such as bread and sugar, becoming extremely hard; and by the preservation of the skin and parts of the flesh of the beasts, which had perished on the road. To the same cause we must attribute the singular facility with which electricity is excited. My flannel-waistcoat, when rubbed in the dark, appeared as if it had been washed with phosphorus;— every hair on a dog's back crackled;—even the linen sheets, and leathern straps of the saddle, when handled, emitted sparks.

March 23rd.—The descent on the eastern side of the Cordillera is much shorter or steeper than on the Pacific side; in other words, the mountains rise more abruptly from the plains than from the alpine country of Chile. A level and brilliantly white sea of clouds was stretched out beneath our feet, shutting out the view of the equally level Pampas. We soon entered the band of clouds, and did not again emerge from it that day. About noon, finding pasture for the animals and bushes for firewood at Los Arenales, we stopped for the night. This was near the uppermost limit of bushes, and the elevation, I suppose, was between seven and eight thousand feet.

I was much struck with the marked difference between the vegetation of these eastern valleys and those on the Chilian side: yet the climate, as well as the kind of soil, is nearly the same, and the difference of longitude very trifling. The same remark holds good with the quadrupeds, and in a lesser degree with the birds and insects. I may instance the mice, of which I obtained thirteen species on the shores of the Atlantic, and five on the Pacific, and not one of them is identical. We must except all those species, which habitually or occasionally frequent elevated mountains; and certain birds, which range as far south as the Strait of Magellan. This fact is in perfect accordance with the geological history of the Andes; for these mountains have existed as a great barrier, since the present races of animals have appeared; and therefore, unless we suppose the same species to have been created in two different places, we ought not to expect any closer similarity between the organic beings on the opposite sides of the Andes, than on the opposite shores of the ocean. In both cases, we must leave out of the question those kinds which have been able to cross the barrier, whether of solid rock or salt-water.[7]

A great number of the plants and animals were absolutely the same as, or most closely allied to those of Patagonia. We here have the agouti, bizcacha, three species of armadillo, the ostrich, certain kinds of partridges and other birds, none of

[7] [Darwin] This is merely an illustration of the admirable laws, first laid down by Mr. Lyell, on the geographical distribution of animals, as influenced by geological changes. The whole reasoning, of course, is founded on the assumption of the immutability of species; otherwise the difference in the species in the two regions, might be considered as superinduced during a length of time.

which are ever seen in Chile, but are the characteristic animals of the desert plains of Patagonia. We have likewise many of the same (to the eyes of the person who is not a botanist) thorny stunted bushes, withered grass, and dwarf plants. Even the black slowly-crawling beetles are closely similar, and some, I believe, on rigorous examination, absolutely identical. It had always been to me a subject of regret, that we were unavoidably compelled to give up the ascent of the S. Cruz river, before reaching the mountains: I always had a latent hope of meeting with some great change in the features of the country; but I now feel sure, that it would only have been following the plains of Patagonia up a mountainous ascent.

March 24th.—Early in the morning I climbed up a mountain on one side of the valley, and enjoyed a far extended view over the Pampas. This was a spectacle to which I had always looked forward with interest, but I was disappointed: at the first glance it much resembled a distant view of the ocean, but in the northern parts many irregularities were soon distinguishable. The most striking feature consisted in the rivers, which, facing the rising sun, glittered like silver threads, till lost in the immensity of the distance. At midday we descended the valley, and reached a hovel, where an officer and three soldiers were posted to examine passports. One of these men was a thoroughbred Pampas Indian: he was kept much for the same purpose as a bloodhound, to track out any person who might pass by secretly, either on foot or horseback. Some years ago, a passenger endeavoured to escape detection, by making a long circuit over a neighbouring mountain; but this Indian, having by chance crossed his track, followed it for the whole day over dry and very stony hills, till at last he came on his prey hidden in a gully. We here heard that the silvery clouds, which we had admired from the bright region above, had poured down torrents of rain. The valley from this point gradually opened, and the hills became mere water-worn hillocks compared to the giants behind: it then expanded into a gently-sloping plain of shingle, covered with low trees and bushes. This talus, although appearing narrow, must be nearly ten miles wide before it blends into the apparently dead level Pampas. We passed the only house in this neighbourhood, the Estancia of Chaquaio; and at sunset we pulled up in the first snug corner, and there bivouacked.

March 25th.—I was reminded of the Pampas of Buenos Ayres, by seeing the disk of the rising sun, intersected by an

horizon, level as that of the ocean. During the night a heavy
dew fell, a circumstance which we did not experience within
the Cordillera. The road proceeded for some distance due east
across a low swamp; then meeting the dry plain, it turned to the
north towards Mendoza. The distance is two very long days'
journey. Our first day's journey was called fourteen leagues to
Estacado, and the second seventeen to Luxan, near Mendoza.
The whole distance is over a level desert plain, with not more
than two or three houses. The sun was exceedingly powerful,
and the ride devoid of all interest. There is very little water in
this "traversia," and in our second day's journey we found only
one little pool. Little water flows from the mountains, and it
soon becomes absorbed by the dry and porous soil; so that, although we travelled at the distance of only ten or fifteen miles
from the outer range of the Cordillera, we did not cross a single stream. In many parts the ground was incrusted with a
saline efflorescence; hence we had the same salt-loving plants,
which are common near Bahia Blanca. The landscape has a
uniform character from the Strait of Magellan, along the whole
eastern coast of Patagonia, to the Rio Colorado; and it appears
that the same kind of country extends inland from this river, in
a sweeping line as far as San Luis, and perhaps even further
north. To the eastward of this curved line, lies the basin of the
comparatively damp and green plains of Buenos Ayres. The
sterile plains of Mendoza and Patagonia consist of a bed of
shingle, worn smooth and accumulated by the waves of the sea;
while the Pampas, covered by thistles, clover, and grass, have
been formed by the ancient estuary mud of the Plata.

After our two days' tedious journey, it was refreshing to see
in the distance the rows of poplars and willows growing round
the village and river of Luxan. Shortly before we arrived at
this place, we observed to the south a ragged cloud of a dark
reddish-brown colour. At first we thought that it was smoke
from some great fire on the plains; but we soon found that it
was a swarm of locusts. They were flying northward; and with
the aid of a light breeze, they overtook us at a rate of ten or
fifteen miles an hour. The main body filled the air from a
height of twenty feet, to that, as it appeared, of two or three
thousand above the ground; "and the sound of their wings was
as the sound of chariots of many horses running to battle:"
or rather, I should say, like a strong breeze passing through
the rigging of a ship. The sky, seen through the advanced
guard, appeared like a mezzotinto engraving, but the main

body was impervious to sight; they were not, however, so thick together, but that they could escape a stick waved backwards and forwards. When they alighted, they were more numerous than the leaves in the field, and the surface became reddish instead of being green: the swarm having once alighted, the individuals flew from side to side in all directions. Locusts are not an uncommon pest in this country: already during this season, several smaller swarms had come up from the south, where, as apparently in all other parts of the world, they are bred in the deserts. The poor cottagers in vain attempted by lighting fires, by shouts, and by waving branches to avert the attack. This species of locust closely resembles, and perhaps is identical with the famous Gryllus migratorius of the East.

We crossed the Luxan, which is a river of considerable size, though its course towards the sea-coast is very imperfectly known: it is even doubtful whether, in passing over the plains, it is not evaporated and lost. We slept in the village of Luxan, which is a small place surrounded by gardens, and forms the most southern cultivated district in the Province of Mendoza; it is five leagues south of the capital. At night I experienced an attack (for it deserves no less a name) of the *Benchuca*, a species of Reduvius, the great black bug of the Pampas.[8] It is most disgusting to feel soft wingless insects, about an inch long, crawling over one's body. Before sucking they are quite thin, but afterwards they become round and bloated with blood, and in this state are easily crushed. One which I caught at Iquique, (for they are found in Chile and Peru) was very empty. When placed on a table, and though surrounded by people, if a finger was presented, the bold insect would immediately protrude its sucker, make a charge, and if allowed, draw blood. No pain was caused by the wound. It was curious to watch its body during the act of sucking, as in less than ten minutes it changed from being as flat as a wafer to a globular form. This one feast, for which the benchuca was indebted to one of the officers, kept it fat during four whole months; but, after the first fortnight, it was quite ready to have another suck.

March 27th.—We rode on to Mendoza. The country was beautifully cultivated, and resembled Chile. This neighbourhood is celebrated for its fruit; and certainly nothing could

8 [Editor] This is the occasion on which Darwin may have contracted Chagas' disease, an ailment that could have caused the symptoms that plagued Darwin almost from the time of his return to England to the end of his life. See discussion on pages xx–xxi.

appear more flourishing than the vineyards and the orchards of figs, peaches, and olives. We bought water-melons nearly twice as large as a man's head, most deliciously cool and well-flavoured, for a halfpenny apiece; and for the value of three-pence, half a wheelbarrowful of peaches. The cultivated and enclosed part of this province is very small; there is little more than that which we passed through between Luxan and the Capital. The land, as in Chile, owes its fertility entirely to artificial irrigation; and it is really wonderful to observe how extraordinarily productive a barren traversia is thus rendered.

We stayed the ensuing day in Mendoza. The prosperity of the place has much declined of late years. The inhabitants say "it is good to live in, but very bad to grow rich in." The lower orders have the lounging, reckless manners of the Gauchos of the Pampas; and their dress, riding-gear, and habits of life, are nearly the same. To my mind the town had a stupid, forlorn aspect. Neither the boasted alameda, nor the scenery, is at all comparable with that of Santiago; but to those who, coming from Buenos Ayres, have just crossed the unvaried Pampas, the gardens and orchards must appear delightful. Sir F. Head, speaking of the inhabitants, says, "They eat their dinners, and it is so very hot, they go to sleep—and could they do better?" I quite agree with Sir F. Head: the happy doom of the Mendozinos is to eat, sleep, and be idle.

March 29th.—We set out on our return to Chile, by the Uspallata pass situated north of Mendoza. We had to cross a long and most sterile traversia of fifteen leagues. The soil in parts was absolutely bare, in others covered by numberless dwarf cacti, armed with formidable spines, and called by the inhabitants "little lions." There were, also, a few low bushes. Although the plain is nearly three thousand feet above the sea, the sun was very powerful; and the heat, as well as the clouds of impalpable dust, rendered the travelling extremely irksome. Our course during the day lay nearly parallel to the Cordillera, but gradually approaching them. Before sunset we entered one of the wide valleys, or rather bays, which open on the plain: this soon narrowed into a ravine, where a little higher up the house of Villa Vicencio is situated. As we had ridden all day without a drop of water, both our mules and selves were very thirsty, and we looked out anxiously for the stream which flows down this valley. It was curious to observe how gradually the water made its appearance: on the plain the course was quite dry; by degrees it became a little damper; then puddles of water appeared; these soon became connected; and at Villa Vicencio there was a nice little rivulet.

30th.—The solitary hovel which bears the imposing name of Villa Vicencio, has been mentioned by every traveller who has crossed the Andes. I stayed here and at some neighbouring mines during the two succeeding days. The geology of the surrounding country is very curious. The Uspallata range is separated from the main Cordillera by a long narrow plain or basin, like those so often mentioned in Chile, but higher, being six thousand feet above the sea. This range has nearly the same geographical position with respect to the Cordillera, which the gigantic Portillo line has, but it is of a totally different origin: it consists of various kinds of submarine lava, alternating with volcanic sandstones and other remarkable sedimentary deposits; the whole having a very close resemblance to some of the tertiary beds on the shores of the Pacific. From this resemblance I expected to find silicified wood, which is generally characteristic of those formations. I was gratified in a very extraordinary manner. In the central part of the range, at an elevation of about seven thousand feet, I observed on a bare slope some snow-white projecting columns. These were petrified trees, eleven being silicified, and from thirty to forty converted into coarsely-crystallized white calcareous spar. They were abruptly broken off, the upright stumps projecting a few feet above the ground. The trunks measured from three to five feet each in circumference. They stood a little way apart from each other, but the whole formed one group. Mr. Robert Brown has been kind enough to examine the wood: he says it belongs to the fir tribe, partaking of the character of the Araucarian family, but with some curious points of affinity with the yew. The volcanic sandstone in which the trees were embedded, and from the lower part of which they must have sprung, had accumulated in successive thin layers around their trunks; and the stone yet retained the impression of the bark.

It required little geological practice to interpret the marvellous story which this scene at once unfolded; though I confess I was at first so much astonished, that I could scarcely believe the plainest evidence. I saw the spot where a cluster of fine trees once waved their branches on the shores of the Atlantic, when that ocean (now driven back 700 miles) came to the foot of the Andes. I saw that they had sprung from a volcanic soil which had been raised above the level of the sea, and that subsequently this dry land, with its upright trees, had been let down into the depths of the ocean. In these depths, the formerly dry land was covered by sedimentary beds, and these again by enormous streams of submarine lava—one such mass attaining the thickness of a thousand feet; and these deluges of molten stone and aqueous deposits five times alternately had been spread out. The ocean which received such thick masses, must have been profoundly deep; but again the subterranean forces exerted themselves, and I now beheld the bed of that ocean, forming a chain of mountains more than seven thousand feet in height. Nor had those antagonist forces been dormant, which are always at work wearing down the surface of the land: the great piles of strata had been intersected by many wide valleys, and the trees, now changed into silex, were exposed projecting from the volcanic soil, now changed into rock, whence formerly, in a green and budding state, they had raised their lofty heads. Now, all is utterly irreclaimable and desert; even the lichen cannot adhere to the stony casts of former trees. Vast, and scarcely comprehensible as such changes must ever appear, yet they have all occurred within a period, recent when compared with the history of the Cordillera; and the Cordillera itself is absolutely modern as compared with many of the fossiliferous strata of Europe and America.

April 1st.—We crossed the Uspallata range, and at night slept at the custom-house—the only inhabited spot on the plain. Shortly before leaving the mountains, there was a very extraordinary view; red, purple, green, and quite white sedimentary rocks, alternating with black lavas, were broken up and thrown into all kinds of disorder by masses of porphyry of every shade of colour, from dark brown to the brightest lilac. It was the first view I ever saw, which really resembled those pretty sections which geologists make of the inside of the earth.

The next day we crossed the plain, and followed the course of the same great mountain stream which flows by Luxan. Here it was a furious torrent, quite impassable, and appeared larger than in the low country, as was the case with the rivulet of Villa Vicencio. On the evening of the succeeding day, we reached the Rio de las Vacas, which is considered the worst stream in the Cordillera to cross. As all these rivers have a rapid and short course, and are formed by the melting of the snow, the hour of the day makes a considerable difference in their volume. In the evening the stream is muddy and full, but about daybreak it becomes clearer and much less impetuous. This we found to be the case with the Rio Vacas, and in the morning we crossed it with little difficulty.

The scenery thus far was very uninteresting, compared with that of the Portillo pass. Little can be seen beyond the bare walls of the one grand, flat-bottomed valley, which the road follows up to the highest crest. The valley and the huge rocky mountains are extremely barren: during the two previous nights the poor mules had absolutely nothing to eat, for excepting a few low resinous bushes, scarcely a plant can be seen. In the course of this day we crossed some of the worst passes in the Cordillera, but their danger has been much exaggerated. I was told that if I attempted to pass on foot, my head would turn giddy, and that there was no room to dismount; but I did not see a place where any one might not have walked over backwards, or got off his mule on either side. One of the bad passes, called *las Animas* (the Souls), I had crossed, and did not find out till a day afterwards, that it was one of the awful dangers. No doubt there are many parts in which, if the mule should stumble, the rider would be hurled down a great precipice; but of this there is little chance. I dare say, in the spring, the "ladcras," or roads, which each year are formed anew across the piles of fallen detritus, are very bad; but from what I saw, I suspect the real danger is nothing. With cargo-mules the case is rather different, for the loads project so far, that the animals, occasionally running against each other, or against a point of rock, lose their balance, and are thrown down the precipices. In crossing the rivers I can well believe that the difficulty may be very great: at this season there was little trouble, but in the summer they must be very hazardous. I can quite imagine, as Sir F. Head describes, the different expressions of those who *have* passed the gulf, and those who *are* passing. I never heard of any man being drowned, but with loaded mules it frequently happens. The arriero tells you to show your mule the best line, and allow her to cross as she likes: the cargo-mule takes a bad line, and is often lost.

April 4th.—From the Rio de las Vacas to the Puente del Incas, half a day's journey. As there was pasture for the mules, and geology for me, we bivouacked here for the night. When one hears of a natural Bridge, one pictures to oneself some deep and narrow ravine, across which a bold mass of rock has fallen; or a great arch hollowed out like the vault of a cavern. Instead of this, the Incas Bridge consists of a crust of stratified shingle, cemented together by the deposits of the neighbouring hot springs. It appears, as if the stream had scooped out a channel on one side, leaving an overhanging ledge, which was met by earth and stones falling down from the opposite cliff. Certainly an oblique junction, as would happen in such a case, was very distinct on one side. The Bridge of the Incas is by no means worthy of the great monarchs whose name it bears.

5th.—We had a long day's ride across the central ridge, from the Incas Bridge to the Ojos del Agua, which are situated near the lowest *casucha* on the Chilian side. These casuchas are round little towers, with steps outside to reach the floor, which is raised some feet above the ground on account of the snow-drifts. They are eight in number, and under the Spanish government were kept during the winter well stored with food and charcoal, and each courier had a master-key. Now they only answer the purpose of caves, or rather dungeons. Seated on some little eminence, they are not, however, ill suited to the surrounding scene of desolation. The zigzag ascent of the Cumbre, or the partition of the waters, was very steep and tedious; its height, according to Mr. Pentland, is 12,454 feet. The road did not pass over any perpetual snow, although there were patches of it on both hands. The wind on the summit was exceedingly cold, but it was impossible not to stop for a few minutes to admire, again and again, the colour of the heavens, and the brilliant transparency of the atmosphere. The scenery was grand: to the westward there was a fine chaos of mountains, divided by profound ravines. Some snow generally falls before this period of the season, and it has even happened that the Cordillera have been finally closed by this time. But we were most fortunate. The sky, by night and by day, was cloudless, excepting a few round little masses of vapour, that floated over the highest pinnacles. I have often seen these islets in the sky, marking the position of the Cordillera, when the far-distant mountains have been hidden beneath the horizon.

April 6th.—In the morning we found some thief had stolen one of our mules, and the bell of the madrina. We therefore rode only two or three miles down the valley, and staid there the ensuing day in hopes of recovering the mule, which the arriero thought had been hidden in some ravine. The scenery in this part had assumed a Chilian character: the lower sides of the mountains, dotted over with the pale evergreen Quillay tree, and with the great chandelier-like cactus, are certainly more to be admired than the bare eastern valleys; but I cannot quite agree with the admiration expressed by some travellers.

The extreme pleasure, I suspect, is chiefly owing to the prospect of a good fire and of a good supper, after escaping from the cold regions above: and I am sure I most heartily participated in these feelings.

8th.—We left the valley of the Aconcagua, by which we had descended, and reached in the evening a cottage near the Villa de St. Rosa. The fertility of the plain was delightful: the autumn being advanced, the leaves of many of the fruit-trees were falling; and of the labourers,—some were busy in drying figs and peaches on the roofs of their cottages, while others were gathering the grapes from the vineyards. It was a pretty scene; but I missed that pensive stillness which makes the autumn in England indeed the evening of the year. On the 10th we reached Santiago, where I received a very kind and hospitable reception from Mr. Caldcleugh. My excursion only cost me twenty-four days, and never did I more deeply enjoy an equal space of time. A few days afterwards I returned to Mr. Corfield's house at Valparaiso.

CHAPTER XVI

NORTHERN CHILE AND PERU

Coast-road to Coquimbo — Great Loads carried by the Miners —
Coquimbo — Earthquake — Step-formed Terraces — Absence of
recent Deposits — Contemporaneousness of the Tertiary Formations — Excursion up the Valley — Road to Guasco — Deserts —
Valley of Copiapó — Rain and Earthquakes — Hydrophobia — The
Despoblado — Indian Ruins — Probable Change of Climate — River-
bed arched by an Earthquake — Cold Gales of Wind — Noises from
a Hill — Iquique — Salt Alluvium — Nitrate of Soda — Lima —
Unhealthy Country — Ruins of Callao, overthrown by an Earthquake — Recent Subsidence — Elevated Shells on San Lorenzo,
their decomposition — Plain with embedded Shells and fragments
of Pottery — Antiquity of the Indian Race

April 27th.—I set out on a journey to Coquimbo, and thence
through Guasco to Copiapó, where Captain Fitz Roy kindly
offered to pick me up in the *Beagle*.[1] The distance in a straight
line along the shore northward is only 420 miles; but my mode

[1] [Editor] The *Beagle* returned to Valparaiso from the Concepción area on April 17. When the survey vessel sent a boat ashore,
Darwin was able to pass on the welcome news, received from
England, that Fitz Roy had been promoted. While Darwin proceeded overland to Coquimbo and thence to Copiapó, the *Beagle*
surveyed the coast to the north of Valparaiso, moored in a small
bay near Coquimbo for beaching and refit before crossing the
Pacific, and then returned to Valparaiso for stores. In Valparaiso,
Fitz Roy heard that a British man-of-war, H.M.S. *Challenger*, had
been lost on the Chilean coast. Fitz Roy recalled talking with the
officers of a Swedish ship who spoke of seeing the wreckage of an
"American brig" near an uninhabited coastal island to the South.
Fitz Roy put two and two together, guessed that the Swedes had
seen *Challenger* with one of her masts gone and only the red and

of travelling made it a very long journey. I bought four horses and two mules, the latter carrying the luggage on alternate days. The six animals together only cost the value of twenty-five pounds sterling, and at Copiapó I sold them again for twenty-three. We travelled in the same independent manner as before, cooking our own meals, and sleeping in the open air. As we rode towards the Viño del Mar, I took a farewell view of Valparaiso, and admired its picturesque appearance. For geological purposes I made a detour from the high road to the foot of the Bell of Quillota. We passed through an alluvial district rich in gold, to the neighbourhood of Limache, where we slept. Washing for gold supports the inhabitants of numerous hovels, scattered along the sides of each little rivulet; but, like all those whose gains are uncertain, they are unthrifty in their habits, and consequently poor.

28th.—In the afternoon we arrived at a cottage at the foot of the Bell mountain. The inhabitants were freeholders, which is not very usual in Chile. They supported themselves on the produce of a garden and a little field, but were very poor. Capital is here so deficient, that the people are obliged to sell their green corn[2] while standing in the field, in order to buy necessaries for the ensuing year. Wheat in consequence was dearer in the very district of its production than at Valparaiso, where the contractors live. The next day we joined the main road to Coquimbo. At night there was a very light shower of rain: this was the first drop that had fallen since the heavy rain of September 11th and 12th, which detained me a prisoner at the Baths of Cauquenes. The interval was seven and a half months; but the rain this year in Chile was rather later than usual. The distant Andes were now covered by a thick mass of snow; and were a glorious sight.

May 2nd.—The road continued to follow the coast, at no

---

white of her ensign visible (so making it look like a U.S. flag). Hastening to the Post Office in the hope of obtaining further news, he found a packet of dispatches from the wrecked ship, all but two of whose officers and men had made it safely ashore and had set up camp to await rescue. Fitz Roy took two of his officers and a whale-boat, joined another British warship, H.M.S. Blonde, in the rescue. The Beagle in the meantime went north under Fitz Roy's second in command, Lieutenant John Wickham, and continued the survey with the aid of a 35-ton vessel loaned by a wealthy Chilean. Fitz Roy rejoined his ship in Callao, Peru.

[2] [Editor] In nineteenth-century England, wheat was called corn.

great distance from the sea. The few trees and bushes which are common in central Chile decreased rapidly in numbers, and were replaced by a tall plant, something like a yucca in appearance. The surface of the country, on a small scale, was singularly broken and irregular; abrupt little peaks of rock rising out of small plains or basins. The indented coast and the bottom of the neighbouring sea, studded with breakers, would, if converted into dry land, present similar forms; and such a conversion without doubt has taken place in the part over which we rode.

3rd.—Quilimari to Conchalee. The country became more and more barren. In the valleys there was scarcely sufficient water for any irrigation; and the intermediate land was quite bare, not supporting even goats. In the spring, after the winter showers, a thin pasture rapidly springs up, and cattle are then driven down from the Cordillera to graze for a short time. It is curious to observe how the seeds of the grass and other plants seem to accommodate themselves, as if by an acquired habit, to the quantity of rain which falls on different parts of this coast. One shower far northward at Copiapó produces as great an effect on the vegetation, as two at Guasco, and as three or four in this district. At Valparaiso a winter so dry as greatly to injure the pasture, would at Guasco produce the most unusual abundance. Proceeding northward, the quantity of rain does not appear to decrease in strict proportion to the latitude. At Conchalee, which is only 67 miles north of Valparaiso, rain is not expected till the end of May; whereas, at Valparaiso some generally falls early in April: the annual quantity is likewise small in proportion to the lateness of the season at which it commences.

4th.—Finding the coast-road devoid of interest of any kind, we turned inland towards the mining district and valley of Illapel. This valley, like every other in Chile, is level, broad, and very fertile: it is bordered on each side, either by cliffs of stratified shingle, or by bare rocky mountains. Above the straight line of the uppermost irrigating ditch, all is brown as on a high road; while all below is of as bright a green as verdigris, from the beds of alfarfa, a kind of clover. We proceeded to Los Hornos, another mining district, where the principal hill was drilled with holes, like a great ants'-nest. The Chilian miners are a peculiar race of men in their habits. Living for weeks together in the most desolate spots, when they descend to the villages on feast-days, there is no excess or extravagance into which they do not run. They sometimes gain a considerable sum, and then, like sailors with prize-money, they try how soon they can contrive to squander it. They drink excessively, buy quantities of clothes, and in a few days return penniless to their miserable abodes, there to work harder than beasts of burden. This thoughtlessness, as with sailors, is evidently the result of a similar manner of life. Their daily food is found them, and they acquire no habits of carefulness; moreover, temptation and the means of yielding to it are placed in their power at the same time. On the other hand, in Cornwall, and some other parts of England, where the system of selling part of the vein is followed, the miners, from being obliged to act and think for themselves, are a singularly intelligent and well-conducted set of men.

The dress of the Chilian miner is peculiar and rather picturesque. He wears a very long shirt of some dark-coloured baize, with a leathern apron; the whole being fastened round his waist by a bright-coloured sash. His trowsers are very broad, and his small cap of scarlet cloth is made to fit the head closely. We met a party of these miners in full costume, carrying the body of one of their companions to be buried. They marched at a very quick trot, four men supporting the corpse. One set having run as hard as they could for about two hundred yards, were relieved by four others, who had previously dashed on ahead on horseback. Thus they proceeded, encouraging each other by wild cries: altogether the scene formed a most strange funeral.

We continued travelling northward, in a zigzag line; sometimes stopping a day to geologise. The country was so thinly inhabited, and the track so obscure, that we often had difficulty in finding our way. On the 12th I stayed at some mines. The ore in this case was not considered particularly good, but from being abundant it was supposed the mine would sell for about thirty or forty thousand dollars (that is, 6000 or 8000 pounds sterling); yet it had been bought by one of the English Associations for an ounce of gold (3l. 8s.). The ore is yellow pyrites, which, as I have already remarked, before the arrival of the English, was not supposed to contain a particle of copper. On a scale of profits nearly as great as in the above instance, piles of cinders, abounding with minute globules of metallic copper, were purchased; yet with these advantages, the mining associations, as is well known, contrived to lose immense sums of money. The folly of the greater number of the commissioners and shareholders amounted to infatuation;—a thousand pounds per annum given in some cases to entertain the Chilian authorities; libraries of well-bound geological books; miners brought out for particular metals, as tin, which are not found in Chile; contracts to supply the miners with milk, in parts where there are no cows; machinery, where it could not possibly be used; and a hundred similar arrangements, bore witness to our absurdity, and to this day afford amusement to the natives. Yet there can be no doubt, that the same capital well employed in these mines would have yielded an immense return: a confidential man of business, a practical miner and assayer, would have been all that was required.

Captain Head has described the wonderful load which the "Apires," truly beasts of burden, carry up from the deepest mines. I confess I thought the account exaggerated; so that I was glad to take an opportunity of weighing one of the loads, which I picked out by hazard. It required considerable exertion on my part, when standing directly over it, to lift it from the ground. The load was considered under weight when found to be 197 pounds. The apire had carried this up eighty perpendicular yards,—part of the way by a steep passage, but the greater part up notched poles, placed in a zigzag line up the shaft. According to the general regulation, the apire is not allowed to halt for breath, except the mine is six hundred feet deep. The average load is considered as rather more than 200 pounds, and I have been assured that one of 300 pounds (twenty-two stone and a half) by way of a trial has been brought up from the deepest mine! At this time the apires were bringing up the usual load twelve times in the day; that is, 2400 pounds from eighty yards deep; and they were employed in the intervals in breaking and picking ore.

These men, excepting from accidents, are healthy, and appear cheerful. Their bodies are not very muscular. They rarely eat meat once a week, and never oftener, and then only the hard dry charqui. Although with a knowledge that the labour was voluntary, it was nevertheless quite revolting to see the state in which they reached the mouth of the mine; their bodies bent forward, leaning with their arms on the steps, their legs bowed, their muscles quivering, the perspiration streaming from their faces over their breasts, their nostrils distended, the corners of their mouth forcibly drawn back, and the expulsion of their breath most laborious. Each time they draw their breath, they utter an articulate cry of "ay-ay," which ends in a sound rising from deep in the chest, but shrill like the note of a fife. After staggering to the pile of ore, they emptied the "carpacho;" in two or three seconds recovering their breath, they wiped the sweat from their brows, and apparently quite fresh descended the mine again at a quick pace. This appears to me a wonderful instance of the amount of labour which habit, for it can be nothing else, will enable a man to endure.

In the evening, talking with the mayor-domo of these mines, about the number of foreigners now scattered over the whole country, he told me that, though quite a young man, he remembers when he was a boy at school at Coquimbo, a holiday being given to see the captain of an English ship, who was brought to the city to speak to the governor. He believes that nothing would have induced any boy in the school, himself included, to have gone close to the Englishman; so deeply had they been impressed with an idea of the heresy, contamination, and evil to be derived from contact with such a person. To this day they relate the atrocious actions of the bucaniers; and especially of one man, who took away the figure of the Virgin Mary, and returned the year after for that of St. Joseph, saying it was a pity the lady should not have a husband. I heard also of an old lady who, at a dinner in Coquimbo, remarked how wonderfully strange it was that she should have lived to dine in the same room with an Englishman; for she remembered as a girl, that twice, at the mere cry of "Los Ingleses," every soul, carrying what valuables they could, had taken to the mountains.

14th.—We reached Coquimbo, where we stayed a few days. The town is remarkable for nothing but its extreme quietness. It is said to contain from 6000 to 8000 inhabitants. On the morning of the 17th it rained lightly, the first time this year, for about five hours. The farmers, who plant corn near the sea-coast where the atmosphere is more humid, taking advantage of this shower, would break up the ground; after a second they would put the seed in; and if a third shower should fall, they would reap a good harvest in the spring. It was interesting to watch the effect of this trifling amount of moisture. Twelve hours afterwards the ground appeared as dry as ever; yet after an interval of ten days, all the hills were faintly tinged with green patches; the grass being sparingly scattered in hair-like fibres a full inch in length. Before this shower every part of the surface was bare as on a high road.

In the evening, Captain Fitz Roy and myself were dining with Mr. Edwards, an English resident well known for his hospitality by all who have visited Coquimbo, when a sharp earthquake happened. I heard the forecoming rumble, but from the screams of the ladies, the running of the servants, and the rush of several of the gentlemen to the doorway, I could not distinguish the motion. Some of the women afterwards were crying with terror, and one gentleman said he should not be able to sleep all night, or if he did, it would only be to dream of falling houses. The father of this person had lately lost all his property at Talcahuano, and he himself had only just escaped a falling roof at Valparaiso, in 1822. He mentioned a curious coincidence which then happened: he was playing at cards, when a German, one of the party, got up, and said he would never sit in a room in these countries with the door shut, as, owing to his having done so, he had nearly lost his life at Copiapó. Accordingly he opened the door; and no sooner had he done this, than he cried out, "Here it comes again!" and the famous shock commenced. The whole party escaped. The danger in an earthquake is not from the time lost in opening a door, but from the chance of its becoming jammed by the movement of the walls.

It is impossible to be much surprised at the fear which natives and old residents, though some of them known to be men of great command of mind, so generally experience during earthquakes. I think, however, this excess of panic may be partly attributed to a want of habit in governing their fear, as it is not a feeling they are ashamed of. Indeed, the natives do not like to see a person indifferent. I heard of two Englishmen who, sleeping in the open air during a smart shock, knowing that there was no danger, did not rise. The natives cried out indignantly, "Look at those heretics, they will not even get out of their beds!"

I spent some days in examining the step-formed terraces of shingle, first noticed by Captain B. Hall, and believed by Mr. Lyell to have been formed by the sea, during the gradual rising of the land. This certainly is the true explanation, for I found numerous shells of existing species on these terraces. Five narrow, gently sloping, fringe-like terraces rise one behind the other, and where best developed are formed of shingle: they front the bay, and sweep up both sides of the valley. At Guasco, north of Coquimbo, the phenomenon is displayed on a much grander scale, so as to strike with surprise even some of the inhabitants. The terraces are there much broader, and may be called plains; in some parts there are six of them, but generally only five; they run up the valley for thirty-seven miles from the coast. These step-formed terraces or fringes closely resemble those in the valley of S. Cruz, and except in being on a smaller scale, those great ones along the whole coast-line of Patagonia. They have undoubtedly been formed by the denuding power of the sea, during long periods of rest in the gradual elevation of the continent.

Shells of many existing species not only lie on the surface of the terraces at Coquimbo (to a height of 250 feet), but are embedded in a friable calcareous rock, which in some places is as much as between twenty and thirty feet in thickness, but is of little extent. These modern beds rest on an ancient tertiary formation containing shells, apparently all extinct. Although I examined so many hundred miles of coast on the Pacific, as well as Atlantic side of the continent, I found no regular strata containing sea-shells of recent species, excepting at this place, and at a few points northward on the road to Guasco. This fact appears to me highly remarkable; for the explanation generally given by geologists, of the absence in any district of stratified ossiliferous deposits of a given period, namely, that the surface then existed as dry land, is not here applicable; for we know from the shells strewed on the surface and embedded in loose sand or mould, that the land for thousands of miles along both coasts has lately been submerged. The explanation, no doubt, must be sought in the fact, that the whole southern part of the continent has been for a long time slowly rising; and therefore that all matter deposited along shore in shallow water, must have been soon brought up and slowly exposed to the wearing action of the sea-beach; and it is only in comparatively shallow water that the greater number of marine organic beings can flourish, and in such water it is obviously impossible that strata of any great thickness can accumulate. To show the vast power of the wearing action of sea-beaches, we need only appeal to the great cliffs along the present coast of Patagonia, and to the escarpments or ancient sea-cliffs at different levels, one above another, on that same line of coast.

The old underlying tertiary formation at Coquimbo, appears to be of about the same age with several deposits on the coast of Chile (of which that of Navedad is the principal one), and with the great formation of Patagonia. Both at Navedad and in Patagonia there is evidence, that since the shells (a list of which has been seen by Professor E. Forbes) there intombed were living, there has been a subsidence of several hundred feet, as well as an ensuing elevation. It may naturally be asked, how it comes that, although no extensive fossiliferous deposits of the recent period, nor of any period intermediate between it and the ancient tertiary epoch, have been preserved on either side of the continent, yet that at this ancient tertiary epoch, sedimentary matter containing fossil remains, should have been deposited and preserved at different points in north and south lines, over a space of 1100 miles on the shores of the Pacific, and of at least 1350 miles on the shores of the Atlantic, and in an east and west line of 700 miles across the widest part of the continent? I believe the explanation is not difficult, and that it is perhaps applicable to nearly analogous facts observed in other quarters of the world. Considering the enormous power of denudation which the sea possesses, as shown by numberless facts, it is not probable that a sedimentary deposit, when being upraised, could pass through the ordeal of the beach, so as to be preserved in sufficient masses to last to a distant period, without it were originally of wide extent and of considerable thickness: now it is impossible on a moderately shallow bottom, which alone is favourable to most living creatures, that a thick and widely extended covering of sediment could be spread out, without the bottom sank down to receive the successive layers. This seems to have actually taken place at about the same period in southern Patagonia and Chile, though these places are a thousand miles apart. Hence, if prolonged movements of approximately contemporaneous subsidence are generally widely extensive, as I am strongly inclined to believe from my examination of the Coral Reefs of the great oceans—or if, confining our view to South America, the subsiding movements have been coextensive with those of elevation, by which, within the same period of existing shells, the shores of Peru, Chile, Tierra del Fuego, Patagonia, and La Plata have been upraised—then we can see that at the same time, at far distant points, circumstances would have been favourable to the formation of fossiliferous deposits, of wide extent and of considerable thickness; and such deposits, consequently, would have a good chance of resisting the wear and tear of successive beach-lines, and of lasting to a future epoch.

May 21*st*.—I set out in company with Don Jose Edwards to the silver-mine of Arqueros, and thence up the valley of Coquimbo. Passing through a mountainous country, we reached by nightfall the mines belonging to Mr. Edwards. I enjoyed my night's rest here from a reason which will not be fully appreciated in England, namely, the absence of fleas! The rooms in Coquimbo swarm with them; but they will not live here at the height of only three or four thousand feet: it can scarcely be the trifling diminution of temperature, but some other cause which destroys these troublesome insects at this place. The mines are now in a bad state, though they formerly yielded about 2000 pounds in weight of silver a year. It has been said that "a person with a copper-mine will gain; with silver he may gain; but with gold he is sure to lose." This is not true: all the large Chilian fortunes have been made by mines of the more precious metals. A short time since an English physician returned to England from Copiapó, taking with him the profits of one share in a silver-mine, which amounted to about 24,000 pounds sterling. No doubt a copper-mine with care is a sure game, whereas the other is gambling, or rather taking a ticket in a lottery. The owners lose great quantities of rich ores; for no precautions can prevent robberies. I heard of a gentleman laying a bet with another, that one of his men should rob him before his face. The ore when brought out of the mine is broken into pieces, and the useless stone thrown on one side. A couple of the miners who were thus employed, pitched, as if by accident, two fragments away at the same moment, and then cried out for a joke, "Let us see which rolls furthest." The owner, who was standing by, bet a cigar with his friend on the race. The miner by this means watched the very point amongst the rubbish where the stone lay. In the evening he picked it up and carried it to his master, showing him a rich mass of silver-ore, and saying, "This was the stone on which you won a cigar by its rolling so far."

May 23rd.—We descended into the fertile valley of Coquimbo, and followed it till we reached an Hacienda belonging to a relation of Don Jose, where we stayed the next day. I then rode one day's journey further, to see what were declared to be some petrified shells and beans, which latter turned out to be small quartz pebbles. We passed through several small villages; and the valley was beautifully cultivated, and the whole scenery very grand. We were here near the main Cordillera, and the surrounding hills were lofty. In all parts of northern Chile, fruit-trees produce much more abundantly at a considerable height near the Andes than in the lower country. The figs and grapes of this district are famous for their excellence, and are cultivated to a great extent. This valley is, perhaps, the most productive one north of Quillota: I believe it contains, including Coquimbo, 25,000 inhabitants. The next day I returned to the Hacienda, and thence, together with Don Jose, to Coquimbo.

June 2nd.—We set out for the valley of Guasco, following the coast-road, which was considered rather less desert than the other. Our first day's ride was to a solitary house, called Yerba Buena, where there was pasture for our horses. The shower mentioned as having fallen a fortnight ago, only reached about halfway to Guasco; we had, therefore, in the first part of our journey a most faint tinge of green, which soon faded quite away. Even where brightest, it was scarcely sufficient to remind one of the fresh turf and budding flowers of the spring of other countries. While travelling through these deserts one feels like a prisoner shut up in a gloomy court, who longs to see something green and to smell a moist atmosphere.

June 3rd.—Yerba Buena to Carizal. During the first part of the day we crossed a mountainous rocky desert, and afterwards a long deep sandy plain, strewed with broken sea-shells. There was very little water, and that little saline: the whole country, from the coast to the Cordillera, is an uninhabited desert. I saw traces only of one living animal in abundance, namely, the shells of a Bulimus, which were collected together in extraordinary numbers on the driest spots. In the spring one humble little plant sends out a few leaves, and on these the snails feed. As they are seen only very early in the morning, when the ground is slightly damp with dew, the Guasos believe that they are bred from it. I have observed in other places that extremely dry and sterile districts, where the soil is calcareous, are extraordinarily favourable to land-shells. At Carizal there were a few cottages, some brackish water, and a trace of cultivation: but it was with difficulty that we purchased a little corn and straw for our horses.

4th.—Carizal to Sauce. We continued to ride over desert plains, tenanted by large herds of guanaco. We crossed also the valley of Chañeral; which, although the most fertile one between Guasco and Coquimbo, is very narrow, and produces so little pasture, that we could not purchase any for our horses. At Sauce we found a very civil old gentleman, superintending a copper-smelting furnace. As an especial favour, he allowed me to purchase at a high price an armful of dirty straw, which was all the poor horses had for supper after their long day's journey. Few smelting-furnaces are now at work in any part of Chile; it is found more profitable, on account of the extreme scarcity of firewood, and from the Chilian method of reduction being so unskilful, to ship the ore for Swansea. The next day we crossed some mountains to Freyrina, in the valley of Guasco. During each day's ride further northward, the vegetation became more and more scanty; even the great chandelier-like cactus was here replaced by a different and much smaller species. During the winter months, both in northern Chile and in Peru, a uniform bank of clouds hangs, at no great height, over the Pacific. From the mountains we had a very striking view of this white and brilliant aërial-field, which sent arms up the valleys, leaving islands and promontories in the same manner, as the sea does in the Chonos archipelago and in Tierra del Fuego.

We stayed two days at Freyrina. In the valley of Guasco there are four small towns. At the mouth there is the port, a spot entirely desert, and without any water in the immediate neighbourhood. Five leagues higher up stands Freyrina, a long straggling village, with decent whitewashed houses. Again, ten leagues further up Ballenar is situated; and above this Guasco Alto, a horticultural village, famous for its dried fruit. On a clear day the view up the valley is very fine; the straight opening terminates in the far-distant snowy Cordillera; on each side an infinity of crossing lines are blended together in a beautiful haze. The foreground is singular from the number of parallel and step-formed terraces; and the included strip of green valley, with its willow-bushes, is contrasted on both hands with the naked hills. That the surrounding country was most barren will be readily believed, when it is known that a shower of rain had not fallen during the last thirteen months. The inhabitants heard with the greatest envy of the rain at Coquimbo; from the appearance of the sky they had hopes of equally good fortune, which, a fortnight afterwards, were realized. I was at Copiapó at the time; and there the people, with equal envy, talked of the abundant rain at Guasco. After two or three very dry years, perhaps with not more than one shower during the whole time, a rainy year generally follows; and this does more harm than even the drought. The rivers swell, and cover with gravel and sand the narrow strips of ground, which alone are fit for cultivation. The floods also injure the irrigating ditches. Great devastation had thus been caused three years ago.

June 8th.—We rode on to Ballenar, which takes its name from Ballenagh in Ireland, the birthplace of the family of O'Higgins, who, under the Spanish government, were presidents and generals in Chile. As the rocky mountains on each hand were concealed by clouds, the terrace-like plains gave to the valley an appearance like that of Santa Cruz in Patagonia. After spending one day at Ballenar I set out, on the 10th, for the upper part of the valley of Copiapó. We rode all day over an uninteresting country. I am tired of repeating the epithets barren and sterile. These words, however, as commonly used, are comparative; I have always applied them to the plains of Patagonia, which can boast of spiny bushes and some tufts of grass; and this is absolute fertility, as compared with northern Chile. Here again, there are not many spaces of two hundred yards square, where some little bush, cactus or lichen, may not be discovered by careful examination; and in the soil seeds lie dormant ready to spring up during the first rainy winter. In Peru real deserts occur over wide tracts of country. In the evening we arrived at a valley, in which the bed of the streamlet was damp: following it up, we came to tolerably good water. During the night, the stream, from not being evaporated and absorbed so quickly, flows a league lower down than during the day. Sticks were plentiful for firewood, so that it was a good place of bivouac for us; but for the poor animals there was not a mouthful to eat.

June 11th.—We rode without stopping for twelve hours, till we reached an old smelting-furnace, where there was water and firewood; but our horses again had nothing to eat, being shut up in an old courtyard. The line of road was hilly, and the distant views interesting from the varied colours of the bare mountains. It was almost a pity to see the sun shining constantly over so useless a country; such splendid weather ought to have brightened fields and pretty gardens. The next day we reached the valley of Copiapó. I was heartily glad of it; for the whole journey was a continued source of anxiety; it was most disagreeable to hear, whilst eating our own suppers, our horses gnawing the posts to which they were tied, and to have no means of relieving their hunger. To all appearance, however, the animals were quite fresh; and no one could have told that they had eaten nothing for the last fifty-five hours.

I had a letter of introduction to Mr. Bingley, who received

me very kindly at the Hacienda of Potrero Seco. This estate is between twenty and thirty miles long, but very narrow, being generally only two fields wide, one on each side the river. In some parts the estate is of no width, that is to say, the land cannot be irrigated, and therefore is valueless, like the surrounding rocky desert. The small quantity of cultivated land in the whole line of valley, does not so much depend on inequalities of level, and consequent unfitness for irrigation, as on the small supply of water. The river this year was remarkably full: here, high up the valley, it reached to the horse's belly, and was about fifteen yards wide, and rapid; lower down it becomes smaller and smaller, and is generally quite lost, as happened during one period of thirty years, so that not a drop entered the sea. The inhabitants watch a storm over the Cordillera with great interest; as one good fall of snow provides them with water for the ensuing year. This is of infinitely more consequence than rain in the lower country. Rain, as often as it falls, which is about once in every two or three years, is a great advantage, because the cattle and mules can for some time afterwards find a little pasture on the mountains. But without snow on the Andes, desolation extends throughout the valley. It is on record that three times nearly all the inhabitants have been obliged to emigrate to the south. This year there was plenty of water, and every man irrigated his ground as much as he chose; but it has frequently been necessary to post soldiers at the sluices, to see that each estate took only its proper allowance during so many hours in the week. The valley is said to contain 12,000 souls, but its produce is sufficient only for three months in the year; the rest of the supply being drawn from Valparaiso and the south. Before the discovery of the famous silver-mines of Chanuncillo, Copiapó was in a rapid state of decay; but now it is in a very thriving condition; and the town, which was completely overthrown by an earthquake, has been rebuilt.

The valley of Copiapó, forming a mere ribbon of green in a desert, runs in a very southerly direction; so that it is of considerable length to its source in the Cordillera. The valleys of Guasco and Copiapó may both be considered as long narrow islands, separated from the rest of Chile by deserts of rock instead of by salt water. Northward of these, there is one other very miserable valley, called Paposo, which contains about two hundred souls; and then there extends the real desert of Atacama—a barrier far worse than the most turbulent ocean. After staying a few days at Potrero Seco, I proceeded up the valley to the house of Don Benito Cruz, to whom I had a letter of introduction. I found him most hospitable; indeed it is impossible to bear too strong testimony to the kindness, with which travellers are received in almost every part of South America. The next day I hired some mules to take me by the ravine of Jolquera into the central Cordillera. On the second night the weather seemed to foretell a storm of snow or rain, and whilst lying in our beds we felt a trifling shock of an earthquake.

The connexion between earthquakes and the weather has been often disputed: it appears to me to be a point of great interest, which is little understood. Humboldt has remarked in one part of the Personal Narrative,[3] that it would be difficult for any person who had long resided in New Andalusia, or in Lower Peru, to deny that there exists some connexion between these phenomena: in another part, however, he seems to think the connexion fanciful. At Guayaquil, it is said that a heavy shower in the dry season is invariably followed by an earthquake. In Northern Chile, from the extreme infrequency of rain, or even of weather foreboding rain, the probability of accidental coincidences becomes very small; yet the inhabitants are here most firmly convinced of some connexion between the state of the atmosphere and of the trembling of the ground: I was much struck by this, when mentioning to some people at Copiapó that there had been a sharp shock at Coquimbo: they immediately cried out, "How fortunate! there will be plenty of pasture there this year." To their minds an earthquake foretold rain, as surely as rain foretold abundant pasture. Certainly it did so happen that on the very day of the earthquake, that shower of rain fell, which I have described as in ten days' time producing a thin sprinkling of grass. At other times, rain has followed earthquakes, at a period of the year when it is a far greater prodigy than the earthquake itself: this happened after the shock of November, 1822, and again in 1829, at Valparaiso; also after that of September, 1833,

[3] [Darwin] Vol. iv. p. 11, and vol. ii. p. 217. For the remarks on Guayaquil see Silliman's Journ. vol. xxiv. p. 384. For those on Tacna by Mr. Hamilton, see Trans. of British Association, 1840. For those on Coseguina see Mr. Caldcleugh in Phil. Trans., 1835. In the former edition, I collected several references on the coincidences between sudden falls in the barometer and earthquakes; and between earthquakes and meteors.

at Tacna. A person must be somewhat habituated to the climate of these countries, to perceive the extreme improbability of rain falling at such seasons, except as a consequence of some law quite unconnected with the ordinary course of the weather. In the cases of great volcanic eruptions, as that of Coseguina, where torrents of rain fell at a time of the year most unusual for it, and "almost unprecedented in Central America," it is not difficult to understand that the volumes of vapour and clouds of ashes might have disturbed the atmospheric equilibrium. Humboldt extends this view to the case of earthquakes unaccompanied by eruptions; but I can hardly conceive it possible, that the small quantity of aëriform fluids which then escape from the fissured ground, can produce such remarkable effects. There appears much probability in the view first proposed by Mr. P. Scrope, that when the barometer is low, and when rain might naturally be expected to fall, the diminished pressure of the atmosphere over a wide extent of country, might well determine the precise day on which the earth, already stretched to the utmost by the subterranean forces, should yield, crack, and consequently tremble. It is, however, doubtful how far this idea will explain the circumstance of torrents of rain falling in the dry season during several days, after an earthquake unaccompanied by an eruption; such cases seem to bespeak some more intimate connexion between the atmospheric and subterranean regions.

Finding little of interest in this part of the ravine, we retraced our steps to the house of Don Benito, where I stayed two days collecting fossil shells and wood. Great prostrate silicified trunks of trees, embedded in a conglomerate, were extraordinarily numerous. I measured one, which was fifteen feet in circumference: how surprising it is that every atom of the woody matter in this great cylinder should have been removed and replaced by silex so perfectly, that each vessel and pore is preserved! These trees flourished at about the period of our lower chalk; they all belonged to the fir-tribe. It was amusing to hear the inhabitants discussing the nature of the fossil shells which I collected, almost in the same terms as were used a century ago in Europe,—namely, whether or not they had been thus "born by nature." My geological examination of the country generally created a good deal of surprise amongst the Chilenos: it was long before they could be convinced that I was not hunting for mines. This was sometimes troublesome: I found the most ready way of explaining my employment, was to ask them how it was that they themselves were not curious concerning earthquakes and volcanoes?—why some springs were hot and others cold?—Why there were mountains in Chile, and not a hill in La Plata? These bare questions at once satisfied and silenced the greater number; some, however (like a few in England who are a century behindhand), thought that all such inquiries were useless and impious; and that it was quite sufficient that God had thus made the mountains.

An order had recently been issued that all stray dogs should be killed, and we saw many lying dead on the road. A great number had lately gone mad, and several men had been bitten and had died in consequence. On several occasions hydrophobia has prevailed in this valley. It is remarkable thus to find so strange and dreadful a disease, appearing time after time in the same isolated spot. It has been remarked that certain villages in England are in like manner much more subject to this visitation than others. Dr. Unanùe states that hydrophobia was first known in South America in 1803: this statement is corroborated by Azara and Ulloa having never heard of it in their time. Dr. Unanùe says that it broke out in Central America, and slowly travelled southward. It reached Arequipa in 1807; and it is said that some men there, who had not been bitten, were affected, as were some negroes, who had eaten a bullock which had died of hydrophobia. At Ica forty-two people thus miserably perished. The disease came on between twelve and ninety days after the bite; and in those cases where it did come on, death ensued invariably within five days. After 1808, a long interval ensued without any cases. On inquiry, I did not hear of hydrophobia in Van Dieman's Land, or in Australia; and Burchell says, that during the five years he was at the Cape of Good Hope, he never heard of an instance of it. Webster asserts that at the Azores hydrophobia has never occurred; and the same assertion has been made with respect to Mauritius and St. Helena.[4] In so strange a disease, some information might possibly be gained by considering the circumstances under which it originates in distant climates; for it is

[4] [Darwin] Observa. sobre el clima de Lima, p. 67.—Azara's Travels, vol. i. p. 381.—Ulloa's Voyage, vol. ii. p. 28.—Burchell's Travels, vol. ii. p. 524.—Webster's Description of the Azores, p. 124. —Voyage à l'Isle de France par un Officier du Roi, tome i. p. 248. —Description of St. Helena, p. 123.

improbable that a dog already bitten, should have been brought to these distant countries.

At night, a stranger arrived at the house of Don Benito, and asked permission to sleep there. He said he had been wandering about the mountains for seventeen days, having lost his way. He started from Guasco, and being accustomed to travelling in the Cordillera, did not expect any difficulty in following the track to Copiapó; but he soon became involved in a labyrinth of mountains, whence he could not escape. Some of his mules had fallen over precipices, and he had been in great distress. His chief difficulty arose from not knowing where to find water in the lower country, so that he was obliged to keep bordering the central ranges.

We returned down the valley, and on the 22nd reached the town of Copiapó. The lower part of the valley is broad, forming a fine plain like that of Quillota. The town covers a considerable space of ground, each house possessing a garden: but it is an uncomfortable place, and the dwellings are poorly furnished. Every one seems bent on the one object of making money, and then migrating as quickly as possible. All the inhabitants are more or less directly concerned with mines; and mines and ores are the sole subjects of conversation. Necessaries of all sorts are extremely dear; as the distance from the town to the port is eighteen leagues, and the land carriage very expensive. A fowl costs five or six shillings; meat is nearly as dear as in England; firewood, or rather sticks, are brought on donkeys from a distance of two and three days' journey within the Cordillera; and pasturage for animals is a shilling a day: all this for South America is wonderfully exorbitant.

June 26th.—I hired a guide and eight mules to take me into the Cordillera by a different line from my last excursion. As the country was utterly desert, we took a cargo and a half of barley mixed with chopped straw. About two leagues above the town, a broad valley called the "Despoblado," or uninhabited, branches off from that one by which we had arrived. Although a valley of the grandest dimensions, and leading to a pass across the Cordillera, yet it is completely dry, excepting perhaps for a few days during some very rainy winter. The sides of the crumbling mountains were furrowed by scarcely any ravines; and the bottom of the main valley, filled with shingle, was smooth and nearly level. No considerable torrent could ever have flowed down this bed of shingle; for if it had, a great cliff-bounded channel, as in all the southern valleys, would assuredly have been formed. I feel little doubt that this valley, as well as those mentioned by travellers in Peru, were left in the state we now see them by the waves of the sea, as the land slowly rose. I observed in one place, where the Despoblado was joined by a ravine (which in almost any other chain would have been called a grand valley), that its bed, though composed merely of sand and gravel, was higher than that of its tributary. A mere rivulet of water, in the course of an hour, would have cut a channel for itself; but it was evident that ages had passed away, and no such rivulet had drained this great tributary. It was curious to behold the machinery, if such a term may be used, for the drainage, all, with the last trifling exception, perfect, yet without any signs of action. Every one must have remarked how mud-banks, left by the retiring tide, imitate in miniature a country with hill and dale; and here we have the original model in rock, formed as the continent rose during the secular retirement of the ocean, instead of during the ebbing and flowing of the tides. If a shower of rain falls on the mud-bank, when left dry, it deepens the already-formed shallow lines of excavation; and so is it with the rain of successive centuries on the bank of rock and soil, which we call a continent.

We rode on after it was dark, till we reached a side ravine with a small well, called "Agua amarga." The water deserved its name, for besides being saline it was most offensively putrid and bitter; so that we could not force ourselves to drink either tea or maté. I suppose the distance from the river of Copiapó to this spot was at least twenty-five or thirty English miles; in the whole space there was not a single drop of water, the country deserving the name of desert in the strictest sense. Yet about halfway we passed some old Indian ruins near Punta Gorda: I noticed also in front of some of the valleys, which branch off from the Despoblado, two piles of stones placed a little way apart, and directed so as to point up the mouths of these small valleys. My companions knew nothing about them, and only answered my queries by their imperturbable "quien sabe?"

I observed Indian ruins in several parts of the Cordillera: the most perfect, which I saw, were the Ruinas de Tambillos, in the Uspallata Pass. Small square rooms were there huddled together in separate groups: some of the doorways were yet standing; they were formed by a cross slab of stone only about three feet high. Ulloa has remarked on the lowness of the doors in the ancient Peruvian dwellings. These houses, when perfect, must have been capable of containing a considerable number of persons. Tradition says, that they were used as halting places for the Incas, when they crossed the mountains. Traces of Indian habitations have been discovered in many other parts, where it does not appear probable that they were used as mere resting-places, but yet where the land is as utterly unfit for any kind of cultivation as it is near the Tambillos or at the Incas Bridge, or in the Portillo Pass, at all which places I saw ruins. In the ravine of Jajuel, near Aconcagua, where there is no pass, I heard of remains of houses situated at a great height, where it is extremely cold and sterile. At first I imagined that these buildings had been places of refuge, built by the Indians on the first arrival of the Spaniards; but I have since been inclined to speculate on the probability of a small change of climate.

In this northern part of Chile, within the Cordillera, old Indian houses are said to be especially numerous: by digging amongst the ruins, bits of woollen articles, instruments of precious metals, and heads of Indian corn, are not unfrequently discovered: an arrow-head made of agate, and of precisely the same form with those now used in Tierra del Fuego, was given me. I am aware that the Peruvian Indians now frequently inhabit most lofty and bleak situations; but at Copiapó I was assured by men who had spent their lives in travelling through the Andes, that there were very many (*muchisimas*) buildings at heights so great as almost to border on the perpetual snow, and in parts where there exist no passes, and where the land produces absolutely nothing, and what is still more extraordinary, where there is no water. Nevertheless it is the opinion of the people of the country (although they are much puzzled by the circumstance), that, from the appearance of the houses, the Indians must have used them as places of residence. In this valley, at Punta Gorda, the remains consisted of seven or eight square little rooms, which were of a similar form with those at Tambillos, but built chiefly of mud, which the present inhabitants cannot, either here or, according to Ulloa, in Peru, imitate in durability. They were situated in the most conspicuous and defenceless position, at the bottom of the flat broad valley. There was no water nearer than three or four leagues, and that only in very small quantity, and bad: the soil was absolutely sterile; I looked in vain even for a lichen adhering to the rocks. At the present day, with the advantage of beasts of burden, a mine, unless it were very rich, could scarcely be worked here with profit. Yet the Indians formerly chose it as a place of residence! If at the present time two or three showers of rain were to fall annually, instead of one, as now is the case, during as many years, a small rill of water would probably be formed in this great valley; and then, by irrigation (which was formerly so well understood by the Indians), the soil would easily be rendered sufficiently productive to support a few families.

I have convincing proofs that this part of the continent of South America has been elevated near the coast at least from 400 to 500, and in some parts from 1000 to 1300 feet, since the epoch of existing shells; and further inland the rise possibly may have been greater. As the peculiarly arid character of the climate is evidently a consequence of the height of the Cordillera, we may feel almost sure that before the later elevations, the atmosphere could not have been so completely drained of its moisture as it now is; and as the rise has been gradual, so would have been the change in climate. On this notion of a change of climate since the buildings were inhabited, the ruins must be of extreme antiquity, but I do not think their preservation under the Chilian climate any great difficulty. We must also admit on this notion, (and this perhaps is a greater difficulty) that man has inhabited South America for an immensely long period, inasmuch as any change of climate effected by the elevation of the land must have been extremely gradual. At Valparaiso, within the last 220 years, the rise has been somewhat less than 19 feet: at Lima a sea-beach has certainly been upheaved from 80 to 90 feet, within the Indio-human period: but such small elevations could have had little power in deflecting the moisture-bringing atmospheric currents. Dr. Lund, however, found human skeletons in the caves of Brazil, the appearance of which induced him to believe that the Indian race has existed during a vast lapse of time in South America.

When at Lima, I conversed on these subjects[5] with Mr. Gill,

---

[5] [Darwin] Temple, in his travels through Upper Peru, or Bolivia, in going from Potosi to Oruro, says, "I saw many Indian villages or dwellings in ruins, up even to the very tops of the mountains, attesting a former population where now all is desolate." He makes similar remarks in another place; but I cannot tell whether this desolation has been caused by a want of population, or by an altered condition of the land.

a civil engineer, who had seen much of the interior country. He told me that a conjecture of a change of climate had sometimes crossed his mind; but that he thought that the greater portion of land, now incapable of cultivation, but covered with Indian ruins, had been reduced to this state by the water-conduits, which the Indians formerly constructed on so wonderful a scale, having been injured by neglect and by subterranean movements. I may here mention, that the Peruvians actually carried their irrigating streams in tunnels through hills of solid rock. Mr. Gill told me, he had been employed professionally to examine one; he found the passage low, narrow, crooked, and not of uniform breadth, but of very considerable length. Is it not most wonderful that men should have attempted such operations, without the use of iron or gunpowder? Mr. Gill also mentioned to me a most interesting, and, as far as I am aware, quite unparalleled case, of a subterranean disturbance having changed the drainage of a country. Travelling from Casma to Huaraz (not very far distant from Lima), he found a plain covered with ruins and marks of ancient cultivation, but now quite barren. Near it was the dry course of a considerable river, whence the water for irrigation had formerly been conducted. There was nothing in the appearance of the water-course, to indicate that the river had not flowed there a few years previously; in some parts, beds of sand and gravel were spread out; in others, the solid rock had been worn into a broad channel, which in one spot was about 40 yards in breadth and 8 feet deep. It is self-evident that a person following up the course of a stream, will always ascend at a greater or less inclination: Mr. Gill, therefore, was much astonished, when walking up the bed of this ancient river, to find himself suddenly going down hill. He imagined that the downward slope had a fall of about 40 or 50 feet perpendicular. We here have unequivocal evidence that a ridge had been uplifted right across the old bed of a stream. From the moment the river-course was thus arched, the water must necessarily have been thrown back, and a new channel formed. From that moment, also, the neighbouring plain must have lost its fertilizing stream, and become a desert.

June 27th.—We set out early in the morning, and by midday reached the ravine of Paypote, where there is a tiny rill of water, with a little vegetation, and even a few algarroba trees, a kind of mimosa. From having firewood, a smelting-furnace had formerly been built here: we found a solitary man in charge of it, whose sole employment was hunting guanacos. At night it froze sharply; but having plenty of wood for our fire, we kept ourselves warm.

28*th.*—We continued gradually ascending, and the valley now changed into a ravine. During the day we saw several guanacos, and the track of the closely-allied species, the Vicuña: this latter animal is pre-eminently alpine in its habits; it seldom descends much below the limit of perpetual snow, and therefore haunts even a more lofty and sterile situation than the guanaco. The only other animal which we saw in any number was a small fox: I suppose this animal preys on the mice and other small rodents, which, as long as there is the least vegetation, subsist in considerable numbers in very desert places. In Patagonia, even on the borders of the salinas, where a drop of fresh water can never be found, excepting dew, these little animals swarm. Next to lizards, mice appear to be able to support existence on the smallest and driest portions of the earth,—even on islets in the midst of great oceans.

The scene on all sides showed desolation, brightened and made palpable by a clear, unclouded sky. For a time such scenery is sublime, but this feeling cannot last, and then it becomes uninteresting. We bivouacked at the foot of the "primera linea," or the first line of the partition of the waters. The streams, however, on the east side do not flow to the Atlantic, but into an elevated district, in the middle of which there is a large salina, or salt lake;—thus forming a little Caspian Sea at the height, perhaps, of ten thousand feet. Where we slept, there were some considerable patches of snow, but they do not remain throughout the year. The winds in these lofty regions obey very regular laws: every day a fresh breeze blows up the valley, and at night, an hour or two after sunset, the air from the cold regions above descends as through a funnel. This night it blew a gale of wind, and the temperature must have been considerably below the freezing-point, for water in a vessel soon became a block of ice. No clothes seemed to oppose any obstacle to the air; I suffered very much from the cold, so that I could not sleep, and in the morning rose with my body quite dull and benumbed.

In the Cordillera further southward, people lose their lives from snow-storms; here, it sometimes happens from another cause. My guide, when a boy of fourteen years old, was passing the Cordillera with a party in the month of May; and while in the central parts, a furious gale of wind arose, so that the men could hardly cling on their mules, and stones were flying along the ground. The day was cloudless, and not a speck of snow fell, but the temperature was low. It is probable that the thermometer would not have stood very many degrees below the freezing-point, but the effect on their bodies, ill protected by clothing, must have been in proportion to the rapidity of the current of cold air. The gale lasted for more than a day; the men began to lose their strength, and the mules would not move onwards. My guide's brother tried to return, but he perished, and his body was found two years afterwards, lying by the side of his mule near the road, with the bridle still in his hand. Two other men in the party lost their fingers and toes; and out of two hundred mules and thirty cows, only fourteen mules escaped alive. Many years ago the whole of a large party are supposed to have perished from a similar cause, but their bodies to this day have never been discovered. The union of a cloudless sky, low temperature, and a furious gale of wind, must be, I should think, in all parts of the world, an unusual occurrence.

June 29th.—We gladly travelled down the valley to our former night's lodging, and thence to near the Agua amarga. On July 1st we reached the valley of Copiapó. The smell of the fresh clover was quite delightful, after the scentless air of the dry sterile Despoblado. Whilst staying in the town I heard an account from several of the inhabitants, of a hill in the neighbourhood which they called "El Bramador,"—the roarer or bellower. I did not at the time pay sufficient attention to the account; but, as far as I understood, the hill was covered by sand, and the noise was produced only when people, by ascending it, put the sand in motion. The same circumstances are described in detail on the authority of Seetzen and Ehrenberg,[6] as the cause of the sounds which have been heard by many travellers on Mount Sinai near the Red Sea. One person with whom I conversed, had himself heard the noise; he described it as very surprising; and he distinctly stated that, although he could not understand how it was caused, yet it was necessary to set the sand rolling down the acclivity. A horse walking over dry and coarse sand, causes a peculiar chirping

6 [Darwin] Edinburgh Phil. Journ., Jan. 1830, p. 74; and April, 1830, p. 258.—Also Daubeny on Volcanoes, p. 438; and Bengal Journ., vol. vii. p. 324.

noise from the friction of the particles; a circumstance which I several times noticed on the coast of Brazil.

Three days afterwards I heard of the *Beagle's* arrival at the Port, distant eighteen leagues from the town. There is very little land cultivated down the valley; its wide expanse supports a wretched wiry grass, which even the donkeys can hardly eat. This poorness of the vegetation is owing to the quantity of saline matter with which the soil is impregnated. The Port consists of an assemblage of miserable little hovels, situated at the foot of a sterile plain. At present, as the river contains water enough to reach the sea, the inhabitants enjoy the advantage of having fresh water within a mile and a half. On the beach there were large piles of merchandise, and the little place had an air of activity. In the evening I gave my adios, with a hearty good-will, to my companion Mariano Gonzales, with whom I had ridden so many leagues in Chile. The next morning the *Beagle* sailed for Iquique.

July 12*th*.—We anchored in the port of Iquique, in lat. 20° 12′, on the coast of Peru. The town contains about a thousand inhabitants, and stands on a little plain of sand at the foot of a great wall of rock, 2000 feet in height, here forming the coast. The whole is utterly desert. A light shower of rain falls only once in very many years; and the ravines consequently are filled with detritus, and the mountain-sides covered by piles of fine white sand, even to a height of a thousand feet. During this season of the year a heavy bank of clouds, stretched over the ocean, seldom rises above the wall of rocks on the coast. The aspect of the place was most gloomy; the little port, with its few vessels, and small group of wretched houses, seemed overwhelmed and out of all proportion with the rest of the scene.

The inhabitants live like persons on board a ship: every necessary comes from a distance: water is brought in boats from Pisagua, about forty miles northward, and is sold at the rate of nine reals (4*s.* 6*d.*) an eighteen-gallon cask: I bought a wine-bottle full for threepence. In like manner firewood, and of course every article of food, is imported. Very few animals can be maintained in such a place: on the ensuing morning I hired with difficulty, at the price of four pounds sterling, two mules and a guide to take me to the nitrate of soda works. These are at present the support of Iquique. This salt was first exported in 1830: in one year an amount in value of one hundred thousand pounds sterling, was sent to France and England. It is principally used as a manure and in the manufacture of nitric acid: owing to its deliquescent property it will not serve for gunpowder. Formerly there were two exceedingly rich silver-mines in this neighbourhood, but their produce is now very small.

Our arrival in the offing caused some little apprehension. Peru was in a state of anarchy;[7] and each party having demanded a contribution, the poor town of Iquique was in tribulation, thinking the evil hour was come. The people had also their domestic troubles; a short time before, three French carpenters had broken open, during the same night, the two churches, and stolen all the plate: one of the robbers, however, subsequently confessed, and the plate was recovered. The convicts were sent to Arequipa, which, though the capital of this province, is two hundred leagues distant; the government there thought it a pity to punish such useful workmen, who could make all sorts of furniture; and accordingly liberated them. Things being in this state, the churches were again broken open, but this time the plate was not recovered. The inhabitants became dreadfully enraged, and declaring that none but heretics would thus "eat God Almighty," proceeded to torture some Englishmen, with the intention of afterwards shooting them. At last the authorities interfered, and peace was established.

13*th*.—In the morning I started for the saltpetre-works, a distance of fourteen leagues. Having ascended the steep coast-mountains by a zigzag sandy track, we soon came in view of the mines of Guantajaya and St. Rosa. These two small villages are placed at the very mouths of the mines; and being perched up on hills, they had a still more unnatural and desolate ap-

[7] [Editor] Peru had the misfortune to be the seat of Spanish power in South America. As a result, it was beyond her power to win independence by her own unaided efforts; it was won for her by Argentine and Chilean troops under General San Martín of Argentina and Colombians under Simon Bolivar. (Britishers helped, too; San Martín's army was transported to Peru by a Chilean fleet officered by Englishmen and commanded by Lord Cochrane, a remarkable sea fighter who had been dropped from the British Navy and expelled from Parliament because of his involvement in a stock market scandal.) In the first year of Peruvian independence—1825—Bolivar served as head of the government, then returned to his own country, Colombia. Thereafter, Peru seethed for years with plot and counterplot as his successors jockeyed for power.

pearance than the town of Iquique. We did not reach the saltpetre-works till after sunset, having ridden all day across an undulating country, a complete and utter desert. The road was strewed with the bones and dried skins of the many beasts of burden which had perished on it from fatigue. Excepting the Vultur aura, which preys on the carcasses, I saw neither bird, quadruped, reptile, nor insect. On the coast-mountains, at the height of about 2000 feet, where during this season the clouds generally hang, a very few cacti were growing in the clefts of rock; and the loose sand was strewed over with a lichen, which lies on the surface quite unattached. This plant belongs to the genus Cladonia, and somewhat resembles the reindeer lichen. In some parts it was in sufficient quantity to tinge the sand, as seen from a distance, of a pale yellowish colour. Further inland, during the whole ride of fourteen leagues, I saw only one other vegetable production, and that was a most minute yellow lichen, growing on the bones of the dead mules. This was the first true desert which I had seen: the effect on me was not impressive; but I believe this was owing to my having become gradually accustomed to such scenes, as I rode northward from Valparaiso, through Coquimbo, to Copiapó. The appearance of the country was remarkable, from being covered by a thick crust of common salt, and of a stratified saliferous alluvium, which seems to have been deposited as the land slowly rose above the level of the sea. The salt is white, very hard, and compact: it occurs in water-worn nodules projecting from the agglutinated sand, and is associated with much gypsum. The appearance of this superficial mass very closely resembled that of a country after snow, before the last dirty patches are thawed. The existence of this crust of a soluble substance over the whole face of the country, shows how extraordinarily dry the climate must have been for a long period.

At night I slept at the house of the owner of one of the saltpetre mines. The country is here as unproductive as near the coast; but water, having rather a bitter and brackish taste, can be procured by digging wells. The well at this house was thirty-six yards deep: as scarcely any rain falls, it is evident the water is not thus derived; indeed if it were, it could not fail to be as salt as brine, for the whole surrounding country is incrusted with various saline substances. We must therefore conclude that it percolates under ground from the Cordillera, though distant many leagues. In that direction there are a few small villages, where the inhabitants, having more water, are enabled to irrigate a little land, and raise hay, on which the mules and asses, employed in carrying the saltpetre, are fed. The nitrate of soda was now selling at the ship's side at fourteen shillings per hundred pounds: the chief expense is its transport to the sea-coast. The mine consists of a hard stratum, between two and three feet thick, of the nitrate mingled with a little of the sulphate of soda and a good deal of common salt. It lies close beneath the surface, and follows for a length of one hundred and fifty miles the margin of a grand basin or plain; this, from its outline, manifestly must once have been a lake, or more probably an inland arm of the sea, as may be inferred from the presence of iodic salts in the saline stratum. The surface of the plain is 3300 feet above the Pacific.

19th.—We anchored in the Bay of Callao, the seaport of Lima, the capital of Peru. We stayed here six weeks,[8] but from the troubled state of public affairs, I saw very little of the country. During our whole visit the climate was far from being so delightful, as it is generally represented. A dull heavy bank of clouds constantly hung over the land, so that during the first sixteen days I had only one view of the Cordillera behind Lima. These mountains, seen in stages, one above the other, through openings in the clouds, had a very grand appearance. It is almost become a proverb, that rain never falls in the lower part of Peru. Yet this can hardly be considered correct; for during almost every day of our visit there was a thick drizzling mist, which was sufficient to make the streets muddy and one's clothes damp: this the people are pleased to call Peruvian dew. That much rain does not fall is very certain, for the houses are covered only with flat roofs made of hardened mud; and on the mole ship-loads of wheat were piled up, being thus left for weeks together without any shelter.

I cannot say I liked the very little I saw of Peru: in summer,

[8] [Editor] Much of the time was spent in waiting for Fitz Roy to return from the rescue of the *Challenger*. When he reached Callao, Fitz Roy stayed long enough to buy—despite his previous experiences with the Admiralty—the small vessel that had been loaned to Fitz Roy in Chile; Fitz Roy wanted the vessel to extend the survey northward while the *Beagle* herself went to the Galapagos Islands and across the Pacific. (The Admiralty refused to reimburse Fitz Roy for this vessel, too—and the messages from the Lords of the Admiralty to Fitz Roy grew sharper.)

however, it is said that the climate is much pleasanter. In all seasons, both inhabitants and foreigners suffer from severe attacks of ague. This disease is common on the whole coast of Peru, but is unknown in the interior. The attacks of illness which arise from miasma never fail to appear most mysterious. So difficult is it to judge from the aspect of a country, whether or not it is healthy, that if a person had been told to choose within the tropics a situation appearing favourable for health, very probably he would have named this coast. The plain round the outskirts of Callao is sparingly covered with a coarse grass, and in some parts there are a few stagnant, though very small, pools of water. The miasma, in all probability, arises from these: for the town of Arica was similarly circumstanced, and its healthiness was much improved by the drainage of some little pools. Miasma is not always produced by a luxuriant vegetation with an ardent climate; for many parts of Brazil, even where there are marshes and a rank vegetation, are much more healthy than this sterile coast of Peru. The densest forests in a temperate climate, as in Chiloe, do not seem in the slightest degree to affect the healthy condition of the atmosphere.

The island of St. Jago, at the Cape de Verds, offers another strongly-marked instance of a country, which any one would have expected to find most healthy, being very much the contrary. I have described the bare and open plains as supporting, during a few weeks after the rainy season, a thin vegetation, which directly withers away and dries up: at this period the air appears to become quite poisonous; both natives and foreigners often being affected with violent fevers. On the other hand, the Galapagos Archipelago, in the Pacific, with a similar soil, and periodically subject to the same process of vegetation, is perfectly healthy. Humboldt has observed, that, "under the torrid zone, the smallest marshes are the most dangerous, being surrounded, as at Vera Cruz and Carthagena, with an arid and sandy soil, which raises the temperature of the ambient air."[9] On the coast of Peru, however, the temperature is not hot to any excessive degree; and perhaps in consequence, the intermittent fevers are not of the most malignant order. In all unhealthy countries the greatest risk is run by sleeping on shore. Is this owing to the state of the body during sleep, or to a greater abundance of miasma at such times? It appears

[9] [Darwin] Political Essay on the Kingdom of New Spain, vol. iv. p. 199.

certain that those who stay on board a vessel, though anchored at only a short distance from the coast, generally suffer less than those actually on shore. On the other hand, I have heard of one remarkable case where a fever broke out among the crew of a man-of-war some hundred miles off the coast of Africa, and at the very same time that one of those fearful periods[10] of death commenced at Sierra Leone.[11]

No State in South America, since the declaration of independence, has suffered more from anarchy than Peru. At the time of our visit, there were four chiefs in arms contending for supremacy in the government: if one succeeded in becoming for a time very powerful, the others coalesced against him; but no sooner were they victorious, than they were again hostile to each other. The other day, at the Anniversary of the Independence, high mass was performed, the President partaking of the sacrament: during the *Te Deum laudamus,* instead of each regiment displaying the Peruvian flag, a black one with death's head was unfurled. Imagine a government under which such a scene could be ordered, on such an occasion, to be typical of their determination of fighting to death! This state of affairs happened at a time very unfortunately for me, as I was precluded from taking any excursions much beyond the limits of the town. The barren island of S. Lorenzo, which forms the harbour, was nearly the only place where one could walk securely. The upper part, which is upwards of 1000 feet in height, during this season of the year (winter), comes within the lower limit of the clouds; and in consequence, an abundant cryptogamic vegetation, and a few flowers, cover the summit. On the hills near Lima, at a height but little greater, the ground is carpeted with moss, and beds of beautiful yellow lilies, called Amancaes. This indicates a very much greater degree of humidity, than at a corresponding height at Iquique.

[10] [Darwin] A similar interesting case is recorded in the Madras Medical Quart. Journ., 1839, p. 340. Dr. Ferguson, in his admirable Paper (see 9th vol. of Edinburgh Royal Trans.), shows clearly that the poison is generated in the drying process; and hence that dry hot countries are often the most unhealthy.

[11] [Editor] The disease Darwin is discussing is malaria. The observations he reports are easily explained by emergence of mosquitoes in many areas after a period of rain; the freedom of many oceanic islands (like the Galapagos) from mosquitoes; and the smaller numbers of mosquitoes that would reach a ship lying offshore. But the discovery that malaria is transmitted by Anopheline mosquitoes lay two generations in the future.

Proceeding northward of Lima, the climate becomes damper, till on the banks of the Guyaquil, nearly under the equator, we find the most luxuriant forests. The change, however, from the sterile coast of Peru to that fertile land is described as taking place rather abruptly in the latitude of Cape Blanco, two degrees south of Guyaquil.

Callao is a filthy, ill-built, small seaport. The inhabitants, both here and at Lima, present every imaginable shade of mixture, between European, Negro, and Indian blood. They appear a depraved, drunken set of people. The atmosphere is loaded with foul smells, and that peculiar one, which may be perceived in almost every town within the tropics, was here very strong. The fortress, which withstood Lord Cochrane's long siege, has an imposing appearance. But the President, during our stay, sold the brass guns, and proceeded to dismantle parts of it. The reason assigned was, that he had not an officer to whom he could trust so important a charge. He himself had good reasons for thinking so, as he had obtained the presidentship by rebelling while in charge of this same fortress. After we left South America, he paid the penalty in the usual manner, by being conquered, taken prisoner, and shot.

Lima stands on a plain in a valley, formed during the gradual retreat of the sea. It is seven miles from Callao, and is elevated 500 feet above it; but from the slope being very gradual, the road appears absolutely level; so that when at Lima it is difficult to believe one has ascended even one hundred feet: Humboldt has remarked on this singularly deceptive case. Steep, barren hills rise like islands from the plain, which is divided, by straight mud-walls, into large green fields. In these scarcely a tree grows excepting a few willows, and an occasional clump of bananas and of oranges. The city of Lima is now in a wretched state of decay: the streets are nearly unpaved; and heaps of filth are piled up in all directions, where the black gallinazos, tame as poultry, pick up bits of carrion. The houses have generally an upper story, built, on account of the earthquakes, of plastered woodwork; but some of the old ones, which are now used by several families, are immensely large, and would rival in suites of apartments the most magnificent in any place. Lima, the City of the Kings, must formerly have been a splendid town. The extraordinary number of churches gives it, even at the present day, a peculiar and striking character, especially when viewed from a short distance.

One day I went out with some merchants to hunt in the

immediate vicinity of the city. Our sport was very poor; but I had an opportunity of seeing the ruins of one of the ancient Indian villages, with its mound like a natural hill in the centre. The remains of houses, enclosures, irrigating streams, and burial mounds, scattered over this plain, cannot fail to give one a high idea of the condition and number of the ancient population. When their earthenware, woollen clothes, utensils of elegant forms cut out of the hardest rocks, tools of copper, ornaments of precious stones, palaces, and hydraulic works, are considered, it is impossible not to respect the considerable advance made by them in the arts of civilization. The burial mounds, called Huacas, are really stupendous; although in some places they appear to be natural hills incased and modelled.

There is also another and very different class of ruins, which possesses some interest, namely, those of old Callao, overwhelmed by the great earthquake of 1746, and its accompanying wave. The destruction must have been more complete even than at Talcahuano. Quantities of shingle almost conceal the foundations of the walls, and vast masses of brickwork appear to have been whirled about like pebbles by the retiring waves. It has been stated that the land subsided during this memorable shock: I could not discover any proof of this; yet it seems far from improbable, for the form of the coast must certainly have undergone some change since the foundation of the old town; as no people in their senses would willingly have chosen for their building place, the narrow spit of shingle on which the ruins now stand. Since our voyage, M. Tschudi has come to the conclusion, by the comparison of old and modern maps, that the coast both north and south of Lima has certainly subsided.

On the island of San Lorenzo, there are very satisfactory proofs of elevation within the recent period; this of course is not opposed to the belief, of a small sinking of the ground having subsequently taken place. The side of this island fronting the Bay of Callao, is worn into three obscure terraces, the lower one of which is covered by a bed a mile in length, almost wholly composed of shells of eighteen species, now living in the adjoining sea. The height of this bed is eighty-five feet. Many of the shells are deeply corroded, and have a much older and more decayed appearance than those at the height of 500 or 600 feet on the coast of Chile. These shells are associated with much common salt, a little sulphate of lime (both probably left by the evaporation of the spray, as the land slowly rose), together with sulphate of soda and muriate of lime. They rest on fragments of the underlying sandstone, and are covered by a few inches thick of detritus. The shells, higher up on this terrace, could be traced scaling off in flakes, and falling into an impalpable powder; and on an upper terrace, at the height of 170 feet, and likewise at some considerably higher points, I found a layer of saline powder of exactly similar appearance, and lying in the same relative position. I have no doubt that this upper layer originally existed as a bed of shells, like that on the eighty-five-feet ledge; but it does not now contain even a trace of organic structure. The powder has been analyzed for me by Mr. T. Reeks; it consists of sulphates and muriates both of lime and soda, with very little carbonate of lime. It is known that common salt and carbonate of lime left in a mass for some time together, partly decompose each other; though this does not happen with small quantities in solution. As the half-decomposed shells in the lower parts are associated with much common salt, together with some of the saline substances composing the upper saline layer, and as these shells are corroded and decayed in a remarkable manner, I strongly suspect that this double decomposition has here taken place. The resultant salts, however, ought to be carbonate of soda and muriate of lime; the latter is present, but not the carbonate of soda. Hence I am led to imagine that by some unexplained means, the carbonate of soda becomes changed into the sulphate. It is obvious that the saline layer could not have been preserved in any country in which abundant rain occasionally fell: on the other hand, this very circumstance, which at first sight appears so highly favourable to the long preservation of exposed shells, has probably been the indirect means, through the common salt not having been washed away, of their decomposition and early decay.

I was much interested by finding on the terrace, at the height of eighty-five feet, *embedded* amidst the shells and much sea-drifted rubbish, some bits of cotton thread, plaited rush, and the head of a stalk of Indian corn: I compared these relics with similar ones taken out of the Huacas, or old Peruvian tombs, and found them identical in appearance. On the mainland in front of San Lorenzo, near Bellavista, there is an extensive and level plain about a hundred feet high, of which the lower part is formed of alternating layers of sand and impure clay, together with some gravel, and the surface, to the depth of from three to six feet, of a reddish loam, containing a few scattered sea-shells and numerous small fragments of coarse red earthenware, more abundant at certain spots than at others. At first I was inclined to believe that this superficial bed, from its wide extent and smoothness, must have been deposited beneath the sea; but I afterwards found in one spot, that it lay on an artificial floor of round stones. It seems, therefore, most probable that at a period when the land stood at a lower level, there was a plain very similar to that now surrounding Callao, which being protected by a shingle beach, is raised but very little above the level of the sea. On this plain, with its underlying red-clay beds, I imagine that the Indians manufactured their earthen vessels; and that, during some violent earthquake, the sea broke over the beach, and converted the plain into a temporary lake, as happened round Callao in 1713 and 1746. The water would then have deposited mud, containing fragments of pottery from the kilns, more abundant at some spots than at others, and shells from the sea. This bed with fossil earthenware, stands at about the same height with the shells on the lower terrace of San Lorenzo, in which the cotton-thread and other relics were embedded. Hence we may safely conclude, that within the Indo-human period there has been an elevation, as before alluded to, of more than eighty-five feet; for some little elevation must have been lost by the coast having subsided since the old maps were engraved. At Valparaiso, although in the 220 years before our visit, the elevation cannot have exceeded nineteen feet, yet subsequently to 1817 there has been a rise, partly insensible and partly by a start during the shock of 1822, of ten or eleven feet. The antiquity of the Indo-human race here, judging by the eighty-five feet rise of the land since the relics were embedded, is the more remarkable, as on the coast of Patagonia, when the land stood about the same number of feet lower, the Macrauchenia was a living beast; but as the Patagonian coast is some way distant from the Cordillera, the rising there may have been slower than here. At Bahia Blanca, the elevation has been only a few feet since the numerous gigantic quadrupeds were there entombed; and, according to the generally received opinion, when these extinct animals were living, man did not exist. But the rising of that part of the coast of Patagonia, is perhaps noways connected with the Cordillera, but rather with a line of old volcanic rocks in Banda Oriental, so that it may have been infinitely slower than on the shores of Peru. All these speculations, however, must be vague; for who will pretend to say, that there may not have been several periods of subsidence, intercalated between the movements of elevation; for we know that along the whole coast of Patagonia, there have certainly been many and long pauses in the upward action of the elevatory forces.

CHAPTER XVII

GALAPAGOS ARCHIPELAGO

Galapagos Archipelago — The whole Group Volcanic — Number of Craters — Leafless Bushes — Colony at Charles Island — James Island — Salt-lake in Crater — Natural History of the Group — Ornithology, curious Finches — Reptiles — Great Tortoises, habits of — Marine Lizard, feeds on Sea-weed — Terrestrial Lizard, burrowing habits, herbivorous — Importance of Reptiles in the Archipelago — Fish, Shells, Insects — Botany — American type of organization — Differences in the Species or Races on different Islands — Tameness of the Birds — Fear of Man, an acquired instinct

September 15th.—This archipelago consists of ten principal islands, of which five exceed the others in size.[1] They are situated under the Equator, and between five and six hundred miles westward of the coast of America. They are all formed of volcanic rocks; a few fragments of granite curiously glazed and altered by the heat, can hardly be considered as an exception. Some of the craters, surmounting the larger islands, are of immense size, and they rise to a height of between three and four thousand feet. Their flanks are studded by innumerable smaller orifices. I scarcely hesitate to affirm, that there must be in the whole archipelago at least two thousand craters. These consist either of lava and scoriæ, or of finely-stratified,

[1] [Editor] The Galapagos Islands belong to Ecuador. They were discovered early in the sixteenth century by Spanish navigators, who named them for the Galapagos tortoises (*galapago*, a tortoise). The English names of most of the individual islands were given them by English buccaneers, who found them a convenient retreat. A few hundred people, engaged chiefly in the guano industry, live in the Galapagos now.

sandstone-like tuff. Most of the latter are beautifully symmetrical; they owe their origin to eruptions of volcanic mud without any lava: it is a remarkable circumstance that every one
of the twenty-eight tuff-craters which were examined, had their
southern sides either much lower than the other sides, or quite
broken down and removed. As all these craters have apparently been formed when standing in the sea, and as the waves

from the trade-wind and the swell from the open Pacific here
unite their forces on the southern coasts of all the islands, this
singular uniformity in the broken state of the craters, composed of the soft and yielding tuff, is easily explained.

Considering that these islands are placed directly under the
equator, the climate is far from being excessively hot; this
seems chiefly caused by the singularly low temperature of the
surrounding water, brought here by the great southern Polar
current. Excepting during one short season, very little rain falls,
and even then it is irregular; but the clouds generally hang
low. Hence, whilst the lower parts of the island are very sterile,
the upper parts, at a height of a thousand feet and upwards,
possess a damp climate and a tolerably luxuriant vegetation.
This is especially the case on the windward sides of the islands, which first receive and condense the moisture from the
atmosphere.

In the morning (17th) we landed on Chatham Island, which,
like the others, rises with a tame and rounded outline, broken
here and there by scattered hillocks, the remains of former
craters. Nothing could be less inviting than the first appear-

ance. A broken field of black basaltic lava, thrown into the most rugged waves, and crossed by great fissures, is every where covered by stunted, sunburnt brushwood, which shows little signs of life. The dry and parched surface, being heated by the noonday sun, gave to the air a close and sultry feeling, like that from a stove: we fancied even that the bushes smelt unpleasantly. Although I diligently tried to collect as many plants as possible, I succeeded in getting very few; and such wretched-looking little weeds would have better become an arctic than an equatorial Flora. The brushwood appears, from a short distance, as leafless as our trees during winter; and it was some time before I discovered that not only almost every plant was now in full leaf, but that the greater number were in flower. The commonest bush is one of the Euphorbiaceæ: an acacia and a great odd-looking cactus are the only trees which afford any shade. After the season of heavy rains, the islands are said to appear for a short time partially green. The volcanic island of Fernando Noronha, placed in many respects under nearly similar conditions, is the only other country where I have seen a vegetation at all like this of the Galapagos islands.

The *Beagle* sailed round Chatham Island, and anchored in several bays. One night I slept on shore on a part of the island, where black truncated cones were extraordinarily numerous: from one small eminence I counted sixty of them, all surmounted by craters more or less perfect. The greater number consisted merely of a ring of red scoriæ or slags, cemented together: and their height above the plain of lava was not more than from fifty to a hundred feet: none had been very lately active. The entire surface of this part of the island seems to have been permeated, like a sieve, by the subterranean vapours: here and there the lava, whilst soft, has been blown into great bubbles; and in other parts, the tops of caverns similarly formed have fallen in, leaving circular pits with steep sides. From the regular form of the many craters, they gave to the country an artificial appearance, which vividly reminded me of those parts of Staffordshire, where the great iron-foundries are most numerous. The day was glowing hot, and the scrambling over the rough surface and through the intricate thickets, was very fatiguing; but I was well repaid by the strange Cyclopean scene. As I was walking along I met two large tortoises, each of which must have weighed at least two hundred pounds: one was eating a piece of cactus, and as I approached, it stared at me and slowly stalked away; the other gave a deep hiss, and drew in its head. These huge reptiles, surrounded by the black lava, the leafless shrubs, and large cacti, seemed to my fancy like some antediluvian animals. The few dull-coloured birds cared no more for me, than they did for the great tortoises.

23rd.—The *Beagle* proceeded to Charles Island. This archipelago has long been frequented, first by the Bucaniers, and latterly by whalers, but it is only within the last six years, that a small colony has been established here. The inhabitants are between two and three hundred in number: they are nearly all people of colour, who have been banished for political crimes from the Republic of the Equator, of which Quito is the capital.[2] The settlement is placed about four and a half miles inland, and at a height probably of a thousand feet. In the first part of the road we passed through leafless thickets, as in Chatham Island. Higher up, the woods gradually became greener: and as soon as we crossed the ridge of the island, we were cooled by a fine southerly breeze, and our sight refreshed by a green and thriving vegetation. In this upper region coarse grasses and ferns abound; but there are no tree-ferns: I saw nowhere any member of the Palm family, which is the more singular, as 360 miles northward, Cocos Island takes its name from the number of cocoa-nuts. The houses are irregularly scattered over a flat space of ground, which is cultivated with sweet potatoes and bananas. It will not easily be imagined how pleasant the sight of black mud was to us, after having been so long accustomed to the parched soil of Peru and northern Chile. The inhabitants, although complaining of poverty, obtain, without much trouble, the means of subsistence. In the woods there are many wild pigs and goats; but the staple article of animal food is supplied by the tortoises. Their numbers have of course been greatly reduced in this island, but the people yet count on two days' hunting giving them food for the rest of the week. It is said that formerly single vessels have taken away as many as seven hundred, and that the ship's company of a frigate some years since brought down in one day two hundred tortoises to the beach.[3]

September 29th.—We doubled the south-west extremity of

---

[2] [Editor] The last penal settlement in the Galapagos Islands was shut down in 1959.

[3] [Editor] The tortoises have been exterminated on the larger islands, but sizable populations remain on a few of the smaller islands.

Albemarle Island, and the next day were nearly becalmed between it and Narborough Island. Both are covered with immense deluges of black naked lava, which have flowed either over the rims of the great caldrons, like pitch over the rim of a pot in which it has been boiled, or have burst forth from smaller orifices on the flanks; in their descent they have spread over miles of the sea-coast. On both of these islands, eruptions are known to have taken place; and in Albemarle, we saw a small jet of smoke curling from the summit of one of the great craters. In the evening we anchored in Bank's Cove, in Albemarle Island. The next morning I went out walking. To the south of the broken tuff-crater, in which the *Beagle* was anchored, there was another beautifully symmetrical one of an elliptic form; its longer axis was a little less than a mile, and its depth about 500 feet. At its bottom there was a shallow lake, in the middle of which a tiny crater formed an islet. The day was overpoweringly hot, and the lake looked clear and blue: I hurried down the cindery slope, and choked with dust eagerly tasted the water—but, to my sorrow, I found it salt as brine.

The rocks on the coast abounded with great black lizards, between three and four feet long; and on the hills, an ugly yellowish-brown species was equally common. We saw many of this latter kind, some clumsily running out of our way, and others shuffling into their burrows. I shall presently describe in more detail the habits of both these reptiles. The whole of this northern part of Albemarle Island is miserably sterile.

October 8th.—We arrived at James Island; this island, as well as Charles Island, were long since thus named after our kings of the Stuart line. Mr. Bynoe, myself, and our servants were left here for a week, with provisions and a tent, whilst the *Beagle* went for water. We found here a party of Spaniards, who had been sent from Charles Island to dry fish, and to salt tortoise-meat. About six miles inland, and at the height of nearly 2000 feet, a hovel had been built in which two men lived, who were employed in catching tortoises, whilst the others were fishing on the coast. I paid this party two visits, and slept there one night. As in the other islands, the lower region was covered by nearly leafless bushes, but the trees were here of a larger growth than elsewhere, several being two feet and some even two feet nine inches in diameter. The upper region being kept damp by the clouds, supports a green and flourishing vegetation. So damp was the ground, that there were large beds of a coarse cyperus, in which great numbers of a very small water-rail lived and bred. While staying in this upper region, we lived entirely upon tortoise-meat: the breast-plate roasted (as the Gauchos do *carne con cuero*), with the flesh on it, is very good; and the young tortoises make excellent soup; but otherwise the meat to my taste is indifferent.

One day we accompanied a party of the Spaniards in their whale-boat to a salina, or lake from which salt is procured. After landing, we had a very rough walk over a rugged field of recent lava, which has almost surrounded a tuff-crater, at the bottom of which the salt-lake lies. The water is only three or four inches deep, and rests on a layer of beautifully crystallized, white salt. The lake is quite circular, and is fringed with a border of bright green succulent plants; the almost precipitous walls of the crater are clothed with wood, so that the scene was altogether both picturesque and curious. A few years since, the sailors belonging to a sealing-vessel murdered their captain in this quiet spot; and we saw his skull lying among the bushes.

During the greater part of our stay of a week, the sky was cloudless, and if the trade-wind failed for an hour, the heat became very oppressive. On two days, the thermometer within the tent stood for some hours at 93°; but in the open air, in the wind and sun, at only 85°. The sand was extremely hot; the thermometer placed in some of a brown colour immediately rose to 137°, and how much above that it would have risen, I do not know, for it was not graduated any higher. The black sand felt much hotter, so that even in thick boots it was quite disagreeable to walk over it.

The natural history of these islands is eminently curious, and well deserves attention. Most of the organic productions are aboriginal creations, found nowhere else; there is even a difference between the inhabitants of the different islands; yet all show a marked relationship with those of America, though separated from that continent by an open space of ocean, between 500 and 600 miles in width. The archipelago is a little world within itself, or rather a satellite attached to America, whence it has derived a few stray colonists, and has received the general character of its indigenous productions. Considering the small size of these islands, we feel the more astonished at the number of their aboriginal beings, and at their confined range. Seeing every height crowned with its crater, and the boundaries of most of the lava-streams still distinct, we are led to believe that within a period, geologically recent, the unbroken ocean was here spread out. Hence, both in space and time, we seem to be brought somewhat near to that great fact —that mystery of mysteries—the first appearance of new beings on this earth.

Of terrestrial mammals, there is only one which must be considered as indigenous, namely, a mouse (Mus Galapagoensis), and this is confined, as far as I could ascertain, to Chatham Island, the most easterly island of the group. It belongs, as I am informed by Mr. Waterhouse, to a division of the family of mice characteristic of America. At James Island, there is a rat sufficiently distinct from the common kind to have been named and described by Mr. Waterhouse; but as it belongs to the old-world division of the family, and as this island has been frequented by ships for the last hundred and fifty years, I can hardly doubt that this rat is merely a variety, produced by the new and peculiar climate, food, and soil, to which it has been subjected. Although no one has a right to speculate without distinct facts, yet even with respect to the Chatham Island mouse, it should be borne in mind, that it may possibly be an American species imported here; for I have seen, in a most unfrequented part of the Pampas, a native mouse living in the roof of a newly-built hovel, and therefore its transportation in a vessel is not improbable: analogous facts have been observed by Dr. Richardson in North America.

Of land-birds I obtained twenty-six kinds, all peculiar to the group and found nowhere else, with the exception of one lark-like finch from North America (Dolichonyx oryzivorus), which ranges on that continent as far north as 54°, and generally frequents marshes. The other twenty-five birds consist, firstly, of a hawk, curiously intermediate in structure between a Buzzard and the American group of carrion-feeding Polybori; and with these latter birds it agrees most closely in every habit and even tone of voice. Secondly, there are two owls, representing the short-eared and white barn-owls of Europe. Thirdly, a wren, three tyrant fly-catchers (two of them species of Pyrocephalus, one or both of which would be ranked by some ornithologists as only varieties), and a dove—all analogous to, but distinct from, American species. Fourthly, a swallow, which though differing from the Progne purpurea of both Americas, only in being rather duller coloured, smaller, and slenderer, is considered by Mr. Gould as specifically distinct.

Fifthly, there are three species of mocking-thrush—a form
highly characteristic of America. The remaining land-birds
form a most singular group of finches, related to each other in
the structure of their beaks, short tails, form of body, and
plumage: there are thirteen species, which Mr. Gould has divided into four sub-groups. All these species are peculiar to
this archipelago; and so is the whole group, with the exception of one species of the sub-group Cactornis, lately brought
from Bow Island, in the Low Archipelago. Of Cactornis, the
two species may be often seen climbing about the flowers of
the great cactus-trees; but all the other species of this group
of finches, mingled together in flocks, feed on the dry and
sterile ground of the lower districts. The males of all, or certainly of the greater number, are jet black; and the females
(with perhaps one or two exceptions) are brown. The most
curious fact is the perfect gradation in the size of the beaks
in the different species of Geospiza, from one as large as that
of a hawfinch to that of a chaffinch, and (if Mr. Gould is
right in including his sub-group, Certhidea, in the main group),
even to that of a warbler. The largest beak in the genus
Geospiza is shown in Fig. 1, and the smallest in Fig. 3; but
instead of their being only one intermediate species, with a
beak of the size shown in Fig. 2, there are no less than six
species with insensibly graduated beaks. The beak of the sub-

group Certhidea, is shown in Fig. 4. The beak of Cactornis is somewhat like that of a starling; and that of the fourth sub-group, Camarhynchus, is slightly parrot-shaped. Seeing this gradation and diversity of structure in one small, intimately related group of birds, one might really fancy that from an original paucity of birds in this archipelago, one species had been taken and modified for different ends. In a like manner it might be fancied that a bird originally a buzzard, had been induced here to undertake the office of the carrion-feeding Polybori of the American continent.

Of waders and water-birds I was able to get only eleven kinds, and of these only three (including a rail confined to the damp summits of the islands) are new species. Considering the wandering habits of the gulls, I was surprised to find that the species inhabiting these islands is peculiar, but allied to one from the southern parts of South America. The far greater peculiarity of the land-birds, namely, twenty-five out of twenty-six being new species or at least new races, compared with the waders and web-footed birds, is in accordance with the greater range which these latter orders have in all parts of the world. We shall hereafter see this law of aquatic forms, whether marine or fresh-water, being less peculiar at any given point of the earth's surface than the terrestrial forms of the same classes, strikingly illustrated in the shells, and in a lesser degree in the insects of this archipelago.

Two of the waders are rather smaller than the same species brought from other places: the swallow is also smaller, though it is doubtful whether or not it is distinct from its analogue. The two owls, the two tyrant fly-catchers (Pyrocephalus) and the dove, are also smaller than the analogous but distinct species, to which they are most nearly related; on the other hand, the gull is rather larger. The two owls, the swallow, all three species of mocking-thrush, the dove in its separate colours though not in its whole plumage, the Totanus, and the gull, are likewise duskier coloured than their analogous species; and in the case of the mocking-thrush and Totanus, than any other species of the two genera. With the exception of a wren with a fine yellow breast, and of a tyrant fly-catcher with a scarlet tuft and breast, none of the birds are brilliantly coloured, as might have been expected in an equatorial district. Hence it would appear probable, that the same causes which here make the immigrants of some species smaller, make most of the peculiar Galapageian species also smaller, as well as very generally more dusky coloured. All the plants have a wretched, weedy appearance, and I did not see one beautiful flower. The insects, again, are small sized and dull coloured, and, as Mr. Waterhouse informs me, there is nothing in their general appearance which would have led him to imagine that they had come from under the equator. The birds, plants, and insects have a desert character, and are not more brilliantly coloured than those from southern Patagonia; we may, therefore, conclude that the usual gaudy colouring of the intertropical productions, is not related either to the heat or light of those zones, but to some other cause, perhaps to the conditions of existence being generally favourable to life.

We will now turn to the order of reptiles, which gives the most striking character to the zoology of these islands. The species are not numerous, but the numbers of individuals of each species are extraordinarily great. There is one small lizard belonging to a South American genus, and two species (and probably more) of the Amblyrhynchus—a genus confined to the Galapagos Islands. There is one snake which is numerous; it is identical, as I am informed by M. Bibron, with the Psammophis Temminckii from Chile. Of sea-turtle I believe there is more than one species; and of tortoises there are, as we shall presently show, two or three species or races. Of toads and frogs there are none: I was surprised at this, considering how well suited for them the temperate and damp upper woods appeared to be. It recalled to my mind the remark made by Bory St. Vincent,[4] namely, that none of this family are found on any of the volcanic islands in the great oceans. As far as I can ascertain from various works, this seems to hold good throughout the Pacific, and even in the large islands of the Sandwich archipelago. Mauritius offers an apparent exception, where I saw the Rana Mascariensis in abundance: this frog is said now to inhabit the Seychelles, Madagascar, and Bourbon; but on the other hand, Du Bois, in his voyage of 1669, states that there were no reptiles in Bourbon except tortoises; and the Officier du Roi asserts that before

[4] [Darwin] Voyage aux Quatre Iles d'Afrique. With respect to the Sandwich Islands, see Tyerman and Bennett's Journal, vol. i. p. 434. For Mauritius, see Voyage par un Officier, &c., Part i. p. 170. There are no frogs in the Canary Islands (Webb et Berthelot, Hist. Nat. des Iles Canaries). I saw none at St. Jago in the Cape de Verds. There are none at St. Helena.

1768 it had been attempted, without success, to introduce frogs into Mauritius—I presume, for the purpose of eating: hence it may be well doubted whether this frog is an aboriginal of these islands. The absence of the frog family in the oceanic islands is the more remarkable, when contrasted with the case of lizards, which swarm on most of the smallest islands. May this difference not be caused, by the greater facility with which the eggs of lizards, protected by calcareous shells, might be transported through salt-water, than could the slimy spawn of frogs?

I will first describe the habits of the tortoise (Testudo nigra, formerly called Indica), which has been so frequently alluded to. These animals are found, I believe, on all the islands of the Archipelago; certainly on the greater number. They frequent in preference the high damp parts, but they likewise live in the lower and arid districts. I have already shown, from the numbers which have been caught in a single day, how very numerous they must be. Some grow to an immense size: Mr. Lawson, an Englishman, and vice-governor of the colony, told us that he had seen several so large, that it required six or eight men to lift them from the ground; and that some had afforded as much as two hundred pounds of meat. The old males are the largest, the females rarely growing to so great a size: the male can readily be distinguished from the female by the greater length of its tail. The tortoises which live on those islands where there is no water, or in the lower and arid parts of the others, feed chiefly on the succulent cactus. Those which frequent the higher and damp regions, eat the leaves of various trees, a kind of berry (called guayavita) which is acid and austere, and likewise a pale green filamentous lichen (Usnera plicata), that hangs in tresses from the boughs of the trees.

The tortoise is very fond of water, drinking large quantities, and wallowing in the mud. The larger islands alone possess springs, and these are always situated towards the central parts, and at a considerable height. The tortoises, therefore, which frequent the lower districts, when thirsty, are obliged to travel from a long distance. Hence broad and well-beaten paths branch off in every direction from the wells down to the sea-coast; and the Spaniards by following them up, first discovered the watering-places. When I landed at Chatham Island, I could not imagine what animal travelled so methodically along well-chosen tracks. Near the springs it was a curious spectacle to behold many of these huge creatures, one set eagerly travelling onwards with outstretched necks, and another set returning, after having drunk their fill. When the tortoise arrives at the spring, quite regardless of any spectator, he buries his head in the water above his eyes, and greedily swallows great mouthfuls, at the rate of about ten in a minute. The inhabitants say each animal stays three or four days in the neighbourhood of the water, and then returns to the lower country; but they differed respecting the frequency of these visits. The animal probably regulates them according to the nature of the food on which it has lived. It is, however, certain, that tortoises can subsist even on those islands, where there is no other water than what falls during a few rainy days in the year.

I believe it is well ascertained, that the bladder of the frog acts as a reservoir for the moisture necessary to its existence: such seems to be the case with the tortoise. For some time after a visit to the springs, their urinary bladders are distended with fluid, which is said gradually to decrease in volume, and to become less pure. The inhabitants, when walking in the lower district, and overcome with thirst, often take advantage of this circumstance, and drink the contents of the bladder if full: in one I saw killed, the fluid was quite limpid, and had only a very slightly bitter taste. The inhabitants, however, always first drink the water in the pericardium, which is described as being best.

The tortoises, when purposely moving towards any point, travel by night and day, and arrive at their journey's end much sooner than would be expected. The inhabitants, from observing marked individuals, consider that they travel a distance of about eight miles in two or three days. One large tortoise, which I watched, walked at the rate of sixty yards in ten minutes, that is 360 yards in the hour, or four miles a day,—allowing a little time for it to eat on the road. During the breeding season, when the male and female are together, the male utters a hoarse roar or bellowing, which, it is said, can be heard at the distance of more than a hundred yards. The female never uses her voice, and the male only at these times; so that when the people hear this noise, they know that the two are together. They were at this time (October) laying their eggs. The female, where the soil is sandy, deposits them together, and covers them up with sand; but where the ground is rocky she drops them indiscriminately in any hole: Mr. Bynoe found seven placed in a fissure. The egg is white and spherical; one which I measured was seven inches and three-eighths in circumference, and therefore larger than a hen's egg. The young tortoises, as soon as they are hatched, fall a prey in great numbers to the carrion-feeding buzzard. The old ones seem generally to die from accidents, as from falling down precipices: at least, several of the inhabitants told me, that they had never found one dead without some evident cause.

The inhabitants believe that these animals are absolutely deaf; certainly they do not overhear a person walking close behind them. I was always amused when overtaking one of these great monsters, as it was quietly pacing along, to see how suddenly, the instant I passed, it would draw in its head and legs, and uttering a deep hiss fall to the ground with a heavy sound, as if struck dead. I frequently got on their backs, and then giving a few raps on the hinder part of their shells, they would rise up and walk away;—but I found it very difficult to keep my balance. The flesh of this animal is largely employed, both fresh and salted; and a beautifully clear oil is prepared from the fat. When a tortoise is caught, the man makes a slit in the skin near its tail, so as to see inside its body, whether the fat under the dorsal plate is thick. If it is not, the animal is liberated; and it is said to recover soon from this strange operation. In order to secure the tortoises, it is not sufficient to turn them like turtle, for they are often able to get on their legs again.

There can be little doubt that this tortoise is an aboriginal inhabitant of the Galapagos; for it is found on all, or nearly all, the islands, even on some of the smaller ones where there is no water; had it been an imported species, this would hardly have been the case in a group which has been so little frequented. Moreover, the old Bucaniers found this tortoise in greater numbers even than at present: Wood and Rogers also, in 1708, say that it is the opinion of the Spaniards, that it is found nowhere else in this quarter of the world. It is now widely distributed; but it may be questioned whether it is in any other place an aboriginal. The bones of a tortoise at Mauritius, associated with those of the extinct Dodo, have generally been considered as belonging to this tortoise: if this had been so, undoubtedly it must have been there indigenous; but M. Bibron informs me that he believes that it was distinct, as the species now living there certainly is.

The Amblyrhynchus, a remarkable genus of lizards, is confined to this archipelago: there are two species, resembling each other in general form, one being terrestrial and the other

aquatic. This latter species (A. cristatus) was first characterized by Mr. Bell, who well foresaw, from its short, broad
head, and strong claws of equal length, that its habits of life
would turn out very peculiar, and different from those of its
nearest ally, the Iguana. It is extremely common on all the
islands throughout the group, and lives exclusively on the rocky
sea-beaches, being never found, at least I never saw one, even
ten yards in-shore. It is a hideous-looking creature, of a dirty
black colour, stupid, and sluggish in its movements. The usual
length of a full-grown one is about a yard, but there are some
even four feet long; a large one weighed twenty pounds: on
the island of Albemarle they seem to grow to a greater size
than elsewhere. Their tails are flattened sideways, and all four
feet partially webbed. They are occasionally seen some hundred yards from the shore, swimming about; and Captain Collnett, in his Voyage, says, "They go to sea in herds a-fishing,
and sun themselves on the rocks; and may be called alligators
in miniature." It must not, however, be supposed that they live
on fish. When in the water this lizard swims with perfect ease
and quickness, by a serpentine movement of its body and flat-

Amblyrhynchus cristatus. *Insert*: Tooth of natural size, and likewise
magnified.

tened tail—the legs being motionless and closely collapsed on
its sides. A seaman on board sank one, with a heavy weight
attached to it, thinking thus to kill it directly; but when, an
hour afterwards, he drew up the line, it was quite active. Their
limbs and strong claws are admirably adapted for crawling
over the rugged and fissured masses of lava, which everywhere
form the coast. In such situations, a group of six or seven of
these hideous reptiles may oftentimes be seen on the black

rocks, a few feet above the surf, basking in the sun with out-stretched legs.

I opened the stomachs of several, and found them largely distended with minced sea-weed (Ulvæ), which grows in thin foliaceous expansions of a bright green or a dull red colour. I do not recollect having observed this sea-weed in any quantity on the tidal rocks; and I have reason to believe it grows at the bottom of the sea, at some little distance from the coast. If such be the case, the object of these animals occasionally going out to sea is explained. The stomach contained nothing but the sea-weed. Mr. Bynoe, however, found a piece of a crab in one; but this might have got in accidentally, in the same manner as I have seen a caterpillar, in the midst of some lichen, in the paunch of a tortoise. The intestines were large, as in other herbivorous animals. The nature of this lizard's food, as well as the structure of its tail and feet, and the fact of its having been seen voluntarily swimming out at sea, absolutely prove its aquatic habits; yet there is in this respect one strange anomaly, namely, that when frightened it will not enter the water. Hence it is easy to drive these lizards down to any little point overhanging the sea, where they will sooner allow a person to catch hold of their tails than jump into the water. They do not seem to have any notion of biting; but when much frightened they squirt a drop of fluid from each nostril. I threw one several times as far as I could, into a deep pool left by the retiring tide; but it invariably returned in a direct line to the spot where I stood. It swam near the bottom, with a very graceful and rapid movement, and occasionally aided itself over the uneven ground with its feet. As soon as it arrived near the edge, but still being under water, it tried to conceal itself in the tufts of sea-weed, or it entered some crevice. As soon as it thought the danger was past, it crawled out on the dry rocks, and shuffled away as quickly as it could. I several times caught this same lizard, by driving it down to a point, and though possessed of such perfect powers of diving and swimming, nothing would induce it to enter the water; and as often as I threw it in, it returned in the manner above described. Perhaps this singular piece of apparent stupidity may be accounted for by the circumstance, that this reptile has no enemy whatever on shore, whereas at sea it must often fall a prey to the numerous sharks. Hence, probably, urged by a fixed and hereditary instinct that the shore is its place of safety, whatever the emergency may be, it there takes refuge.

During our visit (in October), I saw extremely few small individuals of this species, and none I should think under a year old. From this circumstance it seems probable that the breeding season had not then commenced. I asked several of the inhabitants if they knew where it laid its eggs: they said that they knew nothing of its propagation, although well acquainted with the eggs of the land kind—a fact, considering how very common this lizard is, not a little extraordinary.

We will now turn to the terrestrial species (A. Demarlii), with a round tail, and toes without webs. This lizard, instead of being found like the other on all the islands, is confined to the central part of the archipelago, namely to Albemarle, James, Barrington, and Indefatigable islands. To the southward, in Charles, Hood, and Chatham islands, and to the northward, in Towers, Bindloes, and Abingdon, I neither saw nor heard of any. It would appear as if it had been created in the centre of the archipelago, and thence had been dispersed only to a certain distance. Some of these lizards inhabit the high and damp parts of the islands, but they are much more numerous in the lower and sterile districts near the coast. I cannot give a more forcible proof of their numbers, than by stating that when we were left at James Island, we could not for some time find a spot free from their burrows on which to pitch our single tent. Like their brothers the sea-kind, they are ugly animals, of a yellowish orange beneath, and of a brownish red colour above: from their low facial angle they have a singularly stupid appearance. They are, perhaps, of a rather less size than the marine species; but several of them weighed between ten and fifteen pounds. In their movements they are lazy and half torpid. When not frightened, they slowly crawl along with their tails and bellies dragging on the ground. They often stop, and doze for a minute or two, with closed eyes and hind legs spread out on the parched soil.

They inhabit burrows, which they sometimes make between fragments of lava, but more generally on level patches of the soft sandstone-like tuff. The holes do not appear to be very deep, and they enter the ground at a small angle; so that when walking over these lizard-warrens, the soil is constantly giving way, much to the annoyance of the tired walker. This animal, when making its burrow, works alternately the opposite sides of its body. One front leg for a short time scratches up the soil, and throws it towards the hind foot, which is well placed so as to heave it beyond the mouth of the hole. That side of the body being tired, the other takes up the task, and so on alternately. I watched one for a long time, till half its body was buried; I then walked up and pulled it by the tail; at this it was greatly astonished, and soon shuffled up to see what was the matter; and then stared me in the face, as much as to say, "What made you pull my tail?"

They feed by day, and do not wander far from their burrows; if frightened, they rush to them with a most awkward gait. Except when running down hill, they cannot move very fast, apparently from the lateral position of their legs. They are not at all timorous: when attentively watching any one, they curl their tails, and, raising themselves on their front legs, nod their heads vertically, with a quick movement, and try to look very fierce: but in reality they are not at all so; if one just stamps on the ground, down go their tails, and off they shuffle as quickly as they can. I have frequently observed small fly-eating lizards, when watching anything, nod their heads in precisely the same manner; but I do not at all know for what purpose. If this Amblyrhynchus is held and plagued with a stick, it will bite it very severely; but I caught many by the tail, and they never tried to bite me. If two are placed on the ground and held together, they will fight, and bite each other till blood is drawn.

The individuals, and they are the greater number, which inhabit the lower country, can scarcely taste a drop of water throughout the year; but they consume much of the succulent cactus, the branches of which are occasionally broken off by the wind. I several times threw a piece to two or three of them when together; and it was amusing enough to see them trying to seize and carry it away in their mouths, like so many hungry dogs with a bone. They eat very deliberately, but do not chew their food. The little birds are aware how harmless these creatures are: I have seen one of the thick-billed finches picking at one end of a piece of cactus (which is much relished by all the animals of the lower region), whilst a lizard was eating at the other end; and afterwards the little bird with the utmost indifference hopped on the back of the reptile.

I opened the stomachs of several, and found them full of vegetable fibres and leaves of different trees, especially of an acacia. In the upper region they live chiefly on the acid and astringent berries of the guayavita, under which trees I have seen these lizards and huge tortoises feeding together. To obtain the acacia-leaves they crawl up the low stunted trees; and it is not uncommon to see a pair quietly browsing, whilst seated on a branch several feet above the ground. These lizards, when cooked, yield a white meat, which is liked by those whose stomachs soar above all prejudices. Humboldt has remarked that in intertropical South America, all lizards which inhabit dry regions are esteemed delicacies for the table. The inhabitants state that those which inhabit the upper damp parts drink water, but that the others do not, like the tortoises, travel up for it from the lower sterile country. At the time of our visit, the females had within their bodies numerous large, elongated eggs, which they lay in their burrows: the inhabitants seek them for food.

These two species of Amblyrhynchus agree, as I have already stated, in their general structure, and in many of their habits. Neither have that rapid movement, so characteristic of the genera Lacerta and Iguana. They are both herbivorous, although the kind of vegetation on which they feed is so very different. Mr. Bell has given the name to the genus from the shortness of the snout; indeed, the form of the mouth may almost be compared to that of the tortoise: one is led to suppose that this is an adaptation to their herbivorous appetites. It is very interesting thus to find a well-characterized genus, having its marine and terrestrial species, belonging to so confined a portion of the world. The aquatic species is by far the most remarkable, because it is the only existing lizard which lives on marine vegetable productions. As I at first observed, these islands are not so remarkable for the number of the species of reptiles, as for that of the individuals; when we remember the well-beaten paths made by the thousands of huge tortoises—the many turtles—the great warrens of the terrestrial Amblyrhynchus—and the groups of the marine species basking on the coast-rocks of every island—we must admit that there is no other quarter of the world where this Order replaces the herbivorous mammalia in so extraordinary a manner. The geologist on hearing this will probably refer back in his mind to the Secondary epochs, when lizards, some herbivorous, some carnivorous, and of dimensions comparable only with our existing whales, swarmed on the land and in the sea. It is, therefore, worthy of his observation, that this archipelago, instead of possessing a humid climate and rank vegetation, cannot be considered otherwise than extremely arid, and, for an equatorial region, remarkably temperate.

To finish with the zoology: the fifteen kinds of sea-fish which

I procured here are all new species; they belong to twelve genera, all widely distributed, with the exception of Prionotus, of which the four previously known species live on the eastern side of America. Of land-shells I collected sixteen kinds (and two marked varieties), of which, with the exception of one Helix found at Tahiti, all are peculiar to this archipelago: a single fresh-water shell (Paludina) is common to Tahiti and Van Diemen's Land. Mr. Cuming, before our voyage, procured here ninety species of sea-shells, and this does not include several species not yet specifically examined, of Trochus, Turbo, Monodonta, and Nassa. He has been kind enough to give me the following interesting results: of the ninety shells, no less than forty-seven are unknown elsewhere—a wonderful fact, considering how widely distributed sea-shells generally are. Of the forty-three shells found in other parts of the world, twenty-five inhabit the western coast of America, and of these eight are distinguishable as varieties; the remaining eighteen (including one variety) were found by Mr. Cuming in the Low archipelago,[5] and some of them also at the Philippines. This fact of shells from islands in the central part of the Pacific occurring here, deserves notice, for not one single sea-shell is known to be common to the islands of that ocean and to the west coast of America. The space of open sea running north and south off the west coast, separates two quite distinct conchological provinces; but at the Galapagos Archipelago we have a halting-place, where many new forms have been created, and whither these two great conchological provinces have each sent several colonists. The American province has also sent here representative species; for there is a Galapageian species of Monoceros, a genus only found on the west coast of America; and there are Galapageian species of Fissurella and Cancellaria, genera common on the west coast, but not found (as I am informed by Mr. Cuming) in the central islands of the Pacific. On the other hand, there are Galapageian species of Oniscia and Stylifer, genera common to the West Indies and to the Chinese and Indian seas, but not found either on the west coast of America or in the central Pacific. I may here add, that after the comparison by Messrs. Cuming and Hinds of about 2000 shells from the eastern and western coasts of America, only one single shell was found in common, namely, the Purpura patula, which in-

[5] [Editor] A group of Pacific islands not far from Tahiti belonging to France.

habits the West Indies, the coast of Panama, and the Galapagos. We have, therefore, in this quarter of the world, three great conchological sea-provinces, quite distinct, though surprisingly near each other, being separated by long north and south spaces either of land or of open sea.

I took great pains in collecting the insects, but, excepting Tierra del Fuego, I never saw in this respect so poor a country. Even in the upper and damp region I procured very few, excepting some minute Diptera and Hymenoptera, mostly of common mundane forms. As before remarked, the insects, for a tropical region, are of very small size and dull colours. Of beetles I collected twenty-five species (excluding a Dermestes and Corynetes imported, wherever a ship touches); of these, two belong to the Harpalidæ, two to the Hydrophilidæ, nine to three families of the Heteromera, and the remaining twelve to as many different families. This circumstance of insects (and I may add plants), where few in number, belonging to many different families, is, I believe, very general. Mr. Waterhouse, who has published[6] an account of the insects of this archipelago, and to whom I am indebted for the above details, informs me that there are several new genera; and that of the genera not new, one or two are American, and the rest of mundane distribution. With the exception of a wood-feeding Apate, and of one or probably two water-beetles from the American continent, all the species appear to be new.

The botany of this group is fully as interesting as the zoology. Dr. J. Hooker will soon publish in the "Linnean Transactions" a full account of the Flora, and I am much indebted to him for the following details. Of flowering plants there are, as far as at present is known, 185 species, and 40 cryptogamic species, making together 225; of this number I was fortunate enough to bring home 193. Of the flowering plants, 100 are new species, and are probably confined to this archipelago. Dr. Hooker conceives that, of the plants not so confined, at least 10 species found near the cultivated ground at Charles Island, have been imported. It is, I think, surprising that more American species have not been introduced naturally, considering that the distance is only between 500 and 600 miles from the continent; and that (according to Collnett, p. 58) drift-wood, bamboos, canes, and the nuts of a palm, are

[6] [Darwin] Ann. and Mag. of Nat. Hist., vol. xvi. p. 19.

often washed on the south-eastern shores. The proportion of 100 flowering plants out of 185 (or 175 excluding the imported weeds) being new, is sufficient, I conceive, to make the Galapagos Archipelago a distinct botanical province; but this Flora is not nearly so peculiar as that of St. Helena, nor, as I am informed by Dr. Hooker, of Juan Fernandez. The peculiarity of the Galapageian Flora is best shown in certain families;—thus there are 21 species of Compositæ,[7] of which 20 are peculiar to this archipelago; these belong to twelve genera, and of these genera no less than ten are confined to the archipelago! Dr. Hooker informs me that the Flora has an undoubted Western American character; nor can he detect in it any affinity with that of the Pacific. If, therefore, we except the eighteen marine, the one fresh-water, and one land-shell, which have apparently come here as colonists from the central islands of the Pacific, and likewise the one distinct Pacific species of the Galapageian group of finches, we see that this archipelago, though standing in the Pacific Ocean, is zoologically part of America.

If this character were owing merely to immigrants from America, there would be little remarkable in it; but we see that a vast majority of all the land animals, and that more than half of the flowering plants, are aboriginal productions. It was most striking to be surrounded by new birds, new reptiles, new shells, new insects, new plants, and yet by innumerable trifling details of structure, and even by the tones of voice and plumage of the birds, to have the temperate plains of Patagonia, or the hot dry deserts of Northern Chile, vividly brought before my eyes. Why, on these small points of land, which within a late geological period must have been covered by the ocean, which are formed of basaltic lava, and therefore differ in geological character from the American continent, and which are placed under a peculiar climate,—why were their aboriginal inhabitants, associated, I may add, in different proportions both in kind and number from those on the continent, and therefore acting on each other in a different manner—why were they created on American types of organization? It is probable that the islands of the Cape de Verd group resemble, in all their physical conditions, far more closely the Galapagos Islands

[7] [Editor] Trees, shrubs and herbs having flowers composed of many individual florets. A group that takes in a large proportion of all higher plants.

than these latter physically resemble the coast of America; yet the aboriginal inhabitants of the two groups are totally unlike; those of the Cape de Verd Islands bearing the impress of Africa, as the inhabitants of the Galapagos Archipelago are stamped with that of America.

I have not as yet noticed by far the most remarkable feature in the natural history of this archipelago; it is, that the different islands to a considerable extent are inhabited by a different set of beings. My attention was first called to this fact by the Vice-Governor, Mr. Lawson, declaring that the tortoises differed from the different islands, and that he could with certainty tell from which island any one was brought. I did not for some time pay sufficient attention to this statement, and I had already partially mingled together the collections from two of the islands. I never dreamed that islands, about fifty or sixty miles apart, and most of them in sight of each other, formed of precisely the same rocks, placed under a quite similar climate, rising to a nearly equal height, would have been differently tenanted; but we shall soon see that this is the case. It is the fate of most voyagers, no sooner to discover what is most interesting in any locality, than they are hurried from it; but I ought, perhaps, to be thankful that I obtained sufficient material to establish this most remarkable fact in the distribution of organic beings.

The inhabitants, as I have said, state that they can distinguish the tortoises from the different islands; and that they differ not only in size, but in other characters. Captain Porter has described[8] those from Charles and from the nearest island to it, namely, Hood Island, as having their shells in front thick and turned up like a Spanish saddle, whilst the tortoises from James Island are rounder, blacker, and have a better taste when cooked. M. Bibron, moreover, informs me that he has seen what he considers two distinct species of tortoise from the Galapagos, but he does not know from which islands. The specimens that I brought from three islands were young ones; and probably owing to this cause, neither Mr. Gray nor myself could find in them any specific differences. I have remarked that the marine Amblyrhynchus was larger at Albemarle Island than elsewhere; and M. Bibron informs me that he has seen two distinct aquatic species of this genus; so that the dif-

8 [Darwin] Voyage in the U. S. ship *Essex*, vol. i. p. 215.

ferent islands probably have their representative species or races of the Amblyrhynchus, as well as of the tortoise. My attention was first thoroughly aroused, by comparing together the numerous specimens, shot by myself and several other parties on board, of the mocking-thrushes, when, to my astonishment, I discovered that all those from Charles Island belonged to one species (Mimus trifasciatus); all from Albemarle Island to M. parvulus; and all from James and Chatham Islands (between which two other islands are situated, as connecting links) belonged to M. melanotis. These two latter species are closely allied, and would by some ornithologists be considered as only well-marked races or varieties; but the Mimus trifasciatus is very distinct. Unfortunately most of the specimens of the finch tribe were mingled together; but I have strong reasons to suspect that some of the species of the sub-group Geospiza are confined to separate islands. If the different islands have their representatives of Geospiza, it may help to explain the singularly large number of the species of this sub-group in this one small archipelago, and as a probable consequence of their numbers, the perfectly graduated series in the size of their beaks. Two species of the sub-group Cactornis, and two of Camarhynchus, were procured in the archipelago; and of the numerous specimens of these two sub-groups shot by four collectors at James Island, all were found to belong to one species of each; whereas the numerous specimens shot either on Chatham or Charles Island (for the two sets were mingled together) all belonged to the two other species: hence we may feel almost sure that these islands possess their representative species of these two sub-groups. In land-shells this law of distribution does not appear to hold good. In my very small collection of insects, Mr. Waterhouse remarks, that of those which were ticketed with their locality, not one was common to any two of the islands.

If we now turn to the Flora, we shall find the aboriginal plants of the different islands wonderfully different. I give all the following results on the high authority of my friend Dr. J. Hooker. I may premise that I indiscriminately collected everything in flower on the different islands, and fortunately kept my collections separate. Too much confidence, however, must not be placed in the proportional results, as the small collections brought home by some other naturalists, though in some respects confirming the results, plainly show that much remains to be done in the botany of this group: the Leguminosæ, moreover, have as yet been only approximately worked out:—

Name of Island.	Total No. of Species.	No. of Species found in other parts of the world.	No. of Species confined to the Galapagos Archipelago.	No. confined to the one Island.	No. of Species confined to the Galapagos Archipelago, but found on more than the one Island.
James Island	71	33	38	30	8
Albemarle Island	46	18	26	22	4
Chatham Island	32	16	16	12	4
Charles Island	68	39 (or 29, if the probably imported plants be subtracted)	29	21	8

Hence we have the truly wonderful fact, that in James Island, of the thirty-eight Galapageian plants, or those found in no other part of the world, thirty are exclusively confined to this one island; and in Albemarle Island, of the twenty-six aboriginal Galapageian plants, twenty-two are confined to this one island, that is, only four are at present known to grow in the other islands of the archipelago; and so on, as shown in the above table, with the plants from Chatham and Charles Islands. This fact will, perhaps, be rendered even more striking, by giving a few illustrations:—thus, Scalesia, a remarkable arborescent genus of the Compositæ, is confined to the archipelago: it has six species; one from Chatham, one from Albemarle, one from Charles Island, two from James Island, and the sixth from one of the three latter islands, but it is not known from which: not one of these six species grows on any two islands. Again, Euphorbia, a mundane or widely distributed genus, has here eight species, of which seven are confined to the archipelago, and not one found on any two islands: Acalypha and Borreria, both mundane genera, have respectively six and seven species, none of which have the same species on two islands, with the exception of one Borreria, which does occur on two islands.[9] The species of the Compositæ are particularly local; and Dr. Hooker has furnished me with several other most striking illustrations of the difference of the species on the different islands. He remarks that this law of distribution holds good both with those genera confined to the archipelago, and those distributed in other quarters of the world: in like manner we have seen that the different islands have their proper species of the mundane genus of tortoise, and of the widely distributed American genus of the mocking-thrush, as well as of two of the Galapageian sub-groups of finches, and almost certainly of the Galapageian genus Amblyrhynchus.

The distribution of the tenants of this archipelago would not be nearly so wonderful, if, for instance, one island had a mocking-thrush, and a second island some other quite distinct genus;—if one island had its genus of lizard, and a second island another distinct genus, or none whatever;—or if the different islands were inhabited, not by representative species of the same genera of plants, but by totally different genera, as does to a certain extent hold good; for, to give one instance, a large berry-bearing tree at James Island has no representative species in Charles Island. But it is the circumstance, that several of the islands possess their own species of the tortoise, mocking-thrush, finches, and numerous plants, these species having the same general habits, occupying analogous situations, and obviously filling the same place in the natural economy of this archipelago, that strikes me with wonder. It may be suspected that some of these representative species, at least in the case of the tortoise and of some of the birds, may hereafter prove to be only well-marked races; but this would be of equally great interest to the philosophical naturalist. I have said that most of the islands are in sight of each other: I may specify that Charles Island is fifty miles from the nearest part of Chatham Island, and thirty-three miles from the nearest part of Albemarle Is-

9 [Editor] Euphorbia and Acalypha: large genera of cactus-like plants. Borreria: a genus of herbs and shrubs of the madder family.

land. Chatham Island is sixty miles from the nearest part of James Island, but there are two intermediate islands between them which were not visited by me. James Island is only ten miles from the nearest part of Albemarle Island, but the two points where the collections were made are thirty-two miles apart. I must repeat, that neither the nature of the soil, nor height of the land, nor the climate, nor the general character of the associated beings, and therefore their action one on another, can differ much in the different islands. If there be any sensible difference in their climates, it must be between the windward group (namely Charles and Chatham Islands), and that to leeward; but there seems to be no corresponding difference in the productions of these two halves of the archipelago.

The only light which I can throw on this remarkable difference in the inhabitants of the different islands, is, that very strong currents of the sea running in a westerly and W.N.W. direction must separate, as far as transportal by the sea is concerned, the southern islands from the northern ones; and between these northern islands a strong N.W. current was observed, which must effectually separate James and Albemarle Islands. As the archipelago is free to a most remarkable degree from gales of wind, neither the birds, insects, nor lighter seeds, would be blown from island to island. And lastly, the profound depth of the ocean between the islands, and their apparently recent (in a geological sense) volcanic origin, render it highly unlikely that they were ever united; and this, probably, is a far more important consideration than any other, with respect to the geographical distribution of their inhabitants. Reviewing the facts here given, one is astonished at the amount of creative force, if such an expression may be used, displayed on these small, barren, and rocky islands; and still more so, at its diverse yet analogous action on points so near each other. I have said that the Galapagos Archipelago might be called a satellite attached to America, but it should rather be called a group of satellites, physically similar, organically distinct, yet intimately related to each other, and all related in a marked, though much lesser degree, to the great American continent.

I will conclude my description of the natural history of these islands, by giving an account of the extreme tameness of the birds.

This disposition is common to all the terrestrial species; namely, to the mocking-thrushes, the finches, wrens, tyrant-fly-catchers, the dove, and carrion-buzzard. All of them often approached sufficiently near to be killed with a switch, and sometimes, as I myself tried, with a cap or hat. A gun is here almost superfluous; for with the muzzle I pushed a hawk off the branch of a tree. One day, whilst lying down, a mocking-thrush alighted on the edge of a pitcher, made of the shell of a tortoise, which I held in my hand, and began very quietly to sip the water; it allowed me to lift it from the ground whilst seated on the vessel: I often tried, and very nearly succeeded, in catching these birds by their legs. Formerly the birds appear to have been even tamer than at present. Cowley (in the year 1684) says that the "Turtle-doves were so tame, that they would often alight upon our hats and arms, so as that we could take them alive: they not fearing man, until such time as some of our company did fire at them, whereby they were rendered more shy." Dampier also, in the same year, says that a man in a morning's walk might kill six or seven dozen of these doves. At present, although certainly very tame, they do not alight on people's arms, nor do they suffer themselves to be killed in such large numbers. It is surprising that they have not become wilder; for these islands during the last hundred and fifty years have been frequently visited by bucaniers and whalers; and the sailors, wandering through the woods in search of tortoises, always take cruel delight in knocking down the little birds.

These birds, although now still more persecuted, do not readily become wild: in Charles Island, which had then been colonized about six years, I saw a boy sitting by a well with a switch in his hand, with which he killed the doves and finches as they came to drink. He had already procured a little heap of them for his dinner; and he said that he had constantly been in the habit of waiting by this well for the same purpose. It would appear that the birds of this archipelago, not having as yet learnt that man is a more dangerous animal than the tortoise or the Amblyrhynchus, disregard him, in the same manner as in England shy birds, such as magpies, disregard the cows and horses grazing in our fields.

The Falkland Islands offer a second instance of birds with a similar disposition. The extraordinary tameness of the little Opetiorhynchus has been remarked by Pernety, Lesson, and other voyagers. It is not, however, peculiar to that bird: the Polyborus, snipe, upland and lowland goose, thrush, bunting, and even some true hawks, are all more or less tame. As the birds are so tame there, where foxes, hawks, and owls occur, we may infer that the absence of all rapacious animals at the Galapagos, is not the cause of their tameness here. The upland geese at the Falklands show, by the precaution they take in building on the islets, that they are aware of their danger from the foxes; but they are not by this rendered wild towards man. This tameness of the birds, especially of the waterfowl, is strongly contrasted with the habits of the same species in Tierra del Fuego, where for ages past they have been persecuted by the wild inhabitants. In the Falklands, the sportsman may sometimes kill more of the upland geese in one day than he can carry home; whereas in Tierra del Fuego, it is nearly as difficult to kill one, as it is in England to shoot the common wild goose.

In the time of Pernety (1763), all the birds there appear to have been much tamer than at present; he states that the Opetiorhynchus would almost perch on his finger; and that with a wand he killed ten in half an hour. At that period the birds must have been about as tame, as they now are at the Galapagos. They appear to have learnt caution more slowly at these latter islands than at the Falklands, where they have had proportionate means of experience; for besides frequent visits from vessels, those islands have been at intervals colonized during the entire period. Even formerly, when all the birds were so tame, it was impossible by Pernety's account to kill the black-necked swan—a bird of passage, which probably brought with it the wisdom learnt in foreign countries.

I may add that, according to Du Bois, all the birds at Bourbon in 1571-72, with the exception of the flamingoes and geese, were so extremely tame, that they could be caught by the hand, or killed in any number with a stick. Again, at Tristan d'Acunha in the Atlantic, Carmichael[10] states that the only two land-birds, a thrush and a bunting, were "so tame as

10 [Darwin] Linn. Trans., vol. xii. p. 496. The most anomalous fact on this subject which I have met with, is the wildness of the small birds in the Arctic parts of North America (as described by Richardson, Fauna Bor., vol. ii. p. 332), where they are said never to be persecuted. This case is the more strange, because it is asserted that some of the same species in their winter-quarters in the United States are tame. There is much, as Dr. Richardson well remarks, utterly inexplicable connected with the different degrees of shyness and care with which birds conceal their nests. How strange it is that the English wood-pigeon, generally so wild a bird, should very frequently rear its young in shrubberies close to houses!

to suffer themselves to be caught with a hand-net." From these several facts we may, I think, conclude, first, that the wildness of birds with regard to man, is a particular instinct directed against *him*, and not dependent on any general degree of caution arising from other sources of danger; secondly, that it is not acquired by individual birds in a short time, even when much persecuted; but that in the course of successive generations it becomes hereditary. With domesticated animals we are accustomed to see new mental habits or instincts acquired and rendered hereditary; but with animals in a state of nature, it must always be most difficult to discover instances of acquired hereditary knowledge. In regard to the wildness of birds towards man, there is no way of accounting for it, except as an inherited habit: comparatively few young birds, in any one year, have been injured by man in England, yet almost all, even nestlings, are afraid of him; many individuals, on the other hand, both at the Galapagos and at the Falklands, have been pursued and injured by man, but yet have not learned a salutary dread of him. We may infer from these facts, what havoc the introduction of any new beast of prey must cause in a country, before the instincts of the indigenous inhabitants have become adapted to the stranger's craft or power.

CHAPTER XVIII

TAHITI AND NEW ZEALAND

Pass through the Low Archipelago — Tahiti — Aspect — Vegetation on the Mountains — View of Eimeo — Excursion into the Interior — Profound Ravines — Succession of Waterfalls — Number of wild useful Plants — Temperance of the Inhabitants — Their moral state — Parliament convened — New Zealand — Bay of Islands — Hippahs — Excursion to Waimate — Missionary Establishment — English Weeds now run wild — Waiomio — Funeral of a New Zealand Woman — Sail for Australia

October 20*th*.—The survey of the Galapagos Archipelago being concluded, we steered towards Tahiti and commenced our long passage of 3200 miles. In the course of a few days we sailed out of the gloomy and clouded ocean-district which extends during the winter far from the coast of South America. We then enjoyed bright and clear weather, while running pleasantly along at the rate of 150 or 160 miles a day before the steady trade-wind. The temperature in this more central part of the Pacific is higher than near the American shore. The thermometer in the poop cabin, by night and day, ranged between 80° and 83°, which feels very pleasant; but with one degree or two higher, the heat becomes oppressive. We passed through the Low or Dangerous Archipelago, and saw several of those most curious rings of coral land, just rising above the water's edge, which have been called Lagoon Islands. A long and brilliantly-white beach is capped by a margin of green vegetation; and the strip, looking either way, rapidly narrows away in the distance, and sinks beneath the horizon. From the mast-head a wide expanse of smooth water can be seen within the ring. These low hollow coral islands bear no proportion to the vast ocean out of which they abruptly rise; and it seems wonderful, that such weak invaders are not overwhelmed, by the all-powerful and never-tiring waves of that great sea, miscalled the Pacific.

November 15th.—At daylight, Tahiti, an island which must for ever remain classical to the voyager in the South Sea, was in view. At a distance the appearance was not attractive. The luxuriant vegetation of the lower part could not yet be seen, and as the clouds rolled past, the wildest and most precipitous peaks showed themselves towards the centre of the island. As soon as we anchored in Matavai Bay, we were surrounded by canoes. This was our Sunday, but the Monday of Tahiti: if the case had been reversed, we should not have received a single visit; for the injunction not to launch a canoe on the sabbath is rigidly obeyed. After dinner we landed to enjoy all the delights produced by the first impressions of a new country, and that country the charming Tahiti. A crowd of men, women, and children, was collected on the memorable Point Venus, ready to receive us with laughing, merry faces. They marshalled us towards the house of Mr. Wilson, the missionary of the district, who met us on the road, and gave us a very friendly reception. After sitting a short time in his house, we separated to walk about, but returned there in the evening.

The land capable of cultivation, is scarcely in any part more than a fringe of low alluvial soil, accumulated round the base of the mountains, and protected from the waves of the sea by a coral reef, which encircles the entire line of coast. Within the reef there is an expanse of smooth water, like that of a lake, where the canoes of the natives can ply with safety and where ships anchor. The low land which comes down to the beach of coral-sand, is covered by the most beautiful productions of the intertropical regions. In the midst of bananas, orange, cocoa-nut, and bread-fruit trees, spots are cleared where yams, sweet potatoes, the sugar-cane, and pine-apples, are cultivated. Even the brushwood is an imported fruit-tree, namely, the guava, which from its abundance has become as noxious as a weed. In Brazil I have often admired the varied beauty of the bananas, palms, and orange-trees contrasted together; and here we also have the bread-fruit, conspicuous from its large, glossy, and deeply digitated leaf. It is admirable to behold groves of a tree, sending forth its branches with the vigour of an English oak, loaded with large and most nutritious fruit. However seldom the usefulness of an object can account for the pleasure of beholding it, in the case of these beautiful woods, the knowledge of their high productiveness no doubt enters largely into the feeling of admiration. The little winding paths, cool from the surrounding shade, led to the scattered houses; the owners of which every where gave us a cheerful and most hospitable reception.

I was pleased with nothing so much as with the inhabitants. There is a mildness in the expression of their countenances which at once banishes the idea of a savage; and an intelligence which shows that they are advancing in civilization. The common people, when working, keep the upper part of their bodies quite naked; and it is then that the Tahitians are seen to advantage. They are very tall, broad-shouldered, athletic, and well-proportioned. It has been remarked, that it requires little habit to make a dark skin more pleasing and natural to the eye of an European than his own colour. A white man bathing by the side of a Tahitian, was like a plant bleached by the gardener's art compared with a fine dark green one growing vigorously in the open fields. Most of the men are tattooed, and the ornaments follow the curvature of the body so gracefully, that they have a very elegant effect. One common pattern, varying in its details, is somewhat like the crown of a palm-tree. It springs from the central line of the back, and gracefully curls round both sides. The simile may be a fanciful one, but I thought the body of a man thus ornamented was like the trunk of a noble tree embraced by a delicate creeper.

Many of the elder people had their feet covered with small figures, so placed as to resemble a sock. This fashion, however, is partly gone by, and has been succeeded by others. Here, although fashion is far from immutable, every one must abide by that prevailing in his youth. An old man has thus his age for ever stamped on his body, and he cannot assume the airs of a young dandy. The women are tattooed in the same manner as the men, and very commonly on their fingers. One unbecoming fashion is now almost universal: namely, shaving the hair from the upper part of the head, in a circular form, so as to leave only an outer ring. The missionaries have tried to persuade the people to change this habit; but it is the fashion, and that is a sufficient answer at Tahiti, as well as at Paris. I was much disappointed in the personal appearance of the women: they are far inferior in every respect to the men. The custom of wearing a white or scarlet flower in the back of the head, or through a small hole in each ear, is pretty. A crown of woven cocoa-nut leaves is also worn as a shade for the eyes.

The women appear to be in greater want of some becoming costume even than the men.

Nearly all the natives understand a little English—that is, they know the names of common things; and by the aid of this, together with signs, a lame sort of conversation could be carried on. In returning in the evening to the boat, we stopped to witness a very pretty scene. Numbers of children were playing on the beach, and had lighted bonfires which illumined the placid sea and surrounding trees; others, in circles, were singing Tahitian verses. We seated ourselves on the sand, and joined their party. The songs were impromptu, and I believe related to our arrival: one little girl sang a line, which the rest took up in parts, forming a very pretty chorus. The whole scene made us unequivocally aware that we were seated on the shores of an island in the far-famed South Sea.

17th.—This day is reckoned in the log-book as Tuesday the 17th, instead of Monday the 16th, owing to our, so far, successful chase of the sun. Before breakfast the ship was hemmed in by a flotilla of canoes; and when the natives were allowed to come on board, I suppose there could not have been less than two hundred. It was the opinion of every one that it would have been difficult to have picked out an equal number from any other nation, who would have given so little trouble. Everybody brought something for sale: shells were the main article of trade. The Tahitians now fully understand the value of money, and prefer it to old clothes or other articles. The various coins, however, of English and Spanish denomination puzzle them, and they never seemed to think the small silver quite secure until changed into dollars. Some of the chiefs have accumulated considerable sums of money. One chief, not long since, offered 800 dollars (about 160*l*. sterling) for a small vessel; and frequently they purchase whale-boats and horses at the rate of from 50 to 100 dollars.

After breakfast I went on shore, and ascended the nearest slope to a height of between two and three thousand feet. The outer mountains are smooth and conical, but steep; and the old volcanic rocks, of which they are formed, have been cut through by many profound ravines, diverging from the central broken parts of the island to the coast. Having crossed the narrow low girt of inhabited and fertile land, I followed a smooth steep ridge between two of the deep ravines. The vegetation was singular, consisting almost exclusively of small dwarf ferns, mingled, higher up, with coarse grass; it was not very dissimilar from that on some of the Welsh hills, and this so close above the orchard of tropical plants on the coast was very surprising. At the highest point, which I reached, trees again appeared. Of the three zones of comparative luxuriance, the lower one owes its moisture, and therefore fertility, to its flatness; for, being scarcely raised above the level of the sea, the water from the higher land drains away slowly. The intermediate zone does not, like the upper one, reach into a damp and cloudy atmosphere, and therefore remains sterile. The woods in the upper zone are very pretty, tree-ferns replacing the cocoa-nuts on the coast. It must not, however, be supposed that these woods at all equal in splendour the forests of Brazil. The vast number of productions, which characterize a continent, cannot be expected to occur in an island.

From the highest point which I attained, there was a good view of the distant island of Eimeo, dependent on the same sovereign with Tahiti. On the lofty and broken pinnacles, white massive clouds were piled up, which formed an island in the blue sky, as Eimeo itself did in the blue ocean. The island, with the exception of one small gateway, is completely encircled by a reef. At this distance, a narrow but well-defined brilliantly white line was alone visible, where the waves first encountered the wall of coral. The mountains rose abruptly out of the glassy expanse of the lagoon, included within this narrow white line, outside which the heaving waters of the ocean were dark-coloured. The view was striking: it may aptly be compared to a framed engraving, where the frame represents the breakers, the marginal paper the smooth lagoon, and the drawing the island itself. When in the evening I descended from the mountain, a man, whom I had pleased with a trifling gift, met me, bringing with him hot roasted bananas, a pineapple, and cocoa-nuts. After walking under a burning sun, I do not know anything more delicious than the milk of a young cocoa-nut. Pine-apples are here so abundant that the people eat them in the same wasteful manner as we might turnips. They are of an excellent flavour—perhaps even better than those cultivated in England; and this I believe is the highest compliment which can be paid to any fruit. Before going on board, Mr. Wilson interpreted for me to the Tahitian who had paid me so adroit an attention, that I wanted him and another man to accompany me on a short excursion into the mountains.

18th.—In the morning I came on shore early, bringing with me some provisions in a bag, and two blankets for myself and servant. These were lashed to each end of a long pole, which was alternately carried by my Tahitian companions on their shoulders. These men are accustomed thus to carry, for a whole day, as much as fifty pounds at each end of their poles. I told my guides to provide themselves with food and clothing; but they said that there was plenty of food in the mountains, and for clothing, that their skins were sufficient. Our line of march was the valley of Tia-auru, down which a river flows into the sea by Point Venus. This is one of the principal streams in the island, and its source lies at the base of the loftiest central pinnacles, which rise to a height of about 7000 feet. The whole island is so mountainous that the only way to penetrate into the interior is to follow up the valleys. Our road, at first, lay through woods which bordered each side of the river; and the glimpses of the lofty central peaks, seen as through an avenue, with here and there a waving cocoa-nut tree on one side, were extremely picturesque. The valley soon began to narrow, and the sides to grow lofty and more precipitous. After having walked between three and four hours, we found the width of the ravine scarcely exceeded that of the bed of the stream. On each hand the walls were nearly vertical; yet from the soft nature of the volcanic strata, trees and a rank vegetation sprung from every projecting ledge. These precipices must have been some thousand feet high; and the whole formed a mountain gorge far more magnificent than anything which I had ever before beheld. Until the mid-day sun stood vertically over the ravine, the air felt cool and damp, but now it became very sultry. Shaded by a ledge of rock, beneath a façade of columnar lava, we ate our dinner. My guides had already procured a dish of small fish and fresh-water prawns. They carried with them a small net stretched on a hoop; and where the water was deep and in eddies, they dived, and like otters, with their eyes open followed the fish into holes and corners, and thus caught them.

The Tahitians have the dexterity of amphibious animals in the water. An anecdote mentioned by Ellis shows how much they feel at home in this element. When a horse was landing for Pomarre in 1817, the slings broke, and it fell into the wa-ter: immediately the natives jumped overboard, and by their cries and vain efforts at assistance almost drowned it. As soon, however, as it reached the shore, the whole population took to flight, and tried to hide themselves from the man-carrying pig, as they christened the horse.

A little higher up, the river divided itself into three little streams. The two northern ones were impracticable, owing to a succession of waterfalls which descended from the jagged summit of the highest mountain; the other to all appearance was equally inaccessible, but we managed to ascend it by a most extraordinary road. The sides of the valley were here nearly precipitous; but, as frequently happens with stratified rocks, small ledges projected, which were thickly covered by wild bananas, liliaceous plants, and other luxuriant productions of the tropics. The Tahitians, by climbing amongst these ledges, searching for fruit, had discovered a track by which the whole precipice could be scaled. The first ascent from the valley was very dangerous; for it was necessary to pass a steeply-inclined face of naked rock, by the aid of ropes which we brought with us. How any person discovered that this formidable spot was the only point where the side of the mountain was practicable, I cannot imagine. We then cautiously walked along one of the ledges till we came to one of the three streams. This ledge formed a flat spot, above which a beautiful cascade, some hundred feet in height, poured down its waters, and beneath, another high cascade fell into the main stream in the valley below. From this cool and shady recess we made a circuit to avoid the overhanging waterfall. As before, we followed little projecting ledges, the danger being partly concealed by the thickness of the vegetation. In passing from one of the ledges to another, there was a vertical wall of rock. One of the Tahitians, a fine active man, placed the trunk of a tree against this, climbed up it, and then by the aid of crevices reached the summit. He fixed the ropes to a projecting point, and lowered them for our dog and luggage, and then we clambered up ourselves. Beneath the ledge on which the dead tree was placed, the precipice must have been five or six hundred feet deep; and if the abyss had not been partly concealed by the overhanging ferns and lilies, my head would have turned giddy, and nothing should have induced me to have attempted it. We continued to ascend, sometimes along ledges, and sometimes along knife-edged ridges, having on each hand profound ravines. In the Cordillera I have seen mountains on a far grander scale, but for abruptness, nothing at all comparable with this. In the evening we reached a flat little spot on the banks of the same stream, which we had continued to follow, and which descends in a chain of waterfalls: here we bivouacked for the night. On each side of the ravine there were great beds of the mountain-banana, covered with ripe fruit. Many of these plants were from twenty to twenty-five feet high, and from three to four in circumference. By the aid of strips of bark for rope, the stems of bamboos for rafters, and the large leaf of the banana for a thatch, the Tahitians in a few minutes built us an excellent house; and with withered leaves made a soft bed.

They then proceeded to make a fire, and cook our evening meal. A light was procured, by rubbing a blunt-pointed stick in a groove made in another, as if with intention of deepening it, until by the friction the dust became ignited. A peculiarly white and very light wood (the Hibiscus tiliaceus) is alone used for this purpose: it is the same which serves for poles to carry any burden, and for the floating outriggers to their canoes. The fire was produced in a few seconds: but to a person who does not understand the art, it requires, as I found, the greatest exertion; but at last, to my great pride, I succeeded in igniting the dust. The Gaucho in the Pampas uses a different method: taking an elastic stick about eighteen inches long, he presses one end on his breast, and the other pointed end into a hole in a piece of wood, and then rapidly turns the curved part, like a carpenter's centre-bit. The Tahitians having made a small fire of sticks, placed a score of stones, of about the size of cricket-balls, on the burning wood. In about ten minutes the sticks were consumed, and the stones hot. They had previously folded up in small parcels of leaves, pieces of beef, fish, ripe and unripe bananas, and the tops of the wild arum. These green parcels were laid in a layer between two layers of the hot stones, and the whole then covered up with earth, so that no smoke or steam could escape. In about a quarter of an hour, the whole was most deliciously cooked. The choice green parcels were now laid on a cloth of banana leaves, and with a cocoa-nut shell we drank the cool water of the running stream; and thus we enjoyed our rustic meal.

I could not look on the surrounding plants without admiration. On every side were forests of banana; the fruit of which, though serving for food in various ways, lay in heaps decaying on the ground. In front of us there was an extensive brake of wild sugar-cane; and the stream was shaded by the dark green knotted stem of the Ava,—so famous in former days for its powerful intoxicating effects.[1] I chewed a piece, and found that

[1] [Editor] Ava is a variety of pepper, Piper methysticum, that grows throughout the South Pacific. Once widely chewed, but may also be grated and infused to make a beverage with properties

it had an acrid and unpleasant taste, which would have induced any one at once to have pronounced it poisonous. Thanks to the missionaries, this plant now thrives only in these deep ravines, innocuous to every one. Close by I saw the wild arum, the roots of which, when well baked, are good to eat, and the young leaves better than spinach. There was the wild yam, and a liliaceous plant called Ti, which grows in abundance, and has a soft brown root, in shape and size like a huge log of wood: this served us for dessert, for it is as sweet as treacle, and with a pleasant taste. There were, moreover, several other wild fruits, and useful vegetables. The little stream, besides its cool water, produced eels and cray-fish. I did indeed admire this scene, when I compared it with an uncultivated one in the temperate zones. I felt the force of the remark, that man, at least savage man, with his reasoning powers only partly developed, is the child of the tropics.

As the evening drew to a close, I strolled beneath the gloomy shade of the bananas up the course of the stream. My walk was soon brought to a close, by coming to a waterfall between two and three hundred feet high; and again above this there was another. I mention all these waterfalls in this one brook, to give a general idea of the inclination of the land. In the little recess where the water fell, it did not appear that a breath of wind had ever blown. The thin edges of the great leaves of the banana, damp with spray, were unbroken, instead of being, as is so generally the case, split into a thousand shreds. From our position, almost suspended on the mountain-side, there were glimpses into the depths of the neighbouring valleys; and the lofty points of the central mountains, towering up within sixty degrees of the zenith, hid half the evening sky. Thus seated, it was a sublime spectacle to watch the shades of night gradually obscuring the last and highest pinnacles.

Before we laid ourselves down to sleep, the elder Tahitian fell on his knees, and with closed eyes repeated a long prayer in his native tongue. He prayed as a Christian should do, with fitting reverence, and without the fear of ridicule or any ostentation of piety. At our meals neither of the men would taste food, without saying beforehand a short grace. Those travel-

somewhat similar to alcohol, that is "stimulating" in small doses, stupefying in large, but its narcotic effects are more pronounced than those of alcohol. Is drunk at gatherings much like cocktail parties. Also called Awa, Kawa, or Kava.

lers who think that a Tahitian prays only when the eyes of the missionary are fixed on him, should have slept with us that night on the mountain-side. Before morning it rained very heavily; but the good thatch of banana-leaves kept us dry.

November 19*th*.—At daylight my friends, after their morning prayer, prepared an excellent breakfast in the same manner as in the evening. They themselves certainly partook of it largely; indeed I never saw any men eat near so much. I suppose such enormously capacious stomachs must be the effect of a large part of their diet consisting of fruit and vegetables, which contain, in a given bulk, a comparatively small portion of nutriment. Unwittingly, I was the means of my companions breaking, as I afterwards learned, one of their own laws and resolutions: I took with me a flask of spirits, which they could not refuse to partake of; but as often as they drank a little, they put their fingers before their mouths, and uttered the word "Missionary." About two years ago, although the use of the ava was prevented, drunkenness from the introduction of spirits became very prevalent. The missionaries prevailed on a few good men, who saw that their country was rapidly going to ruin, to join with them in a Temperance Society. From good sense or shame, all the chiefs and the queen were at last persuaded to join. Immediately a law was passed, that no spirits should be allowed to be introduced into the island, and that he who sold and he who bought the forbidden article should be punished by a fine. With remarkable justice, a certain period was allowed for stock in hand to be sold, before the law came into effect. But when it did, a general search was made, in which even the houses of the missionaries were not exempted, and all the ava (as the natives call all ardent spirits) was poured on the ground. When one reflects on the effect of intemperance on the aborigines of the two Americas, I think it will be acknowledged that every well-wisher of Tahiti owes no common debt of gratitude to the missionaries. As long as the little island of St. Helena remained under the government of the East India Company, spirits, owing to the great injury they had produced, were not allowed to be imported; but wine was supplied from the Cape of Good Hope. It is rather a striking, and not very gratifying fact, that in the same year that spirits were allowed to be sold in St. Helena, their use was banished from Tahiti by the free will of the people.

After breakfast we proceeded on our journey. As my object was merely to see a little of the interior scenery, we returned by another track, which descended into the main valley lower down. For some distance we wound, by a most intricate path, along the side of the mountain which formed the valley. In the less precipitous parts we passed through extensive groves of the wild banana. The Tahitians, with their naked, tattooed bodies, their heads ornamented with flowers, and seen in the dark shade of these groves, would have formed a fine picture of man inhabiting some primeval land. In our descent we followed the line of ridges; these were exceedingly narrow, and for considerable lengths steep as a ladder; but all clothed with vegetation. The extreme care necessary in poising each step rendered the walk fatiguing. I did not cease to wonder at these ravines and precipices: when viewing the country from one of the knife-edged ridges, the point of support was so small, that the effect was nearly the same as it must be from a balloon. In this descent we had occasion to use the ropes only once, at the point where we entered the main valley. We slept under the same ledge of rock where we had dined the day before: the night was fine, but from the depth and narrowness of the gorge, profoundly dark.

Before actually seeing this country, I found it difficult to understand two facts mentioned by Ellis; namely, that after the murderous battles of former times, the survivors on the conquered side retired into the mountains, where a handful of men could resist a multitude. Certainly half-a-dozen men, at the spot where the Tahitian reared the old tree, could easily have repulsed thousands. Secondly, that after the introduction of Christianity, there were wild men who lived in the mountains, and whose retreats were unknown to the more civilized inhabitants.

November 20th.—In the morning we started early, and reached Matavai at noon. On the road we met a large party of noble athletic men, going for wild bananas. I found that the ship, on account of the difficulty in watering, had moved to the harbour of Papawa, to which place I immediately walked. This is a very pretty spot. The cove is surrounded by reefs, and the water as smooth as in a lake. The cultivated ground, with its beautiful productions, interspersed with cottages, comes close down to the water's edge.

From the varying accounts which I had read before reaching these islands, I was very anxious to form, from my own observation, a judgment of their moral state,—although such judgment would necessarily be very imperfect. First impressions at all times very much depend on one's previously-acquired ideas.

My notions were drawn from Ellis's "Polynesian Researches" —an admirable and most interesting work, but naturally looking at every thing under a favourable point of view; from Beechey's Voyage; and from that of Kotzebue, which is strongly adverse to the whole missionary system. He who compares these three accounts will, I think, form a tolerably accurate conception of the present state of Tahiti. One of my impressions, which I took from the two last authorities, was decidedly incorrect; viz., that the Tahitians had become a gloomy race, and lived in fear of the missionaries. Of the latter feeling I saw no trace, unless, indeed, fear and respect be confounded under one name. Instead of discontent being a common feeling, it would be difficult in Europe to pick out of a crowd half so many merry and happy faces. The prohibition of the flute and dancing is inveighed against as wrong and foolish; —the more than presbyterian manner of keeping the sabbath is looked at in a similar light. On these points I will not pretend to offer any opinion, in opposition to men who have resided as many years as I was days on the island.

On the whole, it appears to me that the morality and religion of the inhabitants are highly creditable. There are many who attack, even more acrimoniously than Kotzebue, both the missionaries, their system, and the effects produced by it. Such reasoners never compare the present state with that of the island only twenty years ago; nor even with that of Europe at this day; but they compare it with the high standard of Gospel perfection. They expect the missionaries to effect that which the Apostles themselves failed to do. In as much as the condition of the people falls short of this high standard, blame is attached to the missionary, instead of credit for that which he has effected. They forget, or will not remember, that human sacrifices, and the power of an idolatrous priesthood—a system of profligacy unparalleled in any other part of the world—infanticide a consequence of that system—bloody wars, where the conquerors spared neither women nor children—that all these have been abolished; and that dishonesty, intemperance, and licentiousness have been greatly reduced by the introduction of Christianity. In a voyager to forget these things is base ingratitude; for should he chance to be at the point of shipwreck on some unknown coast, he will most devoutly pray that the lesson of the missionary may have extended thus far.

In point of morality, the virtue of the women, it has been often said, is most open to exception. But before they are

blamed too severely, it will be well distinctly to call to mind
the scenes described by Captain Cook and Mr. Banks, in which
the grandmothers and mothers of the present race played a
part. Those who are most severe, should consider how much of
the morality of the women in Europe, is owing to the system
early impressed by mothers on their daughters, and how much
in each individual case to the precepts of religion. But it is
useless to argue against such reasoners;—I believe that, disappointed in not finding the field of licentiousness quite so open
as formerly, they will not give credit to a morality which they
do not wish to practise, or to a religion which they undervalue,
if not despise.

Sunday, 22nd.—The harbour of Papiéte, where the queen
resides, may be considered as the capital of the island: it is
also the seat of government, and the chief resort of shipping.
Captain Fitz Roy took a party there this day to hear divine
service, first in the Tahitian language, and afterwards in our
own. Mr. Pritchard, the leading missionary in the island, performed the service. The chapel consisted of a large airy framework of wood; and it was filled to excess by tidy, clean people,
of all ages and both sexes. I was rather disappointed in the
apparent degree of attention; but I believe my expectations
were raised too high. At all events the appearance was quite
equal to that in a country church in England. The singing of
the hymns was decidedly very pleasing; but the language from
the pulpit, although fluently delivered, did not sound well: a
constant repetition of words, like *"tata ta, mata mai,"* rendered
it monotonous. After English service, a party returned on foot
to Matavai. It was a pleasant walk, sometimes along the sea-
beach and sometimes under the shade of the many beautiful
trees.

About two years ago, a small vessel under English colours
was plundered by some of the inhabitants of the Low Islands,
which were then under the dominion of the Queen of Tahiti. It
was believed that the perpetrators were instigated to this act
by some indiscreet laws issued by her majesty. The British government demanded compensation; which was acceded to, and
a sum of nearly three thousand dollars was agreed to be paid
on the first of last September. The Commodore at Lima ordered Captain Fitz Roy to inquire concerning this debt, and to
demand satisfaction if it were not paid. Captain Fitz Roy accordingly requested an interview with the Queen Pomarre,
since famous from the ill-treatment she has received from the

French;[2] and a parliament was held to consider the question, at which all the principal chiefs of the island, and the queen, were assembled. I will not attempt to describe what took place, after the interesting account given by Captain Fitz Roy. The money, it appeared, had not been paid; perhaps the alleged reasons were rather equivocal; but otherwise I cannot sufficiently express our general surprise at the extreme good sense, the reasoning powers, moderation, candour, and prompt resolution, which were displayed on all sides. I believe we all left the meeting with a very different opinion of the Tahitians, from what we entertained when we entered. The chiefs and people resolved to subscribe and complete the sum which was wanting; Captain Fitz Roy urged that it was hard that their private property should be sacrificed for the crimes of distant islanders. They replied, that they were grateful for his consideration, but that Pomarre was their Queen, and that they were determined to help her in this her difficulty. This resolution and its prompt execution, for a book was opened early the next morning, made a perfect conclusion to this very remarkable scene of loyalty and good feeling.

After the main discussion was ended, several of the chiefs took the opportunity of asking Captain Fitz Roy many intelligent questions on international customs and laws, relating to the treatment of ships and foreigners. On some points, as soon as the decision was made, the law was issued verbally on the spot. This Tahitian parliament lasted for several hours; and when it was over Captain Fitz Roy invited Queen Pomarre to pay the *Beagle* a visit.

November 25th.—In the evening four boats were sent for her majesty; the ship was dressed with flags, and the yards manned on her coming on board. She was accompanied by most of the chiefs. The behaviour of all was very proper: they begged for nothing, and seemed much pleased with Captain Fitz Roy's presents. The Queen is a large awkward woman, without any beauty, grace, or dignity. She has only one royal attribute: a perfect immoveability of expression under all circumstances, and that rather a sullen one. The rockets were most admired; and a deep "Oh!" could be heard from the shore, all round

2 [Editor] In 1842, the French attempted to depose Queen Pomarre when she protested against the act of several Tahitian chiefs in asking that Tahiti be taken under French protection. The attempt to oust her was halted by the French courts. In 1852, she abdicated in favor of a son.

the dark bay, after each explosion. The sailors' songs were also much admired; and the queen said she thought that one of the most boisterous ones certainly could not be a hymn! The royal party did not return on shore till past midnight.

26th.—In the evening, with a gentle land-breeze, a course was steered for New Zealand; and as the sun set, we had a farewell view of the mountains of Tahiti—the island to which every voyager has offered up his tribute of admiration.

December 19th.—In the evening we saw in the distance New Zealand. We may now consider that we have nearly crossed the Pacific. It is necessary to sail over this great ocean to comprehend its immensity. Moving quickly onwards for weeks together, we meet with nothing but the same blue, profoundly deep, ocean. Even within the archipelagoes, the islands are mere specks, and far distant one from the other. Accustomed to look at maps drawn on a small scale, where dots, shading, and names are crowded together, we do not rightly judge how infinitely small the proportion of dry land is to the water of this vast expanse. The meridian of the Antipodes has likewise been passed; and now every league, it made us happy to think, was one league nearer to England. These Antipodes call to one's mind old recollections of childish doubt and wonder. Only the other day I looked forward to this airy barrier as a definite point in our voyage homewards; but now I find it, and all such resting-places for the imagination, are like shadows, which a man moving onwards cannot catch. A gale of wind lasting for some days, has lately given us full leisure to measure the future stages in our long homeward voyage, and to wish most earnestly for its termination.

December 21st.—Early in the morning we entered the Bay of Islands,[3] and being becalmed for some hours near the mouth, we did not reach the anchorage till the middle of the day. The country is hilly, with a smooth outline, and is deeply intersected by numerous arms of the sea extending from the bay. The surface appears from a distance as if clothed with coarse pasture, but this in truth is nothing but fern. On the more distant hills, as well as in parts of the valleys, there is a good deal of woodland. The general tint of the landscape is not

[3] [Editor] A small bay near the northern tip of New Zealand's North Island, and relatively remote from New Zealand's present centers of population around Auckland (near the center of the island) and Wellington (on Cook Strait, between North and South Islands).

a bright green; and it resembles the country a short distance to the south of Concepcion in Chile. In several parts of the bay, little villages of square tidy-looking houses are scattered close down to the water's edge. Three whaling-ships were lying at anchor, and a canoe every now and then crossed from shore to shore; with these exceptions, an air of extreme quietness reigned over the whole district. Only a single canoe came alongside. This, and the aspect of the whole scene, afforded a remarkable, and not very pleasing contrast, with our joyful and boisterous welcome at Tahiti.

In the afternoon we went on shore to one of the larger groups of houses, which yet hardly deserves the title of a village. Its name is Pahia: it is the residence of the missionaries; and there are no native residents except servants and labourers. In the vicinity of the Bay of Islands, the number of Englishmen, including their families, amounts to between two and three hundred. All the cottages, many of which are whitewashed and look very neat, are the property of the English. The hovels of the natives are so diminutive and paltry, that they can scarcely be perceived from a distance. At Pahia, it was quite pleasing to behold the English flowers in the gardens before the houses; there were roses of several kinds, honeysuckle, jasmine, stocks, and whole hedges of sweetbriar.

December 22nd.—In the morning I went out walking; but I soon found that the country was very impracticable. All the hills are thickly covered with tall fern, together with a low bush which grows like a cypress; and very little ground has been cleared or cultivated. I then tried the sea-beach; but proceeding towards either hand, my walk was soon stopped by salt-water creeks and deep brooks. The communication between the inhabitants of the different parts of the bay, is (as in Chiloe) almost entirely kept up by boats. I was surprised to find that almost every hill which I ascended, had been at some former time more or less fortified. The summits were cut into steps or successive terraces, and frequently they had been protected by deep trenches. I afterwards observed that the principal hills inland in like manner showed an artificial outline. These are the Pas, so frequently mentioned by Captain Cook under the name of "hippah;" the difference of sound being owing to the prefixed article.

That the Pas had formerly been much used, was evident from the piles of shells, and the pits in which, as I was informed, sweet potatoes used to be kept as a reserve. As there was no water on these hills, the defenders could never have anticipated a long siege, but only a hurried attack for plunder, against which the successive terraces would have afforded good protection. The general introduction of fire-arms has changed the whole system of warfare; and an exposed situation on the top of a hill is now worse than useless. The Pas in consequence are, at the present day, always built on a level piece of ground. They consist of a double stockade of thick and tall posts, placed in a zigzag line, so that every part can be flanked. Within the stockade a mound of earth is thrown up, behind which the defenders can rest in safety, or use their fire-arms over it. On the level of the ground little archways sometimes pass through this breastwork, by which means the defenders can crawl out to the stockade to reconnoitre their enemies. The Rev. W. Williams, who gave me this account, added, that in one Pas he had noticed spurs or buttresses projecting on the inner and protected side of the mound of earth. On asking the chief the use of them, he replied, that if two or three of his men were shot, their neighbours would not see the bodies, and so be discouraged.

These Pas are considered by the New Zealanders as very perfect means of defence: for the attacking force is never so well disciplined as to rush in a body to the stockade, cut it down, and effect their entry. When a tribe goes to war, the chief cannot order one party to go here and another there; but every man fights in the manner which best pleases himself; and to each separate individual to approach a stockade defended by fire-arms must appear certain death. I should think a more warlike race of inhabitants could not be found in any part of the world than the New Zealanders. Their conduct on first seeing a ship, as described by Captain Cook, strongly illustrates this: the act of throwing volleys of stones at so great and novel an object, and their defiance of "Come on shore and we will kill and eat you all," shows uncommon boldness. This warlike spirit is evident in many of their customs, and even in their smallest actions. If a New Zealander is struck, although but in joke, the blow must be returned; and of this I saw an instance with one of our officers.

At the present day, from the progress of civilization, there is much less warfare, except among some of the southern tribes. I heard a characteristic anecdote of what took place some time ago in the south. A missionary found a chief and his tribe in preparation for war;—their muskets clean and bright, and their ammunition ready. He reasoned long on the inutility of the war, and the little provocation which had been given for it. The chief was much shaken in his resolution, and seemed in doubt: but at length it occurred to him that a barrel of his gunpowder was in a bad state, and that it would not keep much longer. This was brought forward as an unanswerable argument for the necessity of immediately declaring war: the idea of allowing so much good gunpowder to spoil was not to be thought of; and this settled the point. I was told by the missionaries that in the life of Shongi, the chief who visited England, the love of war was the one and lasting spring of every action. The tribe in which he was a principal chief, had at one time been much oppressed by another tribe, from the Thames River. A solemn oath was taken by the men, that when their boys should grow up, and they should be powerful enough, they would never forget or forgive these injuries. To fulfil this oath appears to have been Shongi's chief motive for going to England; and when there it was his sole object. Presents were valued only as they could be converted into arms; of the arts, those alone interested him which were connected with the manufacture of arms. When at Sydney, Shongi, by a strange coincidence, met the hostile chief of the Thames River at the house of Mr. Marsden: their conduct was civil to each other; but Shongi told him that when again in New Zealand he would never cease to carry war into his country. The challenge was accepted; and Shongi on his return fulfilled the threat to the utmost letter. The tribe on the Thames River was utterly overthrown, and the chief to whom the challenge had been given was himself killed. Shongi, although harbouring such deep feelings of hatred and revenge, is described as having been a good-natured person.

In the evening I went with Captain Fitz Roy and Mr. Baker, one of the missionaries, to pay a visit to Kororadika: we wandered about the village, and saw and conversed with many of the people, both men, women, and children. Looking at the New Zealander, one naturally compares him with the Tahitian; both belonging to the same family of mankind. The comparison, however, tells heavily against the New Zealander. He may, perhaps, be superior in energy, but in every other respect his character is of a much lower order. One glance at their respective expressions, brings conviction to the mind that one is a savage, the other a civilized man. It would be vain to seek in the whole of New Zealand a person with the face and mien of the old Tahitian chief Utamme. No doubt the extraordinary manner in which tattooing is here practised, gives a disagreeable expression to their countenances. The complicated but symmetrical figures covering the whole face, puzzle and mislead an unaccustomed eye: it is moreover probable, that the deep incisions, by destroying the play of the superficial muscles, give an air of rigid inflexibility. But, besides this, there is a twinkling in the eye, which cannot indicate any thing but cunning and ferocity. Their figures are tall and bulky; but not comparable in elegance with those of the working-classes in Tahiti.

Both their persons and houses are filthily dirty and offensive: the idea of washing either their bodies or their clothes never seems to enter their heads. I saw a chief, who was wearing a shirt black and matted with filth, and when asked how it came to be so dirty, he replied, with surprise, "Do not you see it is an old one?" Some of the men have shirts; but the common dress is one or two large blankets, generally black with dirt, which are thrown over their shoulders in a very inconvenient and awkward fashion. A few of the principal chiefs have decent suits of English clothes; but these are only worn on great occasions.

December 23rd.—At a place called Waimate, about fifteen miles from the Bay of Islands, and midway between the eastern and western coasts, the missionaries have purchased some land for agricultural purposes. I had been introduced to the Rev. W. Williams, who, upon my expressing a wish, invited me to pay him a visit there. Mr. Bushby, the British resident, offered to take me in his boat by a creek, where I should see a pretty waterfall, and by which means my walk would be shortened. He likewise procured for me a guide. Upon asking a neighbouring chief to recommend a man, the chief himself offered to go; but his ignorance of the value of money was so complete, that at first he asked how many pounds I would give him, but afterwards was well contented with two dollars. When I showed the chief a very small bundle, which I wanted carried, it became absolutely necessary for him to take a slave. These feelings of pride are beginning to wear away; but formerly a leading man would sooner have died, than undergone the indignity of carrying the smallest burden. My companion was a light active man, dressed in a dirty blanket, and with his face completely tattooed. He had formerly been a great warrior. He appeared to be on very cordial terms with Mr. Bushby; but at various times they had quarrelled violently. Mr. Bushby remarked that a little quiet irony would frequently silence any one of these natives in their most blustering moments. This chief has come and harangued Mr. Bushby in a hectoring manner, saying, "A great chief, a great man, a friend of mine, has come to pay me a visit—you must give him something good to eat, some fine presents, &c." Mr. Bushby has allowed him to finish his discourse, and then has quietly replied by some such answer as, "What else shall your slave do for you?" The man would then instantly, with a very comical expression, cease his braggadocio.

Some time ago, Mr. Bushby suffered a far more serious attack. A chief and a party of men tried to break into his house in the middle of the night, and not finding this so easy, commenced a brisk firing with their muskets. Mr. Bushby was slightly wounded; but the party was at length driven away. Shortly afterwards it was discovered who was the aggressor; and a general meeting of the chiefs was convened to consider the case. It was considered by the New Zealanders as very atrocious, inasmuch as it was a night attack, and that Mrs. Bushby was lying ill in the house: this latter circumstance, much to their honour, being considered in all cases as a protection. The chiefs agreed to confiscate the land of the aggressor to the King of England. The whole proceeding, however, in thus trying and punishing a chief was entirely without precedent. The aggressor, moreover, lost caste in the estimation of his equals; and this was considered by the British as of more consequence than the confiscation of his land.

As the boat was shoving off, a second chief stepped into her, who only wanted the amusement of the passage up and down the creek. I never saw a more horrid and ferocious expression than this man had. It immediately struck me I had somewhere seen his likeness: it will be found in Retzsch's outlines to Schiller's ballad of Fridolin, where two men are pushing Robert into the burning iron furnace. It is the man who has his arm on Robert's breast. Physiognomy here spoke the truth; this chief had been a notorious murderer, and was an arrant coward to boot. At the point where the boat landed, Mr. Bushby accompanied me a few hundred yards on the road: I could not help admiring the cool impudence of the hoary old villain, whom we left lying in the boat, when he shouted to Mr. Bushby, "Do not you stay long, I shall be tired of waiting here."

We now commenced our walk. The road lay along a well-beaten path, bordered on each side by the tall fern, which covers the whole country. After travelling some miles, we came to a little country village, where a few hovels were collected together, and some patches of ground cultivated with potatoes. The introduction of the potato has been the most essential benefit to the island; it is now much more used than any native vegetable. New Zealand is favoured by one great natural advantage; namely, that the inhabitants can never perish from famine. The whole country abounds with fern; and the roots of this plant, if not very palatable, yet contain much nutriment. A native can always subsist on these, and on the shell-fish, which are abundant on all parts of the sea-coast. The villages are chiefly conspicuous by the platforms which are raised on four posts ten or twelve feet above the ground, and on which the produce of the fields is kept secure from all accidents.

On coming near one of the huts I was much amused by seeing in due form the ceremony of rubbing, or, as it ought to be called, pressing noses. The women, on our first approach, began uttering something in a most dolorous voice, they then squatted themselves down and held up their faces; my companion standing over them, one after another, placed the bridge of his nose at right angles to theirs, and commenced pressing. This lasted rather longer than a cordial shake of the hand with us; and as we vary the force of the grasp of the hand in shaking, so do they in pressing. During the process they uttered comfortable little grunts, very much in the same manner as two pigs do, when rubbing against each other. I noticed that the slave would press noses with any one he met, indifferently either before or after his master the chief. Although among these savages, the chief has absolute power of life and death over his slave, yet there is an entire absence of ceremony between them. Mr. Burchell has remarked the same thing in Southern Africa, with the rude Bachapins. Where civilization has arrived at a certain point, complex formalities soon arise between the different grades of society: thus at Tahiti all were formerly obliged to uncover themselves as low as the waist in presence of the king.

The ceremony of pressing noses having been duly completed with all present, we seated ourselves in a circle in the front of one of the hovels, and rested there half-an-hour. All the hovels have nearly the same form and dimensions, and all agree in being filthily dirty. They resemble a cow-shed with one end open, but having a partition a little way within, with a square hole in it, making a small gloomy chamber. In this the inhabitants keep all their property, and when the weather is cold they sleep there. They eat, however, and pass their time in the open part in front. My guides having finished their pipes, we continued our walk. The path led through the same undulating country, the whole uniformly clothed as before with fern. On our right hand we had a serpentine river, the banks of which were fringed with trees, and here and there on the hill sides there was a clump of wood. The whole scene, in spite of its green colour, had rather a desolate aspect. The sight of so much fern impresses the mind with an idea of sterility: this, however, is not correct; for wherever the fern grows thick and breast-high, the land by tillage becomes productive. Some of the residents think that all this extensive open country originally was covered with forests, and that it has been cleared by fire. It is said, that by digging in the barest spots, lumps of the kind of resin which flows from the kauri pine are frequently found. The natives had an evident motive in clearing the country; for the fern, formerly a staple article of food, flourishes only in the open cleared tracks. The almost entire absence of associated grasses, which forms so remarkable a feature in the vegetation of this island, may perhaps be accounted for by the land having been aboriginally covered with forest-trees.

The soil is volcanic; in several parts we passed over slaggy lavas, and craters could clearly be distinguished on several of the neighbouring hills. Although the scenery is nowhere beautiful, and only occasionally pretty, I enjoyed my walk. I should have enjoyed it more, if my companion, the chief, had not possessed extraordinary conversational powers. I knew only three words; "good," "bad," and "yes:" and with these I answered all his remarks, without of course having understood one word he said. This, however, was quite sufficient: I was a good listener, an agreeable person, and he never ceased talking to me.

At length we reached Waimate. After having passed over so many miles of an uninhabited useless country, the sudden appearance of an English farm-house, and its well-dressed fields, placed there as if by an enchanter's wand, was exceedingly pleasant. Mr. Williams not being at home, I received in Mr. Davies's house a cordial welcome. After drinking tea with his family party, we took a stroll about the farm. At Waimate there are three large houses, where the missionary gentlemen, Messrs. Williams, Davies, and Clarke, reside; and near them are the huts of the native labourers. On an adjoining slope, fine crops of barley and wheat were standing in full ear; and in another part, fields of potatoes and clover. But I cannot attempt to describe all I saw; there were large gardens, with every fruit and vegetable which England produces; and many belonging to a warmer clime. I may instance asparagus, kidney beans, cucumbers, rhubarb, apples, pears, figs, peaches, apricots, grapes, olives, gooseberries, currants, hops, gorse for fences, and English oaks; also many kinds of flowers. Around the farm-yard there were stables, a thrashing-barn with its winnowing machine, a blacksmith's forge, and on the ground ploughshares and other tools: in the middle was that happy mixture of pigs and poultry, lying comfortably together, as in every English farm-yard. At the distance of a few hundred yards, where the water of a little rill had been dammed up into a pool, there was a large and substantial water-mill.

All this is very surprising, when it is considered that five years ago nothing but the fern flourished here. Moreover, native workmanship, taught by the missionaries, has effected this change;—the lesson of the missionary is the enchanter's wand. The house had been built, the windows framed, the fields ploughed, and even the trees grafted, by the New Zealander. At the mill, a New Zealander was seen powdered white with flour, like his brother miller in England. When I looked at this whole scene, I thought it admirable. It was not merely that England was brought vividly before my mind; yet, as the evening drew to a close, the domestic sounds, the fields of corn, the distant undulating country with its trees might well have been mistaken for our father-land: nor was it the triumphant feeling at seeing what Englishmen could effect; but rather the high hopes thus inspired for the future progress of this fine island.

Several young men, redeemed by the missionaries from slavery, were employed on the farm. They were dressed in a shirt, jacket, and trousers, and had a respectable appearance. Judging from one trifling anecdote, I should think they must be honest. When walking in the fields, a young labourer came up to Mr. Davies, and gave him a knife and gimlet, saying that he had found them on the road, and did not know to whom they belonged! These young men and boys appeared very merry and good-humoured. In the evening I saw a party of them at cricket: when I thought of the austerity of which the missionaries have been accused, I was amused by observing one of their own sons taking an active part in the game. A more decided and pleasing change was manifested in the young women, who acted as servants within the houses. Their clean, tidy, and healthy appearance, like that of dairy-maids in England, formed a wonderful contrast with the women of the filthy hovels in Kororadika. The wives of the missionaries tried to persuade them not to be tattooed; but a famous operator having arrived from the south, they said, "We really must just have a few lines on our lips; else when we grow old, our lips will shrivel, and we shall be so very ugly." There is not nearly so much tattooing as formerly; but as it is a badge of distinction between the chief and the slave, it will probably long be practised. So soon does any train of ideas become habitual, that the missionaries told me that even in their eyes a plain face looked mean, and not like that of a New Zealand gentleman.

Late in the evening I went to Mr. Williams's house, where I passed the night. I found there a large party of children, collected together for Christmas-day, and all sitting round a table at tea. I never saw a nicer or more merry group; and to think that this was in the centre of the land of cannibalism, murder, and all atrocious crimes! The cordiality and happiness so plainly pictured in the faces of the little circle, appeared equally felt by the older persons of the mission.

December 24*th.*—In the morning, prayers were read in the native tongue to the whole family. After breakfast I rambled about the gardens and farm. This was a market-day, when the natives of the surrounding hamlets bring their potatoes, Indian corn, or pigs, to exchange for blankets, tobacco, and sometimes, through the persuasions of the missionaries, for soap. Mr. Davies's eldest son, who manages a farm of his own, is the man of business in the market. The children of the missionaries, who came while young to the island, understand the language better than their parents, and can get anything more readily done by the natives.

A little before noon Messrs. Williams and Davies walked with me to part of a neighbouring forest, to show me the famous kauri pine. I measured one of these noble trees, and found it thirty-one feet in circumference above the roots. There was another close by, which I did not see, thirty-three feet; and I heard of one no less than forty feet. These trees are remarkable for their smooth cylindrical boles, which run up to a height of sixty, and even ninety feet, with a nearly equal diameter, and without a single branch. The crown of branches at the summit is out of all proportion small to the trunk; and the leaves are likewise small compared with the branches. The forest was here almost composed of the kauri; and the largest trees, from the parallelism of their sides, stood up like gigantic columns of wood. The timber of the kauri is the most valuable production of the island; moreover, a quantity of resin oozes from the bark, which is sold at a penny a pound to the Americans, but its use was then unknown. Some of the New Zealand forests must be impenetrable to an extraordinary degree. Mr. Matthews informed me that one forest only thirty-four miles in width, and separating two inhabited districts, had only lately, for the first time, been crossed. He and another missionary, each with a party of about fifty men, undertook to open a road; but it cost them more than a fortnight's labour! In the woods I saw very few birds. With regard to animals, it is a most remarkable fact, that so large an island, extending over more than 700 miles in latitude, and in many parts ninety broad, with varied stations, a fine climate, and land of all heights, from 14,000 feet downwards, with the exception of a small rat, did not possess one indigenous animal.[4] The several species of that gigantic genus of birds, the Deinornis,[5] seem here to have replaced mammiferous quadrupeds, in the same manner as the reptiles still do at the Galapagos archipelago. It is said that the common Norway rat, in the short space of two years, annihilated in this northern end of the island, the New Zealand species. In many places I noticed several sorts of weeds, which, like the rats, I was forced to own as countrymen. A leek has overrun whole districts, and will prove very troublesome, but it was imported as a favour by a French vessel. The common dock is also widely disseminated, and will, I fear, for ever remain a proof of the rascality of an Englishman, who sold the seeds for those of the tobacco plant.

On returning from our pleasant walk to the house, I dined with Mr. Williams; and then, a horse being lent me, I returned

[4] [Editor] Most authorities believe the "native" rat of New Zealand is not indigenous either, but was brought by the Maoris when they came to New Zealand from Polynesia about the eleventh century.

[5] [Editor] A genus of huge flightless birds, including the extinct moas. Another type of flightless New Zealand bird, the kiwi, was once included in Dinornis but is now classed as a separate genus, Apteryx.

to the Bay of Islands. I took leave of the missionaries with thankfulness for their kind welcome, and with feelings of high respect for their gentlemanlike, useful, and upright characters. I think it would be difficult to find a body of men better adapted for the high office which they fulfil.

Christmas-Day.—In a few more days the fourth year of our absence from England will be completed. Our first Christmas-day was spent at Plymouth; the second at St. Martin's Cove, near Cape Horn; the third at Port Desire, in Patagonia; the fourth at anchor in a wild harbour in the peninsula of Tres Montes; this fifth here; and the next, I trust in Providence, will be in England. We attended divine service in the chapel of Pahia; part of the service being read in English, and part in the native language. Whilst at New Zealand we did not hear of any recent acts of cannibalism; but Mr. Stokes found burnt human bones strewed round a fire-place on a small island near the anchorage; but these remains of a comfortable banquet might have been lying there for several years. It is probable that the moral state of the people will rapidly improve. Mr. Bushby mentioned one pleasing anecdote as a proof of the sincerity of some, at least, of those who profess Christianity. One of his young men left him, who had been accustomed to read prayers to the rest of the servants. Some weeks afterwards, happening to pass late in the evening by an outhouse, he saw and heard one of his men reading the Bible with difficulty by the light of the fire, to the others. After this the party knelt and prayed: in their prayers they mentioned Mr. Bushby and his family, and the missionaries, each separately in his respective district.

December 26th.—Mr. Bushby offered to take Mr. Sulivan and myself in his boat some miles up the river to Cawa-Cawa; and proposed afterwards to walk on to the village of Waiomio, where there are some curious rocks. Following one of the arms of the bay, we enjoyed a pleasant row, and passed through pretty scenery, until we came to a village, beyond which the boat could not pass. From this place a chief and a party of men volunteered to walk with us to Waiomio, a distance of four miles. The chief was at this time rather notorious from having lately hung one of his wives and a slave for adultery. When one of the missionaries remonstrated with him he seemed surprised, and said he thought he was exactly following the English method. Old Shongi, who happened to be in England during the Queen's trial, expressed great disapprobation at the whole proceeding: he said he had five wives, and he would rather cut off all their heads than be so much troubled about one. Leaving this village, we crossed over to another, seated on a hill-side at a little distance. The daughter of a chief, who was still a heathen, had died there five days before. The hovel in which she had expired had been burnt to the ground: her body being enclosed between two small canoes, was placed upright on the ground, and protected by an enclosure bearing wooden images of their gods, and the whole was painted bright red, so as to be conspicuous from afar. Her gown was fastened to the coffin, and her hair being cut off was cast at its foot. The relatives of the family had torn the flesh of their arms, bodies, and faces, so that they were covered with clotted blood; and the old women looked most filthy, disgusting objects. On the following day some of the officers visited this place, and found the women still howling and cutting themselves.

We continued our walk, and soon reached Waiomio. Here there are some singular masses of limestone, resembling ruined castles. These rocks have long served for burial-places, and in consequence are held too sacred to be approached. One of the young men, however, cried out, "Let us all be brave," and ran on ahead; but when within a hundred yards, the whole party thought better of it, and stopped short. With perfect indifference, however, they allowed us to examine the whole place. At this village we rested some hours, during which time there was a long discussion with Mr. Bushby, concerning the right of sale of certain lands. One old man, who appeared a perfect genealogist, illustrated the successive possessors by bits of stick driven into the ground. Before leaving the houses a little basketful of roasted sweet potatoes was given to each of our party; and we all, according to the custom, carried them away to eat on the road. I noticed that among the women employed in cooking, there was a man-slave: it must be a humiliating thing for a man in this warlike country to be employed in doing that which is considered as the lowest woman's work. Slaves are not allowed to go to war; but this perhaps can hardly be considered as a hardship. I heard of one poor wretch who, during hostilities, ran away to the opposite party; being met by two men, he was immediately seized; but as they could not agree to whom he should belong, each stood over him with a stone hatchet, and seemed determined that the other at least should not take him away alive. The poor man, almost dead with fright, was only saved by the address of a chief's wife. We afterwards enjoyed a pleasant walk back to the boat, but did not reach the ship till late in the evening.

December 30*th*.—In the afternoon we stood out of the Bay of Islands, on our course to Sydney. I believe we were all glad to leave New Zealand. It is not a pleasant place. Amongst the natives there is absent that charming simplicity which is found at Tahiti; and the greater part of the English are the very refuse of society. Neither is the country itself attractive. I look back but to one bright spot, and that is Waimate, with its Christian inhabitants.

CHAPTER XIX

AUSTRALIA

January 12*th*, 1836.—Early in the morning a light air carried us towards the entrance of Port Jackson. Instead of beholding a verdant country, interspersed with fine houses, a straight line of yellowish cliff brought to our minds the coast of Patagonia. A solitary lighthouse, built of white stone, alone told us that we were near a great and populous city. Having entered the harbour, it appears fine and spacious, with cliff-formed shores of horizontally stratified sandstone. The nearly level country is covered with thin scrubby trees, bespeaking the curse of sterility. Proceeding further inland, the country improves: beautiful villas and nice cottages are here and there scattered along the beach. In the distance stone houses, two and three stories high, and windmills standing on the edge of a bank, pointed out to us the neighbourhood of the capital of Australia.

At last we anchored within Sydney Cove. We found the little basin occupied by many large ships, and surrounded by warehouses. In the evening I walked through the town, and returned full of admiration at the whole scene. It is a most magnificent testimony to the power of the British nation. Here, in a less promising country, scores of years have done many times more than an equal number of centuries have effected in South America. My first feeling was to congratulate myself that I was born an Englishman. Upon seeing more of the town afterwards, perhaps my admiration fell a little; but yet it is a fine town. The streets are regular, broad, clean, and kept in excellent order; the houses are of a good size, and the shops well furnished. It may be faithfully compared to the large suburbs which stretch out from London and a few other great towns in England; but not even near London or Birmingham is there an appearance of such rapid growth. The number of large houses and other buildings just finished was truly surprising; nevertheless, every one complained of the high rents and difficulty in procuring a house. Coming from South America, where in the towns every man of property is known, no one thing surprised me more than not being able to ascertain at once to whom this or that carriage belonged.

I hired a man and two horses to take me to Bathurst, a village about one hundred and twenty miles in the interior, and the centre of a great pastoral district. By this means I hoped to gain a general idea of the appearance of the country. On the morning of the 16th (January) I set out on my excursion. The first stage took us to Paramatta, a small country town, next to Sydney in importance. The roads were excellent, and made upon the MacAdam principle, whinstone having been brought for the purpose from the distance of several miles. In all respects there was a close resemblance to England: perhaps the ale-houses here were more numerous. The iron gangs, or parties of convicts who have committed here some offence, appeared the least like England: they were working in chains, under the charge of sentries with loaded arms. The power which the Government possesses, by means of forced labour, of at once opening good roads throughout the country, has been, I believe, one main cause of the early prosperity of this colony. I slept at night at a very comfortable inn at Emu ferry, thirty-five miles from Sydney, and near the ascent of the Blue Mountains. This line of road is the most frequented, and has been the longest inhabited of any in the colony. The whole land is enclosed with high railings, for the farmers have not succeeded in rearing hedges. There are many substantial houses and good cottages scattered about; but although considerable pieces of land are under cultivation, the greater part yet remains as when first discovered.

The extreme uniformity of the vegetation is the most remarkable feature in the landscape of the greater part of New South Wales. Everywhere we have an open woodland, the ground being partially covered with a very thin pasture, with little appearance of verdure. The trees nearly all belong to one family, and mostly have their leaves placed in a vertical, instead of, as in Europe, in a nearly horizontal position: the foliage is scanty, and of a peculiar pale green tint, without any gloss. Hence the woods appear light and shadowless: this, although a loss of comfort to the traveller under the scorching rays of summer, is of importance to the farmer, as it allows grass to grow where it otherwise would not. The leaves are not shed periodically: this character appears common to the entire southern hemisphere, namely, South America, Australia, and the Cape of Good Hope. The inhabitants of this hemisphere, and of the intertropical regions, thus lose perhaps one of the most glorious, though to our eyes common, spectacles in the world—the first bursting into full foliage of the leafless tree. They may, however, say that we pay dearly for this by having the land covered with mere naked skeletons for so many months. This is too true; but our senses thus acquire a keen relish for the exquisite green of the spring, which the eyes of those living within the tropics, sated during the long year with the gorgeous productions of those glowing climates, can never experience. The greater number of the trees, with the exception of some of the Blue-gums, do not attain a large size; but they grow tall and tolerably straight, and stand well apart. The bark of some of the Eucalypti falls annually, or hangs dead in long shreds which swing about with the wind, and give to the woods a desolate and untidy appearance. I cannot imagine a more complete contrast, in every respect, than between the forests of Valdivia or Chiloe, and the woods of Australia.

At sunset, a party of a score of the black aborigines passed by, each carrying, in their accustomed manner, a bundle of spears and other weapons. By giving a leading young man a shilling, they were easily detained, and threw their spears for my amusement. They were all partly clothed, and several could speak a little English: their countenances were good-humoured and pleasant, and they appeared far from being such utterly degraded beings as they have usually been represented. In their own arts they are admirable. A cap being fixed at thirty yards distance, they transfixed it with a spear, delivered by the throwing-stick with the rapidity of an arrow from the bow of a practised archer. In tracking animals or men they show most wonderful sagacity; and I heard of several of their remarks which manifested considerable acuteness. They will not, however, cultivate the ground, or build houses and remain stationary, or even take the trouble of tending a flock of sheep when given to them. On the whole they appear to me to stand some few degrees higher in the scale of civilization than the Fuegians.

It is very curious thus to see in the midst of a civilized people, a set of harmless savages wandering about without knowing where they shall sleep at night, and gaining their livelihood by hunting in the woods. As the white man has travelled onwards, he has spread over the country belonging to several tribes. These, although thus enclosed by one common people, keep up their ancient distinctions, and sometimes go to war with each other. In an engagement which took place lately, the two parties most singularly chose the centre of the village of Bathurst for the field of battle. This was of service to the defeated side, for the runaway warriors took refuge in the barracks.

The number of aborigines is rapidly decreasing. In my whole ride, with the exception of some boys brought up by Englishmen, I saw only one other party. This decrease, no doubt, must be partly owing to the introduction of spirits, to European diseases (even the milder ones of which, such as the measles,[1] prove very destructive), and to the gradual extinction of the wild animals. It is said that numbers of their children invariably perish in very early infancy from the effects of their wandering life; and as the difficulty of procuring food increases, so must their wandering habits increase; and hence the population, without any apparent deaths from famine, is repressed in a manner extremely sudden compared to what happens in civilized countries, where the father, though in adding to his labour he may injure himself, does not destroy his offspring.

Besides these several evident causes of destruction, there appears to be some more mysterious agency generally at work. Wherever the European has trod, death seems to pursue the

[1] [Darwin] It is remarkable how the same disease is modified in different climates. At the little island of St. Helena, the introduction of scarlet-fever is dreaded as a plague. In some countries, foreigners and natives are as differently affected by certain contagious disorders, as if they had been different animals; of which fact some instances have occurred in Chile; and, according to Humboldt, in Mexico. (Polit. Essay, New Spain, vol. iv.)

aboriginal. We may look to the wide extent of the Americas, Polynesia, the Cape of Good Hope, and Australia, and we find the same result. Nor is it the white man alone that thus acts the destroyer; the Polynesian of Malay extraction has in parts of the East Indian archipelago, thus driven before him the dark-coloured native. The varieties of man seem to act on each other in the same way as different species of animals—the stronger always extirpating the weaker. It was melancholy at New Zealand to hear the fine energetic natives saying, that they knew the land was doomed to pass from their children. Every one has heard of the inexplicable reduction of the population in the beautiful and healthy island of Tahiti since the date of Captain Cook's voyages: although in that case we might have expected that it would have been increased; for infanticide, which formerly prevailed to so extraordinary a degree, has ceased, profligacy has greatly diminished, and the murderous wars become less frequent.[2]

The Rev. J. Williams, in his interesting work,[3] says, that the first intercourse between natives and Europeans, "is invariably attended with the introduction of fever, dysentery, or some other disease, which carries off numbers of the people." Again he affirms, "It is certainly a fact, which cannot be controverted, that most of the diseases which have raged in the islands during my residence there, have been introduced by ships;[4] and

[2] [Editor] Like the pureblooded natives of Hawaii, the pure-blooded natives of Tahiti are disappearing. White man's diseases no longer kill off the great number of natives they once did. However, admixture with European and Chinese blood continues to whittle away at the Polynesian population.

The Maoris of New Zealand appear to be almost the only indigenous population in the Pacific that is flourishing. From a low of 42,000 in 1896, the number of Maoris of half-blood or more increased to 137,000 by 1956. In Australia, about 70,000 aborigines of pure or mixed blood were living on reservations (as against a total aboriginal population of 150,000 to 300,000 before the coming of white settlers). As Darwin notes later in this chapter, the natives of Tasmania were forcibly removed to an island in the strait separating Tasmania from Australia; they have since entirely died out.

[3] [Darwin] Narrative of Missionary Enterprise, p. 282.

[4] [Darwin] Captain Beechey (chap. iv. vol. i.) states that the inhabitants of Pitcairn Island are firmly convinced that after the arrival of every ship they suffer cutaneous and other disorders. Captain Beechey attributes this to the change of diet during the time of the visit. Dr. Macculloch (Western Isles, vol. ii. p. 32)

what renders this fact remarkable is, that there might be no appearance of disease among the crew of the ship which conveyed this destructive importation." This statement is not quite so extraordinary as it at first appears; for several cases are on record of the most malignant fevers having broken out, although the parties themselves, who were the cause, were not affected. In the early part of the reign of George III., a prisoner who had been confined in a dungeon, was taken in a coach with four constables before a magistrate; and, although the man himself was not ill, the four constables died from a short putrid fever; but the contagion extended to no others. From these facts it would almost appear as if the effluvium of one set of men shut up for some time together was poisonous when inhaled by others; and possibly more so, if the men be of different races. Mysterious as this circumstance appears to be, it is not more surprising than that the body of one's fellow-creature, directly after death, and before putrefaction has commenced, should often be of so deleterious a quality, that the mere puncture from an instrument used in its dissection, should prove fatal.

17*th*.—Early in the morning we passed the Nepean in a ferry-boat. The river, although at this spot both broad and deep, had a very small body of running water. Having crossed a low piece of land on the opposite side, we reached the slope of the

---

says, "It is asserted, that on the arrival of a stranger (at St. Kilda) all the inhabitants, in the common phraseology, catch a cold." Dr. Macculloch considers the whole case, although often previously affirmed, as ludicrous. He adds, however, that "the question was put by us to the inhabitants who unanimously agreed in the story." In Vancouver's Voyage, there is a somewhat similar statement with respect to Otaheite. Dr. Dieffenbach, in a note to his translation of this Journal, states that the same fact is universally believed by the inhabitants of the Chatham Islands, and in parts of New Zealand. It is impossible that such a belief should have become universal in the northern hemisphere, at the Antipodes, and in the Pacific, without some good foundation. Humboldt (Polit. Essay on King of New Spain, vol. iv.) says, that the great epidemics at Panama and Callao are "marked" by the arrival of ships from Chile, because the people from that temperate region, first experience the fatal effects of the torrid zones. I may add, that I have heard it stated in Shropshire, that sheep which have been imported from vessels, although themselves in a healthy condition, if placed in the same fold with others, frequently produce sickness in the flock.

Blue Mountains. The ascent is not steep, the road having been cut with much care on the side of a sandstone cliff. On the summit an almost level plain extends, which, rising imperceptibly to the westward, at last attains a height of more than 3000 feet. From so grand a title as Blue Mountains, and from their absolute altitude, I expected to have seen a bold chain of mountains crossing the country; but instead of this, a sloping plain presents merely an inconsiderable front to the low land near the coast. From this first slope, the view of the extensive woodland to the east was striking, and the surrounding trees grew bold and lofty. But when once on the sandstone platform, the scenery becomes exceedingly monotonous; each side of the road is bordered by scrubby trees of the never-failing Eucalyptus family; and with the exception of two or three small inns, there are no houses or cultivated land: the road, moreover, is solitary; the most frequent object being a bullock-waggon, piled up with bales of wool.

In the middle of the day we baited our horses at a little inn, called the Weatherboard. The country here is elevated 2800 feet above the sea. About a mile and a half from this place there is a view exceedingly well worth visiting. Following down a little valley and its tiny rill of water, an immense gulf unexpectedly opens through the trees which border the pathway, at the depth of perhaps 1500 feet. Walking on a few yards, one stands on the brink of a vast precipice, and below one sees a grand bay or gulf, for I know not what other name to give it, thickly covered with forest. The point of view is situated as if at the head of a bay, the line of cliff diverging on each side, and showing headland behind headland, as on a bold sea-coast. These cliffs are composed of horizontal strata of whitish sandstone; and are so absolutely vertical, that in many places a person standing on the edge and throwing down a stone, can see it strike the trees in the abyss below. So unbroken is the line of cliff, that in order to reach the foot of the waterfall, formed by this little stream, it is said to be necessary to go sixteen miles round. About five miles distant in front, another line of cliff extends, which thus appears completely to encircle the valley; and hence the name of bay is justified, as applied to this grand amphitheatrical depression. If we imagine a winding harbour, with its deep water surrounded by bold cliff-like shores, to be laid dry, and a forest to spring up on its sandy bottom, we should then have the appearance and structure here exhibited. This kind of view was to me quite novel, and extremely magnificent.

In the evening we reached the Blackheath. The sandstone plateau has here attained the height of 3400 feet; and is covered, as before, with the same scrubby woods. From the road, there were occasional glimpses into a profound valley, of the same character as the one described; but from the steepness and depth of its sides, the bottom was scarcely ever to be seen. The Blackheath is a very comfortable inn, kept by an old soldier; and it reminded me of the small inns in North Wales.

18*th*.—Very early in the morning, I walked about three miles to see Govett's Leap: a view of a similar character with that near the Weatherboard, but perhaps even more stupendous. So early in the day the gulf was filled with a thin blue haze, which, although destroying the general effect of the view, added to the apparent depth at which the forest was stretched out beneath our feet. These valleys, which so long presented an insuperable barrier to the attempts of the most enterprising of the colonists to reach the interior, are most remarkable. Great arm-like bays, expanding at their upper ends, often branch from the main valleys and penetrate the sandstone platform; on the other hand, the platform often sends promontories into the valleys, and even leaves in them great, almost insulated, masses. To descend into some of these valleys, it is necessary to go round twenty miles; and into others, the surveyors have only lately penetrated, and the colonists have not yet been able to drive in their cattle. But the most remarkable feature in their structure is, that although several miles wide at their heads, they generally contract towards their mouths to such a degree as to become impassable. The Surveyor-General, Sir T. Mitchell,[5] endeavoured in vain, first walking and then by crawling between the great fallen fragments of sandstone, to ascend through the gorge by which the river Grose joins the Nepean; yet the valley of the Grose in its upper part, as I saw, forms a magnificent level basin some miles in width, and is on all sides surrounded by cliffs, the summits of which are believed to be nowhere less than 3000 feet above the level of the sea. When cattle are driven into the valley of the Wolgan by a path (which I descended), partly natural and partly made

[5] [Darwin] Travels in Australia, vol. i. p. 154. I must express my obligation to Sir T. Mitchell, for several interesting personal communications, on the subject of these great valleys of New South Wales.

by the owner of the land, they cannot escape; for this valley
is in every other part surrounded by perpendicular cliffs, and
eight miles lower down, it contracts from an average width of
half a mile, to a mere chasm, impassable to man or beast.
Sir T. Mitchell states that the great valley of the Cox river
with all its branches, contracts, where it unites with the Nepean,
into a gorge 2200 yards in width, and about 1000 feet in
depth. Other similar cases might have been added.

The first impression, on seeing the correspondence of the
horizontal strata on each side of these valleys and great amphitheatrical depressions, is that they have been hollowed out,
like other valleys, by the action of water; but when one reflects
on the enormous amount of stone, which on this view must
have been removed through mere gorges or chasms, one is led
to ask whether these spaces may not have subsided. But considering the form of the irregularly branching valleys, and of
the narrow promontories projecting into them from the platforms, we are compelled to abandon this notion. To attribute
these hollows to the present alluvial action would be preposterous; nor does the drainage from the summit-level always
fall, as I remarked near the Weatherboard, into the head of
these valleys, but into one side of their bay-like recesses. Some
of the inhabitants remarked to me that they never viewed one
of those bay-like recesses, with the headlands receding on both
hands, without being struck with their resemblance to a bold
sea-coast. This is certainly the case; moreover, on the present
coast of New South Wales, the numerous fine, widely-branch-
ing harbours, which are generally connected with the sea by a
narrow mouth worn through the sandstone coast-cliffs, varying from one mile in width to a quarter of a mile, present a
likeness, though on a miniature scale, to the great valleys of the
interior. But then immediately occurs the startling difficulty,
why has the sea worn out these great, though circumscribed
depressions on a wide platform, and left mere gorges at the
openings, through which the whole vast amount of triturated
matter must have been carried away? The only light I can
throw upon this enigma, is by remarking that banks of the
most irregular forms appear to be now forming in some seas,
as in parts of the West Indies and in the Red Sea, and that their
sides are exceedingly steep. Such banks, I have been led to
suppose, have been formed by sediment heaped by strong currents on an irregular bottom. That in some cases the sea, instead of spreading out sediment in a uniform sheet, heaps it

round submarine rocks and islands, it is hardly possible to doubt, after examining the charts of the West Indies; and that the waves have power to form high and precipitous cliffs, even in land-locked harbours, I have noticed in many parts of South America. To apply these ideas to the sandstone platforms of New South Wales, I imagine that the strata were heaped by the action of strong currents, and of the undulations of an open sea, on an irregular bottom; and that the valley-like spaces thus left unfilled had their steeply sloping flanks worn into cliffs, during a slow elevation of the land; the worn-down sandstone being removed, either at the time when the narrow gorges were cut by the retreating sea, or subsequently by alluvial action.

Soon after leaving the Blackheath, we descended from the sandstone platform by the pass of Mount Victoria. To effect this pass, an enormous quantity of stone has been cut through; the design, and its manner of execution, being worthy of any line of road in England. We now entered upon a country less elevated by nearly a thousand feet, and consisting of granite. With the change of rock, the vegetation improved; the trees were both finer and stood farther apart; and the pasture between them was a little greener and more plentiful. At Hassan's Walls, I left the high road, and made a short détour to a farm called Walerawang; to the superintendent of which I had a letter of introduction from the owner in Sydney. Mr. Browne had the kindness to ask me to stay the ensuing day, which I had much pleasure in doing. This place offers an example of one of the large farming, or rather sheep-grazing, establishments of the colony. Cattle and horses are, however, in this case rather more numerous than usual, owing to some of the valleys being swampy and producing a coarser pasture. Two or three flat pieces of ground near the house were cleared and cultivated with corn, which the harvest-men were now reaping: but no more wheat is sown than sufficient for the annual support of the labourers employed on the establishment. The usual number of assigned convict-servants here is about forty, but at the present time there were rather more. Although the farm was well stocked with every necessary, there was an apparent absence of comfort; and not one single woman resided here. The sunset of a fine day will generally cast an air of happy contentment on any scene; but here, at this retired farm-house, the brightest tints on the surrounding woods could not make me forget that forty hardened, profligate men were ceasing from their daily labours, like the slaves from Africa, yet without their holy claim for compassion.

Early on the next morning, Mr. Archer, the joint superintendent, had the kindness to take me out kangaroo-hunting. We continued riding the greater part of the day, but had very bad sport, not seeing a kangaroo, or even a wild dog. The greyhounds pursued a kangaroo rat into a hollow tree, out of which we dragged it: it is an animal as large as a rabbit, but with the figure of a kangaroo. A few years since this country abounded with wild animals; but now the emu is banished to a long distance, and the kangaroo is become scarce; to both the English greyhound has been highly destructive. It may be long before these animals are altogether exterminated, but their doom is fixed. The aborigines are always anxious to borrow the dogs from the farm-houses: the use of them, the offal when an animal is killed, and some milk from the cows, are the peace-offerings of the settlers, who push farther and farther towards the interior. The thoughtless aboriginal, blinded by these trifling advantages, is delighted at the approach of the white man, who seems predestined to inherit the country of his children.

Although having poor sport, we enjoyed a pleasant ride. The woodland is generally so open that a person on horseback can gallop through it. It is traversed by a few flat-bottomed valleys, which are green and free from trees: in such spots the scenery was pretty like that of a park. In the whole country I scarcely saw a place without the marks of a fire; whether these had been more or less recent—whether the stumps were more or less black, was the greatest change which varied the uniformity, so wearisome to the traveller's eye. In these woods there are not many birds; I saw, however, some large flocks of the white cockatoo feeding in a corn-field, and a few most beautiful parrots; crows like our jackdaws were not uncommon, and another bird something like the magpie. In the dusk of the evening I took a stroll along a chain of ponds, which in this dry country represented the course of a river, and had the good fortune to see several of the famous Ornithorhynchus paradoxus.[6] They were diving and playing about the surface of the water, but showed so little of their bodies, that they might easily have been mistaken for water-rats. Mr. Browne shot one: certainly it is a most extraordinary animal; a stuffed

[6] [Editor] The duckbill platypus.

specimen does not at all give a good idea of the appearance of the head and beak when fresh; the latter becoming hard and contracted.[7]

20*th*.—A long day's ride to Bathurst. Before joining the high road we followed a mere path through the forest; and the country, with the exception of a few squatters' huts, was very solitary. We experienced this day the sirocco-like wind of Australia, which comes from the parched deserts of the interior. Clouds of dust were travelling in every direction; and the wind felt as if it had passed over a fire. I afterwards heard that the thermometer out of doors had stood at 119°, and in a closed room at 96°. In the afternoon we came in view of the downs of Bathurst. These undulating but nearly smooth plains are very remarkable in this country, from being absolutely destitute of trees. They support only a thin brown pasture. We rode some miles over this country, and then reached the township of Bathurst, seated in the middle of what may be called either a very broad valley, or narrow plain. I was told at Sydney not to form too bad an opinion of Australia by judging of the country from the road-side, nor too good a one from Bathurst; in this latter respect, I did not feel myself in the least danger of being prejudiced. The season, it must be owned, had been one of great drought, and the country did not wear a favourable aspect; although I understand it was incomparably worse two or three months before. The secret of the rapidly growing prosperity of Bathurst is, that the brown pasture which appears to the stranger's eye so wretched, is excellent for sheep-grazing. The town stands, at the height of 2200 feet above the sea, on the banks of the Macquarie: this is one of the rivers flowing into the vast and scarcely known interior. The line of water-shed, which divides the inland streams from those on the coast, has a height of about 3000 feet, and runs in a north and south direction at the distance of from eighty to a hundred miles

[7] [Darwin] I was interested by finding here the hollow conical pitfall of the lion-ant, or some other insect; first a fly fell down the treacherous slope and immediately disappeared; then came a large but unwary ant; its struggles to escape being very violent, those curious little jets of sand, described by Kirby and Spence (Entomol., vol. i. p. 425) as being flirted by the insect's tail, were promptly directed against the expected victim. But the ant enjoyed a better fate than the fly, and escaped the fatal jaws which lay concealed at the base of the conical hollow. This Australian pitfall was only about half the size of that made by the European lion-ant.

from the sea-side. The Macquarie figures in the map as a respectable river, and it is the largest of those draining this part of the water-shed; yet to my surprise I found it a mere chain of ponds, separated from each other by spaces almost dry. Generally a small stream is running; and sometimes there are high and impetuous floods. Scanty as the supply of the water is throughout this district, it becomes still scantier further inland.

22nd.—I commenced my return, and followed a new road called Lockyer's Line, along which the country is rather more hilly and picturesque. This was a long day's ride; and the house where I wished to sleep was some way off the road, and not easily found. I met on this occasion, and indeed on all others, a very general and ready civility among the lower orders, which, when one considers what they are, and what they have been, would scarcely have been expected. The farm where I passed the night, was owned by two young men who had only lately come out, and were beginning a settler's life. The total want of almost every comfort was not very attractive; but future and certain prosperity was before their eyes, and that not far distant.

The next day we passed through large tracts of country in flames, volumes of smoke sweeping across the road. Before noon we joined our former road, and ascended Mount Victoria. I slept at the Weatherboard, and before dark took another walk to the amphitheatre. On the road to Sydney I spent a very pleasant evening with Captain King at Dunheved; and thus ended my little excursion in the colony of New South Wales.

Before arriving here the three things which interested me most were—the state of society amongst the higher classes, the condition of the convicts, and the degree of attraction sufficient to induce persons to emigrate. Of course, after so very short a visit, one's opinion is worth scarcely anything; but it is as difficult not to form some opinion, as it is to form a correct judgment. On the whole, from what I heard, more than from what I saw, I was disappointed in the state of society. The whole community is rancorously divided into parties on almost every subject. Among those who, from their station in life, ought to be the best, many live in such open profligacy that respectable people cannot associate with them. There is much jealousy between the children of the rich emancipist and the free settlers, the former being pleased to consider honest men as interlopers. The whole population, poor and rich, are bent on acquiring wealth: amongst the higher orders, wool and sheep-grazing form the constant subject of conversation. There are many serious drawbacks to the comforts of a family, the chief of which, perhaps, is being surrounded by convict servants. How thoroughly odious to every feeling, to be waited on by a man who the day before, perhaps, was flogged, from your representation, for some trifling misdemeanour. The female servants are of course much worse: hence children learn the vilest expressions, and it is fortunate, if not equally vile ideas.

On the other hand, the capital of a person, without any trouble on his part, produces him treble interest to what it will in England; and with care he is sure to grow rich. The luxuries of life are in abundance, and very little dearer than in England, and most articles of food are cheaper. The climate is splendid, and perfectly healthy; but to my mind its charms are lost by the uninviting aspect of the country. Settlers possess a great advantage in finding their sons of service when very young. At the age of from sixteen to twenty, they frequently take charge of distant farming stations. This, however, must happen at the expense of their boys associating entirely with convict servants. I am not aware that the tone of society has assumed any peculiar character; but with such habits, and without intellectual pursuits, it can hardly fail to deteriorate. My opinion is such, that nothing but rather sharp necessity should compel me to emigrate.

The rapid prosperity and future prospects of this colony are to me, not understanding these subjects, very puzzling. The two main exports are wool and whale-oil, and to both of these productions there is a limit. The country is totally unfit for canals, therefore there is a not very distant point, beyond which the land-carriage of wool will not repay the expense of shearing and tending sheep. Pasture everywhere is so thin that settlers have already pushed far into the interior: moreover, the country further inland becomes extremely poor. Agriculture, on account of the droughts, can never succeed on an extended scale: therefore, so far as I can see, Australia must ultimately depend upon being the centre of commerce for the southern hemisphere, and perhaps on her future manufactories. Possessing coal, she always has the moving power at hand. From the habitable country extending along the coast, and from her English extraction, she is sure to be a maritime nation. I formerly imagined that Australia would rise to be as grand and powerful a country as North America, but now it appears to me that such future grandeur is rather problematical.

With respect to the state of the convicts, I had still fewer opportunities of judging than on the other points. The first question is, whether their condition is at all one of punishment: no one will maintain that it is a very severe one. This, however, I suppose, is of little consequence as long as it continues to be an object of dread to criminals at home. The corporeal wants of the convicts are tolerably well supplied: their prospect of future liberty and comfort is not distant, and after good conduct certain. A "ticket of leave," which, as long as a man keeps clear of suspicion as well as of crime, makes him free within a certain district, is given upon good conduct, after years proportional to the length of the sentence; yet with all this, and overlooking the previous imprisonment and wretched passage out, I believe the years of assignment are passed away with discontent and unhappiness. As an intelligent man remarked to me, the convicts know no pleasure beyond sensuality, and in this they are not gratified. The enormous bribe which Government possesses in offering free pardons, together with the deep horror of the secluded penal settlements, destroys confidence between the convicts, and so prevents crime. As to a sense of shame, such a feeling does not appear to be known, and of this I witnessed some very singular proofs. Though it is a curious fact, I was universally told that the character of the convict population is one of arrant cowardice: not unfrequently some become desperate, and quite indifferent as to life, yet a plan requiring cool or continued courage is seldom put into execution. The worst feature in the whole case is, that although there exists what may be called a legal reform, and comparatively little is committed which the law can touch, yet that any moral reform should take place appears to be quite out of the question. I was assured by well-informed people, that a man who should try to improve, could not while living with other assigned servants;—his life would be one of intolerable misery and persecution. Nor must the contamination of the convict-ships and prisons, both here and in England, be forgotten. On the whole, as a place of punishment, the object is scarcely gained; as a real system of reform it has failed, as perhaps would every other plan; but as a means of making men outwardly honest,—of converting vagabonds, most useless in one hemisphere, into active citizens of another, and thus giving birth to a new and splendid country—a grand centre of civilization—it has succeeded to a degree perhaps unparalleled in history.

30th.—The *Beagle* sailed for Hobart Town in Van Diemen's Land. On the 5th of February, after a six days' passage, of which the first part was fine, and the latter very cold and squally, we entered the mouth of Storm Bay: the weather justified this awful name. The bay should rather be called an estuary, for it receives at its head the waters of the Derwent. Near the mouth, there are some extensive basaltic platforms; but higher up the land becomes mountainous, and is covered by a light wood. The lower parts of the hills which skirt the bay are cleared; and the bright yellow fields of corn, and dark green ones of potatoes, appeared very luxuriant. Late in the evening we anchored in the snug cove, on the shores of which stands the capital of Tasmania. The first aspect of the place was very inferior to that of Sydney; the latter might be called a city, this only a town. It stands at the base of Mount Wellington, a mountain 3100 feet high, but of little picturesque beauty: from this source, however, it receives a good supply of water. Round the cove there are some fine warehouses, and on one side a small fort. Coming from the Spanish settlements, where such magnificent care has generally been paid to the fortifications, the means of defence in these colonies appeared very contemptible. Comparing the town with Sydney, I was chiefly struck with the comparative fewness of the large houses, either built or building. Hobart Town, from the census of 1835, contained 13,826 inhabitants, and the whole of Tasmania 36,505.

All the aborigines have been removed to an island in Bass's Straits, so that Van Diemen's Land enjoys the great advantage of being free from a native population. This most cruel step seems to have been quite unavoidable, as the only means of stopping a fearful succession of robberies, burnings, and murders, committed by the blacks; and which sooner or later would have ended in their utter destruction. I fear there is no doubt, that this train of evil and its consequences, originated in the infamous conduct of some of our countrymen. Thirty years is a short period, in which to have banished the last aboriginal from his native island,—and that island nearly as large as Ireland. The correspondence on this subject, which took place between the government at home and that of Van Diemen's Land, is very interesting. Although numbers of natives were shot and taken prisoners in the skirmishing, which was going on at inter-

vals for several years; nothing seems fully to have impressed
them with the idea of our overwhelming power, until the whole
island, in 1830, was put under martial law, and by proclama-
tion the whole population commanded to assist in one great
attempt to secure the entire race. The plan adopted was nearly
similar to that of the great hunting-matches in India: a line
was formed reaching across the island, with the intention of
driving the natives into a *cul-de-sac* on Tasman's peninsula.
The attempt failed; the natives, having tied up their dogs, stole
during one night through the lines. This is far from surprising,
when their practised senses, and usual manner of crawling after
wild animals is considered. I have been assured that they can
conceal themselves on almost bare ground, in a manner which
until witnessed is scarcely credible; their dusky bodies being
easily mistaken for the blackened stumps which are scattered
all over the country. I was told of a trial between a party of
Englishmen and a native, who was to stand in full view on the
side of a bare hill; if the Englishmen closed their eyes for less
than a minute, he would squat down, and then they were never
able to distinguish him from the surrounding stumps. But to
return to the hunting-match; the natives understanding this
kind of warfare, were terribly alarmed, for they at once perceived the power and numbers of the whites. Shortly afterwards a party of thirteen belonging to two tribes came in; and,
conscious of their unprotected condition, delivered themselves
up in despair. Subsequently by the intrepid exertions of Mr.
Robinson, an active and benevolent man, who fearlessly visited
by himself the most hostile of the natives, the whole were induced to act in a similar manner. They were then removed to
an island, where food and clothes were provided them. Count
Strzelecki states,[8] that "at the epoch of their deportation in
1835, the number of natives amounted to 210. In 1842, that
is after the interval of seven years, they mustered only fifty-
four individuals; and, while each family of the interior of New
South Wales, uncontaminated by contact with the whites,
swarms with children, those of Flinders' Island had during eight
years, an accession of only fourteen in number!"

The *Beagle* staid here ten days, and in this time I made several pleasant little excursions, chiefly with the object of examining the geological structure of the immediate neighbourhood.

[8] [Darwin] Physical Description of New South Wales and Van
Diemen's Land, p. 354.

The main points of interest consist, first in some highly fossiliferous strata, belonging to the Devonian or Carboniferous
period; secondly, in proofs of a late small rise of the land; and
lastly, in a solitary and superficial patch of yellowish limestone
or travertin, which contains numerous impressions of leaves of
trees, together with land-shells, not now existing. It is not improbable that this one small quarry, includes the only remaining record of the vegetation of Van Diemen's Land during one
former epoch.

The climate here is damper than in New South Wales, and
hence the land is more fertile. Agriculture flourishes: the cultivated fields look well, and the gardens abound with thriving
vegetables and fruit-trees. Some of the farm-houses, situated in
retired spots, had a very attractive appearance. The general
aspect of the vegetation is similar to that of Australia; perhaps
it is a little more green and cheerful; and the pasture between
the trees rather more abundant. One day I took a long walk
on the side of the bay opposite to the town: I crossed in a
steam-boat, two of which are constantly plying backwards and
forwards. The machinery of one of these vessels was entirely
manufactured in this colony, which, from its very foundation,
then numbered only three and thirty years! Another day I ascended Mount Wellington; I took with me a guide, for I failed
in a first attempt, from the thickness of the wood. Our guide,
however, was a stupid fellow, and conducted us to the southern
and damp side of the mountain, where the vegetation was very
luxuriant; and where the labour of the ascent, from the number of rotten trunks, was almost as great as on a mountain
in Tierra del Fuego or in Chiloe. It cost us five and a half
hours of hard climbing before we reached the summit. In many
parts the Eucalypti grew to a great size, and composed a noble
forest. In some of the dampest ravines, tree-ferns flourished in
an extraordinary manner; I saw one which must have been at
least twenty feet high to the base of the fronds, and was in
girth exactly six feet. The fronds forming the most elegant
parasols, produced a gloomy shade, like that of the first hour
of night. The summit of the mountain is broad and flat, and
is composed of huge angular masses of naked greenstone. Its
elevation is 3100 feet above the level of the sea. The day was
splendidly clear, and we enjoyed a most extensive view; to the
north, the country appeared a mass of wooded mountains, of
about the same height with that on which we were standing,
and with an equally tame outline: to the south the broken land

and water, forming many intricate bays, was mapped with clearness before us. After staying some hours on the summit, we found a better way to descend, but did not reach the *Beagle* till eight o'clock, after a severe day's work.

February 7th.—The *Beagle* sailed from Tasmania, and, on the 6th of the ensuing month, reached King George's Sound, situated close to the S.W. corner of Australia. We staid there eight days; and we did not during our voyage pass a more dull and uninteresting time. The country, viewed from an eminence, appears a woody plain, with here and there rounded and partly bare hills of granite protruding. One day I went out with a party, in hopes of seeing a kangaroo hunt, and walked over a good many miles of country. Everywhere we found the soil sandy, and very poor; it supported either a coarse vegetation of thin, low brushwood and wiry grass, or a forest of stunted trees. The scenery resembled that of the high sandstone platform of the Blue Mountains; the Casuarina (a tree somewhat resembling a Scotch fir) is, however, here in greater number, and the Eucalyptus in rather less. In the open parts there were many grass-trees,—a plant which, in appearance, has some affinity with the palm; but, instead of being surmounted by a crown of noble fronds, it can boast merely of a tuft of very coarse grass-like leaves. The general bright green colour of the brushwood and other plants, viewed from a distance, seemed to promise fertility. A single walk, however, was enough to dispel such an illusion; and he who thinks with me will never wish to walk again in so uninviting a country.

One day I accompanied Captain Fitz Roy to Bald Head; the place mentioned by so many navigators, where some imagined that they saw corals, and others that they saw petrified trees, standing in the position in which they had grown. According to our view, the beds have been formed by the wind having heaped up fine sand, composed of minute rounded particles of shells and corals, during which process branches and roots of trees, together with many land-shells, became enclosed. The whole then became consolidated by the percolation of calcareous matter; and the cylindrical cavities left by the decaying of the wood, were thus also filled up with a hard pseudostalactitical stone. The weather is now wearing away the softer parts, and in consequence the hard casts of the roots and branches of the trees project above the surface, and, in a singularly deceptive manner, resemble the stumps of a dead thicket.

A large tribe of natives, called the White Cockatoo men,

happened to pay the settlement a visit while we were there. These men, as well as those of the tribe belonging to King George's Sound, being tempted by the offer of some tubs of rice and sugar, were persuaded to hold a "corrobery," or great dancing-party. As soon as it grew dark, small fires were lighted, and the men commenced their toilet, which consisted in painting themselves white in spots and lines. As soon as all was ready, large fires were kept blazing, round which the women and children were collected as spectators; the Cockatoo and King George's men formed two distinct parties, and generally danced in answer to each other. The dancing consisted in their running either sideways or in Indian file into an open space, and stamping the ground with great force as they marched together. Their heavy footsteps were accompanied by a kind of grunt, by beating their clubs and spears together, and by various other gesticulations, such as extending their arms and wriggling their bodies. It was a most rude, barbarous scene, and, to our ideas, without any sort of meaning; but we observed that the black women and children watched it with the greatest pleasure. Perhaps these dances originally represented actions, such as wars and victories; there was one called the Emu dance, in which each man extended his arm in a bent manner, like the neck of that bird. In another dance, one man imitated the movements of a kangaroo grazing in the woods, whilst a second crawled up, and pretended to spear him. When both tribes mingled in the dance, the ground trembled with the heaviness of their steps, and the air resounded with their wild cries. Every one appeared in high spirits, and the group of nearly naked figures, viewed by the light of the blazing fires, all moving in hideous harmony, formed a perfect display of a festival amongst the lowest barbarians. In Tierra del Fuego, we have beheld many curious scenes in savage life, but never, I think, one where the natives were in such high spirits, and so perfectly at their ease. After the dancing was over, the whole party formed a great circle on the ground, and the boiled rice and sugar was distributed, to the delight of all.

After several tedious delays from clouded weather, on the 14th of March, we gladly stood out of King George's Sound on our course to Keeling Island. Farewell, Australia! you are a rising child, and doubtless some day will reign a great princess in the South: but you are too great and ambitious for affection, yet not great enough for respect. I leave your shores without sorrow or regret.

CHAPTER XX

KEELING ISLAND:—
CORAL FORMATIONS

Keeling Island — Singular appearance — Scanty Flora — Transport
of Seeds — Birds and Insects — Ebbing and flowing Wells — Fields
of dead Coral — Stones transported in the Roots of Trees — Great
Crab — Stinging Corals — Coral-eating Fish — Coral Formations —
Lagoon Islands, or Atolls — Depth at which reef-building Corals
can live — Vast Areas interspersed with low Coral Islands — Sub-
sidence of their Foundations — Barrier Reefs — Fringing Reefs —
Conversion of Fringing Reefs into Barrier Reefs, and into Atolls
— Evidence of Changes in Level — Breaches in Barrier Reefs —
Maldiva Atolls; their peculiar structure — Dead and submerged
Reefs — Areas of Subsidence and Elevation — Distribution of Vol-
canoes — Subsidence slow, and vast in amount

April 1*st*.—We arrived in view of the Keeling or Cocos Islands, situated in the Indian Ocean, and about six hundred
miles distant from the coast of Sumatra. This is one of the
lagoon-islands (or atolls) of coral formation, similar to those
in the Low Archipelago which we passed near. When the ship
was in the channel at the entrance, Mr. Liesk, an English resident, came off in his boat. The history of the inhabitants of
this place, in as few words as possible, is as follows. About
nine years ago, Mr. Hare, a worthless character, brought from
the East Indian archipelago a number of Malay slaves, which
now, including children, amount to more than a hundred.
Shortly afterwards, Captain Ross, who had before visited these
islands in his merchant-ship, arrived from England, bringing
with him his family and goods for settlement: along with him
came Mr. Liesk, who had been a mate in his vessel. The Malay
slaves soon ran away from the islet on which Mr. Hare was
settled, and joined Captain Ross's party. Mr. Hare upon this
was ultimately obliged to leave the place.

The Malays are now nominally in a state of freedom, and certainly are so, as far as regards their personal treatment; but in most other points they are considered as slaves. From their discontented state, from the repeated removals from islet to islet, and perhaps also from a little mismanagement, things are not very prosperous. The island has no domestic quadruped, excepting the pig, and the main vegetable production is the cocoa-nut. The whole prosperity of the place depends on this tree: the only exports being oil from the nut, and the nuts themselves, which are taken to Singapore and Mauritius, where they are chiefly used, when grated, in making curries. On the cocoa-nut, also, the pigs, which are loaded with fat, almost entirely subsist, as do the ducks and poultry. Even a huge land-crab is furnished by nature with the means to open and feed on this most useful production.[1]

[1] [Editor] Fitz Roy gives an interesting account of the Keeling Islands history and state at the time of the *Beagle's* visit:

"These lonely islands (also called Cocos) were discovered in 1608–9 by Captain William Keeling, who was in the East India Company's service, and held a commission from King James I. Little or no notice was taken of them from that time till 1823, when one Alexander Hare, a British subject, established himself a small party of Malays, upon the Southern Keeling Island, which he thought a favourable place for commerce, and for maintaining a seraglio of Malay women, whom he confined to one island,—almost to one house.

"In 1826, or within a year of that time, Mr. J. C. Ross, some time master of a merchant ship, took up his abode on the south-eastern islet of the group; and in a very short time Hare's Malay slaves, aggrieved by his harsh treatment of them, especially by his taking away the women, and shutting them up on an island which the Malay men might not approach, deserted in a body, and claimed protection from Mr. Ross. Hare then left the Keelings, and about a year afterwards was arrested in his lawless career by death, while establishing another harem at Batavia.

"From that time Mr. Ross and the Malays lived peaceably, collecting cocoa-nut oil, turtle, tortoise-shell, and bicho do mar; and occasionally sailing to the Mauritius, Singapore, or Batavia, to dispose of them, and buy necessaries with their produce. Another Englishman, Mr. C. Liesk, who had served as mate of Mr. Ross's ship, lived with him, and they both had wives (English) and children, the whole party residing together in a large house of Malay build—just such a structure as one sees represented upon old japanned work. At the time of our visit Mr. Ross was absent on one of their trading excursions, and his deputy, Liesk, was left in charge of everything.

"By some strange misconception, not intentional act of injustice,

The ring-formed reef of the lagoon-island is surmounted in the greater part of its length by linear islets. On the northern or leeward side, there is an opening through which vessels can pass to the anchorage within. On entering, the scene was very curious and rather pretty; its beauty, however, entirely depended on the brilliancy of the surrounding colours. The shallow, clear, and still water of the lagoon, resting in its greater part on white sand, is, when illumined by a vertical sun, of the most vivid green. This brilliant expanse, several miles in width, is on all sides divided, either by a line of snow-white breakers from the dark heaving waters of the ocean, or from the blue vault of heaven by the strips of land, crowned by the level tops of the cocoa-nut trees. As a white cloud here and there affords a pleasing contrast with the azure sky, so in the lagoon, bands of living coral darken the emerald green water.

The next morning after anchoring, I went on shore on Direction Island. The strip of dry land is only a few hundred yards in width; on the lagoon side there is a white calcareous beach, the radiation from which under this sultry climate was very oppressive; and on the outer coast, a solid broad flat of coral-rock served to break the violence of the open sea. Excepting near the lagoon, where there is some sand, the land is entirely composed of rounded fragments of coral. In such a loose, dry, stony soil, the climate of the intertropical regions alone could produce a vigorous vegetation. On some of the

---

Mr. Ross had refused to give Hare's slaves their freedom, for fear that the executors of that man should demand their value from him; but he paid them each two rupees a week, in goods (at his own valuation), provided that they worked for him, both men and women, as he thought proper. Mr. Liesk told me this, and said that 'many of the Malays were very discontented, and wanted to leave the island.' 'No wonder,' thought I, 'for they are still slaves, and only less ill used than they were by the man who purchased them.'

"These Malays were allowed to rear poultry, which they sometimes sold to shipping. They were also allowed to have the produce of a certain number of cocoa-nut trees, and might catch fish and turtle for their own use; but the sale of turtle to shipping, when they touched there, and the immense crops of cocoa-nuts which are produced annually on all the islets of the group were monopolized by Mr. Ross for his sole advantage. One daily task imposed upon the Malay women was to 'husk' a hundred nuts, collected for them by the men, who extract a gallon of oil from every ten."

smaller islets, nothing could be more elegant than the manner in which the young and full-grown cocoa-nut trees, without destroying each other's symmetry, were mingled into one wood. A beach of glittering white sand formed a border to these fairy spots.

I will now give a sketch of the natural history of these islands, which, from its very paucity, possesses a peculiar interest. The cocoa-nut tree, at the first glance, seems to compose the whole wood; there are, however, five or six other trees. One of these grows to a very large size, but, from the extreme softness of its wood, is useless; another sort affords excellent timber for ship-building. Besides the trees, the number of plants is exceedingly limited, and consists of insignificant weeds. In my collection, which includes, I believe, nearly the perfect Flora, there are twenty species, without reckoning a moss, lichen, and fungus. To this number two trees must be added; one of which was not in flower, and the other I only heard of. The latter is a solitary tree of its kind, and grows near the beach, where, without doubt, the one seed was thrown up by the waves. A Guilandina also grows on only one of the islets. I do not include in the above list the sugar-cane, banana, some other vegetables, fruit-trees, and imported grasses. As the islands consist entirely of coral, and at one time must have existed as mere water-washed reefs, all their terrestrial productions must have been transported here by the waves of the sea. In accordance with this, the Florula has quite the character of a refuge for the destitute: Professor Henslow informs me that of the twenty species nineteen belong to different genera, and these again to no less than sixteen families![2]

In Holman's[3] Travels an account is given, on the authority of Mr. A. S. Keating, who resided twelve months on these islands, of the various seeds and other bodies which have been known to have been washed on shore. "Seeds and plants from Sumatra and Java have been driven up by the surf on the windward side of the islands. Among them have been found the Kimiri, native of Sumatra and the peninsula of Malacca; the cocoa-nut of Balci, known by its shape and size; the Dadass, which is planted by the Malays with the pepper-vine, the latter intwining round its trunk, and supporting itself by the prickles on its stem; the soap-tree; the castor-oil plant; trunks of the

[2] [Darwin] These plants are described in the Annals of Nat. Hist., vol. i. 1838, p. 337.

[3] [Darwin] Holman's Travels, vol. iv. p. 378.

sago palm; and various kinds of seeds unknown to the Malays settled on the islands. These are all supposed to have been driven by the N.W. monsoon to the coast of New Holland,[4] and thence to these islands by the S.E. trade-wind. Large masses of Java teak and Yellow wood have also been found, besides immense trees of red and white cedar, and the blue gumwood of New Holland, in a perfectly sound condition. All the hardy seeds, such as creepers, retain their germinating power, but the softer kinds, among which is the mangostin, are destroyed in the passage. Fishing-canoes, apparently from Java, have at times been washed on shore." It is interesting thus to discover how numerous the seeds are, which, coming from several countries, are drifted over the wide ocean. Professor Henslow tells me, he believes that nearly all the plants which I brought from these islands, are common littoral species in the East Indian archipelago. From the direction, however, of the winds and currents, it seems scarcely possible that they could have come here in a direct line. If, as suggested with much probability by Mr. Keating, they were first carried towards the coast of New Holland, and thence drifted back together with the productions of that country, the seeds, before germinating, must have travelled between 1800 and 2400 miles.

Chamisso,[5] when describing the Radack Archipelago,[6] situated in the western part of the Pacific, states that "the sea brings to these islands the seeds and fruits of many trees, most of which have not yet grown here. The greater part of these seeds appear to have not yet lost the capability of growing." It is also said that palms and bamboos from somewhere in the torrid zone, and trunks of northern firs, are washed on shore: these firs must have come from an immense distance. These facts are highly interesting. It cannot be doubted that if there were land-birds to pick up the seeds when first cast on shore, and a soil better adapted for their growth than the loose blocks of coral, that the most isolated of the lagoon-islands would in time possess a far more abundant Flora than they now have.

The list of land animals is even poorer than that of the plants. Some of the islets are inhabited by rats, which were brought in a ship from the Mauritius, wrecked here. These rats are considered by Mr. Waterhouse as identical with the Eng-

[4] [Editor] An old name for Australia, dating back to the era of Dutch exploration in the Far East.

[5] [Darwin] Kotzebue's First Voyage, vol. iii. p. 155.

[6] [Editor] Radak Group of the Marshall Islands.

lish kind, but they are smaller, and more brightly coloured. There are no true land-birds; for a snipe and a rail (Rallus Phillippensis), though living entirely in the dry herbage, belong to the order of Waders. Birds of this order are said to occur on several of the small low islands in the Pacific. At Ascension, where there is no land bird, a rail (Porphyrio simplex) was shot near the summit of the mountain, and it was evidently a solitary straggler. At Tristan d'Acunha,[7] where, according to Carmichael, there are only two land birds, there is a coot. From these facts I believe that the waders, after the innumerable web-footed species, are generally the first colonists of small isolated islands. I may add, that whenever I noticed birds, not of oceanic species, very far out at sea, they always belonged to this order; and hence they would naturally become the earliest colonists of any remote point of land.

Of reptiles I saw only one small lizard. Of insects I took pains to collect every kind. Exclusive of spiders, which were numerous, there were thirteen species.[8] Of these, one only was a beetle. A small ant swarmed by thousands under the loose dry blocks of coral, and was the only true insect which was abundant. Although the productions of the land are thus scanty, if we look to the waters of the surrounding sea, the number of organic beings is indeed infinite. Chamisso has described[9] the natural history of a lagoon-island in the Radack Archipelago; and it is remarkable how closely its inhabitants, in number and kind, resemble those of Keeling Island. There is one lizard and two waders, namely, a snipe and curlew. Of plants there are nineteen species, including a fern; and some of these are the same with those growing here, though on a spot so immensely remote, and in a different ocean.

The long strips of land, forming the linear islets, have been raised only to that height to which the surf can throw fragments of coral, and the wind heap up calcareous sand. The solid flat of coral rock on the outside, by its breadth, breaks the first violence of the waves, which otherwise, in a day, would sweep away these islets and all their productions. The ocean and the

---

[7] [Editor] At latitude 38° South in the South Atlantic Ocean.

[8] [Darwin] The thirteen species belong to the following orders: —In the *Coleoptera*, a minute Elater; *Orthoptera*, a Gryllus and a Blatta; *Hemiptera*, one species; *Homoptera*, two; *Neuroptera*, a Chrysopa; *Hymenoptera*, two ants; *Lepidoptera nocturna*, a Diopæa, and a Pterophorus (?); *Diptera*, two species.

[9] [Darwin] Kotzebue's First Voyage, vol. iii. p. 222.

land seem here struggling for mastery: although terra firma
has obtained a footing, the denizens of the water think their
claim at least equally good. In every part one meets hermit
crabs of more than one species,[10] carrying on their backs
the shells which they have stolen from the neighbouring beach.
Overhead, numerous gannets, frigate-birds, and terns, rest on
the trees; and the wood, from the many nests and from the
smell of the atmosphere, might be called a sea-rookery. The
gannets, sitting on their rude nests, gaze at one with a stupid
yet angry air. The noddies, as their name expresses, are silly
little creatures. But there is one charming bird: it is a small
snow-white tern, which smoothly hovers at the distance of a
few feet above one's head, its large black eye scanning, with
quiet curiosity, your expression. Little imagination is required
to fancy that so light and delicate a body must be tenanted by
some wandering fairy spirit.

Sunday, April 3rd.—After service I accompanied Captain Fitz
Roy to the settlement, situated at the distance of some miles,
on the point of an islet thickly covered with tall cocoa-nut
trees. Captain Ross and Mr. Liesk live in a large barn-like
house open at both ends, and lined with mats made of woven
bark. The houses of the Malays are arranged along the shore
of the lagoon. The whole place had rather a desolate aspect,
for there were no gardens to show the signs of care and cultivation. The natives belong to different islands in the East Indian archipelago, but all speak the same language: we saw the
inhabitants of Borneo, Celebes, Java, and Sumatra. In colour
they resemble the Tahitians, from whom they do not widely
differ in features. Some of the women, however, show a good
deal of the Chinese character. I liked both their general expressions and the sound of their voices. They appeared poor, and
their houses were destitute of furniture; but it was evident, from
the plumpness of the little children, that cocoa-nuts and turtle
afford no bad sustenance.

On this island the wells are situated, from which ships obtain water. At first sight it appears not a little remarkable that
the fresh water should regularly ebb and flow with the tides;

[10] [Darwin] The large claws or pincers of some of these crabs
are most beautifully adapted, when drawn back, to form an opercu-
lum to the shell, nearly as perfect as the proper one originally belonging to the molluscous animal. I was assured, and as far as my
observation went I found it so, that certain species of the hermit-
crabs always use certain species of shells.

and it has even been imagined that sand has the power of filtering the salt from the sea-water. These ebbing wells are common on some of the low islands in the West Indies. The compressed sand, or porous coral rock, is permeated like a sponge with the salt water; but the rain which falls on the surface must sink to the level of the surrounding sea, and must accumulate there, displacing an equal bulk of the salt water. As the water in the lower part of the great sponge-like coral mass rises and falls with the tides, so will the water near the surface; and this will keep fresh, if the mass be sufficiently compact to prevent much mechanical admixture; but where the land consists of great loose blocks of coral with open interstices, if a well be dug, the water, as I have seen, is brackish.

After dinner we stayed to see a curious half superstitious scene acted by the Malay women. A large wooden spoon dressed in garments, and which had been carried to the grave of a dead man, they pretend becomes inspired at the full of the moon, and will dance and jump about. After the proper preparations, the spoon, held by two women, became convulsed, and danced in good time to the song of the surrounding children and women. It was a most foolish spectacle; but Mr. Liesk maintained that many of the Malays believed in its spiritual movements. The dance did not commence till the moon had risen, and it was well worth remaining to behold her bright orb so quietly shining through the long arms of the cocoa-nut trees as they waved in the evening breeze. These scenes of the tropics are in themselves so delicious, that they almost equal those dearer ones at home, to which we are bound by each best feeling of the mind.

The next day I employed myself in examining the very interesting, yet simple structure and origin of these islands. The water being unusually smooth, I waded over the outer flat of dead rock as far as the living mounds of coral, on which the swell of the open sea breaks. In some of the gullies and hollows there were beautiful green and other coloured fishes, and the forms and tints of many of the zoophytes were admirable. It is excusable to grow enthusiastic over the infinite numbers of organic beings with which the sea of the tropics, so prodigal of life, teems; yet I must confess I think those naturalists who have described, in well-known words, the submarine grottoes decked with a thousand beauties, have indulged in rather exuberant language.

April 6th.—I accompanied Captain Fitz Roy to an island at

the head of the lagoon: the channel was exceedingly intricate, winding through fields of delicately branched corals. We saw several turtle, and two boats were then employed in catching them. The water was so clear and shallow, that although at first a turtle quickly dives out of sight, yet in a canoe or boat under sail, the pursuers after no very long chase come up to it. A man standing ready in the bow, at this moment dashes through the water upon the turtle's back; then clinging with both hands by the shell of its neck, he is carried away till the animal becomes exhausted and is secured. It was quite an interesting chase to see the two boats thus doubling about, and the men dashing head foremost into the water trying to seize their prey. Captain Moresby informs me that in the Chagos archipelago in this same ocean, the natives, by a horrible process, take the shell from the back of the living turtle. "It is covered with burning charcoal, which causes the outer shell to curl upwards; it is then forced off with a knife, and before it becomes cold flattened between boards. After this barbarous process the animal is suffered to regain its native element, where, after a certain time, a new shell is formed; it is, however, too thin to be of any service, and the animal always appears languishing and sickly."

When we arrived at the head of the lagoon, we crossed a narrow islet, and found a great surf breaking on the windward coast. I can hardly explain the reason, but there is to my mind much grandeur in the view of the outer shores of these lagoon-islands. There is a simplicity in the barrier-like beach, the margin of green bushes and tall cocoa-nuts, the solid flat of dead coral-rock, strewed here and there with great loose fragments, and the line of furious breakers, all rounding away towards either hand. The ocean throwing its waters over the broad reef appears an invincible, all-powerful enemy; yet we see it resisted, and even conquered, by means which at first seem most weak and inefficient. It is not that the ocean spares the rock of coral; the great fragments scattered over the reef, and heaped on the beach, whence the tall cocoa-nut springs, plainly bespeak the unrelenting power of the waves. Nor are any periods of repose granted. The long swell caused by the gentle but steady action of the trade-wind, always blowing in one direction over a wide area, causes breakers, almost equalling in force those during a gale of wind in the temperate regions, and which never cease to rage. It is impossible to behold these waves without feeling a conviction that an island, though built of the hardest rock, let it be porphyry, granite, or quartz, would ultimately yield and be demolished by such an irresistible power. Yet these low, insignificant coral-islets stand and are victorious: for here another power, as an antagonist, takes part in the contest. The organic forces separate the atoms of carbonate of lime, one by one, from the foaming breakers, and unite them into a symmetrical structure. Let the hurricane tear up its thousand huge fragments; yet what will that tell against the accumulated labour of myriads of architects at work night and day, month after month? Thus do we see the soft and gelatinous body of a polypus, through the agency of the vital laws, conquering the great mechanical power of the waves of an ocean which neither the art of man nor the inanimate works of nature could successfully resist.

We did not return on board till late in the evening, for we staid a long time in the lagoon, examining the fields of coral and the gigantic shells of the chama, into which, if a man were to put his hand, he would not, as long as the animal lived, be able to withdraw it. Near the head of the lagoon, I was much surprised to find a wide area, considerably more than a mile square, covered with a forest of delicately branching corals, which, though standing upright, were all dead and rotten. At first I was quite at a loss to understand the cause; afterwards it occurred to me that it was owing to the following rather curious combination of circumstances. It should, however, first be stated, that corals are not able to survive even a short exposure in the air to the sun's rays, so that their upward limit of growth is determined by that of lowest water at spring tides. It appears, from some old charts, that the long island to windward was formerly separated by wide channels into several islets; this fact is likewise indicated by the trees being younger on these portions. Under the former condition of the reef, a strong breeze, by throwing more water over the barrier, would tend to raise the level of the lagoon. Now it acts in a directly contrary manner; for the water within the lagoon not only is not increased by currents from the outside, but is itself blown outwards by the force of the wind. Hence it is observed, that the tide near the head of the lagoon does not rise so high during a strong breeze as it does when it is calm. This difference of level, although no doubt very small, has, I believe, caused the death of those coral-groves, which under the former and more open condition of the outer reef had attained the utmost possible limit of upward growth.

A few miles north of Keeling there is another small atoll,
the lagoon of which is nearly filled up with coral-mud. Captain
Ross found embedded in the conglomerate on the outer coast,
a well-rounded fragment of greenstone, rather larger than a
man's head: he and the men with him were so much surprised
at this, that they brought it away and preserved it as a curiosity.
The occurrence of this one stone, where every other particle
of matter is calcareous, certainly is very puzzling. The island
has scarcely ever been visited, nor is it probable that a ship
had been wrecked there. From the absence of any better explanation, I came to the conclusion that it must have come
entangled in the roots of some large tree: when, however, I
considered the great distance from the nearest land, the combination of chances against a stone thus being entangled, the
tree washed into the sea, floated so far, then landed safely, and
the stone finally so embedded as to allow of its discovery, I
was almost afraid of imagining a means of transport apparently so improbable. It was therefore with great interest that I
found Chamisso, the justly distinguished naturalist who accompanied Kotzebue, stating that the inhabitants of the Radack
archipelago, a group of lagoon-islands in the midst of the Pacific, obtained stones for sharpening their instruments by
searching the roots of trees which are cast upon the beach. It
will be evident that this must have happened several times,
since laws have been established that such stones belong to the
chief, and a punishment is inflicted on any one who attempts
to steal them. When the isolated position of these small islands
in the midst of a vast ocean—their great distance from any
land excepting that of coral formation, attested by the value
which the inhabitants, who are such bold navigators, attach
to a stone of any kind,[11]—and the slowness of the currents
of the open sea, are all considered, the occurrence of pebbles
thus transported does appear wonderful. Stones may often be
thus carried; and if the island on which they are stranded is
constructed of any other substance besides coral, they would
scarcely attract attention, and their origin at least would never
be guessed. Moreover, this agency may long escape discovery
from the probability of trees, especially those loaded with
stones, floating beneath the surface. In the channels of Tierra
del Fuego large quantities of drift timber are cast upon the

---

[11] [Darwin] Some natives carried by Kotzebue to Kamtschatka
collected stones to take back to their country.

beach, yet it is extremely rare to meet a tree swimming on the water. These facts may possibly throw light on single stones, whether angular or rounded, occasionally found embedded in fine sedimentary masses.

During another day I visited West Islet, on which the vegetation was perhaps more luxuriant than on any other. The cocoa-nut trees generally grow separate, but here the young ones flourished beneath their tall parents, and formed with their long and curved fronds the most shady arbours. Those alone who have tried it, know how delicious it is to be seated in such shade, and drink the cool pleasant fluid of the cocoa-nut. In this island there is a large bay-like space, composed of the finest white sand: it is quite level, and is only covered by the tide at high water; from this large bay smaller creeks penetrate the surrounding woods. To see a field of glittering white sand, representing water, with the cocoa-nut trees extending their tall and waving trunks round the margin, formed a singular and very pretty view.

I have before alluded to a crab which lives on the cocoa-nuts: it is very common on all parts of the dry land, and grows to a monstrous size: it is closely allied or identical with the Birgos latro. The front pair of legs terminate in very strong and heavy pincers, and the last pair are fitted with others weaker and much narrower. It would at first be thought quite impossible for a crab to open a strong cocoa-nut covered with the husk; but Mr. Liesk assures me that he has repeatedly seen this effected. The crab begins by tearing the husk, fibre by fibre, and always from that end under which the three eye-holes are situated; when this is completed, the crab commences hammering with its heavy claws on one of the eye-holes till an opening is made. Then turning round its body, by the aid of its posterior and narrow pair of pincers, it extracts the white albuminous substance. I think this is as curious a case of instinct as ever I heard of, and likewise of adaptation in structure between two objects apparently so remote from each other in the scheme of nature, as a crab and a cocoa-nut tree. The Birgos is diurnal in its habits; but every night it is said to pay a visit to the sea, no doubt for the purpose of moistening its branchiæ. The young are likewise hatched, and live for some time, on the coast. These crabs inhabit deep burrows, which they hollow out beneath the roots of trees; and where they accumulate surprising quantities of the picked fibres of the cocoa-nut husk, on which they rest as on a bed. The Malays

sometimes take advantage of this, and collect the fibrous mass
to use as junk. These crabs are very good to eat; moreover,
under the tail of the larger ones there is a great mass of fat,
which, when melted, sometimes yields as much as a quart bottle full of limpid oil. It has been stated by some authors that
the Birgos crawls up the cocoa-nut trees for the purpose of
stealing the nuts: I very much doubt the possibility of this; but
with the Pandanus[12] the task would be very much easier. I
was told by Mr. Liesk that on these islands the Birgos lives
only on the nuts which have fallen to the ground.

Captain Moresby informs me that this crab inhabits the
Chagos and Seychelle groups, but not the neighbouring Maldiva archipelago. It formerly abounded at Mauritius, but only
a few small ones are now found there. In the Pacific, this
species, or one with closely allied habits, is said[13] to inhabit
a single coral island, north of the Society group. To show the
wonderful strength of the front pair of pincers, I may mention, that Captain Moresby confined one in a strong tin-box,
which had held biscuits, the lid being secured with wire; but
the crab turned down the edges and escaped. In turning down
the edges, it actually punched many small holes quite through
the tin!

I was a good deal surprised by finding two species of coral
of the genus Millepora (M. complanata and alcicornis), possessed of the power of stinging. The stony branches or plates,
when taken fresh from the water, have a harsh feel and are
not slimy, although possessing a strong and disagreeable smell.
The stinging property seems to vary in different specimens:
when a piece was pressed or rubbed on the tender skin of the
face or arm, a pricking sensation was usually caused, which
came on after the interval of a second, and lasted only for a
few minutes. One day, however, by merely touching my face
with one of the branches, pain was instantaneously caused; it
increased as usual after a few seconds, and remaining sharp
for some minutes, was perceptible for half an hour afterwards.
The sensation was as bad as that from a nettle, but more like
that caused by the Physalia or Portuguese man-of-war. Little
red spots were produced on the tender skin of the arm, which
appeared as if they would have formed watery pustules, but
did not. M. Quoy mentions this case of the Millepora; and I

12 [Darwin] See Proceedings of Zoological Society, 1832, p. 17.
13 [Darwin] Tyerman and Bennett. Voyage, &c., vol. ii. p. 33.

have heard of stinging corals in the West Indies. Many marine animals seem to have this power of stinging: besides the Portuguese man-of-war, many jelly-fish, and the Aplysia or sea-slug of the Cape de Verd Islands, it is stated in the voyage of the *Astrolabe*, that an Actinia or sea-anemone, as well as a flexible coralline allied to Sertularia, both possess this means of offence or defence. In the East Indian sea, a stinging sea-weed is said to be found.

Two species of fish, of the genus Scarus, which are common here, exclusively feed on coral: both are coloured of a splendid bluish-green, one living invariably in the lagoon, and the other amongst the outer breakers. Mr. Liesk assured us, that he had repeatedly seen whole shoals grazing with their strong bony jaws on the tops of the coral branches: I opened the intestines of several, and found them distended with yellowish calcareous sandy mud. The slimy disgusting Holuthuriæ (allied to our star-fish), which the Chinese gourmands are so fond of, also feed largely, as I am informed by Dr. Allan, on corals; and the bony apparatus within their bodies seems well adapted for this end. These holuthuriæ, the fish, the numerous burrowing shells, and nereidous worms, which perforate every block of dead coral, must be very efficient agents in producing the fine white mud which lies at the bottom and on the shores of the lagoon. A portion, however, of this mud, which when wet strikingly resembled pounded chalk, was found by Professor Ehrenberg to be partly composed of siliceous-shielded infusoria.

April 12*th*.—In the morning we stood out of the lagoon on our passage to the Isle of France.[14] I am glad we have visited these islands: such formations surely rank high amongst the wonderful objects of this world. Captain Fitz Roy found no bottom with a line 7200 feet in length, at the distance of only 2200 yards from the shore; hence this island forms a lofty submarine mountain, with sides steeper even than those of the most abrupt volcanic cone. The saucer-shaped summit is nearly ten miles across; and every single atom,[15] from the least particle to the largest fragment of rock, in this great pile, which

14 [Editor] Mauritius.

15 [Darwin] I exclude, of course, some soil which has been imported here in vessels from Malacca and Java, and likewise some small fragments of pumice, drifted here by the waves. The one block of green-stone, moreover, on the northern island must be excepted.

however is small compared with very many other lagoon-islands, bears the stamp of having been subjected to organic arrangement. We feel surprise when travellers tell us of the vast dimensions of the Pyramids and other great ruins, but how utterly insignificant are the greatest of these, when compared to these mountains of stone accumulated by the agency of various minute and tender animals! This is a wonder which does not at first strike the eye of the body, but, after reflection, the eye of reason.

I will now give a very brief account of the three great classes of coral-reefs; namely, Atolls, Barrier, and Fringing-reefs, and will explain my views[16] on their formation. Almost every voyager who has crossed the Pacific has expressed his unbounded

astonishment at the lagoon-islands, or as I shall for the future call them by their Indian name of atolls, and has attempted some explanation. Even as long ago as the year 1605, Pyrard de Laval well exclaimed, "C'est une meruille de voir chacun de ces atollons, enuironné d'un grand banc de pierre tout autour, n'y ayant point d'artifice humain."[17] The accompanying sketch of Whitsunday Island in the Pacific, copied from Capt. Beechey's admirable Voyage, gives but a faint idea of the singular aspect of an atoll: it is one of the smallest size, and has its narrow islets united together in a ring. The immensity of the ocean, the fury of the breakers, contrasted with the

[16] [Darwin] These were first read before the Geological Society in May, 1837, and have since been developed in a separate volume on the "Structure and Distribution of Coral Reefs."

[17] [Editor] "It is a marvel to see each of these atolls, surrounded by a great bank of stone involving no human artifice at all."

lowness of the land and the smoothness of the bright green water within the lagoon, can hardly be imagined without having been seen.

The earlier voyagers fancied that the coral-building animals instinctively built up their great circles to afford themselves protection in the inner parts; but so far is this from the truth, that those massive kinds, to whose growth on the exposed outer shores the very existence of the reef depends, cannot live within the lagoon, where other delicately-branching kinds flourish. Moreover, on this view, many species of distinct genera and families are supposed to combine for one end; and of such a combination, not a single instance can be found in the whole of nature. The theory that has been most generally received is, that atolls are based on submarine craters; but when we consider the form and size of some, the number, proximity, and relative positions of others, this idea loses its plausible character: thus, Suadiva atoll is 44 geographical miles in diameter in one line, by 34 miles in another line; Rimsky is 54 by 20 miles across, and it has a strangely sinuous margin; Bow atoll is 30 miles long, and on an average only 6 in width; Menchicoff atoll consists of three atolls united or tied together. This theory, moreover, is totally inapplicable to the northern Maldiva atolls in the Indian Ocean (one of which is 88 miles in length, and between 10 and 20 in breadth), for they are not bounded like ordinary atolls by narrow reefs, but by a vast number of separate little atolls; other little atolls rising out of the great central lagoon-like spaces. A third and better theory was advanced by Chamisso, who thought that from the corals growing more vigorously where exposed to the open sea, as undoubtedly is the case, the outer edges would grow up from the general foundation before any other part, and that this would account for the ring or cup-shaped structure. But we shall immediately see, that in this, as well as in the crater-theory, a most important consideration has been overlooked, namely, on what have the reef-building corals, which cannot live at a great depth, based their massive structures?

Numerous soundings were carefully taken by Captain Fitz Roy on the steep outside of Keeling atoll, and it was found that within ten fathoms, the prepared tallow at the bottom of the lead, invariably came up marked with the impressions of living corals, but as perfectly clean as if it had been dropped on a carpet of turf; as the depth increased, the impressions became less numerous, but the adhering particles of sand more and more numerous, until at last it was evident that the bottom consisted of a smooth sandy layer: to carry on the analogy of the turf, the blades of grass grew thinner and thinner, till at last the soil was so sterile, that nothing sprang from it. From these observations, confirmed by many others, it may be safely inferred that the utmost depth at which corals can construct reefs is between 20 and 30 fathoms. Now there are enormous areas in the Pacific and Indian Oceans, in which every single island is of coral formation, and is raised only to that height to which the waves can throw up fragments, and the winds pile up sand. Thus the Radack group of atolls is an irregular square, 520 miles long and 240 broad; the Low archipelago is elliptic-formed, 840 miles in its longer, and 420 in its shorter axis: there are other small groups and single low islands between these two archipelagoes, making a linear space of ocean actually more than 4000 miles in length, in which not one single island rises above the specified height. Again, in the Indian Ocean there is a space of ocean 1500 miles in length, including three archipelagoes, in which every island is low and of coral formation. From the fact of the reef-building corals not living at great depths, it is absolutely certain that throughout these vast areas, wherever there is now an atoll, a foundation must have originally existed within a depth of from 20 to 30 fathoms from the surface. It is improbable in the highest degree that broad, lofty, isolated, steep-sided banks of sediment, arranged in groups and lines hundreds of leagues in length, could have been deposited in the central and profoundest parts of the Pacific and Indian Oceans, at an immense distance from any continent, and where the water is perfectly limpid. It is equally improbable that the elevatory forces should have uplifted throughout the above vast areas, innumerable great rocky banks within 20 to 30 fathoms, or 120 to 180 feet, of the surface of the sea, and not one single point above that level; for where on the whole face of the globe can we find a single chain of mountains, even a few hundred miles in length, with their many summits rising within a few feet of a given level, and not one pinnacle above it? If then the foundations, whence the atoll-building corals sprang, were not formed of sediment, and if they were not lifted up to the required level, they must of necessity have subsided into it; and this at once solves the difficulty. For as mountain after mountain, and island after island, slowly sank beneath the water, fresh bases would be successively afforded for the growth of the corals. It is impossible here to enter into all the necessary details, but I venture to defy[18] any one to explain in any other manner, how it is possible that numerous islands should be distributed throughout vast areas—all the islands being low—all being built of corals, absolutely requiring a foundation within a limited depth from the surface.

Before explaining how atoll-formed reefs acquire their peculiar structure, we must turn to the second great class, namely, Barrier-reefs. These either extend in straight lines in front of the shores of a continent or of a large island, or they encircle smaller islands; in both cases, being separated from the land by a broad and rather deep channel of water, analogous to the lagoon within an atoll. It is remarkable how little attention has been paid to encircling barrier-reefs; yet they are truly wonderful structures. The following sketch represents part of

the barrier encircling the island of Bolabola in the Pacific, as seen from one of the central peaks. In this instance the whole line of reef has been converted into land; but usually a snow-white line of great breakers, with only here and there a single low islet crowned with cocoa-nut trees, divides the dark heaving waters of the ocean from the light-green expanse of the lagoon-channel. And the quiet waters of this channel generally bathe a fringe of low alluvial soil, loaded with the most beau-

18 [Darwin] It is remarkable that Mr. Lyell, even in the first Edition of his "Principles of Geology," inferred that the amount of subsidence in the Pacific must have exceeded that of elevation, from the area of land being very small relatively to the agents there tending to form it, namely, the growth of coral and volcanic action.

tiful productions of the tropics, and lying at the foot of the wild, abrupt, central mountains.

Encircling barrier-reefs are of all sizes, from three miles to no less than forty-four miles in diameter; and that which fronts one side, and encircles both ends, of New Caledonia, is 400 miles long. Each reef includes one, two, or several rocky islands of various heights; and in one instance, even as many as twelve separate islands. The reef runs at a greater or less distance from the included land; in the Society archipelago generally from one to three or four miles; but at Hogoleu the reef is 20 miles on the southern side, and 14 miles on the opposite or northern side, from the included islands. The depth within the lagoon-channel also varies much; from 10 to 30 fathoms may be taken as an average; but at Vanikoro there are spaces no less than 56 fathoms or 336 feet deep. Internally the reef either slopes gently into the lagoon-channel, or ends in a perpendicular wall sometimes between two and three hundred feet under water in height: externally the reef rises, like an atoll, with extreme abruptness out of the profound depths of the ocean. What can be more singular than these structures? We see an island, which may be compared to a castle situated on the summit of a lofty submarine mountain, protected by a great wall of coral-rock, always steep externally and sometimes internally, with a broad level summit, here and there breached by narrow gateways, through which the largest ships can enter the wide and deep encircling moat.

As far as the actual reef of coral is concerned, there is not the smallest difference, in general size, outline, grouping, and even in quite trifling details of structure, between a barrier and an atoll. The geographer Balbi has well remarked, that an encircled island is an atoll with high land rising out of its lagoon; remove the land from within, and a perfect atoll is left.

But what has caused these reefs to spring up at such great distances from the shores of the included islands? It cannot be that the corals will not grow close to the land; for the shores within the lagoon-channel, when not surrounded by alluvial soil, are often fringed by living reefs; and we shall presently see that there is a whole class, which I have called Fringing-reefs from their close attachment to the shores both of continents and of islands. Again, on what have the reef-building corals, which cannot live at great depths, based their encircling structures? This is a great apparent difficulty, analogous to that in the case of atolls, which has generally been overlooked. It will be perceived more clearly by inspecting the following sections, which are real ones, taken in north and south lines, through the islands with their barrier-reefs, of Vanikoro, Gambier, and Maurua; and they are laid down, both vertically and horizontally, on the same scale of a quarter of an inch to a mile.

It should be observed that the sections might have been taken in any direction through these islands, or through many other encircled islands, and the general features would have been the same. Now bearing in mind that reef-building coral cannot live at a greater depth than from 20 to 30 fathoms, and that the scale is so small that the plummets on the right hand show a depth of 200 fathoms, on what are these barrier-

1. Vanikoro.   2. Gambier Islands.   3. Maurua.

The horizontal shading shows the barrier-reefs and lagoon-channels. The inclined shading above the level of the sea (AA), shows the actual form of the land; the inclined shading below this line, shows its probable prolongation under water.

reefs based? Are we to suppose that each island is surrounded by a collar-like submarine ledge of rock, or by a great bank of sediment, ending abruptly where the reef ends? If the sea had formerly eaten deeply into the islands, before they were protected by the reefs, thus having left a shallow ledge round them under water, the present shores would have been invariably bounded by great precipices; but this is most rarely the case. Moreover, on this notion, it is not possible to explain why the corals should have sprung up, like a wall, from the extreme outer margin of the ledge, often leaving a broad space of water within, too deep for the growth of corals. The ac-

cumulation of a wide bank of sediment all round these islands,
and generally widest where the included islands are smallest,
is highly improbable, considering their exposed positions in the
central and deepest parts of the ocean. In the case of the
barrier-reef of New Caledonia, which extends for 150 miles
beyond the northern point of the island, in the same straight
line with which it fronts the west coast, it is hardly possible to
believe, that a bank of sediment could thus have been straightly
deposited in front of a lofty island, and so far beyond its termination in the open sea. Finally, if we look to other oceanic
islands of about the same height and of similar geological constitution, but not encircled by coral-reefs, we may in vain
search for so trifling a circumambient depth as 30 fathoms,
except quite near to their shores; for usually land that rises
abruptly out of water, as do most of the encircled and non-
encircled oceanic islands, plunges abruptly under it. On what
then, I repeat, are these barrier-reefs based? Why, with their
wide and deep moat-like channels, do they stand so far from
the included land? We shall soon see how easily these difficulties disappear.

We come now to our third class of Fringing-reefs, which
will require a very short notice. Where the land slopes abruptly
under water, these reefs are only a few yards in width, forming a mere ribbon or fringe round the shores: where the land
slopes gently under the water the reef extends further, sometimes even as much as a mile from the land; but in such cases
the soundings outside the reef, always show that the submarine
prolongation of the land is gently inclined. In fact the reefs
extend only to that distance from the shore, at which a foundation within the requisite depth from 20 to 30 fathoms is found.
As far as the actual reef is concerned, there is no essential
difference between it and that forming a barrier or an atoll:
it is, however, generally of less width, and consequently few
islets have been formed on it. From the corals growing more
vigorously on the outside, and from the noxious effect of the
sediment washed inwards, the outer edge of the reef is the
highest part, and between it and the land there is generally a
shallow sandy channel a few feet in depth. Where banks of
sediment have accumulated near to the surface, as in parts
of the West Indies, they sometimes become fringed with corals,
and hence in some degree resemble lagoon-islands or atolls;
in the same manner as fringing-reefs, surrounding gently-
sloping islands, in some degree resemble barrier-reefs.

No theory on the formation of coral-reefs can be considered satisfactory which does not include the three great classes. We have seen that we are driven to believe in the subsidence of these vast areas, interspersed with low islands, of which not one rises above the height to which the wind and waves can throw up matter, and yet are constructed by animals requiring a foundation, and that foundation to lie at no great depth. Let us then take an island surrounded by fringing-reefs, which offer no difficulty in their structure; and let this island with its reef,

AA. Outer edges of the fringing-reef, at the level of the sea. BB. The shores of the fringed island.

A'A'. Outer edges of the reef, after its upward growth during a period of subsidence, now converted into a barrier, with islets on it. B'B'. The shores of the now encircled island. CC. Lagoon-channel.

N.B. In this and the following woodcut, the subsidence of the land could be represented only by an apparent rise in the level of the sea.

represented by the unbroken lines in the woodcut, slowly subside. Now as the island sinks down, either a few feet at a time or quite insensibly, we may safely infer, from what is known of the conditions favourable to the growth of coral, that the living masses, bathed by the surf on the margin of the reef, will soon regain the surface. The water, however, will encroach little by little on the shore, the island becoming lower and smaller, and the space between the inner edge of the reef and the beach proportionally broader. A section of the reef and island in this state, after a subsidence of several hundred feet, is given by the dotted lines. Coral islets are supposed to have been formed on the reef; and a ship is anchored in the lagoon-channel. This channel will be more or less deep, according to the rate of subsidence, to the amount of sediment accumulated in it, and to the growth of the delicately branched corals which can live there. The section in this state resembles in every respect one drawn through an encircled island: in fact, it is a real section (on the scale of .517 of an inch to a mile) through Bolabola in the Pacific. We can now at once see why encircling barrier-reefs stand so far from the shores which they front. We can also perceive, that a line drawn perpendicularly down from the outer edge of the new reef, to the foundation of solid rock beneath the old fringing-reef, will exceed by as many feet as there have been feet of subsidence, that small limit of depth at which the effective corals can live:—the little architects having built up their great wall-like mass, as the whole sank down, upon a basis formed of other corals

A′A′. Outer edges of the barrier-reef at the level of the sea, with islets on it. B′B′. The shores of the included island. CC. The lagoon-channel.

A″A″. Outer edges of the reef, now converted into an atoll. C′. The lagoon of the new atoll.

N.B. According to the true scale, the depths of the lagoon-channel and lagoon are much exaggerated.

and their consolidated fragments. Thus the difficulty on this head, which appeared so great, disappears.

If, instead of an island, we had taken the shore of a continent fringed with reefs, and had imagined it to have subsided, a great straight barrier, like that of Australia or New Caledonia, separated from the land by a wide and deep channel, would evidently have been the result.

Let us take our new encircling barrier-reef, of which the section is now represented by unbroken lines, and which, as I have said, is a real section through Bolabola, and let it go on subsiding. As the barrier-reef slowly sinks down, the corals will go on vigorously growing upwards; but as the island sinks, the water will gain inch by inch on the shore—the separate mountains first forming separate islands within one great reef—and finally, the last and highest pinnacle disappearing. The instant this takes place, a perfect atoll is formed: I have said, remove the high land from within an encircling barrier-reef, and an atoll is left, and the land has been removed. We can now perceive how it comes that atolls, having sprung from encircling barrier-reefs, resemble them in general size, form, in the manner in which they are grouped together, and in their arrangement in single or double lines; for they may be called rude outline charts of the sunken islands over which they stand. We can further see how it arises that the atolls in the Pacific and Indian oceans extend in lines parallel to the generally prevailing strike of the high islands and the great coast-lines of those oceans. I venture, therefore, to affirm, that on the theory of the upward growth of the corals during the sinking of the land,[19] all the leading features in those wonderful structures, the lagoon-islands or atolls, which have so long excited the attention of voyagers, as well as in the no less wonderful barrier-reefs, whether encircling small islands or stretching for hundreds of miles along the shores of a continent, are simply explained.

It may be asked, whether I can offer any direct evidence of the subsidence of barrier-reefs or atolls; but it must be borne in mind how difficult it must ever be to detect a movement, the tendency of which is to hide under water the part affected. Nevertheless, at Keeling atoll I observed on all sides of the lagoon old cocoa-nut trees undermined and falling; and in one place the foundation-posts of a shed, which the inhabitants asserted had stood seven years before just above high-water mark, but now was daily washed by every tide: on inquiry I found that three earthquakes, one of them severe, had been felt here during the last ten years. At Vanikoro, the lagoon-channel is remarkably deep, scarcely any alluvial soil has accumulated at the foot of the lofty included mountains, and remarkably few islets have been formed by the heaping of fragments and sand on the wall-like barrier-reef; these facts, and some analogous ones, led me to believe that this island

[19] [Darwin] It has been highly satisfactory to me to find the following passage in a pamphlet by Mr. Couthouy, one of the naturalists in the great Antarctic Expedition of the United States:— "Having personally examined a large number of coral-islands, and resided eight months among the volcanic class having shore and partially encircling reefs, I may be permitted to state that my own observations have impressed a conviction of the correctness of the theory of Mr. Darwin."—The naturalists, however, of this expedition differ with me on some points respecting coral formations.

must lately have subsided and the reef grown upwards: here again earthquakes are frequent and very severe. In the Society archipelago, on the other hand, where the lagoon-channels are almost choked up, where much low alluvial land has accumulated, and where in some cases long islets have been formed on the barrier-reefs—facts all showing that the islands have not very lately subsided—only feeble shocks are most rarely felt. In these coral formations, where the land and water seem struggling for mastery, it must be ever difficult to decide between the effects of a change in the set of the tides and of a slight subsidence: that many of these reefs and atolls are subject to changes of some kind is certain; on some atolls the islets appear to have increased greatly within a late period; on others they have been partially or wholly washed away. The inhabitants of parts of the Maldiva archipelago know the date of the first formation of some islets; in other parts, the corals are now flourishing on water-washed reefs, where holes made for graves attest the former existence of inhabited land. It is difficult to believe in frequent changes in the tidal currents of an open ocean; whereas, we have in the earthquakes recorded by the natives on some atolls, and in the great fissures observed on other atolls, plain evidence of changes and disturbances in progress in the subterranean regions.

It is evident, on our theory, that coasts merely fringed by reefs cannot have subsided to any perceptible amount; and therefore they must, since the growth of their corals, either have remained stationary or have been upheaved. Now it is remarkable how generally it can be shown, by the presence of upraised organic remains, that the fringed islands have been elevated: and so far, this is indirect evidence in favour of our theory. I was particularly struck with this fact, when I found to my surprise, that the descriptions given by MM. Quoy and Gaimard were applicable, not to reefs in general as implied by them, but only to those of the fringing-class; my surprise, however, ceased when I afterwards found that, by a strange chance, all the several islands visited by these eminent naturalists, could be shown by their own statements to have been elevated within a recent geological era.

Not only the grand features in the structure of barrier-reefs and of atolls, and of their likeness to each other in form, size, and other characters, are explained on the theory of subsidence—which theory we are independently forced to admit in the very areas in question, from the necessity of finding bases for the corals within the requisite depth—but many details in structure and exceptional cases can thus also be simply explained. I will give only a few instances. In barrier-reefs it has long been remarked with surprise, that the passages through the reef exactly face valleys in the included land, even in cases where the reef is separated from the land by a lagoon-channel so wide and so much deeper than the actual passage itself, that it seems hardly possible that the very small quantity of water or sediment brought down could injure the corals on the reef. Now, every reef of the fringing-class is breached by a narrow gateway in front of the smallest rivulet, even if dry during the greater part of the year, for the mud, sand, or gravel, occasionally washed down, kills the corals on which it is deposited. Consequently, when an island thus fringed subsides, though most of the narrow gateways will probably become closed by the outward and upward growth of the corals, yet any that are not closed (and some must always be kept open by the sediment and impure water flowing out of the lagoon-channel) will still continue to front exactly the upper parts of those valleys, at the mouths of which the original basal fringing-reef was breached.

We can easily see how an island fronted only on one side, or on one side with one end or both ends encircled by barrier-reefs, might after long-continued subsidence be converted either into a single wall-like reef, or into an atoll with a great straight spur projecting from it, or into two or three atolls tied together by straight reefs—all of which exceptional cases actually occur. As the reef-building corals require food, are preyed upon by other animals, are killed by sediment, cannot adhere to a loose bottom, and may be easily carried down to a depth whence they cannot spring up again, we need feel no surprise at the reefs both of atolls and barriers becoming in parts imperfect. The great barrier of New Caledonia is thus imperfect and broken in many parts; hence, after long subsidence, this great reef would not produce one great atoll 400 miles in length, but a chain or archipelago of atolls, of very nearly the same dimensions with those in the Maldiva archipelago. Moreover, in an atoll once breached on opposite sides, from the likelihood of the oceanic and tidal currents passing straight through the breaches, it is extremely improbable that the corals, especially during continued subsidence, would ever be able again to unite the rim; if they did not, as the whole sank downwards, one atoll would be divided into two or more. In the

Maldiva archipelago there are distinct atolls so related to each other in position, and separated by channels either unfathomable or very deep (the channel between Ross and Ari atolls is 150 fathoms, and that between the north and south Nillandoo atolls is 200 fathoms in depth), that it is impossible to look at a map of them without believing that they were once more intimately related. And in this same archipelago, Mahlos-Mahdoo atoll is divided by a bifurcating channel from 100 to 132 fathoms in depth, in such a manner, that it is scarcely possible to say whether it ought strictly to be called three separate atolls, or one great atoll not yet finally divided.

I will not enter on many more details; but I must remark that the curious structure of the northern Maldiva atolls receives (taking into consideration the free entrance of the sea through their broken margins) a simple explanation in the upward and outward growth of the corals, originally based both on small detached reefs in their lagoons, such as occur in common atolls, and on broken portions of the linear marginal reef, such as bounds every atoll of the ordinary form. I cannot refrain from once again remarking on the singularity of these complex structures—a great sandy and generally concave disk rises abruptly from the unfathomable ocean, with its central expanse studded, and its edge symmetrically bordered with oval basins of coral-rock just lipping the surface of the sea, sometimes clothed with vegetation, and each containing a lake of clear water!

One more point in detail: as in two neighbouring archipelagoes corals flourish in one and not in the other, and as so many conditions before enumerated must affect their existence, it would be an inexplicable fact if, during the changes to which earth, air, and water are subjected, the reef-building corals were to keep alive for perpetuity on any one spot or area. And as by our theory the areas including atolls and barrier-reefs are subsiding, we ought occasionally to find reefs both dead and submerged. In all reefs, owing to the sediment being washed out of the lagoon or lagoon-channel to leeward, that side is least favourable to the long-continued vigorous growth of the corals; hence dead portions of reef not unfrequently occur on the leeward side; and these, though still retaining their proper wall-like form, are now in several instances sunk several fathoms beneath the surface. The Chagos group appears from some cause, possibly from the subsidence having been too rapid, at present to be much less favourably circumstanced for the growth of reefs than formerly: one atoll has a portion of its marginal reef, nine miles in length, dead and submerged; a second has only a few quite small living points which rise to the surface; a third and fourth are entirely dead and submerged; a fifth is a mere wreck, with its structure almost obliterated. It is remarkable that in all these cases, the dead reefs and portions of reef lie at nearly the same depth, namely, from six to eight fathoms beneath the surface, as if they had been carried down by one uniform movement. One of these "half-drowned atolls," so called by Capt. Moresby (to whom I am indebted for much invaluable information), is of vast size, namely, ninety nautical miles across in one direction, and seventy miles in another line; and is in many respects eminently curious. As by our theory it follows that new atolls will generally be formed in each new area of subsidence, two weighty objections might have been raised, namely, that atolls must be increasing indefinitely in number; and secondly, that in old areas of subsidence each separate atoll must be increasing indefinitely in thickness, if proofs of their occasional destruction could not have been adduced. Thus have we traced the history of these great rings of coral-rock, from their first origin through their normal changes, and through the occasional accidents of their existence, to their death and final obliteration.

In my volume on "Coral Formations" I have published a map, in which I have coloured all the atolls dark-blue, the barrier-reefs pale-blue, and the fringing-reefs red. These latter reefs have been formed whilst the land has been stationary, or, as appears from the frequent presence of upraised organic remains, whilst it has been slowly rising: atolls and barrier-reefs, on the other hand, have grown up during the directly opposite movement of subsidence, which movement must have been very gradual, and in the case of atolls so vast in amount as to have buried every mountain-summit over wide ocean-spaces. Now in this map we see that the reefs tinted pale and dark blue, which have been produced by the same order of movement, as a general rule manifestly stand near each other. Again we see, that the areas with the two blue tints are of wide extent; and that they lie separate from extensive lines of coast coloured red, both of which circumstances might naturally have been inferred, on the theory of the nature of the reefs having been governed by the nature of the earth's move-

ment. It deserves notice, that in more than one instance where
single red and blue circles approach near each other, I can
show that there have been oscillations of level; for in such
cases the red or fringed circles consist of atolls, originally by
our theory formed during subsidence, but subsequently upheaved; and on the other hand, some of the pale-blue or encircled islands are composed of coral-rock, which must have
been uplifted to its present height before that subsidence took
place, during which the existing barrier-reefs grew upwards.

Authors have noticed with surprise, that although atolls are
the commonest coral-structures throughout some enormous
oceanic tracts, they are entirely absent in other seas, as in the
West Indies: we can now at once perceive the cause, for where
there has not been subsidence, atolls cannot have been formed;
and in the case of the West Indies and parts of the East Indies,
these tracts are known to have been rising within the recent
period. The larger areas, coloured red and blue, are all elongated; and between the two colours there is a degree of rude
alternation, as if the rising of one had balanced the sinking of
the other. Taking into consideration the proofs of recent elevation both on the fringed coasts and on some others (for instance, in South America) where there are no reefs, we are
led to conclude that the great continents are for the most part
rising areas; and from the nature of the coral-reefs, that the
central parts of the great oceans are sinking areas.[20] The East
Indian archipelago, the most broken land in the world, is in
most parts an area of elevation, but surrounded and penetrated, probably in more lines than one, by narrow areas of
subsidence.

I have marked with vermilion spots all the many known
active volcanoes within the limits of this same map. Their entire absence from every one of the great subsiding areas, coloured either pale or dark blue, is most striking; and not less so
is the coincidence of the chief volcanic chains with the parts
coloured red, which we are led to conclude have either long

[20] [Editor] Darwin supposed that the deep ocean basins are sinking in order to account for the submergence of volcanic islands required by his theory of atoll formation. Modern instruments for
charting the ocean bottom have revealed that the islands themselves, not the ocean basins as a whole, are sinking. Thus, many
oceanic islands stand in saucerlike depressions in the ocean floor.
The sinking is due to the great weight of the island pressing down
on the earth's crust.

remained stationary, or more generally have been recently up-raised. Although a few of the vermilion spots occur within no great distance of single circles tinted blue, yet not one single active volcano is situated within several hundred miles of an archipelago, or even small group of atolls. It is, therefore, a striking fact that in the Friendly Archipelago, which consists of a group of atolls upheaved and since partially worn down, two volcanoes, and perhaps more, are historically known to have been in action. On the other hand, although most of the islands in the Pacific which are encircled by barrier-reefs, are of volcanic origin, often with the remnants of craters still distinguishable, not one of them is known to have ever been in eruption. Hence in these cases it would appear, that volcanoes burst forth into action and become extinguished on the same spots, according as elevatory or subsiding movements prevail there. Numberless facts could be adduced to prove that up-raised organic remains are common wherever there are active volcanoes; but until it could be shown that in areas of subsidence, volcanoes were either absent or inactive, the inference, however probable in itself, that their distribution depended on the rising or falling of the earth's surface, would have been hazardous. But now, I think, we may freely admit this important deduction.

Taking a final view of the map, and bearing in mind the statement made with respect to the upraised organic remains, we must feel astonished at the vastness of the areas, which have suffered changes in level either downwards or upwards, within a period not geologically remote. It would appear, also, that the elevatory and subsiding movements follow nearly the same laws. Throughout the spaces interspersed with atolls, where not a single peak of high land has been left above the level of the sea, the sinking must have been immense in amount. The sinking, moreover, whether continuous, or recurrent with intervals sufficiently long for the corals again to bring up their living edifices to the surface, must necessarily have been extremely slow. This conclusion is probably the most important one which can be deduced from the study of coral formations;—and it is one which it is difficult to imagine, how otherwise could ever have been arrived at. Nor can I quite pass over the probability of the former existence of large archipelagoes of lofty islands, where now only rings of coral-rock scarcely break the open expanse of the sea, throwing some light on the distribution of the inhabitants of the other high islands, now left standing so immensely remote from each other in the midst of the great oceans. The reef-constructing corals have indeed reared and preserved wonderful memorials of the subterranean oscillations of level; we see in each barrier-reef a proof that the land has there subsided, and in each atoll a monument over an island now lost. We may thus, like unto a geologist who had lived his ten thousand years and kept a record of the passing changes, gain some insight into the great system by which the surface of this globe has been broken up, and land and water interchanged.

CHAPTER XXI

MAURITIUS TO ENGLAND

Mauritius, beautiful appearance of — Great crateriform Ring of Mountains — Hindoos — St. Helena — History of the Changes in the Vegetation — Cause of the Extinction of Land-shells — Ascension — Variation in the Imported Rats — Volcanic Bombs — Beds of Infusoria — Bahia — Brazil — Splendour of Tropical Scenery — Pernambuco — Singular Reef — Slavery — Return to England — Retrospect on our Voyage

April 29th.—In the morning we passed round the northern end of Mauritius, or the Isle of France. From this point of view the aspect of the island equalled the expectations raised by the many well-known descriptions of its beautiful scenery. The sloping plain of the Pamplemousses, interspersed with houses, and coloured by the large fields of sugar-cane of a bright green, composed the foreground. The brilliancy of the green was the more remarkable, because it is a colour which generally is conspicuous only from a very short distance. Towards the centre of the island groups of wooded mountains rose out of this highly-cultivated plain; their summits, as so commonly happens with ancient volcanic rocks, being jagged into the sharpest points. Masses of white clouds were collected around these pinnacles, as if for the sake of pleasing the stranger's eye. The whole island, with its sloping border and central mountains, was adorned with an air of perfect elegance: the scenery, if I may use such an expression, appeared to the sight harmonious.

I spent the greater part of the next day in walking about the town, and visiting different people. The town is of considerable size, and is said to contain 20,000[1] inhabitants; the streets are

---

[1] [Editor] Port Louis has grown to a city of over 50,000, but has lost a good deal of the trade it had a century ago as a result of the opening of the Suez Canal.

very clean and regular. Although the island has been so many years under the English government, the general character of the place is quite French: Englishmen speak to their servants in French, and the shops are all French; indeed I should think that Calais or Boulogne was much more Anglified. There is a very pretty little theatre, in which operas are excellently performed. We were also surprised at seeing large booksellers' shops, with well-stored shelves;—music and reading bespeak our approach to the old world of civilization; for in truth both Australia and America are new worlds.

The various races of men walking in the streets afford the most interesting spectacle in Port Louis. Convicts from India are banished here for life; at present there are about 800, and they are employed in various public works. Before seeing these people, I had no idea that the inhabitants of India were such noble-looking figures. Their skin is extremely dark, and many of the older men had large mustaches and beards of a snow-white colour; this, together with the fire of their expression, gave them quite an imposing aspect. The greater number had been banished for murder and the worst crimes; others for causes which can scarcely be considered as moral faults, such as for not obeying, from superstitious motives, the English laws. These men are generally quiet and well conducted; from their outward conduct, their cleanliness, and faithful observance of their strange religious rites, it was impossible to look at them with the same eyes as on our wretched convicts in New South Wales.

May 1*st*.—Sunday. I took a quiet walk along the sea-coast to the north of the town. The plain in this part is quite uncultivated; it consists of a field of black lava, smoothed over with coarse grass and bushes, the latter being chiefly Mimosas. The scenery may be described as intermediate in character between that of the Galapagos and of Tahiti; but this will convey a definite idea to very few persons. It is a very pleasant country, but it has not the charms of Tahiti, or the grandeur of Brazil. The next day I ascended La Pouce, a mountain so called from a thumb-like projection, which rises close behind the town to a height of 2600 feet. The centre of the island consists of a great platform, surrounded by old broken basaltic mountains, with their strata dipping seawards. The central platform, formed of comparatively recent streams of lava, is of an oval shape, thirteen geographical miles across, in the line of its shorter axis. The exterior bounding mountains come into that class of structures called Craters of Elevation, which are supposed to have been formed not like ordinary craters, but by a great and sudden upheaval. There appears to me to be insuperable objections to this view: on the other hand, I can hardly believe, in this and in some other cases, that these marginal crateriform mountains are merely the basal remnants of immense volcanoes, of which the summits either have been blown off, or swallowed up in subterranean abysses.

From our elevated position we enjoyed an excellent view over the island. The country on this side appears pretty well cultivated, being divided into fields and studded with farmhouses. I was however assured that of the whole land, not more than half is yet in a productive state; if such be the case, considering the present large export of sugar, this island, at some future period when thickly peopled, will be of great value. Since England has taken possession of it, a period of only twenty-five years, the export of sugar is said to have increased seventy-five fold. One great cause of its prosperity is the excellent state of the roads. In the neighbouring Isle of Bourbon, which remains under the French government, the roads are still in the same miserable state as they were here only a few years ago. Although the French residents must have largely profited by the increased prosperity of their island, yet the English government is far from popular.

3rd.—In the evening Captain Lloyd, the Surveyor-general so well known from his examination of the Isthmus of Panama, invited Mr. Stokes and myself to his country-house, which is situated on the edge of Wilheim Plains, and about six miles from the Port. We staid at this delightful place two days; standing nearly 800 feet above the sea, the air was cool and fresh, and on every side there were delightful walks. Close by, a grand ravine has been worn to a depth of about 500 feet through the slightly inclined streams of lava, which have flowed from the central platform.

5th.—Captain Lloyd took us to the Rivière Noire, which is several miles to the southward, that I might examine some rocks of elevated coral. We passed through pleasant gardens, and fine fields of sugar-cane growing amidst huge blocks of lava. The roads were bordered by hedges of Mimosa, and near many of the houses there were avenues of the mango. Some of the views, where the peaked hills and the cultivated farms were seen together, were exceedingly picturesque; and we were constantly tempted to exclaim, "How pleasant it would be to pass one's life in such quiet abodes!" Captain Lloyd possessed an elephant, and he sent it half way with us, that we might enjoy a ride in true Indian fashion. The circumstance which surprised me most was its quite noiseless step. This elephant is the only one at present on the island; but it is said others will be sent for.

May 9th.—We sailed from Port Louis, and, calling at the Cape of Good Hope, on the 8th of July we arrived off St. Helena. This island, the forbidding aspect of which has been so often described, rises abruptly like a huge black castle from the ocean. Near the town, as if to complete nature's defence, small forts and guns fill up every gap in the rugged rocks. The town runs up a flat and narrow valley; the houses look respectable, and are interspersed with a very few green trees. When approaching the anchorage there was one striking view: an irregular castle perched on the summit of a lofty hill, and surrounded by a few scattered fir-trees, boldly projected against the sky.

The next day I obtained lodgings within a stone's throw of Napoleon's tomb:[2] it was a capital central situation, whence I could make excursions in every direction. During the four days I staid here, I wandered over the island from morning to night, and examined its geological history. My lodgings were situated at a height of about 2000 feet; here the weather was cold and boisterous, with constant showers of rain; and every now and then the whole scene was veiled in thick clouds.

Near the coast the rough lava is quite bare: in the central and higher parts, feldspathic rocks by their decomposition have produced a clayey soil, which, where not covered by vegetation, is stained in broad bands of many bright colours. At this season, the land moistened by constant showers, produces a singularly bright green pasture, which lower and lower down, gradually fades away and at last disappears. In latitude 16°, and at the trifling elevation of 1500 feet, it is surprising to behold a vegetation possessing a character decidedly British. The hills are crowned with irregular plantations of Scotch firs; and the sloping banks are thickly scattered over with thickets of

[2] [Darwin] After the volumes of eloquence which have poured forth on this subject, it is dangerous even to mention the tomb. A modern traveller, in twelve lines, burdens the poor little island with the following titles,—it is a grave, tomb, pyramid, cemetery, sepulchre, catacomb, sarcophagus, minaret, and mausoleum!

gorse, covered with its bright yellow flowers. Weeping-willows are common on the banks of the rivulets, and the hedges are made of the blackberry, producing its well-known fruit. When we consider that the number of plants now found on the island is 746, and that out of these fifty-two alone are indigenous species, the rest having been imported, and most of them from England, we see the reason of the British character of the vegetation. Many of these English plants appear to flourish better than in their native country; some also from the opposite quarter of Australia succeed remarkably well. The many imported species must have destroyed some of the native kinds; and it is only on the highest and steepest ridges, that the indigenous Flora is now predominant.

The English, or rather Welsh character of the scenery, is kept up by the numerous cottages and small white houses; some buried at the bottom of the deepest valleys, and others mounted on the crests of the lofty hills. Some of the views are striking, for instance that from near Sir W. Doveton's house, where the bold peak called Lot is seen over a dark wood of firs, the whole being backed by the red water-worn mountains of the southern coast. On viewing the island from an eminence, the first circumstance which strikes one, is the number of the roads and forts: the labour bestowed on the public works, if one forgets its character as a prison, seems out of all proportion to its extent or value. There is so little level or useful land, that it seems surprising how so many people, about 5000, can subsist here. The lower orders, or the emancipated slaves, are I believe extremely poor: they complain of the want of work. From the reduction in the number of public servants, owing to the island having been given up by the East India Company, and the consequent emigration of many of the richer people, the poverty probably will increase. The chief food of the working class is rice with a little salt meat; as neither of these articles are the products of the island, but must be purchased with money, the low wages tell heavily on the poor people. Now that the people are blessed with freedom, a right which I believe they value fully, it seems probable that their numbers will quickly increase: if so, what is to become of the little state of St. Helena?[8]

8 [Editor] Darwin's gloomy prediction has not been quite fulfilled. The population of St. Helena has remained nearly constant, being just under 5000 today. Fishing and the raising of flax have been successfully established as the principal occupations.

My guide was an elderly man, who had been a goatherd when a boy, and knew every step amongst the rocks. He was of a race many times crossed, and although with a dusky skin, he had not the disagreeable expression of a mulatto. He was a very civil, quiet old man, and such appears the character of the greater number of the lower classes. It was strange to my ears to hear a man, nearly white and respectably dressed, talking with indifference of the times when he was a slave. With my companion, who carried our dinners and a horn of water, which is quite necessary, as all the water in the lower valleys is saline, I every day took long walks.

Beneath the upper and central green circle, the wild valleys are quite desolate and untenanted. Here, to the geologist, there were scenes of high interest, showing successive changes and complicated disturbances. According to my views, St. Helena has existed as an island from a very remote epoch: some obscure proofs, however, of the elevation of the land are still extant. I believe that the central and highest peaks form parts of the rim of a great crater, the southern half of which has been entirely removed by the waves of the sea: there is, moreover, an external wall of black basaltic rocks, like the coast-mountains of Mauritius, which are older than the central volcanic streams. On the higher parts of the island, considerable numbers of a shell, long thought a marine species, occur embedded in the soil. It proves to be a Cochlogena, or land-shell of a very peculiar form;[4] with it I found six other kinds; and in another spot an eighth species. It is remarkable that none of them are now found living. Their extinction has probably been caused by the entire destruction of the woods, and the consequent loss of food and shelter, which occurred during the early part of the last century.

The history of the changes, which the elevated plains of Longwood and Deadwood have undergone, as given in General Beatson's account of the island, is extremely curious. Both plains, it is said, in former times were covered with wood, and were therefore called the Great Wood. So late as the year 1716 there were many trees, but in 1724 the old trees had mostly fallen; and as goats and hogs had been suffered to range about, all the young trees had been killed. It appears also from the official records, that the trees were unexpectedly, some years

[4] [Darwin] It deserves notice, that all the many specimens of this shell found by me in one spot differ, as a marked variety, from another set of specimens procured from a different spot.

afterwards, succeeded by a wire grass, which spread over the whole surface.[5] General Beatson adds that now this plain "is covered with fine sward, and is become the finest piece of pasture on the island." The extent of surface, probably covered by wood at a former period, is estimated at no less than two thousand acres; at the present day scarcely a single tree can be found there. It is also said that in 1709 there were quantities of dead trees in Sandy Bay; this place is now so utterly desert, that nothing but so well attested an account could have made me believe that they could ever have grown there. The fact, that the goats and hogs destroyed all the young trees as they sprang up, and that in the course of time the old ones, which were safe from their attacks, perished from age, seems clearly made out. Goats were introduced in the year 1502; eighty-six years afterwards, in the time of Cavendish, it is known that they were exceedingly numerous. More than a century afterwards, in 1731, when the evil was complete and irretrievable, an order was issued that all stray animals should be destroyed. It is very interesting thus to find, that the arrival of animals at St. Helena in 1501, did not change the whole aspect of the island, until a period of two hundred and twenty years had elapsed: for the goats were introduced in 1502, and in 1724 it is said "the old trees had mostly fallen." There can be little doubt that this great change in the vegetation affected not only the land-shells, causing eight species to become extinct, but likewise a multitude of insects.

St. Helena, situated so remote from any continent, in the midst of a great ocean, and possessing a unique Flora, excites our curiosity. The eight land-shells, though now extinct, and one living Succinea, are peculiar species found nowhere else. Mr. Cuming, however, informs me that an English Helix is common here, its eggs no doubt having been imported in some of the many introduced plants. Mr. Cuming collected on the coast sixteen species of sea-shells, of which seven, as far as he knows, are confined to this island. Birds and insects,[6] as might

---

[5] [Darwin] Beatson's St. Helena. Introductory chapter, p. 4.

[6] [Darwin] Among these few insects, I was surprised to find a small Aphodius (*nov. spec.*) and an Oryctes, both extremely numerous under dung. When the island was discovered it certainly possessed no quadruped, excepting *perhaps* a mouse; it becomes, therefore, a difficult point to ascertain, whether these stercovorous insects have since been imported by accident, or if aborigines, on what food they formerly subsisted. On the banks of the Plata,

have been expected, are very few in number; indeed I believe all the birds have been introduced within late years. Partridges and pheasants are tolerably abundant: the island is much too English not to be subject to strict game-laws. I was told of a more unjust sacrifice to such ordinances than I ever heard of even in England. The poor people formerly used to burn a plant, which grows on the coast-rocks, and export the soda from its ashes; but a peremptory order came out prohibiting this practice, and giving as a reason that the partridges would have nowhere to build!

In my walks I passed more than once over the grassy plain, bounded by deep valleys, on which Longwood stands. Viewed from a short distance, it appears like a respectable gentleman's country-seat. In front there are a few cultivated fields, and

---

where, from the vast number of cattle and horses, the fine plains of turf are richly manured, it is vain to seek the many kinds of dung-feeding beetles, which occur so abundantly in Europe. I observed only an Oryctes (the insects of this genus in Europe generally feed on decayed vegetable matter) and two species of Phanæus, common in such situations. On the opposite side of the Cordillera in Chiloe, another species of Phanæus is exceedingly abundant, and it buries the dung of the cattle in large earthen balls beneath the ground. There is reason to believe that the genus Phanæus, before the introduction of cattle, acted as scavengers to man. In Europe, beetles, which find support in the matter which has already contributed towards the life of other and larger animals, are so numerous, that there must be considerably more than one hundred different species. Considering this, and observing what a quantity of food of this kind is lost on the plains of La Plata, I imagined I saw an instance where man had disturbed that chain, by which so many animals are linked together in their native country. In Van Diemen's Land, however, I found four species of Onthophagus, two of Aphodius, and one of a third genus, very abundant under the dung of cows; yet these latter animals had been then introduced only thirty-three years. Previously to that time, the Kangaroo and some other small animals were the only quadrupeds; and their dung is of a very different quality from that of their successors introduced by man. In England the greater number of stercovorous beetles are confined in their appetites; that is, they do not depend indifferently on any quadruped for the means of subsistence. The change, therefore, in habits, which must have taken place in Van Diemen's Land, is highly remarkable. I am indebted to the Rev. F. W. Hope, who, I hope, will permit me to call him my master in Entomology, for giving me the names of the foregoing insects.

beyond them the smooth hill of coloured rocks called the Flag-staff, and the rugged square black mass of the Barn. On the whole the view was rather bleak and uninteresting. The only inconvenience I suffered during my walks was from the impetuous winds. One day I noticed a curious circumstance: standing on the edge of a plain, terminated by a great cliff of about a thousand feet in depth, I saw at the distance of a few yards right to windward, some tern, struggling against a very strong breeze, whilst, where I stood, the air was quite calm. Approaching close to the brink, where the current seemed to be deflected upwards from the face of the cliff, I stretched out my arm, and immediately felt the full force of the wind: an invisible barrier, two yards in width, separated perfectly calm air from a strong blast.

I so much enjoyed my rambles among the rocks and mountains of St. Helena, that I felt almost sorry on the morning of the 14th to descend to the town. Before noon I was on board, and the *Beagle* made sail.

On the 19th of July we reached Ascension. Those who have beheld a volcanic island, situated under an arid climate, will at once be able to picture to themselves the appearance of Ascension. They will imagine smooth conical hills of a bright red colour, with their summits generally truncated, rising separately out of a level surface of black rugged lava. A principal mound in the centre of the island, seems the father of the lesser cones. It is called Green Hill; its name being taken from the faintest tinge of that colour, which at this time of the year is barely perceptible from the anchorage. To complete the desolate scene, the black rocks on the coast are lashed by a wild and turbulent sea.

The settlement is near the beach; it consists of several houses and barracks placed irregularly, but well built of white freestone. The only inhabitants are marines, and some negroes liberated from slave-ships, who are paid and victualled by government. There is not a private person on the island. Many of the marines appeared well contented with their situation; they think it better to serve their one-and-twenty years on shore, let it be what it may, than in a ship; in this choice, if I were a marine, I should most heartily agree.

The next morning I ascended Green Hill, 2840 feet high, and thence walked across the island to the windward point. A good cart-road leads from the coast-settlement to the houses, gardens, and fields, placed near the summit of the central mountain. On the roadside there are milestones, and likewise cisterns, where each thirsty passer-by can drink some good water. Similar care is displayed in each part of the establishment, and especially in the management of the springs, so that a single drop of water may not be lost: indeed the whole island may be compared to a huge ship kept in first-rate order. I could not help, when admiring the active industry which had created such effects out of such means, at the same time regretting that it had been wasted on so poor and trifling an end. M. Lesson has remarked with justice, that the English nation alone would have thought of making the island of Ascension a productive spot; any other people would have held it as a mere fortress in the ocean.

Near this coast nothing grows; further inland, an occasional green castor-oil plant, and a few grasshoppers, true friends of the desert, may be met with. Some grass is scattered over the surface of the central elevated region, and the whole much resembles the worse parts of the Welsh mountains. But scanty as the pasture appears, about six hundred sheep, many goats, a few cows and horses, all thrive well on it. Of native animals, land-crabs and rats swarm in numbers. Whether the rat is really indigenous, may well be doubted; there are two varieties as described by Mr. Waterhouse; one is of a black colour, with fine glossy fur, and lives on the grassy summit; the other is brown-coloured and less glossy, with longer hairs, and lives near the settlement on the coast. Both these varieties are one-third smaller than the common black rat (M. rattus); and they differ from it both in the colour and character of their fur, but in no other essential respect. I can hardly doubt that these rats (like the common mouse, which has also run wild) have been imported, and, as at the Galapagos, have varied from the effect of the new conditions to which they have been exposed: hence the variety on the summit of the island differs from that on the coast. Of native birds there are none; but the guinea-fowl, imported from the Cape de Verd Islands, is abundant, and the common fowl has likewise run wild. Some cats, which were originally turned out to destroy the rats and mice, have increased, so as to become a great plague. The island is entirely without trees, in which, and in every other respect, it is very far inferior to St. Helena.

One of my excursions took me towards the S.W. extremity of the island. The day was clear and hot, and I saw the island,

not smiling with beauty, but staring with naked hideousness.
The lava streams are covered with hummocks, and are rugged
to a degree which, geologically speaking, is not of easy explanation. The intervening spaces are concealed with layers
of pumice, ashes, and volcanic tuff. Whilst passing this end of
the island at sea, I could not imagine what the white patches
were with which the whole plain was mottled; I now found that
they were sea-fowl, sleeping in such full confidence, that even
in mid-day a man could walk up and seize hold of them. These
birds were the only living creatures I saw during the whole day.
On the beach a great surf, although the breeze was light, came
tumbling over the broken lava rocks.

The geology of this island is in many respects interesting.
In several places I noticed volcanic bombs, that is, masses of
lava which have been shot through the air whilst fluid, and
have consequently assumed a spherical or pear-shape. Not only
their external form, but, in several cases, their internal structure shows in a very curious manner that they have revolved
in their aërial course. The internal structure of one of these
bombs, when broken, is represented very accurately in the
wood-cut on the next page. The central part is coarsely cellular, the cells decreasing in size towards the exterior; where
there is a shell-like case about the third of an inch in thickness,
of compact stone, which again is overlaid by the outside crust
of finely cellular lava. I think there can be little doubt, first,
that the external crust cooled rapidly in the state in which we
now see it; secondly, that the still fluid lava within, was packed
by the centrifugal force, generated by the revolving of the
bomb, against the external cooled crust, and so produced the
solid shell of stone; and lastly, that the centrifugal force, by
relieving the pressure in the more central parts of the bomb,
allowed the heated vapours to expand their cells, thus forming
the coarsely cellular mass of the centre.

A hill, formed of the older series of volcanic rocks, and
which has been incorrectly considered as the crater of a volcano, is remarkable from its broad, slightly hollowed, and circular summit having been filled up with many successive
layers of ashes and fine scoriæ. These saucer-shaped layers
crop out on the margin, forming perfect rings of many different colours, giving to the summit a most fantastic appearance;
one of these rings is white and broad, and resembles a course
round which horses have been exercised; hence the hill has
been called the Devil's Riding School. I brought away speci-

mens of one of the tufaceous layers of a pinkish colour; and it is a most extraordinary fact, that Professor Ehrenberg[7] finds it almost wholly composed of matter which has been organized: he detects in it some siliceous-shielded, fresh-water infusoria, and no less than twenty-five different kinds of the siliceous tissue of plants, chiefly of grasses. From the absence of all carbonaceous matter, Professor Ehrenberg believes that these organic bodies have passed through the volcanic fire, and have been erupted in the state in which we now see them. The appearance of the layers induced me to believe that they had been deposited under water, though from the extreme dryness of the climate I was forced to imagine, that torrents of rain had probably fallen during some great eruption, and that thus a temporary lake had been formed, into which the ashes fell. But it may now be suspected that the lake was not a temporary one. Anyhow, we may feel sure, that at some former epoch, the climate and productions of Ascension were very different from

[7] [Darwin] Monats. der König. Akad. d. Wiss. zu Berlin. Vom April, 1845.

what they now are. Where on the face of the earth can we find a spot, on which close investigation will not discover signs of that endless cycle of change, to which this earth has been, is, and will be subjected?

On leaving Ascension we sailed for Bahia, on the coast of Brazil, in order to complete the chronometrical measurement of the world. We arrived there on August 1st, and stayed four days, during which I took several long walks. I was glad to find my enjoyment in tropical scenery had not decreased from the want of novelty, even in the slightest degree. The elements of the scenery are so simple, that they are worth mentioning, as a proof on what trifling circumstances exquisite natural beauty depends.

The country may be described as a level plain of about three hundred feet in elevation, which in all parts has been worn into flat-bottomed valleys. This structure is remarkable in a granitic land, but is nearly universal in all those softer formations of which plains are usually composed. The whole surface is covered by various kinds of stately trees, interspersed with patches of cultivated ground, out of which houses, convents, and chapels arise. It must be remembered that within the tropics, the wild luxuriance of nature is not lost even in the vicinity of large cities; for the natural vegetation of the hedges and hill-sides overpowers in picturesque effect the artificial labour of man. Hence, there are only a few spots where the bright red soil affords a strong contrast with the universal clothing of green. From the edges of the plain there are distant views either of the ocean, or of the great Bay with its low-wooded shores, and on which numerous boats and canoes show their white sails. Excepting from these points, the scene is extremely limited; following the level pathways, on each hand, only glimpses into the wooded valleys below can be obtained. The houses, I may add, and especially the sacred edifices, are built in a peculiar and rather fantastic style of architecture. They are all white-washed; so that when illumined by the brilliant sun of mid-day, and as seen against the pale-blue sky of the horizon, they stand out more like shadows than real buildings.

Such are the elements of the scenery, but it is a hopeless attempt to paint the general effect. Learned naturalists describe these scenes of the tropics by naming a multitude of objects, and mentioning some characteristic feature of each. To a learned traveller this possibly may communicate some definite ideas: but who else from seeing a plant in an herbarium can imagine its appearance when growing in its native soil? Who from seeing choice plants in a hothouse, can magnify some into the dimensions of forest trees, and crowd others into an entangled jungle? Who when examining in the cabinet of the entomologist the gay exotic butterflies, and singular cicadas, will associate with these lifeless objects, the ceaseless harsh music of the latter, and the lazy flight of the former,—the sure accompaniments of the still, glowing noonday of the tropics? It is when the sun has attained its greatest height, that such scenes should be viewed: then the dense splendid foliage of the mango hides the ground with its darkest shade, whilst the upper branches are rendered from the profusion of light of the most brilliant green. In the temperate zones the case is different— the vegetation there is not so dark or so rich, and hence the rays of the declining sun, tinged of a red, purple, or bright yellow colour, add most to the beauties of those climes.

When quietly walking along the shady pathways, and admiring each successive view, I wished to find language to express my ideas. Epithet after epithet was found too weak to convey to those who have not visited the intertropical regions, the sensation of delight which the mind experiences. I have said that the plants in a hothouse fail to communicate a just idea of the vegetation, yet I must recur to it. The land is one great wild, untidy, luxuriant hothouse, made by Nature for herself, but taken possession of by man, who has studded it with gay houses and formal gardens. How great would be the desire in every admirer of nature to behold, if such were possible, the scenery of another planet! yet to every person in Europe, it may be truly said, that at the distance of only a few degrees from his native soil, the glories of another world are opened to him. In my last walk I stopped again and again to gaze on these beauties, and endeavoured to fix in my mind for ever, an impression which at the time I knew sooner or later must fail. The form of the orange-tree, the cocoa-nut, the palm, the mango, the tree-fern, the banana, will remain clear and separate; but the thousand beauties which unite these into one perfect scene must fade away; yet they will leave, like a tale heard in childhood, a picture full of indistinct, but most beautiful figures.

August 6th.—In the afternoon we stood out to sea, with the intention of making a direct course to the Cape de Verd Islands. Unfavourable winds, however, delayed us, and on the 12th we ran into Pernambuco,[8]—a large city on the coast of Brazil, in latitude 8° south. We anchored outside the reef; but in a short time a pilot came on board and took us into the inner harbour, where we lay close to the town.

Pernambuco is built on some narrow and low sand-banks, which are separated from each other by shoal channels of salt water. The three parts of the town are connected together by two long bridges built on wooden piles. The town is in all parts disgusting, the streets being narrow, ill-paved, and filthy; the houses, tall and gloomy. The season of heavy rains had hardly come to an end, and hence the surrounding country, which is scarcely raised above the level of the sea, was flooded with water; and I failed in all my attempts to take long walks.

The flat swampy land on which Pernambuco stands is surrounded, at the distance of a few miles, by a semi-circle of low hills, or rather by the edge of a country elevated perhaps two hundred feet above the sea. The old city of Olinda stands on one extremity of this range. One day I took a canoe, and proceeded up one of the channels to visit it; I found the old town from its situation both sweeter and cleaner than that of Pernambuco. I must here commemorate what happened for the first time during our nearly five years' wandering, namely, having met with a want of politeness: I was refused in a sullen manner at two different houses, and obtained with difficulty from a third, permission to pass through their gardens to an uncultivated hill, for the purpose of viewing the country. I feel glad that this happened in the land of the Brazilians, for I bear them no good will—a land also of slavery, and therefore of moral debasement. A Spaniard would have felt ashamed at the very thought of refusing such a request, or of behaving to a stranger with rudeness. The channel by which we went to and returned from Olinda, was bordered on each side by mangroves, which sprang like a miniature forest out of the greasy mud-banks. The bright green colour of these bushes always reminded me of the rank grass in a churchyard: both are nourished by putrid exhalations; the one speaks of death past, and the other too often of death to come.

The most curious object which I saw in this neighbourhood, was the reef that forms the harbour. I doubt whether in the whole world any other natural structure has so artificial an ap-

[8] [Editor] Now better known as Recife.

pearance.[9] It runs for a length of several miles in an absolutely straight line, parallel to, and not far distant from, the shore. It varies in width from thirty to sixty yards, and its surface is level and smooth; it is composed of obscurely-stratified hard sandstone. At high water the waves break over it; at low water its summit is left dry, and it might then be mistaken for a breakwater erected by Cyclopean workmen. On this coast the currents of the sea tend to throw up in front of the land, long spits and bars of loose sand, and on one of these, part of the town of Pernambuco stands. In former times a long spit of this nature seems to have become consolidated by the percolation of calcareous matter, and afterwards to have been gradually upheaved; the outer and loose parts during this process having been worn away by the action of the sea, and the solid nucleus left as we now see it. Although night and day the waves of the open Atlantic, turbid with sediment, are driven against the steep outside edges of this wall of stone, yet the oldest pilots know of no tradition of any change in its appearance. This durability is much the most curious fact in its history: it is due to a tough layer, a few inches thick, of calcareous matter, wholly formed by the successive growth and death of the small shells of Serpulæ, together with some few barnacles and nulliporæ. These nulliporæ, which are hard, very simply-organized sea-plants, play an analogous and important part in protecting the upper surfaces of coral-reefs, behind and within the breakers, where the true corals, during the outward growth of the mass, become killed by exposure to the sun and air. These insignificant organic beings, especially the Serpulæ, have done good service to the people of Pernambuco; for without their protective aid the bar of sandstone would inevitably have been long ago worn away, and without the bar, there would have been no harbour.

On the 19th of August we finally left the shores of Brazil. I thank God, I shall never again visit a slave-country. To this day, if I hear a distant scream, it recalls with painful vividness my feelings, when passing a house near Pernambuco, I heard the most pitiable moans, and could not but suspect that some poor slave was being tortured, yet knew that I was as powerless as a child even to remonstrate. I suspected that these moans were from a tortured slave, for I was told that this was the case

9 [Darwin] I have described this Bar in detail, in the Lond. and Edin. Phil. Mag., vol. xix. (1841) p. 257.

in another instance. Near Rio de Janeiro I lived opposite to an old lady, who kept screws to crush the fingers of her female slaves. I have staid in a house where a young household mulatto, daily and hourly, was reviled, beaten, and persecuted enough to break the spirit of the lowest animal. I have seen a little boy, six or seven years old, struck thrice with a horse-whip (before I could interfere) on his naked head, for having handed me a glass of water not quite clean; I saw his father tremble at a mere glance from his master's eye. These latter cruelties were witnessed by me in a Spanish colony, in which it has always been said, that slaves are better treated than by the Portuguese, English, or other European nations. I have seen at Rio de Janeiro a powerful negro afraid to ward off a blow directed, as he thought, at his face. I was present when a kind-hearted man was on the point of separating for ever the men, women, and little children of a large number of families who had long lived together. I will not even allude to the many heart-sickening atrocities which I authentically heard of;—nor would I have mentioned the above revolting details, had I not met with several people, so blinded by the constitutional gaiety of the negro, as to speak of slavery as a tolerable evil. Such people have generally visited at the houses of the upper classes, where the domestic slaves are usually well treated; and they have not, like myself, lived amongst the lower classes. Such enquirers will ask slaves about their condition; they forget that the slave must indeed be dull, who does not calculate on the chance of his answer reaching his master's ears.

It is argued that self-interest will prevent excessive cruelty; as if self-interest protected our domestic animals, which are far less likely than degraded slaves, to stir up the rage of their savage masters. It is an argument long since protested against with noble feeling, and strikingly exemplified, by the ever il-lustrious Humboldt. It is often attempted to palliate slavery by comparing the state of slaves with our poorer countrymen: if the misery of our poor be caused not by the laws of nature, but by our institutions, great is our sin; but how this bears on slav-ery, I cannot see; as well might the use of the thumbscrew be defended in one land, by showing that men in another land suffered from some dreadful disease. Those who look tenderly at the slave-owner, and with a cold heart at the slave, never seem to put themselves into the position of the latter;—what a cheerless prospect, with not even a hope of change! picture to yourself the chance, ever hanging over you, of your wife and your little children—those objects which nature urges even the slave to call his own—being torn from you and sold like beasts to the first bidder! And these deeds are done and palliated by men, who profess to love their neighbours as themselves, who believe in God, and pray that his Will be done on earth! It makes one's blood boil, yet heart tremble, to think that we Englishmen and our American descendants, with their boastful cry of liberty, have been and are so guilty: but it is a consolation to reflect, that we at least have made a greater sacrifice, than ever made by any nation, to expiate our sin.

On the last day of August we anchored for the second time at Porto Praya in the Cape de Verd archipelago; thence we proceeded to the Azores, where we staid six days. On the 2nd of October we made the shores of England; and at Falmouth I left the *Beagle*, having lived on board the good little vessel nearly five years.

Our Voyage having come to an end, I will take a short retrospect of the advantages and disadvantages, the pains and pleasures, of our circumnavigation of the world. If a person asked my advice, before undertaking a long voyage, my answer would depend upon his possessing a decided taste for some branch of knowledge, which could by this means be advanced. No doubt it is a high satisfaction to behold various countries and the many races of mankind, but the pleasures gained at the time do not counterbalance the evils. It is necessary to look forward to a harvest, however distant that may be, when some fruit will be reaped, some good effected.

Many of the losses which must be experienced are obvious; such as that of the society of every old friend, and of the sight of those places with which every dearest remembrance is so intimately connected. These losses, however, are at the time partly relieved by the exhaustless delight of anticipating the long wished-for day of return. If, as poets say, life is a dream, I am sure in a voyage these are the visions which best serve to pass away the long night. Other losses, although not at first felt, tell heavily after a period: these are the want of room, of seclusion, of rest; the jading feeling of constant hurry; the privation of small luxuries, the loss of domestic society, and even of music and the other pleasures of imagination. When such trifles are mentioned, it is evident that the real grievances, excepting from accidents, of a sea-life are at an end. The short space of sixty years has made an astonishing difference in the facility of distant navigation. Even in the time of Cook, a man who left his fireside for such expeditions underwent severe privations. A yacht now, with every luxury of life, can circumnavigate the globe. Besides the vast improvements in ships and naval resources, the whole western shores of America are thrown open, and Australia has become the capital of a rising continent. How different are the circumstances to a man shipwrecked at the present day in the Pacific, to what they were in the time of Cook! Since his voyage a hemisphere has been added to the civilized world.

If a person suffer much from sea-sickness, let him weigh it heavily in the balance. I speak from experience: it is no trifling evil, cured in a week. If, on the other hand, he take pleasure in naval tactics, he will assuredly have full scope for his taste. But it must be borne in mind, how large a proportion of the time, during a long voyage, is spent on the water, as compared with the days in harbour. And what are the boasted glories of the illimitable ocean? A tedious waste, a desert of water, as the Arabian calls it. No doubt there are some delightful scenes. A moonlight night, with the clear heavens and the dark glittering sea, and the white sails filled by the soft air of a gently-blowing trade-wind; a dead calm, with the heaving surface polished like a mirror, and all still except the occasional flapping of the canvas. It is well once to behold a squall with its rising arch and coming fury, or the heavy gale of wind and mountainous waves. I confess, however, my imagination had painted something more grand, more terrific in the full-grown storm. It is an incomparably finer spectacle when beheld on shore, where the waving trees, the wild flight of the birds, the dark shadows and bright lights, the rushing of the torrents, all proclaim the strife of the unloosed elements. At sea the albatross and little petrel fly as if the storm were their proper sphere, the water rises and sinks as if fulfilling its usual task, the ship alone and its inhabitants seem the objects of wrath. On a forlorn and weather-beaten coast, the scene is indeed different, but the feelings partake more of horror than of wild delight.

Let us now look at the brighter side of the past time. The pleasure derived from beholding the scenery and the general aspect of the various countries we have visited, has decidedly been the most constant and highest source of enjoyment. It is probable that the picturesque beauty of many parts of Europe

exceeds anything which we beheld. But there is a growing
pleasure in comparing the character of the scenery in different countries, which to a certain degree is distinct from merely
admiring its beauty. It depends chiefly on an acquaintance with
the individual parts of each view: I am strongly induced to
believe that, as in music, the person who understands every
note will, if he also possesses a proper taste, more thoroughly
enjoy the whole, so he who examines each part of a fine view,
may also thoroughly comprehend the full and combined effect.
Hence, a traveller should be a botanist, for in all views plants
form the chief embellishment. Group masses of naked rock
even in the wildest forms, and they may for a time afford a
sublime spectacle, but they will soon grow monotonous. Paint
them with bright and varied colours, as in Northern Chile, they
will become fantastic; clothe them with vegetation, they must
form a decent, if not a beautiful picture.

When I say that the scenery of parts of Europe is probably
superior to anything which we beheld, I except, as a class by
itself, that of the intertropical zones. The two classes cannot be
compared together; but I have already often enlarged on the
grandeur of those regions. As the force of impressions generally depends on preconceived ideas, I may add, that mine were
taken from the vivid descriptions in the Personal Narrative of
Humboldt, which far exceed in merit anything else which I
have read. Yet with these high-wrought ideas, my feelings were
far from partaking of a tinge of disappointment on my first
and final landing on the shores of Brazil.

Among the scenes which are deeply impressed on my mind,
none exceed in sublimity the primeval forests undefaced by
the hand of man; whether those of Brazil, where the powers of
Life are predominant, or those of Tierra del Fuego, where
Death and Decay prevail. Both are temples filled with the varied
productions of the God of Nature:—no one can stand in these
solitudes unmoved, and not feel that there is more in man than
the mere breath of his body. In calling up images of the past, I
find that the plains of Patagonia frequently cross before my
eyes; yet these plains are pronounced by all wretched and useless. They can be described only by negative characters; without habitations, without water, without trees, without mountains, they support merely a few dwarf plants. Why then, and
the case is not peculiar to myself, have these arid wastes taken
so firm a hold on my memory? Why have not the still more
level, the greener and more fertile Pampas, which are service-

able to mankind, produced an equal impression? I can scarcely analyze these feelings: but it must be partly owing to the free scope given to the imagination. The plains of Patagonia are boundless, for they are scarcely passable, and hence unknown: they bear the stamp of having lasted, as they are now, for ages, and there appears no limit to their duration through future time. If, as the ancients supposed, the flat earth was surrounded by an impassable breadth of water, or by deserts heated to an intolerable excess, who would not look at these last boundaries to man's knowledge with deep but ill-defined sensations?

Lastly, of natural scenery, the views from lofty mountains, though certainly in one sense not beautiful, are very memorable. When looking down from the highest crest of the Cordillera, the mind, undisturbed by minute details, was filled with the stupendous dimensions of the surrounding masses.

Of individual objects, perhaps nothing is more certain to create astonishment than the first sight in his native haunt of a barbarian,—of man in his lowest and most savage state. One's mind hurries back over past centuries, and then asks, could our progenitors have been men like these?—men, whose very signs and expressions are less intelligible to us than those of the domesticated animals; men, who do not possess the instinct of those animals, nor yet appear to boast of human reason, or at least of arts consequent on that reason. I do not believe it is possible to describe or paint the difference between savage and civilized man. It is the difference between a wild and tame animal: and part of the interest in beholding a savage, is the same which would lead every one to desire to see the lion in his desert, the tiger tearing his prey in the jungle, or the rhinoceros wandering over the wild plains of Africa.

Among the other most remarkable spectacles which we have beheld, may be ranked the Southern Cross, the cloud of Magellan, and the other constellations of the southern hemisphere—the water-spout—the glacier leading its blue stream of ice, overhanging the sea in a bold precipice—a lagoon-island raised by the reef-building corals—an active volcano—and the overwhelming effects of a violent earthquake. These latter phenomena, perhaps, possess for me a peculiar interest, from their intimate connexion with the geological structure of the world. The earthquake, however, must be to every one a most impressive event: the earth, considered from our earliest childhood as the type of solidity, has oscillated like a thin crust beneath our feet; and in seeing the laboured works of man in a moment overthrown, we feel the insignificance of his boasted power.

It has been said, that the love of the chase is an inherent delight in man—a relic of an instinctive passion. If so, I am sure the pleasure of living in the open air, with the sky for a roof and the ground for a table, is part of the same feeling; it is the savage returning to his wild and native habits. I always look back to our boat cruises, and my land journeys, when through unfrequented countries, with an extreme delight, which no scenes of civilization could have created. I do not doubt that every traveller must remember the glowing sense of happiness which he experienced, when he first breathed in a foreign clime, where the civilized man had seldom or never trod.

There are several other sources of enjoyment in a long voyage, which are of a more reasonable nature. The map of the world ceases to be a blank; it becomes a picture full of the most varied and animated figures. Each part assumes its proper dimensions: continents are not looked at in the light of islands, or islands considered as mere specks, which are, in truth, larger than many kingdoms of Europe. Africa, or North and South America, are well-sounding names, and easily pronounced; but it is not until having sailed for weeks along small portions of their shores, that one is thoroughly convinced what vast spaces on our immense world these names imply.

From seeing the present state, it is impossible not to look forward with high expectations to the future progress of nearly an entire hemisphere. The march of improvement, consequent on the introduction of Christianity throughout the South Sea, probably stands by itself in the records of history. It is the more striking when we remember that only sixty years since, Cook, whose excellent judgment none will dispute, could foresee no prospect of a change. Yet these changes have now been effected by the philanthropic spirit of the British nation.

In the same quarter of the globe Australia is rising, or indeed may be said to have risen, into a grand centre of civilization, which, at some not very remote period, will rule as empress over the southern hemisphere. It is impossible for an Englishman to behold these distant colonies, without a high pride and satisfaction. To hoist the British flag, seems to draw with it as a certain consequence, wealth, prosperity, and civilization.

In conclusion, it appears to me that nothing can be more improving to a young naturalist, than a journey in distant countries. It both sharpens, and partly allays that want and craving, which, as Sir J. Herschel remarks, a man experiences although every corporeal sense be fully satisfied. The excitement from the novelty of objects, and the chance of success, stimulate him to increased activity. Moreover, as a number of isolated facts soon become uninteresting, the habit of comparison leads to generalization. On the other hand, as the traveller stays but a short time in each place, his descriptions must generally consist of mere sketches, instead of detailed observations. Hence arises, as I have found to my cost, a constant tendency to fill up the wide gaps of knowledge, by inaccurate and superficial hypotheses.

But I have too deeply enjoyed the voyage, not to recommend any naturalist, although he must not expect to be so fortunate in his companions as I have been, to take all chances, and to start, on travels by land if possible, if otherwise on a long voyage. He may feel assured, he will meet with no difficulties or dangers, excepting in rare cases, nearly so bad as he beforehand anticipates. In a moral point of view, the effect ought to be, to teach him good-humoured patience, freedom from selfishness, the habit of acting for himself, and of making the best of every occurence. In short, he ought to partake of the characteristic qualities of most sailors. Travelling ought also to teach him distrust; but at the same time he will discover, how many truly kind-hearted people there are, with whom he never before had, or ever again will have any further communication, who yet are ready to offer him the most disinterested assistance.

NOTE. [Darwin]—The snake, described at page 97, with the curious habit of vibrating its tail, is a new species of Trigonocephalus, which M. Bibron proposes to call T. crepitans.

Selected List of Darwin's Formal Scientific Works

The Structure and Distribution of Coral Reefs. (First part of the *Geology of the Voyage of the Beagle*.) London, 1842.

Zoology of H.M.S. Beagle. London, 1839–43.

Geological Observations on the Volcanic Islands visited during The Voyage of H.M.S. Beagle. (Second part of the *Geology of the Voyage of the Beagle*.) London, 1844.

Geological Observations on South America. (Third part of the *Geology of the Voyage of the Beagle*.) London, 1846.

On the Origin of Species by Means of Natural Selection, or the Preservation of Favoured Races in the Struggle for Life. Reprint of the first edition (originally issued 1859). Watts & Co., London, 1950.

The Origin of Species by Means of Natural Selection, or the Preservation of Favored Races in the Struggle for Life. Reprint of the sixth edition (the last edition revised by Darwin, originally issued 1872). Dolphin Books, Doubleday & Co., Inc., New York, 1959.

The Variation of Animals and Plants under Domestication. London, 1868.

The Descent of Man, and Selection in Relation to Sex. London, 1871.

The Expression of the Emotions in Man and Animals. London, 1872.

The Power of Movement in Plants. London, 1880.

Selected Works. D. Appleton & Co., New York and London, 1887.

Darwiniana

The Autobiography of Charles Darwin. Edited with appendix and notes by Nora Barlow. Harcourt, Brace & Co., New York, 1958.

Charles Darwin's Diary of the Voyage of H.M.S. Beagle. Unpublished letters and notebooks. Edited by Nora Barlow. Philosophical Library, New York, 1946.

Evolution by Natural Selection. Darwin and Wallace. A centenary commemorative volume containing Darwin's sketch of

1842 and essay of 1844, the joint papers of 1858 and a foreword by Sir Gavin de Beer. Cambridge University Press, New York, 1958.

Journal of Researches into the Natural History and Geology of the Countries Visited during the Voyage of H.M.S. Beagle round the World, under the Command of Capt. Fitz Roy, R.N. (Revised version of *The Voyage of the Beagle.*) John Murray, London, 1845.

Life and Letters. Edited by Francis Darwin. London, 1887.

More Letters. Edited by Francis Darwin and A. C. Seward. London, 1903.

Narrative of the Surveying Voyages of His Majesty's Ships Adventure and Beagle, between the years 1826 and 1836, describing their examination of the Southern Shores of South America, and the Beagle's Circumnavigation of the Globe. Henry Colburn, London, 1839.

 Vol. I. Mainly by Philip Parker King and contains narrative of first expedition.

 Vol. II. with Appendix Volume. By Robert Fitz Roy. Contains general narrative of second expedition.

 Vol. III. Titled "Journal and Remarks," 1832–1836. By Charles Darwin. (First published form of *The Voyage of the Beagle.*)

Additional Suggestions for Further Reading

GENERAL

Barnett, Samuel A., editor. *Century of Darwin.* Harvard University Press, Cambridge, Mass., 1958.

Bates, Marston and Humphrey, Philip S. *Darwin Reader.* Charles Scribner's Sons, New York, 1956.

Bell, Peter R. *Darwin's Biological Works: Some Aspects Reconsidered.* Cambridge University Press, New York, 1959.

Eiseley, Loren. *Darwin's Century: Evolution and the Men Who Discovered It.* Doubleday & Co., Inc., New York, 1958.

Simpson, George Gaylord. *The Meaning of Evolution.* (Yale Y-23) Yale University Press, New Haven, 1960.

OTHER BOOKS OF INTEREST

Bates, Henry Walter. *The Naturalist on the Amazon.* (Everyman's 446) E. P. Dutton & Co., New York.

Belt, Thomas. *The Naturalist in Nicaragua.* (Everyman's 561) E. P. Dutton & Co., New York.

Bridges, E. Lucas. *The Uttermost Part of the Earth.* E. P. Dutton & Co., New York, 1949.

Buchsbaum, Ralph. *Animals without Backbones: An Introduction to the Invertebrates.* University of Chicago Press, Chicago, 1948.

Dobzhansky, Theodosius G. *Genetics and the Origin of Species.* Columbia University Press, New York, 1951.

Eibl-Eibesfeldt, Irenäus. *Galapagos: The Noah's Ark of the Pacific.* Doubleday & Co., Inc., New York, 1961.

Ford, Edmund B. *Butterflies.* (New Naturalist series) The Macmillan Company, New York, 1957.

Ford, Edmund B. *Moths.* (New Naturalist series) The Macmillan Company, New York, 1955.

Hardy, Alister C. *The Open Sea.* Vol. I, World of Plankton, 1957. Vol. II, Fish and Fisheries, 1959. Houghton Mifflin Co., Boston.

Humboldt, Alexander, Freiherr von. *Personal Narrative of Travels to the Equinoctial Regions of America, during the Years 1799–1804.* (Bohn's scientific library) G. Bell & Sons, London, 1894–1900.

Huxley, Julian. *Evolution, the Modern Synthesis,* Harper & Bros., New York, 1942.

Lack, David. *Darwin's Finches.* Cambridge University Press, New York, 1947.

Rensch, Bernhard. *Evolution above the Species Level.* Columbia University Press, New York, 1960.

Romer, Alfred S. *The Vertebrate Story.* University of Chicago Press, Chicago, 1959.

Sears, Paul B. *Charles Darwin: The Naturalist as a Cultural Force.* Charles Scribner's Sons, New York, 1950.

Sheppard, Philip MacDonald. *Natural Selection and Heredity.* (Torchbooks 528) Harper & Brothers, New York.

Simpson, George Gaylord. *Horses: The Story of the Horse Family in the Modern World and through Sixty Million Years of History.* The Natural History Library, Doubleday Anchor Books, Garden City, New York, 1961.

Simpson, George Gaylord. *Principles of Animal Taxonomy.* Columbia University Press, New York, 1961.

Von Hagen, Victor W. *South America Called Them.* Alfred A. Knopf, New York, 1945.

Waterton, Charles. *Wanderings in South America.* (Everyman's 772) E. P. Dutton & Co., New York.

INDEX